LONDON : PRINTED BY
SPOTTISWOODE AND CO., NEW-STREET SQUARE
AND PARLIAMENT STREET

A MANUAL

OF

ENGLISH LITERATURE

HISTORICAL AND CRITICAL:

WITH AN APPENDIX ON ENGLISH METRES.

BY

THOMAS ARNOLD, M.A.

OF UNIV. COLL. OXFORD.

FOURTH EDITION, REVISED.

LONDON:

LONGMANS, GREEN, AND CO.

1877.

PREFACE

TO

THE FOURTH EDITION.

———◦◦◦———

CONSIDERABLE additions have been made in the prior, or historical, portion of this work, particularly in the 'Norman Period.' Among these are :—A view of the legend of St. Graal, and of its incorporation in the cycle of Arthurian Romance (pp. 54–61) ; notices of Wireker and Richard of Bury ; and a fuller account of the earliest English remains, in poetry and prose, such as the verses of St. Godric (p. 46), 'The Owl and the Nightingale' (p. 74), the rhythmic gospels of Ormin (p. 71), and the 'Ancren Riwle' (p. 75). In the chapter on the 'Early English Period,' a separate notice of Alliterative Poems (p. 81), from the thirteenth to the sixteenth century, has been introduced ; and the review of Chaucer's works (pp. 88–122) has been re-cast and largely extended. In the following chapter the notices of Hawes, Lyndsay, Colet, and More have been enlarged, and new articles added on Warham, Tyndale, &c. In the chapter on the 'Elizabethan Period,' I have endeavoured to do more justice to the genius of Sidney (pp. 186 and 217), and have added more detailed notices (199–208) of Shakspere's various plays than had been given in former editions. In the

CONTENTS.

HISTORICAL SECTION.

PRELIMINARY CHAPTER.

CHAPTER IV.

CIVIL WAR PERIOD: 1625-1700.

CHAPTER V.

EIGHTEENTH CENTURY: 1700-1800.

CHAPTER II.

HISTORY

OF

ENGLISH LITERATURE.

----◆----

PRELIMINARY CHAPTER.

SECTION I.

ANGLO-SAXON PERIOD.

1. ANGLO-SAXON LITERATURE forms of itself a special department of study. It is one of those exceptional products of the human mind, working with scanty materials, imperfect tools, and under adverse circumstances, which, like stars scattered over a dark portion of the sky, stud the dreary period that intervenes between the break-up of the ancient civilization and literature, and the rise of those of modern times. It is a thing apart, like the Irish or the Icelandic literature, and requires to be studied in connection with the fossil remains of other extinct cognate languages, such as the Old Saxon, the Mœsogothic, and the Frisian. It is a chapter in Palæontology. Yet, since the present English tongue is in its essential elements derived from the Anglo-Saxon, and since the existence of an Anglo-Saxon literature probably stimulated our earliest English writers to persist in the use of the vernacular, when interest, fashion, and the torrent of literary example would have led them to adopt the Norman French, it seems desirable to commence with a brief sketch of that literature.

2. We know of no Anglo-Saxon composition, produced in England, that can be traced back with certainty to the times of Paganism. We must not look to the dwellers on the muddy Elbe, or the inhabitants of the plains of Holstein, for the teem-

B

ing imagination which characterized the Northmen of Iceland and Scandinavia, and which—ages before the stirring stimulus of Christianity was applied to them—produced the wonderful mythology of the Edda. In 596, St. Augustine, sent by Gregory the Great, brought the faith to the Anglo-Saxon tribes; and the moral ferment which the introduction of this new spiritual element occasioned, acting upon a towardly and capable race, full of dormant power and energy of every kind, induced also such intellectual exertion as the times permitted, and as the partial communication by the missionaries of the literature of the ancient world tended to enkindle and to sustain. The Angles of Northumbria received Christianity, not from Rome, but from Iona, the island-monastery of the Culdees, or 'servants of God,' founded by Columba, an Irish saint, in 565. Aidan, a monk of Iona, having come into Northumbria about the year 635, at the invitation of the pious king Oswald, converted great numbers of the Angles, and fixed his episcopal see at Lindisfarne or Holy Isle.[1] From this period until the Norman Conquest (and in one memorable instance beyond it), the Anglo-Saxon mind was ever labouring, so far as intestine war and Danish inroad would allow, and executed a very creditable amount of work. Its chief successes, it is true, were obtained through the medium of the Latin, which was then and long after the common language of Europe, and which a generous and expansive mind, sick of irrational or semi-rational local usages, and material isolation, would rejoice to employ.

3. The Venerable Bede (673–735), in whom the Saxon intellect culminated, wrote all his extant works in Latin. Incomparably the most valuable of these is his *Historia Ecclesiastica Gentis Anglorum*, which gives us professedly a connected history of the Church and religion of England down to his own times, and incidentally throws a flood of light upon the secular history also. Among his other works may be named, *De Ratione Temporum*, a *Martyrology*, the *Life of St. Cuthbert*, a poem in leonine verse on St. Justin's martyrdom, *Commentaries* both on the Old and on the New Testament, and a sort of chronicle of universal history called *De Sex Ætatibus Sæculi*. Alcuin, Eddi Stephanus, and Ethelwerd also wrote in Latin. But the rough vernacular was employed in popular poetry, and in all such prose writings as had a didactic purpose which included the laity within its scope. Such writings were naturally for the most part translations, since it was evidently safer and wiser to gain an insight into, and acquaintance with, the wisdom of

---

[1] Bede, *Eccl. Hist.* book iii. ch. 5.

antiquity, before essaying, under less favourable conditions, to make conquests in the realm of original thought.

4. I. Poetry.—Of Anglo-Saxon poetry there remains to us on the whole a considerable mass. By far the larger portion of it dates, both in original conception and in extant form, from a period subsequent to the introduction of Christianity. One poem, of 143 lines, *The Gleeman's Song*, bears on the face of it that the writer lived in the time of Attila, in the early part of the fifth century; nor does there seem any sufficient reason to doubt that such was the fact. Another, *Beowulf*, the longest and most important of all, though in its present form manifestly the composition of a Christian writer, points to, and proves the existence of, earlier Sagas and songs, containing the substance of the narrative, which must have been produced in pre-Christian times. In others, again, as *Andreas*, *Elene*, and *Judith*, although the narrative itself deals with a Christian subject-matter, the zeal of Grimm in the investigation of the old Teutonic world has elicited numerous traces of heathen customs and modes of thought, which to us, and to all Teutonic races, possess the deepest historical interest. The last and least interesting class consists of metrical translations from the Psalms, and other parts of the Bible, the only value of which lies in any additional illustration which they may bring to the study of the language.

5. The earliest in date of all the Anglo-Saxon poems appears to be *The Gleeman's Song*. It forms a part of the well-known Exeter MS., given to the cathedral of that city by Bishop Leofric in the time of Edward the Confessor.[1] In this poem (printed by Mr. Kemble, together with *Beowulf*, in 1833, by Dr. Guest in his *History of English Rhythms*, and by Mr. Thorpe, along with *Beowulf*, in 1855), we undoubtedly possess, to pass over the mere mention of the name of the Angli by Tacitus,[2] the earliest existing notices of the country, government, and political relations of our Angle progenitors. When the Gleeman has to speak of 'Ongle,' the land of the 'Engle,' he tells us that it was ruled over by a king named Offa; that this king, with the help of the Myrgings (apparently a tribe bearing kindred to the Angles,—the poet himself was a Myrging, see l. 87), enlarged his borders after the battle of Fifel-dór (a name for the Eider —literally 'gate of terror'); and that the Engle and Swæfe (Suevi) held their respective lands thenceforward, as Offa appointed to them. The Angles, at the date of the poem, still

---

[1] The Codex Exoniensis was printed for the Society of Antiquaries in 1842, under the editorship of Mr. Thorpe.
[2] *Germania*, xl.

lived in Germany; the abode of the great Eormanric or Hermanric, King of the East Goths, was to be sought for 'eastan of Ongle;' it lay in and around 'Wistla-wudu,' the forest of the Vistula, where the Gothic warriors, with their hard swords, turned to bay in defence of their ancient seats against the hordes of Attila :[1]

> heardum sweordum
> Ymb Wistla-wudu wergan sceoldon
> Ealdne eðel-stol Ætlan leodum.

Again, the nations under the sway of the empire are designated by the singular name of Rum-walas—strangers of Rome,—and part of the dominions of the 'Cæser,' or emperor, is called Wala-ríce. Evidently we have here the Wälsch, Wälsch-land, Walloon, Welsh, of the Teutonic tribes; names by which they described the races, strange to themselves in blood and language, by which they were surrounded, and especially the inhabitants of Italy. But the Anglo-Saxon, after his conversion at the end of the seventh century, never again applied this name to the subjects of the Roman empire; Rome was then too near and dear a name to him to allow of his using any term importing estrangement with reference to her people. Here again, then, we have an evidence of the early date of the present poem. But it may be objected that the author speaks of 'heathens' (l. 73), and therefore may be presumed to have been a Christian; and if there were Angle Christians early in the fifth century, how came it that at the time of their transmigration to Britain, and for more than a century after, they are represented to us as purely Pagan? Many lines of thought and inquiry suggest themselves in reply, which cannot here be followed up. But it may be observed that Christianity admits of many degrees; that of the Peruvians, after the Spanish conquest, bore but a faint resemblance to that of the Jesuit converts in Paraguay; and the thin varnish of Arian Christianity thrown over the barbarism of Alaric and his Visigoths, shares the name, but not the influence or the durability, of the religious system which softened the manners and the hearts of Ethelbert and Edwin. Besides the East and West Goths, the Burgundians, and many other Teutonic

---

[1] It seems a difficulty at first sight to understand how Hermanric (see Gibbon, *Decline and Fall*, chs. xxv. and xxvi.) and Attila could be brought in conjunction as contemporaries of the same poet. But this was perfectly possible; Hermanric was assassinated in the year 375, and Attila, though not known in the Roman world till many years later, succeeded his uncle as ruler, jointly with his brother Blæda, of the Hunnish tribes, in 403. Now the whole tenor of the poem points to a long course of wanderings continued through mary years, so that the Gleeman, at diffcrent parts of his career, may easily have known both Hermanric and Attila.

races, professed Christianity in the fifth century; and there is nothing improbable in the conjecture that the Angles may have derived from their neighbourhood to the Goths of East Prussia the same kind of nominal Christianity which the latter possessed. This loose profession they may easily have lost, after their colonizing enterprise had established them firmly in Britain; nor would the circumstance that the Britons were Christians have tended at all to attach them to Christianity, but rather the contrary. For, besides the proverbial 'odisse quem læseris,' no fact is more certain than that the Angles thoroughly despised the Celts whom they dislodged; and as the latter carefully refrained from imparting to their conquerors that faith, without which they believed them to be under the sentence of eternal perdition, so the former must have been disposed to involve the religion of the Britons in the same sweeping contempt which they entertained for themselves.

6. The essential charm of the Anglo-Saxon, as of the Icelandic poetry—though it appertains to the former in a lower degree—is in the glimpses which it gives us into the old Teutonic world, when Odin was still worshipped in the sacred wood, when the wolf, the eagle, and the raven were held in reverence as noble and fearless creatures, bringers of good luck, and specially dear to the gods; and when the battle and the banquet were the only forms of life in which the hero could or cared to shine. In this *Gleeman's Song*, though in the main a mere catalogue of the nations and persons visited by the writer, traces of this primitive state of things may be gathered. From the following lines it would seem that the Goths knew not as yet how to coin money :—

> And ic wæs mid Eormanrice ealle þrage;
> Þær me Gotena cyning gode dohte,
> Se me beag forgeaf, burg-warena fruma.
> On þam siex hund wæs smætes goldes
> Gescyred sceatta, scilling-rime.
> Þone ic Eadgilse on æht sealde
> Minum hleo-drihtne, þa ic to ham bicwom,
> Leofum to leane; þæs þe he me lond forgeaf,
> Mines fæder eðel, frea Myrginga.[1]

> * And I was with Eormanric a whole season;
> There the King of the Goths endowed me with good things:
> He—chief of the burgh-dwellers—gave me a ring; *
> For it were cut off six hundred shots [*i.e.* pieces]

---

[1] The ring of metal, large or small, was a customary form of present among the Germans. Tacitus (*Germ.* xv.) mentions 'torques' among the gifts which they delighted to receive from neighbouring nations.

7. But the features of the antique world are more distinctly and variously exhibited to us in the poem of *Beowulf.* Unfortunately the single manuscript on which we are dependent for the text was injured in the fire at the Cotton Library in 1731, and a not inconsiderable number of lines remain from this cause more or less unintelligible. The MS. was first edited, in 1815, by Thorkelin, keeper of the Royal Archives at Copenhagen. In 1833 the text with annotations, and in 1837 a translation with a learned introduction, were produced by J. M. Kemble, under the auspices of the English Historical Society. The poem has been studied most attentively by German scholars, as Grimm, Ettmüller, Leo, and others, for the sake of the light which it throws upon the origins of the Teutonic race. Many different theories have been advanced respecting its age and import of which I have elsewhere given an account.[1] After explaining what the poem is about, I shall briefly state my own view of its origin.

8. The main actions of the poem are three : first, the fight of the hero, Beowulf, with the fiendish monster, Grendel, who had long infested the approaches to Heorot,[2] the palace of Hrothgar, king of Denmark, and killed many noble Danes; secondly, the fight of the same hero with Grendel's mother, whom he kills; thirdly, the deadly conflict between Beowulf, now an old man, and king both of Denmark and Gautland, and a huge dragon, keeper of a large treasure-hoard by the seashore. Beowulf, who was a prince of the Geatas (the people of Gautland or Gotland in the south of Sweden), came by sea to the aid of Hrothgar, attacked Grendel, and after a tremendous struggle, compelled him to flee, leaving one of his arms torn off in Beowulf's hands, to his home at the bottom of a pool, where he soon afterwards died. His mother, to revenge his defeat, visited Heorot by night, and carried off Æschere, Hrothgar's favourite thane. Beowulf goes in pursuit, traces the creature to her watery abode, goes down into the pool, and after a hard

> Of beaten gold, reckoning by shillings.*
> That ring I delivered into the possession of Eadgils
> My sheltering lord lit. 'lee-lord ', when I came home,
> As a gift to the dear one ; for which he gave me land,
> The native place of my father—be, Lord of the Myrgings.

   * The 'sceat' (a word that still survives in the phrase 'scot and lot ') seems to have been equivalent to the smaller penny, twelve of which went to the 'scilling.' 600 sceatta then were equal to 50 scillingas.

---

   [1] See the Introduction to the author's, *Beowulf, a Heroic Poem of the English Century*; Longmans, 1876.
   [2] The name of Heorot is thought to be preserved in Hjorthelm, a village of Zealand, not far from Copenhagen.

fight despatches her. Returning to his own land, he succeeds after a while to the kingdom, and reigns for many years in all prosperity. In his old age, hearing of the ravages of a fiery dragon on the sea-board of his kingdom, he undertakes the perilous adventure, shunned by all but himself, of attacking and destroying him. He succeeds, but receives in the struggle a mortal wound. The plundering of the dragon-hoard, the burning of Beowulf's body on a funeral pile by the seashore, and the raising of a large beacon-mound over his ashes, 'easy to behold by the sailors over the waves,' are the concluding events of the poem.

9. The following view of the origin and relations of the poem is briefly summarized from the Introduction to the edition above cited. The date of composition was the early part of the eighth century. This conclusion arises from a number of converging considerations,—such as, 1. the language, which in its general cast, and also in certain peculiar terms and expressions, closely resembles that of *Guðlac, Andreas,* and *Elene,* poems which must be unquestionably referred to that century; 2. certain historical allusions contained in the work. The most important of these refers to the expedition, mentioned several times in *Beowulf,* of Hygelac king of the Geatas to Friesland, where he was slain by the Franks. This expedition has been satisfactorily identified with a marauding raid, described by the chronicler Gregory of Tours under the year 511, in which a king 'Chocilaicus' (Frankish-Latin for Hygelac) met his death in Friesland under precisely similar circumstances. The poem itself contains incidents which are supposed to happen some sixty years after this expedition, and has expressions which indicate that after the latest of those incidents the writer conceived of a long period of time intervening between it and his own day. These facts completely demolish a theory which has been often advanced, that *Beowulf* was written in Anglen or Holstein before the Angles and Saxons had migrated to Britain in the fifth century. The poem contains another allusion helping to determine its date, in the words of the Geat, who, after mentioning Hygelac's raid, adds (l. 2921), 'To us never after that was granted the favour of the Merovingians.' The Merovingian dynasty among the Franks became extinct in 752; and since the poem contains no mention whatever of the great family which succeeded it, the Carolingians or Karlings, it may be reasonably inferred that it was written before that date. Dr. Grein of Marburg, who by his *Bibliothek der Angelsächsischen Poesie,* and admirable *Glossar,* or Dictionary, accompanying it, has laid all students of old Teutonic literature under an in-

estimable obligation,—and also Ludwig Ettmüller of Zurich, agree with the general result embodied in the above view, namely that *Beowulf* must be placed in the eighth century.

10. With regard to the authorship, it must be premised that in the judgment of the best critics the poem—apart from two or three passages, not necessary to the connection of the story, which may be the interpolations of a later age—forms one whole, composed about the same time, and by one author. That author was undoubtedly a Christian. If the conclusion above given as to the date of the poem be sound, the re-flection at once arises that the early part of the eighth century was a period of great literary activity for the West Saxons (in whose language the work is written), as is proved by the writings of St. Aldhelm, and the letters of St. Boniface and others. It was also an age in which West Saxon missionaries, led by SS. Wilfrid and Willibrord, were actively engaged in spreading the light of Christianity among the still Pagan nations of their own blood living to the eastward—the Frisians, Old Saxons, and Danes. Alcuin, in his *Vita S. Willibrordi*, mentions that thirty young Danes were placed in the missionary's hands, in 695, and sent to be educated in Friesland. By means of some communication of this kind, it is conjectured that the legends and traditions of Scandinavia may have become known to a West-Saxon priest or clerk of a poetic turn, and by him worked up into the poem before us.

11. Another theory—that of Mr. Thorpe—is to this effect : that we have here no original Anglo-Saxon poem in any sense, but only a metrical paraphrase of an old Swedish poem of un-certain date, composed in England under the Danish dynasty, between the years 1010 and 1050, by some one who was of Danish parentage, but a native of England. Yet why any one should take so much trouble to make a translation which would be unintelligible to his Danish, and uninteresting to his English countrymen, it is not easy to understand.

12. *Cædmon's Paraphrase.*—The unique MS. containing this poem belonged to Archbishop Usher, and is now in the Bodleian library. No author's name is to be found in the MS. itself; but Francis Junius, who published the first edition of the poem in 1655, observing the remarkable general agree-ment of its contents with the summary given by Beda [1] of the substance of the religious poetry written by Cædmon, the lay brother of Whitby, who flourished about 680 A.D., assumed the identity of the two works. Later critics have generally held

---

[1] *Hist. Eccl.* vi. 24.

the contrary opinion.   Hickes led the way, by maintaining that
the language of the work published by Junius was full of
Dano-Saxon peculiarities, and therefore could not be referred to
so early a date as the seventh century.   But he did not succeed
in establishing the fact of these peculiarities ; and even if they
existed, there is no reason why they should not be laid to the
charge of some later transcriber, rather than of the author.
Rask, however, the learned Dane to whom Anglo-Saxon
scholars owe so much, was decidedly of opinion that the work
was not written by Beda's Cædmon ; he always speaks of its
author as the 'pseudo-Cædmon.'   This also seems to be the
general opinion in Germany.   On the other hand, Thorpe[1] and
Guest[2] are disposed to uphold the correctness of the designation
assigned by Junius.

13. If there were no means of trying the question, other
than a comparison of Junius's poem with the meagre description
of Cædmon given by Beda will furnish, I do not see why we
should not hold with considerable confidence the opinion that
the two are identical.   But the reader shall judge for himself.
Beda writes of Cædmon thus :—' He sang of the creation of
the world and the origin of the human race, and the whole
history as found in Genesis, concerning the going forth of Israel
out of Egypt, and their entrance into the land of promise ; of
very many other narratives in Holy Scripture, of the Incarnation of our Lord, his Passion, Resurrection, and Ascension
into heaven ; of the descent of the Holy Ghost, and the teaching
of the Apostles.   He also composed many verses concerning
the terror of the judgment to come, and the fearfulness of the
punishments of hell, and the sweetness of the heavenly kingdom ; besides a great many others on the loving-kindnesses and
judgments of God ; and in all his compositions he strove to
wean men from the love of vice, and stimulate them to the love
and right understanding of virtue.'

14. The following rough notes of the contents of the ' Paraphrase,' as printed by Mr. Thorpe, were made without any
reference to the passage in Beda :—

15. ' Book I.—The Creation ; Revolt of the Angels ; they
are hurled into hell ; the Fall ; Expulsion from Eden (pp. 1–59).
From Cain and Abel to the Flood (pp. 59–93).   From the
Flood to the destruction of Sodom and Gomorrah, and thence
regularly on to the Sacrifice of Isaac (pp. 94–177).   Here is a
break ; Canto xlii. makes a fresh start on the subject of

---

[1] Thorpe's *Cædmon*, Edited for the Society of Antiquaries, 1832.
[2] *History of English Rhythms*, ii. 24.

" Moyses dómas," the Statutes of Moses; but the story of Moses
is told very concisely down to the passage of the Red Sea, on
which the writer descants lengthily. The passage from page
200 to page 206 reads like an interpolation of later date; it
goes back again to Noah and Abraham's sacrifice. At page 207
the narrative of the passage of the Red Sea resumes, and continues to page 216. The remainder of the first book (pp. 216—
263) is a paraphrase of parts of the Book of Daniel; the
Three Children in the Fiery Furnace; their Song; Daniel's
Dream-wisdom; Belshazzar.

16. ' Book II.—The complaints of the fallen angels and
other inhabitants of hell; the descent of Christ; his intercourse with the twelve before the Ascension; his Ascension;
description of the Last Judgment. (pp. 264–313.) '

17. From this analysis it is manifest that the contents of the
MS. printed by Junius and Thorpe correspond very well as far
as they go, allowing for gaps and omissions, with Beda's description of the writings of Cædmon. There is, however, one other
piece of evidence producible, which bears, though perhaps with
no great force, the other way. Beda professes to give the substance, in Latin, of the opening of Cædmon's poem. After
speaking of the manner in which the verses were, so to speak,
given to him, he continues, ' quorum iste est sensus :—Nunc
laudare debemus auctorem regni cœlestis, potentiam Creatoris,
et consilium illius, facta patris gloriæ. Quomodo ille, cum sit
eternus Deus, omnium miraculorum auctor extitit; qui primo
filiis hominum cœlum pro culmine tecti, dehinc terram custos
humani generis omnipotens creavit. Hic est sensus,' he continues, ' non autem *ordo ipse verborum*, quæ dormiens ille
canebat; neque enim possunt carmina, quamvis optime compo-
sita, ex alia in aliam linguam, ad verbum, sine detrimento sui
decoris ac dignitatis, transferri.' In King Alfred's translation
of Beda, a metrical rendering of the above Latin version of
Cædmon's opening is given, introduced by the words, para ende-
byrdnes is þis, 'their order is this.' At the close of his version,
Alfred, who, though he omits much, generally adheres closely
to his original in the parts which he translates, forbears to
translate the passage from ' Hic est sensus ' to ' transferri.'
This he would naturally do, if the lines which he had just
written down were really known by him to have been taken
from the actual work of Cædmon; for in that case he *had*
given the ' ordo ipse verborum '; and it would seem absurd to
insert in his translation words importing the exact contrary.
But if the lines inserted were, as some suppose, his own composition—not the *ipsissima verba* of Cædmon at all, but a more

metrical rendering of Beda's Latin—would he not have felt
himself bound to append to them, though not the exact expressions of Beda, yet some analogous explanatory or justificatory
statement ?　Again, the substitution of ' their order is this,' as
introductory words, instead of ' their meaning is this' (quorum
iste est sensus), taken in connection with Beda's disclaimer of
having given the ' ordo ipse,' certainly agrees better with the
supposition that Alfred was quoting the very words of Cædmon,
and knew it, than with any other.　And yet, if we adopt this
conclusion, how can we any longer identify Cædmon with the
Paraphrast ?　For the version of the opening of the poem, as
given by Alfred, stands very far apart from that in the Paraphrase, though with a general agreement in tenor.　The following is a literal translation of Alfred's version :—

'Now must we praise the warden of the heavenly kingdom, the might of the Creator, and his purpose, the work of the
Father of glory ; how he, the eternal Lord, established the
beginning of each one of his marvels.　He first, the holy Creator,
framed for the children of earth heaven to be their roof ; then
afterwards he, the eternal Lord, the King almighty, guardian of
mankind, formed the earth, a home for men.'

18.　On the other hand the opening of the Paraphrase runs
as follows :—

' For us it is very right that we praise with our words,
love in our souls, the warden of the heavens, the glorious king
of hosts ; he is of powers the essence, head of all high creations,
the Ruler Almighty.　There was never for him first beginning,
nor cometh now end for the eternal Lord ; but he is in his
kingdom above heaven-thrones, in high majesty, sooth-fast and
very firm.'

19.　To this it may be added, that in a very ancient and
valuable MS. of the *Historia Ecclesiastica*, written in the eighth
century, preserved in the University library at Cambridge,
something like positive evidence to the genuineness of Alfred's
version is on record.　At the end of the history, on the back of
the last leaf of the MS., occur, without any preface, some Anglo-
Saxon lines, written in an eighth-century hand.　They commence, ' Nu scylun hergean hefaen-ricaes ward,' and end,
' firum foldu frea allmaectig.'　Then come the words, ' Primo
cantavit Cædmon istud carmen ' (Cædmon first sang this song,
or poem).　On comparing the lines with Alfred's version of the
opening of Cædmon, we find that they exactly agree with it, the
only difference being that this is in the Northumbrian, Alfred's
in the West-Saxon dialect.　It certainly looks as if the writer
of these lines had Cædmon's poem before him, or was setting them

down from memory. But it is very unfortunate that he stops just where Beda stops; one more line of Anglo-Saxon, followed by the Latin note quoted above, would have left it out of doubt that we were reading Cædmon's own words. As it is, there is just the possibility that this writer, and Alfred also, were only translating from Beda; but I think that the probability lies the other way.

20. *Andreas* and *Elene* constitute the principal portion of the poetry of the Codex Vercellensis, a manuscript discovered by Blume in the library at Vercelli, in the year 1836, printed in the appendix to the report of the Record Commission in 1837, published with an excellent introduction and notes by Jacob Grimm, at Cassel, in 1840, and edited by J. M. Kemble, for the Ælfric Society, in 1853. The two poems are, though in the same handwriting, quite unconnected with one another. *Andreas*, containing 1722 lines, is a narrative of some of the remarkable adventures of the apostle St. Andrew, in aid of the evangelist St. Matthew, who had fallen into the hands of a tribe of idolatrous cannibals in the land of Mermedonia. The *Codex Apocryphus Novi Testamenti*, published by Fabricius, contains a brief abstract of this legend; but a Greek MS. at Paris, entitled Πράξεις 'Ανδρέου καὶ Ματθαίου, furnishes a narrative approaching very closely to that of the Anglo-Saxon poem.

21. The chief incidents of the poem are as follows. St. Andrew, while preaching in Achaia, is warned by a voice from heaven to go to the aid of his fellow-labourer and friend St. Matthew, who was in Mermedonia, and in great danger. He comes down to the shore, and embarks in a boat in which the Deity himself and two angels are the rowers. A storm arises, and gives occasion to much edifying talk between the boatmen and the passengers. Andrew and his friends fall asleep, and next morning find themselves lying on the beach in Mermedonia. Unseen, Andrew walks up to the castle where the prisoner is confined; the seven guards before the prison-door fall down dead; the door flies open; the friends embrace. St. Matthew and his fellow-prisoners depart immediately; Andrew returns to the city. About this time the Mermedonians send for a fat prisoner to the jail, and their disappointment upon discovering that the birds have flown is inconsolable. But a breakfast must be had, so they at length resolve upon casting lots amongst themselves, to determine who shall be sacrificed to the appetites of the rest. The lot falls on a young man; but, at the prayer of Andrew, all weapons lifted against him become like wax. The devil now appears, and reveals the presence of the saint; Andrew is seized, and dragged all day over the hard roads and rocks,—

drogon deormode æfter dunscræfum,
ymb stanhleoðo stearcedferhðe,
efne swa wide swa wegas to lagon,
enta ærgeweorc innan burgum,
stræte stanfage. storm upp aras
æfter ceasterhofum, cirm unlytel
hæðnes heriges.[1]

This lingering martyrdom is renewed during several days, the saint being healed of his wounds each night, and strengthened to endurance by his Almighty protector. At length, after various astounding miracles, the persecutors are all overawed into baptism, and the saint, after appointing a pious bishop over them, named Plato, commits them to the grace of God, and departs, to their infinite sorrow, for his own country.

22. The subject of *Elene*, that is, Helena, the mother of the Emperor Constantine, is the finding of the true cross at Jerusalem. The well-known story is adhered to pretty closely in its main features, though with much amplification in details. The discovery of the holy nails used in the Crucifixion receives especial prominence; indeed, it almost throws the Invention of the Cross into the shade. The poem contains 1,321 lines.

23. Both stories, then, in substance and in details, are taken from church tradition; yet the spirit of the time and the people is manifest, perhaps, in the very choice of the subjects, especially in that of *Elene*. A Teuton loved before all things to hear of war and fighting; now Constantine in the story only embraces Christianity because it has brought him victory in war; nor is the cross on the sacred Labarum sufficient for him—out of the holy nails must be fashioned a bit for his bridle, which victory ever waits upon. In *Andreas* there is indeed no fighting; but there is a striking picture of a solemn Volks-thing, or national assembly; and in the account of the divine ferryman, we cannot but trace the sagas about the Saxon Woden, according to which he was wont, in the disguise of a ferryman, to transport and deliver men from danger. The patient, almost monotonous, endurance of the saint, is indeed a purely Christian feature; but when we find him with all the wounds and bruises of the day miraculously healed before the morning, we are reminded of the fact that the sagas attribute the same marvel to the 'Hiadningar,' the ancient heroes of the north, though indeed with this difference, that the latter have fought valiantly, and not got more hard blows than they have given.

[1] 'They dragged the beloved one among the mountain dens, the strong-souled round the rocky summits, even as wide as ways lay, the old work of giants within the burgh, in the street paved with stones of many colours. A storm arose at the castle court, no small clamour of the heathen host.'

24. With regard to the authorship of these poems, Jacob Grimm (from whose excellent introduction my account of them is mainly taken) enters into an interesting speculation. The name of the author of *Elene* is given in *runic* letters at the close of the poem—it is Cynewulf. But who was Cynewulf? and who wrote *Andreas*? Grimm now proceeds to weave a pretty theory. Towards the end of *Andreas* occur the lines (l. 1487),—

> Hwæðre ȝit sceolon
> lytlum sticcum leoð worda dæl
> furður reccan.[1]

The 'git,' ye two, refers, he thinks, to a king and queen. These were, he conjectures, Ina, king of Wessex (688–725), and Ethelburga, his queen; if so, the poet was probably Bishop Aldhelm, Ina's friend and counsellor, who is known to have written Saxon poems, though they were supposed to be lost, and who, as educated under Archbishop Theodore in the school of Canterbury, might easily have become acquainted with the Greek legend embodied in *Andreas*. Cynewulf was perhaps a disciple of Aldhelm. *Crist*, a long poem on the threefold coming of Christ, and *Juliana*, which is the legend of the martyrdom of the saint of that name, derived from her Acts,[2] are also proved, by runes inserted in the body of each poem, to have been written by Cynewulf. All four poems seem to point to a time when only some hundred years, or less, had elapsed since the nation renounced the faith of its forefathers, so that it still retained many vestiges of its wild heathen past.

25. *Judith*, a fragment of which only has come down to us, found in the same unique MS. volume which contains *Beowulf*, is not inaptly described by Mr. Turner[3] as an Anglo-Saxon romance, since, like many of the romances of a later age, while the outline of the story is taken from Jewish history, the tone, the descriptions, and many of the incidents, present the broadest local colouring, and breathe the full Teutonic spirit. The opening of the poem, down to the middle of the ninth section, is lost. The exact date is unascertainable, but Grimm seems to treat it as belonging to the great literary age of Wessex, the eighth century.

26. Several remarkable poems are preserved to us in the *Anglo-Saxon Chronicle*, presently to be described. The chief of these are, the Brunanburgh War-song, and the Elegy on King

---

[1] 'Yet must ye two, in little pieces, further con over a portion of my verses.'
[2] Printed in the *Acta Sanctorum*, February 16.
[3] Turner's *Anglo-Saxons*, iii. 302.

Edgar, given under the years 938 and 975 respectively. The first—the 'Waterloo ode' of the ninth century—is a triumphal chant occasioned by the great victory won by Athelstan, over the Danes from Ireland under Anlaf, and the Scots under their king Constantine, at Brunanburgh.[1] Never, says the Gleeman, since the Angles and Saxons came hither from the eastward, had they gained a bloodier victory :—

> Ne wearð wæl mare
> On ðise iȝlande æfer ȝyta
> folces ȝefylled beforan þissum,
> sweordes ecȝum, þæs þe us secȝað bec
> ealde uðwitan, siððan eastan hider
> Enȝle and Seaxe up becomon
> ofer brymum brad Brytene sohton
> wlance wiȝ-smiðas Wealas ofer-comon
> eorlas arhwate eard beȝeaton.

'Nor was there ever yet a greater slaughter of people brought about in this island before this with the edge of the sword, according to that which old sages tell us by book, since Angles and Saxons came up hither from the east, sought Britain over the broad main, as proud artificers of war overcame the alien race [Welsh], got possession—the earls keen after glory!—of the land.'

27. The Elegy on King Edgar belongs to the waning period of Anglo-Saxon poetry. Some of the homely, vivid metaphors of the old gleemen are still retained ; the sea is still 'the gannet's bath,' 'the home of the whale,' and so on ; but the fire and the swift movement are gone. It is short, and yet diffuse—meagre, but obscure.

28. II. The extant prose writings, though numerous, are, with one exception, valuable not so much for any literary merits as for the light which they throw on the labours of the historian and the antiquary. There exists in the public Record-offices an immense body of documents—charters, conveyances, declarations,

---

[1] There should be little hesitation in identifying Brunanburgh with Brom-borrow, a place on the Mersey in the Wirral of Cheshire. Various allusions in the song establish : 1. That the field of battle was close to the water side, so that the routed Danes immediately took to their ships. 2. That the place of refuge which they sought was *Dublin*. Both these conditions suit Brom-borrow exactly, but ill agree with the supposition, either of Camden, that Broomridge in Northumberland, or of Ingram, that 'Bromby in Lincolnshire, was the scene of the contest ; since each of those places is some miles distant from the sea or a navigable river, and one would hardly expect to find Ireland mentioned as the place of refuge for a Danish fleet defeated on the eastern coast. Florence of Worcester, and later writers copying from him, do indeed locate the battle on or near the Humber, but the earlier authorities, the Chronicle and Ethelwerd, say nothing to warrant him in so doing.

laws, edicts, &c.—many of which have been arranged and translated by the labours of Thorpe and Kemble, and have greatly
contributed to deepen our knowledge of the way of life of our
forefathers.   All the more valuable Anglo-Saxon charters, to
the number of many hundreds, were published by Mr. Kemble
in his invaluable *Codex Diplomaticus*.   But such documents are
of course not literature, and therefore need not be here considered.   Another large portion of the extant works consists of
translations, many of which proceed from the pen of Alfred
himself, who has explained his own motives for undertaking the
work.   The views of an 'Educational Reformer' in the ninth
century are worthy of our careful attention.   His object is, he
says, 'the translation of useful books into the language which
we all understand; so that all the youth of England, but more
especially those who are of gentle kind and at ease in their
circumstances, may be grounded in letters,—for they cannot
profit in any pursuit until they are well able to read English.'
With these views Alfred translated the work of Pope Gregory,
De Curâ Pastorali, the epitome of universal history by Orosius,
the work of Boethius *De Consolatione Philosophiæ*, and the
Ecclesiastical History of Bede.

29. But by far the most important prose work that has
come down to us is the *Saxon Chronicle*, which gives a connected history of Britain, in the form of annals, from the
Christian era to the year 1154.   The oldest MS. in existence
dates from about the year 891, and is thought, with much
probability, to have been partly composed, partly transcribed
from earlier annals, by or under the direction of Archbishop
Plegmund.   From this time the Chronicle seems to have been
continued under succeeding Archbishops of Canterbury to the
time of the Conquest, when the task was transferred, under
what circumstances we do not know, to the monks of Peterborough.

It seems possible to trace two principal hands in the
composition of the *Chronicle* prior to the time of Plegmund—
one that of a Northumbrian, the other of a West-Saxon writer.
The traces of the Northumbrian hand are most evident,
especially in the earlier portion; *e.g.* under the year 449 occurs
the passage, 'From this Woden sprang all *our* royal kindred,
and that of the South-Humbrians also.'   Other indications
occur under the years 697 and 702; and the comparative fulness with which Northumbrian affairs are recorded, as contrasted with all the other Anglo-Saxon kingdoms except Wessex, points to the same conclusion.   The Northumbrian work
was very likely performed at Lindisfarne; at any rate, soon

after the touching notice of the destruction of the monastery
in the year 793, this writer disappears, and Northumbrian
history sinks back into a cloud of impenetrable darkness. Of
the MSS. which contain these Northumbrian annals, the
Laudian MS. in the Bodleian Library (the E of Mr. Earle's late
edition) is the most important and complete. Mr. Earle has
shown cause for supposing that this MS. was compiled at the
monastery of Peterborough, in or soon after the year 1116.
The other great MS., known as the Benet MS. (the A of Mr.
Earle), represents almost exclusively the historic view and
literary interest of the South and West of England; thus,
while the history of Alfred, on which the Laud MS. is almost
silent, is minutely and lengthily told in the Benet, hundreds of
notices of Northumbrian affairs which are found in the former
are entirely omitted in the latter. The analysis of all the
leading MSS. of the *Chronicle* has been ably made by Mr.
Earle;[1] but it is singular that he should have overlooked the
significant entry in the Laud MS. under the year 449 above
noticed: since that entry demonstrates, not merely that a
Worcester scribe obtained Northumbrian information, which is
Mr. Earle's theory (Introduction, p. xl.), but that part of the
Chronicle itself comes from a Northumbrian hand.

30. Considered as a whole, the literature of the Anglo-
Saxons conveys the impression that they were a prosaic and
practical race, solid but slow thinkers, without much imagination
or mental fire. What they might have made of it, had they
been allowed to develop their literature uninterruptedly, it is,
of course, impossible to say. But it seems reasonable to suppose
that, for ulterior ends of higher good, it was ordered that the
Saxon commonwealth should not repose in unmolested prosperity. A vein of sluggishness, of Bœotian enjoyment, of
coarse indulgence, with forgetfulness of the higher aims of life,
ran through the Saxon character. Their transference from the
sandy barrens and marshes of Holstein, from the peaty plains
and stunted forests of Hanover, to the rich soil and milder
climate of England, tended to develop this weak side—this
proneness to ease. In their old dwelling-place they were
at least stimulated by the necessity of contending with the un-
fruitfulness of nature and the encroachments of the sea; in
comparison with it, England must have been a terrestrial
paradise—a very land of Cockaigne. This tendency to relapse
into habits of indolence, which Sir Walter Scott has portrayed
in the character of Athelstan in *Ivanhoe*, extended to the

---

[1] *Two of the Saxon Chronicles parallel;* Oxford, 1865.

C

learned class, and to the churchmen no less than the laity.
The influence of such a man as Beda should have been enough
to inaugurate a long era of literary energy; yet William of
Malmesbury assures us that, with the exception of the brief
Saxon annals and the barbarous epitome of Ethelwerd, he had
not been able to discover any historical work composed by an
Anglo-Saxon upon the affairs of Britain, from the death of
Beda to his own time.   To form the future English character,
it was necessary that the harder and sterner elements which
belonged to the Scandinavian races, should be mingled and
gradually fused with the softer Germanic type.   The Danish
invasions and immigrations, which commenced in 787, and terminated with the establishment of the Danish dynasty in 1017,
effected this.   But in the process, the existing literary culture,
and nearly all the establishments which had been founded to
promote it, were swept away.   In a country reduced to the
dismal condition described by Bishop Lupus in a sermon
preached to his flock [1] about the year 1012, it was impossible
that men's thoughts should be efficaciously turned to any subjects save such as bore upon their personal security.   Canute,
indeed, after he had restored internal peace and order, showed
a desire to patronise literary men, and, by rebuilding the monasteries, to open asylums for learning.   But the glory and
greatness of his reign gave an impulse rather to the Scandinavian than to the Saxon genius.   No English poet sang of
his victories; that task was left to the *scalds*, whom he brought
with him from Denmark.   By this time large advances had
been made towards the amalgamation of the races.   Writing
of the year 1036, Malmesbury [2] says that the citizens of London,
'from long intercourse with these barbarians' (the Danes),
'had almost entirely adopted their customs.'   The Danes
adopted with facility the Anglo-Saxon tongue, though importing
into it many Danish words, and probably breaking down to a
great degree its grammatical structure.   The secular laws of
Canute, addressed to both races equally, are written in Anglo-
Saxon.   All that the cold North could supply, the English
nationality had now received.   The stubborn hardihood and
perseverance which were illustrated in the Drakes, the Cooks,
the Stephensons, of later days, were, by this large infusion of
Danish blood, made a part of the English nature.   The intellectual activity and literary culture of the South, together with
the great Roman tradition of political order and vigorous administration, were still wanting; and these were supplied by
means of the Norman Conquest.

[1] Turner, *Ang.-Sax.* Book vi. ch. xiv.
[2] Malmesbury, p. 205 (Bohn's series).

PRELIMINARY CHAPTER.

SECTION II.

THE NORMAN PERIOD.

10€6-1350.

1. In the age at which we are arrived, two classes of men only cultivated literature, the clergy and the minstrels. The local centres at which learning was to be obtained were of two kinds, the universities and the monasteries. Poetry and light literature were comparatively independent of such aids ; yet the form and development even of these could not but be largely dependent on the social and moral condition of the classes amongst which they were circulated. The intellectual achievements, therefore, of the clergy—both Saxon and Norman—the means of self-culture which they had at their disposal, and the degree of success with which they availed themselves of those means—the different classes of poets, their nationality, the traditional or other materials upon which they worked, and the furtherance or obstruction which they met with in the temper and habits of the time—all these matters must now be successively touched upon. What we have named the Norman period embraces more than two centuries and a half, and includes the long conflict between two opposing elements, which terminated, on the whole, in favour of what was English, yet so that the national language, literature, and prevailing opinions, were all deeply coloured by French words and French thoughts.

2. For many years after the Conquest the Saxon clergy were in no mood or condition to betake themselves to the tranquil pursuits of learning. Before that catastrophe, religious fervour and rigour of discipline had long been on the wane amongst them. We read of much laxity of manners, of bishops holding two or more sees at once, of priests so ignorant of Latin as to be unable to say mass without innumerable blunders. The Conqueror, who, with all his cruelty and pride, hated hypocrisy and empty profession with all his heart, would not tolerate these relaxed ecclesiastics, and by the nomination of Lanfranc (a native

of Italy, but for many years prior of Bec, in Normandy) to the
see of Canterbury, inaugurated a great reformation in Church
matters.   Some few of the Saxon bishops, as the noble St. Wul-
stan of Worcester, Agelric of Chichester, and one or two others,
were left in possession of their sees; the rest had to make way
for Normans.   Nor was this all.   Had the unworthy only been
deposed, and the worthy still allowed to look forward to advancement to be obtained through desert, the Saxon clergy might
still have held together, and with renewed strictness of life a
revival of learning might have taken place among them.   But
the repeated insurrections of the English exasperated the fiery
temper of the Conqueror; and after having quelled them, and
thus 'overturned the power of the laity, he made an ordinance
that no monk or clergyman of that nation should be suffered to
aspire to any dignity whatever.'[1]   Thus cut off from the hope of
due recognition for merit, the Saxon clergy were deprived of one
of the chief incentives to study.   One may be sure that from
that time the more ambitious among them would make haste to
learn French, and would rather disguise their nationality than
avow it.   Yet there was at least one monastery, in which a
literary work, begun in happier times two centuries before, was
carried on by Saxon monks, and in the Saxon tongue.   This
was the continuation of the *Saxon Chronicle*, composed in the
monastery of Peterborough.   It ends abruptly in the first year
of the reign of Henry II. (1154), the writer or writers being by
that time probably unable to resist any longer the universal
fashion of employing Latin for any serious prose work.   William
of Malmesbury, Henry of Huntingdon, Geoffrey of Monmouth,
Caradoc,—all these, and many others, were writing history at
this very time, and all, as a matter of course, wrote in Latin.
The Anglo-Saxon, too, being no longer taught in schools, nor
spoken in the higher circles of society, had lost very much of
its original harmony and precision of structure; and when the
annalist found himself using one inflection for another, or dropping inflections altogether, he may well have thought it high
time to exchange a tongue which seemed crumbling and disin-
tegrating under his hands, for one whose forms were fixed and
its grammar rational.   Little did the down-hearted monk anticipate the future glories, which, after a crisis of transformation
and fusion, would surround his rude ancestral tongue.

3. Yet literature and learning were not negligently or even
unsuccessfully prosecuted in England during this which we call
the Norman period; and this is a fact which we must learn to

---

[1] Malmesbury p. 287.

see in its true light, in order to understand aright the rise of
English literature in the fourteenth century. Again, the intellectual awakening which spread to England in the eleventh and
twelfth, and produced valuable literary results there in the
thirteenth century, cannot be understood except in connection
with the general European movement of mind which ensued
upon the consolidation of society following the long troubled
night of the dark ages. Something must therefore be said about
the origin of that movement, about the course it took, and about
the great thinkers whose names are for ever associated with it.

4. Strange as it may seem, the revival of intellectual activity
at the end of the eleventh and in the twelfth century is clearly
traceable to the labours and the example of Mahometans.
Charlemagne, indeed, had made a noble effort in the ninth
century to systematize education, and to make literature and
science the permanent denizens of his empire, but the wars and
confusion of every kind which ensued upon the partition of that
empire among his sons extinguished the still feeble light. A
happier lot had befallen the powerful and populous kingdoms
founded by the successors of Mahomet. Indoctrinated with a
knowledge of the wonderful fertility and energy of the Greek
mind, as exemplified especially in Aristotle and Plato, by Syrian
Nestorians (whose forefathers, fleeing from persecution into
Persia after the council of Chalcedon, carried with them Syriac
versions of the chief works of the Greek philosophers, and
founded a school at Gondisapor, near Bagdad), Haroun-al-Ra-
schid (whose reign was contemporary with that of Charlemagne),
and Al Mamoun, his successor, saw and assisted in the commencement of a brilliant period of literary activity in the nations
of Arabian race, which lasted from the ninth to the fourteenth
century. Among the Arabian kingdoms none entered into this
movement with more earnestness and success than the Moorish
kingdoms in Spain.[1] We hear of the Universities of Cordova,
Seville, and Granada; and the immense number of Arabic
manuscripts on almost every subject contained at this day in
the library of the Escurial at Madrid attests the eagerness with
which the Moorish writers sought after knowledge, and the uni-
versality of their literary tastes. Of their poetry, and the effect
which it had on that of Christian Europe, we shall speak presently. Their proficiency in science is evidenced by the remarkable facts which William of Malmesbury relates of Gerbert,
afterwards Pope Sylvester II. After having put on the monastic
habit at Flory, in France, his thirst for knowledge led him to

---

[1] Sismondi's *Literature of the South of Europe.*

quit his cloister and betake himself to the Moorish community
in Spain, about the year 1000. At Seville, we are told, he
'satisfied his desires,' becoming an adept, not only in astrology
and magic, but also in the 'lawful sciences' of music and astronomy, arithmetic and geometry. 'These,' says Malmesbury,
'with great perseverance he revived in Gaul, where they had
for a long time been wholly obsolete.' Allowing for some exaggeration in this statement, since the studies of the Trivium
and Quadrivium,[1] among which the said lawful sciences were
included, had never been wholly discontinued in the West since
the fall of the Roman Empire, we may yet easily conceive that
Gerbert was the first who popularized in Gaul the use of the
Arabic numerals, without which arithmetic could never have
made any considerable progress; and that by importing the
astronomical instruments used by the Moors, together with a
knowledge of the mechanical principles on which they were constructed, he may have placed the study of astronomy on a new
footing. He became a public professor on his return into Gaul,
and had many eminent persons among his scholars.

5. Our next forward step transports us to the monastery of
Bec, in Normandy. There the abbots Herluin, Lanfranc, and
St. Anselm, formed a line of great teachers, whose lectures were
eagerly attended, both by laymen and ecclesiastics. Whether
the intellectual life of Bec was directly influenced by the writings
of the great Arabian thinkers, it is difficult to ascertain. Avi-
cenna, the physician and philosopher, died in 1037; therefore in
point of time, his expositions of the Aristotelian philosophy
might have become known to Lanfranc and Anselm. The
Organon, however, which was translated by Boethius and was
known to Bede and Alcuin, had never ceased to be used in the
schools, and the writings of St. Anselm do not, we believe, contain any proof that he was acquainted with any other of the
works of the Stagirite besides the Aristotelian logic. Still, it is
not only possible, but probable, that the reports brought by
Gerbert and others of the palmy state of literature among the
Moors, and of the zeal both of teachers and students in their universities, may have indirectly had a stimulating effect on the
studies of Bec.

6. St. Anselm, abbot of Bec after Lanfranc had been called
into England in 1070, is considered by many the founder of
the scholastic philosophy. At any rate, he seems to have been
the first to apply, on a large scale, philosophy and its formulæ

---

[1] The Trivium consisted of grammar, logic, and rhetoric; the Quadrivium
of arithmetic, geometry, music, and astronomy.

to the doctrines of religion. Yet, as he did not originate a method, and his writings do not form a systematic whole, it would seem that he cannot fairly be called the founder of scholasticism. What the true scholastic method was, and by whom originated, we shall presently see. St. Anselm merely handles, with great subtlety and dialectical skill, certain special subjects, such as the divine essence, the Trinity, original sin, &c., but does not treat of theology as one connected whole. For these doctrines he endeavours to find irrefragable intellectual proof, and to show that they must be as necessarily accepted on grounds of reason as on grounds of faith. Thus he defines his *Proslogium*, a treatise on the existence of God, to be 'faith seeking understanding' (fides quærens intellectum), and says that he has framed the work 'under the character of one endeavouring to lift up his mind to the contemplation of the Deity, *and seeking to understand what he believes.*' Yet we may be certain that St. Anselm himself, like all the saints, derived the certainty of his religious convictions through the will rather than through the reason; he believed and loved, therefore he knew. He, and those who were like-minded to him, could safely philosophize upon the doctrines of faith, because they already possessed, and firmly grasped, the conclusions to which their argumentation was to lead. But what if a thinker were to arise, who should follow the same path without the same preservative? What if a being of brilliant genius, of captivating eloquence, of immense ambition, should undertake to philosophize upon religion, without the safeguard of personal sanctity?

7. Such a being was the famous Abelard. This is not the place to enlarge upon his story, which in every subsequent age has attracted the regards alike of the poet and the philosopher.[1] Suffice it to say that he developed a great scheme, of what we should now call rationalism, through taking up St. Anselm's argumentative way of proving religious doctrine, without his spirit of docile submission to authority. He made faith and reason identical (charitas Dei per fidem *sive rationis donum* infusa), and his scholars demanded from him, he informs us,—evidently placing his own sentiments in their mouths,—not words but ideas, not bare dogmatic statements, but clear enunciations of their philosophical import. His lectures, at Paris, Melun, and Troyes, were attended by enthusiastic multitudes. Roused from its long intellectual slumber, the Western world, like a man whose limbs have been numbed by long inaction, delighted in the vigorous exercise of its mental powers for the

---

[1] It has been handled by Bayle, Cousin, Pope, Cawthorn, &c.

mere exercise's sake; or else was eager to try their edge upon
whatever subject came in their way. Hence, on the one hand,
the endless logical combats, the twistings and turnings of the
syllogism in every shape, the invention of innumerable sophisms
and solutions of sophisms; on the other hand, that undue
extension of rational methods to objects of faith which we have
ascribed to Abelard. The danger was great; already Abelard's
definitions and explanations trembled on the verge of heresy, if
they did not go beyond it; but the ground-tone of his philosophy
was still more inconsistent with a traditional scheme of belief
than any particular expressions.

8. At this crisis St. Bernard appeared to check the growing
evil. He turned back the stream of philosophy, or rather he
forced it back within its own limits, and forbade it to encroach
upon a domain which did not belong to it. In answering
Abelard, he denied that Faith and Reason were identical, or
that the doctrines of faith could be discovered and proved
independently by any argumentative process. The objects of
faith, he said, are given to us from above; they are revealed
by God exactly because it is impossible that they should
be discovered by man. 'Quid magis contra rationem, quam
ratione rationem conari transcendere?' A conference between
the two, to be held at Soissons, was agreed to; but when the
time came for vindicating his philosophy, Abelard's heart failed
him, and he appealed to the Pope. He was on the whole
leniently treated; he seems to have had misgivings that he had
wandered into a wrong path; and his life of struggle and
suffering found its close in the peaceful seclusion of Cluny,
whose abbot, Peter the Venerable, generously sheltered and
protected his unhappy friend.

We must not suppose, however, that St. Bernard's influence as a thinker was mainly of a negative sort. On the
contrary, this last, and not least eloquent, of the Fathers,
scarcely ever employed his penetrating and versatile genius
except for some end of practical edification. Whether he
addresses his own monks at Clairvaux, or writes to Pope Euge-
nius, or kindles the crusading zeal of nations, or counsels the
Knights of the Temple, or composes Latin hymns, the evident
aim of his labours is always to enlighten, animate, and do good
to his neighbour. His Latin is admirable; far superior to that
of St. Anselm; and the charm of genius unites with the halo of
saintliness in giving attractiveness to his writings.

9. Scholasticism, then, made what we may call a false start
in the school of Bec; its true commencement dates a little
later, and from Paris. Peter Lombard, the Master of the

Sentences, hit upon the most convenient method of presenting theology under philosophical forms. The *data* of religion—the substance of revealed truth—be took from tradition; and reserved to philosophy the subordinate office of presenting it in a connected form, of deducing inferences, solving difficulties, and harmonizing apparent discrepancies. The *Book of Sentences*, which appeared in 1151, is a complete body of theology in four books. It commences with God—His being and attributes;— then treats of the Creation, first of angels, then of man; of the Fall, and original and actual sin. In the third book it treats of the remedy of the Fall, the Incarnation; of the theological virtues, and the gifts of the Holy Spirit. In the fourth, of the sacraments, purgatory, the resurrection, the last judgment, and the state of the blessed. All these doctrines are given in the form of 'sentences,' extracted from the writings of the Fathers. The sentences are interspersed with numerous 'quæstiones,' in which the author proposes and attempts to solve any difficulties that may arise. The conveniences of this plan are manifest, and it was at once adopted. Alexander Hales, Albertus Magnus, St. Bonaventure, and St. Thomas Aquinas, in the thirteenth century,—Duns Scotus, and William of Occam in the fourteenth,—whatever may be their differences, agree in treating theology as a whole, in seeking its *data* from authority, not from speculation, and in confining themselves to the discussion of special questions. Extraneous impulses were not wanting. The metaphysical and ethical works of Aristotle became known in the West about this period, chiefly through the commentaries of the celebrated Spanish Arab Averrhoes (1120–1198), and powerfully stimulated the speculative genius of the schoolmen. But the admiration of the Greek philosopher degenerated into an extravagance, and his authority was at last considered *infallible* in the schools. It was as if the age, in its horror of losing its way, would have a sheet anchor for the mind as well as for the soul, and chain the progressive intellect of man to the Aristotelian philosophy, because the unchanging interests of the soul demanded fixity and certainty in the eternal Gospel. So it ever is, that a true and valuable principle, once found, is sure to be strained in the application.

10. The scholastic method, having thus taken its rise in Paris, soon spread to England, and was prosecuted there with equal ardour. Some of the greatest of the schoolmen were British-born, although they reaped their highest honours, and spent the greater part of their lives, abroad. Alexander Hales, the Irrefragable, the master of St. Bonaventure, was the author of the first important commentary on the work of Peter Lombard,

and died at Paris in 1245. Duns Scotus, the subtle doctor whose birthplace, and even the date of whose death, are no certainly known, but who was, at any rate, a native of the British Isles, after lecturing at Paris with extraordinary success, is said to have died at Bologna in 1308. William o Occam, styled the Invincible, passed the greater part of his manhood at the court of the Emperor in Germany, and died there in the year 1347. In the great struggle then proceeding between imperial and papal claims, Occam sided with the Emperors. He was also in his day the head of the school o the Nominalists, a section of the schoolmen which maintained that our abstract ideas had no realities corresponding to them in external existence, but merely corresponded in thought to universal terms in language, that is to generalized expressions arrived at by the abstraction of differences.

Historians and Chroniclers.

11. The great intellectual movement which we have been describing expended its force chiefly on questions of theology and philosophy; but it also caused other subjects to be treated more intelligently and studied more earnestly. A great number of historians and chroniclers flourished in England during this period. All of these were ecclesiastics, most of them monks and all wrote in the Latin language. With the exception o Marianus Scotus, Ordericus Vitalis, and Ranulph Higden, they all confined themselves to recording the succession of events in their own country. There is no occasion to seek out motives and particular inducements impelling the learned of any country to historical composition. All men are eager to know the past to hear about the deeds of their forefathers; to take their bear ings, as it were, from the elevation to which history raises them and from a survey of the road along which their nation, or race or class, have come, deduce more trustworthy conclusions as to the unknown future which lies before them. If, however, in regard to the principal writers, any special reasons must be given, it might be mentioned that William of Malmesbury, and his con temporary, Henry of Huntingdon, took as their literary model the Venerable Bede, the father of modern history in the West that Richard the Canon records with natural complacency the chivalrous adventures of King Richard, in whose train he visited Palestine at the time of the third Crusade; and that Geoffrey of Monmouth and Caradoc, when clothing in a grave historic dress the floating fictions which had come down the

stream of their popular poetry, may have thought to indemnify their Welsh countrymen for recent defeat and present inferiority, by telling them of the imaginary victories of Arthur over Saxon hosts.

Some account must be given of the chief historians or chroniclers in each century of our period. The twelfth century is the richest; then flourished Eadmer, William of Malmesbury, Ordericus Vitalis, Geoffrey of Monmouth, Simeon of Durham, Florence of Worcester, Henry of Huntingdon, Giraldus Cambrensis, Benedictus Abbas, Ralph de Diceto, and Roger de Hoveden. In the thirteenth century the leading names are Roger of Wendover, and Matthew Paris; in the fourteenth, Nicholas Trivet, and Ranulph Higden.

12. **Eadmer**, the faithful and trusted follower of St. Anselm, wrote a chronicle to which he gave the name *Historia Novorum*, terminating in 1122. For the reigns of the two sons of the Conqueror it is the most valuable work that we possess; it was printed by Selden in 1623.

13. The chronicle of **Ingulfus**, with its various continuations, extends from about 650 to 1486. It is chiefly occupied with the history of Croyland, an abbey founded in the eighth century by Ethelbald King of Mercia, at the place where had stood the cell of his friend and confessor, St. Guthlac the anchorite. Ingulfus was abbot from 1075 to 1109, but the part of the chronicle which he wrote ends in 1090. The first continuation was by Peter of Blois, archdeacon of Bath, who died at a great age about the year 1198; a letter to him from the abbot, Henry de Longchamp, asking him to undertake the work, with his reply, in which he explicitly states his purpose of continuing the work of Ingulfus, are still extant. When therefore we find Sir Francis Palgrave setting down the said work as ' a historical novel,' ' a monkish forgery of the thirteenth or fourteenth century,' we can only wonder at this extravagance of scepticism; at the same time there can be little doubt that nearly all the charters and deeds of grant, in which the chronicle abounds, are spurious.

14. **William of Malmesbury**, a monk in the famous monastery of that name, founded by the Irish St. Maidulf in the seventh century, dedicated his *Historia Regum Angliæ* to Robert, Earl of Gloucester, a natural son of Henry I., and the chief patron of literature in those times. He congratulates himself on being the ' first who, since Beda, has arranged a continuous history of the English.' Being, as he tells us, of Norman descent by one parent, and of Saxon by the other, he writes of the actions of both impartially. Certain modern historians

have, perhaps, made too much of the alienation caused between Saxon and Norman by the difference of race. The English knew that William of Normandy professed to have as good a title to the crown as Harold; it was chiefly the unjust laws, not the persons, of him and his sons, to which they had a rooted objection; and it was as the 'tyrants of their fields,' not as Normans, that they detested his followers. Malmesbury himself, though half Norman, evidently regards himself as a thorough Englishman; the history of England, from the landing of Hengist and Horsa, is his history. Archbishop Lanfranc has a special devotion to Dunstan, a Saxon saint; and even the Saxon chronicler can freely praise the Norman abbot of Peterborough, if he is a man of worth and stands up for the rights of the monastery. Malmesbury's history comes down to the year 1142;—he is supposed to have died soon afterwards. Besides writing the history of the English kings, he also compiled an account of the English bishops,—*De Gestis Pontificum*,—composed biographies of St. Aldhelm and other saints, and left behind him various other works, of which some are still in MS., while several are not now known to exist.

15. **Ordericus Vitalis**, though his father was a native of Orleans, and he himself lived the greater part of his life in Normandy, speaks of himself as 'an Englishman' (Bk. v. ch. 1). His father Odelirius, a clerk, and a member of the household of Roger of Montgomeri, accompanied his lord to England at the time of the Conquest. He seems to have married an Englishwoman, by whom he had three sons, Orderic (born in 1075), Everard, and Benedict. His wife died, and Odelirius soon afterwards resolved to give up the remainder of his own life, as well as two of his sons, to the service of God. With Benedict, he took the monastic habit in a convent founded on his own land near Shrewsbury; Orderic, when but a boy ten years old, was given over to the monks of St. Evroult in Normandy. Writing some fifty-five years afterwards, the historian says: ' Wherefore, O glorious God, who badest Abraham to depart from his own land and his father's house, and the society of his kinsmen, thou didst put it into the heart of my father Odelirius to separate me entirely from himself, and devote me, in body and soul, to thee. He therefore, amidst floods of tears, delivered me, also weeping bitterly, to the monk Reynold, and, sending me into exile for the love of thee, never saw me afterwards. Being then a young boy, it was not for me to oppose my father's will; and he promised me, for his part, that if I became a monk I should partake with the Innocents the joys of Paradise. . . . I was ten years old when I crossed the British sea, and arrived in Normandy, an exile,

unknown to all, and knowing no one.　Like Joseph in Egypt, I heard a language to which I was an utter stranger.　But, supported by thy merciful goodness, I found the utmost kindness and attention amongst these foreigners.'

The *Ecclesiastical History* of Orderic, though extremely desultory, is of great value for the light which it reflects on the state of society in Normandy both before and after the reign of the Conqueror.　It is in thirteen books.　The first two treat of the life of Christ and the ministry of the Apostles, and bring down the successions of secular princes and Roman pontiffs from the Christian era to 1141 or 1142.　The five books which follow treat of all sorts of things; the life of St. Evroult; the history of his monastery; the lands which it possessed; the history of religion in Normandy from the time when it was first planted there; the story of St. Nicholas, and the translation of his relics; the careers of Hildebrand and Robert Guiscard; a short sketch of French history, and many other matters, terminating with a description of the death and funeral of William the Conqueror in 1187.　The remaining six books carry on the history of events in England and Normandy, with tolerable regularity, from that date to 1141.

16. **Geoffrey of Monmouth**, author of the famous *Historia Britonum*, was a Welshman, as his name implies, and was raised in 1152 to the bishopric of St. Asaph.　He also dedicated his history to Robert, Earl of Gloucester.　It professes to be a translation of 'a very ancient book in the British tongue,' brought out of Brittany by Walter, Archdeacon of Oxford, in which the actions of all the kings of Britain were related, from the Trojan Brutus ' down to Cadwallader, the son of Cadwallo.'　Nothing further is known of this ' very ancient book,' and not a single page of the history will stand the test of criticism.　What amount of truth may be mixed up with the mass of falsehood it is impossible now to determine.　But the book must ever possess an abiding literary interest, because, like the pretended history of Charlemagne by Archbishop Turpin, it furnished a rich mine of materials to the romance writers, of whom we shall have to speak presently.　It is to Geoffrey's ardent Welsh nationality, and disregard of historic precision, that we owe the raw material of the undying story of Arthur and the Knights of the Round Table.

17. Of **Simeon of Durham** little is known, and that little is not to his advantage.　He had no hand, it seems, in the composition of the curious *History of the Church of Durham*, which bears his name—at least of the greater portion of it—but appropriated the work and the credit of the real author, a

monk called Turgot. Yet it is but fair to say that an edition
of this history appeared in 1732, with a learned dissertation
by Rud prefixed to it, undertaking to prove that not Turgot
but Simeon was the real author. The remarkable story of the
peregrinations, during many centuries, of the bones of St.
Cuthbert, and of their finding a final resting-place on the hill
of Dunholme, thus forming the nucleus round which grew up
the city of Durham, was first told in this history. Simeon is
the undoubted author of a *Historia de Gestis Regum Anglorum*
closing in 1129, but a large portion of this is said to be literally
copied from Florence of Worcester; its sole value consists in
its preserving a number of notices of northern affairs not found
elsewhere.[1]

18. **Florence,** a monk of Worcester, taking for the foundation of his work the voluminous annals of the Irish monk,
Marianus Scotus, composed the *Chronicle* which bears his name,
commencing with the Creation and terminating in 1117, the
year before the author's death. This work, in all the early
portion, is substantially taken from Beda, Asser's *Life of Alfred*,
and the *Saxon Chronicle*; but as Florence approaches his own
time he becomes really valuable, preserving to us the knowledge
of many facts, especially in relation to Worcester and the parts
adjoining, including Wales, which no other writer mentions.
His lists of Saxon kings and bishops are also for the most part
peculiar to himself, and of great value, since they are derived
from sources, some of which are unknown and inaccessible.
Another monk of Worcester, named John, took up the work
where Florence left it, and continued the annals to the year
1141. This John has, under the year 1118, the following entry;
it is the one gleam of light but for which Florence of Worcester
would be to us a bare name :—' Dom Florence, the monk of
Worcester, died on the nones of July. His keen intelligence
and perseverance in studious toil have rendered this Chronicle
of Chronicles pre-eminent above all others.

> Corpus terra tegit, spiritus astra petit,
> Quo cernendo Deum cum sanctis regnet in ævum.'

A second continuation, made quite independently, by two monks
of Bury St. Edmunds, brings down the narrative of events to
1295, with a gap, however, from 1141 to 1152.

19. Of **Henry of Huntingdon,** personally, we know next to
nothing, but his tendencies and qualifications as a writer may
be well judged of from the *Chronicle,* extending to the death of

[1] See Wright's *Biog. Brit. Literaria, Anglo-Norman Period.*

Stephen, which bears his name. He was Archdeacon of Huntingdon, which was then in the diocese of Lincoln, and a friend of the Bishop Alexander, who held the see next before the great and noble St. Hugh of Lincoln, with the incidents of whose life one of the recent publications of the Rolls series has made us familiar. Henry is rhetorical and sometimes diffuse; he has at the same time the tastes of an antiquary, and the heart of a thorough Englishman; he delights in those old Saxon chronicles and poems which the polished Latinists of the twelfth century generally regarded as beneath their notice, and he actually took the trouble to translate into Latin prose the war-song on the battle of Brunanburgh, which he found in the *Saxon Chronicle*.

20. The chronicle which passes under the name of ' **Benedictus Abbas**,' i.e. Benedict, Abbot of Peterborough between 1177 and 1193,—a record of the highest importance for the reigns of Henry II. and Richard I.—has been conjectured by the latest editor, Professor Stubbs, to be the work of Richard Fitzneal, treasurer to Henry II., the author of the treatise *Dialogus de Scaccario*. It certainly was not *written* by Benedictus, for there is distinct evidence of its having been *transcribed* by his order.

21. The chronicle of **William of Newbury** (called also Neubrigensis and Gulielmus Parvus) relates to the same reigns, and terminates in 1197. It is in five books; the first of which, after briefly retracing the history of the Norman kings, treats of the reign of Stephen; the second and third deal with the times of Henry II.; and the fourth and fifth with those of Richard I. William was a monk of some enlightenment; he protests in his preface against the practice of muddling history and mythology together, after the fashion which had been set by Geoffrey of Monmouth.

22. **Ralph de Diceto**, Dean of St. Paul's in London, is the author of an important chronicle called *Imagines Historiarum*, extending from 1147 to 1202, about which year he died, and also of an historical abridgment called *Abbreviationes Chronicorum*. In his later years Ralph was a friend of Walter Map, a canon of the same cathedral.

23. **Giraldus de Barri**, surnamed Cambrensis to mark his nationality, was one of the ablest and most stirring spirits produced in a remarkable century. Born in 1147, the child of William de Barri, a powerful Norman baron of Pembrokeshire, and a Welsh lady of royal descent, Giraldus united in himself, in a notable degree, the good and bad qualities of either race; he was energetic, proud, and grasping with the Norman; imaginative, genial, vain, and flighty with the Celt. He re-

ceived his education at the University of Paris, whence he returned to Wales in 1172, and, as Archdeacon of Brecknock, discharged with the utmost zeal and ability the duties of a vigilant pastor of souls. His uncle, who was Bishop of St. David's, died in 1176, and the chapter elected Giraldus to the vacant see, but Henry II., to whom his Welsh connection and sympathies were no recommendation, insisted upon the appointment of a safer man. The king, however, than whom none could better recognise or gauge the worth of a man of capacity, employed Giraldus on several missions of importance. He sent him, in 1185, in the train of his son John to Ireland, where he stayed about a year, and it is to this visit that we owe two works of the greatest historical and antiquarian value, the *Topographia Hiberniæ*, and the *Vaticinalis Expugnationis Historia*, under which strange name the conquest of Ireland by Strongbow and his followers is graphically and minutely described. He was again employed by the king in 1188 to preach the crusade in Wales, in company with Archbishop Baldwin, and his well-known *Itinerarium Cambriæ* was the literary result of his labours on this occasion, which were also highly successful in regard to their immediate object, for the fervid eloquence of Giraldus was exactly calculated to touch the hearts of his susceptible countrymen. Again, in 1198, there was a vacancy in the see of St. David's, and the canons again nominated Giraldus. But the Archbishop of Canterbury, who probably knew of his design, if elected, to claim metropolitan rights for the see of St. David's, resolutely opposed their choice. A furious struggle ensued, the steps of which are detailed, partly in Giraldus's autobiography, the work entitled *De Rebus a se Gestis*, partly in his historico-legal treatise on the see of St. David's, *De Jure et Statu Menevensis Ecclesiæ*. He visited Rome more than once, and had repeated interviews with Innocent III., the master-mind of Christendom in that age ; but, after all, the Archbishop was too strong for him, and another man was appointed. After this great disappointment we hear little more of our fiery friend, who appears to have lived some eighteen years longer, in retirement, but in easy circumstances, dying about the year 1217.[1]

24. **Roger de Hoveden**, one of the many ornaments of the great reign of Henry II., was a churchman devoted to legal and technical studies, who acted as one of the king's clerks or secretaries. Thus is explained the manner in which his *Annals*

---

[1] See Mr. Brewer's excellent Introduction to the works of Giraldus, edited by him for the Rolls series in 1861.

are encumbered with copies of charters, letters, bulls, briefs, and other documents. Being a native of Yorkshire, he naturally treats with somewhat disproportionate fulness the affairs of the northern counties. He intended his history to form in some sense a continuation of that of Beda, and therefore made it commence from the year 732, carrying it down to 1201, the events of the last twenty years being told in very great detail, so as to form one half of the entire work.

25. **Roger of Wendover**, a monk of St. Albans, Prior of Belvoir at the time of his death, in 1237, left behind him a chronicle entitled *Flores Historiarum*, which is considered to be divided into three parts. The first, extending from the Creation to the year A.D. 447, is entirely copied from older authors, and is of no value. The second part, which reaches to about the year 1200, is in the main copied from other chroniclers, but is valuable inasmuch as it preserves to us many extracts from lost works. The third part, recording the history of Roger's own times, is exceedingly valuable as an original authority.

26. **Matthew Paris**, also a monk of St. Albans, wrote, under the title of *Historia Major*, a History of England, commencing from the remotest times, and coming down to 1259, the year in which he died. It was long believed that the entire work was original, but it has been lately discovered that the whole of the earlier portion, down to 1235, is taken from the *Flores Historiarum* of Roger of Wendover. So far as it is a contemporary authority, this bulky work has always been considered as of the highest value. Allowance must, however, be made for the prejudices of a monk when he writes of the secular clergy; perhaps for those of an Englishman when he writes of the court of Rome. With the *Historia Major* is printed a continuation to the year 1272, supposed to be by Rishanger. Paris also wrote the *Historia Minor*, from the Conquest to 1253, lately printed in the Rolls series.

27. **Thomas Wikes**, said by Bale to have been an Augustinian canon of Oseney, near Oxford, is one of Gale's *Quinque Scriptores*. His chronicle, from the Conquest down to 1260, gives a brief summary of events; from that point to 1289, where he breaks off suddenly, he is very full and interesting.

28. **William Rishanger**, a monk of St. Albans, wrote a chronicle which he seems to have intended should serve for a continuation of the history of Matthew Paris; it extends from 1259 to 1307.

29. **Nicholas Trivet**, a Dominican, and **Ranulph Higden**, a monk of St. Werburgh's, in Chester, composed, the one a

D

valuable and well-written series of Annals, extending from 1135 to 1307, the other a work entitled *Polychronicon*, which comes down to 1357.

This was the standard work on general history and geography towards the end of the fourteenth and all through the fifteenth century. The Latin MSS. of it are prodigiously numerous. No doubt Chaucer made use of it; it is quoted by writers in the Wyclif controversy,[1] and Henry of Knyghton, writing about the year 1400, excerpts largely from it. It is divided into seven books, of which the first is a sketch of Universal Geography, taken from Pliny, Solinus, Beda, &c., and the second contains a summary of Universal History from the Creation to the destruction of the Jewish temple. The entire work is being edited by Mr. Babington for the Master of the Rolls, and will fill many volumes of the series.

30. Many chronicles, giving the history of particular monasteries or dioceses, and assigning to political events only the second place in point of importance, have been edited in recent years for the Rolls series. Such are the chronicles of Abingdon, St. Albans, Bermondsey, Burton, Canterbury, Dunstable, Durham, Evesham, Gloucester, Hyde, Melsa or Meaux (an abbey in Holderness), Oseney, Tewkesbury, Winton, and Worcester. Gale, nearly two hundred years ago, published the chronicle of Melrose, and the annals of Margan, Ramsay, and Waverley. There are treasures in these ample records which as yet are far from having been fully utilised by English historians. Among such compilations, none hitherto has excited a wider interest than the *Chronicle of Jocelin de Brakelond*, paraphrased and commented upon by Mr. Carlyle in his *Past and Present*. Jocelin was a monk of the great monastery which had arisen over the sacred remains of the East Anglian king, St. Edmund, slain by heathen Danes in the ninth century. The old Beodricsworth had become 'St. Edmund's Bury,' the town of St. Edmund; the abbey was richly endowed; its abbot wore the mitre, and was summoned to Parliament as one of the magnates of the land. Jocelin, commencing from the year (1173) in which he took the Benedictine habit, gives us the history of the abbey, interweaving many a passage helping to bring before our eyes, as they stood in the flesh, King Richard and his baser brother, down to 1203. Here he abruptly breaks off, for what reason it is impossible to say, since he is known to have lived some years longer, and to have been almoner of the convent in 1211. The chief interest of the chronicle lies in the account of the election

[1] *Fasciculi Zizaniorum* (Rolls series), p. 256.

of Abbot Samson in 1282, and in the narrative, so forcibly
translated into the language of the nineteenth century by Mr.
Carlyle, of the success with which that strong, just, patient
ruler gradually raised out of a confusion and indebtedness
which seemed inextricable the affairs of the convent, and made
the good name of St. Edmund and of his house once more re-
spected throughout England.

Law and Medicine : other Prose Writings.

31. Early in our period the study of laws and jurisprudence
was revived, and carried on with the eagerness and exclusiveness
which are incidental to revivals. Up to the twelfth century
the Roman law had been known either by tradition or imperfect copies. But the Pisans, when they took Amalfi in 1137,
are said [1] to have discovered an entire copy of the Pandects of
Justinian—the work in which (together with its sister publications, the Codex and Institute) the laws of the Roman empire
were by the orders of that emperor (about the year 534)
collected, classified, and explained. Copies of the treasure were
soon multiplied, and it was studied, among others, by Gratian,
a monk of Bologna, who conceived the idea of collecting and
arranging in a similar way what may be called the statutory
and traditional law of the Christian Church. He published, in
1151, under the name of *Decretum*, a collection of the canons
of councils, the decrees of popes, and the maxims of the more
ancient Fathers, all which branches are included under the
general term of Canon Law. The fame of Gratian and his
work drew students to Bologna from all parts of Europe, and
noted schools of canonists and civilians (for the Roman, or civil,
was studied there *pari passu* with the canon law) grew up at
that city. English ecclesiastics resorted there in great numbers, and imported the legal knowledge thus gained into the
ecclesiastical courts of their own country. These courts, both on
account of the greater simplicity and clearness of the law administered in them, and as less open to be tampered with by royal
or aristocratic influences, were much resorted to by the laity in
preference to the temporal or common law courts. They were
consequently the object of keen ill-will among the lawyers, and
of jealousy or opposition on the part of the crown. But they
seem to have had this good effect, if no other—that their rivalry
stimulated the lawyers to polish, digest, and present in a
rational and consistent form, the ancient common law of the

---

[1] See, however, Hallam's *Literature of Europe*, vol. i. p. 62.

land, which otherwise could not have stood its ground against
its twin foreign rivals.   Hence arose, near the end of the twelfth
century, the work of chief justiciary **Ranulf de Glanville**, *On
the Laws and Customs of England*,[1] the earliest extant treatise
upon English law.   The well-known work of **Bracton**, bearing
the same title, was written about the middle of the thirteenth
century.

32. The chief seat of medical science during this period was
the University of Salerno in Italy.   This university was in
existence before the time of Charlemagne, who founded a college
in it.   It was known as 'the city or commonwealth of Hippo-
crates' (civitas Hippocratica), and was at the zenith of its
reputation in the twelfth century; early in which the *Schola
Salernitana*, a learned poem in leonine, *i.e.* riming Latin verses,
on the mode of preserving health, was composed and published.
In 1225 the University received from the Emperor, Frederick
II., the exclusive right of granting medical degrees in his
dominions.   Like all other sciences at this period, medicine was
greatly indebted to the researches of the Arabians, for profiting
by which, Salerno, from its position on the Mediterranean, was
singularly well fitted.

33. **John of Salisbury**, born about 1120, passed fifteen years
of his youth and manhood, between 1136 and 1151, in studying
and teaching in France.   In the latter year he was made secretary
to Theobald, archbishop of Canterbury, and continued to hold
the same office under Thomas à Becket, whose violent death he
is said to have narrowly escaped sharing.   In 1176 he was
appointed bishop of Chartres, where he died in 1180.   His
works are miscellaneous in their contents, and seem to proceed
upon no well-defined general plan.   The *Polycraticus de Nugis
Curialium et Vestigiis Philosophorum* was completed in 1156.
The 'frivolities of the courtiers,' by which he means all that
Bunyan would describe as merchandise in the markets of the
city of Vanity, are examined and censured with a prolix
seriousness which is more edifying than entertaining.   By the
'footsteps of the philosophers' are meant those philosophical
doctrines which were worthy to be generally received and
followed.   A treatise in Latin elegiacs, entitled *Entheticus de
Dogmate Philosophorum*, has much the same argument as the
Polycraticus.   The *Metalogicus*, composed about 1160, is a
prose treatise in six books, and, according to Mr. Wright,
'contains valuable materials for the history of scholastic
philosophy during the twelfth century, and furnishes portraits

---

[1] *Tractatus de Legibus et Consuetudinibus regni Angliæ.*

of the leaders of the different sects by one who had lived and
studied in their society.'

34. Geoffrey Vinsauf's *Itinerarium Regis Anglorum Rich-
ardi et aliorum in terram Hierosolymorum* (printed by Gale in
1687) is a detailed narrative of the third crusade, from the pen
of an eye-witness. As such, it is a work of the highest value.
It may be said to close with Richard's departure from Palestine; a few lines suffice the author to describe, by way of brief
allusion, the king's captivity, redemption, return, and re-
appearance in France. The work seems to have been completed
in 1197 or 1198. In assigning it to Vinsauf, Gale thought himself justified by the heading of a nearly contemporary MS. of
the work, preserved at Cambridge. But Professor Stubbs, in
his edition of the *Itinerarium* prepared for the Rolls series, has
shown cause for believing pretty confidently that Vinsauf had
nothing to do with it, but that it was the work of one **Richard**,
canon and prior of the Holy Trinity in London.

35. **Walter Map**, writing of himself, says, 'qui marchio
sum Wallensibus;' he was probably a native of Herefordshire
or Gloucestershire, but of Welsh extraction, for Map or Mab is
Welsh for 'son;' 'Mabinogion,' 'tales for children.' He
pursued his studies under Girard la Pucelle at the University of
Paris. His masterly intellect and his wit recommended him to
Henry II., who employed him on several important missions,
and made him one of his itinerant justices. Giraldus de Barri
(from whose *Speculum Ecclesiæ* almost all that is known of
Walter Map is derived) tells us that he was for many years
the parson of Westbury, near Bristol, and had a stiff contest
with a neighbouring Cistercian convent, to protect from them
the immunities and property of his benefice. He had no love
therefore for the white habit of that order; and when the king
was once sending him out on circuit, and charging him to deal
equal justice to all men, Map quietly replied, 'Except Jews and
white monks.' St. Thomas à Becket once asked him what
reliance could be placed on the Welsh, to which Map replied in
his own dry way by telling a good story. In 1176 he was
made a canon of St. Paul's, and twenty years later he became
archdeacon of Oxford. That he had much to do with extending
and improving the organisation of the infant university, may be
reasonably surmised. Nothing later is recorded of him; but
we know from Giraldus's *Expugnatio Hiberniæ* that he was
dead in 1209.

Of his prose writings in French we shall speak presently;
in Latin, he is the author of *De Nugis Curialium*, a gossiping
book, in five 'distinctions,' on the history of the English Court,

and the employments of the courtiers. It is a disconnected record of his experiences of life as a courtier, and was evidently written at odd times during the course of many years. A passage in the first distinction pathetically bewails the conquest of Jerusalem by the Saracens, which happened in 1187. Besides a history of the court, from William Rufus to Henry II., the book contains accounts of modern heretics and recent miracles, a collection of fairy legends or 'apparitiones fantasticæ,' the dissuasion against marriage addressed by Valerius to Rufinus the philosopher, and tales, dealing much in the marvellous, about various persons. The work was edited by Mr. T. Wright for the Camden Society in 1850.

36. Of **Sæwulf**, whose name shows his English birth, we have a short narrative of a voyage to Palestine in 1102. This was printed in D'Avezac's *Recueil de Voyages*, and a translation has appeared in Bohn's Antiquarian Library.

37. **Richard Aungervile**, of Bury, Bishop of Durham, wrote a little book, called *Philobiblon*, towards the middle of the fourteenth century. He was a distinguished public man in the reigns of Edward II. and Edward III. Having furthered the designs of Isabella, near the close of her unhappy husband's reign, he was, on the accession of her son, loaded with honours and rewards. In 1333, the see of Durham being vacant, Richard, though the chapter elected another person, was, by the support of the king and the pope, placed in the chair of St. Cuthbert. In 1334 he was made Chancellor. In 1338 he carried to Paris Edward III.'s declaration of war; but he did so with a heavy heart, for he loved France, and was accustomed to call Paris the 'paradise of the world.' Some negotiations with David Bruce in 1345 were the last public business in which he was engaged. Remaining thenceforth quietly at his see, he wrote the *Philobiblon*, and died shortly afterwards.

The treatise is in twenty chapters; it is the fruit of the author's love of books and zeal in collecting them. Chapter IV. is the unhappy history of a book, told by itself; among all its enemies, woman, that 'bestia bipedalis,' with her propensity to clean and put in order, is one of the worst. Severe language is used respecting the monks and the corruption prevalent among the orders; in reading which, it need hardly be said that the almost universal prejudice of a secular clergyman against the regulars must be taken into the account. In several chapters he maintains the superiority of the ancient classical authors, with whose works he shows considerable familiarity, over modern writers. This suggests to M. Cocheris, the French editor of the *Philobiblon*, the true and weighty remark, that a series of 'little

revivals' of ancient literature may be traced through the whole
course of the middle ages, and that it is not true that antiquity
was discovered at any given epoch, for 'antiquity had never
been lost.' Speaking of his mania for collecting, Richard says (ch.
viii.), 'When I held high office, and it became generally known
that I preferred books to money, books of all sorts flowed in
upon me—cœnulenti quaterni et decrepiti codices—dirty quartos
and shaky folios.' In another place he says, 'Wisdom, thou art
better than all other treasure, but where shall we find thee?
In libris quidem procul dubio posuisti tabernaculum desidera-
bile tuum, ubi te fundavit Altissimus, lumen luminum, liber
vitæ.' He tells us that monks and friars, especially the Dominicans, masters of arts, scholars, and professors, all of either sex
—of every degree, estate, or dignity—whose pursuits were in
any way connected with books—all came to know him, and
helped to gratify his passion for accumulation. And when he
himself could visit Paris, that seat of learning and splendour,
the joy was almost too great for utterance. 'O beate Deus
Deorum in Sion, quantus fluminis impetus voluptatis lætificavit
cor nostrum, quoties paradysum mundi Parisiis visitare vaca-
vimus, ibi moraturi, ubi nobis semper dies pauci præ amoris
magnitudine videbantur.' Richard writes not seldom in a
strange bantering tone, which in a modern would savour of
scepticism. But the eloquent and feeling words with which he
concludes the treatise show that this was not so with him. His
love of books was but a whim after all, and he knew it to be so;
deep in his soul lay that faith which is the root of the whole
matter, and his religion was sound, intelligent, and pervading.

Science: Adelard, Roger Bacon.

38. **Adelard** of Bath (in English, Æthelheard) is described
by Mr. Wright[1] as 'the greatest name in English science before
Robert Grosseteste and Roger Bacon.' He lived in the reign
of Henry I. He travelled for seven years, chiefly in the East,
and studied mathematics in the Arabian schools, which, though
verging to their decline, were still the depositories of more of
the science of the Greeks and Chaldees than could be found elsewhere. Before 1116 he wrote *De Eodem et Diverso*, an allegory
on the relative attractions of philosophy and the world. His
other works are, *Quæstiones Naturales*, the preface to which was
printed by Dom Martenne in 1717, and *Regulæ Abaci*. He also
translated Euclid from the Arabic.

---

[1] *Biogr. Brit. Lit.*, Norman period.

39. The thirteenth century is illustrated in the history of science by the name of a great Englishman, **Roger Bacon.** We have seen how astronomy, and the subsidiary sciences of arithmetic and geometry, were included in the old Quadrivium, the course of study which had struggled down from the Roman Empire. The reason of this lay in the absolute necessity of the thing; for without some degree of astronomical knowledge the calendar could not be computed, and the very church feasts could not be fixed to their proper dates. Moreover, the *ignis fatuus* of astrology—the delusive belief that human events were influenced by the aspects and conjunctions of the heavenly bodies —led on the student, duped for the benefit of his race, to a more careful study of the phenomena of the heavens than he would otherwise have bestowed. But, besides these long-established studies, scientific teaching in other branches had been ardently commenced in France by Gerbert, as we have seen, early in the eleventh century. But in spite of the intrinsic attractiveness of such studies, they languished and dwindled away. One cause of this is to be found in the suspicion and dislike with which they were popularly regarded. Gerbert was believed to have been a magician, and to have sold his soul to the evil one. Roger Bacon was popularly regarded in England as a sorcerer down to the reign of James I. To trace this feeling to its sources would be a very curious inquiry, but it is one foreign to our present purpose. The second principal cause of this scientific sterility lay in the superior attractiveness of scholasticism. It was pleasanter to be disputatious than to be thoughtful; easier to gain a victory in dialectics than to solve a problem in mechanics. Moreover, men could not distinguish between the applicability of the scholastic method to a subject, such as theology, in which the postulates or first principles were fixed, and its applicability to subjects of which the postulates either had to be discovered, or were liable to progressive change. They tried nature, not by an appeal to facts, but by certain physical or metaphysical canons which they supposed to be impregnable. Thus Roger Bacon says that it was the general belief in his time that hot water exposed to a low temperature in a vessel would freeze sooner than the same quantity of cold water, because, say the metaphysicians, *contrarium excitatur per contrarium*—contraries reciprocally produce each other. ' But I have tried it,' he says, with amusing earnestness, ' and it is not the fact, but the very reverse.' It thus happened that Roger Bacon, one of the most profound and penetrating thinkers that ever existed, had no disciples, and left no school behind him. This great anticipator of modern science only serves as a gauge whereby to

test the depth and strength of the mediæval intellect; the circumstances of the time did not permit the seed which he cast abroad to fructify.

But few particulars are known of his life. He was born at Ilchester, in Somersetshire, in 1214; received his education at the universities of Oxford and Paris; and, after taking the Franciscan habit, commenced a long life of unbroken study at Oxford. Among his numerous works the most important is the *Opus Majus*, which he dedicated and presented in 1267 to Clement IV. This high-minded and enlightened Pope he had known when formerly, as Guido, Bishop of Sabina, he had visited England in the capacity of Legate. Clamours and accusations were already beginning to be raised against him, for dabbling in unlawful arts; but the Pope promised him his protection, and kept his word. But after the death of Clement the efforts to silence him were renewed, and at a chapter of Franciscans held at Paris, his writings were condemned, and he himself was placed in confinement. For ten years, dating from 1278, he remained a prisoner, and was liberated at last owing to the intercession of some English noblemen with the Pope. He died, according to Anthony Wood, in 1292.

40. The *Opus Majus* is an investigation of what he calls ' the roots of wisdom.' The introductory portion discusses at great length, and with masterly handling, the relations between philosophy and religion. Then he treats of *grammatica*, or the study of languages, the first and not the least essential of the roots of wisdom, since from 'these [languages] the sciences of the Latins have been translated.' By 'Latins' he means literary men in general, to whom the Latin language was then the medium of thought in all subjects except poetry. Nay, the ' Latins' threatened at one time, as we shall see, to engross even the field of poetry. The second 'root' is mathematical science, the key, as he justly says, to all other sciences, 'the neglect of which now, for these thirty or forty years, has vitiated all the studies of the Latins; for whoever is ignorant of it cannot know the rest of the sciences.' Metaphysical disputation, as we have seen, had proved more exciting and attractive. To this part of the work is appended a long geographical treatise, followed by an account of the planets and their influences, which shows that on this point Bacon had succumbed to the solemn nonsense of the Arabian astrologers. The third root is *perspectiva*, or optics, a study to which Bacon had especially devoted himself. The fourth is experimental science, a source of knowledge which, he says, 'by the common herd of students is utterly ignored.' The whole work is remarkably characterised by that spirit of

system in which later English philosophers have been singularly deficient. The study of each of these 'roots of wisdom' is recommended, not for its own sake, not for mere intellectual improvement, but on account of the relation which it bears to, and the light which it is able to throw on, the supreme science, Theology. The reasoning is sometimes singular : the study of optics, for instance, is stated to be essential to the right understanding of Holy Scripture, because in such passages as ' Guard us, Lord, as the apple of an eye,' we cannot fully enter into the meaning of the inspired writer, unless we have learned from this science *how*, and with what a multiplicity of precautions, the apple of the eye is secured from injury.

Means of Education.

41. We have now to inquire what were the principal means of education which students had at their command during this period. The most important among these were the two universities of Oxford and Cambridge. There seems good reason to believe that the school which Alfred founded was established at Oxford. A more central situation could not be found; it was a royal residence, and the scene of many a great council of the notables of the kingdom in the period intervening between Alfred and the Conquest; nor was it in those times a slight matter, that, standing on the Thames, and commanding by the bridge enclosed in its fortifications the passage of the river, it was equally accessible to those who lived north of Thames, and those who lived south. The distinction is clearly recognised in the Saxon Chronicle, and it probably gave rise to the division of all the students of Oxford into the 'nations' of North Englishmen and South Englishmen, a division apparently as old as the University itself. Once established, we may be certain that the school would continue to exist in a precarious way, even in the troubled reigns of Alfred's successors. Perhaps it was at Oxford that Ethelwerd learnt the exceedingly bad Latin in which, about the year 930, he addressed his cousin Matilda, daughter of the Emperor Otho, with the view of supplying her with information as to the early history of their common country. A charter of Ethelred, dated in 1006, proves at any rate the existence of valuable *books* in a monastery at Oxford at that time. But at the Conquest the dissolution of the University, if it had ever existed, seems to have been nearly complete. Towards the end of the eleventh century it revived, and all during the twelfth century was making slow upward progress.

42. The lectures of Abelard, the most active thinker of his day, were attended by crowds of Englishmen — John of Salisbury for one, who has left us a curious account of them —and some of his hearers must undoubtedly have opened lectures on similar subjects in the halls of Oxford. But it is not till the thirteenth century that we hear of Oxford as an important educational centre. A great stimulus seems to have been applied in 1229 by the migration of a large body of students from Paris to Oxford. The connection between these two universities was during all this period most intimate;—identity of religion, common studies, and the use of Latin as a common language, produced and maintained it;—they might almost be regarded as two national colleges in an European university. Some of the great men who lectured at Oxford have been already noticed, but there is one, whose connection with the university in this century was long and important, whom we have yet to mention. Robert Grossetête, Bishop of Lincoln, was long a teacher at Oxford, afterwards chancellor, and finally, in his episcopal capacity, *ex officio* head of the University. A man of varied learning, and. a great and liberal nature, he was the warm friend and patron of Roger Bacon, and is mentioned by him in terms of high admiration in the *Opus Majus*. The number of students who flocked to Oxford in this and the following century far surpassed anything that has been seen in later times. ' We are told that there were in Oxford in 1209 three thousand members of the University, in 1231 thirty thousand, in 1263 fifteen thousand, in 1350 between three and four thousand, and in 1360 six thousand.'[1] All national and local antipathies, all political tendencies, all existing schools of thought, found numerous and ardent representatives at Oxford. We are not therefore surprised to read of a succession of furious fights between the university ' nations,' and also between the student-body and the townspeople. The mendicant orders, though regarded at first by the scholastic body with vehement dislike, both in Oxford and Paris, all at last established houses in, and furnished teachers to, the University;—and it was in the Franciscan monastery that Bacon prosecuted his experiments in physical science. ' Halls' and ' Inns,' unendowed, but licensed by the University, were the primitive arrangement for the accommodation of students ;—the first colleges, the main intention of which was to facilitate the education of poor students, were founded in the latter half of the thirteenth century.

---

[1] Newman's *Office and Work of Universities*, p. 267.

Merton and University are the first instances of such foundations.

43. Cambridge, which has trained so many minds of the highest order in more recent times, was comparatively uninfluential in the Middle Ages. About the year 1109 the monks of Croyland, at the instigation apparently of their abbot, Goisfred, who had studied at Orleans, opened a school in a barn at Cambridge. The scheme succeeded; the number of scholars gradually increased; and a large migration of Oxonians in the year 1209 seems to have established the rising university on a permanent basis.[1]

44. *Monasteries.*—Next in importance to the universities as seats of education were the monasteries. These arose rapidly in every part of England after the Norman Conquest. William himself was a zealous promoter of the monastic institution. ' Scarcely did his own munificence,' says Malmesbury, ' or that of his nobility, leave any monastery unnoticed. . . . Thus in his time the monastic flock increased on every side;—monasteries arose, ancient in their form, but modern in building.' And in a previous passage he had said, speaking of the consequences of the Norman invasion, ' You might see churches rise in every village, and monasteries in the towns and cities, built in a style unknown before.' This style was of course the round-arched Norman architecture, of which the specimens in England are so numerous and so magnificent. Nearly all the monasteries in England, till the introduction of the mendicant orders about 1230, belonged to the Benedictine order, or some branch of it, and the devotion of the Benedictines to learning is well known. Among the houses especially distinguished for the learned men whom they produced were St. Albans, Malmesbury, Canterbury, and Peterborough. Besides the original works composed by monks at this period, we are indebted to their systematic diligence for the preservation of the ancient authors. Every large monastery had its *scriptorium,* in which manuscripts were kept, and the business of transcribing was regularly carried on, by monks appointed for the purpose.

45. *Paper.*—Among literary helps, few have a more practically powerful influence on the circulation and stimulation of ideas than a plentiful supply of writing material. Literature was grievously hampered up to nearly the end of our period owing to the costliness and scarcity of paper. For the first seven centuries after the Christian era, the material generally used was the papyrus, imported from Egypt. But after the

---

[1] See Huber's *English Universities,* edited by F. Newman.

conquest of Egypt by the Mahomedans, towards the end of the seventh century, this importation ceased. The place of the papyrus was now supplied by parchment, in itself a much better and more durable material, but so costly that the practice became common of erasing the writing on an old parchment, in order to make room for a new work. A manuscript thus treated was called a *palimpsest*. When the characters had become much faded through lapse of time, the same motive—scarcity of material—led to the practice of writing a new work across the old one without resorting to erasure. A manuscript so dealt with was called a *codex rescriptus*. But since, in manuscripts of the first kind, the process of erasure was often imperfectly performed, and in those of the second, the old faded letters can often, with a little trouble, be distinguished beneath the newer ones, it has happened that valuable copies, or fragments of ancient works, have in both these ways been recovered.[1] Paper made from linen or cotton rags is an Arabian invention; and the first paper, nearly resembling that which we now use, was made at Mecca in the year 706. The knowledge of the art soon passed into Spain, and by the Moors was communicated to the Christians. But it was not till towards the close of the thirteenth century that paper mills were established in the Christian states of Spain, whence, in the following century, the art passed into Italy, and became generally diffused.

Poetry :—Early English Fragments; Latin Poems.

46. From the Conquest to the year 1200, the vernacular poetry is represented only by a few scraps and fragments of verse. These are—

(1) The Song of Canute.
(2) Archbishop Aldred's curse.
(3) St. Godric's verses.
(4) The Prophecy of Here.

Thomas, a monk of Ely, who wrote about 1170, relates that King Canute was once in his barge on the river Nen near Ely, with his queen Emma. As they drew near the monastery, which stood on the river bank, the monks happened to be singing the hours; the religious harmony filled the house and floated over the waters; and Canute, standing up in the barge

---

[1] The *Codex Ephraemi Rescriptus*, at Paris, a manuscript of the Greek Testament of the highest value, written over with a work of St. Ephrem, is a case in point.

in the jubilation of his soul, 'composed a song in English, the beginning of which runs as follows : '—

> Merie sungen ðe muneches binnen Ely,
> ða Cnut ching reu ðerby :
> Roweð, cnites, noer the land,
> And here we þes muneches sæng.

That is,—

> Merrily sang the monks within Ely,
> When Cnut the king rowed thereby :
> ' Row, my men, nearer the land,
> And let us hear these monks' song.'

Doubtless Canute's poem was in many stanzas, but this is the only one which has come down to us. 'These verses,' adds Thomas, 'are to this day publicly sung at merry-makings, and quoted as proverbs.' Thomas' chronicle is in Gale's *Scriptores Quindecim*, 1691.

47. William of Malmesbury, in his *Gesta Pontificum*, tells us that Aldred, Archbishop of York, who died in 1069, said to Urse, the Norman Sheriff of Worcester, who had built his castle close to the monastery at that town,—

> Hattest þu Urs ;
> Have þu Godes kurs.

> Thou art called Urse ;
> Have thou God's curse !

48. St. Godric lived as a hermit at Finchale, near Durham, for sixty years, dying in 1170. In a MS. life of him in the King's library, written not long after his death at the request of Thomas, prior of Finchale, are found (besides a few other detached verses) the following lines, which are not without a certain rude beauty ; they are said to have been composed by St. Godric :—

> Sainte Marie virgine,
> Moder Jesus Cristes Nazarene,
> Onfo, schild, help þin Godric ;
> Onfang, bring hegilich wið þe in Godes riche.
> Sainte Marie, Xristes bur,
> Maidenes clenhad, moderes flur,
> Dilie min sinne, rix in min mod,
> Bring me to winne wið þe selfd God.

> Saint Mary the Virgin,
> Mother of Jesus Christ of Nazareth,
> Receive, shield, help thy Godric ;
> Receive, bring [him] quickly with thee to God's kingdom.

Saint Mary, Christ's bower,
Maiden's purity, mother's flower,
Raze out my sin, reign in my mood,
Bring me to joy with the same God.

49. The Prophecy of Here (perhaps Harford in Devonshire) is less interesting; it consists of five rude lines, containing a prophecy (supposed to have been fulfilled in the reign of Richard I.), that Englishmen should be divided into three parts, ' in thre ydeled.' It is found in the chronicle of Benedictus Abbas.

50. It may be stated broadly, that from the eleventh to the thirteenth century inclusive, the prose literature of Europe came from churchmen, the poetry from laymen. But in one direction the churchmen made incursions into the domain of their rivals without fear of competition or reprisals. We refer to the Latin poetry of the Middle Ages. Much of this owed its existence to a spirited but hopeless endeavour—one which even Erasmus was disposed to repeat a hundred and fifty years later—to make the Latin the universal language of literature. All the existing vernacular tongues—though some were more advanced than others—were not to be compared in respect of regularity and euphony to the Latin; and the poets of the cloister preferred to write elegant hexameters and elegiacs after the model of their beloved Virgil and Ovid rather than engage in a struggle with the difficulties of their native speech in its then condition of fluidity and rapid change. One concession they did make to the fashion of their own age, when, forsaking the classic metres, they sought for that measured melody which is the essential form of poetry, in the Arabic—or possibly Celtic—invention of rime, by this time (1100) completely naturalised in the south of Europe. These Latin rimes were called Leonine verses.[1] The solemn hymns of the Church —some of which are unsurpassed even as literary compositions —were composed in these riming measures; among their authors were St. Anselm, St. Bernard, St. Thomas Aquinas, and Pope Innocent III. The majority of these were written in the twelfth and thirteenth centuries.

51. No Latin poems of this elevated class were composed by English ecclesiastics, but leonine verse was largely used in this country as a vehicle for satire and humour. There is among

---

[1] The term seems to have been originally applied only to rimed hexa meters or elegiacs, and afterwards to have been extended to any Latin rimed poems. The name comes from the inventor, Leoninus or Leonine, a monk of Marseilles, who flourished about 1135. See Warton, vol. i. p. cl. n.

the publications of the Camden Society a thick volume of such Latin poems,[1] the authorship of which was long ascribed, though upon the authority of no MS. of earlier date than the fourteenth century, to Walter Map, archdeacon of Oxford, the friend of Giraldus de Barri, and the composer of several of the great prose romances concerning Arthur, who flourished towards the end of the twelfth century. But Mr. Wright doubts whether Map had really any hand in them; he thinks that they were 'probably written at different periods from the latter half of the twelfth century to the middle of the thirteenth;' and that they emanated from, and circulated amongst, university men, to whom attacks on ecclesiastical irregularities were always welcome. Most of them pass under the name of 'Bishop Golias,' an imaginary personage representing episcopal and clerical vice and irregularity, and also a satirist of the same. The *Apocalypsis Goliæ* is a general onslaught on the shortcomings of the clergy; it maintained its popularity down to the time of the Reformation. The *Confessio Goliæ* is the poem out of which a few stanzas were extracted to form the famous drinking-song —so called—beginning

> Meum est propositum in tabernâ mori,

on the strength of which Walter Map obtained the *sobriquet* of 'the jovial Archdeacon,' the fact being, even assuming him to be the author of it, that the poem is ironical and satirical throughout. In a third poem, *Golias in Romanam Curiam*, occurs the following ludicrous account of the effect on a well-filled purse of the transaction of business at the papal court:—

> Des istis, das aliis, addis dona datis,
> Et cum satis dederis, quærunt ultra satis;
> O vos, bursæ turgidæ, Romam veniatis,
> Romæ viget physica bursis constipatis.
>
> Prædantur marsupium singuli paulatim;
> Magna, major, maxima, præda fit gradatim.
> Quid irem per singula? Colligam summatim:
> Omnes bursam strangulant, et expirat statim.

52. Two or three other poems, which it is strange to find in company with the satirical verses just described, are of a serious cast. Such is the *Predicatio Goliæ*, in which Golias is supposed to preach to his clerical brethren; but the thread of

----

[1] Edited by Mr. Wright in 1841.

address and admonition gradually widens into a magnificent *ébauche* of the Catholic creed. Man, it says,—

> Dignitate præminet universæ rei,
> Factus ad imaginem majestatis Dei ;
> Cuncta sibi serviunt ; ipse servit ei,
> Quem nox nocti prædicat et dies diei.
>
> Obligavit omnia nostræ servituti,
> Alia deliciis, alia saluti ;
> Sciunt evangelicis regulis induti,
> Quibus frui convenit, quibus fas est uti.
>
> His nos beneficiis voluit ditari,
> Et adjecit cumulum muneris præclari,
> Cum pro nobis Filium misit incarnari,
> Ut uniret hominem suo salutari.
>
> Est inenarrabilis ista genitura, &c.

53. But the strict Latinists scouted the idea of any such concessions to a corrupt modern taste as were implied in the practice of riming ; when they wrote poetry, they used the metres as well as the language of the Latin poets. Thus **Geoffrey de Vinsauf** wrote a Latin poem, entitled *De Novâ Poetriâ*, and addressed to Innocent III., the intention of which was to recommend and illustrate the legitimate mode of versification in opposition to the leonine or barbarous species. Actuated by the same prepossessions, **Josephus Iscanus**, a monk of Exeter, who flourished about the year 1210, wrote a long poem in Latin hexameters, entitled *De bello Trojano*, which, to judge of it from the extracts printed by Warton, must have possessed great literary merit. Though now forgotten, it enjoyed so great a popularity, even as late as the fifteenth century, as to be thumbed by school-boys in every grammar-school, and ranked by teachers side by side with the genuine poets of Rome.

54. A classical metre was also employed by **Nigellus Wireker**, a monk of Canterbury and precentor of the cathedral, in his satire entitled *Speculum Stultorum*, written about 1190. The poem is in Latin elegiacs, which, though full of what we should call false quantities, are easy and flowing. It has so much point and humour that the reader will not be sorry to have an abstract of its contents :—

The hero of the *Speculum Stultorum* is Brunellus or Burnellus (little brown ass), the property of Bernardus, an Italian farmer. He runs away from his master, and begins to speculate on self-improvement. He considers that the fundamental misery of his condition lies in the shortness of his tail, and, to remedy this defect, he seeks counsel and assistance from all quarters. He goes to consult a physician named Galienus. Galienus tells him he is a fool; why not be content with his tail as it is? Louis, King of France, is obliged to be content with his tail; so are his bishops and barons: why not Burnellus? At last, to get rid of him, Galienus tells him that the only way is to go to Salerno, and get the necessary recipe and drugs from the great medical school there. The journey into Italy gives occasion for many satirical descriptions. Burnellus studies at Salerno; is cheated there by a London merchant; at last, laden with phials, medicines, and prescriptions, he sets out for home. Misfortunes, chiefly caused by monks, overtake him. The Benedictine monk Fromundus sets his dogs on him; they bite off half his tail; his baggage is thrown off, the phials broken, and the medicines lost. He is in despair; at last he resolves to go to Paris, that he may at least return home a scholar. To the University of Paris, of which a satirical description follows, he is accompanied by Arnoldus, who has joined him on the road, and tells a curious story.

Burnellus joins himself to the scholars of the English nation. He is thick-headed, and does not get on, so he resolves to turn monk. He passes in review all the orders; the Hospitallers of the White Cross, the Black Monks (Cluniacs), the White Monks (Cistercians), the monks of Grandmont, the Carthusians, the Black Canons, the Premonstratensians or Norbertines, the Secular Canons, and the Gilbertines of Sempringham. Not one of them pleases him entirely, and the modest idea occurs to him of founding a new order, which shall combine the good points and avoid the defects of all the rest. But suddenly his nose bursts out bleeding, and he takes this as a sign of coming evil. Bernardus his master appears, claims his property, and drives him off, after he has been on the loose for some five-and-twenty years. His master tells him that he shall have light work; only a few faggots, two brass panniers, two sacks of flour, and himself on the top of all. For greater security, he cuts off both the ears of poor Burnellus:—

> Funditus abscidit aurem Bernardus utramque,
> Cautior ut fieret, cauteriatus ita.

Cured of ambition, our hero thenceforth subsides into the normal existence of donkeys.

55. In the interesting volumes which contain Wireker's *Speculum* (*Anglo-Latin Satirical Poets of the Twelfth Century*, ed. by T. Wright, Rolls series) may be read the Epigrams of Henry of Huntingdon, and an elegiac poem of about 800 lines, *De Vitâ Monachorum*, by **Alexander Neckam**. This Neckam was the foster-brother of Richard I. He studied at Paris, and was known as one of the most brilliant scholars of his day, his special subjects being Grammar, Elocution, and Prosody.

But the preference of a dead language, even as the medium for poetry, could not in the nature of things hold its ground. In poetry, the originality of the thought, the vigour and aptness of the expression, are what constitutes the charm: we read it, not that we may learn about *things*, but that we may come in contact with thoughts. But no one can think with perfect freedom except in his native tongue, nor express himself with remarkable degrees of force and fire, unless upon subjects coming closely home to his feelings. To an ecclesiastic, whose home is the church, the church's language might perhaps be considered almost as his natural speech, so long as his thoughts are busied with religious objects. Thus no poem more startlingly real, more tender, more awe-inspiring, exists in any language, than the wonderful sequence ' Dies iræ, dies illa.' But for the themes of love, or war, or gaiety, with which poetry is principally conversant, the Latin could not be so apt a medium as the roughest of the vernacular tongues, since to the ear accustomed to the vivid and expressive utterances on these subjects to which the converse of daily life of necessity gives rise, its phrases must always have seemed cold, flat, and indirect. Hence, as the Trouvères and their imitators rise and multiply, the school of Latin poetry dwindles away, and after the middle of the thirteenth century nearly disappears.

The poetry which, strong in its truth to nature, supplanted its more polished rival, was the growth of France ; and to trace its origin, and analyse its many developments, is no part of the task of the historian of English literature. It is necessary, however, that the English student should have some general knowledge of the matter ; otherwise he would very imperfectly understand the course of English poetry in this and in the following period.

French Poetry.

56. The French poetry of the age was divided into two schools, the Norman and the Provençal. The poets of the one were called Trouvères ; those of the other, Troubadours. The language of the one was the *Langue d'oil*, that of the other the *Langue d'oc*.[1] The poetry of the Trouvères was mostly epic in its character ; that of the Troubadours mostly lyric. Each most probably arose independently of the other, although that of the Troubadours sprang the soonest into full maturity, as it was also the first to decline and pass away. The origin of the Provençal literature is to be sought in the amicable intercourse which subsisted during the ninth and tenth centuries between the Moorish and the Christian states of Spain, resulting for the latter in their acquaintance with, and imitation of, the Arabic poetry and prose

---

[1] So called from the different words signifying ' yes' in the two languages.

fiction. The poems of those children of the burning South were
distinguished by an almost idolatrous exaltation of the female
sex, and an inexhaustible inventiveness in depicting every phase,
and imagining every condition, of the passion of love.   The
Catalan minstrels took up the strain in their own language,
which was a variety of the *langue d'oc*; and from Catalonia,
upon its being united to a portion of Provence, in 1092, under
Raymond Berenger, Count of Barcelona, the newly kindled flame
of romantic sentiment and idealising passion passed into the
south of France, and gave birth to the poetry of the Troubadours.   Of this poetry, love is the chief, though not the sole,
inspiration.   It neglects the realities of life; it is impatient of
historical themes which require learning and toil; it is essentially
fugitive—subjective—conventional.   In a certain sense it may
be called *abstract* poetry, since throughout a large portion of it
the reader is removed from the world of concrete existences, and
placed in an imaginary realm, peopled by beings who own no
laws but the conventional decrees of a Court of Love, and know
no higher ambition than that of being a successful suitor. Such
a style evidently contains within itself the germ of a certain
dissolution, unless it admit of change and enrichment from without.   But external circumstances accelerated the fall of the literature of the Troubadours; the bloody wars of which the south
of France was the theatre during the early part of the thirteenth
century, silenced the minstrel's lute, and substituted the wail of
the mourner for the song of the lover.   Attempts were subsequently made, down even to the fifteenth century, to revive
the ancient style; but they failed to impart to it more than a
transient and factitious vitality.   But in its flourishing time the
Gay Science was eagerly cultivated in every part of Western
Europe, and kings were proud to rank themselves among its
members.   Our own **Richard Cœur-de-Lion** not only entertained at his court some of the most celebrated Troubadours
of Provence, but himself composed several *sirventes* which
are still extant.   A *tenson*, the joint composition of himself
and his favourite minstrel Blondel, is said, according to the
well-known story in Matthew Paris, to have been the means
of Blondel's discovering the place of the king's confinement in
Germany.

57. Almost the whole of the poetry of the Troubadours falls
under two heads : the *tenson* and the *sirvente*.[1] The former was
a kind of literary duel, or dialogue controversial, between two

---

[1] *Tenson* is connected by Raynouard with 'contention.' Ducange explains *sirventes* as ' poemata in quibus *servientium*, seu militum, facta et *servitia*
referuntur.'

rival Troubadours, on some knotty point of amatory ethics, and often took place before, and was decided by, a Court of Love. To these courts we shall again have occasion to refer when we come to speak of Chaucer. The latter was employed on themes of war or politics or satire. Among the most eminent composers of *sirventes* were Bertrand de Born, the gifted knight of Périgord, whose insidious suggestions kept alive for years the feud which divided our Henry II. and his sons,—Peyrols, a knight of Auvergne,—and Sordello of Mantua. Bertrand and Sordello both figure in the great poem of Dante, the one in the *Inferno*, the other in the *Purgatorio*. Poems by these, and many other Troubadours, may be found in the great work of M. Raynouard on the Provençal poetry.

58. But the poetry of the Trouvères had a far more important and lasting influence over our early English literature than that of the Troubadours. We may arrange it under four heads: —Romances, Fabliaux, Satires, and Historical Poetry. To the first head belong, besides a great number of poems on separate subjects, four great epic cycles of romance; the first relating to Charlemagne, the second to Arthur and the Round Table, the third to the crusades for the recovery of the Holy Sepulchre, and the fourth to the ancient world and its heroes, especially Alexander the Great.

Of the romances relating to Charlemagne, the oldest is the *Chanson de Roland*, a narrative of the last battle and death of the brave Roland on the field of Roncesvalles. This poem, although, in the shape in which we now have it, it was not written down earlier than the eleventh century, in its primitive form is believed to date from the reign of Louis le Débonnaire.[1] As it stands, it was written by Turold, a Norman, whom some identify with the abbot of Peterborough of the same name, who governed the convent from 1069 to 1098, or else with Turold, his father, the Conqueror's tutor. The oldest MS. of this noble poem is in the Bodleian Library. It is written in stanzas of varying length, in riming lines of eleven or ten syllables; each stanza ends with the war-cry 'Aoi.' It has been ably edited by M. Génin, and, more recently, by M. Gautier, professor of the École des Chartes.

59. Among the other celebrated pieces in this cycle are the *Four Sons of Aymon, Roland and Ferrabras*, and *Ogier le Danois*. A direct proof of the high antiquity of some portions at least of the Charlemagne romance is found in the lines in which Robert Wace, in the *Roman de Rou*, completed about 1160, describes

---

[1] Démogeot, *Hist. de la Lit. Française.*

the proceedings of the Norman minstrel Taillefer, just before the battle of Hastings :—

> Taillefer, ki mult bien cantout,
> Sor un cheval ki tost alout,
> Devant li Dus alout cantant
> De Karlemaine è de Rollant,
> E d'Oliver è des vassals
> Ki morurent en Renchevals.[1]

The Arthur Legend; The Saint Graal.

60. The next cycle, that of Arthur, was unquestionably founded upon the national and patriotic songs of Wales and Brittany. At the courts of the petty kingdoms of Wales, which for centuries, while the Saxons were fighting with each other or struggling against the Danes, seem to have enjoyed comparative prosperity and peace, the Welsh bards, feeding their imagination on the memory of the gallant stand made by their patriotic prince against the Teutonic hordes, gradually wove a beautiful tissue of romantic poetry, of which the central figure was Arthur. The songs in which his exploits were celebrated naturally made their way among their self-exiled brethren in Brittany, and, perhaps, were by them added to and embellished. From Brittany they easily passed into the rest of France, and by the congenial imaginations of the Norman poets were eagerly welcomed. This is the *direct* influence of Brittany upon the formation of the Arthur cycle; and it is exemplified in the romance of *Iwain* or *Owen*, composed in French by Chrétien of Troyes, about the year 1160, after the Breton original by Jehann Vaour. There was also an *indirect* or reflex influence, communicated through the British history of Geoffrey of Monmouth, which, as we have seen, is stated by its author to have been translated from a work in the Breton language. Geoffrey reproduced this work in Latin, adding probably a good deal from original Welsh sources, and the result was the *Historia Britonum*. This Latin history became exceedingly popular, and was resorted to by the Trouvères as a secondary mine of information respecting Arthur and the Round Table.

61. The steps by which the Arthur legend gradually reached the complex form which it wore in the thirteenth century, can be made out with tolerable clearness. Gildas the Wise, writing about 550, mentions a great victory won by the Britons over

---

[1] That is :—' Taillefer, who sang very well, on a horse which went quickly, went before the Duke, singing of Charlemagne, and of Roland, and of Olivier, and of the vassals, who perished at Roncevaux.'

the Saxons at the ' mons Badonicus,' but does not give the name
of the victorious chief.   Nennius, writing either at the end of
the seventh, or in the ninth century, mentions the same victory
as one of twelve gained at various times by the ' magnanimous
Arthur' over the Saxon invaders. This is the earliest mention
of Arthur.   Nennius also mentions a boy named Ambrosius,
born in a preternatural manner, who became a great magician,
and had more than mortal knowledge.   We pass over three or
four centuries, and in the *Historia Britonum* of Geoffrey of
Monmouth we find that the story of Arthur has grown enormously.   His birth and parentage are fully explained, and his
victorious career, both on the continent and in the British Isles,
is described.   The Ambrosius of Nennius now appears as Merlin
the enchanter, the contemporary not only of Vortigern, but of
Uther Pendragon and his son Arthur.   Concerning the Round
Table, however, Geoffrey is silent.   That splendid feature of the
legend first appears in the *Brut* of Robert Wace, which may be
some ten or twelve years later than the *Historia Britonum*.
Wace probably derived it from Breton poems or traditions to
which Geoffrey had not had access.   ' For the noble barons that
he had, of whom each thought himself to be the superior, each
accounted himself to be the better man, and none knew fear,—

> Fist reis Ertur la Runde Table,
> Dunt Bretun dient meint fable.'

(King Arthur made the Round Table, of which the Bretons tell
many a fable.)   Laȝamon, in his version of Wace, enters into
fuller particulars on the construction of the Table, which, by
giving no one the precedence, was to put an end to the bloody
conflicts for the uppermost seats which had been waged in
Arthur's court.   He ends by saying,—

> þis wes þat ilke bord
> þat Bruttes of ȝelpeð ;
> and sugeð feole cunne lesinge,
> bi Ardure þan kinge.

(This was that same Board, that the Bretons boast of, and tell
many kinds of leasings concerning Arthur the king.)
   62. The legend had now attained a rich development ; but
popular as it was, it certainly contained little that was edifying.
The Celtic nationality of its framers appeared in the manner in
which Arthur's frequent slaughters of the Saxons were gloated
over ; the diablerie and magic of the old pagan North found
expression in the stories of giants, serpents, enchanters, and
wizards engrafted upon it.   As it stood, it bore no *Christian*

impress ; nay, by the revengefulness which it breathed, and the
grotesque superstitions which it harboured, it must tend to lead
away from religion the crowds that heard it recited.   What if
the legend were, so to speak, converted and baptised ?   What if
the guilt of Arthur and the licentiousness of his barons were to
be visited with chastisement and expiated by penance ?   What if
a religious idea were introduced into it, which should form a
kind of *plot*, in connection with which both the existing forms
and any future developments of the legend might be arranged ?

63. Some such thoughts as these must have passed through
the mind of the great churchman who, towards the end of the
twelfth century, inwove into the Arthur legend the immortal
conception of the Saint Graal.   Whether it was Walter Map, or
some other, will never be known with certainty; the reader is
referred for fuller speculation on this point to Sir F. Madden's
edition of *Sir Gawayne* (printed for the Bannatyne Club in 1839),
and the learned and profound observations of M. Paulin Paris.[1]
From the literary point of view, the change may be said to
consist in the incorporation of the legend of Joseph of Arimathea
with that of Arthur.   Tradition had long connected Glastonbury
with Joseph ; there he was said to have established himself, and
built a chapel after landing in Britain ; the Christmas flowering
thorn which he planted is said to have flourishing descendants
to this day.   Taking the first suggestion of his story from the
apocryphal ' Gospel of Nicodemus,' in which he and Nicodemus
are said to have been thrown into prison at Jerusalem soon after
the Ascension, but miraculously delivered from confinement,
some inventive mind imagined a long series of adventures for
Joseph, terminating with his arrival in Britain.   Chief among
these adventures figure the marvellous incidents arising from his
guardianship of the Holy Graal.   In order to comprehend the
manner in which this new element is worked into and colours
the whole mass of romances relating to Arthur, it is necessary
to examine the circumstances under which it first appears.

64. In several of the oldest MSS. of romances of the Round
Table, existing in the national libraries of England and France,
distinct mention is made of an original Latin history of the
Holy Graal, from which the various French romances forming
the Arthurian cycle, including *Merlin, Tristan,* and *Lancelot,*
were, with more or less of amplification, translated.   This is
asserted in so many words by Hélie de Borron, in the preface to
his *Gyron le Courtois.*   This Latin original does not now exist,
and some critics have doubted whether it ever existed, and was

---

[1] *Les Manuscrits de la Bibliothèque Royale,* Paris, 1888.

not *assumed* merely, in order to give an air of authority and veracity to the romances said to be translated from it. Yet as the Latin original from which Wace translated his *Brut* certainly existed, it seems unreasonable to deny, in the face of positive statements by contemporaries, that there was some Latin treatise on which the romances of the Round Table were similarly founded. Luc de Gast, the author of the French romance of *Tristan*, says that he had 'read, and re-read, and many a time examined the great book in Latin which treats openly of the history of the Holy Graal.'[1] This Latin book may have been so utterly thrown into the shade by the celebrity of the French romances taken from it, that copies of it ceased to be made. In that case the few copies that ever existed may easily have been lost.

65. If this Latin book existed, it was probably written by **Walter Map**, a genius of the highest order, with that design of converting the Arthur legends, and employing them in the service of Christ, which has been already explained. His mode of proceeding was conceived of, perhaps by himself but certainly by others, in the following manner. The adventures of Lancelot and his fellows in the Quest of the Holy Graal, and the history of the Graal itself, were originally set down in writing in the Breton tongue by King Arthur's order, and the records thereof preserved in Salisbury Abbey. There Walter Map found them, and translated them, at King Henry's command, into Latin. So Geoffrey claimed to have founded his history of the Bretons on a Breton original. The MS. which we are here quoting goes on to say that Henry II. also caused the history of the Graal to be turned from Latin into French ;[2] this was done by Robert Borron. On the whole, I am inclined to believe that the Latin book of the Graal (*Historia de Gradali*) really existed, and that it was written by Map. The first part of it, the account of the Saint Graal, as containing the new element which it was his object to infuse into the cycle, he probably composed with great fulness and care. The legends of Merlin, Arthur's acts and death, of Lancelot, Tristan, and Palamedes, were already in existence when he began to write, some in a Welsh, some in a Breton, some even in a French dress; for the *Chevalier au Lion* at least, by Chrétien of Troyes, must have been written before any of the Graal romances appeared. That Map knew Welsh, we may, considering his Welsh extraction and long residence near the Welsh border, regard as certain ; it

[1] Paulin Paris, i. 118.
[2] Reg. 14 E. III., in the British Museum.

is probable therefore that he understood Breton also, and could read the legends of *Tristan* in the language in which they were then circulating. Fusing all these legends of the Round Table into one, connecting the very Round Table itself with the loss of the Holy Vessel and its Quest, interwining the threads of love and war, in the life of each Arthurian knight, with a golden mystic thread of more or less proximity to the Saint Graal, Map probably forbore to write in Latin with any great fulness the lives of these popular heroes. It was enough for him to have brought them and their actions into connection with the Saint Graal ; the Romance poets, working on the grand outlines which he had chalked out for them, might be trusted to fill in the details.

66. What then was the story of the Saint Graal? It was briefly this :—While Christ still hung upon the cross, Joseph of Arimathea, desiring to have some object which the Saviour's hands had touched for a memorial of Him, went to the house where He had held the last supper with His disciples, and found there the bowl or dish from which he had eaten the paschal lamb. This dish is the Graal.[1] After the deposition from the cross, Joseph, as the body of Christ is being laid in the tomb, receives into the Graal all the drops of blood that he can collect, as they flow from the sacred wounds. From this time all that happens to the Graal, and to those who come near it, is in the supernatural order. Thrown into prison, Joseph is nourished for many years by the Holy Graal alone, which appears to him in visions, and as an oracle reveals to him heavenly things. After he is released, he, at the command of Christ, departs from Palestine, taking with him nothing but the Graal, and after a series of marvellous adventures in many lands arrives in Britain. The Graal is kept in an ark, and the ark placed in a castle built for its reception. For several generations Britain prospers ; its kings are obedient to the faith ; and beatific glimpses of the Saint Graal are frequently vouchsafed. But a moral change comes on ; lust, cruelty, and irreligion reign everywhere unrebuked, and the land is desolated by factious strife. At last the sins of the people are so multiplied that the

---

[1] *Graal*, or *graalz*, means vessel of pleasure ; compare our ' loving-cup.' M. Fauriel refers it to the Provençal *grazul* ; in Ducange the forms *grasala, grassellus, graletus*, are found, all having the general meaning of ' vessel.' It must have been a word in common use ; for Helinand, a French chronicler who died early in the thirteenth century (the last date in his chronicle is 1204), after describing the Gradalis, says, ' Dicitur vulgari nomine *graalz*, quia grata et acceptabilis est in ea comedenti, tum propter continens . . . . tum propter contentum . . . .' With this agrees the explanation of Luc de Gast (MS. Reg. 20 D. III.) : ' Ce est l'escuelle qi a servise a touz ceus que je ai trove en mon servise, et por ce est elle apelle graals.' The etymology has not yet been satisfactorily explained.

Graal is withdrawn into heaven; at any rate it blesses human eyes no more. Yet a persuasion exists that it is not very far off, and may by diligent search be found; and Uther Pendragon, Arthur's father, institutes the order of knights of the Round Table for the express purpose of undertaking the quest of the Graal. This quest thenceforth influences the actions, and colours the legend, of each of the principal Arthurian heroes. Even when not seen, the Graal sometimes makes its presence felt in wonderful ways. In Sir Thomas Malory's version (Book x. part 2, ch. 4) we are told how the Holy Graal entered into the hall at Camelot, covered with white samite, while all the knights were seated at the Round Table; it passed by amid thunders and blinding flashes of sunlight: 'then had every knight such meat and drink as he best loved;' but there was none that might see it. Lancelot, Gawayne, Tristan, Bort, Agrawaine, and many others undertake the quest; they brave many perils, surmount many obstacles, but to none of them is the beatific vision granted, because they were not clean of heart. At last Sir Galahad, Lancelot's son, the type of Christian holiness and knightly honour, 'achieves the Saint Graal.' The holy vessel is manifested to him, with Joseph of Arimathea vested as a bishop kneeling before it. Galahad receives communion from the hands of Joseph, and entrusts to his companions a loving message for his father. 'And therewith he kneeled down before the table and made his prayers; and then suddenly his soul departed unto Jesus Christ. And a great multitude of angels bare his soul up to heaven, that his two fellows might behold it; also they saw come down from heaven a hand, but they saw not the body; and then it came right to the vessel, and took it and the spear, and so bare it up to heaven. Sithence was there never no man so hardy for to say that he had seen the Sancgreal (Saint Graal).'

67. It is evident that whoever conceived the idea of the Saint Graal had for his principal design to enforce the dignity and fruitfulness of the eucharistic mystery. The chalice on the Catholic altar is the Saint Graal; the treasure which it contains, like that in the Saint Graal, is present for brief intervals and disappears again; after 'the sakering of the Mass,' to use the words of old Malory, it is there; in a short space it vanishes, and is there no more. The only difference is, that whereas the ordinary chalice has not, as such, any peculiar sacredness, the Saint Graal is itself sacred, from having been held in the hands of Christ, and used by Him in celebrating the paschal feast. This distinction superadds to the religious significance of the conception an element of poetry and imagination, which brings

it within the sphere, and adapts it to the purposes, of literature. Nevertheless it remains true that a full comprehension of the Catholic doctrine of the eucharist is the proper key to understanding the pregnant import of this legend of the Saint Graal.

68. The number and order of the Graal romances may be thus represented :—

I. A Latin *Historia de Gradali* by Walter Map, written probably between 1160 and 1170, in which the commencements of the history of the Saint Graal were minutely given, and all the chief branches of Arthurian legend, Lancelot, Tristan, Perceval, &c., introduced with more or less of detail, and connected with the Saint Graal.

II. The *Saint Graal*, a romance in French prose, translated by **Robert Borron** (whom there is some reason to believe to have been a native of Nottinghamshire, and an ancestor of Lord Byron) from the Latin of Map. It has been printed for the Roxburghe Society, under the editorial care of Mr. Furnivall.

III. *Merlin* ; in French prose ; translated by Robert Borron.

IV. *Quest of the Saint Graal* ; in French prose ; by Walter Map ; see MS. Reg. 14 E. III. This is sometimes regarded as a branch of *Lancelot*.

V. *Lancelot* ; in French prose ; by Walter Map, as distinctly stated by Hélie de Borron.

VI. *Tristan* ; Part I. ; by **Luces, or Luc, de Gast**, a castle near Salisbury.

     „   Part II. ; by **Hélie de Borron**, a kinsman of Robert.

VII. *Mort Artur* ; by Walter Map.

VIII. *Gyron le Courtois* or *Palamedes* ; by Hélie de Borron. All these eight romances, except the first, are in French prose, and the dates of their composition probably range between 1160 and 1230. To these we must add—

IX. *Perceval* ; in French verse, by Chrétien of Troyes. This romance, which, with its continuations, extended to more than 20,000 lines, was founded on the prose *Tristan* of Luc de Gast, and probably written between 1190 and 1198, in which year Chrétien is thought to have died.

X. *Parzival*, with its prelude *Titurel* ; in German verse, by Wolfram von Eschenbach. Wolfram followed partly Chrétien of Troyes, partly a Provençal poet whom he names Kyot. The *Titurel* is thought to have been written in the last years of the twelfth century ; the *Parzival* between 1200 and 1207.

The earliest in order of time of all the French romances of the Graal, according to the express testimony of Hélie de Borron, was the *Tristan* of Luc de Gast.

69. That this legend of the Graal arose on British ground, there seems, on the whole, no ground for doubting. Yet M. Fauriel, in the work above cited,[1] concludes it to have been of Provençal origin, and Dr. Simrock in his edition of the *Parzival* takes the same view. With regard to M. Fauriel it is difficult to argue seriously with a writer who believes, not *Perceval* only, but *the whole series of Arthur legends*, to have been of Provençal origin. Dr. Simrock considers that the mention of Kyot, the Provençal poet, by Wolfram von Eschenbach, as the writer on the Graal whom he had chiefly followed, compels us to believe that the Graal legend had a Provençal origin. But in reply it may be argued:—

(1) Wolfram interlards what he says about Kyot with so many fabulous touches, that it is impossible to know how much of his words is to be believed. Kyot, he says, found the story of the Graal at Dolet (Toledo); it had first been written down by one Flegetanis, an astrologer, who, having a heathen father, worshipped a calf for his god, but on the mother's side was descended from Solomon. Flegetanis found out by the stars that the wondrous thing called the Graal was brought down to the earth by a band of angels, who then flew back to heaven. Evidently we are not on the ground of authentic statement here. But (2) Kyot, after all, is said by Wolfram to have found the Latin version of the work of Flegetanis which he used for his poem, not anywhere in the south of France, but in *Anjou*; a province belonging to Henry II., to which the work of Map might easily have come from England. Moreover, he is stated to have written in *French*, not in Provençal. It is needless to add that no one has ever seen a line of Kyot's poem. M. Fauriel lays much stress on allusions to the Saint Graal in the works of Provençal poets of early date. But the earliest clear allusion that I have seen is in a poem by Richard of Barbezieux, a troubadour of the thirteenth century, who might, of course, have read the French prose romances above enumerated. It seems to me that much stronger arguments than any hitherto adduced must be brought forward, before the glory of having originated the sublime conception of the Saint Graal can be justly withheld from Britain.

Other Epopees : Fabliaux : Riming Chronicles.

70. Of the third cycle, that relating to the crusades, the most important piece is the famous romance of Richard Cœur-

---

[1] *Histoire de la Poésie Provençale*, ii.

de-Lion. The French original is not known to exist, but there is an English metrical translation, dating probably from the reign of Edward I., which is of great interest. It abounds in marvellous or miraculous details, which, however, there is reason to suppose, were not in the original romance (which was of the nature of a true heroic poem, and contemporaneous with the crusade itself), but added by succeeding Norman minstrels in the course of the thirteenth century.[1]

71. The leading poem of the fourth cycle, that relating to the ancient world, is the *Alexandreis*, the joint work of Lambert li Cors and Alexandre de Bernay, which appeared in 1184. The extraordinary popularity of this romance caused the metre in which it was composed (rimed lines of twelve syllables) to drive out the heroic pentameters which had previously been employed for epic poetry in France, and to be known thenceforth by the name of *Alexandrine*. It shares with many other French poems of this period the peculiarity of continuing the same rime through a whole paragraph, or for as many lines as the poet can find fresh instances of it. For instance, in the first twenty-three lines there is but one rime, -*ir*; the next thirty-one lines have the rime -*ie*; the next six end in -*ele*, and so on. Some idea of the monotony resulting from this practice may be obtained from the following extract :—

> Por prendre bon exemple de proecce aquellir,
> De connoistre raison d'amer et de hair,
> De ses amis garder, et cierement tenir,
> Ses anemis grever, c'uns n'en puist avancir,
> Les laidures vengier, et les bienfaits merir,
> De canter, quant lius est, et a terme s'ofrir,
> Oies donques l'estore boinement, a l'oisir ;
>   *   *   *   *   *
> Cou est de l'millor roi que Dex laisast morir.
> D'Alixandre vus voel l'estore rafrescir,
> Cui Dex donna fierte et e l'cuer grant air,
> Qui par mer et par tierre osa gent envair, &c.

The poem opens with a dream which Alexander had, when a boy of ten years old, about an egg, out of which issued a serpent. The main points of the historical outline are preserved with tolerable fidelity; we read of the siege of Tyre, the defeat and death of Darius, of Porus the Indian king, and the death of the great conqueror at Babylon ; but the frame is filled in, and sometimes overlaid, with an infinite amount of Gothic embroidery. The poem extends to upwards of 12,000 lines.

[1] See Ellis's *Specimens of Early English Romances*, vol. ii. p. 93.

72. The Fabliau, or Metrical Tale, aimed, not at singing the actions of heroes, but at describing, in an amusing striking way, the course of real life. It was to the chivalrous romance what comedy is to tragedy—comedy, that is to say, like that of Menander, not like that of Aristophanes; it is not political, and does not attack individuals, but paints society and phases of character. With a frequent touch of satire, or flavour of cynicism, the Fabliau is upon the whole a true account of the everyday life and manners of the time, of which it conveys no very pleasing or edifying impression. Many fabliaux were drawn from eastern sources; *e.g.* the famous Indian tale of the *Seven Wise Masters*, which has been rendered or imitated in so many different languages.

73. The glaring inconsistencies which this world presents between promise and performance—between theory and practice—give rise in every age to satire. Every village has its satirist, who with greater or less skill exposes the hypocrite, and ridicules the dupe. It is quite a secondary question whether the satire current in any particular age finds or misses literary expression. In the Middle Ages the great literary movement of France, which we are now considering, could not fail to extend to satire also. And as deficient practice and performance are nowhere so offensive as when they accompany the grandest theories and the most uncompromising professions, it was natural that the vices of ministers of the Church, that one powerful European institution, the very grandeur of which made it a more obvious mark, should be the principal theme of mediæval satirists. The continuation of the *Roman de la Rose*, by Jean de Meung, composed about the end, and the famous tale of *Reynard the Fox*,[1] composed about the middle, of the thirteenth century, are full of satirical attacks upon men in high places and established institutions, in all which the clergy come in for the principal share of invective.

74. The period which produced so many Latin chronicles for circulation among the clergy, gave birth also to French chronicles in verse for the entertainment of the laity. In verse —because few laymen could read, and a history in rime was easier and more agreeable to remember, both for the reciter and for the hearer. We do not hear of prose chronicles in French, still less in English, until the next period, by which time a reading and cultivated lay audience had been formed. The chief name of note among these French metrical chroniclers is that of Maître Wace, a learned clerk, born in Jersey, near the

---

[1] See p. 425.

end of the eleventh century, and educated in Normandy. His first history, the *Brut d'Angleterre* (Chronicle of England), is in the main a translation of Geoffrey of Monmouth's *Historia Britonum* before mentioned, and ends with the year 680. His second work, the *Roman de Rou* (Rollo), is a history of the Dukes of Normandy, reaching down to 1170, the sixteenth year of Henry II. Part of this latter work is in the Alexandrine measure; the remaining portion, and all the *Brut d'Angleterre*, are in the eight-syllable romance metre. Another chronicler, Benoit, composed, at the desire of Henry II., a history of the Dukes of Normandy, which appeared some years after that of Wace. Wace died about the year 1175. Geffroy Gaimar wrote his *Estorie des Engles*, a metrical history of the Anglo-Saxon kings, about the middle of the twelfth century. His materials were,—a Latin history of the British kings lent him by Robert, Earl of Gloucester, who had caused it to be trans-lated from the *Welsh* (it was different, therefore, from the history in *Breton* of the same kings which had been used by Geoffrey of Monmouth); an 'estoire de Wincestre,' and an English book kept at 'Wassinburc,' *i.e.* Washingborough in Lincolnshire. The following couplet shows the metre :—

> Coment chescous maintint la terre,
> Quel ama pes, e li quel guerre.

English Poets and Translators; 'Havelok;' Lazamon, and other Riming Chroniclers; Religious Poems; Ormin. Hampole : Other Poems; Battle of Lewes, Owl and Nightingale.

75. The English poetry of the period from 1200 to 1350 bears witness, as we have said, in almost every line, to the powerful foreign influences amid which it grew up, and to which it owed the chief part of its inspiration. It may be arranged, therefore, under the same four heads as the French poetry ; to these, however, we will add two others, religious poems, and occasional poems; since it is in these compositions that we first find a marked originality, a promise of an independent growth to come.

Romances.—English versions or imitations of the popular French romances began to be multiplied towards the end of the thirteenth and beginning of the fourteenth centuries. For a particular account of these English romances, the reader may consult the work of Ellis.[1] Besides the two heroic sub-

---

[1] See also p 69.

jects, Charlemagne and Arthur, (the heroes of classical antiquity seem to have been less popular with the English versifiers), the crusades, particularly the one in which King Richard was engaged, and many miscellaneous topics, are handled by these writers. Yet even *Guy of Warwick, Bevis of Hamptoun,* and *Richard Cœur-de-Lion,* though the names have such a local and national sound, were founded upon French originals, the authors of which, indeed, were probably Englishmen, but derived from France their literary culture.

76. The earliest, or one of the earliest, and perhaps the most remarkable, of these English romances is the Anglo-Danish legend of *Havelok,* the unique MS. of which, discovered not many years ago in the middle of a volume of Lives of Saints in the Bodleian Library, was of course unknown to Ellis. This MS. dates from about the end of the thirteenth century. But we possess a French version of the same story about a hundred and fifty years earlier in the *Estorie des Engles* by Geffrei de Gaimar, who evidently derived it from an English chronicle—the book of 'Wassinburc' (Washingborough, near Lincoln)—which he mentions among his authorities. It would be interesting to know whether this book was in verse or prose; but Gaimar does not say. The substance of the story, according to the English version, is briefly this. The sovereigns of England and Denmark, dying about the same time, leave to inherit their kingdoms, the one a daughter, Goldeboro', the other a son, Havelok. The guardians of the children, Godrich in England, and Godard in Denmark, are both false to their trust; Goldeboro' is placed in Dover castle, and Havelok is given by Godard to the fisherman Grim, to be drowned in the sea. But a miraculous light issuing from the child causes Grim to spare him; and soon after, taking all his family with him, together with the young prince, he sails for England, and landing on the coast of Lincolnshire founds the town of Grimsby, which still bears his name. Twelve years pass, and Havelok has become a youth of marvellous size, strength, and beauty; Goldeboro', too, has become the loveliest of English maidens. Going to Lincoln for work in a time of scarcity, Havelok by feats of strength attracts the notice of Godrich; the traitor resolves to force Goldeboro' to marry him, as a kind of fulfilment of his promise to her father, to marry her to the 'best, fairest, and strongest man' in England. The marriage takes place in spite of the resistance of both; but Goldeboro' is soon comforted by beholding one night the marvellous splendour issuing out of Havelok's mouth. At her suggestion he sails for Denmark; there, after a long train of adventures, which the reader must imagine, he is recognised as

F

king, and defeats and slays Godard. Returning with a Danish
army to England, he visits Godrich with the like retribution.
Goldeboro' and he are crowned, reign over England for sixty
years, and have fifteen children, of whom all the sons live to be
kings, and all the daughters queens. Finally, the poet beseeches
all who have heard his tale—

> Þat ilke of you, with gode wille,
> Seye a Paternoster stille
> For him þat haveth þe ryme maked,
> And þerfore fele nihtes waked ;
> Þat Jhesu Crist his soule bringe
> Bi-fore his Fader at his endinge.

77. Another Anglo-Danish romance, the materials for which may also
have been taken from the book of Washingborough or some similar
compilation, is *King Horn*. It has come down to us both in English
and in French, and of each version there are but three extant manuscripts, all in English libraries. No MS. of the English version is of
earlier date than about 1290; but the poem itself must have been composed at least a hundred years earlier. I should not hesitate in dating,
with Mr. Wright, the English before the French version. The latter
is longer and more elaborate; it contains, besides the names of the
principal personages, which are the same as in the English version,
many names which are found in other French romances of the thirteenth
century. The English story has in it only names of pure Anglo-Danish
origin. The tale, which bears a considerable resemblance to that of
Havelok, tells how Horn, the son of the King of Suddene or Suthdene
(Surrey), while in exile at the Court of Westernesse (Devonshire),
won the love of Rymenhild, the king's daughter, and, after passing
through a thousand perils, in which he was aided by knights from
Westene-londe (Ireland), finally married her. The versification, though
rude, is often very pleasing. The following is the opening, as found in
the MS. in the Bodleian Library :—

> Alle ben he bliþe
> Þat to me wilen liþe :
> A song ich wille you singe
> Of Morye þe kinge.
> King he was bi westen,
> Wel þat hise dayes lesten ;
> And Godild hise gode quene,
> Feyrer non micte bene.
> Here sone havede to name Horn,
> Feyrer child ne micte ben born ;
> Ne reyn ne micte upon-reyne
> Ne no sonne by-schine,
> Fayrer child þanne he was,
> Brict so evere any glas,
> Whit so any lili flour,
> So rose red was hys colur.

King Horn has been edited in English by Ritson, Mr.

Lumby, and Dr. Horstmann, and in French and English by M. Francisque Michel.

78. .To a somewhat later date (1320–30) is assigned the legend of *Sir Gawayne and the Green Knight*, published by the Early English Text Society.

79. Scarcely any English versions of fabliaux are known to exist of earlier date than 1350. The raillery and more refined touches which belong to this class of compositions were not suited to the rude intelligences of the English-speaking popula-tion in the Norman period, and would have been utterly thrown away upon them. The only instance of a fabliau given by Ellis is the version of the Indian story before mentioned of the *Seven Wise Masters*, supposed to have been made from the French about the year 1330.

80. Under the head of satire, there exists a curious poem, entitled the *Land of Cockaygne*, the date of which is not cer-tainly known, though Warton is undoubtedly wrong in placing it as early as the twelfth century. It is a biting satire on the monastic orders, and bears the stamp of the flippant age of Boccaccio rather than that of the grave and earnest century of St. Bernard. Nothing is known about the author, nor is the French original, from which it was evidently taken, in existence.

81. Of the metrical chroniclers, who, in imitation of Wace and his fellow-labourers, related the history of England in English verse for the entertainment of the laity, the earliest in date is **Laȝamon**, priest of Ernley-on-Severn, now Areley, in Worcestershire, who about the close of the twelfth century pro-duced an amplified imitation of Wace's *Brut d'Angleterre*. This curious work, the earliest existing poem of considerable magni-tude in the English language, extends to about 16,000 long lines of four accents. To produce the effect of metre, Laȝamon employs both alliteration and rime, each of the rudest descrip-tion; sometimes, too, he seems unable to achieve either the one or the other. The writer seems to have been balancing be-tween the example of his French prototype, who uses rime, and the attractions of the old native Saxon poets, who employed nothing but alliteration. In the opening passage he tells of his parentage, and what induced him to write :—

> An preost wes on leoden[1] :
> Laȝamon wes ihoten[2].
> he wes Leovenaȶes sone :
> liȶe[3] him beo Drihten[4].
>   *   *   *   *

---

[1] in the land.   [2] called.   [3] gracious.   [4] the Lord.

Hit com him on mode :
and on his mern[1] þonke.
þet he wolde of Engle ;
þa æðelæn[2] tellen.
wat heo ihoten weoren :
and wonene[3] heo comen.
þa Englene londe :
ærest ahten.[4]

He goes on to say that he travelled over the land in search of
materials, and found three 'noble books,' which he used for his
guidance, the 'English book' of St. Beda, the Latin book written
by St. Albin and 'the fair Austin, who brought baptism in
hither,' and the French book by Wace.   By the first two books,
he seems merely to have meant the *Ecclesiastical History* of St.
Beda, in its English and in its Latin shape.   The English version is that which bears the name of Alfred.   By some misappre-
hension he appears to have confounded Albinus, abbot of Canterbury, who is mentioned in Beda's preface as having supplied
him largely with materials, with the author of the history.

82. Two MSS. of Laȝamon's *Brut* exist, both in the British
Museum.   The oldest of these is in every way the most interesting ; it is held to have been written, or completed, about 1205.
The later version is considerably shorter, and the MS. containing it was much damaged by the fire at the Cottonian Library in
1731, a portion of it being destroyed, and another portion made
illegible.   In the earlier text not so many as fifty words of
French origin have been found.   Of these, the later text, which
is assigned to the middle of the thirteenth century, retains
thirty, and adds to them rather more than forty.   The two texts
together contain more than 28,000 lines, and only about ninety
French words; from this fact may be inferred the great slow-
ness with which, at any rate in remote country districts like the
corner of Worcestershire where Laȝamon wrote, the speech of the
people was mingled with that of their conquerors.

Laȝamon is considerably fuller than Wace whom he imitates,
and a complete inquiry into the sources whence he drew his
additional matter has yet to be made.   The valuable edition of
the *Brut*, with translation and notes, which bears the name of
Sir F. Madden, was printed in 1847 for the Society of Antiquaries.

83. The poem relates how Brutus, the great-grandson of
Æneas, collecting a band of his Trojan kinsmen, descended from
the exiles who had settled in Greece after the destruction of
Troy, put himself at their head, and after a voyage full of peril
and vicissitude landed at Dartmouth in Totnes.   He became the

[1] chief.   [2] noble deeds.   [3] whence.   [4] first owned.

ancestor of the kings of Britain, among whom Lud, Bladud, Lear, Gorboduc, and Lucius are reckoned. The last king mentioned in the poem is Cadwalader, whose date is 689 A.D. The exploits of Uther Pendragon and his more famous son Arthur are, as mentioned above,[1] related with great fulness.

84. An interval of nearly a hundred years separates Laȝamon from the next of the riming chroniclers, **Robert of Gloucester.** Robert, as he follows Geoffrey of Monmouth, travels partly over the same ground as Laȝamon, whose prototype, Wace, also followed Geoffrey. But in everything else but their subject, the difference between the two chroniclers is enormous. Divest Robert of his strange orthography, and he becomes a readable, intelligible English writer. A monk of a great monastery in an important frontier city, his style is that of a man who is fully up to the level of the civilization, and familiar with the literature of his age, while Laȝamon's bespeaks the simple parish priest, moving among a rustic population, whose barbarous dialect he with a meritorious audacity adapts as best he can to literary purposes. Robert's chronicle, which is in long twelve-syllable lines, is continued to the year 1272.

85. To Robert of Gloucester succeeds **Robert Manning,** a native of Brunne, or Bourn, in South Lincolnshire, and a monk of the Gilbertine monastery of Sixhill. Manning composed a riming chronicle in two parts: the first, a translation, in the ordinary octosyllabic verse of the romance writers, of the everlasting *Brut* by Wace, of which the reader has already heard so much; the second, a version in Alexandrine verse of a French metrical chronicle by Peter Langtoft, a canon regular of St. Austin at Bridlington in Yorkshire, ending with the death of Edward I. in 1307. The Prologue to the second part explains so simply and clearly the motives which induced the riming chroniclers to employ themselves on a task which to our modern notions involves a strange misapplication of poetical power, that it seems advisable to insert it here :—

> Lordynges that be now here,
> If ye wille listen and lere [learn]
> All the story of Inglande,
> Als Robert Mannyng wryten [written] it fand,
> And on Inglysch has it schewed,
> Not for the lerid bot for the lewed [lay people],
> For tho [those] that on this lond wonn [dwell]
> That the Latyn ne Frankys conn [know neither Latin nor French],
> For to haf solace and gamen
> In felauschip when tha sitt samen [together].

---

[1] See *ante*, § 61.

And it is wisdom for to wytten [know]
The state of the land, and haf it wryten,
What manere of folk first it wan,
And of what kynde it first began.
And gude it is for many thynges
For to here the dedis of kynges,
Whilk [which] were foles, and whilk were wyse,
And whilk of tham couth [knew] most quantyse [quaintness,
    i.e. artfulness] ;
And whilk did wrong, and whilk ryght,
And whilk mayntend pes [peace] and fyght.
Of thare dedes salle be my sawe [story],
In what tyme, and of what law,
I salle you schewe, fro gre to gre [degree, *i.e.* step by step],
Sen [since] the tyme of Sir Noe.

In this same Prologue, Manning speaks of the ' geste' of
Tristrem, as written in verse by Thomas of Ercildoune, complaining that it is commonly not said as Thomas made it. A
note at the end of the MS. states that this part of his chronicle
was finished by Manning in 1338.

Another poem by the same author, *Meditacyuns of the Soper of oure
Lorde Jesus,* translated from St. Bonaventure's *Vita Christi* between
the years 1315 and 1330, has been lately printed for the Early English
Text Society. It opens thus :—

Allemyghty God yn trynyte,
Now and ever wyth us be ;
For thy Sones passyun
Save alle þys congregacyun ;   •
And graunte us grace of gode lyvyng,
To wynne us blysse wythouten endyng.

But the most interesting of all Manning's works is his
Handlyng Synne, translated, with the addition of many original
passages, from the *Manuel des Pechés* of William de Waddington,
written about thirty years before. The *Handlyng Synne* has
been printed for the Roxburghe Club. The modern character
of the language, and the large admixture of French words in this
poem, have been well pointed out by Mr. Kington Oliphant.[1]
It was written in 1303, as the following lively passage shows :—

To alle Crystyn men undir sunne,
And to gode men of Brunne,
And speciali alle bi name
The felaushepe of Symprynghame,
Roberd of Brunne greteth yow
In all godenèsse that may to prow [benefit].

[1] *Sources of Standard English,* p. 182.

Of Brymwake yn Kestevene,
Syxé myle besyde Sympryngham evene [plain]
Y dwellede yn the pryorye
Fyftene yere yn companye.

* * * * * * *

Dane Felyp was mayster that tyme
That Y begau thys Englysch ryme.
The yeres of grace fyl [fell] than to be
A thousynd and thre hundrede and thre.
In that tyme turnede Y thys
On Englysshe tunge out of Frankys.

86. **Religious Poems.**—Among those that remain to us, the most important is Ormin's work on the Gospels, usually called the *Ormulum*. It has been carefully edited by Dr. R. M. White, formerly the Oxford professor of Anglo-Saxon. Ormin and his brother Walter, to whom he dedicates the work, were both regular canons of St. Austin. To what part of England he belonged is unknown; but the dialect which he uses is considered to point to the district surrounding Peterborough. There are no means of fixing the date with certainty; it is roughly set down as the middle of the thirteenth century. The work is described by Dr. White as ' a series of Homilies, in an imperfect state, composed in metre without alliteration, and (except in very few cases) also without rime; the subjects of the Homilies being ' the gospels daily read at the mass. The unique MS. is in the Bodleian Library; it is in a sadly mutilated condition. Ormin's plan was to paraphrase the gospel of the day, and then give a commentary upon it. He gives the heads of 230 gospels and twelve lessons from the Acts, but the part of the poem now extant only comes down to the thirty-second gospel, and is imperfect. In his prologue Ormin (whose system of orthography, invented by himself, requires the doubling of every consonant that follows a short vowel) thus describes his plan:—

Ic hafe sammnedd [1] o þiss boc
Þa Goddspelless neh [2] alle,
Þatt sinndenn [3] o þe messe-boc [4]
Inn all þe ȝer [5] att messe
And aȝȝ [6] affterr þe Goddspell stant
Þatt tatt te Goddspell meneþþ,
Þatt mann birrþ spellenn [7] to þe follc,
Off þeȝȝre [8] sawle nede.

87. The *Proverbs of Hendyng*, written in the southern dialect, near the end of the thirteenth century, are of unknown author-

---

[1] collected. [2] nigh. [5] are. [4] mass-book. [5] year.
[6] eke, also. [7] ought to declare. [8] their.

ship. They consist of forty stanzas of seven lines, each ending
with a proverb, followed by 'Quoth Hendyng.' They have been
printed in *Reliquiæ Antiquæ*.

88. The *Cursor Mundi* (date about 1320), a 'metrical version
of Old and New Testament History,'[1] in which are interwoven
many legends of Saints, has never yet been printed entire; it
was once very popular, as is shown by the existence of numerous
MSS.

89. Richard Rolle, who lived as a hermit at Hampole near
Doncaster, and died in 1349, is the author of a metrical version
of the Psalms in the northern dialect, which obtained a wide
notoriety, and also of a curious moral poem called *The Pricke
of Conscience*. This he wrote both in Latin and English. The
following passage[2] on the joys of Heaven is a favourable specimen of Hampole's manner :—

> Alle manere of joyes er in that stede.
> Thare es ay lyfe withouten dede ;
> Thare es yhowthe ay withouten elde,
> Thare es al kyn welth ay to welde.
> Thare es rest ay, withouten travayle ;
> Thare es alle gudes that never sal fayle ;
> Thare es pese ay, withouten stryf ;
> Thare es alle manere of lykyng of lyfe ;
> Thare es, withouten myrknes, lyght ;
> Thare es ay day and never nyght,
> Thare es ay somer fulle bryght to se,
> And never mare wynter in that contre.

90. Of the other religious poems in English which remain to us
from this period, some (as the two by Manning before described)
are didactic poems on points of Christian doctrine or morality ;
some, Lives of Saints ; some, lastly, short poems on devotional
topics, such as the *Crucifixion* and the *Blessed Virgin under
the Rood*. Many interesting relics of this kind have been lately
published by the Early English Text Society, *e.g.* the metrical
lives of *St. Marherete* [Margaret] and *St. Juliana*, and the *Story
of Genesis and Exodus*.

91. The religious poems were probably written by ecclesiastics ; but the *occasional* and *miscellaneous* poems of the period are
evidently for the most part the productions of laymen. There
is one of these which the certainty of its date, and the remarkable character of its contents, render so important from an historical point of view, that it must be noticed here. This is a piece
(given by Warton *in extenso*) composed after the battle of Lewes

---

[1] *Specimens of Early English*, Morris and Skeat, Part II.
[2] Ibid. p. 124.

in 1264, by an adherent of Simon de Montfort. The number of French words which it contains, and the easy way in which they are employed, unite to prove that the new English language was well on in the process of formation, conditioned always by the necessity, which this writer frankly accepts, of incorporating a vast number of French words, expressive of the ideas which England owed to the Norman invasion. Again, the broad, hearty satire, the strong anti-royalist, or rather anti-foreigner, prejudices of the writer, the energy of resolution which the lines convey, point unmistakably to the rise, which indeed must any way be dated from this century, of a distinct English nationality, uniting and reconciling the Norman and Saxon elements. A portion of this poem is subjoined :—

> Sitteth alle still, and herkneth to me ;
> The kyng of Alemaigne, bi mi leautè,
> Thritti thousent pound askede he,
> For te make the pees in the countrè,
>   And so he dude more.
> Richard, thah thou be ever trichard,[1]
>   Tricthen shalt thou never more.
>   *   *   *   *   *
> The kyng of Alemaigne wende [2] do ful wel,
> He saisede the mulne [3] for a castel,
> With hare [4] sharpe swerdes he grounde the stel,
> He wende that the sayles were mangonel,[5]
>   To help Wyndesore.
> Richard, &c.
>   *   *   *   *   *
> Sire Simond de Mountfort hath suore bi ys chyn,
> Hevede [6] he now here the erl of Waryn,
> Should he never more come to is yn,[7]
> Ne with sheld, ne with spere, ne with other gyn,[8]
>   To helpe of Wyndesore.
> Richard, &c.
>
> Sire Simond de Montfort hath suore bi ys fot,
> Hevede he nou here sire Hue de Bigot,
> Al he shulde grante here twelf-moneth scot,
> Shulde he never more with his sot pot,
>   To helpe Wyndesore.
> Richard, &c.
>
> Be the luef, be the loht,[9] sire Edward,
> Thou shalt ride sporeless o' thy lyard,[10]
> Al the ryhte way to Dovere-ward,
> Shalt thou nevermore breke foreword,[11]
>   Ant that reweth sore ;

[1] Treacherous. [2] Weened. [3] Mill. [4] Their. [5] A military engine.
[6] Had. [7] His inn. [8] Engine.
[9] Be thou lief, be thou loth. [10] Grey horse. [11] Promise.

Edward, thou dudest ase a shreward,
Forsoke thyn emes lore,[1]
Richard, thah thou be ever trichard,
Tricthen shalt thou never more.

92. To the reign of Henry III. (1216–1272) is supposed to belong the remarkable poem of *The Owl and Nightingale*, written probably by the 'Maister Nichole of Guldeforde' (Guildford), who is named in it, or else by his brother John of Guildford, the author of the piece which, in the Cottonian MS., precedes that which we have under consideration. Perched on a spray, whence she looks down with sovereign contempt on her un-melodious adversary, the Nightingale challenges the Owl to a contest and controversy regarding their respective qualities of song. The Owl consents; a dialogue follows, in which the Owl stands chiefly on the defensive, maintaining that her song is less harsh, and her appetite for mice and small birds less ravenous, than the proud Nightingale would allow. In the end they agree to go to Portesham, and submit their dispute to Master Nicholas of Guildford. The Owl says that she can repeat all that has been said :—

' Telle ich con word after worde;
And ʒef þe þincþ þat ich mis-rempe,
Þu stonde aʒein, and dome crempe.'
Mid þisse worde forþ hi ferden,
Al bute here and bute verðe,
To Portesham þat heo bi-come;
Ah hu heo spedde of heore dome
Ne chan ich eu namore telle;
Her nis namore of þis spelle.

('I can tell word after word, and if it seemeth to thee that I mis-state, do thou stand against me and stop judgment.' With these words forth they fared, all without army and without followers, until they reached Portesham. But how they sped in their judgment, I can no more tell you; here is no more of this story.)

The poem is nearly 1,800 lines long; it is in the dialect of the South of England, with many Danish forms. It was probably imitated from the *Roman de Rose*, or rather suggested by it. In that famous and widely influential poem, frequent mention is made of birds and their singing powers. The garden which the poet sees in his dream is alive with them:

In many places were nyghtyngales,
Alpes, fynches, and wodewales,

[1] Forsake thine uncle's teaching.

and various other birds,—

> That songen for to wynne hem prys,
> *And eke to sormounte in her songe*
> *That other briddes hem amonge.*[1]

93. In Hickes' *Thesaurus*, part of a moral poem of 119 stanzas is given, which the learned editor placed just after the Conquest, and to which Warton (*Eng. Poetry*, § 1) would assign a still earlier date. The progressive changes in the language being now better understood, no modern critic would think of placing this poem much before the middle of the thirteenth century. From a MS. in the Bodleian the following specimen is taken :

> Ic am elder þanne ic wes
> a winter and ec a lore ;[2]
> ic ealdi more þanne ic dede,
> mi wit oȝhte to bi more.

> Wel longe ic habbe child ibien[3]
> on worde and on dede ;
> Þeȝh[4] ic bi on wintren eald,
> to ȝiung[5] ic am on rede.
> *   *   *   *   *

> Deað com on þis midelard,[6]
> þurð þes defies onde ;[7]
> and senne and sorȝe[8] and iswinc[9]
> on se and on londe.

Early English Prose : The Ancren Riwle ; Ayenbite of Inwyt.

94. It would not be easy to point out any considerable work in English prose, belonging to the period between the cessation of the Peterborough Chronicle in 1154 and the end of the twelfth century. Early in the thirteenth, the *Ancren Riwle*, or Rule for Anchorites, was written. This interesting treatise partakes of three characters ; it is a rule of daily life, a manual of instruction in those portions of the Christian doctrine which relate to counsels of perfection, and a guide to devotion. It was edited for the Camden Society in 1853. It has been ascribed to

---

[1] *Romaunt of the Rose*, as translated by Chaucer.
[2] In winters and also in learning.   [3] been.   [4] though.
[5] young. The reader will observe how this letter ȝ, which represented a guttural sound in the early language, was replaced in course of time, in some words by *g* or *gh*, in others by *y*.
[6] earth ; A.S. *middangeard*.
[7] through the devil's rancour ; A.S. *anda*. [8] sorrow.   [9] toil.

Simon of Ghent, who died in 1315; but considering the very archaic character of the language, the opinion which holds a former bishop of Salisbury, Richard le Poore, to be the author, appears to me preferable. Bishop le Poore, the commencer, and in great part the builder, of the glorious cathedral at Salisbury, died in 1237.

The work was written for a small society, consisting of three religious ladies, residing at Tarente, now Tarrant-Kaimes, in Dorsetshire. At a later period their house received the Cistercian rule, but at this time they appear not to have belonged to any regular order. The dialect is considered to be West of England; it much resembles that of Laȝamon, but differs from it in respect of the large number of French and Latin words which it admits. I quote a sentence from the extract printed in Mr. Kington Oliphant's *Standard English:*—

'A lefdi [lady] was, þet was mid hire voan [foes] biset al abuten, and hire lond al destrued, and heo [she] al povre, wiðinnen one eorðene castle. On [a] mihti kinges luve was þauh [however] biturned upon hire, so un-imete [measureless] swuðe [very], þet he vor [for] wouhlecchunge [wooing] sende hire his sonden [messengers], on efter oðer, and ofte somed [at once] monie [many]: and sende hire beaubelet [baubles, jewels] boðe veole [many] and feire, and sukurs of liveneð [victuals], and help of his heie hird [army] to holden hire castel.'

95. The *Ayenbite of Inwyt*, or Remorse of Conscience, is a translation by Dan Michel, of Northgate, Kent, made in 1340, of the French treatise, 'Le Somme des Vices et des Vertus,' composed near the end of the thirteenth century by Frère Lorens. The dialect is the Kentish, and exceedingly rough. It was edited by Dr. Morris for the Early English Text Society in 1866.

CHAPTER I.

EARLY ENGLISH PERIOD.

1350—1450.

1. Hitherto such English writers as we have met with since the Conquest have generally appeared in the humble guise of translators or imitators. In the period before us we at last meet with original invention applied on a large scale : this, therefore, is the point at which English literature takes its true commencement.

The Latin and French compositions, which engaged so much of our attention in the previous period, may in this be disposed of in a few words. That Englishmen still continued to write French poetry, we have the proof in many unprinted poems by Gower, and might also infer from a passage, often quoted, in the prologue to the *Testament of Love.*[1] But few such pieces are of sufficient merit to bear printing. In French prose scarcely anything can be mentioned besides the despatches, treaties, &c., contained in Rymer's *Fœdera* and similar compilations, and the original draft of Sir John Maundevile's *Travels in the Holy Land.* Froissart's famous *Chronicle* may, indeed, be considered as partly belonging to us, since it treats largely of English feats of arms, and its author—the son of a painter of armorial bearings—entered in early youth the service of Queen Philippa in the capacity of secretary, and held for many years a post in the household of Edward III.

2. In Latin poetry there is nothing that deserves mention except the *Liber Metricus* of **Thomas Elmham**, concerning the career of Henry V., edited by Mr. Cole for the Rolls series in 1858. Elmham, who flourished about the year 1440, was a Benedictine monk in the monastery of St. Austin's, Canterbury. The poem contains 1,349 lines, and is, as Byron would have

---

[1] 'Lette than clerkes enditen in Latin, for they have the propertie of science, and the knowing in that facultie : and lette Frenchmen in their Frenche also enditen their queinte termes, for it is kyndely to their mouthes, and let us showe our fantasies in soche wordes as we lerneden of our dames tonge.'

said, not so much poetry as ' prose run mad ; ' in proof of which
let these lines suffice :—

> Hic Jon Oldcastel Christi fuit insidiator,
> Amplectens hæreses, in scelus omne ruens ;
> Fautor perfidiæ, pro sectâ Wiclivianâ,
> Obicibus Regis fert mala vota sacris.

Whether the last line means ' he wishes ill to the king's devout
objects,' or what else it means, it is hard to say.

3. In Latin prose, we have a version, made by himself, of
Maundevile's Travels, and the chroniclers (amongst others of
less note), Robert de Avesbury, Henry Knyghton, Thomas
Walsingham, and John Fordun. **Robert de Avesbury** was
registrar of the Archbishop of Canterbury's Court, and wrote a
fair and accurate history of the reign of Edward III. (published
by Hearne in 1720) coming down to the year 1356, in which or
in the following year he died. **Henry Knyghton**, the date of
whose death is unknown, was a canon regular of Leicester ; he
is the author of *Compilatio de Eventibus Angliæ a tempore
Regis Edgari usque ad mortem Regis Ricardi II.* His account
of the rise of Lollardism, though written with a strong anti-
Wycliffite bias, is highly interesting and valuable.

4. The *Historia Anglicana* of **Thomas Walsingham**, a
work to which all modern historians continually refer in writing
of the events of the fourteenth and earlier portion of the fifteenth
centuries, was edited by Mr. Riley for the Rolls series in 1864.
Scarcely anything is known of Walsingham except that he was
a monk of St. Albans, that he compiled, besides the *Historia*,
an account of Normandy, called *Ypodigma Neustriæ*, and that
he was still alive in 1419. The *Historia*, as it stands, extends
from 1272 to 1422 ; but Mr. Riley shows some ground for supposing that the portion compiled by Walsingham himself may
reach no further than to 1392, the only really original and valuable part even of this being the fifteen years between 1377 and
1392, while the concluding thirty years were added by some
unknown hand.

5. **John Fordun**, a secular priest of Kincardineshire, is the
author of the *Scotichronicon*, a history of Scotland in Latin
prose, written towards the close of the fourteenth century. The
entire work contains sixteen books ; but of these only five and
part of the sixth were composed by Fordun, the remainder
being the work of Abbot Bower, who brings down the story to
the death of James I. in 1437.[1]

---

[1] Irving's *History of Scottish Poetry*, edited by Dr. Carlyle, p. 116.

6. In theology and philosophy occurs the name of **John Wyclif**, the ablest schoolman of his day in England, admired by his contemporaries as an expert logician and prolific system-monger, long before he wrote those attacks on the hierarchy, the mendicant friars, and the received doctrine concerning the Eucharist, which gained for him with posterity the name of the first English reformer. His numerous Latin works, very few of which have ever been printed, are classed by Dr. Shirley in his excellent *Catalogue of the original Works of John Wyclif*,[1] under six heads: 1. Philosophy and Systematic Theology; 2. Sermons, Expositions, and Practical Theology; 3. Protests, Disputations, and Epistles; 4. On Church Government and Endowments; 5. On the Monastic Orders; 6. On the Secular Clergy. Under the first head is included the *Summa Theologiæ*, a body of Divinity of stupendous magnitude, the substance of which he afterwards reproduced in the *Trialogus, sive Summa Summæ*, the best known of all his works, printed at Basle by the Swiss reformers in 1525.[2] Two or three of his shorter Latin tracts are contained in the *Fasciculi Zizaniorum*, which, in spite of its enigmatical title, is a volume of remarkable interest, in respect of the light which it throws on the ecclesiastical history of the last half of the fourteenth century. Here are described in detail the first bickerings between Wyclif and the friars his opponents, the synodical proceedings taken by the bishops against the rising heresy, the turbulent sympathy of the masters at Oxford with the accused, and the steps taken by the Government, on a scale of ever increasing severity, to enforce submission to the hierarchy. Dr. Shirley's introduction to the volume, which was edited by him for the Rolls series in 1858, explains the acts and tendencies of Wyclif, in a spirit characterised alike by penetration and fairness.

7. Early in the fifteenth century the Wycliffite opinions were examined by a theologian of far greater power than Wyclif —**Thomas of Walden**, author of the *Doctrinale Fidei*. Thomas was a Carmelite, a member of one of those orders of friars which Wyclif pursued with incessant malediction. He was confessor to Henry V., and was summoned as a theologian to attend the sessions of the Council of Constance, at which the views of Wyclif were condemned. But finding that the Lollard party was still widely spread through the country, Walden undertook to combat their innovations once for all in a systematic treatise, which he dedicated to Pope Martin V. The *Doctrinale*, which

[1] Clarendon Press, 1865.
[2] And lately carefully edited by Dr. Lechler, of Leipsic, for the Clarendon Press. 1869.

appeared in 1428, is in three parts—1. 'De Deo, Christo, Petro, Ecclesia, et Religionibus;' 2. 'De Sacramentis;' 3. 'De Sacramentalibus.' In the first, Wyclif's unsound views on the divine nature, on the prerogatives of the see of Peter, on the authority of the Church, and on the nature and objects of the monastic profession, are powerfully and eloquently rebutted. In the second part, his novel opinions on the Eucharist are discussed. The third part, on Sacramentals, deals with the externals and accessories of religion, and is directed rather against the Lollards than against Wyclif himself. The style of the work has great merits; and to this probably it is owing that it was printed on the continent in the sixteenth century (Venice, 1571), although in this country, owing to the change of religion, it has been allowed to lie in manuscript. It is certain, sooner or later, to receive more adequate recognition than has hitherto been its lot.

8. The obvious cause of the decline of French and Latin composition in England was the growing prevalence, social and literary, of the native speech. To this many circumstances contributed. The gradual consolidation of nationalities, which had long been making steady progress throughout Europe, had been constantly drawing the Norman barons and the English commonalty closer together, and separating both from the rival nationality of France. Nor had the nation at any time lost, so to speak, its personal identity : it was *England* for which the Norman Richard fought at Acre; and even William of Malmesbury, writing not a hundred years after the Conquest, speaks of that event rather as a change of dynasty occurring in English history, than as of a complete social revolution. The influence of the Church must have pressed powerfully in the same direction. Though the Conqueror filled nearly all the sees with Normans, it was not long before native Englishmen, through that noble respect for and recognition of human equality which were—theoretically always, and often practically—maintained in the midst of feudalism by the Church of the Middle Ages, obtained a fair proportion of them. The political and official power of bishops in those days was great, and the native tongue of an English Archbishop of Canterbury could not, even by the proud Norman barons, his compeers in Parliament, be treated with disrespect. Again, since 1340, England and France had been constantly at war : in this war the English-speaking archers, not the French-speaking barons, had won the chief laurels : and the tongue of a humbled beaten enemy was likely to be less attractive to the mass of Englishmen than ever. The well-known law of Edward III., passed in 1362, directing the

English language to be used thenceforward in judicial pleadings, was merely an effect of the slow but resistless operation of these and other cognate causes. Again, it must not be lost sight of, that a sort of tacit compromise passed between the English and French-speaking portions of the population : the former were to retain the entire grammar—so much, at least, as was left of it—of the native speech ; all the conjunctions, prepositions, and pronouns,—the osseous structure, so to speak, of the language, —were to be English ; while, in return, the Normans were to be at liberty to import French nouns, adjectives, and verbs at discretion, without troubling themselves to hunt for the corresponding terms in the old literary Anglo-Saxon. Finally, this English language, so re-cast, became in the fourteenth century the chosen instrument of thought and expression for a great poet ; and, after Chaucer, no Englishman could feel ashamed of his native tongue, nor doubt of its boundless capabilities.

But the literary influences which had been long at work, united to the stubbornness of the popular preference for rhythms which had come down to them from their forefathers of at least eight centuries before, found ruder and, in a sense, more congenial expression than through the mouth of Chaucer. This is also the age of Langland, the author of the long alliterative poems which sounded so musically in the ears of the countrymen of Caedmon, and to the consideration of which we now proceed. Before, however, examining the *Vision of William concerning Piers the Plowman*, with Langland's other works, some notice must be taken of other alliterative poems of earlier date.

9. **Alliterative Poems.**—One of the lives of St. Margaret, noticed above at p. 72, is of very early date, about 1200, and alliterative. The Rev. O. Cockayne, who edited it in 1866 for the Early English Text Society, printed it as prose, in order to ' abide by the example of our forefathers ! ' It did not strike him that our forefathers wrote down verse in this way, on account of the scarcity and dearness of parchment : they could not afford to leave so much of their material uncovered, as they must have done had they written verse as we do. The poem opens :—

> Efter ure Laverdes pine, and his passiun,
> Ant his deð on rode, ant his ariste of deað.

The legend appears to be translated from a contemporary life by Theotimus of Antioch, and, though full of marvels, makes no allusion to that particular one which is represented in Raphael's exquisite picture of the saint.

10. Of Laȝamon's *Brut*, which is partly alliterative partly

rimed, we have already spoken. A long period follows, to which no alliterative poems have as yet been certainly assigned; but that such poems will yet be recognised among the unprinted MSS. of our libraries, seems exceedingly probable. The alliterative romance of *Sir Gawayne and the Green Knight*, first printed by Sir F. Madden in 1839 for the Bannatyne Club, and re-edited by Dr. Morris for the Early English Text Society, is deemed by the last editor to have been written about 1320. Sir Gawayne, Arthur's nephew, was the favourite hero of many a worker in the vast and splendid field of Arthurian romance. Passages in this particular poem can be traced to the *Perceval* of Chrétien de Troyes. The dialect is Northern, and not a little barbarous. The letter ȝ, which we have hitherto met with only as a guttural, occurs often in this poem with a sibilant sound, which led, in innumerable poems of later date, to its being confounded, or used interchangeably, with *z*. Thus we read at the opening :—

> Siþen þe sege and þe assaut watȝ sesed at Troye,
> Þe borȝ brittened and brent to brondeȝ and askeȝ

(After that the siege and the assault was ceased at Troy, the burgh ruined and burnt to brands and ashes).

11. *Joseph of Arimathie*, an alliterative poem of about 1350, has been edited by Mr. Skeat for the Early English Text Society. It consists of 709 lines, but is incomplete, some ninety lines at the end being lost. So far as it goes, it follows pretty closely the story of Joseph, as developed in the romance of the *Saint Graal* by Robert Borron. The only known copy, the language of which has both Midland and Southern forms, is in the ponderous volume in the Bodleian Library, known as the Vernon MS.

12. Dr. Morris places the alliterative romance of *William of Palerne*, translated by an Englishman named William from the French poem 'Guillaume de Palerne' (Palermo) for Humphrey de Bohun, nephew to Edward II., between the years 1350 and 1360. 'The story is, that Prince William of Palermo, son of Embrous, king of Sicily, was stolen when a child by a werwolf, who hid him in a forest in Apulia, and tended him with great care. He was there found by a shepherd, who adopted him; but he was afterwards adopted by no less a person than the Emperor of Rome, whom he succeeded on the throne. The wer-wolf was Prince Alphonse, who was afterwards disenchanted, and became King of Spain.'[1] The poem was first edited by Sir F. Madden for the Roxburghe Club, and afterwards by Mr.

----

[1] Morris.

Skeat for the Early English Text Society. It is in a Midland dialect, full of French words, and very readable.

13. *Piers the Plowman*, and the other alliterative poems of Langland, come next in order of time ; these we shall examine presently. The esteem in which they were popularly held raised a crop of imitators, not only in England but in Scotland. It must have been the fame of Langland's alliterative verse that caused 'Huchowne of the Awle Ryale' (by whom Sir Hugh Eglintoun, a courtier in the reigns of David II. and Robert II., is believed to be meant) to adopt that metre in writing the ' Gest Hystoriale' of the *Destruction of Troy*. This poem is of enormous length, more than 14,000 lines, and has been lately printed from a MS. at Glasgow for the Early English Text Society. It ends :—

> Now the proses is plainly put to an end :
> He bryng us to the blisse, þat bled for our syn.

This, and other ' Troy books,' will be further considered when we come to speak of Lydgate.

14. In England two alliterative poems, *Clannesse* and *Pacience*, the one of 1,800, the other of 530 lines, written in a rough northern dialect, and edited by Dr. Morris for the same society, may probably be assigned to imitators of Langland, writing towards the end of the fourteenth century. In the first, the anger of heaven against impurity is illustrated by several Scripture narratives, in particular by the story of 'Baltazar' son of ' Nabugodenozar ; ' in the second, the benefits of Patience, and the danger of being without it, are deduced from the history of Jonas the prophet.

15. Another unknown imitator produced *Pierce the Ploughman's Crede*, a poem 850 lines long, written about 1394. The writer, assuming the character of a plain unlettered man, pretends to be ignorant of his creed ; he applies in vain to friars of all the four orders, Franciscans, Dominicans, Carmelites, and Augustinians, from whom he hears little but railing against one another ; at last he obtains all the knowledge that he desires from Pierce, or Peter, an honest ploughman. This satire is much more rancorous in tone than any of those of Langland.

Chaucer held this form of rhythm cheap; it had become, he knew, very popular in the north, but he, with the finer perceptions and better opportunities of ' a sotherne man,' preferred the purer harmony resulting from exact measure and rime. He makes the Persone say [1] :—

> But trusteth wel, I am a sotherne man,
> I cannot geste, *rom, ram, ruf*, by my letter,

[1] *Canterbury Tales* ; Persone's prologue.

G 2

adding, as suitable to the Persone's character :—

> And, God wote, rime hold I but litel better.

It would seem from this passage that so great a number of
romances or 'gestes' written in alliterative verse (such as
those of which we have just given a sample) were in circulation,
that a verb ' to geste,' meaning to write alliteratively, had come
into use.

16. But in spite of the sarcasm of Chaucer, and the deter-
rent influence which must have lain in the fact that he and the
English school of poets formed on him abstained from using it,
alliteration continued to flourish, though chiefly in the north,
all through the fifteenth and into the sixteenth century.   Perhaps the latest alliterative poem that can be cited is *The Twa
Maryit Women and the Wedo,* by Dunbar, who died about 1521.
Even though alliteration was dropped in form, its characteristics
were often retained in substance.   The extreme irregularity of
versification which is noticeable in so much of the English
poetry of the fifteenth century, and down to the time of Surrey,
seems to me to be a legacy from the alliterators.   Where alliteration is, the number of syllables in the verse is little regarded ;
so long as the correspondence of the two halves of the line was
by means of the alliteration—the *rom, ram, ruf,* as Chaucer calls
it—preserved, the effect of poetry was thought to be realised,
and the internal constitution of each half-verse was left pretty
much to itself.   I am speaking not of the alliteration practised
by the Icelandic skalds, but of that used by our native poets ;
and rather of that which is later than that which is earlier
than the Conquest.   In *Beowulf, Andreas,* and all the finer
Anglo-Saxon poems, though no strict rule limited the number
of syllables, the ear and taste of the writers kept them within
due bounds.   After the Conquest this power of control seems
to have been lost.   Now alliteration is, under any circumstances, but a poor substitute for rime; by the side of which it
may be likened to the striking of a note three times on a flat
metal plate, compared with the full ringing sound of the same
note when struck on a bell.   To this poverty of harmony let
complete license of internal structure be joined, and the result
is seen in the rough and rambling alliterative poems, which
their modern admirers, however interesting they may be on
many accounts, find it extremely difficult to read through.
Rime, after Chaucer's day, gradually supplanted alliteration ;
but it was long before the ex-alliterators perceived that riming
lines ought to involve a strict metrical system, and that the one
point of music or harmony at the *end* of a line is not enough to

compensate for anarchy and uncertainty reigning in every other part of it. In this way the intolerable irregularity of versification which annoys us in Lydgate and Occleve, and still-more in inferior writers, such as Hawes, Bradshaw, Hardyng, and Barclay, may most simply be accounted for.

17. *Piers the Plowman.* The labours of Mr. Skeat, who has edited the three varying texts of this work for the Early English Text Society, and a portion of it as a school book for the Clarendon Press, have cleared up many points that were formerly obscure. Yet even now the real name of the author is uncertain. In one manuscript he is described as ' Willielmus de Langlond,' in two others as 'Wilielmus W.' The first-named document describes him as a native of Shipton-under-Whichwood in Oxfordshire. In his poems he often speaks of himself; and from the scattered notices Mr. Skeat has gathered that he was the son of a franklin or freeman, and educated at Malvern Abbey for the priesthood; that he became a clerk and received the tonsure; but that, having married, he could never rise above minor orders. He had to struggle all his life with poverty, gaining a precarious maintenance as a chorister and scrivener. He lived many years in London, with his wife Kitte and his daughter Calote. There is some reason to think that he was at Bristol in 1399, at the time when Richard II. lost his throne; but from that date we entirely lose sight of him.

The *Vision* exists in three different forms or recensions. The first, called by Mr. Skeat the A text, was written about 1362. It contains only 2,567 lines, and in it the vision concerning Piers the Plowman is kept distinct from the *Visio de Do-wel, Do-bet, et Do-best.* In the later recensions the name *Liber de Petro Plowman* is given to the entire work, including the *Visio dè Dowel* &c. The first vision contains a prologue and eight ' Passus' (or chapters), the second a prologue and three Passus. After writing the A text, Langland remained quiet fifteen years. In 1377, the old king was just dead, merited disaster had fallen on the English arms in France, discontent was abroad, the young king was a minor, and his uncle, the hated Duke of Lancaster, was believed to be plotting for the crown. In such troubled times Langland resumed his work and rewrote his poem, putting in, in the Prologue to the first Vision, the well-known version of the apologue of the rats and the cat, and making very large additions. We have the result in the B text, which contains about 7,100 lines. The C text contains additions and variations, made, in the opinion of Mr. Skeat, after 1378. This version shows some tendency to diffuseness and the discussion of subtle points in theology, but does not add more than about 250 lines to the poem as it stood in the B text. The distinction between the Visions is preserved, but the numbering of the Passus is made continuous, so that the C text contains in all twenty-three Passus, of which ten belong to the Vision concerning the Plowman, seven to that of Do-wel, four to that of Do-bet, and two to that of Do-best.

18. When we come to analyse the plot of this long poem, its enormous defects as a work of art become apparent. Nothing more rambling, more discursive, or more disconnected was ever written. The first Vision comprehends, so to speak, two sub-visions ; one is that of the field full of folk ; the other that of the Seven deadly Sins. The author falls asleep on a May morning under a bank beside a brook on Malvern hills, and dreams that he sees ' a faire feld ful of folke,' among whom are 'japers and jangelers' (jesters and babblers), ploughmen, merchants, anchorites, hermits, minstrels, beggars, pilgrims, and palmers. Beyond the field he sees a deep dale, and rising on the other side of it a toft or hill; in the dale there is a dungeon, on the toft a lofty tower. Presently the king, the knighthood, the clergy, and the commons enter the field. The apologue of the rats and the cat is then, very abruptly, introduced :—

> Wiþ þat ran þere a route of ratones at oncs,
> And smale mys myd hem, mo þen a þousande,
> And comen to a conseille for here comune profit ;
> For a cat of a courte cam when hym lyked,
> And overlepe hem lyȝhtlich, and lauȝte hem at his wille,
> And pleyed with hem perilouslych, and possed hem aboute.

Of such hobbling verse this is a sufficient specimen. By the cat is meant John of Gaunt the Duke of Lancaster. The proposition is then made to tie a bell round the cat's neck, but falls through, because not one 'raton' can be found

> þat dorst have ybounden þe belle aboute þe cattis necke.

A sagacious mouse suggests the consoling reflection that things are just as well as they are ; if they killed this cat, there would soon come another ; *i.e.* if all power were taken from John of Gaunt, it would only pass to some other prince of the blood, who might be as proud and tyrannical as he. The boy king is then spoken of,—' Ve terre ubi puer rex est,'—whence it is evident that this passage (which is not found in the A text) was written soon after the accession of Richard II. in 1377. A lovely lady now appears and tells him that she is Holy Church ; the tower, she says, is the abode of the Creator and Father of men ; the dungeon is the castle of Care, wherein dwells Wrong, the Father of Falshood. Soon after the Lady Meed (*i.e.* reward, bribery) comes upon the scene; she is to be married to Falshood the next day. Meed's unblushing and generally successful attempts to corrupt all ranks and orders, both in Church and State, form the chief subject of the remainder of this sub-vision.

In the other sub-vision, the field again appears, with a multitude of people, and Reason preaching to them. In the course of her sermon, Reason makes the famous prediction, much talked of at the time of the dissolution of the monasteries under Henry VIII.—

For þe abbot of Engelonde [in B text Abingdon] and þe abbesse hys nece
Shullen have a knok on here crounes, and incurable þe wounde.

The Seven deadly Sins, represented by different men, repent and confess, and agree to go in search of *Truth*. A Palmer meets them of whom they inquire the road; he says he has never heard of a saint of that name; then Piers the Plowman enters, and undertakes to show them the right way.

In the second Vision, scarcely a pretence to anything like a plan is retained. The author goes about seeking for *Do-wel*, i.e. good life, and gradually discovers what is meant by the word. The Passus on *Do-bet*, i.e. the higher life made possible for man by *Christ*, aim, with some degree of connection and plan, at showing that Jesus is the only Saviour of mankind. *Do-best* describes a strange vision in which Piers the Plowman appears to the people in the likeness of Christ; Conscience makes a moral and political harangue; and Need asserts the right of all men to take, if they cannot earn, the means of bare subsistence. The poet dreams again; Antichrist has visited the earth, with Avarice and Simony in its train; thoughts and images in a confused medley are crowded on the canvas; and everything ends with the expression by Conscience, who is perplexed by casuistry, and assailed by Sloth and other vices, of its determination to become a pilgrim, and seek Piers the Plowman over the world.

19. The general moral impression derived from reading this singular work, with its lame and impotent conclusion, is of a mixed character. Langland's touch is wavering, for his position was undefined, and his mind subject to continual gusts of reaction and reconsideration. In spite of all this satirical writing against the clergy, it would be a great mistake to consider him a puritan, much more a Lollard. Whatever he may say against the monks, he thinks there is no place like the cloister for perfection of life; however he may rail against corruption in

the higher clergy, he strongly inculcates the obedience due to them
and to the pope. His feelings, tastes, and sympathies are not
those of a layman, but those of a clerk. He was an unhappy
man, committed to a false position by a mistake made in early
life, and driven into satire by seeing ecclesiastics who had
avoided that mistake, though perhaps only externally, rising to
heights of dignity and influence from which he, who felt himself
morally their superior, was, as a married clerk, for ever debarred.

The literary value of *Piers Plowman* cannot be rated
very highly. We have seen how destitute it is of anything
like unity of plan; it might be added, that the author shows
no power of creating or describing individual character; that
he sees and imagines much, but nothing very distinctly; and
that he has little skill in painting nature. On the other hand
a certain power of declamation and force of invective cannot be
denied to him; and there are many passages in which the
surface of London life, in the infinitely varied aspects resulting
from the aggregation of so many trades, callings, and professions
in the great city, is vividly enough portrayed.

20. An alliterative poem of 850 lines, on the fall of Richard
II., was printed some years ago for the Camden Society, and
has been reprinted with *Piers the Plowman* by Mr. Skeat,
under the title of 'Richard the Redeless.' No direct evidence
of authorship exists; but Mr. Skeat is strongly disposed, from
the resemblance of style, to assign the poem to Langland.

21. *Chaucer and his Works.*—Of the parentage of Geoffrey
Chaucer nothing is known with certainty. The long-received
assumption, that he was born in 1328, has been of late years
carefully examined, and found to rest on no positive evidence
whatever. It is merely a conjecture of Speght, who (writing
in 1597) couples the date—1400—on Chaucer's tombstone with
Leland's assertion that he lived to the 'period of grey hairs.'
Sir Harris Nicholas and other antiquaries have ransacked with
incredible industry the dusty memorials in the Record Office
(Issue Rolls, Patent Rolls, Pipe Rolls, Closet Rolls, &c.), and
have discovered that in October 1386 Chaucer deposed that he
was then forty years old and upwards. His birth accordingly
must be fixed about the year 1340. Yet this view is not without its difficulties. In the earlier copies of the *Confessio
Amantis* of Gower, which cannot be dated later than 1390, the
Muse, after telling Gower to 'grete well Chaucer' when they
meet, and speaking of the faithful service which he, Chaucer,
had done her in his youth, proceeds :—

> Forthy, *now in his daies olde,*
> Thou shalt him telle this message, &c.

Yet the poet who was 'in his daies olde' in 1390, was then, according to the new view, only fifty years old. Leland, writing in the time of Henry VIII., says that he was 'nobili loco natus,' but he gives no authority for the statement. Godwin's supposition, founded upon a number of minute allusions scattered through his works, that his father was a merchant, or burgess of London, has been confirmed by recent investigations, which show that John Chaucer the father, and Richard the grandfather, were both vintners.

That he was educated at a university may be held as certain, but whether at Oxford or Cambridge is not so clear. There is a passage in the *Court of Love*, line 912 :—

> Philogenet I called am ferre and nere,
> Of Cambridge clerk ;

which seems to tell in favour of Cambridge. On the other hand, it is known that his most intimate friends and disciples, Gower, Strode, and Occleve, were Oxford men, and the poor scholar who makes one of the group of Canterbury pilgrims is a 'clerk of Oxenford.' The *Milleres Tale* is about an Oxford student, and the scene is laid at Oxford ; but this is balanced by the *Reves Tale*, which introduces two Cambridge scholars, and brings us to ' Trompington not fer fro Cantebrigge.' This point, therefore, must be left in doubt. In 1359 Chaucer served in the great army of invasion which Edward III. led over into France. In the course of this bootless expedition Chaucer was taken prisoner, but seems to have been released at the peace of Bretigny in 1360. His marriage with Philippa Roet is thought to have taken place about the year 1366. This lady was a native of Hainault, and maid of honour to Queen Philippa. Her sister Catherine was the third wife of John of Gaunt, Duke of Lancaster. These circumstances readily explain Chaucer's long and close connection with the court, commencing with the year 1367, when the king granted him a pension of twenty marks for life, under the designation of ' *dilectus valettus noster.*' His prudence and practical wisdom seem to have been as conspicuous as his more brilliant gifts, since he was at various times employed by the king on important diplomatic missions. One of these took him to Italy in 1373, in which year he is thought with great probability to have become acquainted with Petrarch, who was then living at Arqua, near Padua. What other sense can be attached to the famous passage in the prologue to the *Clerk's Tale* ?—

> I wil you telle a tale, which that I
> Lerned at Padowe of a worthy clerk,
> As proved by his wordes and his werk ;

He is now dead, and nayled in his chest,
Now God give his soule wel good rest !
Fraunces Petrark, the laureat poete,
Highte this clerk, whose rhetorike swete
Enlumynd all Ytail of poetrie,
As Linian did of philosophie.

Petrarch died in 1374, so that the acquaintance could not have been formed at the time of Chaucer's second visit to Italy, in 1378.

In 1374 Chaucer was appointed to the lucrative office of Comptroller of the Customs in the port of London. About the time of the king's death, in 1377, he was employed on more than one secret and delicate mission, of one of which the object was to negotiate the marriage of Richard II. with a French princess. The new king granted him a second pension of the same amount as the first. In 1386 he sat as a burgess for the county of Kent in the parliament which met at Westminster. John of Gaunt, his friend and patron, was at this time absent upon an expedition to Portugal ; and the Duke of Gloucester, another of the king's uncles, a man of cruel and violent character, succeeded in this parliament in driving the king's friends out of office, and engrossing all political power in the hands of himself and his party. In November of the same year a commission was appointed, through the Duke's influence, armed with general and highly inquisitorial powers extending over the royal household and all the public departments. In December we find that Chaucer was dismissed from his office as comptroller. It is evident that these two circumstances stand to each other in the relation of cause and effect. The Commission may perhaps have seized upon the pretext of some official irregularities (for Chaucer received the appointment under stringent conditions), but it is clear that he suffered in common with the rest of the king's friends and favourites, not on account of his ' connection with the Duke of Lancaster,' but simply as a courtier.[1] This view of the matter is confirmed by the fact that in 1389, in which year Richard broke loose from his uncle's tutelage and dismissed him and his satellites, we find that Chaucer was appointed to the office of Clerk of the King's Works. In the interval he had been reduced to such distress as to be compelled to dispose of his pensions. From some unascertained cause he ceased to hold this new situation some time in the year 1391. Three years afterwards the king conferred on him a fresh pension of twenty pounds a year for life, to which Henry IV. in the first

[1] Mr. Bell, in the Life prefixed to his excellent edition of Chaucer, seems to have misapprehended this transaction.

year of his reign (1399) added a pension of forty marks. Except these dry facts, we have absolutely no certain knowledge respecting the last ten years of Chaucer's life ; but it is satisfactory to reflect that the last days of the father of English poetry were at least spent in external comfort and free from the troubles of poverty.

22. The creative power and the literary talent of Chaucer were both of a very high order ; a worthier founder of a national literature could not be desired. But before we commence the examination of the works which have come down to us under his name, the preliminary question meets us, are all these works authentic ? Of late years, much that used to pass unquestioned as Chaucerian has upon various grounds been held to be unauthentic or doubtful. These grounds, and their validity, must be briefly considered before we proceed further. For this purpose it will be convenient temporarily to arrange the reputed works of Chaucer under three heads, as :—

1. Longer Poems.
2. Dream Poems, and the *Court of Love.*
3. Minor Poems.

23. The first division includes the *Canterbury Tales,* the *Romaunt of the Rose, Troylus and Cryseyde,* and the *Legende of Goode Women.* In the *Canterbury Tales* nothing is now printed that is not Chaucer's, except the Coke's Tale of Gamelyn, which, being found in several good MSS., is printed in Mr. Bell's edition, but with an express disavowal of belief in its authenticity. As for *Troylus* and the *Legende,* I do not know that any one has ever had the hardihood to question Chaucer's claim to them. But doubts have been lately thrown out by Mr. Bradshaw, the learned librarian of Cambridge, and by Mr. Furnivall, and even (according to the testimony of the latter) by Professor ten Brink, as to the genuineness of the *Romaunt.* It is therefore necessary to consider, what evidence have we in its favour ? The belief of the Elizabethan editors and first printers does not count for much, for we know that they ascribed to Chaucer many pieces (*e.g.* the *Testament of Creseyde,* by Henryson) with which he had no concern whatever. There is but one MS. of the poem, that in the Hunterian Museum at Glasgow ; it was written many years after Chaucer's death, and contains no indication of authorship. The evidences in favour of the *Romaunt* being by Chaucer are simply these,—that the style is just such as we should expect in an early work of his, and that the fact of his having made *a* translation of the *Roman de la Rose* is mentioned in the *Legende of Goode Women.* The passage may here be quoted, for we shall probably have occasion to refer to it again.

The God of Love says to Chaucer :—

> For in pleyne text, withouten nede of glose,
> Thou hast translated the Romaunce of the Rose,
> That is an heresye ayeins my lawe,
> And makest wise folke fro me withdrawe ;
> And of Cresyde thou hast seyde as the lyste.
>   *   *   *   *   *   *

But Alcestis stands up for the poet, and says :—

> He made the boke that hight the House of Fame,
> And eke the deeth of Blanche the Duchesse,
> And the Parlement of Foules, as I gesse,
> And al the love of Palamon and Arcite.
> Of Thebes, thogh the storye ys knowen lyte ;
> And many an ympne for your haly dayes,
> That highten Ballades, Roundels, Virelayes.
> And for to speke of other holynesse,
> He hath in prose translated Boece,
> And made the Life also of Seynte Cecile.
> He made also, goon ys a grete while,
> Origenes upon the Maudeleyne.

Lastly, at a previous part of the poem, he had begged lovers

> To forthren me somewhat in my labour,
> Whether ye ben with the Leef or with the Flour.

This evidence is conclusive, unless it be maintained that Chaucer's version of the *Roman de la Rose* is lost, and that the existing *Romaunt* is by some other poet. This is plainly an extravagant and gratuitous supposition, unless evidence can be brought to show that the *Romaunt* could not have been written by Chaucer. Such negative evidence Mr. Bradshaw and Mr. Furnivall think they find in certain metrical tests, particularly in the riming of *y* and *ye* (*curtesye, generaly*), which, they say, in Chaucer's known works never rime together. Without going here very fully into the question, I may remark that this seems but a slight basis on which to found such sweeping conclusions. In an age when orthography and pronunciation were rapidly changing, we cannot be certain that a rule which Chaucer observed at one time of his life, he may not have seen reason to disregard at another portion of it. Nor can we be certain that the transcriber of the one existing MS. of the Romaunt did not sometimes modify his text to bring it into accordance with the forms of speech of his own day. Lastly, the test *y–ye*, if rigorously applied, would prove too much. The only reason why Chaucer should have rejected this rime, if he did reject it, was that he considered such words as *curtesye, villanye,* &c., to be words of four not three syllables. If then, in any work supposed to be his, such a word should be met with so used that it cannot be treated as of more than three syllables, the metrical test would prove that the work in question was not by Chaucer. For instance, take the line :—

> That is an heresye ayeins my lawe.

Here *heresye* is plainly a word of three syllables ; then the work in which this line occurs is not by Chaucer. But the work is the *Legende of Good Women!*—which is very like a *reductio ad absurdum.* On the whole we may conclude that, in spite of the so-called metrical tests, the probability of the existing *Romaunt of the Rose* being identical with the version made by Chaucer is overwhelmingly great.

24. The next division of the works contains the *Court of Love,* the *Assembly of Foules,* the *Flower and the Leaf, Chauceres Dreme,* the *Boke of the Duchesse,* and the *House of Fame.* Against three of these objections of more or less weight have been raised, viz., against *Chauceres Dreme, The Flower and the Leaf,* and the *Court of Love.*

Of *Chauceres Dreme,* a poem of about 2,380 lines in the octosyllabic couplet, there is no MS. extant ; it was first printed by Speght in 1597. This fact I by no means agree with Mr. Furnivall in thinking fatal to its authenticity : the fortunes of manuscripts are so singular, that either from existence or nonexistence it would generally be rash to infer anything confidently. But the internal evidence seems to condemn *Chauceres Dreme.* The hand of the great master is nowhere apparent ; the verse indeed goes jogging on in a not unpleasing fashion, and the writer was certainly trained in Chaucer's school ; but surely it was not Chaucer himself. It is more like Gower, or—except as to the dialect—James I.

25. *The Flower and the Leaf,* though its authenticity is maintained by M. Sandras in his *Etude sur G. Chaucer* (Paris, 1859), must, I think, be abandoned to the attacks of Professor ten Brink.[1] It is not that the versification and imagery are not both more or less of the Chaucerian type ; nor need we, with the Professor, attach much weight to the circumstance that this poem is not among those named by Alcestis in the *Legende.* Nothing proves that the list there given was meant to be exhaustive ; and the argument from omission would condemn *Queen Anelida* and the *Complaynte of Mars and Venus* equally with the *Flower and the Leaf.* But, on the other hand, Professor

[1] *Chaucer: Studien;* Münster, 1870 ; p. 156.

ten Brink well points out, that we miss in this work that
alternation of seriousness and humour which is observable in
every other certainly genuine work of Chaucer's of corresponding length.   The great preponderance, too, of description
over dialogue is not like Chaucer.   Another suspicious circumstance, not mentioned by the Professor, is the large proportion
of faulty lines, compared with those of which the metre is sound.
From a comparison of the first 100 lines of the *Assembly of
Foules* with the first hundred of the *Flower and the Leaf*, it is
found that only seven per cent. of the lines are faulty in the
former case, while twenty-two per cent. are faulty in the
latter.   The rime test is again alleged, as decisive against the
genuineness of the poem; and although I think that the
validity of this test has been much overvalued, yet I am willing
to admit that the *number* of rimes of the type *curtesye–generaly*
far exceeds that which any of the certainly genuine works
exhibit.   Finally—and this is a test which to my mind is more
decisive than the rime test, though the Professor does not notice
it—the use of 'very' in the *Flower and Leaf* is absolutely un-
Chaucerian.   Chaucer could not have written 'So *very* good
and wholsome be the shoures' (*Flower and Leaf*, l. 10), because
his 'veray' or 'verray'—the French *vrai*—is only an adjective;
it is never used as an adverb.   Nor does the apparent reference to
the poem in the *Legende* constitute a real difficulty.   The allegory of the Leaf and the Flower—the one representing the solid
and enduring goods of virtue, the other the surface charm of
transitory pleasure—was one with which the educated classes of
that age, both in France and England, were perfectly familiar ;
an allusion to it, therefore, is no sort of proof that Chaucer ever
wrote a poem bearing that title.

26. With regard to the *Court of Love*, I dissent from the
unfavourable judgment formed by Mr. Furnivall and Professor
ten Brink.   In style, tone, and versification it appears to me
completely Chaucerian.   The rime test is that on which the
impugners of its genuineness chiefly rely ; some sixteen instances
being producible, in a poem of more than 1,400 lines, of rimes
of the *generaly–curtesye* type.   It is certainly a noteworthy
fact that in the *Assembly of Foules*, a poem of undoubted
genuineness, and about half as long as the *Court of Love*, not a
single instance of such a rime can be found.   But may not this
be accounted for by the extraordinary strength and energy of
the verse, leading to a most sparing use of *adverbs*, rather than
by a repudiation of such rimes on principle ?   The rime objected
to almost always occurs where an adverb is used ; when the force
of the poet's thought is such as to discard adverbs, the rime does

not occur. It may be added that the rime *eke–seke* (A.S. *eac, secan*) is really as faulty as the rime *ye–y* which is so much objected to; yet this occurs in the *Assembly of Foules*.

27. The third division, that of the Minor Poems, contains the following pieces, besides a few others not named :—*Quene Anelyda and Fals Arcyte, The Complaynt of Pite, The Ballade de Village, Chauceres A B C, The Complaynte of Mars and Venus, Ballade sent to King Richard, The Complaynte of Chaucer to his Purse, Flee fro the Pres, The firste Fadyr, L'Envoy à Scogan, L'Envoy à Bukton, The Cuckowe and the Nightingale, The Complaynte of a Loveres Life,* or, *of the Black Knight.* All these poems may without hesitation be attributed to Chaucer, except, perhaps, the last two. In the *Cuckowe and Nightingale* the versification is so rough and halting that I do not believe that Chaucer, who had a horror of 'mysmetryng,' [1] could possibly have written it. The same consideration tells against the authenticity of the *Complaynte of a Loveres Life*; of which, too, the language appears to be rather later than Chaucer's time. It contains sundry imitations of passages in the *Assembly of Foules* and in the *Knightes Tale,* but has nothing in it original, nothing worthy of Chaucer.

Chronology of Chaucer's Writings.

28. In the separate notices of the works which follow, whatever evidence may exist, tending to fix this or that composition to a particular period of the poet's life, will be considered. Anticipating this examination, we will now divide Chaucer's writings into three classes, those of his youth, those written in middle life, and those of his mature age. The expression 'old age' is scarcely applicable to the last years of a man who, as is now believed, did not live to be more than sixty.

Early Poems. *The Complaynt of Pite, The Romaunt of the Rose, The Assembly of Foules, The Boke of the Duchesse, Quene Anelyda and Fals Arcyte, Chauceres A B C.*

Poems of Middle Life. *Troylus and Cryseyde, The Court of Love, The House of Fame, The Love of Palamon and Arcite.*

Later Poems. *Legende of Goode Women, Canterbury Tales, Ballade to Richard II., The Complaynte of Mars and Venus, The Complaynte of Chaucer to his Purse, Flee fro the Pres, The firste Fadyr, L'Envoy à Scogan, L'Envoy à Bukton.*

[1] 'And for ther is so grete dyversite
   In Englissh, and in writynge of our tonge,
   So preye I to God, that non myswrite the,
   Ne the mysmetere, for defaute of tonge.'—*Tr. and Crys.* ad fin.

Chaucer's Early Poems.

29. *The Complaynt of the Dethe of Pite* is the composition of a courtly versifier, writing in the French manner. It abounds with that personification of moral qualities which the *Roman de la Rose* had introduced into European literature. Pity has died in the heart of the poet's mistress, and Cruelty now reigns there, having confederated herself with Beauty, Assured-Manner, Wisdom, and other virtues, with whom the poet remonstrates against the unholy league into which they have entered with a tyrannous feeling which is their natural enemy.

30. *Romaunt of the Rose.* The only MS. of this poem known to exist is in the Hunterian Museum at Glasgow. It is a translation of the long allegorical work written in octosyllabic verse by two French poets, Guillaume de Lorris and Jean de Meung, under the name of *Roman de la Rose*. The originator of the design, Lorris—who died in 1260—composed about 4,000 verses, than which nothing, according to the taste of those days, could be conceived more exquisite in sentiment or more refined in diction. Jean de Meung continued the work in a very different strain. A born satirist, he lashed with an unflagging pen whatever abuses he found or fancied in the court, the castle, and the convent; but, though a revolutionist in temper, he was a man without an ideal. Chaucer translated the whole of Lorris' portion; but of the 18,000 lines and more which were written by Meung he adopted only about 3,600.

Chaucer has allowed himself no variations from the story of the *Roman de la Rose*, which, in briefest outline, is as follows. Its hero is not the true knight, but the constant lover. L'Amant dreams that he is walking by the side of a river, and comes upon a beautiful garden, the *Vergier du Deduit*. Knocking at the wicket, he is admitted by Idleness, who tells him that the garden belongs to Deduit or Mirth. Courtesy approaches, and invites the new-comer to join the band of revellers by whom Mirth is surrounded. Chief among these is Cupid, the God of Love, who carries five arrows. After sauntering for some time with this agreeable company, L'Amant goes off by himself to explore the garden. He comes to the well of Narcissus, at the bottom of which are two crystal stones, each of which wonderfully reflects to the gazer's eye one half of the garden, with all the trees and flowers growing in it. In this mirror he sees 'a roser (rose-tree) chargid fulle of rosis.' He goes up to it, and admires its beautiful 'knoppes' or flowers. One of these excelled all the rest in vigour of growth and perfection of form and hues :—

Among the knoppes I chese oon
So faire, that of the remenaunt noon
Ne preise I half so welle as it,
Whanne I avise in my wit.
For it so welle was enlumyned
With colour reed, as welle fyned
As Nature couthe it make faire.
And it hath leves wel foure paire,
That Kynde hath sett, thorough his knowyng,
Aboute the rede roses spryngyng.
The stalke was as rish right,[1]
And thereon stode the knoppe upright,
That it ne bowide upon no side.
The swote smelle spronge so wide,
That it dide alle the place aboute.

As L'Amant gazes on the Rose, Love comes up and discharges his five arrows successively into his breast. From this moment L'Amant is inflamed with a passionate desire to possess the Rose, and the rest of the poem may be described as the narrative of his adventures in this pursuit—Danger, Wicked-Tongue, Shame, and Richesse doing their best to drive him out of the garden,—Reason sagely advising him to renounce love and cultivate friendship in its place; while Venus, Genius, Cupid, L'Ami (*i.e.* Friendship), and Bel-Accueil, or Fine Manners, encourage him to constancy, and help him to surmount the various perils by which he is beset. At the point where Lorris breaks off, L'Amant has just succeeded in *kissing* the Rose. At the end of Meung's part he plucks it; but Chaucer does not follow him so far. He stops at line 13105 of the original, where Wicked-Tongue, having been persuaded to kneel down and make his confession, has his tongue cut out by L'Amant's unprincipled allies.

31. With the *Roman de la Rose* came in a new style, which influenced for more than three centuries the imaginative literature of Europe. The period from Lorris to Spenser is the reign of allegory. We have seen how, in the turbulent ages which preceded the crystallisation of European society into separate states, the actions of popular warriors or kings, mixed up with many a wild growth of legend, were sung in *national lays* (Breton lays, the Welsh *Triads*, Frankish lays, &c.); how the Norman trouvères took these lays and worked them up into metrical chronicles and *romances of chivalry*; finally, how the romance of chivalry was in great part spiritualized by the introduction of a religious meaning into the most popular and prolific of its developments, the Arthurian epopee. The theme

[1] As straight as a rush.

H

of war appeared to have been worked out; but an inventive poet might find scope for a fresh and attractive exercise of the imagination, through the expansion of the theme of love. In that delicious valley of the Loire, between Orleans and Tours, where earth herself is like a garden, arose the poet who was to satisfy the refined and more exigent tastes of a courtly and aristocratic world, by removing from his page all the rough personages and violent catastrophes of which the readers of romance had had their fill, and introducing in their stead personages that were not personages at all, but mere abstractions, yet whose words and proceedings were interesting, because engaged upon that unfailing source of interest, the love of man to woman. The machinery of a vision seen in a dream was suggested by the *Somnium Scipionis*, one of the most popular bequests of antiquity. The counsels and warnings to lovers were suggested, and in great part supplied, by the writings of Ovid. Thus we see that the work of Lorris arose out of a partial Renaissance, or reversion to classical images and pagan conceptions. That the *Ars Amandi* should come to spread so wide an influence was a fact of no good omen for the morals of Europe. Vice, it is true, lost a portion of its evil ' by losing all its grossness;'[1] but far too much of the evil remained behind.

The literary *form* chosen by Lorris, that of dream and allegory, attracted Langland and Chaucer as we have seen; it was also adopted by Lydgate and Hawes and many other poets. His theme, and his mode of handling it, were imitated, with a change for the worse, by Gower in the *Confessio Amantis*. The deterioration came from copying the audacious license of Jean de Meung, who developed into a doctrine of anarchy, and the boundless riot of the lower faculties, passages which in Lorris were suggestive of nothing worse than elegant luxury and frivolity.

No means exist for determining the date of the *Romaunt*. Professor ten Brink is inclined to place it in 1366; but there are not wanting reasons why it would be better to place it two or three years earlier. The great number of French words, the level flow of the style, the closeness of the translation, all point to a prelusive period of life, when Chaucer did not yet feel that he was thoroughly master of his own powers. It was probably earlier than, rather than contemporaneous with, the *Assembly of Foules*, which, as we shall presently see, there is good ground for assigning to 1364.

---

[1] Burke's *Reflections*.

32. In the *Assembly of Foules*, a poem of about 700 lines, in the Chaucerian heptastich or seven-lined stanza,[1] the poet begins by saying that he has lately fallen in with a book, written 'wyth lettres olde,' by which he had been completely engrossed. The book was the treatise of Macrobius on the Dream of Scipio, to whom his ancestor 'Aufrikan' appeared in his sleep, and declared to him the nothingness of this world and the greatness of eternity, together with many other wonderful things. The poet then falls asleep, and dreams that Aufrikan comes and leads him to a beautiful park or garden (the description of which is taken from Boccaccio's *Theseide*),—a blessed place, where it is ever day, the air ever calm and sweet, no sickness comes nor age, and all wholesome spices and grasses grow abundantly. After much description of the sights of the garden, the poet tells us that he came to a place where the goddess Nature was seated upon 'an hille of floures.' It was Saint Valentine's day, and all the birds were gathered round her in order to choose their mates for the coming year. She holds on her hand a beautiful 'formel' eagle. The choosing begins, and three 'tercel' eagles, one of which is a 'real' (royal) tercel, dispute which shall have the formel eagle. Nature bids the leaders of the different orders of birds to deliver their verdict in the dispute. The falcon, representing the birds of prey, says that the formel should take the 'worthiest of knyghthode' and 'of blode the gentyleste' among the three tercels. The goose, speaking for the water-fowl, shows his lack of gentle blood and of the romantic spirit, by proposing with vulgar brevity that 'whichever of the tercels she cannot love, let him love another.' But all the 'gentil foules' scout this ignoble idea. The cuckow, for the worm-eating birds, advises that, since they cannot agree, the tercels and the formel shall remain single all their lives. But this advice is flouted and scorned by the merlin. The turtle-dove, for the seed-eating birds, simply urges the lovers to maintain unchauging constancy, and to live on hope—a notion much ridiculed by the duck, who intimates that 'there be mo sterres, God wote, than a paire,' or, as we should say, 'there are as good fish in the sea as ever came out of it.' Embarrassed by these discordant verdicts, Nature tells the formel to choose for herself ; but she asks leave to put off her decision for another year, 'for to avysen me.' The other birds then pair and depart, singing a roundel in Nature's honour, of which the refrain is—

Qui bien ayme tarde oublie.

---

[1] For a description of this stave, see Appendix, 'Stanzas.'

It has been lately suggested by a writer in the *Saturday Review*, that Chaucer is referring in this poem to the courtship of Engelram de Couci and Isabel, daughter of Edward III., who were betrothed in 1364 and married in 1365. Mr. Furnivall[1] thinks that this theory will not hold, because he has satisfied himself, by a search among the grimy treasures of the Record Office, that, in the actual courtship of this princely pair, things cannot have proceeded in the precise manner, nor at the precise dates, that seem to be indicated in the poem. But what if they could not? Chaucer surely was not bound to trammel his imagination within the bounds of strict matter of fact. It is now generally agreed that the courtship intended cannot be that of John of Gaunt and Blanche of Lancaster (married in 1358), according to the view of Godwin and others, because that date is much too early, nor did the circumstances of that courtship resemble in any way those here shadowed forth. Yet it is scarcely possible to believe that *some* real event is not the basis of the poem; and if this be granted, it is certain that no royal marriage in the reign of Edward III. fits the poem half so well as that of Engelram and Isabel.

33. *The Boke of the Duchesse* was formerly called *Chauceres Dreme*, till Speght published the poem which properly bears that name in 1597. It is an elegiac composition of about 1,350 lines, in octosyllabic rime, on the death (1369) of Blanche of Lancaster, the first wife of John of Gaunt. In the *Canterbury Tales*, the Man of Lawe is made to say in his prologue,—

In youthe he [Chaucer] made of Ceys and Alcioun.

Now the first part of the *Boke of the Duchesse* gives the story of Ceyx and Alcyone; we have here therefore clear proof that this was a poem of Chaucer's *youth*; yet this it could not have been, assuming the old date of his birth (1328) to be true; for in that case he would have been more than forty years old at the time of the death of the Duchess Blanche. This, consequently, is an independent argument in favour of the later date now usually assigned to his birth.

There are beautiful lines in this poem, and the description of the hunt in the wood is graphic and stirring. Still M. Sandras, who has pointed out how largely it is made up out of the works of the French poets Lorris, Meung, and Machault, is perhaps right in assigning to it no very high place among Chaucer's works. The slight plot is thus analysed by Mr. Bell[2]:—'Falling asleep over Ovid's story of Ceyx and Alcyone, [the poet] hears

[1] See Mr. Furnivall's *Trial Forewords*.
[2] Chaucer's Poetical Works, vol. vi.

the merry sounds of huntsmen and hounds, and starts from his
bed to follow them to the woods. Here, while awaiting the
unharbouring of the deer, he sees a knight sitting dolefully
under an oak, lamenting the recent death of his lady. Having
ascertained the cause and history of his sorrow, Chaucer rides
home, and is suddenly awakened by the sound of the great clock
of a neighbouring castle striking twelve. The knight is John
of Gaunt ; and the lady his Duchess, Blanche. The identity
of the latter is ascertained by a passage where she is called
"faire White," which, says the mourning knight, "was my ladyes
name righte."' The Lady Blanche died in 1369, and John of
Gaunt married his second wife Constantia, daughter of Pedro
the Cruel, king of Castile, in 1371.

34. *Quene Anelyda and Fals Arcyte* is an unfinished poem,
mostly in the Chaucerian heptastich, in which we seem to have
a rough draught of the story of Theseus and the two noble
kinsmen of Thebes, laid aside by Chaucer when he had resolved
to follow Boccaccio more closely, and complete the tale as we
have it in *The Love of Palamon and Arcite*, or the Knightes
Tale. Some curious specimens of metre found in this poem are
described in the Appendix. Chaucer says that he has followed
in it Statius and Corinna. At the opening Theseus is introduced,
with his Amazonian queen Hippolyta, and her sister Emilie,
making his triumphal entry into Athens, just as in the Knightes
Tale. But then an abrupt transition is made to the affairs of
Thebes ; we hear no more of Theseus, but the rest of the poem
is devoted to the hapless love of Anelyda the queen of Ermony
for her perjured Theban lover, Arcyte. In the Knightes Tale,
on the other hand, the events all follow in a clear and logical
sequence. The poem is named by Lydgate, in the prologue to
his *Falls of Princes*, among Chaucer's works. Its exact date
cannot be given, but it was certainly earlier than the ' Love of
Palamon and Arcite' mentioned in the *Legende*.

35. *Chauceres A B C*, or *La Prière de Nostre Dame*, is a
poem of twenty-three stanzas, each beginning with a different
letter of the alphabet (*j*, *u*, and *w* being omitted), in honour of
the Virgin Mary. It is a translation from a composition of the
same name by the French poet De Guilerville, whose verses are
printed in Mr. Furnivall's One-Text edition of the Minor
Poems of Chaucer, opposite the English text. For the metre,
see the section on 'Stanzas' in the Appendix. There was a
tradition in the time of Speght that Chaucer wrote the *A B C*
at the desire of the Duchess Blanche. However this may be, it
was probably a work of his youth.

Poems of Chaucer's Middle Life.

36. *Troylus and Cryseyde* is a translation, though with many changes and many additions, of the *Filostrato* of Boccaccio. The original inventor of the story (of which no hint is found in Homer, nor in the Greek writers of the Lower Empire, Dares and Dictys, from whose pages Guido delle Colonne supplemented his *Historia Trojana*) was, according to M. Sandras, the Anglo-Norman trouvère, Benoit de Sainte-Maure. This author, a contemporary of Wace, before he wrote, by the commission of Henry II., his metrical history of the Dukes of Normandy, appears to have compiled a *Geste de Troie*, with the view of correcting the errors into which Homer had fallen, and giving the *authentic* history of the siege of Troy! In this work, the sources of which appear to be but imperfectly known, the story of the loves of Troilus, son of Priam, and the faithless Chryseis, daughter of Chryses, the priest of Apollo, appears for the first time. Guido delle Colonne, a Sicilian lawyer of the thirteenth century, either copying Benoit, or using the unknown sources at which Benoit drew, reproduces the story in his *Historia Trojana*. From Guido, and possibly from Benoit also, it was borrowed by Boccaccio, and worked up into the elegant poem of *Filostrato*. But the character of Cressid is very differently drawn by Boccaccio and Chaucer. In the hands of the former she is a light and sensual woman, for whom it is impossible to feel respect or pity; such a Cressid, in short, as we have in Shakespeare's play. But 'Chaucer's Cryseyde is cast in a different mould. She possesses every quality which entitles a woman, not only to love, but to respect. Her delicacy is conspicuous; she is won with difficulty after a long courtship, carried on with consummate address under the direction of Pandarus; and is finally overcome by surprise. The moral beauty of her nature imparts a profound interest to her conduct, and we follow her through the gradual course of her infidelity with sorrow and compassion.'[1]

37. Chaucer speaks of Boccaccio by the pseudonym of *Lollius*, an historian of the third century. In the first book he calls him 'myn autour Lollius;' again in the fifth book near the end of the poem, he says, 'as telleth Lollius.' Lydgate also quotes Lollius as an author on Troy at the end of his Troy book; again, in the *House of Fame*, Chaucer names him after Homer as an historian of Troy. Professor ten Brink, following out a sug-

---

[1] Quoted from Mr. Bell's able Introduction to *Troylus and Cryseyde.*

gestion of Mr. Latham, conjectures that Chaucer may have misread his Horace (*Epist.* I. ii. 1), and instead of

> Trojani belli scriptorem, maxime Lolli,
> .   .   .   .   Præneste relegi,

may have read :—

> Trojani belli scriptorum maxime Lolli,
> .   .   .   .   Præneste te legi—

' I have read thee at Præneste, O Lollius, greatest of the historians of the Trojan war.' This conjecture would be more admissible, were there any evidence that Chaucer was acquainted with Horace; but, so far as I know, he quotes him nowhere in his writings. On the whole, the supposition that Lollius Urbicus, mentioned in ancient lists of Latin authors as an historian of the third age, is the person intended, seems the most probable. But why Chaucer, who freely names Dante and Petrarch, to whom he was far less beholden, should have chosen to avoid all mention of Boccaccio, to whom he was so deeply indebted, remains an unsolved difficulty.

The *Troylus* is written in the Chaucerian heptastich, and is in five books. There is no certain indication of its date, but Lydgate vaguely speaks of it, in the prologue to his *Falls of Princes*, as a translation made in the poet's youth. But there is a marked increase of power, as compared with the *Romaunt*, which may incline us to place it some ten or fifteen years farther on in the poet's life. The noble and eloquent close is worthy of all admiration. In the ' Envoye' at the end, he commends it to the correcting hands of his friends Gower and Strode :—

> O moral Gower, this boke I directe
> To the, and to the philosophical Strode,
> To vouchensauf, ther nede is, to correcte,
> Of youre benignites and zeles good.

38. The *Court of Love* is a poem of about 1,400 lines, written in the Chaucerian heptastich. The only MS. of it known to exist is one lately discovered at Cambridge ; it was first printed by Stowe in 1561. The versification is admirably musical ; nowhere in his works has Chaucer written anything better in this respect. The poet, who describes himself as ' Philogenet, of Cambridge, clerk,'—a name which perhaps contains a modest allusion to Chaucer's connection, in virtue of his confidential position at court, with the royal house of Plantagenet, —says that when he was eighteen years of age, Love compelled him to go on a pilgrimage to the isle of Cythera to do homage to Venus. On reaching the island he finds that its government

is in the hands of Admetus and Alceste, acting as viceroys for Venus—

To whom obeyed the ladies good ninetene.

So, in the *Legende*, Alceste is attended by 'ladies ninetene.' Presently he espies a friend of his, the maiden Philobone 'chamberere unto the queen.' She acts as his guide, and brings him to the temple where Venus and Cupid preside. The god of Love chides him for having come so late to his court, and commands him to read the twenty statutes of love, and swear to observe them. This Philogenet does. The idea of these statutes is taken from the *Roman de la Rose*, but a cynical and immoral turn is given to some of them, of which the good Lorris would never have been guilty. After swearing to observe the statutes, Philogenet makes a long prayer to Venus, in the course of which he petitions that a lovely lady whom he had seen one night in a vision might be given to him as his love. The prayer is granted, and Rosial, in the description of whose beauty the poet draws largely on that with which Boccaccio in the *Theseide* celebrates the charms of Emilie, is revealed to his gaze. He makes his 'bille' to her, suing for her grace, and she after a time looks favourably on his suit. The poem ends with a profane parody, which has nothing to do with the thread of narrative, of the psalms sung at matins on Trinity Sunday,—the birds taking up the chant in succession in praise of the god of Love. In other passages of the poem monks and nuns are introduced, deploring that they had too early committed themselves by vows to a renunciation of the service of Cupid. In appearance nothing can be laxer than the morality of the *Court of Love*; yet the gibes on austerity and the parodies on doctrine do not, in the mouth of Chaucer, mean all that they would mean in the mouth of a modern poet. He is exercising his poetical gift; appropriating and imitating all the witty things, bad and good, that he finds in the pages of his French and Italian compeers. The astonishing immorality of a great deal in the *Decameron*, recommended as it was by all the graces of style, then first attained by the prose of any modern language, is a parallel phenomenon to the cynicism of the *Court of Love*. Yet neither Chaucer nor Boccaccio lost his faith, as the 'Retractions' of the one, and the penitent end of the other, sufficiently demonstrate. 'It was not his intente,' as the fiend said of the poor carter;[1] there was no full and deliberate intention of the will in either poet to depart from the precepts of God and the Church, so that each, culpable as had been too often the exercise of his pen, made a good end at last.

[1] *The Freres Tale.*

M. Sandras considers the *Court of Love* to be a very early work, but in this I cannot agree with him. The perfection of the verse seems to be more suitable to the ease and experience of a practised writer than to the rawness of a beginner. It is also worth noticing that the king of Love, when Philogenet is brought before him, is made to say :—

> What doth this old,
> Thus far ystope in yeres, come so late
> Unto the court ?—

as if the poet was here thinking of himself as he really was, forgetting that he had represented Philogenet, at the time of this adventure, as only eighteen years old. I should be disposed to place the poem between 1370 and 1380. With regard to Philogenet's being a clerk of Cambridge, it is by no means unlikely, as has been often pointed out, that Chaucer studied at both universities.

39. The *House of Fame* is a poem of about 2,170 lines, in octosyllabic couplets, divided into three books. The first 'contains a dissertation on dreams analogous to the opening of the *Roman de la Rose*, an invocation of Sleep imitated from Machault, a reference to the tragical death of Crœsus, as related by Jean de Meung, and a description of the temple of Venus, adorned with paintings which represent the different scenes of the Æneid. . . . This long introduction ends with a vision borrowed from Dante.' [1] As in the ninth canto of the Purgatorio, the poet sees before him an eagle with golden wings, dazzlingly bright. In the second part, he is carried aloft by the eagle, and after a long aerial voyage brought to the House of Fame, a palace founded on a rock of ice. The third part tells us what he saw there. In the great hall he beholds the statues of the famous poets of old, Homer on a pillar of iron, Virgil on one of iron tinned over, Ovid on a pillar of copper, and Claudian on one of sulphur. He sees and describes crowds of people of every rank and calling, and then suddenly wakes up, and finds that it is all a dream :—

> Thus in dreming and in game
> Endeth this lytel booke of Fame.

Many comic and satirical strokes are introduced throughout the poem ; of which one might say in general, that while evidently suggested by the *Divina Commedia*, it substitutes the fantastic English humour and wealth of conception for the austere dignity and serious purpose of the great Italian. The *House of Fame*

---

[1] Sandras, *Étude*, p. 118.

was modernized by Pope. It bears the evidence of a vast and discursive erudition, and should clearly be assigned to the middle period of Chaucer's life, of which it must be deemed the most important monument.

40. *The Love of Palamon and Arcite* appears, from the way in which it is mentioned in the *Legende*, to have been written some time before the latter work, but to have had little circulation. There can be no reasonable doubt that this is substantially the same composition with that which Chaucer has assigned to his Knight among the *Canterbury Tales*. It may therefore be passed over till we come to speak of that collection.

Chaucer's Later Poems.

41. In writing the *Love of Palamon and Arcite*, Chaucer must have perceived that the riming pentameter, or, as we now call it, the heroic couplet, which he then used for the first time, offered advantages for a continuous, serious, and dignified exposition or narrative, which neither any form of stanza, nor the short romance measure which he had used for the *Romaunt* and the *House of Fame*, could justly pretend to. This conviction, we may suppose, led him to choose this metre for the *Legende of Goode Women*, and afterwards for many of the *Canterbury Tales*.

42. The *Legende* is a poem of about 2,600 lines, and is extant in numerous MSS. The name is perhaps derived from the *Legenda Aurea* of Jacobus de Voragine, which is a collection of the lives of saints. For in pursuance of the mocking parody which we witnessed in the *Court of Love*, though in a milder and less cynical temper, the poet still assimilates the service of Christ to the service of Cupid, and celebrates the nine ladies here held up for imitation as the saints and martyrs of Love.

The opening of the *Legende* is very beautiful. The poet tells us how, when May comes round, he leaves his books and his devotion, and goes abroad into the fields to do honour and obeisance to the Daisy, that 'floure of floures alle.' On such an occasion, after returning to his house he fell asleep in an arbour, and dreamed that he saw the god of Love, with Alceste, and nineteen ladies in her train. Love charges him with having written many things in the dispraise of women, and tending to withdraw men from his service, particularly for having translated the *Roman de la Rose*—

> That is an heresye ayeins my lawe.

But Alceste defends him, and obtains his pardon from the god on the following condition :—

> Thou shalt, while that thou lyvest, yere by yere,
> The most partye of thy tyme spende
> In makyng of a glorious Legende,
> Of good wymmen, maydenes, and wyves,
> That weren trewe in lovyng al hire lyves.

In performance of this penance, the poet writes the lives or ' legends' of the following ladies who were eminent in the annals of Love,—Cleopatra, Thisbe, Dido, Medea, Lucretia, Adriana (*i.e.* Ariadne), Philomene, Phyllis, and Hypermnestra. His materials are taken almost entirely from Ovid's *Metamorphoses* and *Heroides*, some passages being pretty close versions of the Latin.

An indication of date is found in the following injunction laid down by Alceste on the poet :—

> And whan this boke ys made, yeve it the Quene
> On my behalf, at Eltham, or at Sheene.

Manifestly this could not be Queen Philippa, who died in 1369, long before most of the works named in the *Legende* were written ; it must therefore be the first queen of Richard II., Anne of Bohemia (the second, Isabella of France, whom he married in 1397, was a mere child), who came over to England in 1382, and died in her palace of Sheen in 1394. Between these two years the *Legende* must have been written.

43. Before examining the *Canterbury Tales*, the remaining productions of Chaucer's later years may be briefly noticed. The *Ballade to Richard II.* may perhaps be his ; but we should with equanimity see it adjudged to Lydgate or Gower. The *Complaynte of Mars and Venus*, a piece of about 350, in stanzas of seven and eight lines, is, at least in part, a translation from the French of Graunson. Chaucer avows it to be the work of his old age :—

> For elde, that in my spirite dulleth me,
> Hath of endyting al the subtilite
> Welnygh berefte out of my remembraunce.

In contemporary MSS. this poem is said to have been written by Chaucer, at the request of John of Gaunt, to celebrate a shameful intrigue between the Duchess of York, Lancaster's sister-in-law, and the Duke of Exeter, her niece's husband. The *Envoy* to Scogan, and that to Bukton, are both late compositions ; in the latter, Chaucer entreats his friend to read 'The Wyfe of Bathe.' *Flee fro the Pres* is a poem of three stanzas, breathing the noble and sad resignation of a great mind which at the end of its course, uncorrupted though not unstained, ' cast down but not subdued,' throws a backward look upon the storms of life :—

> That the is sent receyve in buxomnesse,
> The wrasteling of this world asketh a falle ;
> Her is no home, her is but wyldyrnesse.
> Forth, pilgrime ! forth best out of thy stalle !
> Loke up on hye, and thonke God of alle ;
> Weyve thy lust, and let thy goste the lede,
> And trouthe shal thee delyver, hit is no drede.

The firste Fadyr is a short piece, ascribed to Chaucer by Scogan. The *Complaynte to his Purse*, being addressed to Henry IV., who obtained the crown in 1399, comes at the very end of our poet's life. He says in it that he is ' shave as nye as is a frere,' and throws himself on the benignity of the new king, not without success, as we have seen.

44. The general plan of the *Canterbury Tales* may be said to have been so far suggested by the *Decameron* of Boccaccio, that the later, like the earlier work, consists of a framework created for the purpose of inserting tales in. The ten friends, assembled during the prevalence of the plague in a country house outside the walls of Florence, and beguiling the tedium of a ten days' quarantine by each telling a story daily, are represented in the English poem by the thirty-two pilgrims, bound to the shrine of St. Thomas-à-Becket at Canterbury, each of whom (except the host) binds himself to tell a story for the amusement of the company, both going and returning. Harry Bailey, the host of the Tabard, the inn at Southwark from which the expedition starts, is its guide and chief. He is to tell no tale himself, but to be the judge of those which the other pilgrims tell. If the scheme announced in the Prologue had been fully carried out, it is evident that we should have a hundred and twenty-four tales. In fact, there are but twenty-four, of which two are told by Chaucer, one, the Coke's Tale, is a short fragment, and a fourth is told by the Chanounes Yeman, who is not one of the original party, but, with his master, joins the pilgrims on the road. This incompleteness is in marked contrast to the symmetrical exactness with which the less ambitious plan of the *Decameron* is worked out.

A few general observations on the characteristics of Chaucer's genius, as exhibited in the *Canterbury Tales*, are reserved for the second part of this work.[1] Here I propose, after discussing

[1] See Critical Section, ch. I., *Narrative Poetry*.

the question of the order in which the tales should be arranged, to indicate briefly the character of each, and the source from which it is supposed to be derived.

The following persons besides the Host, out of the thirty-two pilgrims named in the Prologue, have no tales assigned to them : the Yeoman, two out of the three Nun's Priests, the Haber- dasher, the Carpenter, the Webbe (*i.e.* weaver), the Dyer, the Tapiser (tapestry-worker), and the Plowman.

45. The examination and comparison of a great number of MSS., carefully made by Mr. Bradshaw and Mr. Furnivall, have resulted in the re-establishment of the true order in which, if not the whole, at least the great majority of the tales should stand. About the first five tales, — the Knight's, Miller's, Reve's, Cook's, and Man-of-Law's,—there is no difficulty, for they are linked together by their prologues. The Wife of Bath's Prologue and Tale follow in all the printed editions. But a MS. (Arch. Seld. B. 14) has been found in the Bodleian Library, which places the Shipman's Prologue and Tale next after the Man-of-Law's Tale ; and this is unquestionably the right order. To the Shipman's Tale are linked in regular succession the Prioresses Tale, Sir Thopas, Meliboeus, the Monkes Tale, and the Nonnes Preestes Tale. Rochester is mentioned in the Monk's Prologue—

> Lo, Rouchester stondeth here faste by.

After the Nonnes Preestes Tale there is a break, and it is doubtful what tale should come next. Mr. Furnivall wavers between the Doctor's and the Wife of Bath's. But the Doctor's Tale, if the short prologue printed in Mr. Bell's edition be admitted as genuine, must follow the Franklin's Tale. Taking the Wife of Bath's as the next in succession to the Nonnes Preestes Tale, we get a sequence of nine tales, the Wife of Bath's, Frere's, Sompnour's, Clerk's, Merchant's, Squire's, Frank- lin's, Doctor's, and Pardoner's. In the first and third of these Sittingbourne is mentioned, a town ten miles beyond Rochester, and forty miles from London. Between the Sompnour's and the Clerk's Tales there is no positive link, but one follows the other in five out of the six first-class MSS. printed by Mr. Furnivall in the Six-Text Chaucer. All the other tales in this group are linked together by prefatory matter. The Second Nun's Tale, which has no prologue, is placed next by Mr. Fur- nivall. To it is linked the Chanounes Yemans Tale, in which Boughton-under-Blee is mentioned, a village five miles from Canterbury. The Manciple's Prologue and Tale are placed next by Mr. Furnivall, in the former of which the 'litel toun' called Bob-up-and-down, under the Blee, is mentioned. To the Manciple's Tale are linked the Persones Prologue and Tale, which in all the MSS. terminate the work.

46. *Knightes Tale.* This, as we have seen, is a free version of the *Theseide* of Boccaccio, an heroic poem in twelve books, in the *ottava rima*, which appeared in 1341. Theseus, duke of Athens, after his conquest of Scythia, by which he won the hand of Hippolyta the Amazonian queen, returns to his capital. Before entering the city he is beset by a band of wretched women, praying him to avenge them on Creon king of Thebes, who has forbidden the burial of the bodies of their husbands slain during the siege. Theseus at once marches against Creon, defeats and kills him. In the battle two young Thebans, Palamon and Arcite, are left for dead on the field; but, their wounds being not mortal, they are taken to Athens and there imprisoned. From the window of their cell Palamon sees one May morning the faire Emelie, sister of Hippolita, walking in the palace garden. Arcite also sees her; the friends both conceive themselves to be in love with the maiden, who all the time has not seen them, and a bitter quarrel ensues between them. Arcite is released, and Palamon at the end of seven years makes his escape. The rivals meet in the wood near Athens, and agree to fight the next morning. But the combat is interrupted by Theseus, who, after hearing their story, promises that if they return to that spot at the end of fifty weeks, each with a hundred knights in his train, and institute a tournament for the love of Emelie, he will give her hand to the victor. The lists are prepared with great care and expense, oratories and altars being erected to Venus, Mars, and Diana, and enriched with painting and sculpture. The tournament takes place on the appointed day; Arcite is victorious; but just as he is being proclaimed, his horse, startled by a 'fury infernal' sent above ground by Pluto, throws him on his head, and he receives a mortal injury. His farewell to Emelie is one of the most beautiful things in poetry. Palamon of course weds Emelie, and lives with her 'in blisse, in richesse, and in hele.'

Tyrwhitt considered that Chaucer's management of the story was superior to Boccaccio's, because he made Palamon see Emelie first, thereby establishing a kind of prior poetical right to her; and also described jealousy and enmity as springing up between the two young Thebans from the first, whereas Boccaccio makes the tie of friendship between them so strong that for a long time both love Emelie to distraction without being the worse friends. M. Sandras, on the other hand, suggests that the refinement of feeling and sentiment which such friendship implies was beyond the strain of the English poet and his readers. Without pretending to settle so nice a question, we may observe that each poet, in handling this part of the story, was probably guided by his literary instinct to write in the way most in accord with the manners and modes of thought of his own countrymen.

The source from which Boccaccio obtained the story of Palamon and Arcite has not been discovered. From the *Thebais* of the poet Statius (lib. xii.) is taken all the earlier part of the story down to the death of Creon, and also (lib. vii.) the first sketch of the description of the temple of Mars. But this sketch is in Statius hardly more than big words and gaudy swollen images. Boccaccio's description, while preserving all in Statius that is worth preserving, enlarges the theme with much elegance and force of expression. Chaucer departs widely from both, and in the terror and majesty of his lines reminds us, notwithstanding the inferiority of the medium, of the magnificent pictures of Tartarus in the sixth Æneid. M. Sandras thinks that the particular story of Palamon and Arcite was probably the invention of some French trouvère, whose work is now lost, though known to and used by Boccaccio. But there seems to be really no reason why Boccaccio should not have invented it himself. Statius wrote his epic in twelve books, and called it the *Thebaid*. In the last book Theseus, the great mythic hero of Attica, is introduced for the first time, to redress the wrongs and impieties committed by Creon. Boccaccio seems to have thought that here was a great opportunity for continuing, in a certain sense, the work of Statius, by writing another epic in twelve books, to be called the 'Theseid,' with Theseus for its leading character. The name of Palemon he found in Statius; that of Arcita or Arcite he may have taken from the Archytas of Horace (*Od.* i. xxviii.). The element of love was indispensable in a mediæval poem ; he therefore created Emilia, the sister-in-law of Theseus. The self-forgetting friendship of the two young Thebans is a reminiscence of Pylades and Orestes.

47. The *Milleres Tale* relates how a demure Oxford scholar, fair without and false within, leagued with the wife of the carpenter with whom he was lodging against the poor man's honour, and deceived him by a ridiculous tale of a deluge, which his pretended knowledge of astrology enabled him to foresee. The origin of the story, says Mr. Bell, has not been ascertained ; the main incident, that of the tubs, Chaucer probably found in some fabliau. There is great humour both in this and in the Reve's Tale, but at the same time so much that is gross and offensive, that one may well believe Chaucer to have had them

specially in his mind, when revoking those of his Canterbury Tales 'that sounen unto sinne.'

48. The Reve, who was a carpenter by trade, is offended at the slight thrown upon the craft by the Miller's tale. He proceeds to tell a tale, of which the scene is laid at Trumpington, near Cambridge, and which ends with the effectual humbling of the proud miller who thought to cheat the two Cambridge clerks from the north country. Two fabliaux, containing the main incidents of the story, one of which bears the title of *De Gombert et des Deux Clercs*, may have supplied Chaucer with his materials; they are among the publications of the Chaucer Society.

49. The Coke, Roger or Hodge of Ware, after being rallied by the Host on the deleterious quality of his dishes, promises to tell a tale of a 'hosteler.' He begins it, and we see that there is every prospect of hearing a tale coarser than either the Reve's or the Miller's. But at the end of about 60 lines the storyteller suddenly stops. Tyrwhitt is probably right in supposing that 'Chaucer's more mature judgment convinced him that two such tales as the Miller's and the Reeve's were sufficient at a time.' He perhaps bethought himself of the promise made to his readers in the Miller's Prologue :—

> Whoso list it not to heere,
> Turne over the leef, and cheese another tale;
> For he schal fynde ynowe bothe gret and smale,
> Of storial thing that toucheth gentilesse,
> And eek moralite, and holynesse.

50. The Coke holds his peace, and the Host, observing that now

> The schade of every tree
> Was in the lengthe the same quantite
> That was the body erecte, that caused it,

and knowing that the day of the month was the eighteenth of April, infers from his profound astronomical lore that the time of the day is ten o'clock. Announcing this discovery to the pilgrims as a motive for losing no time, he calls upon the Man of Lawe for a tale. The learned serjeant replies that he himself speaks in prose, but that he will borrow a tale in rime from Chaucer, who in his 'large volume' has 'told of lovers up and down;' yet never, he adds, given currency to such wicked stories as those of Canace and her incestuous love, or about such an unnatural monster as the King Antiochus. This is a stroke at Gower, as we shall presently see, and helps to fix the date of

the *Canterbury Tales*.   The Man of Lawe proceeds to tell the
beautiful tale of Constance ; how the Sultan of Surrye, hearing of
the beauty of the daughter of the Roman emperor, obtains her in
marriage from her father on promising to become a Christian;
how, for keeping this promise, he is murdered by his own mother,
who sends Constance away in a ship without a rudder ; how
she is cast on the coast of Northumberland, and, after many
wonderful adventures, becomes the wife of Alla, the king of
that country ; how Alla's wicked mother, Domegyld, turns him
against her, and persuades him to send her afloat again in the
same ship in which she came ; how the ship carries her and her
little son, Mauricius, to Rome, where she lives a holy and retired life ; finally, how Alla, coming to Rome on pilgrimage,
discovers his wife and son, and lives happily with them for
many years.   This tale is in the Chaucerian stanza.   The
saintly character of Constance is touched with indescribable refinement and grace, as well as depth of feeling ; one is reminded
of those lovely female heads which gaze, wistfully and tenderly,
from the canvas of Sassoferrato or Luini.

The story of Constance is also told in Gower's *Confessio
Amantis* ; and as no other source was formerly known, except
for the portion that relates to Domegyld, whose wicked behaviour towards Constance recalls a similar story in the *Two Offas*,
a work ascribed to Matthew Paris, Tyrwhitt and other critics
assumed that Chaucer must have taken the story from Gower.
On this a further argument has been reared : could Chaucer
have meant to say anything severe of Gower, in the passage
about Canace and Antiochus, when he was on the point of borrowing from him the materials of an important tale?   This
question comes to nothing, now that the common source from
which both Gower and Chaucer took the story has been
discovered.   This source is the chronicle of Nicholas Trivet.
The Chaucer Society has printed an old English version of part
of this chronicle, on reading which no one can doubt that here
we have Chaucer's original.   Tiberie Constantyn, says Trivet,
became emperor in 570 A.D., and reigned twenty-three years, at
Constantinople however, not at Rome.   According to one account he gave his daughter in marriage to a knight of Cappa-
docia ; but according to the ' olde cronicles of Saxons,' Constantia
married Alle the second king of Northumber, and had by him a
son Morys.   This Alle is the king in the well-known story of
Gregory the Great and the Angle children whom he saw in the
slave-market.

Since therefore Chaucer took the tale from Trivet, not from
Gower, the reason alleged for doubting his intention of attacking

I

the latter in what he says of Canace falls to the ground. That he had that intention seems to me most evident. If so, the Man of Lawe's prologue, and the Canterbury Tales generally, must be brought down to a date subsequent to 1390, in which year, or in 1389, the *Confessio* first appeared.

51. The Host pronounces the Serjeant's to be 'a thrifty tale,' and, with many pious *jurations*, calls upon the Parish Priest. The Priest says, 'What aileth the man, so synfully to swere?' Whereupon the Host 'smells a Loller (Lollard) in the wind,' and advises the company to stand by, and they will hear a sermon. But the Shipman gravely interposes, and says that there shall be no glosing of the gospel nor preaching here; 'we all believe in the great God,' says he, and no one shall sow cockle (or tares) amidst our clean corn. Perhaps there is a reference here to Wyclif's short sermons on the Gospels read on Sundays and holidays, which were written at Lutterworth towards the close of his life.[1] The Shipman then tells his tale, which is about a French merchant of St. Denis and a monk, named Dan John. This tale, like the Miller's and the Reeve's, belongs to Chaucer's cynical mood. It is followed by that of the Prioress, one strictly in keeping with her character and religious training; it is the story of a little Christian boy killed in some Asiatic town by the cruel Jews, who could not endure to hear the child sing his *Alma Redemptoris Mater* as he went up and down the street. The versification of this tale, which is in the Chaucerian stanza, is here and there rich and musical in the highest degree. In the last stanza there is a reference to the story of 'yonge Hugh of Lincoln,' said to have met a similar fate 'but a litel whyle ago;' the particulars are given in the Chronicle of Matthew Paris, under the year 1255. The tale itself is taken from a source similar to that of the legend of Alphonsus of Lincoln, which greatly resembles it; this story, however (printed by the Chaucer Society), dates only from the second half of the fifteenth century.

52. The Host now looks upon Chaucer, whom he accosts in his rough gibing way :—

> Thou lokest as thou woldest fynde an hare:
> For ever upon the ground I se thee stare.

A 'tale of mirthe' is called for, and Chaucer professes a willingness to comply. Adopting an old romance tripping stanza, he begins to tell the company of the knightly adventures of Sir Thopas :—

---

[1] See *Select English Works of John Wyclif*, vol. i. Oxford, 1871.

Listeth, Lordes, in good entent,
And I wol telle verrayment
    Of mirthe and of solas;
Al of a knyght was fair and gent
In bataille and in tourneyment,
    His name was Sir Thopas.

Sir Thopas rides forth unarmed, and meets with a giant named Sir Olifaunt, who throws stones at him, but Sir Thopas escapes after challenging the giant to fight next day, when he has his armour on. He returns to his castle, and the process of equipment for the fight begins. The description takes up many stanzas; at last all is ready, and the knight sallies forth again. But the patience of the Host is by this time exhausted. 'No more of this,' he says, 'for goddes dignitie.' Of such trashy rimes he will hear no more. Evidently Chaucer meant to quiz the authors of the 'romances of prys,' such as *Horn Child, Guy of Warwick*, and others that he mentions,—which, though still popular, were ever becoming more divorced from the realities of life. The poet pretends to be vexed, but substitutes for the remainder of Sir Thopas the tale (in prose) of Meliboeus and his Dame Prudence, the subject of which is the forgiveness of injuries. This is translated from the *Livre de Melibée et Prudence* of Jean de Meung, which is itself a version, or rather adaptation, of the *Liber Consolationis et Consilii* written by Albertanus of Brescia in 1246.

53. The Host, after drawing a comparison between the patient Prudence and his own wife much to the advantage of the former, turns to the Monk, observes that they are now close to Rochester, and, after much sarcastic compliment on the subject of the worthy Piers's robust and portly appearance, asks for his tale. The Monk proceeds to tell certain *tragedies*, of which, he says, he has a hundred in his cell. He explains a tragedy to mean the history of one who, having 'stood in great prosperitee,' falls into misfortune and ends miserably. Perhaps Chaucer had begun to write a large work on this theme, in imitation of the *De Casibus illustrium virorum* of Boccaccio, and here assigns the seventeen 'tragedies' which he had written to the Monk, as his tale. Or, as Mr. Skeat suggests, the four modern instances—Pedro the Cruel, Pedro of Cyprus, Barnabo Visconti, and Count Ugolino—may have been inserted by an after-thought in the course of a revision of the Tales subsequent to their first publication. The death of Barnabo, which occurred in 1385, is the latest event, the date of which is absolutely certain, mentioned in the work. The sources of the tragedies are—the Bible, Boccaccio's work just named, the

Roman de la Rose (from which come the stories of Nero and Crœsus), and Chaucer's own reading and recollections.   For the terrible tale of Ugolino, whom he calls 'erl Hugelin of Pise,' he refers his readers to Dante, ' the grete poete of Itaille.'

54. The Knight now interposes, saying that they have had enough and too much of these dismal narratives ; and the Host, after enforcing the same thing in his own way, with his usual bitter boldness of tongue, calls upon the Nun's Priest, addressing him with that proper gradation of *dis*-respect which befits the social difference between a dignified monk and the chaplain of a nunnery, for the tale that he had promised.   The amusing tale that follows is ' taken from a fable of about forty lines, " Don Coc et Don Werpil," in the poems of Marie of France, which is amplified in the fifth chapter of the old French metrical Roman de Renart, entitled " Se comme Renart prist Chantecler le Coc." ' [1]

55. After the Nonnes Prestes tale there is a break.   Probably Chaucer, if his life had been prolonged, would have assigned some tale to this place, and linked it properly on to the Wife of Bath's prologue.   As things are, we can do no better (see above, § 45) than place the last-named prologue in succession to the tale of the Cock and the Fox.   The Wife of Bath, a buxom, fresh-complexioned matron, loud of voice and with bold bright eyes, who has had five husbands at the church-door, and whose gay and costly attire is suggestive of the fact, which she ingenuously confesses, that while she married *two* of her husbands for love, she married *three* for money, discourses at great length in praise of matrimony before she commences her tale.   The shrewd biting humour and sententious pithiness of much of this prologue make it a typical passage exhibitive of one side of the great poet—his *esprit moqueur* ; but the handling is too broad and realistic to admit of its being examined in detail.   She does not spare her own sex :—

> Deceite, wepyng, spynnyng, God hath given
> To women kindly [= naturally], while that they may liven.

The outward life of a vain worldly woman in the England of the fourteenth century is mirrored in her voluble talk.   She ever loved to see and to be seen, she says :—

> Therfore made I my visitations
> To vigilies and to processions,
> To prechings eke, and to these pilgrimages,
> To playes of miracles, and mariages.

[1] Dr. Morris.

How unlike almost all these entertainments to the diversions
of a rich tradesman's wife at the present day ! It is curious to
meet here with the rough proverb which drew the attention of
the world a few years back, when used by a great Prussian
statesman of the luckless Parisians :—

> But certeynly I made folk such chere,
> That *in his owne grees I made him frie,*
> For anger, and for verray jalousie.

At the end of the prologue a wrangling arises between the
Sompnour and the Frere, in the course of which we are told
that the pilgrims had got nearly to Sittingbourne, a town ten
miles beyond Rochester. The Wife's tale is illustrative of the
axiom that the thing which women most desire is to have their
own way. The story is the same as that of Sir Florent, in the
first book of Gower's *Confessio Amantis* ; in a later shape we
have it in the *Marriage of Sir Gawayne,* a ballad in Percy's
Reliques. It is not likely that Chaucer took it from Gower ;
but the common source remains as yet undetected.

56. The Friar, after commending the matron's tale, proceeds
to tell a story of a Sompnour, who, having entered into a friendly
league with a fiend, whereby they bind themselves to pursue
misdemeanants and divide the plunder, proves to be more hard-
hearted than his companion ; for the latter is willing to spare a
poor swearing carter who has put himself in his power, because,
as he said, ' it was not his entente,' whereas the Sompnour is
for showing him no mercy. The origin of the tale is supposed
to be some old French fabliau. A Latin story of similar drift
has been published by Mr. Wright in the *Archæologia,* vol.
xxxii.

57. The Sompnour, boiling over with wrath at the uncivil
usage which his profession has received at the Friar's hands,
follows with a tale in which a questing friar is brought to confusion ; it is impossible to go into particulars. The scene is laid
in Holderness, a district of Yorkshire ; but, according to M.
Sandras, the outlines of the story are to be found in a fabliau
by Jacques de Baisieux, the incidents of which take place at
Antwerp. The Sompnour ends by saying :—

> My tale is don, we ben almost at toune—

that is, at Sittingbourne.

58. The Clerk of Oxenford is now invited to open his lips,
which he has kept closed all day; he obeys, and tells the tale
of patient Grisilde, which, he says, he learned at Padua from
Francis Petrarch. This is usually, and with reason, taken as

evidence that Chaucer made the acquaintance of Petrarch when he visited Italy in 1373. It appears also from Petrarch's letters that this particular story was known to him many years before he ever saw the *Decameron*, in which it figures as the last tale. On the other hand it is difficult to believe that Chaucer had not read the story in the *Decameron* before he ever saw Petrarch. For we have seen (*ante*, § 32) that in a poem, probably written in 1364, Chaucer inserted several stanzas translated from the *Theseide* of Boccaccio. If, then, nine years before his interview with Petrarch, Chaucer knew the *Theseide*, is it not likely that he also knew the *Decameron*, which had appeared in 1352 or 1353, and immediately obtained a wide circulation in Italy? Yet, considering the difficulty of multiplying copies of any work before the invention of printing, it would perhaps be easy to exaggerate this probability. At any rate it is now an ascertained fact, that Chaucer, in the Clerk's Tale, follows pretty closely Petrarch's Latin version of the tale in the *Decameron*, and it may be held as certain that he had a copy of this version before him. He may perhaps have *seen* the tale previously in the *Decameron*, and glanced through it without its leaving any impression; coming from the lips of Petrarch himself, it may have seemed to be invested with a peculiar grace.

As if tired of his theme, and *bored* by the invincible patience of his heroine, Chaucer adds an 'Envoy' to the tale, in his sharpest tone of irony and banter, entreating 'noble wives' to beware of falling into that excess of humility which made Grisilde put up with her husband's absurd caprices. The Merchant, whose turn has now come, expresses his lively regret that his own wife was not more of a Grisilde, and then tells the tale of January and May, which was afterwards modernized by Pope. The theme is well worn—an old husband married to, and deceived by, a young wife; the story is found in part, according to Tyrwhitt, in a Latin tale written by one Adolphus early in the fourteenth century.

59. Next comes the beautiful tale of the Squire, concerning Cambuscan, the lord of Tartary, and Canace his daughter. It remains unfinished; but Spenser, who gives to it a sequel of his own invention in the fourth book of the *Faerie Queene*, evidently believed that Chaucer had written the entire tale, but that the concluding portion had been lost. For in the stanzas following the well-known couplet—

> Dan Chaucer, well of English undefyled,
> On fames eternall beadroll worthie to be fyled—

he says :—

Then pardon, O most sacred happie spirit,
That I thy labours *lost* may thus revive,
And steale from thee the meed of thy due merit,
That none durst ever whilest thou wast alive,
And, being dead, in vain now many strive.

But there is no good reason to believe that Chaucer ever completed the tale, and Milton certainly did not think so when he spoke, in the *Penseroso*, of him—

who left half-told
The story of Cambuscan bold.

Of the sources whence Chaucer drew the materials of this tale, a full and satisfactory account is given by Mr. Skeat.[1] They were, 1. The Travels of Marco Polo, 2. a Latin or French version, now lost, of some of the oriental tales which are familiar to us from being included among the *Arabian Nights' Entertainments*. Marco Polo, the adventurous Venetian who in the thirteenth century resided and travelled many years in Tartary and China, describes in his Travels the court of the great Mongol potentate, Kubla Khan, and Chaucer has borrowed from him many points of the description. But the name Cambuscan is a corruption of Chingis (or Gengis) Khan, which was the name of the mighty conqueror who founded the Mongol empire about 1220 A.D. With the horse of brass and the magic mirror, which are brought as presents to Cambuscan by an envoy from the king of Arabie and Inde, may be compared the similar fictions in the *Arabian Nights* of the flying horse which is moved or stopped by turning a peg on its shoulder, and the magic tube given by the fairy Pari-Banou to Prince Ahmed.

60. The Franklin, who represents the class of *vavasours*, or country gentlemen of the second order,—those, namely, who held their lands not directly from the crown, but from some lord who did so hold—praises so warmly and so diffusely the elegance of the last tale and the eloquence of the teller, that the Host interposes, and bids him proceed with his own tale without more delay. The Franklin says that he derives his tale from the 'olde gentil Bretons,' who 'of divers aventures maden laies.' The story is not unpleasing. Dorigene, the faithful wife of Arviragus, has promised conditionally to grant her love to Aurelius; the condition, which she thought impossible of fulfilment, he, by art magic, apparently fulfils, and claims the execution of her promise. She tells Arviragus, who in great

---

[1] Chaucer, *Prioresses Tale, &c.,* Clarendon Press.

sorrow bids her keep her word : she with like sorrow preparés to do so ; but Aurelius, not to be outdone in generosity, releases her from her promise. Lastly, the magician through whose help he had fulfilled the condition, and to whom he had promised a thousand pounds, releases him from his bond. The substance of the story is found in the fifth novel of the tenth day of the *Decameron.*

61. A few lines, which, though wanting in the six MSS. selected by Mr. Furnivall for the Six-Text Chaucer, are found in some inferior MSS., link the Franklin's to the Doctor's tale. This is perhaps the least important in the whole collection. It is the well-known story of Virginia, 'as telleth Titus Livius.' The *Pardoner* follows, and after describing his life as one wholly based on imposture, and trading on the fears of the superstitious, proceeds to tell a very moral tale, containing terrible warnings against drunkenness and covetousness. It is taken from No. 82 of the *Cento Novelle Antiche.*

Having finished his tale, the Pardoner informs the company that he has a good store of relics and pardons in his 'male,' given him by the Pope with his own hand, and that since one or two of them might fall off their horses at any moment and break their necks, it was only common prudence for them all to draw near, make suitable offerings, kiss the relics, and receive pardons. The Host, as the greatest sinner, would do well to set the example. The Host gives a rough answer, which makes the Pardoner very wroth ; but the Knight interposes with a few pacifying words. It should be remembered that the great schism was at this time—the last decade of the fourteenth century—in full operation ; the exchequer of Boniface IX. was, on this account, miserably low, and among other means used to replenish it was a liberal issue of indulgences, which Chaucer calls 'pardons.'

62. After the Pardoner's tale there is a gap, which Chaucer would probably have filled up with one or more tales if he had lived. The next in order is the *Second Nonnes Tale,* a poem in the same metre as that of the Prioress, and, like it, exceedingly beautiful in parts, from the tender fervour which seems to animate the speaker, and the rich imaginative strain of her pious eloquence. It is that story of St. Cecilia, a Roman lady martyred in the second century, upon whose life a learned monograph of the highest value has lately appeared from the pen of Dom Guéranger of Solesme. Chaucer found his materials in the *Legenda Aurea* of Jacobus de Voragine, archbishop of Genoa about 1290.

63. Soon after the conclusion of the Second Nonnes Tale,

the pilgrims reach Boughton-under-Blee, a village five miles from
Canterbury, where the road mounts a long steep hill, and on the
top of it passes for some distance through the broken forest
country called the Blee.   Here they are overtaken by a Canon,
meanly dressed, and his yeoman.   Entering into conversation
with the latter, the Host finds that his master is an alchemist,
who wastes all his own substance, and all that he can beg or
borrow from other people, in the endeavour to transmute the
baser metals into gold.   The Canon, overhearing this, and
fearing exposure, rides away; then the yeoman, after a long
preface, tells a not very interesting tale about another Canon
who practised alchemy, and ruined both himself, and a London
priest who was so deluded as to believe in him.   This tale is of
Chaucer's own invention.

The pilgrims have now climbed Boughton Hill, and, making
their way along the rough and miry road (see l. 17013) through
the forest, have reached the 'litel toun' under the Blee, called
'Bob-up-and-doun.' In Ogilby's plan of the road to Canterbury,
made in 1675, several houses are marked at the fifty-fourth mile
(two miles from Canterbury) after a succession of sharp ups and
downs extending from the fifty-third mile.   This hamlet was
probably 'Bob-up-and-down.'   Here the Host rouses up the
Coke, who is drunk and has fallen asleep on his horse.   The
Manciple also assails him in rough uncivil terms, by which the
Coke is moved to wrath, but appeased by the offer of a drink
of wine from the Manciple's gourd.   Whereat the Host laughs,
and says—

> I see wel it is necessary,
> Wher that we gon, good drinke with us to carry.

Then comes the *Manciple's Tale*, taken from the second book of
Ovid's Metamorphoses.   Phœbus kills his wife Coronis, because
his white crow tells him of her infidelity; afterwards he repents,
hates the crow, turns him black, and flings him out of doors;—

> And for this cause ben alle crowes blake.

64. By the time the Manciple had ended his tale, the position of the sun showed that it was four o'clock.   They begin to
enter the 'tounes ende,' that is, they get into the enclosed land
surrounding the town of Canterbury.   The Host now, since
every one else has told his tale, desires the Persone to tell the
concluding story.   From these words it is evident that Chaucer,
if his life had been spared, would have completed his plan, and
put tales into the mouth of the Plowman, the Haberdasher, the
Webbe, &c., so that the Persone's tale should really have been

the last of thirty-one, instead of, as it now is, the last of twenty-four.   The Persone says that he will tell no fable, nor can he 'geste,' *i.e.* tell them an alliterative tale, nor does he care to rime ; therefore he will—

> Telle a litel tale in prose,
> To knitte up al this fest, and make an ende.

The tale which follows is in fact a treatise on the sacrament of Penance, in its three parts, contrition, confession, and satisfaction ; under the second head is a description of each of the seven deadly sins, and of the chief remedies against them. Chaucer may have intended to enter in this way a practical protest against the irreverent and absurd proceeding of Gower, in using the seven deadly sins as a sort of framework in which to fix all kinds of loose stories about love. The particular treatise from which Chaucer translated the *Persones Tale* (for we cannot doubt that it is a translation) has not yet been discovered. Attached to it, in all the best MSS., is a paragraph in which, referring to some of his works which he has revoked in his ' Retractions ' (a book now lost), he asks pardon of God for having written them, instancing particularly *Troylus,* the *House of Fame,* the 'book of the Leon' (lost), and several others ; but is thankful for having made his translation of Boethius, and ' other bokes of legendes of Saints, and of omelies, and moralite, and devotion.' Thus does the simple noble heart, arrived at the end of life's pilgrimage, endeavour to disburden itself of that corrupt furniture of word and work which would not stand before the pure eyes of Him to whom he was going.

65. Chaucer was the centre of a group of literary men, of whom he was the friend or master ; who admired and loved him, and in most cases strove to imitate him, though with very indifferent success. Of these, **John Gower,** the 'ancient Gower' of Shakespeare, was the chief.   His family belonged to Kent, and was possessed of manors in different parts of the country. Gower himself was a rich man, and his benefactions to the church of St. Mary Overy, Southwark, had a large share in rebuilding the fabric as it now stands.   In that church his ashes lie under a richly decorated tomb. He wrote many French poems, evidently conceiving that by so doing he found a larger audience than by writing in English.   At the end of one of these, he says,— .

> ' *A l'université de tout le monde*
> Johan Gower ceste balade envoie.'

His principal productions were three books, which (though there is no apparent connection between them) are treated in some MSS. as one work,—respectively entitled *Speculum Meditantis, Vox Clamantis,* and *Confessio Amantis.* The *Speculum* is in French rimes, in ten books ; it was never printed, nor is a manuscript of it known to exist. The poem, according to Warton, ' displays the general nature of virtue and vice, enumerates the felicities of conjugal fidelity by examples selected from various authors, and describes the path which the reprobate ought to pursue for the recovery of the divine grace.' The *Vox Clamantis,* a poem in Latin elegiacs, in seven books, edited by Mr. Coxe of the Bodleian Library, in 1850, for the Roxburghe Society, is in substance a history of the insurrection of the Commons, under Wat Tyler, in the reign of Richard II. The *Confessio Amantis,* an English poem in eight books, written in the short romance metre of eight syllables, was finished in 1393. It has been frequently printed. Imitating the affectations of the authors of the *Roman de la Rose,* Gower presents us in this poem with a long colloquy between a lover and his confessor, Genius, the priest of Venus ; the lover confessing, under the several heads of the seven deadly sins, the respects in which he has offended against Love, and the priest giving him instructions in the duties of a lover, under the guise, generally. of relevant anecdotes, collected from his multifarious reading. The Provençal poets had introduced this fashion of deifying Love, and painting him as the sovereign ruler over human life and destiny. A considerable portion of the poem consists of learned disquisitions upon politics, astrology, and physiology, stuffed with all the crude absurdities which suited the coarse palate of that age. The materials of the tales are gathered in part from the Latin classical poets, in part from the *Gesta Romanorum,* the *Pantheon* of Godfrey of Viterbo, the work of Vincent de Beauvais, and other such compilations.

66. In giving an example of Gower's style, we shall choose a passage where he may be compared with Chaucer ; it is where he exposes the alchemists and their dupes. In the fourth book, which treats of the sin of sloth, he takes occasion to praise the great diligence of the men of former times, who. worked unceasingly at the composition of the philosopher's stone, or rather of the ' three stones made through clergy,' the lapis vegetabilis, the lapis animalis, and the lapis mineralis. The first of these preserves a man through life from sickness. The second sharpens and keeps in good order the five senses. The third refines all the baser metals, and imparts to them the nature of gold and silver. But how to make it is the question :—

They speken fast of thilke stone,
But how to make it, now wot none
After the sothe experience.
And netheles great diligence
They setten up thilke dede,
And spillen more than they spede.
For alle way they finde a lette,[1]
Which bringeth in poverte and dette
To hem, that riche were afore.
The loss is had, the lucre is lore.
To get a pound they spenden five,
I not [2] how such a craft shall thrive
In the maner as it is used.

Gower wrote much, particularly in the later books of the *Vox Clamantis*, on the abuses prevailing among the clergy, both secular and regular; but, like Chaucer, he had no sympathy with the Lollards. There is a long passage denouncing them in the fifth book of the *Confessio Amantis*; it begins :—

Beware that thou be nought oppressed
With anticristes Lollardie.

67. **Thomas Occleve**, a clerk in the Exchequer, flourished about the year 1410. His chief work is a version, in the seven-line stanza first employed by Chaucer, of the work of Ægidius *De Regimine Principum*; but far more interesting than the version itself is the long prologue prefixed to it, in which the poet tells us much about his own life and its troubles, and sings the praise of his great master Chaucer. The author describes his meeting with a poor old man, with whom he falls into conversation, and to whom at last he opens his griefs. After suggesting various causes for his despondency the old man says, prettily :—

If thou fele the in any of thise y-greved,
Or ellis what, tel on in Goddis name,
Thou seest, al day the begger is releved,
That syt and beggith, crokyd, blynd, and lame ;
And whi ? for he ne lettith for no shame
His harmes and his povert to bewreye
To folke, as thei goon bi hym bi the weye.

After a long dialogue, the old man suggests that Occleve should write some poem and send it to Prince Henry, to which the poet assents, while lamenting that his great counsellor is dead :—

But wel away ! so is mine hertè wo
That the honour of English tonge is dede,
Of which I wont was han counsel and rede !

---

[1] Hindrance.   [2] Ne wot, know not.

O mayster dere, and fadir reverent,
My mayster Chaucer, floure of eloquence,
Mirrour of fructuous entendement,
O universal fadir in sciènce,
Alas that thou thine excellent prudence
In thy bed mortel mightest not bequethe !
What eyled Death ?   Alas ! why would he sle the ?

68. **John Lydgate**, a Benedictine monk of Bury St. Edmunds, who flourished about 1425, was also an admirer and imitator of Chaucer. He was, as a writer, less gifted than voluminous; Ritson, in his *Bibliographia Poetica*, has enumerated two hundred and fifty-one of his productions; and this list is known to be incomplete.   No writer was ever more popular in his own day ; but it was a popularity which could not last. His versification is rough and inharmonious; as unlike as possible to the musical movement of Chaucer ; his stories are prolix and dull, and his wit seldom very pointed.   Instèad of, like Chaucer, filling his ear, and feeding his imagination with the poetry of Italy, the only country where literature had as yet emerged from barbarism and assumed forms comparable to those of antiquity, Lydgate's attention seems to have been engrossed, partly by the inane Latin literature [1] of the period, partly by the works of the romance writers and Trouvères, whose French was still rude and unpolished, and whose rhythm was nearly as bad as his own.   A selection from his minor poems was edited by Mr. Halliwell for the Percy Society in 1840.   His longer works are,—the *Storie of Thebes*, the *Falls of Princes*, and the *History of the Siege of Troy*.

69. The *Storie of Thebes* is presented in the guise of a new Canterbury Tale.   After a glowing reference to this masterpiece of his great predecessor, so various, so graphic, and so true, Lydgate says that after the pilgrims had reached Canterbury, and while they were still lodging there, under the watchful rule of the Host, before setting out on the return journey, he himself,—having to pay to St. Thomas a vow which he had made to him in sickness,—came to Canterbury, dressed in a black cope, and riding on a lean palfrey, with rusty bridle. He happened to put up at the inn where the pilgrims lay.   The Host immediately accosted him in his rough and ready way, calling him ‘ Dan Piers, Dan Dominike, Dan Godfrey or Clement,’ and insisting that he should sup with them that night, and tell them a tale on the way back to London next day.   Lydgate was fain to consent; and being called upon for his tale immediately on

---

[1] This expression refers to the miscellaneous literature, not, of course, to the theological or philosophical works written in Latin.

their getting clear of the town next morning, he undertakes to tell them of the destruction of Thebes :—

> As wryte myne aucthor, and Bochas bothe two,
> Rede her bookes, and ye shall finde it so.

That is, his sources are the *Thebaid* of Statius, and the *Theseide* of Boccaccio. The poem, which as a whole is extremely dull, tells the whole story of Thebes, from its foundation by Amphion to its destruction by Theseus. When he has to speak of the widowed Grecian matrons complaining that their husbands lie unburied, he naturally refers to Chaucer :—

> As ye have herde to forne
> Wel rehearsed, at Depforde in the vale,
> In the beginning of the Knightes Tale.

The *Storie of Thebes* is in riming ten-syllable couplets, and contains about 4,780 lines.

70. The *Falls of Princes* is founded on a French paraphrase, by an author named Laurence, of the Latin work, *De Casibus Virorum Illustrium*, of Boccaccio, to which reference was made (*ante*, § 53) in speaking of the sources of the Monk's Tale. In the prologue he gives an interesting enumeration of Chaucer's works, among which he names the version of 'Origenes upon the Maudelayn,' and the *Book of the Lyon* (*ante*, § 64), both of which are now lost. The *Falls of Princes* is in nine books, written in the Chaucerian heptastich.

71. Lydgate's Troy-book professes to be a free version of Guido di Colonne's *Historia Trojana*, just as the latter, making no mention of Benoit de Sainte-Maure (see § 36 above), professes to be founded on the genuine narratives of Dares and Dictys, both of whom fought under the walls of Troy, but on different sides ! The poem, which is in heroic verse, opens with an invocation of Mars :—

> O myghty Mars, that with thy sterne lyght
> In armys hast the power and the myght !

Lydgate then tells us that the work was first taken in hand in 1412, at the instance of Henry, Prince of Wales (Shakespeare's Prince Hal) :—

> Because he would that both to highe and lowe
> The noble storye openly were knowe,
> And, in our tunge about in every age,
> Written it were as well in our language,
> As in the Latyn and the Frensbe it is ;
> That of the storye we the truthe not mys,
> No more than doth eche other nacion :
> This was the fine of his entencion.

Far from rushing, like Homer and Virgil, 'in medias res,'
Lydgate and Guido prefer the example of Horace's cyclic poet
who ' gemino orditur ab ovo ; ' and before we get to the siege of
Troy, we have the whole story of the Golden Fleece, and the
loves of Jason and Medea. In the third book we have the
story of Troilus and Cressida, and Lydgate seizes the opportunity to pay a worthy and feeling tribute to his dead master. 'It
is no nede,' he says, to enlarge on the story of false Cressid—

> Syth my maister Chaucer here afore
> In this matter hath so well him bore,
> In his boke of Troylus and Creseyde,
> Whych he mayde longe or that he deyed,
> Rehersinge, &c.

A long panegyric on Chaucer follows, in which he is declared
to be no less worthy than Petrarch of the laurel crown. In
the fifth and last book the returns of the Grecian chiefs from
Troy are described, and we are favoured with an interesting
piece of military statistics ; Dictys the Greek certifying that
800,006 Greeks fell during the siege, while Dares, not to be
outdone in precision, returns 600,086 as the number of slain
Trojans. Then we have a date ; the translation was *finished*,
it seems, in 1420. A fresh reference to Chaucer ascribes to
him just that large-heartedness, that absence of envy, petti-
ness, and ill-nature, which the perusal of his writings suggests.
He was no carper, no fault-finder ; not a man to ' grutche at
every blot : '—

> I have herde tolde, but sayde alway the beste,
> Sufferynge goodly of his gentilnesse
> Ful many thynge embraced with rudenesse.

Nor was there ever, nor is there now, one in England fit to
' holde his ynke-horn.'
In connection with the perplexing mention of *Lollius* made
by Chaucer, as the author whom he followed in his *Troylus*, it
is noteworthy that Lydgate also names him as an historian of
Troy, though not of equal note with Dares and Dictys :—

> And of this syege wrote eke Lollius,
> But tofore all Daretus Frigeus, &c.

72. Lydgate also translated from the French the *Daunce of
Machabre*, or Dance of Death, in a curious octave stanza, of
which the following is a specimen :—

> Owt of the Ffranche I drew it of entent,
> Not word by word, but following the substance,
> And fro Parys to Englonde it sente,
> Only of purposs yow to do plesaunce ;

Rude of langage,—I was not borne in Ffraunce—
Have me excusèd; my name is John Lidgate,
Off here tunge I have no suffisaunce
Her corious metres in Englisshe to translate.

In this poem Death accosts, first the Pope, then the Emperor, then the representatives of every earthly profession and calling in succession; each of these replies in his turn; and all, with more or less of moralizing, own the levelling hand and irresistible might of Death. A poem called *Chichevache and Bycorne* has also been ascribed to him; he is the author, moreover, of a didactic poem in octosyllabics, of immense length and never printed, to which a commentator of the sixteenth century has given the title *Reson and Sensuallyte*; its subject is the rivalry between reason and sense.

73. Among the minor poets of this period, there is none so well deserving of notice as **Lawrence Minot**, whose poems were accidentally discovered by Mr. Tyrwhitt among the Cottonian MSS. in the British Museum, near the close of the last century. They celebrate the martial exploits of Edward III., from the battle of Halidon Hill in 1333 to the taking of Guisnes castle in 1352, and would seem to have been composed contemporaneously with the events described. They are in the same stanza of six short lines, common among the romancers, in which Chaucer's *Rime of Sir Thopas* is written. Nothing is known of Minot's personal history.

Scottish Poets:—Barbour; James I.; Wynton.

74. **John Barbour**, Archdeacon of Aberdeen, is the author of an heroic poem entitled *The Bruce*,[1] containing the history of Robert Bruce, the victor of Bannockburn, and of Scotland, so far as that was influenced by him. The poem is believed to have been completed in the year 1375. It is in the eight-syllable riming measure, and consists of between twelve and thirteen thousand lines. He also wrote a Troy-book in octosyllabic rime, founded probably on Benoit's *Geste de Troie*, of which nothing was known till the discovery of fragments of it, a short time ago, in a MS. of Lydgate's Troy-book, by Mr. Bradshaw, the learned and acute scholar who has charge of the University Library at Cambridge. See the Introduction to the *Geste Hystoriale* of Troy, printed for the Early English Text Society. **James I.** of Scotland, who received his education while retained as a captive in England between the years 1405 and 1420, wrote his principal work, the *King's Quhair* (i.e. quire, or book), in praise of the

---

[1] See Critical Section, ch. I., *Heroic Poetry*.

lady who had won his heart and whom he afterwards married, the Lady Jane Beaufort, daughter of the Duke of Somerset. This poem, which is in a hundred and ninety-seven stanzas, divided into six cantos, contains much interesting matter of the autobiographical sort. **Andrew Wynton**, author of the *Originale Cronykil*, was a canon of St. Andrew's, and prior of St. Serf's, the monastery on the island in Loch Leven. His *Cronykil* begins, as was then thought decorous and fitting, with the Creation, plunges into the history of the angels, discusses general geography, and at the end of five books, filled with this 'pantographical' rubbish, as Dr. Irving amusingly calls it, settles down upon its proper subject, which is the history of Scotland from the earliest ages down to his own time. He died about the year 1420. He incorporates freely the work of preceding writers—three hundred lines from Barbour, and no less than thirty-six chapters by some versifier, whose name, he says, he has not been able to discover. His verse is, like Barbour's, octosyllabic; it is naïve, sense-full, and, in parts, touching.[1]

Prose Writers :—Maundevile ; Chaucer ; Wyclif.

75. The earliest known work in English prose of a secular character, the *Travels of Sir John Maundevile*, dates from this period. As before mentioned, the book had been originally written in French, and afterwards translated into Latin. It was probably about the year 1360 that Sir John prepared and published an English version also, for the benefit of his own countrymen. This is a proof that about this time the knowledge of French, even among the educated classes, was ceasing to be essential or universal.

The author professes not only to have traversed the Holy Land in several directions, but to have visited many countries farther east, including even India; but when we come to the chapters which treat of these countries, we find them filled with preposterous stories, which Maundevile, whose capacity of swallowing was unlimited, must have derived either from hearsay or from the works of travellers equally gullible with himself. When one reflects that Maundevile had as great opportunities as Herodotus, and then observes the use that he made of them, comparisons are forced on the mind not over-favourable to the English and mediæval, as contrasted with the Greek and classical, grade of intelligence. Our author tells of the 'Land of Amazoym,' an island inhabited only by a race of warlike

[1] Irving's *History of Scottish Poetry.*

K

women; of rocks of adamant in the Indian seas, which draw
to them with irresistible force any ships sailing past that have
any iron bolts or nails in them; of a tribe of people with hoofs
like horses, of people with eight toes, of dwarfs, and of a one-
legged race, whose one foot was so large that they used it to
shade themselves from the sun with. The language, as used by
Maundevile, appears almost precisely similar to that of Chaucer
in his prose works. As a physician, Maundevile belonged to a
class of men not usually addicted to superstition, or over-
burdened with religious veneration; a trait which Chaucer,
with his profound knowledge of mankind, hits off in his account
of the ' Doctor of Phisike : '—

His studie was but litel on the Bible.

But the superstitious credulity of Maundevile is unbounded;
nor did it tend to make his work unpopular. On the contrary,
there is scarcely any old English book of which the manuscript
copies are so numerous; and it is certain that it was held in
high estimation all through the fifteenth century—down, in
fact, to the time when, foreign travel having become more
common, the existence of the eight-toed men &c. began to be
doubted.

76. Chaucer's prose works consist, besides the two Canterbury Tales already described,—*the Tale of Melibœus*, and the
Persones Tale,—of a translation of Boethius *De Consolatione
Philosophiæ*, the *Astrolabie*, and the *Testament of Love*. In
translating Boethius, Chaucer was renewing for the men of his
own day the service rendered by Alfred to his West Saxon countrymen. The *Astrolabie* is a treatise on astronomy, composed
in 1391, for the use of the poet's second son, Louis, who was
at the time ten years old. It opens thus : 'Lytel Lowys my
sonne, I perceive well by certain evidences thyne abylytè to
lerne sciences touching nombres and proporcions.' The *Testament of Love* is divided into three parts. It professes to be an
imitation of the work of Boethius. In the first part, Love
bequeaths instructions to her followers, whereby they may
rightly judge of the causes of cross fortune &c. In the second,
'she teacheth the knowledge of one very God, our Creator; as
also the state of grace, and the state of glory.' Throughout these
two parts are scattered allusions, or what seem to be such, to
the circumstances under which Chaucer lost his official employment, and was reduced to poverty. The third part is a remarkable discourse on necessity and free-will, in which the doctrine
laid down by St. Augustine and expounded by the schoolmen
is eloquently set forth. Professor ten Brink believes that the

Testament of Love is wrongly ascribed to Chaucer, 1. because the writer speaks of Chaucer in the third person, 2. because he praises him without measure, 3. because the passage in the *Troylus* about God's foreknowledge and man's free-will is erroneously quoted, 4. on the ground that it is incredible that Chaucer, after having *translated* Boethius, should now *paraphrase* him in this tedious fashion, 5. because with this writer Love is female, but with Chaucer always male. Some of these considerations have much force. On the other hand, Gower, in the passage quoted above, § 21, says that the Muse had bidden him to enjoin Chaucer, that he

Do make his Testament of Love.

Such a work might therefore be looked for from Chaucer's pen. It may be said that the forger adopted this name because of the passage in Gower; but in that case he would surely have taken more care to remove from the work all appearance of its having been written by another than Chaucer.

77. Among the English writings of **John Wyclif,** his translation of the Bible must be first considered. The subject is surrounded with difficulties, and cannot be fully discussed here. A fine edition of the *Wycliffite Versions of the Holy Scriptures* was issued in 1850, under the care of the Rev. J. Forshall and Sir F. Madden, from the Oxford University Press. In the preface to this work the following passage occurs, and represents probably the real state of the case :—

'Down to the year 1360, the Psalter appears to be the only book of Scripture which had been entirely rendered into English. Within less than twenty-five years from this date a prose version of the whole Bible, including as well the apocryphal as the canonical books, had been completed, and was in circulation among the people. For this invaluable gift England is indebted to John Wyclif. It may be impossible to determine with certainty the exact share which his own pen had in the translation, but there can be no doubt that he took a part in the labour of producing it, and that the accomplishment of the work must be attributed mainly to his zeal, encouragement, and direction.'

The version here referred to is the older of the two versions printed by Forshall and Madden. The later one appeared some years after Wyclif's death, being thought necessary by his Lollard followers on account of the inequality existing between different parts of the original work. However, the general agreement between the two versions is very close.

The other English writings of Wyclif consist of Sermons, Exegetical treatises, Controversial treatises, and Letters. A selection of these, edited by the present writer, was published for the Clarendon Press in 1871.[1]   The *Sermons*, which are very short, are based upon the gospels and epistles read in the church service.   The explanations of the New Testament parables are often racy and original; many curious traditional interpretations are given; and now and then, though it is but seldom, the tone rises to real eloquence.   In the case of the other writings, interesting as many of them are, there is unfortunately much difficulty in distinguishing between those which are genuine and those which are more or less doubtful.   The controversial tracts are directed chiefly against the four orders of friars, whose monasteries Wyclif called ' Caym's [*i.e.* Cain's] castles;'—in a minor degree they assail the pope, the monks, and the higher orders of the secular clergy.   Of one of the exegetical tracts, *On the Paternoster,* a portion of the striking peroration is here subjoined :—

' Whanne a man seith, My God, delyvere me fro myn enemyes, what othir thing saith he than this, Delyvere us from yvel?   And if thou rennest aboute bi alle the wordis of holy praieris, thou schalt fynde nothing whiche is not conteyned in this praier of the Lord.   Whoevere seith a thing that may not perteyne to this praier of the Gospel, he praieth bodili and unjustli and unleeffulli, as me thenkith.   Whanne a man saieth in his praier, Lord, multiplie myn richessis, and encreese myn honouris, and seith this, havynge the coveitise of hem, and not purposynge the profit of hem to men, to be bettir to Godward, I gesse that he may not fynde it in the Lordis praier.   Therfore be it schame to aske the thingis whiche it is not leefful to coveyte.   If a man schameth not of this, but coveytise overcometh him, this is askid, that he delyvere fro this yvel of coveytise, to whom we seyn, Delyvere us from yvel.'

[1] *Select English Works of John Wyclif.*   Oxford, 1871.

CHAPTER II.

REVIVAL OF LEARNING.

1450–1558.

1. M. SISMONDI, in his admirable work on the Literature of the South of Europe, has a passage,[1] explaining the decline of Italian literature in the fifteenth century, which is so strictly applicable to the corresponding decline of English literature for a hundred and seventy years after Chaucer, that we cannot forbear quoting it :—

' The century which, after the death of Petrarch, had been devoted by the Italians to the study of antiquity, during which literature experienced no advance, and the Italian language seemed to retrograde, was not, however, lost to the powers of imagination. Poetry, on its first revival, had not received sufficient nourishment. The fund of knowledge, of ideas, and of images, which she called to her aid, was too restricted. The three great men of the fourteenth century, whom we first presented to the attention of the reader, had, by the sole force of their genius, attained a degree of erudition, and a sublimity of thought, far beyond the spirit of their age. These qualities were entirely personal ; and the rest of the Italian bards, like the Provençal poets, were reduced, by the poverty of their ideas, to have recourse to those continual attempts at wit, and to that mixture of unintelligible ideas and incoherent images, which render the perusal of them so fatiguing. The whole of the fifteenth century was employed in extending in every direction the knowledge and resources of the friends of the Muses. Antiquity was unveiled to them in all its elevated characters—its severe laws, its energetic virtue, and its beautiful and engaging mythology ; in its subtle and profound philosophy, its overpowering eloquence, and its delightful poetry. Another age was required to knead afresh the clay for the formation of a nobler race. At the close of the century, a divine breath animated the finished statue, and it started into life.'

[1] Vol. ii. p. 400 (Roscoe).

Mutatis mutandis, these eloquent sentences are exactly applicable to the case of English literature. Chaucer's eminence was purely personal; even more so, perhaps, than that of the great Italians, for the countrymen of Dante, Petrarch, and Boccaccio at least possessed a settled and beautiful language, adapted already to nearly all literary purposes; while the tongue of Chaucer was in so rude and unformed a condition that only transcendent genius could make a work expressed through it endurable. The fifteenth century seems to have been an age of active preparation in every country of Europe. Though no great books were produced in it, it witnessed the invention of the art of printing, the effect of which was so to multiply copies of the masterpieces of Greek and Roman genius, to reduce their price, and to enlarge the circle of their readers, as to supply abundantly new materials for thought, and new models of artistic form, and thus pave the way for the great writers of the close of the next century.

2. Printing, invented at Metz by Gutenberg about the year 1450, was introduced into England by William Caxton, who learned the art in the Low Countries, where he lived for some years in the service of Margaret, Duchess of Burgundy, a sister of our Edward IV. The first books printed in English are believed to have been, 'The Recueil of the Historyes of Troye,' and 'The Game and Play of the Chesse.' These translations from the French were made by Caxton himself, and seem to have been printed under his direction at Bruges in 1475. In the course of the next year he probably came over to England. The first book indisputably printed in England was the 'Dictes and Sayinges of the Philosophers,' on the title-page of which we read, 'Enprynted by me, William Caxton, at Westmestre, the yere of our Lord mcccclxxvii.' His press was set up in the Almonry near Westminster Abbey; it is clear therefore that the Church regarded his proceedings with approval, and was disposed to further them by substantial aid. The patronage also of two enlightened noblemen, Anthony Woodville Earl Rivers, and John Tiptoft Earl of Worcester, greatly aided Caxton in his enterprise.

This century was also signalized by the foundation of many schools and colleges, in which the founders desired that the recovered learning of antiquity should be uninterruptedly and effectually cultivated. Eton, the greatest of the English schools, and King's College at Cambridge, were founded by Henry VI. between 1440 and 1450. Three new universities arose in Scotland—that of St. Andrews in 1410, of Glasgow in 1450, of Aberdeen in 1494;—all under the express authority of different

Popes. Three or four unsuccessful attempts were made in the course of this and the previous century,—the latest in 1496—to establish a university in Dublin. Several colleges were founded at Oxford and Cambridge in the reign of Henry VIII., among which we may specify Christ Church, the largest college at the former university (which, however, was originally planned by the magnificent Wolsey on a far larger scale), and the noble foundation of Trinity College, Cambridge.

In the period now before us our attention will be directed to three subjects ;—the poets, whether English or Scotch,—the state and progress of learning,—and the prose writers. The manner in which the great and complex movement of the Reformation influenced for good or evil the development of literature, is too wide a subject to be fully considered here. Something, however, will be said under this head, when we come to sketch the rise of the 'new learning,' or study of the Humanities, in England, and inquire into the causes which rendered its growth fitful and intermittent.

Poetry and Romance :—Hardyng, Malory, Hawes, Barclay, Skelton, Surrey, Wyat; first Poet Laureate.

3. The poets of this period, at least on the English side of the border, were of small account. The middle of the fifteenth century witnessed the expulsion of the English from France ; and a time of national humiliation is unfavourable to the production of poetry. If, indeed, humiliation become permanent, and involve subjection to the stranger, the plaintive wailings of the elegiac Muse are naturally evoked ; as we see in the instances of Ireland and Wales. But where a nation is merely disgraced, not crushed, it keeps silence, and waits for a better day. For more than thirty years after the loss of the French provinces, England was distracted and weakened by the civil wars of the Roses. This was also a time unfavourable to poetry, the makers of which then and long afterwards depended on the patronage of the noble and wealthy,—a patronage which, in that time of fierce passions, alternate suffering, and universal disquietude, was not likely to be steadily maintained. Why the fifty years which followed the victory of Bosworth should have been so utterly barren of good poetry, it is less easy to see. All that can be said is, that this was an age of preparation, in which men disentombed and learned to appreciate old treasures, judging that they were much better employed than in attempting to produce new matter, with imperfect means and models. Towards the close of the reign of Henry VIII. were produced the *Songs and Sonnettes* of the

friends Lord Surrey and Sir Thomas Wyat; and Sackville wrote
the Induction to the *Mirrour for Magistrates* in the last year of
Mary.

Scotland seems to have been about a century later than England in arriving at the stage of literary culture which Chaucer
and his contemporaries illustrate. Several poets of no mean
order arose in that country during the period now in question.
Of some of these, namely, Dunbar, Gawain Douglas, Lyndsay,
and Henryson, we shall presently have to make particular
mention.

4. **John Hardyng** was in early life an esquire to Harry Percy, commonly called Hotspur. After seeing his lord fall on the field of
Shrewsbury, he took service with Sir Robert Umfravile, and remained
till his death a dependent on that family. He wrote—in that common
seven-line stanza which we have called the 'Chaucerian heptastich'—
a *Chronicle* of Britain, which comes down to 1462, ending with an
address to Edward IV. urging him to be merciful to the Lancastrians,
and to make just allowance for previous circumstances.

5. Romance in one shape or other furnished the educated
classes with intellectual amusement throughout the fifteenth as in
the fourteenth century. The prose romance of the *Saint Graal*
(see Prel. Ch. II. § 68) was translated into English verse by Henry
Lonelich in the middle of the fifteenth century; his version
along with the original, was edited by Mr. Furnivall in 1861
for the Roxburghe Club. Perhaps it was the success of this
translation which led **Sir Thomas Malory**, about 1470, to produce in English prose the remainder of the romances connected
with the Saint Graal, under the title of *The Historie of King
Arthur and his Noble Knights of the Round Table.* He made
his compilation 'out of certeyn bookes of Frensshe,' namely, the
prose romances of *Merlin, Lancelot, Tristan,* the *Queste du Saint
Graal* and the *Mort Artur.* Caxton printed Malory's work in
1485. It has in later times been frequently edited, *e.g.* by
Southey in 1817, by Mr. T. Wright in 1858, and by Mr. Conybeare in 1868.

6. In spite of this prevalent taste for romance, we have seen
that a great mind like Chaucer's could abandon a track of
thought and invention which was leading farther and farther
away from reality, and paint the world which he saw before him;
nor did he spare ridicule for the hackneyed style of the romancist,
as we saw in *Sir Thopas.* **Stephen Hawes**, author of the *Pastime of Pleasure,* had not enough originality and substance in him
to follow such an example. Still, writing for a refined audience
(he was Groom of the Chamber to Henry VII.), he could see
that if battles and courses and the feats of chivalry were to con-

tinue to please, they must be justified by a new treatment.
Scenes, the like of which are going on all round us, need no
excuse for painting; their interest is immediate; they come
home, as Lord Bacon says, 'to our business and bosoms.'   But
when society is no longer in a state of war, when adventures are
fewer and tamer, then, if narratives of strife delight us still, the
poet is tempted to introduce a hidden meaning into his representations, and, under the forms of material war, to paint the
eternal conflict that rages between the faculties and the desires
of the human mind.   Thus arises Allegory, a style which at
once gratifies the poet with the sense of having come to something more profound and real than if he had remained among
externals, and flatters the intelligence of his readers in the same
proportion.   Hawes, therefore, allegorizes ; and while he writes
of giants with three heads, and enchanted castles, and imprisoned damsels, and employs all the gorgeous imagery of old
romance, he offers to the cultivated and intellectual few a feast
of reason ; he invites them to trace, under all the exciting
adventures of his hero, the progress of a mind subjected to a
scientific course of education.

The substance of the poem under consideration is briefly this.
Grand Amour, walking in a meadow, meets with Fame, from
whom he receives a 'swete report' of the beauty and excellence of the fayre lady, La Bell Pucell, who dwells in the
Tower of Musike.   He is eager to see her; but first he
is directed to the Tower of Doctrine, where, and in dependent towers, he is duly instructed in the 'seven sciences,'
which are simply the old Trivium and Quadrivium of the
schools, Grammar, Logic, Rhetoric, Arithmetic, Geometry, Mu
sic, and Astronomy.   In the course of his indoctrination,
he naturally, therefore, visits the Tower of Musike, and meets
La Bell Pucell.   She grants him her love; but her friends,
she tells him, will soon take her home to her palace in a
distant land, where she will be closely guarded by giants and
dragons ; he, on his part, must complete his education in the
Tower of Chivalry, if he hopes to force his way through all
obstacles to her feet. Their parting is thus prettily described :—

'Forth must I [La Pucell] sayle without longer delaye.
It is full see ; my frendes will come soone ;
Therefore I praye you to go hence your waye.
It draweth fast now towarde the none.'
'Madame,' qucd I [Grand Amour], 'your pleasure shall be done.'
Wyth wofull herte and grete syghes, ofte
I kyssed her lyppes, that were swete and softe.

> She unto me nor I to her colde speke,
> And as of that it was no grete wondre,
> Our hertes swelled as that they would breke,
> The fyre of love was so sore kept under.
> Whan I from her should depart asundre,
> Wyth her fayre head she dyd lowe enclyne,
> And in lykewise so dyd I with myne.

Grand Amour duly visits the Tower of Chivalry, and is there trained in martial accomplishments and knightly virtues; he is then dubbed a knight by king Melyzyus, and proceeds on his adventurous journey in quest of La Bell Pucell. This part of the poem much resembles romances of the old simple type, such for instance as those which are given in Ellis's *Specimens*. The last and decisive combat which the hero has to sustain, is with the Monster of the Seven Metals, a dragon named Privy Malice. He runs the creature through after a terrific conflict, and then—

> Ryght ther wythall the dragon to-brast,
> And out ther flew, ryght blacke and tedyous,
> A foule Ethyope, which such smoke did cast,
> That all ye ylond was full tenebrous;
> It thundered loude wyth clappes tempestious,
> Then all the ladyes were full sore adred,
> They thought none other but that I was ded.

But the air clears presently, and he sees his lady's castle. All difficulties being now overcome, Grand Amour marries La Bell Pucell. Here the poem might have been expected to end; but it is not so. After many years of consummate happiness, Grand Amour is one morning startled by the entrance of an unknown guest, who tells him that his name is Age. He introduces two companions, Policy and Avarice, whose society the hero assiduously frequents, till stopped by the visit of Death. Then come Confession, Contrition, and Satisfaction, and he dies. Even this is not all :—

> Out of my body my soul then it went
> To Purgatory, for to be purified,
> That after that it might be glorified.

His name and memory are enrolled by Fame for perpetual honour with those of the 'nine worthies' of whom three are of the pagan order of things, Hector, Alexander, and Cæsar,—three of the Jewish, Joshua, David, and Judas Maccabeus,—and three of the Christian, Arthur, Charlemagne, and Godfrey de Bouillon.

Of the exceeding crudity of the versification of this poem, it is difficult to form a just idea, except by reading a number of pages in succession. Of the degree in which these minions of a court, the affected euphuists of an earlier generation than Lyly, would have Latinized our language could they have had their way, a conception may more easily be gained. The fine old English words which abound in Chaucer, and the loss of many of which in the modern language is deeply to be regretted, do not appear in Hawes; instead of them we are treated to hundreds of such exquisite phrases as are found in the following stanza :—

> Her redolente wordes of swete influence,
> Degouted vapoure moost aromatyke,
> And made conversyon of my complacence;
> Her depurèd and her lusty rhetoryke
> My courage reformed that was so lunatyke,
> My sorowe defeted and my mynde did modefy,
> And my dolourous herte began to pacyfy.

Hawes must have died after the year 1509, since we have among his poems a Coronation ode celebrating the accession of Henry VIII.

7. **Alexander Barclay**, a priest, chaplain to the college of St. Mary Otter/ in Devonshire, translated in 1508, ' out of Laten, Frenche, and Doche,' to use his own words, Sebastian Brandt's then widely popular poem, the ' Ship of Fools.' This work has a purpose partly satirical, partly didactic, but chiefly the latter; it is, in fact, a sermon in many heads on the corrupt manners of the age, and may be said to stand in nearly the same relation to ordinary sermons as that in which the Proverbs stand to the books of the Prophets. Brandt was an eminent professor and jurisconsult of Strasburg, who died in 1520. He composed the poem originally in German, and commenced to translate it into Latin; this task, however, he soon transferred to his disciple Locher, who completed it, and dedicated the translation to his master, in 1497, giving it the title of ' Narragonia,' which seems to be a barbarous compound, made up of *Narr*, the German for fool, and the Greek verb ἄγειν, to conduct. A French version appeared about the same time, under the title of ' La Nef des Folz du Monde.' From these three versions Barclay compiled his English ' Ship of Fools,' printed by Pynson, side by side with Locher's Latin, in 1509. His rendering is by no means literal, and considerably more diffuse than the original; the additions being often characterized by much spirit and graphic power. Most of the work is, like the *Pastime of Pleasure*, in the Chaucerian heptastich, but towards the end he introduces a new octave stanza, with three rimes, thus arranged, 1, 2, 1, 2, 2, 3, 2, 3.

The prose prologue of Brandt and Locher is freely rendered

in verse by Barclay.   It is to the effect that poetry has always
had as its chief office to commend virtue and reprove vice, and
that, inasmuch as this present age abounded in vice and folly of
every kind, Brandt, imitating the example of Dante and Petrarch,
who wrote in their own mother tongue, the ' lingua Hetrusca,'
had undertaken to lash the crimes and foibles of mankind in
vernacular verse.

The main body of the work contains the descriptions of one
hundred Fools, and several supplemental cantos are added, one
of which is headed ' the Unyversall Shypp,' as containing all
fools hitherto unspecified. The opening is spirited ; it is headed—

> ' BARCLAY THE TRANSLATOUR TO THE FOLES.'
>
> To shypp, galantes ! the se is at the ful ;
> The wynde us calleth ; our sayles ar displayed.
> Wher may we best aryve ? at Lyn, or els at Hulle ?
> To us may no haven in Englonde be denayd.
> Why tary we ? the anchors are up wayed ;
> If any corde or cabyl us hurt, let, outher hynder,
> Let slyp the ende, or els hewe it in sonder.

8. **John Skelton**, a secular priest, studied at both universities,
and had a high reputation for scholarship in the early part of
the sixteenth century.   It is certain that his Latin verses are
much superior to his serious attempts in English.   A long
rambling elegy in the seven-line stanza on Henry, fourth Earl
of Northumberland, murdered in 1489, will be found in Percy.
The versification is even worse than that of Hawes. In Skelton's
satires there are a naturalness and a humour, which make them
still readable.   Two of these, entitled *Speke, Parrot*, and *Why
come ye not to Court*, contain vigorous but coarse attacks on
Cardinal Wolsey, to escape from whose wrath Skelton had to
take sanctuary at Westminster, and afterwards was protected
by Bishop Islip till his death in 1529.   He is particularly fond
of short six-syllable lines, which some have named from him
' Skeltonical verse.'   Here is a short specimen, taken from
Phyllyp Sparowe, a strange rambling elegy upon a favourite
sparrow, belonging to a nun, which had been killed by a cat :—

> O cat of carlyshe kinde,
> The fynde was in thy mynde
> When thou my byrde untwynde !
> I wold thou haddest ben blynde !
> The leopardes sauvage,
> The lyons in theyr rage,
> Myght catche thé in theyr pawes,
> And gnawe thé in theyr jawes !
> The serpentes of Lybany

Myght stynge thé venymously !
The dragones with their tongues
Myght poison thy lyver and longes !
The mantycors of the montaynes
Myght fede them on thy braynes ! &c.

Skelton is also the author of a moral play, called *Magnyfycence*, an inane production of between two and three thousand lines, in the same rough 'Saturnian' metre in which, as we shall see, the first known English comedy, by Udall, was composed. There is no division into acts, only into scenes; the characters are mere abstractions, such as Felycyte, Liberte, Measure, Fansy, Foly, &c. His comedy of *Achademios*, enumerated by himself among his works in the *Garland of Laurell*, appears to have perished; should it ever come to light, it might possibly take from *Ralph Roister Doister* the distinction of being the earliest English comedy.[1]

9. Far above these barbarous rimers rose the poetic genius of **Surrey**. Henry Howard, Earl of Surrey, son of the victor of Flodden, was born about the year 1516. At the age of sixteen he was contracted in marriage to the Lady Frances Vere. His Geraldine, to whom so many of his sonnets are addressed, was a daughter of the Earl of Kildare. She slighted his passion; and the rejected lover carried the fiery ardour of his spirit into the scenes of war and diplomacy. Having committed some errors in the conduct of the campaign in France in 1546, he was thrown into prison by order of the 'jealous ruthless tyrant.'[2] who then sat on the throne, brought to trial on a trumpery charge of high treason, and beheaded in January 1547, a few days before Henry's death. His *Songes and Sonnettes*, together with those of Wyat, were first published in 1557. His translation of the second and fourth books of the Æneid is the earliest specimen of blank verse in the language.

Sir Thomas Wyat the elder, a native of Kent, was much employed by Henry VIII. on diplomatic missions, and overexertion in one of these occasioned his early death in 1541. The improvement in grace and polish of style which distinguishes Surrey and Wyat in comparison with their predecessors was plainly due to Italian influences. The very term 'sonnet,' by them first introduced, is taken from the Italian 'sonetto.' Puttenham, in his *Art of Poesie* (1589), says of them, that 'having travelled into Italie, and there tasted the sweet and stately measures and style of the Italian poesie, as novises newly crept out of the school of Dante, Ariosto, and Petrarch,

[1] See Skelton's works, carefully edited by Mr. Dyce, 1843.
[2] Scott's *Lay of the Last Minstrel*, canto vi.

they greatly polished our rude and homely manner of vulgar poesie from that it had been before, and for that cause may justly be sayd the first reformers of our English metre and style.' He reputes them for ' the chief lanternes of light' to all subsequent English poets. ' Their conceits were lofty, their style stately, their conveyance cleanly, their termes proper, their metre sweet and well-proportioned ; in all imitating very naturally and studiously their master, Francis Petrarch.'

But this praise is too unqualified. Surrey's translation of Virgil is as bald and repulsive a version as can well be. Of his famous love poems in honour of Geraldine, nine are written in a metre so uncouth (alternate twelve and fourteen syllable lines) that it would spoil the effect of far better matter ; and the unchanging querulous whine which characterizes the whole series renders it tedious reading. In truth, notwithstanding the encomiums which Dr. Nott lavished on his favourite author, the gems in Surrey are but few, and may be counted on one's fingers. The sonnets beginning ' Give place, ye lovers '—' The sote season '—and ' Set me whereas ' [1]—nearly exhaust the list.

Of the poems of Wyat a large proportion are translated or imitated from the Italian. They relate almost entirely to love, and sometimes attain to a polish and a grace which English verse had not before exhibited. Of this the reader may in some degree judge from the passage quoted further on.[2]

10. To this period rather than to the next, since a portion of it was in type in the year 1555, belongs the extensive poetical work—meritorious in many ways, but inadequate in point of execution to the vastness of the design—entitled the *Myrroure for Magistrates*. Lydgate's *Falls of Princes*, translated from Boccaccio, was reprinted in 1554, and well received by the public. The printer desired that the work should be continued from the date at which Boccaccio left off, and devoted to the 'tragical histories' of famous Englishmen exclusively. **William Baldwin** agreed, if sufficiently aided by other writers, to undertake the work. Owing to difficulties connected with the censorship, the book did not appear till 1559 ; in this its primitive shape it contained nineteen legends, of which twelve were by Baldwin himself, the rest being written by his friends, Ferrers, Phaier, Chaloner, and others. The first legend was that of Tressilian, one of Richard II.'s judges, executed by Gloucester's faction in 1388. The metre is the Chaucerian heptastich. Copious moralizing is the leading characteristic of the whole work ; this note was just suited to the serious, self-inspecting, somewhat melancholy temper of the English mind ; and numerous redactions of the poem, the latest of which appeared in 1610, attest its remarkable popularity. **Sackville's** beautiful *Induction*, with the legend of the Duke of Buckingham who was beheaded in 1521, first appeared in the edition of 1563. The original design, which was merely to

---

[1] See Crit. Sect. ch. I. § 58.   [2] *Ibid.*

continue Boccaccio, was soon departed from ; and a number of legends
were added, which carried back this 'history teaching by biography'
to the fabulous age of the British kings. One great redaction and
rearrangement was effected by John Higgins in his edition of 1587 ;
another by Richard Niccols in the crowning edition of 1610. In this
last no fewer than ninety legends are contained ; among which one,—
the finest perhaps in the whole work—is the legend of Thomas Cromwell by Michael Drayton.[1] It contains a remarkably enlightened
appreciation of the secondary causes which led to the sudden and tremendous fall of the ancient Church in England.

11. The earliest mention of a poet laureate *eo nomine*, occurs
in the reign of Edward IV., by whom **John Kaye** was appointed
to that office.[2] We read of a king's versifier (*versificator*) as
far back as 1251. The change of title admits of a probable
explanation. The solemn crowning of Petrarch on the Capitol,
in the year 1341, made a profound sensation through all literary
circles in Europe. Chaucer, as we have seen, distinguishes
Petrarch as 'the *laureat* poete.' In the next century we find
the dignity of *poeta laureatus* forming one of the recognised
degrees at our universities, and conferred upon proof being given
by the candidate of proficiency in grammar, rhetoric, and versification. It is impossible not to connect this practice of laurea-
tion with the world-famous tribute rendered by the Romans to
the genius of Petrarch. After the institution of the degree, it
is easy to understand that the king would select his poet among
the *poetæ laureati*, and that the modest title of *versificator*
would be dropped.

Scottish Poets:—Henryson; Blind Harry; Dunbar; Gawain Douglas; Lyndsay

12. The present work does not pretend to trace the history of
Scottish poetry ; but in the dearth of genius in England during
this period, the rise of several admirable poets in the sister
country demands our attention. The earliest of these, **Robert
Henryson**, appears to have died about the end of the fifteenth
century. His longest poem, the *Testament of Faire Creseyde*,
a sort of supplement to Chaucer's *Troilus and Cryseyde*, was
printed by Urry, in his edition of that poet. The pastoral,
called *Robin and Makyne*, is given in Percy's *Reliques*. The
pith of the story is exactly that which we find in Burns's *Dun-
can Gray*, only that in Henryson's poem the parts are reversed ;
it is the lady who first makes love in vain, and then growing

[1] See Mr. Haslewood's edition of *The Mirrour for Magistrates*, 1815.
[2] Hazlitt's *Johnson's Lives*, article Kaye.

indifferent, is vainly wooed by the shepherd who has repented of his coldness. The *Abbey Walk* is a beautiful poem of reflection, the moral of which is, the duty and wisdom of submitting to the will of God in all things.

13. At the beginning of this period, or about 1460, **Blind Harry,** or Harry the Minstrel, produced his poem on the adventures of Wallace. Considered as the composition of a blind man, *The Wallace* is a remarkable production. Considered as a work of art, a more execrable poem perhaps was never composed. Yet national resentment and partiality have made the Scotch, from the fifteenth century down to the present time, delight in this tissue of lies and nonsense; a modernized version of it was a horn-book among the peasantry in the last century; Scottish critics, one and all, speak of its poetical beauties; and even one or two English writers, 'carried away by their dissimulation,' have professed to find much in it to admire. It is written in the heroic riming couplet, and professes to be founded on a Latin chronicle by John Blair, a contemporary of Wallace; but as no such chronicle exists, or is anywhere alluded to as existing, it is probable that the whole story is a pure invention of the minstrel's.

14. **William Dunbar,** the greatest of the old Scottish poets, was a native of East Lothian, and born about the middle of the fifteenth century. He studied at the university of St. Andrews, perhaps also at Oxford. In early life he entered the novitiate of the Franciscan order, and preached, chiefly in order to sell indulgences, in many parts of England, and even in Picardy; but he does not appear ever to have taken the vows. James IV. attached him by many favours to his person and court, where we have certain evidence of his having lived from 1500 to 1513, the date of Flodden. After that fatal day, on which his royal patron perished, his name vanishes from the Scottish records, and it is merely a loose conjecture which assigns his death to about the year 1520.

Of Dunbar's poems, none of which are of any great length, the most perfect is *The Thistle and the Rose,*[1] written in 1503 to commemorate the nuptials of James IV. and Margaret, daughter of Henry VII. The metre is the Chaucerian heptastich. The versification is most musical,—superior to that of any poet before Spenser except Chaucer, and better than much of his. The influence, both direct and indirect, of the father of our poetry, is visible, not in this poem alone, but throughout the works of the school of writers now under consideration.

[1] See Critical Section, ch. i., *Allegories.*

The poet, according to the approved mediæval usage, falls asleep and has a dream, in which May—the 'faire frische May' in which Chaucer so delighted—appears to him, and commands him to attend her into a garden and do homage to the flowers, the birds, and the sun.   Nature is then introduced, and commands that the progress of the spring shall no longer be checked by ungenial weather.   Neptune and Æolus give the necessary orders.   Then Nature, by her messengers, summons all organized beings before her, the beasts by the roe, the birds by the swallow, the flowers by the *yarrow*.   The Lion is crowned king of the beasts, the Eagle of the birds, and the Thistle of the flowers.   The Rose, the type of beauty, is wedded to the Thistle, the type of strength, who is commanded well to cherish and guard his Rose.   Such is an outline of the plot of this graceful poem.

'The design of the *Golden Terge*'—another allegoric poem—'is to show the gradual and imperceptible influence of love when too far indulged over reason.'[1]   This poem is in a curious nine-line stanza, having only two rimes.   But Dunbar excelled also in comic and satirical composition.   The *Flyting of Dunbar and Kennedy* is a wit-combat (though perhaps the word 'slanging-match' would better describe it) between the poet and his friend Kennedy.   The *Freiris of Berwick* is a tale, much of the same kind as the Reves Tale of Chaucer, only less witty. There is no early evidence entitling us to ascribe it to Dunbar; this was merely a conjecture of Pinkerton's, which Mr. Paterson, a recent editor of Dunbar's poems, rightly regards as more than doubtful.   The *Dance of the Seven Deadly Sins* is another satirical production, the humour, dash, and broad Scotch of which remind one of Burns.   The metre is that of Chaucer's *Sir Thopas*.   Some Highlanders are introduced at the end, and receive very disrespectful mention:—

> Thae turmagantis[2] with tag and tatter
> Full loud in Ersche [Erse] begout to clatter,
>   And rowp lyk revin and ruke.[3]
> The devil sa devit[4] was with thair yell
> That in the deepest pit of hell
>   He smorit them with smoke.

Among Dunbar's shorter pieces there is none more interesting than his 'Lament for the Makaris.'   ('Makar' is the literal translation of the Greek word for 'poet.')   As Wordsworth, in

---

[1] Warton.
[2] Ptarmigan; to a covey of which he compares the Highlanders.
[3] Croak like raven and rook.   [4] Deafened.

L

those beautiful verses called ' An Extempore Effusion upon the death of James Hogg,' laments for his brother poets, among whom death had been unusually busy, so Dunbar, in the poem before us (written in 1507), avows that when he counts up the poets his countrymen, who have recently passed away, he is troubled by the fear of death,—' timor mortis conturbat me.' These words are the burden of each stanza :—

> No stait in erd heir standis sicker ;
> As with the wynd wavis the wickir,
> So wavis this warldis vanite ;
> Timor Mortis conturbat me.

After complaining that death has reft away Chaucer, Lydgate, and Gower, he adds :—

> The gude Schir Hew of Eglintoun,
> Etrik, Heryot, and Wintoun,
> He has tane out of this cuntré ;
> Timor Mortis conturbat me.

Dunbar proceeds to name a number of Scottish authors deceased, of most of whom very little is known. Among them are, Clerk of Tranent, ' that maid the aunteirs [adventures] of Gawayne,' Sir Gilbert Hay, Barbour, Stobo, and Quintin Schaw. Kennedy, his old rival, was dying ; as for himself, he feels that he has not long to live.

15. **Gawain Douglas,** sprung from a noble family, studied at the university of Paris, and rose to be bishop of Dunkeld. After Flodden Field, the regent Albany drove him from Scotland. Coming into England, he was hospitably received by Henry, who allowed him a liberal pension. He died in London of the plague, in 1521. He is chiefly known for a translation of the Æneid into heroic verse, which is the eariiest English version on record, having been published in 1513. The prologues prefixed to the several books have some poetic beauty ; and the language presents little more difficulty than that of Chaucer. A passage in one of these prologues is subjoined as a specimen ; it is part of an address to the sun :—

> Welcum the birdis beild[1] upon the brere,
> Welcum maister and reulare of the yere,
> Welcum walefare of husbandis at the plewis,
> Welcum reparare of woddis, treis, and bewis.[2]
> Welcum depaynter of the blomyt medis,
> Welcum the lyffe of everything that spredis.
> Welcum storare[3] of all kynd bestial,
> Welcum be thy bricht bemes gladand al.

---

[1] Shelter.　　　[2] Boughs.　　　[3] Restorer.

16. **Sir David Lyndsay** was a satirist of great power and boldness.   He is the Jean de Meung of the sixteenth century; but,
as a layman and a knight, he levels his satire with even greater
directness and impartiality than that extraordinary ecclesiastic.
In his allegorical satire entitled *The Dreme*, which is probably
the earliest of his works, the poet is conducted by Remem-
brance, first to the infernal regions, which he finds peopled with
churchmen of every grade,—then to Purgatory,—then through
the 'three elements,' to the seven planets in their successive
spheres,—then beyond them to the empyrean and the celestial
abodes.   The poetical topography is without doubt borrowed
from Dante.   He is then transported back to earth, and visits
Paradise; whence, by a 'very rapid transition,' as Warton calls
it, he is taken to Scotland, where he meets 'Johne the comoun-
weill,' who treats him to a long general satire on the corrupt
state of that kingdom.   After this the poet is in the usual manner brought back to the cave by the seaside, where he falls
asleep, and wakes up from his dream.   The metre is the Chaucerian heptastich.   There is prefixed to the poem an exhortation
in ten stanzas, addressed to King James V., in which advice and
warning are conveyed with unceremonious plainness.   In 1535,
his 'morality,' named *Ane Satyre of the Thrie Estaits*, was acted
before the Scottish court; it took nine hours in the representation.   It is described by Professor Nichol as a 'well-sustained
invective against the follies and vices of the time, and as being
the first approach to a regular dramatic composition in Scottish
literature.'[1]   Two years afterwards he composed a lament on the
untimely death of Magdalene, the first wife of James V., under
the title of 'The Deploratioun of the Deith of Quene Magdalene.'
She was a French princess, and Lyndsay descants with feeling
and good taste on the universal joy which the celebration of the
marriage at Paris had spread at the time among the people
of both nations :—

> Bot at his mariage maid upon the morne,
> Sic solace and solempnizatioun
> Was never sene afore, sen Christ was borne,
> Nor to Scotland sic consolatioun !
> There selit was the confirmatioun
> Of the weill kepit ancient alliance
> Maid betwix Scotland and the realme of France.

Among the shorter pieces, the 'Testament of the Papyngo' is
well known; under the form of the dying directions of a favourite parrot, addressed to the king, a bitter attack is made on the

---

[1] Preface to *The Minor Poems of Lyndsay*, E. E. T. S.

Catholic clergy. 'Kittes Confessioun' (1541) is a coarse burlesque of the sacrament of Penance. That in which Chaucer could see so much beauty, and on the divisions and applications of which he loved to discourse with the serious minuteness of a theologian, appears as purely evil and corrupt to the ruder northern intellect and impatient puritanism of Lyndsay. His *Historie of the Squyer William Meldrum* (1550) is an attempt to 'weave into the form of a metrical romance the career and exploits of a contemporary Scotch laird.'[1]

The longest and latest of Lyndsay's poems is the *Dialog concerning the Monarché*, which was written in 1553, about five years before his death. It extends to some 6,000 lines, and is partly in seven-line, partly in eight-line stanzas. After describing with great tediousness the rise and fall of the four monarchies mentioned by the prophet Daniel,—the Assyrian, the Persian, the Greek, and the Roman,—he 'prophesies the overthrow of the fifth and worst monarchy of all, the great tyranny of modern times, that of the Church. This gives him an opportunity of once more inveighing against . . . the court of Rome, and again calling aloud for a general reformation.' Lyndsay's incessant attacks on the Scottish clergy, the state of which at that time unfortunately afforded much ground for them, are said to have hastened the religious war in Scotland.

17. The language of all these Scottish writers in their serious compositions closely resembles the English of their contemporaries south of the Tweed ; the chief difference consisting in certain dialectic peculiarities, such as the use of ' quh ' for ' wh,' and of ' it ' and ' and ' for ' ed ' and ' ing ' in the terminations of the past and present participles. But in proportion as they resort to comic expression, and attach their satire to particular places or persons, their language becomes less English and slides into the rough vernacular of their ordinary speech. Exactly the same thing is observable in Burns' poetry.

Learning :—Grocyn, Linacre, Colet, More; State of the Universities.

18. The fifteenth century was, as we have said, pre-eminently an age of accumulation, assimilation, and preparation.

The first two-thirds of the sixteenth century fall under the same general description. England had to bring herself up to the intellectual level of the continent, and to master the treasures of literature and philosophy, which the revival and diffusion

[1] Prof. Nichol.

of Greek, and partly of Roman learning, had placed within her reach, before her writers could attempt to rival the fame of the great ancients.   There is much interest in tracing in detail the numerous minute steps and individual acts which helped on this process.   Many such are related by Wood in his *Athenæ Oxonienses*.   Thus we are told that the first man who publicly taught Greek at Oxford was **William Grocyn**.   Stapleton, a Roman Catholic writer of the age of Elizabeth, says, ' Recens tunc ex Italiâ venerat Grocinus, qui primus in eâ ætate Græcas literas in Angliam invexerat, Oxoniique publice professus fuerat.'   Of course Grocyn had to go abroad to get this new learning.   Born about 1450, and educated at Oxford, he travelled on the continent about the year 1488, and studied both at Rome and Florence. Greek learning flourished then at Florence more than at any place in Europe, owing to the fact that Lorenzo de' Medici had eagerly welcomed to his court many illustrious and learned refugees, who, subsequently to the fall of Constantinople, had been forced to seek shelter from the violence and intolerance of the Mussulmans in Western Europe.   One of these learned Byzantines, Demetrius Chalcocondyles, together with the Italian Angelo Politian, afforded to Grocyn by their public instructions those opportunities which he had left his country to search for,— of penetrating into the sanctuary of classical antiquity, and drinking in at the fountain-head the inspirations of a national genius, whose glories no lapse of time can obscure.   Gibbon,[1] with his usual fulness of learning and wonderful mastery of style, has thus sketched the features of this eventful time :—

19. ' The genius and education of Lorenzo rendered him not only a patron, but a judge and candidate in the literary race. In his palace, distress was entitled to relief, and merit to reward; his leisure hours were delightfully spent in the Platonic academy ; he encouraged the emulation of Demetrius Chalcocondyles and Angelo Politian; and his active missionary, Janus Lascaris, returned from the East with a treasure of two hundred manuscripts, four score of which were as yet unknown in the libraries of Europe.   The rest of Italy was animated by a similar spirit, and the progress of the nation repaid the liberality of her princes. The Latins held the exclusive property of their own literature, and these disciples of Greece were soon capable of transmitting and improving the lessons which they had imbibed.   After a short succession of foreign teachers, the tide of emigration subsided, but the language of Constantinople was spread beyond the Alps ; and the natives of France, Germany, and England, im-

---

[1] *Decline and Fall of the Roman Empire*, ch. lxvi.

parted to their countrymen the sacred fire which they had kindled
in the schools of Florence and Rome.' After noticing the spirit
of imitation which long prevailed, he continues :—'Genius may
anticipate the season of maturity; but in the education of a
people, as in that of an individual, memory must be exercised
before the powers of reason and fancy can be expanded; nor
may the artist hope to equal or surpass, till he has learned to
imitate, the works of his predecessors.'

20. But to return to Grocyn, whose visit to Florence occasioned this quotation. When settled in Oxford again, about the
year 1490, he opened his budget, and taught Greek to all comers.
He lectured afterwards in St. Paul's on the *Hierarchies* of
Dionysius, ascribing them at first to the Areopagite, but re-
tracting that opinion publicly on becoming convinced that it was
an error. He preferred Aristotle to Plato, calling the first
πολυμαθῆ, a man of great knowledge, the second πολυμυθῆ, a man
of many words.[1]

21. Thomas Linacre, the celebrated physician, was in residence and
giving lectures at Oxford about the same time. He, too, had studied
in Italy, chiefly at Florence and Rome, and had become an accomplished Greek scholar; it is to him that we owe the first version of any
Greek author made by an Englishman. This was a Latin translation
published in 1499 of the *Sphæra* of Proclus, an astronomical treatise.
Linacre also wrote a sort of Latin grammar, which he entitled *De
Emendata Structura Latini Sermonis.* Though, from a want of con-
ciseness and of proper arrangement, this grammar could never have
been very available as a primer, it shows great insight into the structure
of the Latin tongue. A new edition of it appeared in 1543, for which
Melanchthon wrote a preface, earnestly recommending the book for the
teaching of youth, if only a brief compendium of the rules of grammar
had been mastered previously. Linacre also translated into Latin the
works of the old Greek physician Galen, and was the leading spirit in
the knot of enlightened men who founded the College of Physicians
(1518).

22. Another active patron of the new learning was Dean
Colet, the founder of St. Paul's School, and the friend of
Erasmus. His life was well written in the last century by
Dr. Samuel Knight, a prebendary of Ely. The name Colet is
probably a corruption of 'acolyte.' The engraving at the beginning of this biography shows us a spare figure in a dark
gown and cassock, with a birretta on the head, bare neck, no
beard or whiskers, large dark eyes, and a glance expressive of
suppressed enthusiasm and strongly guarded self-control. He
was born about the year 1466. When Erasmus visited Oxford
in 1498, Colet, who had travelled before this, and made the

[1] See his letter to Linacre, printed in the preface to the translation by the
latter of the *Sphæra* of Proclus.

acquaintance of the leading scholars in France and Italy, was in residence at Magdalen College. In a letter from the great scholar to his friend Sixtinus may be read a graphic account of a banquet, or *convivium*, at which he, Colet, Prior Charnock, and other Oxford men were assembled one day, when they fell into a warm discussion on the 'sin of Cain.' 'Colet alone,' says Erasmus, 'was more than a match for us all; he seemed to be beside himself with a kind of sacred frenzy; the expression of sublimity and majesty which his countenance wore was almost superhuman. Voice, eyes, looks, aspect,—all seemed to become grander and to suffer a transformation, 'majorque videri, afflatus est numine quando.' In his Italian travels Colet had formed the acquaintance of some of the distinguished men who at that time, having Florence as their centre, were zealously studying and propagating the philosophy of Plato. The chiefs of this school were Pico of Mirandola and Marsilius Ficinus. It was probably these associations that led Colet to the study of the works of the supposed Dionysius the Areopagite. This author, long believed to be the very Dionysius whom St. Paul converted, but about whom now the only controversy among critics is whether he shall be placed in the third century or in the fifth, wrote a book on the *Celestial and Ecclesiastical Hierarchies*, in which he traces out a regular and minute correspondence between the order of the Church on earth and that which prevails among the heavenly spirits. On this book Colet wrote a treatise, which has been lately disentombed from MS., and edited with care and ability by one of the masters of the school which he founded, Mr. Lupton. This work he probably wrote about the year 1500. The editor says:—' Following his author faithfully in the main, both in the arrangement of his subject, and in his conclusions and general tone of thought, Colet pauses at times to treat more fully of some passing topic than is done in the original. Occasionally, too, he passes over a chapter of the *Hierarchies* altogether, that he may stay the longer at some halting-place of greater importance.' Sometimes he breaks forth into an indignant sentence, suggested by something in his author, against the corruption and worldliness which had invaded the Church and held their ground so stubbornly, even in the highest places.

But the work by which Colet deserved best of learning was the foundation and organization of St. Paul's School. He commenced his preparations in 1508, and the school was opened in 1512. All his patrimony—and it was not small, for he was the son of a wealthy knight who had been twice Lord Mayor of London—was given up to the school. He built it in St. Paul's churchyard, on the site which it still occupies. An image of the child Jesus, to whom the school was dedicated, was placed over the raised seat of the head-master, and before this the scholars were to say a prayer, composed by Colet himself, on entering and on leaving school. The estates with which it was endowed, he, with much judgment, vested, not in any ecclesiastical corporation (in which case they would have been confiscated at the Reformation and lost), but in the Mercers' Company of London, to which his father had belonged. For his first head-master he appointed **William Lilye**, formerly a demye of Magdalen College, whom in the course of his roving life Colet had met at Rome, and discerned to be the man that he wanted.

For his school Colet wrote in Latin a short treatise on the Latin syntax, *De Constructione octo partium Orationis* (Pynson, 1513). But this was probably soon superseded by the Latin grammar prepared by Lilye, under the name of *Brevissima Institutio, seu Ratio Grammatices cognoscendæ*. This is the well-known 'Lilly's Grammar,' which, down to a comparatively recent period, was used in all our public schools, and is not even yet discarded at St. Paul's School.

23. Exegetical theology was first introduced into England by Dean Colet. During the middle ages the attractions of metaphysics and dialectic had caused the track of biblical interpretation, which had been cultivated so diligently and successfully by many of the Fathers, to be almost forsaken. Now, the scholastic methods and inquiries being out of favour, the interest in the interpretation of Scripture revived. The energetic dean of St. Paul's lectured regularly at Oxford, and afterwards in London, on the Pauline epistles. These lectures are unfortunately lost; and the only materials for judging of Colet as a theologian—apart from the letter of Erasmus, describing his character and career, to Jodocus Jonas—are, a treatise *De Sacramentis*, lately edited by Mr. Lupton, the work on the *Hierarchies* of Dionysius already noticed, and a trenchant sermon, preached in St. Paul's, by desire of Archbishop Warham, at the opening of the convocation of the province in 1511, on the corruptions which overspread and undermined the Church in his day. This sermon, which has been several times translated into English and reprinted, denounces powerfully the evils of worldly living and lust of gain which were ruining the church through the clergy. The first part is on 'Conformation,' according to the text, 'Be not conformed to this world, but be ye transformed in the spirit of your minds;' the second part is on 'Reformation.' This, he says, depends on the clergy themselves, and principally on the bishops. Let the laws be rehearsed (for *they* are sound and just,

and minute enough to meet all cases), which forbid laying hands
suddenly on men for ordination, condemn simony, enjoin residence, oblige to a seemly and reputable life, and lay down rules
for the pure election of bishops,—for the pure exercise of
patronage.   If the bishops first, and after them the other orders
of clergy, were once duly reformed, it would be an easy matter
to reform the laity, for—corpus sequitur animam,—the body
followeth the soul.

24. A few words must be said about **William Warham**,
the generous patron, the enlightened scholar, the Christian
without reproach, whose name cannot be forgotten while the
letters of Erasmus continue to be read.   For some years before 1501, when he was made bishop of London, he was principal of St. Edward's, or the Civil Law Hall, in the University
of Oxford; and had raised his Hall to the first rank, intellectually, among the colleges, by skilful regulations and a good
selection of tutors.   From London he was translated to Canterbury in 1503 on the death of Archbishop Dean.   From the time
of his first introduction to Erasmus, which was in 1497, he
regarded the great scholar with affection and admiration, and
during many years, after he was raised to the primacy, ministered to his temporal wants with greater liberality than any
other of his patrons.   Besides an annual pension, he seems to
have been continually sending him money, together with other
gifts.   Erasmus was not ungrateful; he is never weary of extol-
ling to his correspondents the 'sanctissimi mores,' the love of
letters, erudition, integrity, and piety, of the English primate.
The Oxford movement in favour of sound learning and 'bonæ
literæ,' to use the phrase then prevalent, he consistently encouraged.   He was the friend of Colet, and supported him on
an important occasion against the unreasonable opposition of the
Bishop of London.   It is related of him that on his death-bed
he asked his steward how much money was left in his coffers.
Being told 'thirty pounds,' he smiled, and said, 'Satis viatici ad
cælum !'[1]

25. Of **Sir Thomas More's** other writings mention will be
made farther on; in this place we shall only speak of the relation
in which he stood to the movement for the extension of learning.
He studied in Oxford somewhere between 1490 and 1500; that
is known, but the exact years cannot be determined; nor, between conflicting statements, can we decide whether he was a
member of Canterbury College (afterwards merged in Christ
Church), or of St. Mary Hall.   His father, Sir John More, an

---

[1] Enough journey-money to heaven.

able and indefatigable judge, is said to have grudged the time
which his gifted son spent at the university, and to have cur-
tailed his allowance to the utmost, that the contraction of the
supplies might involve a quicker return to London, and an
earlier preparation for the bar.   Erasmus, writing in 1517, be-
wailed the comparative estrangement of his friend from a life of
learning : ' What,' said he, ' might not that marvellous felicity
of nature (admirabilis ista naturæ felicitas) have effected, had his
genius received its training in Italy, and devoted its powers
without restraint to the service of the Muse !'   Though it is
often said that he was at Oxford when Erasmus first arrived
there in 1497, the expressions in Erasmus' letters appear to
render this doubtful.   But, however short his university career
may have·been, we know from Stapleton (the writer quoted in
§ 18) that, with the aid of Grocyn and Linacre, he made the
best use of it.   He mastered Greek thoroughly, and became the
most refined Latin scholar, the most expert hand in Latin writing, that England could produce.   Two early compositions attest
this—his *Progymnasmata* and his *Epigrams*.   The former are
a very slight production ; they are translations from Greek
epigrams, chiefly those of Lucian, into Latin elegiacs, each
translation being separately done by More and William Lilye.
More's versions are the most pointed and antithetical ; there is
a want of finish about both.   These Progymnasmata only fill
nine pages.   The epigrams, which are entirely by More, are a
much more considerable work.   They are addressed to Henry
VIII., and appear to have been first published in ·1513, or early
in 1514.   Most of them are in elegiacs, but not a few are in
various Horatian metres ; some are original, others translated.
There is a certain wantonness and luxuriance of tone about
many of them, which is a little surprising to one who only
knows More from his later works.   Not a few are vigorous and
terse in a high degree ; altogether the work would bear re-editing,
better than many old books that are subjected to the process ;
not that the verses have either the polish of Vida, or the severe
grace of Milton.

26. Several epigrams relate to a poem in Latin hexameters,
which had lately appeared in France, entitled *Chordigeræ navis
conflagratio*.   The author was Germanus Brixius, one of the
secretaries of Anne of Bretagne, the Queen of France, whom in
a fulsome dedication he styles ' Frankorum regina Britonumque
dux.'   It seems that in the short war between England and
France, which broke out in 1512, a French ship, the name of
which is latinized by Brixius as ' Chordigera,' came into action
with an English ship of war, the ' Regent.'   According to

Brixius, the 'Regent,' when on the point of surrendering, succeeded in setting fire to her antagonist; and Hervé, the gallant captain of the 'Chordigera,' with all his crew, were either drowned or burnt. It would appear that this magnificent story, like the similar tale about the 'Vengeur' in modern times, had but little foundation in fact; and More in his epigrams makes fun of the valiant Hervé, and discredits the history of his exploits. This brought down on his head from Brixius a torrent of invective and insult, in what is really a very clever Latin poem, the 'Anti-morus.' More thought of replying,—had indeed sent his reply to press; but an urgent request from Erasmus, who was the friend of both, that he would let the quarrel drop, induced him to stifle the intended replication in the birth. The correspondence between More and Erasmus on this matter is exceedingly amusing.

As a good illustration of More's humour, the reader is referred to an epigram, headed 'De Nautis ejicientibus Monachum in tempestate cui fuerant confessi,' on some sailors who threw a monk overboard in a storm after having confessed to him. The translations from Lucian include the following dialogues, the *Cynicus*, the *Necromantia*, the *Philopseudes*, and the *Tyrannicida*. A declamation in reply to this last, by More himself, in really excellent Latin, completes the work.

There is evidence that More took an active interest in the promotion of good learning at Oxford. From a letter of Erasmus to Hutten, we learn that he lectured to a large university audience, when still very young, on the works of St. Augustine. There is also a letter by himself, printed in Jortin's Life of Erasmus, in which, addressing the university of Oxford, he complains warmly of the conduct of those 'scholastics' who, 'calling themselves Trojans,' declaimed against all liberal arts and their cultivators, but especially against the study and the students of Greek. This letter is dated in 1519.

27. In this age of strange excitement, when a new world supposed to teem with wealth had just been discovered in the West, when by the invention of printing thoughts were communicated and their records multiplied with a speed which must have seemed marvellous, and when the astronomical theory of Copernicus was revolutionizing men's ideas as to the very fundamental relations between the earth and the heavens, unsettling those even whom it did not convince, there was a temporary forgetfulness, on the part even of many holding high office in the Church, that this life, dignify it as you may, is, after all, a scene of trial, not of triumph, and that, if Christianity be true, a life of unchequered enjoyment, even though learning and art may

embellish it, is not the ideal towards which man should aspire. The state of things which ensued, especially in Italy, but also in a less degree among all the nations of Western Europe, has been lucidly and unsparingly portrayed by Dr. Newman in his essays on Savonarola. The Reformers seized on this weak point then noticeable in many of the clergy, and made out of it, to use a modern phrase, controversial capital. Human learning, they said—Luther himself originated the cry—was a waste of time as well as a dangerous snare; art was a mere pandering to the passions;—sinful man should be engrossed but by one pursuit, the pursuit of salvation—should study only one book, and that the Bible. When the party that favoured the Reformation came into power under Edward VI., this spirit operated with prejudicial effect on the young plants of learning and culture which had begun to spring up at our universities. To take one well-known instance;—the ecclesiastical commissioners of Edward, in their visitation to Oxford, destroyed or removed a valuable collection, impossible to be replaced, of six hundred manuscripts of the classical authors, presented by Humphrey, the good duke of Gloucester, uncle of Henry VI., to that University. Many members of the hierarchy also, among whom, as in the case of Nicholas V. and Leo X., some of the most intelligent and zealous promoters of the new learning had been found, saw reason, about the middle of the sixteenth century, to change their tactics. In England, at any rate, we know that the bishops, under Queen Mary, discouraged the study of the Humanities, and attempted to revive in their place the old scholastic exercises and disputations. The reformers immediately set up the cry, ' You are trying to shut out enlightenment, to set up the barbarous scholastic, in preference to the Ciceronian, Latinity,— you are enemies of progress, of civilization, of the enlargement of the mind.'

Cambridge soon followed the example of Oxford in introducing the study of Greek. Towards the close of the reign of Henry VIII., Sir John Cheke and Sir Thomas Smith are mentioned in the annals of that university as having been especially active in promoting this study. Milton refers to this in one of his sonnets :—

> Thy age like ours, O soul of Sir John Cheke,
> Hated not learning worse than toad or asp,
> When thou taught'st Cambridge and King Edward Greek.

28. The sense of insecurity induced among all classes by Henry's tyranny in his later years, and the social confusion which prevailed in the following reign, interrupted the peaceful flow of

learned studies. The universities appear to have been sunk in a lower depth of inefficiency and ignorance about the year 1550 than ever before or since. Under Mary, Cardinal Pole, the legate, was personally favourable to the new learning. Sir Thomas Pope, the founder of Trinity College, Oxford, consulted him on the framing of the college statutes, in which it was provided that Greek should form one of the subjects of instruction. In his legatine constitutions, passed at a synod held in 1555, Pole ordered that all archbishops and bishops, as well as holders of benefices in general, should assign a stated portion of their revenues to the support of cathedral schools in connection with every metropolitan and cathedral church throughout the kingdom, into which lay scholars of respectable parentage were to be admitted, together with theological students. These cathedral schools were kept up in the following reign, and seem to have attained considerable importance. But one enlightened and generous mind could not restrain the reactionary violence of the Gardiners and the Bonners. Under their management a system of obscurantism was attempted, if not established, at the universities; the Greek poets and philosophers were to be banished, and scholasticism was to reign once more in the schools. Ascham, in his *Schoolmaster*, thus describes the state of things :—

'The love of good learning began suddenly to wax cold, the knowledge of the tongues was manifestly contemned;—yea, I know that heads were cast together, and counsel devised, that Duns, with all the rabble of barbarous questionists, should have dispossessed of their place and room Aristotle, Plato, Tully, and Demosthenes, whom good Mr. Redman, and those two worthy stars of that university, Cheke and Smith, with their scholars, had brought to flourish as notably in Cambridge as ever they did in France and in Italy.'

Prose Writers : Pecock, Fortescue, Leland, More; Historical Writing : Capgrave, &c. ; Polemical Writing : Tyndale, More : Ascham ; Elyot.

29. Although no prose work produced during this period can be said to hold a place in our standard literature, considerable progress was made in fitting the rough and motley native idiom for the various requirements of prose composition. Through the work of the publication of our early records, which has now been going on for many years under the superintendence of the Master of the Rolls, a curious book, dating from the early part of this period, has been made generally accessible. This is *The*

Repressor of Reginald Pecock, Bishop of St. Asaph. The modern editor of the work, Mr. Babington, calls it, probably with justice, 'the earliest piece of good philosophical disquisition of which our English prose literature can boast.' Pecock was a Welshman; he was born about the end of the fourteenth century, and educated at Oriel College, Oxford. After his appointment to the see of St. Asaph, he took the line of vehement opposition to the teaching of the Lollards, the followers of Wyclif. The design of *The Repressor*, which was first published in a complete shape about the year 1456, was to justify certain practices or 'governances,' as he calls them, then firmly established in the Church, which the Lollards vehemently declaimed against; such as the use of images, pilgrimages to famous shrines, the holding of landed estates by the clergy, &c. Pecock was made Bishop of Chichester in 1450. His method of argument, however, which consisted in appealing rather to reason and common sense, than to Church authority, to justify the practices complained of, was displeasing to most of his brother bishops; and in 1457 his books were formally condemned in a synod held before Henry VI. at Westminster. He was deposed from his bishopric, and only escaped severer treatment by making a full and formal retractation of his opinions.

Pecock wrote several other works in English, of which the following are extant in MS. :—

(1) *The Donet*: written about 1444, an introduction to the chief truths of the Christian religion, in the form of a dialogue between a father and a son.

(2) *The Follower to the Donet*: this is a supplement to that work.

(3) *The Poor Men's Mirror*: this is the *Donet* popularized.

(4) *The Book of Faith* (1456). In this work he gives up the infallibility of the Church as a certain doctrine, but urges that it ought to be practically accepted, until it is proved that the Church is fallible. He also maintains that Scripture is the only standard of supernatural and revealed verities.

(5) *The Rule of Christian Religion*: a folio of 384 pages.

Also the *Abbreviatio Reginaldi Pecock*, in Latin : printed by Mr. Babington.

30. The most interesting work belonging to this period is Sir John Fortescue's treatise on the *Difference between an Absolute and a Limited Monarchy*. The author was Chief Justice of the Court of King's Bench in the time of Henry VI. He was at first a zealous Lancastrian; he fought at Towton, and was

taken prisoner at Tewkesbury in 1471, after which he was attainted. But upon the death of Henry in that year, leaving no son, Fortescue admitted the legality of the claim of the house of York, and thereby obtained the reversal of the attainder. The title of the work mentioned is not very appropriate; it should rather be,—a 'Treatise on the best means of raising a revenue for the King, and cementing his power,'—these, at least, are the points prominently handled. The opening chapters, drawing a contrast between the state and character of the English peasantry under the constitutional crown of England, and those of the French peasantry under the absolute monarchy of France, are full of acute remarks and curious information. It is instructive to notice that Fortescue (ch. xii.) speaks of England's insular position as a source of *weakness*, because it laid her open to attack on every side. The observation reminds us how modern a creation is the powerful British navy, the wooden walls of which have turned that position into our greatest safeguard. This work is in excellent English, and, if freed from the barbarous orthography in which it is disguised, could be read with ease and pleasure at the present day. Fortescue wrote also, about the year 1463, an able Latin treatise, *De Laudibus Legum Angliæ*, designed for the use of the ill-fated Edward Prince of Wales, son of Henry VI. and Margaret, in which he labours to prove the superiority of the common law of England to the civil law. No other prose writer of the fifteenth century deserves notice, unless we except **Caxton**, who wrote a continuation of Trevisa's translation of the *Polychronicon* to the year 1460, and printed the entire work in 1482. His translation of Raoul le Fevre's *Recueil des Histoires de Troye* was 'begonne in Brugis in 1468, and ended in the holy cyte of Colen, 19 September, 1471.' He also printed a translation, made by himself from the Flemish, of the famous mediæval apologue or satire of *Reynard the Fox*. For some eighteen years he continued with untiring industry to bring out popular works, chiefly religious or moral treatises and romances, from the press, and when he died he left able successors to carry on and extend his work.[1]

31. In 1510 More published the *Life of John Picus, Earl of Mirandula*, with his letters, translated from the Latin; the translation is preceded by a beautiful 'Envoy' from More to his sister Joyeuse Leigh. That prodigy of genius, Pico of Mirandola, after having mastered all the learned languages, and

[1] For fuller particulars about Caxton, see the *History of English Literature* by the late learned Professor Craik, of Belfast.

sucked the marrow of all philosophical systems, was cut off by a fever at Florence in 1494, at the age of thirty-one.

The effect of the revival of ancient learning was for a long time to induce our ablest literary men to aim at a polished Latin style, rather than endeavour to improve their native tongue. Erasmus wished that Latin should be the common literary language of Europe; he always wrote in it himself, and held what he termed the barbarous jargon of his Dutch fatherland in utter detestation. So Leland, More, and Pole composed, if not all, yet their most important and most carefully written works in Latin. **John Leland**, the famous antiquary, to whose *Itinerarium* we owe so much interesting topographical and sociological information for the period immediately following the destruction of the monasteries, is the author of a number of Latin elegies, in various metres, upon the death of Sir Thomas Wyat the elder, which evince no common elegance and mastery over the language. More's *Utopia*, published in 1516, was composed in Latin, but has been translated by Burnet and others.

32. Utopia, according to its Greek derivation (*ού not, τόπος, place*), means the *Land of Nowhere*. The manners and customs of the Utopians are described to More and his friend Tonstall, while on a mission in Flanders, by an 'ancient mariner' named Raphael Hythlodaye (*i.e.* prater or gossipper, from βθλος, *idle talk, nonsense*), who has visited their island. The work is a satire on existing society; every important political or social regulation in Utopia is the reverse of what was then to be found in Europe. The condition of the ideal commonwealth rebukes the ambition of kings, the worldliness of priests, and the selfish greed of private persons. The Utopians detest war, and will only take up arms on a plain call of honour or justice. Instead of burning and torturing men for their religion, they tolerate all forms of belief or no-belief, only refusing to those who deny Divine Providence, and the soul's immortality, the right to hold public offices or trusts. They have no money, but the wants of all are fully supplied by the perfect mechanism of their free government; equality prevails among them and is highly prized; idlers are driven out of the commonwealth; and the lands belonging to each city, incapable of appropriation to private owners, are tilled by all its citizens in succession.

33. The regular series of English prose chronicles commences in this period. The earliest is the *Chronicle of England*, by **John Capgrave**, who dedicated the work to Edward IV. It opens with the creation of the world, and comes down to 1416. It appeared about the year 1463, but was never printed till it came out in the Rolls series. **Robert Fabyan** was an alderman and sheriff of London in the reign of Henry VII.; his *Concordance of Storyes*, giving the history of England from the fabulous Brutus to the year 1485, was published after the

author's death in 1516. Successive subsequent editions of this work continued the history to 1559. More published a *History of Richard III.* (or, as it is also called, of Edward V.), unfinished, in 1513. This work, observes Hallam, 'appears to me the first example of good English language; pure and perspicuous, well-chosen, without vulgarisms or pedantry.'[1] **Edward Hall**, an under-sheriff of London, wrote in 1542 a chronicle, entitled the *Union of the Two Noble Families of Lancaster and York*, bringing the narrative down to 1532. **Richard Grafton**, himself the author of two independent chronicles in the reign of Elizabeth, printed in 1548 a new edition of Hall, with a continuation to the end of Henry's reign. A curious biographical work, *Illustrium Majoris Britanniæ Scriptorum Summarium*, was written by **John Bale**, a reformer, afterwards Bishop of Ossory, in 1548. The accuracy of this writer may be judged of by the fact, that in the article on Chaucer, he fixes the date of the poet's death in 1450, and in the list of his works includes the *Falls of Princes* (which was by Lydgate), and omits the *Canterbury Tales*.

34. Not much of the theological writing of the period possessed more than a passing value. Portions of it are indirectly interesting, as illustrating manners and customs, or as tinged with the peculiar humour of the writer. The sermons of Bishop Latimer, one of the leading reformers, who was burnt at the stake under Mary, possess this twofold attraction. Thus, in preaching against covetousness, he complains of the great rise in rents and in the price of provisions that had taken place in his time, winding up his recital of grievances with the singular climax,—' I think, verily, that if it thus continue, we shall at length be constrained to pay for a pig a pound.' The strange humour of the man breaks out in odd similes—in unexpected applications of homely proverbs—in illustrations of the great by the little, and the little by the great. Cranmer's works have but small literary value, though most important—especially the *Letters*—from the historical point of view. John Bale, already mentioned, Becon, Ridley, Hooper, and Tyndale, all composed theological tracts, chiefly controversial. More, Bishop Fisher, and Pole, were the leading writers on the other side.

35. Among these writings we shall select for somewhat more detailed notice those of Tyndale and More. Ranged on opposite sides in the great controversy, both were sincere and earnest men, and both gave testimony of their sincerity with their blood. **William Tyndale**, a native of Gloucestershire, received

[1] *Literature of Europe*, i. 454.

M

his education at Oxford, whence he went to live with a Gloucestershire knight as tutor to his boys. The ecclesiastical condition of the county while he was growing up was such as might well rouse to indignation his fervid spirit. The see of Worcester, in which diocese Gloucestershire was then included, had been held by four Italian prelates in succession, who had never set foot in England, but administered the affairs of the diocese through their chancellors. In 1521, Leo X. nominated to the see Giulio de' Medici, afterwards Clement VII.; and Henry VIII. was not sorry to acquiesce in the appointment, because part of the arrangement was that Wolsey should administer the property of the see; thus the favourite was rewarded, and the king not the poorer. Such shameful abuses of power in the highest places implied no breach in the network of ecclesiastical ordinance and privilege; whatever was done or left undone, not a finger was to be raised, not a tongue to be moved, against the clergy; their immunities were maintained by the State with all its power. Tyndale saw no remedy for all this, except in the circulation of the New Testament amongst the people in their own language; they would then see, he argued, how sweet and easy was the yoke which Christ had imposed on the members of his Church,—how different from the ponderous system which the clergy, aided and instigated by the civil power, had developed. He therefore devoted his life to the task of translating and circulating the Scriptures, especially the New Testament. He was obliged to carry on the work abroad: his first edition of the New Testament was printed in 1527, partly at Cologne and partly at Worms. The impression was then sent over to England, but the bishops endeavoured to suppress it. Warham, and afterwards Tonstall, Bishop of London, bought up all the copies they could lay their hands on and burnt them—a proceeding not likely to answer their purpose, since printer and translator thus obtained a profit on the labour and capital expended, and were greatly encouraged to set to work instantly and print more. On this first version all the later versions were founded. The king, with his usual inconsistency, after having allowed the bishops to suppress Tyndale's Testament, and after having perhaps given the information to the government of the Belgian provinces, which led to the arrest and imprisonment of Tyndale in 1535, and his death at the stake in 1536, from that time changed his mind, and not only allowed the version to circulate freely, but caused it to be printed by his own printer, with the translator's name on the title-page.

Tyndale's theological writings can hardly claim to be regarded as literature. The chief among them are,—his *Answer* to *Sir Thomas More's Dialogue* (1531), his *Practise of Prelates* (1530), and his treatise *On Tracy's Testament*; this last was found among his papers after his death. There is a fund of rough homely force behind all that the man writes; a quality noticeable also in Becon, and Bradford, and others of these early reformers. At the same time he is unspeakably coarse, prone to libellous imputation, and quite devoid of any spirit of justice or charity towards his opponents. Here is a slight sample of his style. More in his *Dialogue* had spoken of faith; Tyndale replies: ' Master More meaneth, of the best faith that ever he felt. By all likelihood he knoweth of none other, but such as may stand with all wickedness, neither in himself nor in his prelates. Wherefore, inasmuch as their faith may stand with all that Christ hateth, I am sure he looketh but for small thanks of God for his defending of them; and therefore he playeth surely, to take his reward here of our holy patriarchs.' He is always harping in this way on the supposed fact of More having been hired by the bishops to write for them. But we have it on the testimony of Roper, More's son-in-law, that when the bishops and clergy in Convocation, probably in 1533, agreed to present More with the sum of four thousand pounds, in acknowledgment of the labour and expense in which his controversial writings had involved him, he refused to accept one farthing, either for himself or for any member of his family.

The *Practise of Prelates* is a vigorous denunciation of the mal-practices of bishops; in it he urges secular princes and lords, as Wycliffe had done before him, to deprive ecclesiastical persons of that temporal power by which they encroached on the rights of the laity. It must have been such writings as this, and the dealings which as chancellor he had had with the writers, joined perhaps to a sense of the weakness of the bishops' harness in more than one important place, that made More once say to Roper, when the latter was talking in a boastful and sanguine way about the prosperous condition of the Commonwealth: ' Trothe it is so indeed, . . . and yet I praie God that some of us, as highe as we seem to sit upon the mountains, treading heretikes under our feet like ants, live not to see the day that we would gladly be at league and composition with them, to let them have their churches quietly to themselves, so that they would be contented to let us have ours quietly to ourselves.'

The pamphlet *On Tracy's Testament* discusses a will made by a Mr. Tracy, a Gloucestershire gentleman, in 1530, in which he directed in a pointed manner that no money should be paid after his death for the benefit of his soul, and that no part of his property should go to the Church. For this the chancellor, and Dr. Parker, who administered the diocese for its Italian bishop, actually caused the body of Tracy to be exhumed and cast forth out of consecrated ground! It was found, however, that the canon law would not sanction this, and the chancellor, being sued by the relatives, was condemned and heavily fined.

36. The controversial and devotional works of **Sir Thomas More** can only be read in black letter, never having been reprinted since they were first collected and published in 1557. The change of religion, and the fact that several of the polemical tracts were written hastily to meet some special occasion, are enough to account for this neglect. Yet the thoughts of so powerful and so cultivated a mind, though here presented in a somewhat crude and unsatisfactory form, are worth more attention than they have received. The following list, therefore, with the descriptions of which some notices of his imprisonment and death are intermixed, will be found not devoid of interest.

(1) *A Treatise on the Four Last Things* (1522).—This is a devotional tract, containing some eloquent passages; it includes notices of the seven deadly sins, and ends unfinished.

(2) *A Dialogue*, in four books, chiefly on the worship of images, on praying to saints, and on pilgrimages,—against 'the pestilent secte of Luther and Tyndale.' It was this work, published in 1528, to which Tyndale wrote the 'Answer,' noticed in § 35.

(3) *The Supplication of Souls.*—This was written in 1529, against those who denied that there was a purgatory, and especially against a book that had recently appeared, entitled *The Supplication of Beggars.* More defends the power of the keys, and the plenitude of authority in binding and loosing given to St. Peter and his successors; he maintains also that souls in pain may be relieved by masses, prayers, and good works.

(4) *The Confutacion of Tyndale's Answere* (1532).—Of this immense treatise, seven books are occupied with the confutation of Tyndale; the eighth is an argument against 'Friar Barnes's church;' the ninth, summing up all that has gone before, is 'a recapitulation and summary proof that the common knowen Catholic Churche is the verye true Churche of Christ.' There is much in this work that is powerfully and eloquently argued. He indulges in much severity of censure and sarcasm against Tyndale, says that several years of late have been 'plentuous of evil bookes,' and names among their writers Jaye, Thorpe, Constantine, Bayfield, and Frith. Friar Barnes's theory of an

invisible church, composed of the elect and the pure, is examined in the eighth book.

(5) *The Apology* (1533), for his previous controversial writings, was written soon after he had resigned the Great Seal, from the fear of coming into collision with the king on the marriage question. In this work he says that it always had been, and still was, his opinion that it was 'a thing very good and profitable, that the Scripture, well and truely translated, should be in the Englishe tongue;' only he did not believe either in the competency or the good faith of those who were at the time engaged in the task.

(6) *The Debellacyon of Salem and Bizance* (1533).—This treatise was occasioned by the appearance of a work called *Salem and Bizance*, by one who styled himself 'the Pacifier,' and impugned More's *Apology*.

(7) *A Dialogue of Comforte against Tribulacyon* (1534) was written in the Tower. After resigning the seals in 1532, More was not molested for some time. In 1533, on the death of Warham, Cranmer was made Archbishop of Canterbury, and by his management the king obtained a divorce, and married Anne Boleyn. An act was passed to regulate the succession, and to this act a form of oath was attached, recognising the king as supreme head of the church in England. All the bishops, except Fisher, Bishop of Rochester, took this oath when tendered to them. More, being known to hold that the oath could not lawfully be taken, was summoned to appear before the primate at Lambeth in April 1534. A letter to his daughter, Margaret Roper, written in that month, tells how he had appeared accordingly before Cranmer and a great number of the clergy; how he had been pressed on all sides to take the oath, but, though not blaming any that took it, had still refused; how the archbishop pressed him with a sophistical argument, to which he did not at the moment see the answer; and how he saw Latimer amusing himself at horse-play with his friends in the Lambeth garden. Soon afterwards he was committed to the Tower, and his property, though he had taken the precaution to convey it to his wife and children, was seized by the king.

The *Dialogue of Comforte, &c.*, is an eloquent composition. It purports to be a translation from a Latin work by an Hungarian author, who, writing at a time when his countrymen were under the continual terror of a Turkish invasion, animates them to face these dangers by the help of religion and divine philosophy. The work has been several times printed.

37. During two years and more, while More was in the Tower, he wrote, so far as opportunities served, continually; when

ink was denied him, he made use of a piece of coal. On the 5th
May, 1535, he writes to his daughter that he had just seen
Raynolds, a Brigittine monk of the Sion convent, and three
Carthusians, led to execution for denying the royal supremacy ;
his reflections on what he had seen are noteworthy. Soon
after this he was indicted of high treason, for ' malitiouslie,
traitorouslie, and divellishlie ' denying the king to be the supreme head of the Church of England. At his trial, the particulars of which were related to Roper, his son-in-law, by some
who were present, he said, among other things, that to give
the king this supremacy involved a manifest violation of Magna,
Charta, the first clause of which provided ' quod Anglicana ecclesia
libera sit, et habeat omnia jura sua integra et illæsa ' (that the
English Church should be free, and have all its rights entire
and inviolate). Audley, the new chancellor, urged upon him
strongly the consent of the bishops and the universities in favour
of the doctrine, but More replied that the majority of the
bishops in Christendom, to say nothing of the saints in heaven,
condemned it. The scene that followed the trial is familiar to
all readers—the condemned man issuing from the hall of unjust
judgment, his Margaret rushing in among the guards and
falling upon his neck, kissing him with a passion of love and
grief, he blessing and comforting her, all the bystanders weeping.

All the letters written by More from the Tower are full of
interest. In one of them he explains to Cromwell the growth of
his present convictions on the authority of the Holy See ; saying
that he was originally little inclined to believe the primacy of
the pope to be of divine institution, but that, after reading the
king's *Assertio Septem Sacramentorum*, he had been led to
examine the question, and, after much study of the Fathers, had
become convinced that the doctrine was true.

(8) *A Treatise upon the Passion of Christ* (1534). The introduction to this unfinished tract, which is founded on the
narratives in all the four Gospels, is very beautiful. In a colo-
phon the editor has appended these words : ' Sir Thomas More
wrote no more of this woorke ; for when he had written this
farre, he was in prison kept so streyght, that all his bokes and
penne and ynke and paper was taken from hym, and sone after
was he putte to death.'

Besides the works above enumerated, there are extant several
Meditations and *Prayers*, written with a coal in the Tower. In
these we see that happy wit, that shaping imagination, though
chastened by long suffering, still keeping their lustre undimmed
even to the glorious close. More was brought to the block on
the 6th July 1535. The Emperor Charles V., on hearing of it,

said to the English ambassador, 'We would rather have lost the best city of our dominions than such a worthy counsellor.'

38. The close of the period was adorned by the scholarship and refined good sense of Roger Ascham. A native of Yorkshire, he was sent at an early age to Cambridge, and during a length-ened residence there diligently promoted the study of the new learning. In 1544 he wrote and dedicated to Henry VIII. his *Toxophilus*, a treatise on Archery, in which, for military and other reasons, he deprecates the growing disuse of that noble art. His exertions were vain; we hear indeed of the bow as still a formidable weapon at the battle of Pinkie in 1547, but from that date it disappears from our military history. In 1550 Ascham went to Germany as secretary to Sir Richard Morrisine, who was then proceeding as ambassador to the Imperial Court; and in 1553, while at Brussels, he wrote, in the form of a letter to a friend in England, a curious unfinished tract, in which the character and career of Maurice of Saxony, whose successful enterprise he had witnessed, and of two or three other German princes, are described with much acute-ness.

In 1553 he was appointed Latin Secretary to Edward VI., and retained the office (the same that Milton held under Crom-well) during the reign of Mary. On the accession of Elizabeth he received the additional appointment of reader in the learned languages to the Queen. Elizabeth used to take lessons from him at a stated hour each day. In 1563 he wrote his *School-master*, a treatise on education. This work was never finished, and was printed by his widow in 1571. The sense and acute-ness of many of his pedagogic suggestions have been much dwelt upon by Johnson. An excellent biography of Ascham may be found in Hartley Coleridge's *Northern Worthies*.

39. Sir Thomas Elyot, a courtier in the time of Henry VIII., is the author of the political treatise called *The Governour*. The book is dedicated to the king, and was first published in 1531. Experience and reading of the ancients, he tells us, have qualified him, and incli-nation incited him, to write of 'the form of a juste publike weale.' Such an opening makes us think of Plato's *Republic*, or More's *Utopia*, or, at the least, Fortescue's *Absolute and Limited Monarchy*. But the promise was not kept, nor could it well have been kept; for who that had any regard for his life, and was not hopelessly servile in nature, could have written freely and fully on political questions under the horrible despotism of Henry VIII.? After the first few pages, the author slides into the subject of education for the remainder of the first book; the second and third books, again, with the exception of a few pages, form an ethical treatise on virtues and vices, with but slight reference to the bearing of these on the work of government. In the brief portion which is political, Elyot argues on behalf of ranks and

degrees among men from the examples of subordination afforded in the kingdoms of nature. Superior knowledge he deems to be, in itself, the best and most legitimate title to superior honour. Monarchy, as a form of government, he sets above aristocracy and democracy. He draws an argument from a beehive :—

'In a little beaste, whiche of all other is most to be mervailed at, I meane the Bee, is lefte to man by nature a perpetual figure of a just governaunce or rule ; who have among them one principall bee for their governour, which excelleth all other in greatnesse, yet hath he no pricke or stinge, but in him is more knowledge than in the residewe.'

CHAPTER III.

ELIZABETHAN PERIOD.

1558–1625.

1. THIS is the golden or Augustan age of English literature. After its brilliant opening under Chaucer, a period of poverty and feebleness had continued for more than a hundred and fifty years. Servile in thought and stiff in expression, it remained unvivified by genius even during the first half of the reign of Elizabeth; and Italy with her Ariosto and Tasso, France with her Marot and Rabelais, Portugal with her Camoens, and even Spain with her Ercilla, appeared to have outstripped England in the race of fame. Hence Sir Philip Sidney in his *Defence of Poesie*, written shortly before his death in 1586, after awarding a certain meed of praise to Sackville, Surrey, and Spenser (whose first work had but lately appeared), does not 'remember to have seen many more [English poets] that have poetical sinews in them.' Gradually a change became apparent. The *Paradise of Dainty Devices*, a collection of poems published in 1578, contains pieces by Richard Edwards, Jasper Heywood, and others, which evince a skill of poetical handling not before met with. *England's Helicon*, a poetical miscellany (comprising fugitive pieces composed between 1580 and 1600), to which Sidney, Raleigh, Lodge, and Marlowe contributed, is full of genuine and native beauties. Spenser published the first three books of the *Faerie Queene* in 1590; Shakspere began to write for the stage about the year 1586; the *Essays* of Francis Bacon were first published in 1597; and the first portion of Hooker's great work on *Ecclesiastical Polity* appeared in 1594.

2. The peaceable and firmly settled state of the country after 1558 was largely instrumental in the rise of this literary greatness. Queen Elizabeth, whose sagacity detected the one paramount political want of the country, concluded in the second year of her reign a rather inglorious peace with France, and devoted all her energies to the work of strengthening the power of her government, passing good laws, and improving the internal administration of the kingdom. The consequences of the

durable internal peace thus established were astonishing. Men began to trade, farm, and build with renewed vigour; a great breadth of forest land was reclaimed; travellers went forth to ' discover islands far away,' and to open new outlets for commerce; wealth, through this multiplied activity, poured into the kingdom; and that general prosperity was the result which led her subjects to invest the sovereign, under whom all this was done, with a hundred virtues and shining qualities not her own. Of this feeling Shakspere became the mouthpiece and mirror :—

> She shall be loved and feared ; her own shall bless her ;
> Her foes shake like a field of beaten corn,
> And hang their heads with sorrow : good grows with her ;
> *In her days every man shall eat in safety*
> *Under his own vine, what he plants, and sing*
> *The merry songs of peace to all his neighbours.*[1]

There is indeed a reverse to the picture. Ireland was devastated in this reign with fire and sword; and the minority in England who adhered to the ancient faith became the victims of an organized system of persecution and plunder. Open a book by Cardinal Allen, and a scene of martyred priests, of harried and plundered laymen, of tortured consciences and bleeding hearts, will blot out from your view the smiling images of peace and plenty above portrayed. The mass of the people, however, went quietly with the government, believing—and the circumstances of the time were such as to lend some colour to the belief—that to adhere to the pope meant something more than merely to accept seven sacraments instead of two ; that it meant sympathy with Spain, disloyalty to England, and aid and comfort to her enemies all over the world.

Wealth and ease brought leisure in their train; and leisure demanded entertainment, not for the body only, but also for the mind. The people, for amusement's sake, took up the old popular drama, which had come down from the very beginning of the middle ages ; and, after a process of gradual transformation and elaboration by inferior hands, developed it, in the mouths of its Shakspere, Jonson, and Fletcher, into the world-famed romantic drama of England. As the reading class increased, so did the number of those who strove to minister to its desires ; and although the religious convulsions which society had undergone had checked the movement towards a complete and profound appreciation of antiquity, which had been commenced by Colet, More, and Erasmus, in the universities, so

[1] *Henry VIII.* act v. sc. 5.

that England could not then, nor for centuries afterwards, produce scholars in any way comparable to those of the Continent,
yet the number of translations which were made of ancient
authors proves that there was a general taste for at least a
superficial learning, and a very wide diffusion of it. Translation
soon led to imitation, and to the projection of new literary works
on the purer principles of art disclosed in the classical authors.
The epics of Ariosto and Tasso were also translated, the former
by Harrington, the latter by Carew and Fairfax; and the fact
shows both how eagerly the Italian literature was studied by
people of education, and how general must have been the diffusion of an intellectual taste. Spenser doubtless framed his
allegory in emulation of the *Orlando* of Ariosto, and the form
and idea of Bacon's *Essays* were probably suggested to him by
the *Essays* of Montaigne.

Let us now briefly trace the progress, and describe the principal achievements, in poetry and in prose writing, during the
period under consideration.

**Poets :—Spenser, Southwell, Warner, Daniel, Drayton, Donne,
Davies, Chapman, Marston, Gascoigne, Sidney, Tusser,
Marlowe, Raleigh ; Translators.**

3. Among the poets of the period, **Spenser** holds the first
rank. The appearance of his *Shepheard's Calender*, in 1579,
was considered by his contemporaries to form an epoch in the
history of English poetry. This poem is dedicated to Sidney,
and in an introductory epistle, feigned to come from a third
hand, addressed to his friend Gabriel Harvey, the poet enters
into some curious particulars respecting the diction of his work.
He commences the epistle by quoting from 'the old famous
poet' Chaucer, and also from Lydgate, whom he calls 'a worthy
scholar of so excellent a master.' The *Calender* itself, partly by
the large use of alliteration, partly by an express allusion in the
epilogue, supplies us with evidence that he was a diligent reader
and admirer of the *Vision of Piers Plowman* by Langland.
These three were his English models : he was young and full of
enthusiasm, and there is little wonder if their poetical diction,
which, if obsolete, was eminently striking and picturesque,
commended itself to his youthful taste more than the composite
English current in his own day. His words are as follows :—

'And first of the wordes to speake, I graunt they bee something hard, and of most men unused, yet both English, and also
used of most excellent authours and most famous poets. In
whom, whereas this our poet hath bin much travailed and

thoroughly read, how could it be (as that worthy oratour sayde), but that walking in the sunne, although for other cause he walked, yet needes he mought be sunburnt; and having the sound of those auncient poets still ringing in his eares, he mought needes in singing hit out some of their tunes? But whether he useth them by such casualtie and custome, or of set purpose and choise, as thinking them fittest for such rusticall rudenesse of shepheards, either for that their rough sound would make his rimes more ragged and rusticall, or else because such old obsolete wordes are most used of country folke, sure I thinke, and thinke I thinke not amisse, that they bring great grace, and, as one would say, authoritie to the verse. . . . But if any will rashly blame his purpose in choise of old and unwonted wordes, him may I more justly blame and condemne, or of witlesse headinesse in judging, or of heedles hardinesse in condemning; for, not marking the compasse of his bent, he will judge of the length of his cast: for, in my opinion, it is one especial praise of many which are due to this poet, that he hath laboured to restore, as to their rightfull heritage, such good and naturall English wordes as have beene long time out of use, and almost clean disherited, which is the only cause that our mother tongue, which truly of itself is both full enough for prose and stately enough for verse, hath long time been counted most bare and barren of both.   Which default, when as some endeavoured to salve and recure, they patched up the holes with pieces and rags of other languages, borrowing here of the French, there of the Italian, everywhere of the Latin; not weighing how ill those tongues accorded with themselves, but much worse with ours; so now they have made our English tongue a gallimaufrey,[1] or hodge-podge of all other speeches.'

The twelve eclogues of the *Shepheard's Calender* (Spenser, relying on an erroneous etymology, spells the word æglogues) are imitations, so far as their form is concerned, of the pastoral poetry of Theocritus and Virgil.   As with these poets, the pastimes, loves, and disappointments of his shepherds, Cuddie, Colin, Hobbinol, and Piers, form the subject-matter of several eclogues.   In others, more serious themes are handled.   In the fifth, seventh, and ninth, for instance, the abuses both of the old and the new Church are discussed, the chief grounds of attack being the laziness and covetousness of prelates and clergy; the fourth is a panegyrical ode on Queen Elizabeth; in the tenth is set forth 'the perfect pattern of a poet;' the eleventh is an elegy on a lady who is named Dido.   In the tenth, the poet anti-

---

[1] From the French *Galimafrée*; but the origin of the word is unknown.

cipates, as Milton afterwards did, the loftier strain to which he felt that his genius would ere long impel him.

4. In 1580, Spenser attained the object of his desires, being appointed Secretary to the Lord Grey of Wilton, on his nomination to the vice-royalty of Ireland. To this stay in Ireland we owe Spenser's only prose work, his *View of the State of Ireland,* which, though presented to the Queen in manuscript in 1596, was for political reasons held back from publication till the year 1633. His connection with great men was now established, and we cannot doubt that his great intellect and remarkable powers of application made him a most efficient public servant. Nor were his services left unrewarded. He received, in 1586, a grant of Kilcolman Castle, in the county of Cork, together with some three thousand acres of land, being part of the forfeited estates of the Earl of Desmond. From this time to his death, in 1599, few particulars are known about him, but he seems to have resided chiefly in Ireland, and there to have composed his greatest work, *The Faerie Queene.* His friend Sir Walter Raleigh, to whom *The Faerie Queene* is dedicated, is thought to have introduced him to Queen Elizabeth, who granted him, in 1591, a pension of fifty pounds a year. In 1598 occurred a rising of the Irish, headed by O'Neill, the famous Earl of Tyrone, which, after the defeat of the English general, Bagnal, extended to Munster; for a time there was no safety for English settlers outside the walls of fortified places. Spenser had to flee from his castle, which was taken and burnt by the insurgents; his infant child is said to have perished in the flames. In the greatest trouble and affliction, he crossed over to England, and died a few months afterwards in a lodging-house in London, being only in his forty-sixth year.

5. Out of the twelve books composing, or which ought to compose, *The Faerie Queene,* we have but six in an entire state, containing the ‘Legends’ of the Red Cross Knight, Sir Guyon, Britomartis, a lady knight, Cambel and Triamond, Sir Artegall, and Sir Calidore. In the characters and adventures of these heroic personages, the virtues of holiness, temperance, chastity, friendship, justice, and courtesy, are severally illustrated and portrayed. Of the remaining six books, we possess, in two cantos on Mutability, a fragment of the Legend on Constancy. Whether any or what other portions of them were ever written, is not certainly known.

It would be vain to attempt, within the limits here prescribed to us, to do justice to the variety and splendour of this poem, which, even in its unfinished state, is more than twice as long as the *Paradise Lost.* The allegorical form, which, as we have seen, was the favourite style of the mediæval poets, is carefully preserved throughout; but the interest of the narrative, as full of action and incident as an old romance, and the charm of the free, vagrant, open-air life described, make one think and care little for the hidden meaning. 'There is something,' said Pope, 'in Spenser, that pleases one as strongly in one's old age as it did in one's youth. I read *The Faerie Queene* when I was about twelve with a vast deal of delight, and I think it gave me as much when I read it over about a year or two ago.'[1] An account in some detail of a portion of the second book will be found at a later page.[2]

Spenser devoted himself with ardour to the support of the religious system and policy adopted by Elizabeth and her ministers. From his youth upwards he was an aspirant for public employment,—at first with little success, if the well-known complaint[3] in *Mother Hubberd's Tale* may be taken to apply to his own case. He would neither have succeeded in entering the public service, nor, having entered it, could he have retained his position, had he not shown himself zealously affected to the new state of things. Again, as a holder of confiscated lands in Ireland, he personally benefited by that great public crime, which, commenced under Elizabeth, was consummated under William of Orange,—the eviction of the Irish people from nearly the whole of its own soil, under the pretext of imposing upon them a purer faith. It need not, therefore, surprise us to find Spenser typifying by 'Una,' first, Truth and its oneness, secondly, the newly established church of England and Ireland, and by 'Duessa,' first, Falsehood and its multiplicity, secondly, the ancient Church, thirdly, Mary Queen of Scots. This last extension of the allegory occurs in the ninth canto of Book V., where Duessa is supposed to be put on her trial, and found guilty of the same heinous crimes that were imputed to Mary, while Mercilla (Queen Elizabeth), out of the goodness of her heart, delays to give effect to the judgment. On the other hand, Spenser seems to have had no sympathy with the Puritans. The religious discipline by which the Red Cross Knight is purified in the house of Cælia (Book I., Canto x.) has not the least savour of the teaching of Geneva, but is borrowed from the rules of ancient piety. By the 'Blatant Beast' (Book VI.), Puritanism, with its destroying hand and railing bitter tongue, appears to be intended. It is said of him that after ransacking the monasteries,—

---

[1] Spence's *Anecdotes*.   [2] See Crit. Sect. ch. I., *Narrative Poetry*.
[3] See the passage beginning 'Full little knoweth he that hath not tried.'

> From thence into the sacred church he broke,
> And rob'd the chancell, and the deskes downe threw,
> And altars fouled, and blasphémy spoke,
> And the images, for all their goodly hew,
> Did cast to ground, whilst none was them to rew;
> So all confounded and disordered there.

He was subdued and bound by Sir Calidore, or Courtesy; but after a time he escaped, and is now, Spenser intimates, pursuing his old trade of detraction and slander, almost unrebuked. This is a clear allusion to the growth of Puritanism in the latter part of Elizabeth's reign, and to the increasing loudness of its clamour against those portions of the established ritual which it disliked.

6. Of the many shorter poems left by Spenser, none are more noteworthy than *The Ruines of Time* and *The Teares of the Muses*. The first, dedicated to Sidney's sister, the Countess of Pembroke, is, in its main intention, a lament over her noble brother's untimely death. The marvellous poetic energy, the perfect finish, the depth of thought, the grace, tenderness, and richness of this poem make it eminently illustrative of Spenser's genius.[1] *The Teares of the Muses*, published in 1591, is an impassioned protest against the depraved state of the public taste, which at this time, according to Spenser, led society in general to despise learning, nobles to sacrifice true fame to vanity and avarice, and authors to substitute servility and personality for wit. Each muse bewails in turn the miserable condition of that particular branch of literary art over which she is supposed to preside. Melpomene, the Muse of Tragedy, frankly owns that her occupation in England is a sinecure:

> But I, that in true tragedies am skilled,
> The flower of wit, find nought to busie me,
> Therefore I mourne, and pitifully mone,
> Because that mourning matter I have none.

This might well be said, when as yet no better tragedy had appeared in England than Sackville's *Gorboduc*.

The complaint of Thalia, the Muse of Comedy, is different. The comic stage *had* flourished, thanks to one gifted 'gentle spirit;' but he was now keeping silence, and ribaldry and folly had possession of the stage. Then comes the following interesting passage:—

> All these, and all that else the comic stage
>   With seasoned wit and goodly pleasance graced,
> By which man's life, in his likest image,
>   Was limned forth, are wholly now defaced;
> And those sweet wits, which wont the like to frame,
> Are now despised, and made a laughing game.

[1] See Crit. Sect. ch. I., *Miscellaneous Poems*.

And he, the man whom Nature's self had made
    To mock herselfe, and truth to imitate,
With kindly counter, under mimic shade,
    Our pleasant Willy, ah ! is dead of late ;—
With whom all joy and jolly merriment
Is also deaded and in dolour drent.

Instead thereof, scoffing scurrilitie
    And scornful folly with contempt is crept,
Rolling in rymes of shameless ribaudry,
    Without regard or due decorum kept,
Each idle wit at will presumes to make,
And doth the learned's task upon him take.

But that same gentle spirit, from whose pen
    Large streams of honnie and sweet nectar flowe,
Scorning the boldness of such base-born men,
    Which dare their follies forth so rashly throwe,
Doth rather choose to sit in idle cell,
Than so himselfe to mockerie to sell.

In spite of Mr. Todd's petty objections, I firmly believe that here we have Spenser's tribute to the mighty genius that had already given *Two Gentlemen of Verona, Love's Labour's Lost, The Comedy of Errors*, and perhaps one or two historical plays, to the English stage.

7. In *Colin Clout's come Home againe*, Spenser, having returned to his Irish home, describes the visit which he paid to England in 1591, the condescension of the Queen, and the ways of the Court ;—all under the mask of a conversation between shepherds and shepherdesses. The *Foure Hymnes* in honour of earthly and heavenly Love, earthly and heavenly Beauty, are written in the Chaucerian heptastich ; the force and harmony of the verse are wonderful. *Mother Hubberd's Tale*, a work of the poet's youth, is in the heroic couplet ; it is in the main a satire, first exposing with a lofty scorn the hypocrisy and self-seeking of the new clergy, and then turning off to paint the meanness, cunning, and hardheartedness which pervade the atmosphere of a Court. It is in this connection that the famous passage occurs, thought to embody his own experience, which describes the miserable life of a suitor for some favour at Court. *Daphnaida* and *Astrophel* are elegies, the last upon the death of Sir Philip Sidney. The lovely nuptial hymn, *Epithalamion*, was written on the occasion of his marriage ; its metre and movement are Pindaric. *Muiopotmos* is an elaborate poem, in the fantastic style, on the fate of a butterfly.

The reader will observe that there is a wide interval, in respect of the polish and modern air of the diction, between the productions of 1579 and those of 1590 and 1591. One may reasonably conjecture that the perusal of such a play as *Two Gentlemen of Verona* had led Spenser to modify considerably his youthful theory, giving the preference to the obsolete English of a former age.

8. The poems of Shakspere all fall within the early part of his life ; they were all composed before 1598. Writing in that year, Meres, in the *Wit's Treasury*, says,—' As the soul of Euphorbus was thought to live in Pythagoras, so the sweet witty soul of Ovid lives in mellifluous honey-tongued Shakespeare. Witness his "Venus and Adonis ;" his "Lucrece ;" his sugared sonnets among his private friends.' These, together with such portions of the *Passionate Pilgrim* and the *Lover's Complaint* as may have been his genuine composition, constitute the whole of Shakspere's poems, as distinguished from his plays.

The sonnets, a hundred and fifty-four in number, were first published by a bookseller, Thomas Thorpe, in 1609, with a dedication to a Mr. W. H., 'the only begetter of these ensuing sonnets.' Yet there are some among them that are evidently addressed to a woman. The tone of self-humiliating adulation which seems to pervade those of which Mr. W. H. was the object, has always been a mystery and a trouble to the admirers of Shakspere, who have been driven to invent various hypotheses to account for it. The subject is fully discussed by Mr. Knight in his *Pictorial Shakspere*, and briefly handled by Hallam in the third volume of his *Literary History*.

It has been thought by some that the Earl of Southampton, born in 1573, by others that William Herbert, born in 1580, who became Earl of Pembroke in 1601, is intended by ' W. H.' The second supposition seems the more probable. Whoever was meant, the mental condition which produced these sonnets is explained, as we think, with great force and probability in a little book called ' An Introduction to the Philosophy of Shakespeare's Sonnets, by Richard Simpson ' (London, 1868). ' Shakespeare,' says Mr. Simpson, ' is always a philosopher, but in his sonnets he is a philosopher of love.' He imagines W. H. to have been ' either the Earl of Southampton or some other young man of birth and wealth, wit and beauty, who had travelled into Italy, and had come back, brimming over with academies and love-philosophy, with Petrarch and Platonism, upon which he disputed with Shakespeare, and by his discussions "begot" the sonnets.' The works of Pico di Mirandola, Marsilius Ficinus, and other Italian Platonists, abound with metaphysical discussions on love, the ground-thesis of which is to be sought in Plato's Symposium. They distinguish the vulgar from the civil love, and both from the chivalrous love ; last and highest of all they place the celestial or ideal love, which, excited originally by the pure admiration of the beauty of some beautiful youth, rather than of any woman, rises gradually upwards to the contemplation of the celestial or ideal beauty. Mr. Simpson's little book is well worth a careful study.

9. Of the minor poets of the Elizabethan age, the earliest in date among those that attained to real distinction, was **Robert Southwell**,[1] the Jesuit, cruelly put to death by the Government

[1] See his *Poetical Works*, edited by the late Mr. Turnbull, 1856.

in 1595, for the crime of having been found in England, endeavouring to supply his family and friends with priestly ministrations. His poems, under the title of *St. Peter's Complaint, with other Poems*, appeared in the same year that he was executed, and were many times reprinted during the next forty years. Southwell, it seems, was the founder of the modern English style of religious poetry; his influence and example are evident in the work of Crashaw, or of Donne, or of Herbert, or Waller, or any of those whose devout lyrics were admired in later times. Chaucer had, it is true, shown in the prologue to the Prioress's Tale, and in the poem called his *A B C* in honour of the blessed Virgin, how much the English tongue was capable of in this direction. But the language was now greatly altered, and Chaucer, though admired, was looked upon as no subject for direct imitation. The poets of the time were much more solicitous to write like Ovid than like Isaiah. We may admit the truth, excluding only Spenser from its application, of Southwell's general censure, that—

'In lieu of solemn and devout matters, to which in duty they owe their abilities, they now busy themselves in expressing such passions as serve only for testimonies to what unworthy affections they have wedded their wills. And because the best course to let them see the error of their works is to weave a new web in their own loom, I have laid a few coarse threads together, to invite some skilfuller wits to go forward in the same, or to begin some finer piece, wherein it may be seen how well verse and virtue suit together.'

The precision of Southwell's language, and its exact adaptation to the original and beautiful conceptions of his verse, are manifest on a careful reading of *St. Peter's Complaint*, the subject of which is the remorse of the apostle after his three denials of Christ. The following stanza is a good illustration of his manner :—

> Titles I make untruths: am I a rock,
>   That with so soft a gale was overthrown?
> Am I fit pastor for the faithful flock,
>   To guide their souls, that murder'd thus mine own?
> A rock of ruin, not a rest to stay;
> A pastor,—not to feed, but to betray.

A little poem called 'Love's Servile Lot' is striking from its clear, cold austerity. Of ordinary human love, or passion, he says—

> The will she robbeth from the wit,
>   The sense from reason's lore;
> She is delightful in the rind,
>   Corrupted in the core;

and concludes with the advice—

> Plough not the seas, sow not the sands,
>   Leave off your idle pain ;
> Seek other mistress for your minds—
>   Love's service is in vain.

10. Southwell was attacked by **Hall**, then an eager rising young man at Cambridge, in the first book of his satires, called *Virgidemiæ* (*i.e.* 'harvests of rods'), published in 1597. Hall's notion seems to have been that verse was too trivial and too worldly a garb wherein to clothe religious thought. But Marston (see *infra*, § 18) smote the smiter, who had railed

> 'Gainst Peter's teares and Marie's moving moane,

and argued the matter out rather forcibly :—

> Shall painims honor their vile falsed gods
> With sprightly wits, and shall not we by odds
> Far far more strive with wit's best quintessence
> To adore that sacred ever-living Essence ?
> Hath not strong reason moved the legist's mind,
> To say that fairest of all nature's kind
> The prince by his prerogative may claim ?
> Why may not then our soules, without thy blame,
> (Which is the best thing that our God did frame),
> Devote the best part to His sacred name,
> And with due reverence and devotion
> Honor His name with our invention ?[1]

11. **William Warner**, by profession an attorney, is said[2] to have first published his *Albion's England* in 1586. This unwieldy poem (which some read and print in long fourteens, and others in short eights and sixes—it makes not the smallest difference) is in the style of the old riming chronicles ; beginning at the Flood, it traces, through twelve books, the history of Britain, loyally and properly terminating with the reign of Elizabeth. The poem opens thus :—

> I tell of things done long ago,
>   Of many things in few ;
> And chiefly of this clyme of ours
>   The accidents pursue.
> Thou high director of the same,
>   Assist mine artlesse pen,
> To write the gests of Britons stout,
>   And actes of English men.

12. Never was a circle of more richly gifted spirits congre-

---

[1] Marston's Works (ed. J. O. Halliwell, 1856). *Satyre IV.*
[2] See Warton, vol. iv. p. 308 *n.*

gated in one city than the company of poets and playwrights
gathered round the court in London between 1590 and 1610.
From Kent came Samuel Chapman, the translator of Homer;
from Somersetshire the gentle and high-thoughted Daniel;
Warwickshire sent Michael Drayton, author of the *Polyolbion*,
and William Shakspere; Raleigh—who shone in poetry as in
everything else he attempted—came from Devonshire; London
itself was the birthplace of Donne, Spenser, and Jonson.   All
these great men, there is reason to believe, were familiarly acquainted and in constant intercourse with one another; but
unhappily the age produced no Boswell; and their table-talk,
brilliant as it must have been, was lost to posterity.   One dim
glimpse of one of its phases has been preserved in the well-known
passage by Thomas Fuller, writing in 1662 :—

'Many were the wit combats between him and Ben Jonson.
Which two I behold like a Spanish great galleon and an English
man-of-war.   Master Jonson, like the former, was built far
higher in learning; solid, but slow in his performances.   Shakespeare, with the English man-of-war, lesser in bulk, but lighter
in sailing, could turn with all tides, tack about, and take advantage of all winds by the quickness of his wit and invention.   He
died A.D. 1616, and was buried at Stratford-upon-Avon, the town
of his nativity.'

13. The great intellectual activity which pervaded the English nation during this period, the sanguine aspiring temper
which prevailed, the enthusiastic looking forward to an expanding and glorious future which filled the hearts of most men, are
certified to us in the works of a crowd of writers of the second
rank, of whom, though scarcely one did not attempt many
things for which he was ill qualified, almost all have left us
something that is worth remembering.   Among these one of the
most remarkable was **Samuel Daniel.**   He had an ambition to
write a great epic, but in this he signally failed.   His *Wars of
the Roses*, a poem in eight books, written in the eight-line stanza
—the *ottava rima* of Italy—is a heavy, lifeless production, in
which there are innumerable descriptions of men's motives and
plans, but not one description of a battle.   He had no eye for a
stirring picturesque scene, no art to make his characters distinct
and natural; the poem, therefore, produces the effect of a sober
and judicious chronicle done into verse, in which the Hotspurs,
Mortimers, and Warwicks are all very much of a piece.   His
eye seems at last to have been opened to the fact that he was
only wasting his time, for the poem breaks off suddenly just
before the battle of Tewkesbury.   But the meditative temper of
Daniel stood him in good stead in other attempts.   His *Epistle*

to the Lady Margaret, Countess of Cumberland, is marked by an elevated idealism. But his best work is certainly the *Muso-philus*. This is in the form of a dialogue between a man of the world, disposed to ridicule and contemn the pursuits of men of letters, and the poet himself. The progressive and hopeful character of the age is well illustrated in the fine passages in which the poet foretells an approaching vast expansion of the field of science, and dreams of great and unimagined destinies (since then how fully realised !) reserved for the English tongue.

14. **Michael Drayton** also was no mean poet; indeed Mr. Hallam considered that he had greater reach of mind than Daniel. And this, nakedly stated, is undoubtedly true ; Drayton had more variety, more energy, more knowledge of mankind, and far more liveliness than Daniel. His *Baron's Wars* are not tame or prosaic ; they are full of action and strife ; swords flash and helmets rattle on every page. But unfortunately, Mortimer, the hero of the poem, the guilty favourite of Edward II.'s queen, is a personage in whom we vainly endeavour to get up an interest. There is much prolixity of description in this poem, due, it would seem, to imitation of Spenser, whose influence on Drayton's mind and style is conspicuous. But it is one thing to be prolix in a work of pure imagination, when the poet detains us thereby in that magic world of unearthly beauty in which his own spirit habitually dwells, and quite another thing to be prolix in a poem founded upon and closely following historical fact. When both the close and the chief turning-points of the story are known to the reader beforehand, the introduction of fanciful episodes and digressions, unless admirably managed, is apt to strike him as laborious trifling. If Drayton had known, like Tasso, how to associate Clorindas and Erminias with his historical personages, he might have been as discursive as he pleased. But this was ' a grace beyond the reach ' of his art; and the *Baron's Wars* remain, therefore, incurably uninteresting. *England's Heroical Epistles*, published in 1598, have a much stronger claim to distinction. This work, which is in the heroic couplet, consists of twelve pairs of epistles, after the manner of Ovid, supposed to be exchanged between so many pairs of royal or noble lovers : among these are Henry II. and Fair Rosamond, Owen Tudor and Queen Catharine, Surrey and Geraldine, Guildford Dudley and Lady Jane Grey. The style is flowing, fiery, and energetic, and withal extremely *modern* ; it seems to anticipate the ' full resounding line ' of Dryden, and to rebuke the presumption of the poets of the Stuart age, who chose to say that English had never been properly and purely written till Waller and Denham arose. The *Mooncalf* is a

strange satire—and one of a higher order than the weak, uncouth attempts of Hall, Donne, and Marston—on the morals and manners of the time.   One of the best known of Drayton's poems is the *Nymphidia*.   This is in a common romance metre, (the same which Chaucer used for his *Sir Thopas*), and has for its subject the amours of the court of fairy land.   It is a work of the liveliest fancy, but not of imagination.   It is interesting to find Don Quixote referred to in a poem published so soon after Cervantes' death :—

> Men talk of the adventures strange
> Of Don Quichot and of their change.

The most celebrated of our author's works still remains to be noticed—the *Polyolbion*.[1]   This is a poem of enormous length, written in the Alexandrine or twelve-syllable riming couplet, and aiming at a complete topographical and antiquarian delineation of England.   The literary merits of this Cyclopean performance are undeniable.   Mr. Hallam thinks that 'there is probably no poem of this kind in any other language comparable together in extent and excellence to the *Polyolbion* ; nor can any one read a portion of it without admiration for its learned and highly gifted author.'   But the historian of literature goes on to say that 'perhaps no English poem, known so well by name, is so little known beyond its name ;' and, on the whole, the verdict of criticism pronounces it to be one huge mistake ; to be a composition possessing neither the unity of a work of art, nor the utility of a topographical dictionary.

15. Of Drayton's personal history we know almost nothing ; but when we come to speak of **John Donne**, the image of a strange wayward life, actuated evermore by a morbid restlessness of the intellect, rises to our thoughts.   This man, whose youthful *Epithalamia* are tainted by a gross sensuality, ended his career as the grave and learned Dean of St. Paul's whose sermons furnish the text for pages of admiring commentary to S. T. Coleridge.[2]   One fancies him a man with a high forehead, but false wavering eye, whose subtlety, one knows, will make any cause that he takes up seem for the moment unimpeachable, but of whose moral genuineness in the different phases he assumes,—of whose sincere love of truth as truth,—one has incurable doubts.   As a writer, the great popularity which he enjoyed in his own day has long since given way before the repulsive harshness and involved obscurity of his style.   The painful puns, the far-fetched similes, the extravagant metaphors, which in

---

[1] See Crit. Sect. ch. I., *Descriptive Poetry.*   [2] In the *Literary Remains*, vol. iii.

Shakspere occur but as occasional blemishes, form the substance of the poetry of Donne; if they were taken out, very
little would be left.   He is the earliest poet of the fantastic or
metaphysical school, of which we shall have more to say in the
next chapter. The term ' metaphysical,' first applied to the school
by Johnson, though not inappropriate, is hardly distinctive
enough. It is not inappropriate, because the philosophizing spirit
pervades their works, and it is the activity of the intellect,
rather than that of the emotions, by which they are characterized.   The mind, the nature of man, any faculty or virtue
appertaining to the mind, and even any external phenomenon,
can hardly be mentioned without being analysed, without
subtle hair-splitting divisions and distinctions being drawn out,
which the poet of feeling could never stop to elaborate.   But
this is equally true of a great deal that Shakspere (especially
in his later years), and even that Milton has written, whom yet
no one ever thought of including among the metaphysical poets.
It is the tendency to conceits,—that is, to an abuse of the imaginative faculty, by tracing resemblances that are fantastic, or
uncalled for, or unseemly—which really distinguishes this school
from other schools.   This point will be further illustrated in
connection with the poetry of Cowley.

Donne's poems are generally short; they consist of elegies,
funeral elegies, satires, letters, divine poems, and miscellaneous
songs.   Besides these, he wrote *Metempsychosis, or the Progress
of the Soul,* a poem published in 1601 ; ' of which,' Jonson told
Drummond, in 1618, ' he now, since he was made Doctor, re-
penteth highlie, and seeketh to destroy all his poems.' In a
man of so much mind, it cannot be but that fine lines and stanzas
occasionally relieve the mass of barbarous quaintness.   Take,
for instance, the following stanza from the *Letter* to Sir H.
Wotton :—

> Believe me, Sir, in my youth's giddiest days,
> When to be like the court was a player's praise,
> Plays were not so like courts, as courts like plays ;

or this, from the letter to R. Woodward :—

> We are but farmers of ourselves, yet may,
> If we can stock ourselves and thrive, up-lay
> Much, much good treasure 'gainst the great rent day.

16. Towards the end of the century a serious reflecting mood
seems to have been the prevailing temper in the educated part
of the nation : our writers loved to dive or soar into abstruse
and sublime speculations.   Among the noblest memorials of

this philosophic bent, is the *Nosce Teipsum* of **Sir John Davies**, Attorney-General for Ireland,—a poem on the soul of man, which it aims to prove immaterial and immortal. It is in the heroic quatrain or four-lined stanza, with alternate rimes, a metre afterwards employed by Davenant, Dryden, and Gray. The philosophy is Christian and Platonic, as opposed to the systems of the materialist and Epicurean. The versification is clear, sonorous, and full of dignity. There is a passage at the end of the introduction which curiously resembles the celebrated meditation in Pascal's *Pensées* upon the greatness and littleness which are conjoined in man :—

> I know my body's of so frail a kind
> As force without, fevers within, can kill;
> I know the heavenly nature of my mind,
> But 'tis corrupted both in wit and will:
>
> I know my soul hath power to know all things,
> Yet is she blind and ignorant in all;
> I know I'm one of Nature's little kings,
> Yet to the least and vilest things am thrall:
>
> I know my life's a pain, and but a span:
> I know my sense is mock'd in every thing;
> And to conclude, I know myself a man,
> Which is a proud, and yet a wretched thing.

17. **George Chapman** and **John Marston** belonged to the same literary set, about which unhappily we know so little, that included Shakspere and Ben Jonson. As a second-rate dramatist, Chapman will receive some notice further on; here a few words must be said about his translation of the *Iliad*, which appeared about 1601. It is written in the same metre as Warner's *Albion's England*, but always printed in long fourteen-syllable riming lines. Considered as exhibiting imaginative power and rapidity of movement, this version does not ill represent the original; the Elizabethan poets well understood how to make words the musical symbols of ideas, and were not given to dawdle or falter on their way. But the simplicity and dignity of the original,—in other words, the points which constitute the unapproached *elevation* of Homer in poetry and art,—these were characteristics which it was beyond the reach of Chapman to reproduce.[1] Still, considering the time at which it appeared, and that this was the first complete metrical version of the *Iliad* in any modern language, it was truly a surprising and

[1] See the Lectures of my brother, the late Professor of Poetry, *On Translating Homer.*

a gallant venture, and well typifies the intensity of force with
which the English intellect, at this strange period, was working
in every direction.

18. **Marston** is the author of five separate satires (1598),
besides three books of satires, collectively named *The Scourge
of Villanie* (1599). The separate satires are not without merit,
as the passage given above (p. 179), which was taken from the
fourth of them, might prove. The second contains an attack on
the Puritans, who first appeared a few years before this time as
a separate party. A Puritan citizen, who said grace for half an
hour, but was a griping usurer, is thus satirized :—

> No Jew, no Turke, would use a Christian
> So inhumanely as this Puritan.
> * * * * * *
> Take heed, O worlde ! take heed advisedly,
> Of these same damnèd anthropophagi.
> I had rather be within an harpie's clawes
> Than trust myself in their devouring jawes,
> Who all confusion to the world would bring
> Under the forme of their new discipline.

The Scourge of Villanie is much inferior to the separate satires.
The author gloats over the immoralities which he pretends to
scourge in a manner which forces one to think of 'Satan re-
proving sin.' All is invective; those delightful changes of hand,
with which Horace wanders back to the scenes of his boyhood,
or gives us his opinion of Lucilius, or sketches the poetical character, or playfully caricatures the Stoic philosophy, are not for
the imitation of such blundering matter-of-fact satirists as Hall,
or Donne, or Marston; with them satire is satire : they begin
to call names in the first line, and, with the tenacity of their
country's bull-dogs, continue to worry their game down to the
very end.

19. **George Gascoigne**, a Cambridge man, is known as the
author of a satire called *The Steele Glas*, published in 1576, and
dedicated to Lord Grey of Wilton. In the dedication he speaks
of himself as one who had 'misgoverned his youth,' but had resolved to take to industry in his riper age. The first part of the
poem, which is in blank verse, is in the style of an old morality.
Satyra, the sister of Poesy, sees the latter married to Vain Delight; she cries out against him, and he cuts out her tongue with
the 'Raysor of Restraynte.' Yet she can still with the stump
of her tongue make some imperfect sound ; and she will now
inveigh against the age, because in its pride it refuses to see
itself truly in the mirrors which are its delight ; she will hold
up before its eyes the *steel glass* of Lucilius, not the crystal glass ;

for this last he bequeathed to those who like to seem rather than to be; but the steel glass to those who wish to see themselves just as they are, whether foul or fair. A general invective against society, and its different classes and orders, succeeds; parts of which are spirited and forcible, but, for want of defined and personal interest, it loses itself in the vague. At last Satire sees in the glass a number of praying priests, to whom she addresses various counsels and requests, admonishing them finally not to cease praying till the time comes when the swarming abuses of the land shall cease :—

> When Lais lives not like a ladie's peare [peer],
> Nor useth art in dying of her heare.

20. The sonnets, songs, and canzonets of **Sir Philip Sidney** are imitated from Italian and Spanish models, but they are freighted by his powerful mind with a burden of thought and passion almost too great for such slight structures to bear: 'gemuit sub pondere cymba sutilis.' *Astrophel and Stella* consists of a hundred and eight love sonnets, with songs interspersed. Astrophel is Sidney; by Stella Lady Rich was meant. As Penelope Devereux she had shone as a leading beauty in Elizabeth's corrupt court; Sidney loved her, but spoke too late; and she became the wife of a man whom she did not love, Lord Rich. Sidney's passion mastered him, and for two years he gave way to a guilty love : it is the one stain on his lofty character. He afterwards married Frances, daughter of Walsingham, the Secretary of State. Three years after his marriage, in 1586, he fell at Zutphen.

Sidney's sonnets are not inartificial, like Shakspere's, but framed upon the right Petrarcan model. In *Astrophel and Stella* let the reader note particularly the fourth :—

> Virtue, alas ! now let me take some rest;

and the eighty-fourth :—

> High-way, since you my chief Parnassus be.

Among his 'Sonnets and Translations' occurs a beautiful poem to which neither name is applicable; it seems to have been written soon after Penelope's marriage. The Shaksperian cast of the thought and imagery is remarkable :—

> Ring out your bells, let mourning shews be spread,
>   For Love is dead :
> All Love is dead, infected
>   With plague of deep disdain :
> Worth, as nought worth, rejected,
>   And Faith fair scorn doth gain.

From so ungrateful fancy;
From such a female frenzy;
From them that use men thus,
Good Lord, deliver us.
  *   *   *   *   *   *

Let dirge be sung, and Trentals rightly read,
  For Love is dead:
Sir Wrong his tomb ordaineth
  My mistress' marble heart;
Which epitaph containeth,
  Her eyes were once his dart.
    From so ungrateful, &c.

Alas! I lye: Rage hath this error bred;
  Love is not dead, but sleepeth
In her unmatched mind:
  Where she his counsel keepeth
Till due deserts she find.
    Therefore from so vile fancy,
    To call such wit a frenzy,
    Who Love can temper thus,
    Good Lord, deliver us.

21. **Thomas Tusser,** a native of Essex, after trying various
callings, turned his hand to farming, and while struggling with
a Suffolk farm, which proved more than a match for him,
published (about 1558) *Five Hundreth Pointes of good Hus-
bandrie, as well for the Champion or open Countrie, as also for
the Woodland or Severall.* The versification is mean and rough;
it is rather favourably represented by the following sample:—

The sun in the southe, or else southlie and west,
Is joie to the hop, as a welcomed guest;
But wind in the north, or else northerlie east,
To the hop is as ill as a fraie in a feast.

Stillingfleet (quoted in Warton's *History of Poetry*) says of
Tusser: ' He throws his precepts into a calendar, and gives
many good rules in general, both in relation to agriculture and
economy; and had he not written in miserable hobbling
and obscure verse, might have rendered more service to his
countrymen.'

22. **Christopher Marlowe,** who for his rare gift of expression might fitly be called the Keats of the sixteenth century,
was born at Canterbury in 1564. Like Keats he was of humble
birth,—the son of a shoemaker; like him he was cut off by an
untimely death. Of his plays we shall hereafter speak; among
his few poems and translations, the fragment of *Hero and Leander*
is remarkable for the exquisite grace and melody of the verse.
As completed by Chapman, the poem has six books, called
' Sestiads;' of these only the first two, and small portions of

the others, are by Marlowe.   Though founded on a Greek poem
of the pseudo-Musæus (a grammarian, who is supposed to have
lived in the fifth century after Christ), *Hero and Leander* has
more of the character of an original work than of a translation.
We will quote the beautiful passage, a line from which is put in
the mouth of Phebe by Shakspere in *As You Like It* (act iii.
sc. 5) :—

> It lies not in our power to love or hate,
> For will in us is over-ruled by fate.
> When two are stript, long ere the course begin,
> We wish that one should lose, the other win ;
> And one especially do we affect
> Of two gold ingots, like in each respect :
> The reason no man knows ; let it suffice,
> What we behold is censured by our eyes.
> Where both deliberate, the love is slight :
> Who ever loved, that loved not at first sight ?

Marlowe, after being known as one of the brightest wits at
Cambridge, launched into the stage-life of London.   According
to the common story, he was killed in a tavern brawl at Dept-
ford in 1593.   Puritan writers held up his death as a divine
judgment, sent to punish the laxity of his opinions.

23. **Sir Walter Raleigh**, the gay courtier, the gallant soldier,
the discoverer of Virginia, the father of English colonization,
the wily diplomatist, the learned historian, the charming poet,
—as he did everything else well by the force of that bright and
incomparable genius of his, so he is the author of a few beautiful and thoughtful poems.[1]   I am persuaded that he wrote *The
Lie*, for I do not believe that any one then living, except Shakspere, was so capable of having written it.[2]

24. Respecting the numerous tribe of translators who were
busy in the reign of Elizabeth ample details are given in the
fourth volume of Warton's ‘History of Poetry.’   Before 1600,
Homer, the pseudo-Musæus, Virgil, Horace, Ovid, and Martial,
were translated into English verse ;   most of the versions appeared
before 1580.   Thomas Phaier brought out seven books of the
Æneid, in the fourteen-syllable or Sternhold metre, in 1558.   A
ridiculous version of four books, executed by Richard Stanihurst,
in English hexameters, to be read and scanned in the same way

---

[1] Printed at the end of vol. viii. of the Oxford edition of Raleigh's Works.
[2] The evidence is not conclusive either way ; it certainly was not written
the night before his execution,' according to the common story, because it
had appeared in Davison's *Poetical Rhapsody* in 1602 ; but Raleigh's name
was given by the printer as one of the contributors to the *Rhapsody*, and to
him, above all the other contributors, in my opinion at least, may *The Lie* most
reasonably be assigned.

as the Latin, appeared in 1583. Abraham Fleming, in 1575 and 1589, published versions in the same metre of the Bucolics and Georgics. Of Chapman's version of Homer we have already spoken. Thomas Drant published in 1566-7 versions of the Satires, Epistles, and Ars Poetica of Horace. In 1575 Arthur Golding brought out a complete version, in fourteen-syllable lines, of Ovid's Metamorphoses ; this remained popular for many years. Marlowe made a version of Ovid's Elegies which was burnt by Archbishop Whitgift's order in 1599. The Heroical Epistles of the same author were englished by George Turberville. Marlowe also left a version, in blank verse, of the first book of Lucan's Pharsalia.

Dramatists :—Origin of the English Drama ; Miracle Plays ; Moral Plays ; Udall, Still, Heywood, Sackville and Norton, Marlowe ; the Dramatic Unities ; Shakspere, Jonson, Beaumont and Fletcher, Greene, Peele, Nash, Massinger, Ford, Webster, Marston, Chapman, Dekker, T. Heywood, Rowley, Tourneur, Shirley.

25. What we have to say on the development of the drama in this period may best be prefaced by a brief sketch of its rise and progress in the middle ages.

Five distinct influences or tendencies are traceable as having co-operated, in various degrees and ways, in the development of the drama. These are: 1, the didactic efforts of the clergy ; 2, mediæval philosophy ; 3, the revival of ancient learning ; 4, the influence of the feeling of nationality ; 5, the influence of continental literature, especially that of Italy.

26. The first rude attempts in this country to revive those theatrical exhibitions, which, in their early and glorious forms, had been involved in the general destruction of the ancient world, were due to the clergy. They arose out of a perception that what we see with our eyes makes a greater impression upon us than what we merely hear with our ears. It was seen that many events in the life of Christ, as well as in the history of the Christian Church, would easily admit of being dramatized, and thus brought home, as it were, to the feelings and consciences of large bodies of men more effectually than by sermons. As to books, they of course were, at the time now spoken of, accessible only to an insignificant minority. The early plays which thus arose were called 'miracles,' or 'miracle plays,' because miraculous narratives, taken from Scripture or from the lives of the saints, formed their chief subject.

The earliest known specimens of these miracle plays, according to Mr. Wright,[1] were composed in Latin by one Hilarius, an English monk, and a disciple of the famous Abelard, in the early part of the twelfth century. The subjects of these are the raising of Lazarus, a miracle of St. Nicholas, and the life of Daniel. Similar compositions in French date from the thirteenth century; but Mr. Wright does not believe that any were composed in English before the fourteenth. The following passage, from Dugdale's *Antiquities of Warwickshire*, will give a general notion of the mode in which they were performed. It relates to the famous *Coventry Mysteries*, of which a nearly complete set has been preserved, and published by the Shakespeare Society :—

Before the suppression of the monasteries, this cittye was very famous for the pageants that were played therein, upon Corpus Christi day. These pageants were acted with mighty state and reverence by the fryers of this house (the Franciscan monastery at Coventry), and conteyned the story of the New Testament, which was composed into old English rime. The theatres for the severall scenes were very large and high; and being placed upon wheels, were drawn to all the eminent places of the cittye, for the better advantage of the spectators.

These travelling show-vans remind one of Thespis, the founder of Greek tragedy, who is said to have gone about in his theatrical cart, from town to town, exhibiting his plays. According to older authorities, the movable theatre itself was originally signified by the term 'pageant,' not the piece performed in it. The *Coventry Mysteries* were performed in Easter week. The set which we have of them is divided into forty-two parts, or scenes, to each of which its own 'pageant,' or moving theatre, was assigned. Traversing, by a prescribed round, the principal streets of the city, each pageant stopped at certain points along the route, and the actors whom it contained, flinging open the doors, proceeded to perform the scenes allotted to them. Stage properties and gorgeous dresses were not wanting; we even meet, in the old corporation accounts, with such items as money advanced for the effective exhibition of hell-fire. Two days were occupied in the performance of the forty-two scenes, and a person standing at any one of the appointed halting-places would be able to witness the entire drama. The following passage presents a fair sample of the roughness of style and homeliness of conception which characterize these mysteries throughout; it is taken from the pageant of the 'Temptation :'—

[1] Introduction to the *Chester Plays*, published for the Shakespeare Society.

'Now if thou be Goddys Sone of might,
  Ryght down to the erthe anon thou falle,
And save thisylf in every plyght
  From harm and hurt and peinys alle;
For it is wretyn, aungelys bright
  That ben in hevyn, thy faderes halle,
Thee to kepe bothe day and nyght,
  Xal be ful redy as thi tharalle,
    Hurt that thou non have:
That thou stomele not ageyn the stone,
And hurt thi fote as thou dost gon,
Aungelle be ready all everychon
    In weyes thee to save.'

'It is wretyn in holy book,
  Thi Lord God thou shalt not tempte ;
All things must obey to Goddys look,
  Out of His might is non exempt;
Out of thi cursydness and cruel crook
  By Godys grace man xal be redempt ;—
Whan thou to helle, thi brennynge brooke,
  To endles peyne xal evyn be dempt,
    Therein alwey to abyde.   &c. &c.

27. The philosophy of the middle ages, which we have named
as the second influence co-operating to the development of the
drama, dealt much in abstract terms, and delighted in definitions
and logical distinctions.   Debarred, partly by external hindrances, partly by its own inexperience, from profitable inquiry
into nature and her laws, the mind was thrown back upon itself,
its own powers, and immediate instruments ; and the fruits
were, an infinite number of metaphysical cobwebs, logical
subtleties, and quips or plays upon words.   Thus, instead of
proceeding onward from the dramatic exhibition of scriptural
personages and scenes to that of real life and character, the
mediæval playwrights perversely went backwards, and refined
away the scriptural personages into mere moral abstractions.
Thus, instead of the Jonathan and Satan of the mystery, we
come to the Friendship and the Vice of the moral play, or morality,—a dramatic form which seems to have become popular
in this country about the middle of the fifteenth century.   How
far this folly would have gone it is impossible to say; fortunately
it was cut short by the third influence mentioned—the revival
of ancient learning.   When the plays of Terence and Sophocles,
nay, even those of Seneca, became generally known, none but a
pedant or a dunce could put up with the insufferable dulness of
a moral play.
28. The earliest known English comedy, *Ralph Roister
Doister*, bears plain marks of the power of this new influence.

Its author was **Nicholas Udall**, master of Eton College; the exact date of its publication is unknown, but it was certainly composed before 1551. It is written in jingling rhyme, the lines being usually of twelve syllables, though frequently shorter. It is divided into acts and scenes, like those plays of Plautus and Terence of which it is a professed imitation. The following is an outline of the plot, which is managed with considerable skill. The heroine, Dame Christian Custance, is betrothed to a merchant, Gawin Goodluck, who is absent on a voyage. Ralph Roister Doister, who is an idler about town and a silly vain fellow, meets her and falls in love with her. His courtship proceeds with·many ludicrous turns and incidents,—the lady spurning it, while Mathew Merrygreek, a sort of follower of Ralph, pretends to further it, but in fact loses no chance of making a fool of his patron. Gawin returns, and after some difficulty, the circumstances of his rival's supposed favourable treatment being all explained, the lovers come to an understanding, the wedding-day is fixed, and Ralph is invited to the marriage.

29. *Gammer Gurton's Needle* and *Misogonus*, both probably composed before 1560, are comedies of the same kind, but of still ruder workmanship. In the first the plot amounts to no more than this : Gammer Gurton has lost her needle in mending the nether garments of her servant Hodge, and after everything has been thrown into confusion, and several persons falsely accused of stealing it, the needle is found just in the place where it might have been expected to be, that is, in the garment itself. The metre is the same as that of *Ralph Roister Doister*; the object of the writers evidently being to reproduce, so far as they could, the effect of the rough iambic senarii of Plautus and Terence. Our dramatists at this period had sufficient sense to admire the ancients, but not enough to make them despise themselves and their own productions. The more flexible French genius had already begun to follow the advice of the poet Du Bellay, who, writing in the year 1548, says : ' Translation is not a sufficient means to elevate our vernacular speech to the level of the most famous languages. What must we do then? Imitate! imitate the Romans as they imitated the Greeks; as Cicero imitated Demosthenes, and Virgil Homer. We must transform the best authors into ourselves, and, after having digested them, convert them into blood and nutriment.' Yet, on the other hand, the sturdy English independence brought with it countervailing advantages; but for it, the Elizabethan literature, while gaining perhaps in polish and correctness, would have lost tenfold more in the free play

of thought, in exuberance and boldness of conception, and in that display of creative genius which invents new forms for modern wants.

30. Before the appearance of comedies properly so called, a sort of intermediate style was introduced by John Heywood, jester and musician at the court of Henry VIII. He produced several short plays which he called Interludes. The name had been in use for some time, and merely signified a dramatic piece performed in the intervals of a banquet, court pageant, or other festivity. Moral plays are thus frequently described by their authors as Interludes. But the novel character of Heywood's plays, and the popularity which they obtained, caused the name of Interlude to be, after his time, reserved for plays of similar aim and construction. The novelty consisted in this: that whereas, in a Moral play, the characters are personified qualities (Felicity, False Semblance, Youth, &c.), in an Interlude they are true persons, but not yet individuals;—they are the representatives of classes. Thus, in Heywood's clever interlude of *The Four P's*, the leading characters are, the Pedlar, the Palmer, the Pardoner, and the Poticary. In another, one of the characters is even named; this is *A Mery Play betwene the Pardonere and the Frere, the Curate and Neighbour Pratte.*

No comedies worthy of mention appeared after the time of Udall and Still for more than twenty years,—not till the time of Greene, Peele, and Marlowe, the immediate predecessors and contemporaries of Shakspere.

31. The earliest known tragedy was brought upon the stage in 1562, under the title of *Gorboduc* or *Ferrex and Porrex*. It was jointly composed by Sackville, afterwards Lord Buckhurst, and Thomas Norton, a Puritan lawyer. It is the first English drama of any kind written in blank verse. The subject, like that of Shakspere's *King Lear*, is taken from the fabulous British annals, originally compiled by Geoffrey of Monmouth in the twelfth century, and innocently copied into the histories of most of the chroniclers down to the time of Milton. The writers were educated men, and it seems probable that they chose an episode taken from the legendary history of Britain as the subject of their tragedy, in imitation of the Greek tragedians, whose constant storehouse of materials was the mythical traditions of Greece. Similarly Milton thought of writing an epic poem on the legend of Arthur and his knights. But this play bears witness also to the influence of the fourth tendency noted above—the desire to deepen and justify the pride of English nationality. The play is full of allusions to the present state of things, enforcing the advantages of peace and settled government, the evils of popular risings and a disputed succession. The same design of illustrating the present by the past is apparent in an old play written so far back as the last years of

O

Henry VIII., the *Kynge Johan* of Bishop Bale, a piece holding an intermediate position between the moral play and the regular drama, some of the situations and ideas of which are, possibly, through the medium of a later play on the same subject published in 1591, worked up in the *King John* of Shakspere. But our first truly historical play seems to have been the *Life of Edward II.*, by Christopher Marlowe. Mr. Hallam calls it ' by far the best,' after [the historical plays of] Shakspere.'

32. The appearance of Marlowe's tragedy of *Tamburlaine the Great*, in 1586, makes an epoch in the history of the English drama. Blank verse is used in it with so much force and ingenuity that from that time the adoption of this as the regular dramatic measure was a settled · question. The gorgeous language, the rants, the bombast, the Asiatic pomp, which deck this dramatic presentation of the Tartar conqueror, though they provoked Shakspere to good-natured satire,[1] did not prevent the play from making an extraordinary impression. Nor was this unpopularity undeserved. ' This play,' says Mr. Hallam, ' has more spirit and poetry than any which upon clear grounds can be shown to have preceded it. We find also more action on the stage, a shorter and more dramatic dialogue, a more figurative style, with a far more varied and skilful versification.'

Marlowe's greatest work, *The Tragedy of Dr. Faustus*, has attracted much attention of late years, owing to the celebrity with which Goethe's great work has invested the old story. Mr. Hazlitt, though deeming it ' an imperfect and unequal performance,' does justice to its power. ' Faustus himself,' he says, ' is a rude sketch, but it is a gigantic one. This character may be considered as a personification of the pride of will and eagerness of curiosity sublimed beyond the reach of fear and remorse. He is hurried away, and, as it were, devoured by a tormenting desire to enlarge his knowledge to the utmost bounds of nature and art, and to extend his power with his knowledge. He would realize all the fictions of a lawless imagination, would solve the most subtle speculations of abstract reason; and for this purpose sets at defiance all mortal consequences, and leagues himself with demoniacal power, with "fate and metaphysical aid." Faustus, in his impatience to fulfil at once and for a moment, for a few short years, all the desires and conceptions of his soul, is willing to give in exchange his soul and body to the great enemy of mankind.'

33. The fondness for seeing the past history of the nation exhibited in dramatic show, conduced, more than any other single cause, to that constant neglect of the dramatic ' unities ' for which our English play-writers are conspicuous. This, therefore, is the place to explain what those unities were, and how our early tragedians came to violate them.

Aristotle, in his *Treatise on Poetry*, collects from the practice of the Greek dramatists certain rules of art, as necessary to be observed, in order that any tragedy may have its full

---

[1] *Henry IV.*, Part II., Act II., Sc. 4.

effect upon the audience. The chief of these relates to the action represented, which, he says, must be *one, complete,* and *important.* This rule has been called the Unity of Action. He also says that tragedy ' for the most part endeavours to conclude itself within one revolution of the sun, or nearly so.' This rule, limiting the time during which the action represented takes place to twenty-four hours, or thereabouts, has been called the Unity of Time. A third rule, not expressly mentioned by Aristotle, but nearly always observed by the Greek tragedians, requires that the entire action shall be transacted in the same locality; this is called the Unity of Place. These three rules were carefully observed by the first Italian tragedians, Rucellai and Trissino ; and also in France, when the drama took root there. In Spain and in England they were neglected, and apparently for the same reason—that both peoples were fervently national, and intensely self-conscious ; and therefore, in order to gratify them, the drama tended to assume the historic form— a form which necessitates the violation of the unities.[1] Marlowe, in his historical tragedy of *Edward II.*, and Shakspere, in his ten historical plays, proceed upon this principle. Shakspere, however, when he wrote to gratify his own taste rather than that of the public, so far showed his recognition of the soundness of the old classical rules, that in the best of his tragedies he carefully observed the unity of action, although he judged it expedient, perhaps with reference partly to the coarser perceptions of his audience, to sacrifice those lesser congruities of place and time which the sensitive Athenian taste demanded, to the requirements of a wider, though looser, conception of the ends of dramatic art.

34. Marlowe, Peele, Greene, Nash, and Lodge, were all young men together, and all writing for the London stage between the years 1585 and 1593. They had all received a university education, and as brother wits and boon companions were on terms of the freest intimacy. But an interloper, an upstart, a mere provincial who had never seen the inside of a college, worse than all, a *player*, who ought to have deemed it sufficient honour to perform the plays which these choice spirits condescended to write, had come up from Warwickshire to confound them all. The grievance is thus alluded to by Greene, in a curious pamphlet called *A Groat's Worth of Wit*, written just before his death in 1592. Addressing three of his brother dramatists, supposed to be Marlowe, Lodge, and Peele, he says : ' Is it not strange that I to whom they [the players] all have

---

[1] See Critical Section, ch. I., *Dramatic Poetry.*

o 2

been beholding—is it not like that you, to whom they all have been beholding, shall, were ye in that case that I am now, be both of them at once forsaken? Yes, trust them not; for there is an upstart crow, beautified with our feathers, that, with his tiger's heart wrapped in a player's hide, supposes he is as well able to bombast out a blank verse as the best of you; and being an absolute Johannes factotum, is in his own conceit *the only Shake-scene in a country.*' We shall have occasion to examine into the meaning of Greene's charge presently. From this passage, besides other slight indications pointing the same way, it may be concluded that Shakspere (for no one has ever doubted that the allusion is aimed at him) had begun to employ himself in dramatic writing before 1592, that he moved in a different circle in society from that which was formed by the educated wits and *literati* of London, and that he had been busy in adapting other men's plays for production at his own theatre.

35. Every one knows how few and meagre are the known facts of Shakspere's biography. ' The two greatest names in poetry,' says Mr. Hallam, ' are to us little more than names. If we are not yet come to question his unity, as we do that of "the blind old man of Scio's rocky isle," an improvement in critical acuteness doubtless reserved for a distant posterity, we as little feel the power of identifying the young man who came up from Stratford, was afterwards an indifferent player in a London theatre, and retired to his native place in middle life, with the author of *Macbeth* and *Lear*, as we can give a distinct historic personality to Homer. . . . It is not the register of his baptism, or the draft of his will, or the orthography of his name, that we seek. No letter of his writing, no record of his conversation, no character of him drawn with any fulness by a contemporary, has been produced.'

Such as they are, however, the chief of those particulars which untiring research has either firmly established or placed on the level of strong probabilities, must here be related. **William Shakspere** was born at Stratford-upon-Avon, in April 1564. He received, so far as we know, no better education than the grammar school of the place afforded; and soon after he had reached his twentieth year, was drawn up to London, probably through the influence of his friend Richard Burbage, a leading actor of the day, and himself a Warwickshire man. Shakspere's name stands twelfth in a list still extant, of the date of 1589, containing the names of sixteen players, who were at the same time joint proprietors of the Blackfriars Theatre. In a similar list, dated in 1596, he stands fourth, having evidently in the interval attained to a much more important position in the partnership. At this latter date the company were in possession, not only of their old theatre at the Blackfriars, but of a new one by the riverside, called the Globe Theatre, which they used for summer performances. Already, before 1592, besides altering old plays, Shakspere had written several independent dramas, to be performed by his company. In 1598—as we learn from a passage in Meres' *Wit's Treasury* published in that year—at least twelve of his plays had appeared; namely, the comedies of the *Two Gentlemen of Verona, Love's Labour's Lost, The Comedy of Errors, Love's Labour Won* (supposed to be *All's Well that Ends Well*), *Midsummer Night's Dream*, and *The Merchant of Venice*; the historical plays of *Richard II., Richard III., Henry IV.*, and *King John*, and the tragedies of *Titus Andronicus* and *Romeo and Juliet*. Shakspere prospered in his profession ; he amassed a considerable fortune, which we find him to have invested in houses and lands at Stratford, whither he retired to live at his ease some years before his death in 1616. During this retirement, he probably wrote the three Roman plays, *Julius Cæsar, Antony and Cleopatra*, and *Coriolanus*.

36. Out of thirty-five plays which Shakspere has left us (excluding *Titus Andronicus*, and *Pericles, Prince of Tyre*, and waiving the difficult question as to his connection with the three parts of *Henry VI.*), fourteen are comedies, eleven tragedies, and ten histories. With reference to Shakspere, the term ' comedy ' simply denotes a play that ends happily ; but it may have abounded, in the development of the plot, with serious and pathetic incidents. This intermediate style was afterwards called by Fletcher ' tragi-comedy,' a term which he appropriated to those plays in which the final issue of the plot is for good, yet in which, while that issue remains in suspense, some of the principal personages are brought so near to destruction that the true tragic interest is excited. Eighteen of the plays of Beaumont and Fletcher answer to this description ; which would also obviously apply to *Measure for Measure, The Merchant of Venice*, or *Winter's Tale*.

37. The influence of the fifth developing cause mentioned above, viz., the study of continental literature, is apparent at once when we turn to Shakspere's comedies. Ariosto's two comedies, the *Cassaria* and the *Suppositi*, first acted in 1512, were, like our own *Roister Doister*, formed upon ancient models; but they were written in flowing blank verse, and in a language already polished and beautiful ; circumstances which, apart from the genius of the writer, would go far to account for the great

popularity which they obtained.   They were translated into
English by George Gascoigne; and it is probable that to these
and other Italian comedies Shakspere owed much.   That he
was well read in Italian tales is certain, since from such tales
the plots of no fewer than six of his comedies were derived.
One, *Love's Labour's Lost*, comes presumably from a French
source; and one, *The Two Gentlemen of Verona*, from a Spanish
source.   But, after all, it is a matter of little consequence from
what source his materials were derived: whether they were
coarse or fine, his transforming touch changed them all alike
into gold; and so infinitely superior are the very earliest in date
of his comedies to any that had appeared before, that one might
truly call all such pieces, even as *The Taming of a Shrew*,[1] and
Greene's *Orlando Furioso*—much more, of course, the performances of Udall and Still—mere rough drafts, or attempts at the
comic style, and say that English comedy really commences with
Shakspere.   Nothing strikes one more than the comparative
simplicity and purity of style even in his early plays.   The dramatists of the day were mostly men who had received a university education, and they seem to have thought that unless
they gave abundant proof of their college learning in their plays,
people would hold them cheap.   So, with the grossest disregard
to dramatic fitness, the speeches of nearly all their characters
are stuffed full with high-flown classical allusions, introducing
us to all the gods of Olympus, and all the principal places of
the world as known to the ancients.   A few lines from the
old *Taming of a Shrew* may serve by way of illustration:—

> Sweet Kate, thou lovelier than Diana's purple robe,
> Whiter than are the snowy Apennines,
> Or icy hair that grows on Boreas' chin.
> Father, I swear by Ibis' golden beak,
> More fair and radiant is my bonny Kate
> Than silver Xanthus, when he doth embrace
> The ruddy Simois at Ida's feet: &c.

The speaker in these lines is Ferando, the character in the
old play corresponding to Shakspere's Petruchio.   If we turn
to Shakspere's play, we see that he, too, makes Petruchio
compare Kate to Diana; but mark the difference:—

> *Pet.*   Did ever Dian so become a grove
>   As Kate this chamber with her princely gait?
>   O be thou Dian, and let her be Kate;
>   And then let Kate be chaste and Dian sportful.
> *Kate.* Where did you study all this goodly speech?
> *Pet.*   It is extempore, from my mother wit.

---

[1] Upon this old play, which Mr. Knight conjectures to have been the work
of Greene, Shakspere modelled his *Taming of* THE *Shrew*.

This is no more than might be naturally and fitly put in the mouth of the eccentric gentleman from Verona, while the former passage is mere rant and fustian. However, it cannot truthfully be denied that Shakspere, too, falls sometimes into extravagant and dramatically inappropriate language, though it is generally in the shape of quips, quibbles, puns, and metaphysical refinements, arising out of the very exuberance of his intellectual energy, that he sins against literary simplicity; very seldom indeed by decking out his verse with proper names, in the fashion above described. As to the surpassing grace, art, and truth to nature, which these comedies in various degrees exhibit, the limits of this work would be soon outstepped if we were to dwell on them.

38. The following list of the fourteen comedies, the titles of which are arranged in alphabetical order, shows the date at or about which they severally appeared, and the source (where it can be traced) from which the plot of each was derived:—

(1) *All's Well that ends Well.* Date uncertain, but before 1598, if the common supposition identifying this play with the *Love's Labour Won* of Meres be correct. The story is found in the ninth novel of the fourth day in Boccaccio's *Decameron*; but Shakspere probably took it from Paynter's *Palace of Pleasure* (1566), where the tale appears in English.

(2) *As You Like It.* Date about 1600. The plot is English, taken from Thomas Lodge's novel of *Rosalynde*, published in 1590.

(3) *Comedy of Errors.* Date about 1590; in any case one of Shakspere's earliest pieces. The plot is classical, being derived from the *Menæchmi* of Plautus, but through one or both of two English versions which had previously appeared.

(4) *Love's Labour's Lost.* One of the earliest of Shakspere's comedies; date before 1590. The source of the plot has never been discovered; perhaps it was Shakspere's own invention, stimulated by what he had heard of the 'Academes' in Italy, the members of some of which were quite flighty and enthusiastic enough to vow a three years' abstinence from female society, with fasting, vigils, and philosophy, like that to which Ferdinand and his three courtiers have bound themselves. Evidently this play and the *Sonnets* belong to the same period of Shakspere's life.

(5) *Measure for Measure.* Date uncertain; probably after 1607; a late play. The source of the plot is the *Promos and Cassandra* of George Whetstone, a play printed in 1578, but never acted. Whetstone found the story in a novel of Giraldi Cinthio; the plot is therefore Italian.

(6) *Merchant of Venice.* Date about 1594. Stephen Gosson, in his pamphlet *The School of Abuse* (1579), describes a play of his time, 'The Jew shown at the Bull,' which showed 'the greedinesse of worldly chusers, and bloody minds of usurers;' it seems likely, therefore, that this was an earlier play, now lost, containing both the main incidents of Shakspere's play, the choosing of the caskets, and the exaction of the pound of flesh. But for these two incidents earlier sources have been

found, one Italian, the other mediæval. The story of the bond and the pound of flesh has been found in a tale called *Il Pecorone*, by Fiorentino, printed in 1558; that of the caskets is in the *Gesta Romanorum*, No. 76.[1]

(7) *Merry Wives of Windsor*. First printed in 1602; but Mr. Knight believes that it was acted ten years earlier. The story is Shakspere's own invention; the manners, language, and characters are those of his own day. The Falstaff of this comedy is an inferior and notably different creation from the Falstaff of *Henry IV*.

(8) *Midsummer Night's Dream*. Date between 1593 and 1597. The materials for the story of this beautiful play were taken by Shakspere from various sources. Theseus, his queen Hippolyta, and their court at Athens, are borrowed from Chaucer's *Knight's Tale*. Puck and the fairies were part of the mystico-moral furniture of the popular mind in the Middle Ages. Harsnet's *Declaration of egregious Popish Impostures* (1603) speaks of 'Robin Good-fellow the frier, and Sisse the dairy-maid.' But no poet had made use of the conception before Shakspere. The name of Oberon comes from a translation by Lord Berners (1579) of the old French romance of *Huon and Auberon*. The name Titania seems to have been invented by Shakspere. Finally, the story of Pyramus and Thisbe was probably taken from Golding's version of Ovid's Metamorphoses (*ante*, § 24), though Shakspere might also have read it in Chaucer's *Legende of Good Women*.

(9) *Much Ado about Nothing*. Date about 1599; it was first printed in 1600. The story is Italian, taken from one of Bandello's novels, in which Fenicia and Timbreo represent the Hero and Claudio of the play.

(10) *Taming of the Shrew*. The original play of unknown authorship, *The Taming of a Shrew*, which Shakspere has followed pretty closely, was printed in 1594. Shakspere's play probably appeared about the same time; one cannot suppose that he would have stooped to this kind of appropriation in his later years. The story of the cure of the shrew is found in the *Notte Piacevole* of Straparola (1550), and in the *Conde Lucanor* of the Spanish author Juan Manuel. But the story is old and widely diffused; it has been traced to a Persian and also to an Old-German source.

(11) *The Tempest*. Date about 1611; it is one of the latest of the plays, though printed the first in the folio of 1623. Professor Ward thinks it probable that the source whence Shakspere derived the story was a German play, *Die schöne Sidea*, by Jacob Ayrer of Nürnberg, who died in 1605. Not that Shakspere could have read German, but that he might have heard of the play from English actors returning from Germany. Some of the details of the storm and the reference to the 'still vex'd Bermoothes' appear to be traceable to the *Discovery of the Bermudas, otherwise called the Isle of Divels*, by Silvester Jourdan, published in 1610.

(12) *Twelfth Night*. Date about 1601. The sources are, an Italian play called *Gli Inganni*, first printed in 1582, and a tale about twins by Bandello. But both the characterization and the plot are to a large extent original.

(13) *Two Gentlemen of Verona*. Date about 1598. The chief source of the play is the romantic novel called *Diana Enamorada*, by the

---

[1] See Sir F. Madden's *Old English Versions of the Gesta Romanorum*, edited for the Roxburghe Club, 1838.

Spanish author Montemayor; a version of this, by Bartholomew Yonge, was published in 1598, and was probably used by Shakspere.

(14) *Winter's Tale.* Date 1610 or 1611. The source of the play is Robert Greene's novel of *Pandosto, the Triumph of Time,* published in 1588.

39. Among the eleven tragedies are included some of the brightest and most wonderful achievements of the human intellect. In *Hamlet,* with its fearful background of guilt, and lingering, yet foreshadowed, retribution, we see the tragic results which follow from—in the words of Goethe—'a great action being laid upon a soul unfit for its performance;' the unfitness consisting, according to Coleridge, in the want of a due balance 'between the impressions from outward objects and the inward operations of the intellect; for if there be an overbalance in the contemplative faculty, man thereby becomes the creature of mere meditation, and loses his natural power of action.' In *Macbeth,* on the other hand, the action of the drama proceeds with a breathless rapidity; the first crime, engendered by that 'vaulting ambition which doth o'erleap itself,' necessitates the commission of others to avert the natural consequences of the first. A large part of a life is presented to our eyes in the light of one great gilded successful crime, until at last it topples over, and is quenched with the suddenness of an expiring rocket. In *King Lear,* with its ever thickening gloom and deepening sorrows, we see the tragic fate which, as the world of man is constituted, too often waits on folly no less than on guilt, and involves the innocent alike with the guilty in the train of terrible consequences. In *Othello,* the drama opens with all the elements of happiness; manly courage, beauty, truth, devoted love, are met together in the pair who have fought against all the powers of social prejudice in order to become one, and have conquered; yet all is marred by the fiendish wickedness of one man, who abuses the resources of a powerful intellect to practise on the open and impulsive nature of Othello, until he crushes in an access of volcanic passion the jewel which an instant after he would give the whole world to restore. In *Romeo and Juliet,* all that is beautiful and all that is excessive are brought together: the loveliness of the Italian sky; the youthful grace of the lovers; the fair palaces and moonlit gardens of Verona; the hereditary and unforgiving hatred of the two noble houses; the whirlwind of passionate love which unites their two last surviving scions in the inextricable bond of an affection stronger than all the hatreds of their ancestors; their final union in the tomb, beyond the reach of severance by angry fathers or the chances of time—these are the materials of a drama which

for pure literary beauty stands perhaps unsurpassed among intellectual creations. It is not, however, our purpose to attempt anything like a general critical analysis of these or any of Shakspere's plays; nor indeed is it necessary. Genius furnished the text, and men of the greatest intellectual gifts have supplied the commentary; the reader will thank us for referring him to their works, rather than attempting to substitute an inferior article of our own.[1]

40. Of the eleven plays of Shakspere which are usually classed as tragedies, two, *Cymbeline* and *Troilus and Cressida*, since they do not end tragically, do not properly deserve the name. We proceed to pass these plays in review, as in the case of the comedies:—

(1) *Antony and Cleopatra.* Date uncertain, but probably late (see § 35). The source of this and of the other Roman plays is the translation of Plutarch's *Lives*, made in 1579 by Sir Thomas North.

(2) *Coriolanus.* (See the preceding article.)

(3) *Cymbeline.* Date uncertain; it was acted in 1610 or 1611, but whether for the first time is not known. The character of Cymbeline was found by Shakspere in Holinshed, whose authority was Geoffrey of Monmouth. According to Geoffrey, 'Kymbelinus' was king of the Britons at the time of the Christian era, and had two sons, Guiderius and Arviragus. The story of Imogen is borrowed from that of Ginevra, in the ninth novel of the second day of the *Decameron*.

(4) *Hamlet.* The time when this great tragedy first appeared is a point still much disputed. A play called *Hamlet* was, according to an entry in Henslowe's Diary, acted at Newington in 1594. In a tract by Lodge entitled 'Wit's Miserie,' and printed in 1596, there is an allusion to 'the ghost which cried so miserably at the Theator like an oister wife, *Hamlet, revenge.*' Mr. Knight believes that this was the first draft of Shakspere's *Hamlet*, and that Lodge, quoting from memory, did not give the exact words used by the ghost in the play, but only the substance of them. Others hold that since no such words as 'Hamlet, revenge' occur in Shakspere's play, Lodge must have been alluding to a play by some other man. On this point we are inclined to go with Mr. Knight. However this may be, the *Hamlet* of Shakspere was certainly entered in the books of the Stationers' Company, as having been recently acted by the Lord Chamberlain's servants, in 1602. It was first printed in 1603. In the following year the play reappeared, with the following title-page: 'The Tragicall Historie of Hamlet, Prince of Denmark. By William Shakespeare. Newly imprinted and enlarged to almost as much againe as it was, according to the true and perfect coppie.' Substantially this quarto of 1604 and the *Hamlet* of the folio of 1623 are the same play, and are greatly expanded and altered from the edition of 1603.

The immediate source of the plot (unless there was an earlier play which Shakspere followed) is the *Cent Histoires Tragiques* of

---

[1] The works particularly referred to as most generally accessible, are Coleridge's *Literary Remains*, Augustus Schlegel's *Dramatic Literature*, the chapters on *Hamlet* in Goethe's *Wilhelm Meister*, and the works of Gervinus, Guizot, and Villemain.

Belleforest, probably in an English version. Belleforest took the story of Hamlet from the *Historia Danica* of Saxo Grammaticus, who flourished about the beginning of the 13th century. Saxo writes the name 'Amleth;' the queen he calls 'Gerutha.'

(5) *Julius Cæsar.* (See the article on *Antony and Cleopatra.*)

(6) *King Lear.* Date between 1603 and 1606. Shakspere found the story of Lear and his daughters in Holinshed's history; Holinshed took it from Geoffrey of Monmouth's Chronicle. In an amplified form it occurs in Laȝamon's *Brut.* Spenser also tells the story in the second book of the *Faerie Queene,* Canto 10. According to Geoffrey, Leir was the fourth king in descent from Brutus, the founder of the British monarchy.

(7) *Macbeth.* Date between 1603 and 1610. Shakspere took the main facts of the story from Holinshed's *History of Scotland.* Macbeth is no mythical personage, like Lear or Cymbeline; his expulsion from Scotland by Earl Siward in the reign of Edward the Confessor is mentioned in one of the *Saxon Chronicles,* and also by Florence of Worcester.

(8) *Othello.* Date about 1602, in which year it was played at Harefield before Queen Elizabeth. The source of the plot is Giraldi Cinthio's novel of *Il Moro di Venezia.*

(9) *Romeo and Juliet.* Date 1596 or 1597. The materials for this play were found by Shakspere in a novel of Bandello translated in Paynter's *Palace of Pleasure* (1567), and also in an English poem by Arthur Brooke founded on the said novel, and published, with the title 'The Tragicall Historye of Romeus and Juliet,' in 1562.

(10) *Timon of Athens.* Date uncertain; it has been assigned both to 1601 and to 1610. The principal source of the plot is the account of Timon the Athenian contained in Plutarch's life of Mark Antony. Another source, in Mr. Knight's opinion, was the Greek dialogue, 'Timon, or the Misanthrope,' by Lucian. Mr. Knight believes that the differences in style, and in the cast of thought, presented in this play are so remarkable as to justify the conclusion that it is not wholly the work of Shakspere.

(11) *Troilus and Cressida.* Date 1609. The materials are taken partly from classical, partly from mediæval sources. The characters of Thersites, Ajax, Menelaus, &c., seem to have been borrowed by Shakspere from Chapman's translation of Homer (1601), but the development is in great part his own. For the loves of Troilus and Cressida he was indebted to Chaucer's poem; but how different is Cryseyde from Cressida! The former, as we saw (ch. I. § 36), loves virtue and honour, but is weak; the latter—quick-witted and keen, without modesty or reverence, loose-tongued and loose-thoughted—is incapable of any affection save of one sort. Yet there are passages in this play as authentically stamped with the transcendent genius of Shakspere as anything which he ever wrote. Some materials seem also to have been furnished by Lydgate's Troy-book, and Caxton's *Recueil des Histoires de Troye.*

41. *Historical Plays.* In the literatures of Greece and Rome, it is not to the dramatic, but to the epic poetry that we must look for the exhibition of the peculiar pride and spirit of either nationality. Thus in the *Iliad,* as Mr. Gladstone has

eloquently shown,[1] the Greek character and the Greek religion
are forcibly and favourably contrasted with those of Asia; and
the *Æneid* is pervaded, as if by a perpetual under-song, by a
constant stream of allusion to the greatness of Rome.   In
English poetry this spirit of nationality has sought its expression
in the historical drama, and preeminently in the historical plays
of Shakspere.   It is a noble series; commencing, in the
chronological order, with *King John*, and ending with *Henry
VIII.*; omitting, however, the reigns of Henry III., the four
Edwards, and Henry VII.   The manful proud spirit of English
freedom is continually making itself visible; and foreign inter-
ference seems to be resented as such, from whatever quarter it
may come, and whether it relate to Church or to State affairs.
Thus in *King John* (act iii. sc. 1), he makes the king say to
Pandulph :—

> Thou canst not, cardinal, devise a name,
> So slight, unworthy, and ridiculous,
> To charge me to an answer as the pope.
> Tell him this tale; and from the mouth of England
> Add thus much more :—That no Italian priest
> Shall tithe or toll in our dominions;
> But as we under heaven are supreme head,
> So, under him, that great supremacy,
> Where we do reign, we will alone uphold,
> Without the assistance of a mortal hand.
> So tell the pope; all reverence set apart
> To him and his usurp'd authority.

And for a more general expression of the same feeling, take the
concluding passage of the same play :—

> This England never did nor never shall
> Lie at the proud foot of a conqueror,
> But when it first did help to wound itself.
> Now these her princes are come home again,
> Come the three corners of the world in arms,
> And we shall shock them.   Nought shall make us rue,
> If England to herself do rest but true.

As a matter of course, the unities of time and place are
disregarded in these historical plays.   The preservation even of
the unity of action, in a number of plays adhering pretty
faithfully to the order and manner of the events, is, as a general
rule, impossible; nor has Shakspere attempted it.   In *Henry
VIII.*, for instance, his object seems merely to have been to
present a succession of remarkable scenes, founded on occur-
rences which happened in the first thirty years of that

---

[1] In his work on *Homer and the Homeric Age.*

reign; these scenes are, the fall of Buckingham, the fall of Wolsey, the divorce and death of Queen Catherine, and the birth of Elizabeth. Patriotic feeling may be held to invest such a play in the spectator's mind, if only it be written in a lofty and worthy spirit, with a unity of design equal to any that art can frame. When, however, the events of a reign group themselves naturally into a dramatic whole, as in the case of Richard III., Shakspere does not lose the opportunity of still further heightening the effect by his art, and there is accordingly not one of his plays more closely bound together in all its parts by the development of one main action than this. The unscrupulous and fearless ambition of Richard III., so different from the same passion as it appears in the conscience-haunted Macbeth, crushes successively beneath his feet, by fair means or foul, all the obstacles in his path; till the general abhorrence, springing out of that very moral sense which Richard despised and denied, swells to such a height as to embrace all classes, and crushes his iron will and indomitable courage, his schemes, throne, and person, beneath a force yet more irresistible.

42. The 'Histories' are ten in number :—

(1, 2) *Henry IV.* In two parts. First printed in 1598, and probably written in the preceding year. *The Famous Victories of Henry V.*, a prose drama written about 1580, was the foundation upon which Shakspere worked, both in *Henry IV.* and in *Henry V.* It is a very poor piece; its Prince Hal is a mere drunken debauchee. In this old play Sir John Oldcastle occurs as one of the prince's companions, but plays no important part, even in the comic portions. Out of this character Shakspere created his incomparable Falstaff, who was called, in the first draft of both parts of *Henry IV.*, Sir John Oldcastle. The name was changed in deference to the Protestant feeling of the Londoners, who regarded the Lollard Oldcastle as a martyr.

The general source whence Shakspere drew materials, for this and for his other histories, is Holinshed's Chronicle.

(3) *Henry V.* Probable date 1599. The sources of this play are the same as those for *Henry IV.*

(4, 5, 6) *Henry VI.* In three parts. Part I. was first printed, so far as is known, in the folio of 1623. Part II. was published in 1594, under the title of the *First Part of the Contention of the two famous Houses of York and Lancaster*; and Part III. in 1595, with the title, *The true Tragedie of Richard Duke of Yorke, and the Death of good King Henrie the Sixt*. The principal source of all three plays is rather the Chronicle of Hall than that of Holinshed.

Since the question was first mooted by Edmund Malone, in his *Dissertation on the Three Parts of Henry VI.*, volumes have been written on the authenticity of these three plays. Malone endeavoured to prove that not one of the three was written by Shakspere; and in this conclusion Coleridge, Hallam, and Gervinus, with certain reservations, agree. On the other hand, Knight and the German critic, Ulrici, argue strongly for the authenticity of all three. It is chiefly a question of internal evidence; and my own opinion, coinciding with that of the impugners, is, that no one of these plays is, *as a whole*, the work of Shakspere, though each has undoubtedly been altered, retouched, and enlarged by him to an extent which it is sometimes easy and sometimes difficult to define. Of all three plays, I am disposed to believe that he had least to do with Part I., which treats of the leading events of the reign, especially those connected with the siege of Orleans and the exploits of Joan of Arc, from 1422 to 1445. In Part II., which covers the period from 1445 to 1455, most of the episode of Jack Cade may be unhesitatingly ascribed to Shakspere; and his hand may surely be traced in the recasting of the death-scene of Cardinal Beaufort, by which the tame and lack-lustre lines of the *First Contention* are transformed into a passage of unequalled sublimity and beauty. In Part III., which takes us to the murder of Henry in 1471, many of the speeches put in the king's mouth, Warwick's dying speech, and the whole of the last scene, appear to me to have been written by Shakspere.

(7) *Henry VIII.* Probable date 1613; a play of *Henry VIII.* was certainly acted at the Globe Theatre on June 29 of that year, and owing to the firing of cannon on the stage (according to the stage direction in act i. sc. 4) the thatch of the theatre caught fire, and it was burnt to the ground. The materials for the plot were supplied by Hall's Chronicle and Cavendish's Life of Wolsey; perhaps also by common tradition.

Of late years grave doubt has been thrown on the authenticity of this play; see a paper by Mr. Spedding, first printed in the *Gentleman's Magazine* for 1850, and reprinted in the Transactions of the New Shakspere Society. Indeed, anyone who has Shakspere's rhythm in his ear cannot but feel that the movement and ring of the verse in the greater part of the play (excepting the first act) are not Shaksperian. The mere abundance of feminine endings (that is, endings which have one or more syllables *beyond* the last accent) is enough to convince one that the chief author was some other than Shakspere. Mr. Fleay, in his *Shakespeare Manual*, has gone fully into this consideration; he shows that whereas *Othello*, e.g., out of about 2,900 lines has 646 with feminine endings, *Henry VIII.*, out of about 2,600 lines, has 1,195 with such endings. If we exclude the first act (which I believe to be Shakspere's) from the comparison, the proportion of feminine endings becomes much greater. Mr. Spedding thinks that the chief author of the play was John Fletcher, and the resemblance of style to some of Fletcher's known plays is certainly considerable. The drama is to a great extent a piece of gorgeous court-pageantry. It ends with the birth of Elizabeth, on which occasion Cranmer delivers a prophecy of the greatness of the maiden-queen, and also of 'him that should succeed,' James I. Anne Boleyn does not appear in the most favourable light, while Catharine of Aragon is represented as an injured saint and a heroic woman; this makes it certain that the play was produced in the reign of James I., whose Spanish sympathies were notorious, and not in that of Elizabeth, who would not have endured such slighting mention of her mother.

(8) *King John.* Date uncertain, but before 1598. The chief source of the plot is an older play of unknown authorship, *The Troublesome Raigne of King John*, which appeared in 1591.

(9) *Richard II.* This play, first printed in 1597, was probably

written about the same time. The period embraced in it extends from January 1398 to February 1400, the supposed date of Richard's murder. The sources of the plot are the Chronicles of Fabyan and Holinshed.

(10) *Richard III.* Date about 1593; it was first printed in 1597. The subject was very popular on the stage. An older play, *The True Tragedie of Richard III.*, appeared in 1594; it has little in common with Shakspere's play. The chief source of the plot is Holinshed's Chronicle. The picture of Richard, with its hardly relieved blackness, was borrowed by Holinshed from Sir Thomas More's *History of Edward V.* (*ante*, ch. ii. § 33). More had strong Lancastrian sympathies and antipathies; hence some modern writers are disposed to infer that the colours are overcharged, and that Richard was not really such a monster as tradition has exhibited him. That he passed several wise and just laws in his short reign is certain.

43. Two plays remain which are usually printed as Shakspere's—*Pericles, Prince of Tyre*, and *Titus Andronicus*.

Pericles. First printed in 1609, with Shakspere's name on the title-page; and probably first acted, at any rate as it now stands, the year before. The source of the plot is the story of Appollinus of Tyre, related in the Seventh Book of Gower's *Confessio Amantis*. Hence 'Ancient Gower' is introduced like a herald at the beginning of each act of the play, to tell the audience the drift of what they are about to see represented.

The most degraded modern audience would scarcely tolerate this play, and if there were good grounds to dispute Shakspere's connection with it, his admirers would most willingly do so. The chief reason for adopting such an opinion lies in the fact that it was not included in the first folio edition of 1623. It first appeared among the collected plays in the third folio, that of 1664. Again, the extremely inartistic construction of the plot, which embraces several separate actions, seems inconsistent with that mastery of his art to which Shakspere had attained long before 1608. This induces Mr. Knight to conjecture that it was a very early work of the poet's, which, having become popular on the stage, was in part newly written and published some fifteen years later. However this may be, the unbroken stage tradition of the seventeenth century (Dryden, for instance, speaks of it as the first birth of Shakspere's muse), and the far stronger evidences of style, manner, and rhythm, force us, however reluctantly, to admit that *Pericles* is probably the authentic work of the poet.

Titus Andronicus. First printed in 1600, without author's name. It is ascribed to Shakspere by Meres, as we have seen, and was included in the folio of 1623. There is a ballad on the same subject in Percy's *Reliques*, with the heading 'Titus Andronicus's Complaint.' Mr. Hallam remarks: '*Titus Andronicus* is now, by common consent, denied to be in any sense a production of Shakespeare; very few passages—I should think not one—resemble his manner.' Without denying that there may be some touches here and there from Shakspere's hand, which it is now impossible to distinguish with certainty, I should cordially subscribe to Mr. Hallam's judgment. But Mr. Knight replies that the 'consent' of all the German critics runs the other way. This does not, however, mean so much as would appear at first sight; for, in a case where the use of language, the general cast of expression, and all that constitutes *manner* are concerned, it is idle to oppose a consensus of foreign to a consensus of English critics. As Mr. Hallam

says, 'res ipsa per se vociferatur.' The versification of the play is
vigorous, but it runs in a different channel, and with a different movement, from that of Shakspere—a movement perhaps even more equably
sustained than his, but without those *ascensions*, those upward springs,
whether of thought or fancy, which characterize his genuine work.
The scraps of Latin, 'sit fas aut nefas,' 'per Styga, per manes vehor,'
&c., point to some university scholar, not to the player who had learned
no more Latin than what the Stratford Grammar School could teach a
truant pupil.

44. *Doubtful or spurious plays.* Of *The Two Noble Kinsmen*, a play
founded on the story of Palamon and Arcite, which was first printed in
1634 with the names of Fletcher and Shakspere on the title-page,
Coleridge says, 'I can scarcely retain a doubt as to the first act's having
been written by Shakespeare.' The titles of other plays that have
been ascribed to him are, *Locrine* (which Professor Ward is inclined to
ascribe to Peele), *Arden of Feversham, Edward III., Sir John Oldcastle,
The London Prodigal,* and *A Yorkshire Tragedy.*

45. It is usual to rank **Ben Jonson** next after Shakspere
among the dramatists of this age, chiefly on the ground of the
merits of his celebrated comedy, *Every Man in his Humour*,
published in 1596.   Yet the inferiority of Jonson to Shakspere is immeasurable.   It is true that he observes the 'unities'
(as he takes care to inform us in the prologue), and that the
character of Captain Bobadil, the bouncing braggart of the
piece, though the original conception of it is found in Terence,
and though it falls far short of the somewhat similar creation of
' Ancient Pistol,' abounds in fine strokes of humour.   But the
characters generally do not impress one as substantial flesh-and-
blood personages like those of Shakspere, but rather as mere
shadows, or personified humours, in which one cannot feel any
lively interest.   Real wit is rare in the piece ; and of pure fun
and merriment there is not a sparkle.   Even the humour,
although it has been so much admired, has scarcely any universal character about it ; local turns of thought, and the passing
mannerisms of the age, are its source and aliment.

Neither of the two completed tragedies which Ben Jonson
left, *Sejanus* and *Catiline*, was of much service to his fame.[1]
The story of Sejanus, the powerful minister of Tiberius, is an
excellent tragic subject ; but Jonson, though he was learned
about Roman manners and the externals of Roman life, failed
to catch the spirit of the Roman character ; its dignity on the
one hand, its cold intellectual hardness on the other, he has not

---

[1] Chief plays of Ben Jonson—*Every Man in his Humour, Every Man out
of his Humour, Volpone* or *The Fox, Epicœne* or *The Silent Woman, The Alchemist, Bartholomew Fair*, comedies ;   *The Poetaster* and *Cynthia's Revels*,
comical satires ;   *Sejanus* and *Catiline*, tragedies ;   *The Sad Shepherd*, a pastoral
drama ;   *Love freed from Ignorance and Folly*, a masque.

reproduced, nor, apparently, appreciated.   The *Poetaster*, a comical satire, is a drama in every way superior to *Sejanus*. The scene is laid at the court of Augustus ; Crispinus (by whom is intended the dramatist, Thomas Dekker) and Demetrius Fannius are arraigned as bad and worthless poets and libellous scribblers ; Crispinus, being condemned, has to swallow a purge, which makes him bring up a string of crude and flatulent words which he had been in the habit of using ; and the two are sworn to keep the peace towards Horace and all other men of genius for the future.   In this play there is more regularity in the verse, more measure in the conceptions, more appropriateness in the expressions, than are met with in *Sejanus* ; the scene in which Augustus invites Virgil to read before the court a passage from the *Æneid*, is really a noble picture.

Among the comedies, *Volpone* and the *Alchemist* are usually placed first.   The first is the story of a wily Venetian nobleman, who, assisted by a confederate, feigns himself to be dying, in order to extract gifts from his rich acquaintances, each of whom is persuaded in his turn that he is named as sole heir in the sick man's will.   It was this Volpone, between whose character and that of Lord Godolphin Dr. Sacheverell, in his celebrated sermon, drew the audacious parallel which probably had a good deal to do with his prosecution.   The workmanship of this piece is good, and the dialogue lively ; but the characters are too uniformly weak or vicious to allow of the play taking a strong hold on the mind.   In the *Alchemist* the knight, Sir Epicure Mammon, is the dupe of Subtle the alchemist, by whom he is being ruined, while supposing himself to be on the brink of the attainment of enormous wealth.

Out of forty-six extant plays, eleven are comedies, three comical satires, one a pastoral drama, only two, besides a fragment of a third, tragedies, and twenty-eight masques or other court entertainments,—short pieces, in which, to a yet greater extent ·than in the modern opera, the words were of less importance than the music, decoration, dumb show, and other theatrical accessories.

46. The plays of **Beaumont and Fletcher** are written in a purer style and finer language, yet in both these respects they fall far below those of Shakspere; and most of them are disfigured by a grossness of thought and expression which became more and more the besetting vice of the English stage.   They are about fifty-four in number, fifteen of which seem to have been produced by the two friends in conjunction; the remainder are understood to have been by Fletcher alone.   There is much fine writing in these plays, but they are marred even for reading,

P

much more for acting, by their utter want of measure and
sobriety, a defect partly due perhaps to the predilection of the
authors for Spanish plots.   The characters in *The Maid's
Tragedy*, one of the most famous among their tragedies, go to
almost inconceivable lengths of extravagance.   In the celebrated
comedy of *Rule a Wife and have a Wife*, the change which
gradually comes over the wife, who has found a master where
she meant to have a submissive tool, is nobly and beautifully
described; but this very change seems grossly improbable, when
ensuing upon the utter moral corruption which possessed her at
the first.   The versification of these plays is, as a general rule,
much less musical and regular than that of Shakspere.[1]

47. **Robert Greene,** who ran through his life and used up his
genius almost as quickly as Marlowe, is the acknowledged author
of several plays, which were edited and published by Mr. Dyce in
1831. These are, *Orlando Furioso, A Looking Glass for London
and England, Friar Bacon and Friar Bungay, The Comicall
Historie of Alphonsus King of Aragon,* and *The Scottish Historie of James IV.*   We have seen that Mr. Knight is disposed
to assign to him the old play of *The Taming of a Shrew (ante,*
§ 37); he has been also conjectured to be the author of *George-
a-Greene, the Pinner of Wakefield,* which has been assigned by
some to Shakspere.

48. **George Peele,** a Christ Church man, was an intimate
friend of Greene, Nash, and Lodge.   His *Arraignment of Paris,*
a court pageant, was exhibited before Elizabeth in 1584.   His
historical play of *Edward I.* (1593) is of little value; but he
shows to considerable advantage in his scriptural drama, *The
Love of King David and Fair Bethsabe.*   The revolt and death
of Absalom are worked into the play, which was first printed in
1599.   The verse is generally flowing and musical,—more equably
so, perhaps, than that of either Ben Jonson or Fletcher.   There
is all the Elizabethan wealth of imagery and illustration, together with that redundance and tendency to excess which are
also of the time.

49. **Thomas Nash,** more effective as a pamphleteer than as a
dramatist, is known as the author of two comedies, *Summer's
Last Will and Testament,* and *The Supplication of Pierce
Penniless,* both printed in 1592, and a serious drama, *Christ's
Tears over Jerusalem* (1593).

50. Of the plays of **Philip Massinger** eighteen are pre-

---

[1] Chief plays of Beaumont and Fletcher—*Philaster,* the *Maid's Tragedy,*
the *Knight of the Burning Pestle, King and no King,* the *Scornful Lady ;* of
Fletcher alone—the *Elder Brother,* the *Beggar's Bush, Rule a Wife and have a
Wife,* the *Faithful Shepherdess.*

served; six tragedies, eight comedies, and four tragi-comedies The famous play of *A New Way to Pay Old Debts* still keeps possession of the stage, for the sake of the finely drawn character of Sir Giles Overreach. Massinger's plays were carefully and ably edited by Gifford in 1813. He seems to have been a retiring amiable man, ill fitted to battle with the rough theatrical world on which he was thrown. He could compose a fine piece of theatrical declamation, and arrange situations which proved very effective on the stage, as we see in the long popular tragedy of the *Virgin Martyr*; but for the creation of character, in the Shaksperian way, he had no vocation; his personages are not fashioned and developed from within outwards, but take up or change a course of action, rather because the exigencies of the plot so require, than because the action and reaction between their natures and external circumstances constrain them so to behave.

The *Virgin Martyr* has telling situations, and was extremely popular in its day. The martyr is Dorothea, a Christian maiden of the age of Diocletian. Antonius, who is in love with Dorothea, is finely drawn. There is little reality in the other characters. There is no intrinsic reason laid in the nature of Theophilus, as developed up to the end of the fourth act, to account for his turning Christian in the fifth, any more than is the case with Sapritius or Sempronius.[1]

51. **John Ford**, a native of Devonshire, and born in 1586, was bred to the law, though he never seems to have made anything of a career in that profession. His first play, *The Lover's Melancholy*, was produced in 1629; his last, *The Lady's Trial*, in 1639. From this date he disappears from our view. The plots of his finest tragedies are so horrible and revolting that it has long ceased to be possible to produce them on the stage. Ford's command of language, and power of presenting and suitably conducting tragic situations, are very great. He wrote a portion of a once famous play, *The Witch of Edmonton*, in conjunction with Rowley and Dekker.

In the *Broken Heart* we have a smooth and cheerful opening, but the fourth and fifth acts bring down a very shower of horrors. In the fourth, King Amyclas dies, Panthea starves herself to death, and Orgilus her lover treacherously kills her brother Ithocles, by whom he had been prevented from marrying her. In the fifth, Calantha the daughter of Amyclas, who had been betrothed to Ithocles, dies of a 'broken heart;' and Orgilus, allowed to choose the manner of his death, opens his veins

---

[1] Chief plays of Massinger—the *Virgin Martyr*, the *Fatal Dowry*, tragedies; the *Maid of Honour*, *A Very Woman*, the *Bashful Lover*, tragi-comedies; *A New Way to Pay Old Debts*, the *City Madam*, comedies.

with his own dagger. The language in this play is often intricate and obscure, which is the less excusable in Ford, because he could write with a beautiful clearness and simplicity. Nine plays by Ford have survived, of which four are tragedies, two tragi-comedies, one a masque, one (*Perkin Warbeck*) an historical play, and one a comedy.[1]

52. Of **John Webster**, the author of a famous tragedy called *The Duchess of Malfi*, not even so much as the year of his birth is known. The period of his greatest popularity and acceptance as a dramatist was about 1620. Eight of his plays have been preserved, of several of which he was only in part author. The three tragedies are exclusively his, and it is upon these that his fame rests. The plot of *The Duchess of Malfi* turns upon the virtuous affection conceived by the Duchess for her steward Antonio,—an affection which, by wounding the pride of her family, involves both its object and herself in ruin.

53. **John Marston** was born about the year 1575. What little is known of him is gathered almost entirely from stray allusions in the works of his contemporaries. In conversation with Drummond of Hawthornden, Ben Jonson spoke contemptuously of Marston, and said that he had fought him several times. He is the author of eight plays, the chief of which is *The Malcontent*, a tragi-comedy. Besides these, he was part-author, with Jonson and Chapman, of the comedy of *Eastward Hoe*, which contained such stinging sarcasms upon the Scotch that all three were thrown into prison.

54. **Chapman** has left us eight comedies and four tragedies, among which the tragedy of *Bussy d'Amboise* is the most noted. Even of this Dryden says, in the dedication to his *Spanish Friar* : ' A famous modern poet used to sacrifice every year a Statius to Virgil's manes; and I have indignation enough to burn a *d'Amboise* annually to the memory of Jonson.'

55. Some mention must be made of **Thomas Dekker**, the butt, as we have seen, of Jonson's satire in the *Poetaster*. Dekker replied vigorously to the attack in his comedy of *Satiro-mastix ; or, the Untrussing the Humorous Poet*, in which Ben Jonson is introduced as ' Young Horace.' He wrote several other plays, in whole or in part; with Webster he produced *Westward Hoe* and *Northward Hoe*, and assisted Middleton in the *Roaring Girl*. Dekker is also the author of several satirical tracts, *e.g.*, *News from Hell*, and the *Guls Hornbooke*, which throw great light on the manners of the age.

56. **Thomas Heywood**, a most prolific writer, is the author of one very famous play, *A Woman Killed with Kindnesse* (1617).

---

[1] Chief plays of Ford—the *Broken Heart*, *Love's Sacrifice*, the *Lover's Melancholy*, the *Lady's Trial*, the *Fancies Chaste and Noble*.

The story closely resembles that of Kotzebue's play of the *Stranger*; an unfaithful wife, overcome by the inexhaustible goodness of her injured but forgiving husband, droops and expires in the rush of contending emotions—shame, remorse, penitence, and gratitude—which distract her soul. Thomas Middleton wrote, in whole or in part, a large number of plays; Mr. Dyce's edition of his works comprises twenty-two dramas and eleven masques. Of these the *Familie of Love* and the *Witch* (from which Shakspere may have derived a suggestion or two for the witches in *Macbeth*) have been singled out for praise. **William Rowley** seems to have preferred writing acts in other men's plays to inventing or adapting plots for himself; thus we find him taking part in the *Old Law* with Massinger and Middleton, and in the *Spanish Gipsie* with Middleton. There is much powerful writing in **Cyril Tourneur's** tragedy of the *Atheist's Revenge*.

57. When we look into the private life of these Elizabethan dramatists, we too often find it a wild scene of irregular activity and unbridled passion, of improvidence and embarrassment, of fits of diligence alternating with the saturnalia of a loose and reckless gaiety, of unavailing regrets cut short by early death. Yet we must not judge them harshly, for they fell upon an age of transition and revolution. The ancient Church, environed as it was with awe and mystery,—spreading into unknown depths and distances in time and space,—which might be resisted, but could not be despised,—had passed from the land like a dream; and the new institution which the will of the nation had substituted for it, whatever might be its merits, could not as yet curb the pride, nor calm the passions, nor dazzle the imagination of England's turbulent and gifted youth. True, Catholicism, in disappearing, had left solid moral traditions behind it, which the better English mind, naturally serious and conscientious, faithfully adhered to and even developed; but the playwrights and wits, or at any rate the great majority of them, plunged in the immunities and irregularities of a great city, and weak with the ductile temperament of the artist, were generally outside the sphere of these traditions.

58. The last of this race of dramatists was **James Shirley.** His first play, *Love Tricks*, appeared in 1625, and scarcely a year passed between that date and 1642 in which he did not bring a new drama upon the stage. In November 1642, the Long Parliament passed a resolution, by which, in consideration of the disturbed state of the country, the London theatres were closed. Out of the thirty dramas comprised in Mr. Dyce's edition, six are tragedies, four tragi-comedies, and twenty comedies. The plots of more than half of these are of Italian or Spanish

origin; most of the rest are drawn from contemporary English life. ' In the greater part of Shirley's dramas,' says Mr. Hallam, ' we find the favourite style of that age, the characters foreign and of elevated rank, the interest serious but not always of buskined dignity, the catastrophe fortunate; all, in short, that has gone under the vague appellation of tragi-comedy.' It must be admitted in Shirley's favour, that though his incidents are often coarse, and his dialogue licentious, his poetical justice is most often soundly administered; in the end vice suffers and virtue is rewarded. He was burnt out in the great fire of 1666, and the discomfort and distress thus brought upon him are said to have caused his death. Besides his regular dramas, Shirley is the author of several moral plays, masques, and short plays for exhibition in private houses or schools. At the end of a performance of this kind, which seems to have been the last dramatic piece he ever wrote,—the *Contention of Ajax and Ulysses*,—occurs the noble choral ode beginning ' The glories of our blood and state,' which is printed in Percy's *Reliques* and many other collections.[1]

The invectives of the Puritans against theatrical entertainments during all this period became ever louder and more vehement, creating by their extravagance a counter license and recklessness in the dramatists, and again justified in their turn, or partly so, by their excesses. At last, as already mentioned, the Puritan party became the masters of the situation, and the theatres were closed. This date brings us down some way into the succeeding period.

Prose Writing: Novels, Lodge's 'Euphues,' Sidney's 'Arcadia,' Hall; Essays: Bacon, Burton: Criticism: Gascoigne, &c.

59. The prose literature of this period is not less abundant and various than the poetry. We meet now with novelists, pamphleteers, and essayists for the first time. **Lodge** wrote several novels or novelettes, from one of which, as we have seen, Shakspere took the plot of *As You Like It*. *Euphues, the Anatomy of Wit*, a didactic romance by **John Lyly**, with several appendices or sequels, appeared in 1579, and *Euphues and his England*, by the same author, in 1580. Both have been lately reprinted by Mr. Edward Arber. *Euphues* is a clever— but not, as Mr. Arber thinks, a *very* clever book—treating of

---

[1] Chief plays of Shirley—the *Maid's Revenge*, the *Politician*, the *Cardinal*, tragedies; the *Ball*, the *Gamester*, the *Bird in a Cage* (which has an ironical dedication to William Prynne), the *Lady of Pleasure*, comedies.

friendship, love, philosophy, education, and religion.   Euphues is a young Athenian who finds himself, on the death of his parents, the possessor of a large fortune, a fine person, a ready wit, and a cultivated mind.   He proceeds to Naples, where he gains the friendship of Philautus, engages in a great deal of philosophical conversation, has one or two love affairs which come to nothing, and at length sails for Athens, leaving a long letter for Philautus inveighing against love, and urging his friend to flee women and their allurements.   To this letter is attached ' Euphues and his Ephebus,' a tract on education, which Professor Rushton, of Cork College, has shown to be almost entirely a translation from Plutarch's treatise on the same subject.   With this tract is connected another called ' Euphues and Atheos '—being a dialogue between Euphues and an atheist.   After being, not so much talked, as railed and browbeaten out of his errors with great ease and celerity, the atheist is made to exclaim : 'O Euphues, howe much am I bounde to the goodnesse of almightie God, which hath made me of an infidell a beleever, of a castaway a Christian, of an heathenly Pagan a heavenly Protestant !'

60. *Euphues and his England* is a much more considerable work.   Euphues visits England in company with Philautus, and several English friends who have been staying at Italy, and writes a ' description of the countrey, the Court, and the manners of the isle.'   In this picture there is not a particle of shadow ; England and the English, as compared with other nations, are all light.   The temper that leads to this kind of writing we now call *Chauvinism*.   There is, of course, an elaborate pane-gyric on Queen Elizabeth, whose beauty is represented, if that were possible, as being equalled by her virtue.   Englishmen are sparing in the use of strong liquor, unlike the men of other nations, ' who never thinke that they have dyned till they be dronken.'   The English ladies 'spend the morning in devout prayer,' whereas the gentlewomen of Greece and Italy use 'sonets for psalmes, and pastymes for prayers.'   Hence the divine favour is reserved for this virtuous people *exclusively*. ' Oh blessed peace ! oh happy Prince ! oh fortunate people! The lyving God is onely the Englysh God.'

61. There is less affectation in the style of *Euphues* than, after reading the *Monastery*, one would be prepared to expect. Antithesis and alliteration are doubtless much resorted to ; the author seems to have regarded them as the chief ornaments of an English style.   He is also fond of bringing in curious or scien-tific terms ; he abounds in similes and illustrations ; and is almost as fond of proverbs as Cervantes, though less happy in applying

them. But, on the whole, the talk of Euphues and his friends is simple and rational compared with the affected pedantic bombast which Scott puts in the mouth of his Sir Piercie Shafton, and calls Euphuism. As for the precise and mincing way of speaking attributed to Holofernes in Shakspere's *Love's Labour's Lost*, the notion that Lodge and *Euphues* are here glanced at has been satisfactorily shown by Mr. Knight to be untenable.

The more the subject is investigated, the more manifest it will be that no great change of literary style is ever so distinctly traceable to one book, or one man, or one set of men, as on a casual survey it would seem plausible to maintain. A pedantic preference for long words of classical origin has often been supposed to be a distinctive mark of 'Euphuism.' But the tendency to the employment of such words showed itself strongly as far back as the time of Hawes (see *ante*, p. 139). The same thing was noticed by a shrewd and forcible writer of the middle of the century, Thomas Wilson. I quote the passage from Mr. Knight's preface to *Love's Labour's Lost*. In his *Arte of Rhetorike* (1553) Wilson cites a letter which he describes as actually written by the applicant for a benefice; it runs as follows: 'Ponderying, expendyng, and revolutyng with myself your ingent affabilitie, and ingenious capacitie for mundane affaires, I cannot but celebrate and extoll your magnificall dexteritie above all other. For how could you have adapted suche illustrate prerogative, and dominicall superioritie, if the fecundite of your ingenie had not been so fertile and wonderfull pregnaunt?' In truth, this sort of thing may be easily explained as an extravagance and excess growing out of the zeal for the revival of classical learning, and varying in intensity according to the development of public or individual taste.

Nevertheless, it must be granted that the writings of Lyly exercised temporarily a considerable influence on style; and this we learn from a witness who attests the far more powerful influence excited by the writer next to be mentioned. Drayton, in an elegy 'Of Poets and Poesie,'[1] praises Sidney for having thoroughly *paced* our language, so that it might run abreast of Greek and Latin. Sidney, he says,

> did first reduce
> Our tongue from Lillie's writing then in use;
> Talking of stones, stars, plants, of fishes, flyes,
> Playing with words, and idle similies.
> As th' English apes and very zanies be
> Of everything that they do hear and see,
> So, imitating his ridiculous tricks,
> They spake and writ all like meere lunatiques.

[1] Quoted by Mr. Arber in his preface to *Euphues*.

62. Just as the sonnets and songs of **Sir Philip Sidney** (*ante*, § 20) are of a merit and power transcending the foreign models on which they were framed, so is it with his celebrated prose romance, *The Countess of Pembroke's Arcadia*. The *Diana* of Montemayor (1580), and the *Arcadia* of Sannazaro (1549), suggested the form of the work ; but a glance at these insipid and artificial productions will show that the intellectual and imaginative *reach* visible in the English work, the richness and beauty of many of the descriptions, the energy, loftiness, and suggestiveness of the thoughts, are solely due to the native genius of the writer. Written about 1584, the *Arcadia* was first published in 1613. It may be described as the record of the adventures of the two friends, Pyrocles and Musidorus, while aspiring to the love of the princesses of Arcadia, Philoclea and Pamela. But long narratives are introduced by way of episode, and many other personages, particularly the parents of the princesses, have a troublesome activity, and a proneness to fall in love with every one whom they ought not to think of ; all which circumstances complicate the plot wonderfully, and make the novel wearisome to modern taste. Eclogues and songs, in all kinds of classic metres—most of which are ridiculously unsuited to English words—are of constant occurrence : we have elegiacs, sapphics, anacreontics, phaleutiacs, asclepiadics, &c. The highly coloured prose, full of trope and metaphor and metonymy, and in the best passages sententious and profound rather than antithetical, is a typical monument of the Elizabethan manner—a manner which is generally rich and forcible, but too often sacrifices simplicity and good taste. The book contains many striking passages on forms of government. For an unlimited democracy Sidney had an unbounded aversion ; but he also condemns oligarchy, particularly that worst form of it, ' when men are governed indeed by a few, and yet are not taught to know what those few be, whom they should obey.' The following word-picture is Sidney's description of Arcadia :—

There were hills which garnished their proud heights with stately trees ; humble valleys whose base estate seemed comforted with the refreshing of silver rivers ; meadows enamel'd with all sorts of eye-pleasing flowers ; thickets which, being lined with most pleasant shade, were witnessed so too by the cheerful disposition of many well-tuned birds ; each pasture stored with sheep, feeding with sober security, while the pretty lambs with bleating oratory craved the dams' comfort ; here a shepherd's boy piping, as though he should never be old ; there a young shepherdess knitting, and withal singing, and it seemed that her voice comforted her hands to work, and her hands kept time to her voice-music.

63. The strange political romance, *Mundus Alter et Idem*,

by **Joseph Hall,** appeared in 1605. The man has taken a great stride since he wrote his satires (*ante,* § 10); he is now a grave divine, pacing on the road to preferment; his style is chastened and improved; he no longer discharges his shafts at haphazard, but keeps them for the adversaries of the divine right and prerogative of kings and bishops. Like Sidney, he dreads a pure democracy; but he is not, like Sidney, a true lover of human freedom. In writing the *Mundus &c.* his object seems to have been to depict the brutal, savage, and debased condition into which, according to his theory, a community would fall if allowed to manage its own affairs and gratify all its caprices. Pure democracy, he means to say, would in time bring man down to the level of the brutes. His 'Terra Australis' has four main territories, *Crapulia, Viraginia, Moronia,* and *Lavernia.* The land altogether is a fool's paradise, a land of Cockayne. 'The whole country groans with eatables of all kinds, and none are permitted to be exported.' The grand-duke or king is elected solely on account of his *eating* powers. In his speech of installation he declares himself an uncompromising foe to fasting, abstinence, short allowance, and leanness. 'Every one is desirous of governing, none willing to obey. Everything is regulated by public suffrage; all speak at once, and none pay any attention to what their neighbour says. They have a *perpetual parliament,* and what is voted to-day may be repealed to-morrow.' The real *animus* of the writer is here unveiled; we have before us a Coryphæus among the clerical advisers who encouraged Charles I. to reign eleven years without a parliament, and who would have suppressed the House of Commons and established regal absolutism, if their power had been equal to their will.

64. In this period, the literature of travel and adventure, which began with old Sir John Maundevile, and has attained to such vast proportions among us in modern times, was placed on a broad and solid pedestal of recorded fact by the work of **Richard Hakluyt,** a Herefordshire man, who in 1589 published a collection of voyages made by Englishmen 'at any time' (as he states on the title-page) 'within the compass of these fifteen hundred years.' Purchas' *Pilgrimage,* of which the third edition is dated 1617, will occur to many as the book in which Coleridge had been reading before he dreamt the dream of *Kubla Khan.* **Samuel Purchas** was the clergyman of St. Martin's, Ludgate, and a staunch upholder of episcopacy. In the epistle dedicatory, addressed to Archbishop Bancroft—after saying that he had consulted above twelve hundred authors in the composition of the work, and explaining what those would find in it who sought for information simply—he proceeds: 'Others may hence

learn . . . two lessons fitting these times, the unnaturalness
of Faction and Atheism; that law of nature having written in
the practice of all men . . . the profession of some religion,
and in that religion, wheresoever any society of priests or religious persons are or have been in the world, no admittance of
Paritie; the angels in heaven, divels in hell (as the royallest of
fathers, the father of our country, hath pronounced), and all
religions on earth, as here we show, being equally subject to inequality, that is, to the equitie of subordinate order.   And if I
live to finish the rest, I hope to show the *Paganism* of anti-
christian popery,' &c.   Without being a follower of M. Comte,
one may be of opinion that the mental condition of those who
could carry on, or assent to the carrying on of, anthropological
researches in the temper of mind avowed by honest Purchas,
needed a large infusion of the *esprit positif*.[1]

65. The genius of Montaigne raised up English imitators of his
famous work, one of whom was afterwards to eclipse his original.
Francis Bacon published a small volume entitled *Essays, Religious Meditations, Places of Perswasion and Disswasion*, in 1597.
The essays were ten in number; they were followed by ' Medi-
tationes Sacræ,' or Religious Meditations, in Latin, and these
by ' The Coulers of Good and Evill,' which are the ' places of
perswasion,' &c., mentioned in the title-page.   The ten essays,
except that of 'Honour and Reputation,' after being much
altered and enlarged, were republished, with the addition of
twenty-nine new essays, in 1612.   The last edition published
in the author's lifetime was that of 1625, under the title of
' Essayes, or Counsels Civill and Moral;'[2] it contained fifty-eight
essays, of which twenty were new, and the rest altered or
enlarged.   In the dedication to this last edition Lord Bacon
writes: ' I do now publish my *Essayes*; which of all my other
workes have beene most currant; for that, as it seemes, they
come home to men's businesse and bossomes.   I have enlarged
them both in number and weight, so that they are indeed a new
work.'   The *Essays* in this their final shape were immediately
translated into French, Italian, and Latin.

66. At the end of the present period an Oxford student,
fond of solitude and the learned dust of great libraries, produced

---

[1] The full title of this curious old book is, ' Purchas, his Pilgrimage, or,
Relations of the World and the Religions observed in all Ages and Places discovered, from the Creation unto this Present.   In four parts.   This First con-
tayneth a Theological and Geographical History of Asia, Africa, and America,
with the islands adjacent.'   Besides the religions, ancient and modern (which,
he says, are his principal aim), he undertakes to describe the chief rarities and
wonders of nature and art in all the countries treated of.

[2] See Crit. Sect. ch. II., *Philosophy*.

a strange multifarious book, which he called *The Anatomy of Melancholy.* Robert Burton lived for some thirty years in his rooms at Christ Church, much like a monk in his cell, reading innumerable books on all conceivable subjects; 'but to little purpose,' as he himself admits, 'for want of good method;' and could hit on no better mode of utilizing his labours than by completing, or attempting to complete, a design which the Greek philosopher Democritus is recorded to have entertained—that of writing a scientific treatise on melancholy! Burton had an odd sort of humour, and an idle hour may be whiled away pleasantly enough by opening his book almost anywhere; but as for science, it is not to writers of his stamp that one must go for that.

67. The deeper culture of the time displayed itself in the earliest attempts in our language at literary and æsthetic criticism. George Gascoigne, the poet, led the way with a short tract, entitled *Notes of Instruction concerning the making of Verse or Rhyme in English* : this appeared in 1575. William Webbe is the author of a *Discourse of English Poetrie*, published in 1586, a work of little value. But in 1589 appeared the *Arte of English Poesie* by Puttenham, a gentleman pensioner at the court of Elizabeth, a work distinguished by much shrewdness and good sense, and containing, as Warton's pages testify, a quantity of minute information about English poetry in the sixteenth century which cannot be found elsewhere. But among all such works, Sir Philip Sidney's *Defence of Poesy*, written about 1584, stands preeminent. Chaucer's diction was antiquated; Surrey and Wyat were refined versifiers rather than poets; the sun of Spenser had but just risen : and, as people are apt to hold cheap that in which they do not excel, it seems that the English literary public at this time were disposed to regard poetry as a frivolous and useless exercise of the mind, unworthy to engage the attention of those who could betake themselves to philosophy or history. A work embodying these opinions, entitled *The School of Abuse*, was written by Stephen Gosson in 1579, and dedicated to Sidney; and it seems not improbable that this work was the immediate occasion which called forth the *Defence of Poesy*. In this really noble and beautiful treatise, which moreover has the merit of being very short, Sir Philip seeks to call his countrymen to a better mind, and vindicates the preeminence of the poet, as a seer, a thinker, and a maker.[1]

68. It has been discovered[2] that from this period dates the

---

[1] See Crit. Sect. ch. II., *Criticism.*   [2] Craik, vol. iv. p. 97.

first regular newspaper, though it did not as yet contain domestic intelligence. 'The first news-pamphlet which came out at regular intervals appears to have been that entitled *The News of the Present Week,* edited by Nathaniel Butler, which was started in 1622, in the early days of the Thirty Years' War, and was continued in conformity with its title as a weekly publication.'

History :—Holinshed, Camden, Bacon, Speed, Knolles, Raleigh, Foxe.

69. Continuing in the track of the Chroniclers mentioned in the last chapter, **Raphael Holinshed** and his colleague, **William Harrison,** produced their well-known *Description and History of England, Scotland, and Ireland,* in 1577. Since the revival of learning, familiarity with the works of Strabo and other Greek geographers had caused geography to become a popular study; and among the evidences of this in England, the topographical portions of this Chronicle are perhaps the most important that we have come to since the *Itinerarium* of Leland, though superseded, a few years later, by the far more celebrated and valuable work known as Camden's *Britannia.* It would be unfair to say a word in dispraise of the style of this Description, since its author, Harrison, throws himself ingenuously on the reader's mercy, in words which remind one of the immortal Dogberry's anxiety to be 'written down an ass.' 'If your honour,' he says (the book is addressed to Lord Cobham), 'regard the substance of that which is here declared, I must needs confesse that it is none of mine owne; but if your lordship have consideration of the barbarous composition showed herein, that I may boldly claime and challenge for mine owne; sith there is no man of any so slender skill, that will defraud me of that reproach, which is due unto me, for the meere negligence, disorder, and evil disposition of matter comprehended in the same.' Of Holinshed, the author of the historical portions, very little is known; but the total absence of the critical spirit in his work seems to show that he could not have belonged to the general literary fraternity of Europe, since that spirit was already rife and operative on the Continent. Ludovicus Vives, for instance, a Spaniard, and a fellow-worker with Erasmus and other emancipators of literature and taste, had expressed disbelief in the fable of Brute, the legendary founder of the British monarchy, many years before; yet Holinshed quietly translates all the trash that he found in Geoffrey of Monmouth,

about that and other mythical personages, as if it were so much
solid history.   The extent to which, in the sixteenth century,
credulity still darkened the historic field, may be judged of from
a few facts.   Thus Holinshed lays it down as probable that
Britain was peopled long before the Deluge.   These primitive
Britons he supposes to have been all drowned in the Flood;
he then attributes the repeopling of the island to Samothes, the
son of Japhet, son of Noah.   The population being scanty, it
was providentially recruited by the arrival of the fifty daughters
of Danaus, a king of Egypt, who, having all killed their
husbands, were sent adrift in a ship, and carried by the winds
to Britain.   This, however, Holinshed admits to be doubtful,
but the arrival of Ulysses on our shores he is ready to vouch
for, and he favourably considers the opinion that the name of
Albion was derived from a huge giant of that name who took
up his abode here, the son of Neptune, god of the seas.   Then,
as to Brute, the great-grandson of Æneas, Holinshed no more
doubts about his existence, nor that from him comes the name
of Britain, than he doubts that Elizabeth succeeded Mary.   Such
were among the consequences of the manner in which the uncritical writers of the Middle Ages had jumbled history, theology,
and philosophy all up together.   Nevertheless the Chronicles of
Holinshed, being written in an easy and agreeable style, became
a popular book.   They were reprinted, with a continuation, in
1587; they found in Shakspere a diligent reader; and they
were again reprinted in 1807.

70. It was not long before the judicial office of the historian
began to be better understood.   **William Camden,** now scarcely
thought of except as an antiquary, was in truth a trained and
ripe scholar, and an intelligent student of history.   England has
more reason to be proud of him than of many whose names are
more familiar to our ears.   The man who won the friendship of
the president De Thou, and corresponded on equal terms with
that eminent historian, as also with Casaubon and Lipsius
abroad, and Usher and Spelman at home, must have possessed
solid and extraordinary merits.   His *Britannia*, a work on the
topography of England, Scotland, and Ireland, with the isles
adjacent, enriched with historical illustrations, first appeared in
1586, while he was an under-master at Westminster School.   In
1604 he published his *Reliquiæ Britannicæ*, a treatise on the
early inhabitants of Britain.   In this work, undeterred by the
sham array of authorities which had imposed upon Holinshed,
he 'blew away sixty British kings with one blast.'[1]   Burleigh,

---

[1] Speed.

the great statesman of the reign of Elizabeth, the Cavour of the sixteenth century, singled out Camden as the fittest man in all England to write the history of the first thirty years of the Queen's reign, and intrusted to him, for that purpose, a large mass of state papers. Eighteen years elapsed before Camden discharged the trust. At last, in 1615, his *History, or Annals of England during the Reign of Queen Elizabeth*, made its appearance. 'The love of truth,' he says in the preface, 'has been the only incitement to me to undertake this work.' The studied impartiality of De Thou had made this language popular among historians, and Camden probably fancied at the moment that he had no other motive; but to say nothing of the 'incitement' administered by Lord Burleigh, his own words, a little further on, show that the 'scandalous libels' published in foreign parts against the late Queen and the English government, formed a powerful stimulus; in short, his History must be taken as a vindication, but in a more moderate tone than was then usual, of the Protestant policy of England since the accession of Elizabeth. Its value would be greater than it is, but for his almost uniform neglect to quote his authorities for the statements he makes. This fact, coupled to the discovery, in our own times, of many new and independent sources of information, to him unknown, has caused his labours to be much disregarded.

71. Sir Francis Bacon's *History of the Reign of Henry VII.*, published in 1622, is in many ways a masterly work. With the true philosophic temper, he seeks, not content with a superficial narrative of events, to trace out and exhibit their causes and connections; and hence he approaches to the modern conception of history, as the record of the development of peoples, rather than of the actions of princes and other showy personages.

72. The writers of literary history have been unjust to **John Speed**, whom it is the custom to speak of as a dull plodding chronicler. Speed was much more than this. His *Historie of Great Britain* exhibits, in a very striking way, the rapid growth of that healthy scepticism which is one of the essential qualifications of the historian. The nonsense which Holinshed, as we have seen, had received from his predecessors,. and innocently retailed, respecting the early history of Britain, Speed disposes of with a few blunt words. A supposed work of Berosus, on which Holinshed, following Bishop Bale, relied for the details he entered into respecting the antediluvian period, had been proved to be an impudent forgery; Speed therefore extinguishes Samothes, the daughters of Danaus, Ulysses, &c., without ceremony. Next, he presumes to doubt, if not to deny, the existence

of 'Albion the Giant.' But a more audacious piece of scepticism remains. Speed does not believe in Brute, and by implication denies that we English are descended from the Trojans; an article which, all through the Middle Ages, was believed in with a firm undoubting faith. After giving the evidence for and against the legend in great detail, and with perfect fairness, he gives judgment himself on the side of reason; and with regard to the Trojan descent, advises Britons to 'disclaim that which bringeth no honour to so renowned a nation.' The same rationality displays itself as the History proceeds. Holinshed speaks in a sort of gingerly way of the miracles attributed to St. Dunstan, as if on the one hand the extraordinary character of some of them staggered even him; while on the other, his natural credulity compelled him to swallow them. But honest Speed brushes out of his path these pious figments. 'As for angels singing familiarly unto him,' he says, 'and divels in the shape of dogs, foxes, and beares, whipped by him, that was but ordinary; as likewise his making the she-divel to roare, when, coming to tempt him in shape of a beautiful lasse, he caught her by the nose with hot burning pincers, and so spoilde a good face. But to leave these figments wherewith our monkish stories are stuffed,' &c.

The complimentary verses printed, as the custom then was, at the beginning of the second edition of the work, show that Speed was warmly admired by a circle of contemporary students, who took an eager interest in his labours. This fact, and the rudiments of a sound historical criticism contained in his History, entitle us to conjecture that, had no disturbing influences intervened, the English school of historians, which numbered at this time men like Speed, and Knolles, and Camden, in its ranks, would have progressively developed its powers, and attained to ever wider views, until it had thought out all those critical principles which it was actually left to Niebuhr and the Germans to discover. But the civil war came, and broke the thread of research. The strong intellects that might otherwise have applied themselves to the task of establishing canons of evidence, and testing the relative credibility of various historical materials, were compelled to enter into the arena of political action, and to work and fight either for King or Parliament. We cannot complain; one nation cannot do all that the race requires. Contented to have immensely accelerated, by our civil war and its incidents, the progress of political freedom in Europe, we must resign to Germany that philosophical preeminence, which, had the English intellect peacefully expanded itself during the seventeenth century, we might possibly have contested with her.

73. Another excellent and painstaking writer of the school was **Richard Knolles**, a former fellow of Lincoln College, Oxford, who published in 1610 his *General Historie of the Turks*. It was the first complete history of this people that had appeared, and the interest of the undertaking lay, in the opinion of the author, in the 'fatal mutations' which this warlike nation had in a short time brought upon a great part of the world. In the mournful list of conquests from Christendom which he records, the only names of countries that have been since reconquered Hungary, Greece, and Algeria; but the European mind had not, in 1610, become indifferent from long custom to the ruin of so many Christian communities, recently flourishing in Asia Minor and Roumelia.

74. The versatility of **Raleigh's** powers was something marvellous; nevertheless it must be admitted that when he undertook to write the *History of the World*,[1] commencing at the Creation, he miscalculated his powers. No one indeed would bear hardly on a work, the labours of which must have relieved many a cheerless and lonely hour in that dark prison-cell in the Tower, in which one may still stand, and muse on the indomitable spirit of its inmate. The book, however, has certainly been overpraised. It is full of that uncritical sort of learning, which, with all its elaborate theories and solemn discussions, we, in the nineteenth century, know to be absolutely worthless. The hundred and thirty-eighth page is reached before the reader is let out of the Garden of Eden. Deucalion's flood is gravely treated as an historical event, the date of which is pretty certain; a similar view is taken of the 'flood of Ogyges,' which, by a stupendous process of argumentation, is *proved* to have taken place exactly five hundred and eighty years after that of Noah. A voluminous disquisition follows, with the object of proving that the ark did *not* rest on Mount Ararat, but upon some part of the Caucasus. At the end of four hundred and eleven pages, we have only reached the reign of Semiramis, B.C. 2000, or thereabouts. Proceeding at this rate, it was obviously impossible, even though the scale of the narrative is gradually contracted, that within the ordinary term of a human life the work should be carried down beyond the Christian era. It closes, in fact, about the year B.C. 170, with the final subjugation of Macedon by the Romans. That there are eloquent and stirring passages in the book, no one will deny; yet they mostly appear in connection with a theory of history which, though commonly held in Raleigh's day, has long ceased to be thought adequate to

[1] See Crit. Sect. ch. ii. § 24.

Q

cover the facts. That theory—a legacy from the times when all departments of human knowledge were overshadowed and intruded upon by theology—is fully stated in the preface. It deals with history as being didactic rather than expository; as if its proper office were to teach moral lessons,—the most important of these being, that God always requites virtuous and vicious princes in this world according to their deserts—that ' ill-doing hath always been attended with ill-success.' History, on this view, became a sort of department of preaching. The one-sidedness of the theory, and the special pleading of its advocates, after eliciting counter-extravagances from Machiavel and Hobbes, drew down, in the *Candide*, the withering mockery of Voltaire.

75. The appearance of the first edition of **Foxe's** *Acts and Monuments*, commonly called the *Book of Martyrs*, in 1561, is yet more an historical than a literary event. Of this work, filling three bulky folio volumes, nine standard editions were called for between its first publication and the year 1684; and it is impossible to exaggerate the effect which its thrilling narratives of the persecutions and burnings of the Protestants under Mary had in weakening the hold of the ancient Church on the general English heart. The style is plain and manly; the language vigorous and often coarse; but it was thereby only rendered the more effective for its immediate purpose. It is now indeed well understood that Foxe was a rampant bigot, and, like all of his class, utterly unscrupulous in assertion; the falsehoods, misrepresentations, and exaggerations to which he gave circulation, are endless. Take for instance his account of the death of Wolsey, which we know from the testimony of George Cavendish, an eye-witness, to be a string of pure unmitigated falsehoods. ' It is testified by one, yet being alive, in whose armes the said Cardinall died, that his body being dead was black as pitch, also was so heavie that six could scarce beare it. Furthermore, it did so stinke above the ground, that they were constrained to hasten the burial thereof in the night season before it was day. At the which burial such a tempest with such a stinke there arose, that all the torches went out, and so hee was throwne into the tombe, and there was laied.' Such foul slanderous hearsays it was Foxe's delight and care to incorporate by dozens in his work: no weapon came amiss, if a Catholic prelate was the object aimed at. Mr. Maitland, in a series of pamphlets,[1] has examined a number of these, proved

---

[1] The first of the series was entitled ' Six Letters on Foxe's *Acts and Monuments*,' 1837.

their falsehood, and established the general unreliability of the martyrologist.

The first volume, beginning with the persecutions directed against the early Church, professes to trace, according to a favourite doctrine of the Reformers, the history of a faithful and suffering remnant, the pure Church of Christ, which retained the unadulterated Gospel in the midst of the idolatrous corruptions introduced by the official Church, down across the dark and middle ages, through the Waldenses, the Albigenses, Wyclif, Huss, and Oldcastle, to the brighter times of Luther and Cranmer.   This volume ends with the accession of Henry VIII.   The second volume includes the reigns of Henry VIII. and Edward VI.; the third is chiefly taken up with the records of the persecution under Mary.

Theology:—Jewel, Hooker, Parsons, Stapleton, James I., Andrewes; Translations of the Bible.

76. In the grave works resulting from profound thought and learning, not less than in the creations of the imaginative faculty, the buoyant and progressive character of the period may be traced.   To speak first of theology: even the Catholic controversialists seem to catch the contagion of the time's enthusiasm.   Allen and Parsons wrote and combated with a hopeful pugnacity not found in the Gothers and Challoners of a later age; driven from the old universities, they founded English colleges for the education of priests at Rome and Douay; they laboured to keep up their communications all over England; they formed plots; they exposed the doctrinal and liturgical compromises in which the new Anglican Church had its beginning; they would not believe but that all would ultimately come right again, and the nation repent of its wild aberrations from Catholic and papal unity.

77. The partisans of the Reformation split, as the reign went on, into two great sections—the Puritans and the Church party, or Prelatists, as they were nick-named by their opponents. The leading men among the former had been in exile during the persecution in Mary's reign, and returned home full of admiration for the doctrines and Church polity of Calvin, which last they had seen in full operation at Geneva.   **Jewel**, Bishop of Salisbury, was one of these:—his famous *Apology*, published in 1562, is Calvinistic in its theology; but the fact of his being able, though with some scruples of conscience, to accept a bishopric, proves that the differences between the two parties about Church government were not as yet held to be vital.

The *Apology*, which was directed against Rome, and originally written in Latin, drew forth a reply from the Jesuit Harding, to which Jewel rejoined in his *Defence of the Apology*, a long and laboured work in English.

78. While Grindal was archbishop, the deviations of the Puritan clergy from the established liturgy were to some extent connived at. But upon the appointment of Whitgift, in 1583, a man of great energy and a strict disciplinarian, uniformity was everywhere enforced; and the Puritans saw no alternative before them, but either to accept a form of Church government of which they doubted the lawfulness, and acquiesce in practices which they detested as relics of 'Popery' (such as the sign of the cross at baptism, the use of vestments, the retention of fast and feast days, &c.), or else to give up their ministry in the Church. Before deciding on the latter course, they tried the effect of putting forth various literary statements of their case. Of these the most important were the *Admonition* of Cartwright, and the *Ecclesiastica Disciplina* of Travers. These works drew forth from the Church party a memorable response, in the *Ecclesiastical Polity* of **Richard Hooker.** This celebrated man, who never attained to a higher ecclesiastical rank than that of a simple clergyman in the diocese of Canterbury, published the first four books of his treatise of *Ecclesiastical Polity* in 1594; the fifth book followed in 1597. His life by Izaak Walton is one of our most popular biographies; but it used to be remarked by the late Dr. Arnold, that the gentle, humble, unworldly pastor brought before us by Walton is quite unlike the strong majestic character suggested by the works themselves. The general object of the treatise was to defend the Established Church, its laws, rites, and ceremonies, from the attacks of the Puritans. These attacks reduced themselves to two principal heads : first, that the episcopal government of the Church and the temporal status of bishops, together with all laws connected with and upholding this system, as not being laid down in Scripture, were therefore unlawful, and ought to be exchanged for the Presbyterian system, which they maintained was so laid down;—secondly, that many of the rites and practices enjoined by the rubric were superstitious and 'popish,' and ought to be abolished. To the first position Hooker replies by establishing the distinction between natural and positive law,—the former being essentially immutable, the latter, even though commanded by God Himself for special purposes and at particular times, essentially mutable. Thence he argues, that even if the Puritans could prove their Presbyterian form of Church government to be laid down in Scripture, it would not follow (since such form

was, after all, a part of positive law), that for cogent reasons and by lawful authority it might not be altered. The philosophical analysis of law which the course of his argument renders necessary, is the most masterly and also the most eloquent portion of the treatise. To the second head of objections Hooker replies by endeavouring to trace all the rites and practices complained of to the primitive and uncorrupted Church of the first four centuries. His great familiarity with the writings of the Fathers gave him an advantage here over his less learned opponents; yet at the same time the minuteness of the details, coupled with the comparative obsoleteness of the questions argued, renders this latter portion of the work less permanently valuable than the first four books. The sixth book, as Mr. Keble has proved,[1] is lost to us, all but a few of the opening paragraphs; the remainder of the book as it now stands being a fragment upon a totally different subject from that treated of in the original, though undoubtedly composed by Hooker. The seventh and eighth books belong to the original design, but were published long after Hooker's death, from MSS. left unrevised and in a disorderly condition.

79. The Catholic writers of this period were very busy with their pens in their different places of exile, and produced a great number of works, both in Latin and in English. We have the names of Stapleton, Sander or Sanders, Walsingham, Harpsfield, More (the historian of the English Jesuits), Campion, and many others. **Robert Parsons**, whose name has been already mentioned, excelled them all in industry and tenacity. A long and candid account of his labours may be read in Wood's *Athenæ*. Among his many treatises, the *Three Conversions of England* (1603) is the most remarkable. The first conversion is supposed to have taken place in the time of the apostles; the second is that effected in the second century, in the days of Pope Eleutherus and the British King Lucius; the third is that commenced by Pope Gregory. The works of **Thomas Stapleton**, collected in four large folio volumes, are now scarcely to be met with outside the walls of a few public libraries. Obliged, with his family, to go into exile at the accession of Elizabeth, Stapleton found shelter, under the rule of Spain, at Louvain, and afterwards at Douay. In the proem to the *Tres Thomæ*, his principal work, containing biographies of St. Thomas the apostle, St. Thomas-à-Becket, and Sir Thomas More, he says that he was born in the same month in which More was martyred, and

---

[1] In the introduction to his excellent edition of Hooker's Works, Oxford, 1842.

that he had obtained authentic information respecting him from a number of other English exiles, and also from the works of many distinguished foreign authors, such as Cochlæus, Paulus Jovius, Budæus, and Rhenanus.

80. In the reign of James, Dr. Donne and Bishop Andrewes were the chief writers of the Episcopalian party. The reaction against the encroaching self-asserting spirit of Puritanism, joined to the perception that the controversy with the Catholics could not be carried on upon the narrow Puritan grounds, nor without reference to the past history of the Church, led back about this time the ablest and best men among the Anglican divines to the study of the primitive ages and the writings of the Fathers. Donne, Andrewes, and Laud, as afterwards Bull, Pearson, Taylor, and Barrow, were deeply read in ecclesiastical literature. **James I.** prided himself on his theological profundity. His *Basilicon Doron*, or advice to his son Prince Henry, published in 1599, contains far more of theological argument than of moral counsel. In 1610 his works were published in folio; they include his often-cited treatise on *Demonology* (in which he assumes the reality and discusses the conditions of the Satanic agency which operates in witches), and a tract against the new practice of smoking, called *A Counterblast to Tobacco*. His *Apology for the Oath of Allegiance,* written in 1605, to justify the imposition upon English Catholics of the new oaths framed after the discovery of the Gunpowder Plot, drew forth an answer from Bellarmine, under the feigned name of Matthew Tortus. To the strictures of the cardinal a reply appeared with the curious title of *Tortura Torti* (1609), from the pen of **Lancelot Andrewes**, bishop of Winchester. This good and able man, in whom an earnest piety was united to a quick and sparkling wit and an unflagging industry, was of humble parentage, but, by sheer weight and force of character, he gained the intimacy and confidence of three sovereigns— Elizabeth, James I., and Charles I. He was one of the translators of the Bible in the time of James; the portion assigned to him and his company being the Pentateuch, and the historical books from Joshua to the end of the Second Book of Kings. He died in 1626, and was lamented in a beautiful Latin elegy by Milton, then a young student at Cambridge.

81. The authorized English version of the Scriptures was the work of the reign of James. 'Forty-seven persons, in six companies, meeting at Westminster, Oxford, and Cambridge, distributed the labour among them; twenty-five being assigned to the Old Testament, fifteen to the New, seven to the Apocrypha. The rules imposed for their guidance by the King were

designed, as far as possible, to secure the text against any novel
interpretation; the translation called *The Bishops' Bible* being
established as the basis, as those still older had been in that;
and the work of each person or company being subjected to the
review of the rest. The translation, which was commenced
in 1607, was published in 1611.'[1] *The Bishops' Bible* named in
the above extract was a translation prepared in the early part
of Elizabeth's reign, under the supervision of Archbishop
Parker, and published in 1567. In this, also, earlier translations had been pretty closely followed; so that there can be no
doubt that the English of the authorized version is considerably
more antique in character than that of the generation in which
it appeared. Of a few expressions—such as 'wist ye not,'
'strait' for narrow, 'strawed,' 'charger,' 'emerods,' 'receipt of
custom,' and the like—the meaning may perhaps be thus
obscured for the uneducated. But, on the whole, the beautiful
simplicity and easy idiomatic flow of the authorized version
render it a people's book, and a model for translators; while
the strength and dignity of its style have probably operated for
good upon English prose-writing ever since.

Philosophy :—Francis Bacon; his Method; The Advancement of Learning

82. In the early part of the seventeenth century, the philosophy and science taught at the intellectual centres of the
country—Oxford and Cambridge—differed little from those
which the great schoolmen of the Middle Age had invented or
transmitted. That is to say, logic and moral philosophy,—the
one investigating the reasoning process, the other the different
qualities of human actions,—were taught according to the system
of Aristotle; rhetoric was studied as a practical application of
logic; and mathematics, more as an intellectual exercise, than
as an instrument for the investigation of nature. The physical
sciences, so far as they were studied at all, were treated in an
off-hand manner, as if they were already tolerably complete;
and being still overlaid with metaphysical notions, which gave
the show without the reality of knowledge, were unable to
make effectual progress. For instance, the old fourfold division
of causes into material, formal, efficient, and final, instead of
being regarded as what it really is—a useful temporary formula
to introduce clearness into our own conceptions—was still supposed to be actually inherent in the nature of things, and was

---

[1] Hallam's *Literature of Europe*, vol. ii. p. 463.

made the basis for the formation of distinct departments of knowledge. In the seventeenth century, the human mind, even among the most advanced communities, had still much of the presumptuous forwardness natural to children and savages. The complexity of natural phenomena was partly unknown, partly under-estimated. Instead of sitting down humbly as a disciple, and endeavouring to decipher here and there a few pages of nature's book, man still conceived himself to stand immeasurably above nature, and to possess within his own resources, if the proper key could only be found, the means of unlocking all her secrets, and compelling her subservience to his wants.

If **Bacon's** philosophical labours had been of no other service than to beat down this presumptuous temper, and explode this notion of the finality of science, they must have been regarded as of inestimable value. He shared to the full in the eager and sanguine temper which we have shown to be characteristic of the age ;—he takes for his motto *Plus ultra*; he revels in the view of the immensity of the field lying open before the human faculties; and the title-page of the original edition of his *Instauratio Magna* bears the meaning portraiture of a ship in full sail, with a consort following in her wake, bearing down to pass between the fabled Pillars of Hercules, the limit of the knowledge, and almost of the aspirations, of the ancient world. He repeats more than once that in the sciences ' opinion of store is found to be one of the chief causes of want.' He is unjust, indeed, in attributing this presumptuous persuasion of the completeness of science to Aristotle, whom he sometimes strangely depreciates, even going so far as to say that in the general wreck of learning consequent upon the invasion of the Empire by the barbarians, the flimsy and superficial character of Aristotle's system buoyed it up, when the more solid and valuable works of the earlier philosophers perished. It is true that those who had attempted to philosophize, ever since the time of Aristotle, had been unduly influenced by his great name, and had often acquiesced blindly in his conclusions. Aristotle, however, is not justly chargeable with the errors of his followers.

It is clear that Bacon was keenly alive to the comparative worthlessness of all that had been done by the philosophers who preceded him towards a real knowledge of nature. What made him prize this knowledge so highly? Not so much its own intrinsic value, nor even its effects on the mind receiving it, as the persuasion which he felt that, if obtained, it would give to man an effective command over nature. For his aim in philosophizing was eminently practical; he loved philosophy chiefly because of the immense utility which he felt certain lay enfolded in it, for the improving and adorning of man's life. This is the meaning of the well-known Baconian axiom, 'Knowledge is power.' To know nature would always involve, he thought, the power to use her for our own purposes; and it seems that he would have cared little for any scientific knowledge of phenomena which remained barren of practical results.

83. The end, therefore, was to know nature in order to make use of her ; from this end all previous philosophy had wandered away and lost itself. Let us try now to conceive distinctly what Bacon believed himself to have accomplished for its realization. In few words, he believed that he had discovered an intellectual instrument of such enormous power, that the skilful application of it would suffice to resolve all the problems which the world of sense presents to us. This 'new instrument,' or *Novum Organum*, he describes in the book so named. Armed with this, he considered that an ordinary intellect would be placed on a par with the most highly gifted minds; and this supposed fact he uses to defend himself from the charge of presumption, since, he says, it is not a question of mental gifts or powers, but of methods ; and just as a weak man, armed with a lever, may, without presumption, think he can raise a greater weight than a strong man using only his bare strength, so the inquirer into nature, who has found out the right road or method, may, without vanity, expect to make greater discoveries than he, however great his original powers, who is proceeding by the wrong road. The instrument thus extolled is the Baconian ' method of instances,' of which it may be well here to give a short account.

Let it be premised that the object of the philosopher is to ascertain the *form*, that is, the fundamental law,[1] of some property common to a variety of natural objects. He must proceed thus : First, he prepares a table of instances, in all of which the property is present; as, for example,—in the case of heat,—the sun's rays, fire, wetted hay, &c. Secondly, he prepares a table of instances, apparently cognate to those in the first table, or some of them, in which, nevertheless, the given property is absent. Thus, the moon's rays, though, like those of the sun, they possess illuminating powers, give out no heat. Thirdly, he prepares a table of degrees, or a comparative table, showing the different degrees in which the property is exhibited in different instances. Fourthly, by means of the materials accumulated in the three preceding tables, he constructs a table

---

[1] *Novum Organum*, book ii. ch. 17 : ' The form of heat, or of light, means exactly the same as the law of heat, or the law of light.'

of exclusions, or a 'rejection of natures;' that is, he successively denies any property to be the *form* of the given property,
which he has not found to be invariably present or absent in
every instance where the latter was present or absent, and to
increase and decrease as the latter increased and decreased. Thus,
in the case of heat, he denies light to be the form of heat, because he has found light to be present in the instance of the
moon's rays, while heat was absent.   The fifth and final step is,
to draw an affirmative conclusion—the 'interpretation of nature
in the affirmative;'—that is, to affirm that residuary property,
which, *if the process has been carried far enough*, will be found
remaining when all others have been excluded, to be the form
of the given property.   Thus he affirms motion to be the form
of heat.

The weak point in this method, or, at any rate, one weak
point, seems to be indicated by the words printed in italics, 'if
the process has been carried far enough.'   There would be no
difficulty in doing this, if it were really such an easy matter to
break up every instance or concrete phenomenon into the 'natures,' or abstract properties, entering into its composition, as
Bacon assumes it to be.   But how far is even modern science,
aided by all the resources of chemistry and electricity, from
having accomplished this: and how hopeless was it then to make
this process the foundation of a philosophic method, when chemistry could not as yet be said to exist!   It seems that Bacon
himself partly fell into that error, to which he rightly ascribes
the sterility of philosophy in his day,[1]—the tendency, namely,
to frame wide generalizations from insufficient data, and to neglect the laborious establishment of partial or medial generalizations.   Thus it is that he is led to attempt to define the in-
most nature of heat, when as yet the materials for so wide and
difficult a generalization had not been collected—as they can
only be collected—by means of a searching investigation into
all the laws which regulate its operation and manifestation.

Considerations of this kind, coupled with the now admitted
fact, that, fond as Bacon was of experiments, he made and multiplied them to little profit, and left no important contribution
to any single branch of physical science, induce the latest editors
of his works,[2] whose admirable performance of their task marks
them out as in every way competent judges, to acknowledge
that nothing can be made of his peculiar system of philosophy.
'If we have not tried it, it is because we feel confident that it

---

[1] *Novum Organum*, book ii.
[2] Bacon's Works, edited by Ellis and Spedding.

would not answer. We regard it as a curious piece of machinery, very subtle, elaborate, and ingenious; but not worth constructing, because all the work it could do may be done more easily another way.'

All this may be true; still the claims of Bacon to the admiration and gratitude of his countrymen rest upon grounds which nothing alleged here, or that can be alleged, will ever weaken. He used his life and his genius in preaching perpetually, that men should go to nature, and investigate the facts; that, in all matters cognizable by the understanding, with the sole exception of revealed religion, experience, not authority, should be taken as the guide to truth. When he himself indeed went to nature, the instrument which he used was too much encumbered with those metaphysical notions, the futility of which it was reserved for a later age to discover, to permit of his effecting much. But his general advice was followed, though his particular method was found unworkable. It may be doubted whether his influence has not been almost too great in this direction: whether he has not led his countrymen too far away from the path of speculation and the consideration of general principles; whether the incessant accumulation of observations and experiments, to which our men of science, as Baconians, have devoted themselves ever since the sixteenth century, has not been too exclusively prosecuted, to the detriment of the departments of pure thought.[1]   But, however this may be, the reality and the greatness of his influence can be denied by none who contemplate the immense material benefits which the prevalence of the inductive spirit, and the resort to experiment, have conferred upon England, and, through England, upon Europe and America.

Again, it must be remembered that if anything was wanting to Bacon in exact scientific faculty, it was more than compensated in moral wisdom. Certainly, when we consider with what a grasp of understanding he took in all the parts of human society,—how he surveyed all its ranks and subdivisions, noting the elements of strength and weakness natural to each; and again, how profoundly he analysed the false appearances, or 'idols,' which beset individual minds and prevent them from attaining to truth,—the idols of the tribe, or false notions common to the race,—the idols of the cave, or false notions proper to the individual,—the idols of the market-place, or the false notions imposed upon us by the ambiguities of language,—

[1] See some valuable remarks on this point in the chapter on the Scottish intellect in the eighteenth century, in the second volume of the lamented Mr. Buckle's *History of Civilization.*

lastly, the idols of the theatre, or the specious theories of false philosophy;—when we review these and many other deep and subtle thoughts that lie thickly scattered through his works, it is impossible not to rank Bacon among the most powerful and sagacious thinkers that have ever instructed mankind.

84. With these general remarks on the Baconian philosophy, we proceed to note down the date of appearance and general scope of Bacon's principal works. Of the *Essays* we have already spoken.[1] His philosophical views are contained in three principal works, besides many detached papers and fragments. The three works are, the *Advancement of Learning*, the *Instauratio Magna*, and the *De Augmentis Scientiarum*. The first was composed in English, and first published in 1605. Its general object was to take a survey of the whole field of human knowledge, showing its actual state in its various departments, and noting what parts had been cultivated, what were lying waste, without, however, entering upon the difficult inquiry as to *erroneous methods* of cultivation; his purpose in this work being only 'to note omissions and deficiencies,' with a view to their being made good by the labours of learned men. It may throw light on what has been said as to the nature of Bacon's method, if his mode of procedure in the work now under consideration be examined somewhat more fully.

After dividing human learning into three parts, history, poetry, and philosophy, corresponding respectively to the three principal faculties of the mind, memory, imagination, and reason, he first examines how far history and poetry have been adequately cultivated. Literary history is noted as deficient, a remark which Bacon certainly would not have made at the present day, Coming to philosophy, he again makes a threefold division into divine, natural, and human philosophy. By divine philosophy he means natural theology, or 'that knowledge or rudiment of knowledge concerning God, which may be obtained by the contemplation of His creatures; which knowledge may be truly termed divine in respect of the object, and natural in respect of the light.'

Natural philosophy he divides into two parts, the inquisition of causes, and the production of effects; speculative and operative; natural science and natural prudence. Now the reader, unacquainted with the precise light in which Bacon regarded his own method, would expect to find him noting down natural science as extremely deficient, and giving some sketch, by way of anticipation, of the improvements which he hoped to introduce

---

[1] See *ante*, § 65.

into its cultivation. But he does nothing of the kind; and for this reason, because the method from which he expected so much did not appear to him in the light of an improvement on old modes of inquiry, but rather as a piece of new intellectual machinery, by him first invented; he does not, therefore, refer it to the philosophy of nature, but, as we shall see, to the philosophy of the human mind. Human philosophy he divides into two parts—knowledge of man as an individual, and knowledge of man in society, or civil knowledge. Again, the knowledge of man, as an individual, is of two kinds, as relating either to the body or to the mind. To the first kind are referred human anatomy, medicine, &c.; the second kind includes knowledge of the substance or nature of the mind, and knowledge of its faculties or functions. And since these faculties are mainly of two kinds, those of the understanding and reason, and those of the will, appetite, and affection, this part of human philosophy naturally falls into the two great leading divisions, rational and moral. What is said of the state of moral or ethical philosophy is exceedingly interesting, but it is with his account of 'rational knowledge, or arts intellectual,' that we have here to do. The first of these, he says, is the 'art of inquiry or invention,' which, in that department of it which deals with arts and sciences, he notes as deficient, and proceeds, in a very striking passage,[1] to explain the grounds of this opinion. Rejecting the syllogistic method as inadequate, he pronounces in favour of the inductive method, as the true art of intellectual invention—the sole genuine interpreter of nature—and promises to expound it on a subsequent occasion.

85. This promise was redeemed, partially at least, by the publication of the *Novum Organum* in 1620. This is the second part of what he intended to be a vast philosophical system, in six divisions, entitled the *Instauratio Philosophiæ*. The *De Augmentis Scientiarum*, which is in the main a Latin version of *The Advancement of Learning*, about one-third of its bulk consisting of new matter, covers most of the ground which the first of these divisions was intended to occupy; the second is the *Novum Organum*. The third division was to consist of a complete *Historia Naturalis*, founded on the most accurate observation and the most diligent and extensive research. To this part Bacon only contributed what he called his *Centuries of Natural History*, containing about one thousand observed facts and experiments; at the same time he enumerated one hundred and thirty particular histories which ought to be prepared under this

---

[1] Vol. iii. p. 392 (Ellis's edition).

head. The *Scala Intellectus*, or history of analytical investigation, was to form the fourth division. By this appears to have been meant a description of the actual processes employed by the intellect in the investigation of truth, with an account of the peculiar difficulties and peculiar facilities which it encounters on the road. Of this part Bacon has only written a few introductory pages. The fifth division was to have contained samples of the new method of philosophizing, and specimens of the results obtained, under the title *Prodromi sive Anticipationes Philosophiæ Secundæ.* Two or three separate tracts under this head are all that Bacon could accomplish. The sixth division, *Philosophia Secunda sive Scientia activa*, which should have been the full system, properly digested and harmoniously ordered, of the new philosophy itself, he despaired of living to accomplish. Indeed, to use Mr. Hallam's words, 'no one man could have filled up the vast outline, which he alone, in that stage of the world, could have so boldly sketched.'

Political Science :—Buchanan, Spenser, Raleigh.

86. It was impossible but that the general intellectual awakening which characterized the period should extend itself to political science. The doctrines of civil freedom now began to be heard from many lips, and in every direction penetrated the minds of men, producing convictions which the next generation was to see brought into action. Not that these opinions were wholly new, even the most advanced of them. To say nothing of the ancients, the great Aquinas, in his treatise *De Regimine Principum*, had said, as far back as the middle of the thirteenth century, that 'Rex datur propter regnum, et non regnum propter regem,'[1] and had declared the constitutional or limited form of monarchy to be superior to the absolute form. But the class to which literature appealed in the thirteenth century was both too small, and too much absorbed in professional interests, to admit of such views becoming fruitful. After the invention of printing and the revival of learning, they were taken up by many thinkers in different parts of Europe, and rapidly circulated through the educated portion of society. In 1579, the stern old **George Buchanan,** James I.'s pedagogue, crowned a long and adventurous life, in which his liberal opinions had brought on him more than one imprisonment, besides innumerable minor persecutions and troubles, by the publication, in his seventy-fourth year, of the

[1] 'The king exists for the sake of the kingdom, not the kingdom for the sake of the king.'

work, *De jure Regni apud Scotos*.[1] This treatise, which is in
Latin, is in the form of a dialogue between the author and
Thomas Maitland, upon the origin and nature of royal authority
in general, and of the authority of the Scottish crown in particular. In either case, he derives the authority, so far as
lawful, entirely from the consent of the governed; and argues
that its abuse—inasmuch as its possessor is thereby constituted
a tyrant—exposes him justly even to capital punishment at the
hands of his people, and that not by public sentence only, but
by the act of any private person. Views so extreme led to the
condemnation and prohibition of the work by the Scottish
parliament in 1584. It may be granted that Buchanan's close
connection with the party of the Regent Murray, whose interest `
it was to create an opinion of the lawfulness of any proceedings,
to whatever lengths they might be carried, against the person and
authority of the unhappy Queen, then in confinement in England, was likely to impart an extraordinary keenness and strin-
gency to the anti-monarchical theories advocated in the book.
Nevertheless similar views were supported in the sixteenth century in the most unexpected quarters; the Jesuit Mariana, for
instance, openly advocates regicide in certain contingencies; and
it was quite in character with the daring temper of the age to
demolish the awe surrounding any power, however venerable,
which thwarted the projects of either the majority or the most
active and influential party in a state.

87. Among the political writings of this period there is none
more remarkable than **Spenser's** *View of the State of Ireland*,
which, though written and presented to Elizabeth about the
year 1596, was not published till 1633. This is the work of an
eye-witness, who was at once a shrewd observer and a profound
thinker, upon the difficulties of the Irish question,—that problem which pressed for solution in the sixteenth century, and is
still unsolved in the nineteenth. Spenser traces the evils afflict-
ing Ireland to three sources, connected respectively with its
laws, its customs, and its religion; examines each source in
turn; suggests specific remedial measures; and, finally, sketches
out a general plan of government calculated to prevent the
growth of similar mischiefs for the future.

88. In England, the active and penetrating mind of **Raleigh**
was employed in this direction among others. It is very interesting to find him, in his *Observations on Trade and Commerce*, advocating the system of low duties on imports, and
explaining the immense advantages which the Dutch, in the few

---

[1] 'Upon Scotch Monarchical Law.' `

years that had elapsed since they conquered their independence from Spain, had derived from free trade and open ports. The treatise on the *Prerogative of Parliament*, written in the Tower, and addressed to the King, was designed to induce James to summon a parliament, as the most certain and satisfactory mode of paying the crown debts.   It is true, he adapts the reasoning in some places to the base and tyrannical mind which he was attempting to influence; saying, for example, that although the King might be obliged to promise reforms to his parliament in return for subsidies, he need not keep his word when parliament was broken up.   But this Machiavelian suggestion may be explained as the desperate expedient of an unhappy prisoner, who saw no hope either for himself or for his country except in the justice of a free Parliament, and, since the King alone could call Parliament together, endeavoured to make the measure as little unpalatable as possible to the contemptible and unprincipled person who then occupied the throne.   Much of the historical inquiry which he institutes into the relations between former parliaments and English kings is extremely acute and valuable.   In the *Maxims of State*, a short treatise, not written, like the one last mentioned, to serve an immediate purpose, Raleigh's naturally honest and noble nature asserts itself.   In this he explicitly rejects all the immoral suggestions of Machiavel, and lays down none but sound and enlightened principles for the conduct of governments.   Thus, among the maxims to be observed by an hereditary sovereign, we read the following :—

15. To observe the laws of his country, and not to encounter them with his prerogative, nor to use it at all where there is a law, for that it maketh a secret and just grudge in the people's hearts, especially if it tend to take from them their commodities, and to bestow them upon other of his courtiers and ministers.

It would have been well for Charles I. if he had laid this maxim to heart before attempting to levy ship-money.   Again :

17. To be moderate in his taxes and impositions; and when need doth require to use the subjects' purse, to do it by parliament, and with their consents, making the cause apparent to them, and showing his unwillingness in charging them.   Finally, so to use it that it may seem rather an offer from his subjects than an exaction by him.

A political essay, entitled *The Cabinet Council*, was left by Raleigh in manuscript at his death, and came into the hands of Milton, by whom it was published with a short preface.   Though acute and shrewd, like all that came from the same hand, this treatise is less interesting than those already mentioned, because it enters little into the consideration of general causes, but consists mainly of practical maxims, suited to that age, for the use of statesmen and commanders.

CHAPTER IV.

CIVIL WAR PERIOD.

1625–1700.

1. THE literature of this period will be better understood after
a brief explanation has been given of the political changes which
attended the fall, restoration, and ultimate expulsion of the
Stuart dynasty.

The Puritan party, whose proceedings and opinions in the
two preceding reigns have been already noticed, continued to
grow in importance, and demanded with increasing loudness a
reform in the Church establishment. They were met at first by
a bigotry at least equal, and a power superior, to their own.
Archbishop Laud, who presided in the High Commission Court,[1]
had taken for his motto the word 'Thorough,' and had persuaded
himself that only by a system of severity could conformity to
the established religion be enforced. Those who wrote against,
or even impugned in conversation, the doctrine, discipline, or
government of the Church of England, were brought before the
High Commission Court and heavily fined; and a repetition
of the offence, particularly if any expressions were used out
of which a seditious meaning could be extracted, frequently
led to an indictment of the offender in the Star Chamber (in
which also Laud had a seat), and to his imprisonment and
mutilation by order of that iniquitous tribunal. Thus Prynne,
a lawyer, Bastwick, a physician, and Burton, a clergyman, after
having run the gauntlet of the High Commission Court, and
been there sentenced to suspension from the practice of their
professions, fined, imprisoned, and excommunicated, were in
1632 summoned before the Star Chamber, and sentenced to
stand in the pillory, to lose their ears, and be imprisoned for life.
In 1633 Leighton, father of the eminent Archbishop Leighton,
was by the same court sentenced to be publicly whipped, to lose
both ears, to have his nostrils slit, to be branded on both cheeks,
and imprisoned for life. In all these cases the offence was of
the same kind;—the publication of some book or tract, gene-

---

[1] Established by Queen Elizabeth to try ecclesiastical offences.

R

rally couched, it must be admitted, in scurrilous and inflammatory language, assailing the government of the Church by bishops, or the Church liturgy and ceremonies, or some of the common popular amusements, such as dancing and playgoing, to which these fanatics imputed most of the vice which corrupted society.

To these ecclesiastical grievances Charles I. took care to add political. By his levies of ship-money, and of tonnage and poundage,—by his stretches of the prerogative,—by his long delay in convoking the Parliament, and many other illegal or irritating proceedings, he estranged most of the leading politicians, —the Pyms, Hampdens, Seldens, and Hydes,—just as by supporting Laud he estranged the commercial and burgher classes, among whom Puritanism had its stronghold. In November 1640 the famous Long Parliament met; the quarrel became too envenomed to be composed otherwise than by recourse to arms; and in 1642 the civil war broke out. Gradually the conduct of the war passed out of the hands of the more numerous section of the Puritan party—the Presbyterians—into those of a section hitherto obscure—the Independents—who were supported by the genius of Milton and Cromwell. This sect originally bore the name of *Brownists*, from their founder, Robert Browne (1549–1630): they went beyond the moderate Puritans in regarding conformity to the Establishment as a sin, and therefore forming, in defiance of the law, separate congregations. But their later writers, such as Milton and Owen, compensated for this indomitable sectarianism by maintaining the doctrine of toleration; against the Presbyterians they argued that the civil magistrate had no right to force the consciences of individuals. They took care, indeed, to make one exception; there was to be no toleration for the Roman Catholic worship. 'As for what you mention about liberty of conscience,' said Cromwell to the delegates from Ross, 'I meddle not with any man's conscience. But if by liberty of conscience you mean a liberty to exercise the mass, I judge it best to use plain dealing, and to let you know, where the Parliament of England have power, that will not be permitted.'[1] Still it was a great thing to have the principle once boldly asserted and partially applied; for Catholics as well as others were sure to benefit sooner or later from its extension.

2. In the civil war, the clergy, four-fifths of the aristocracy and landed gentry, with the rural population depending on them, and some few cities, adhered to the King. The poets,

[1] See Carlyle's *Letters and Speeches of Cromwell.*

wits, and artists, between whom and Puritanism a kind of natural enmity subsisted, sought, with few exceptions, the royal camp, where they were probably more noisy than serviceable. On the other hand, the Parliament was supported by the great middle class, and by the yeomen or small landed proprietors. It had at first but one poet (Wither was then a royalist), but that one was John Milton.

The King's cause became hopeless after the defeat of Naseby in 1645; and after a lengthened imprisonment he was brought to the block by the army and the Independents, ostensibly as a traitor and malefactor against his people; really, because, while he lived, the revolutionary leaders could never feel secure. There is a significant query in one of Cromwell's letters, written in 1648, 'whether "Salus populi summa lex" be not a sound maxim.'

But before the fatal window in Whitehall the reaction in the public sentiment and conscience commenced. Cromwell, indeed, carried on the government with consummate ability and vigour; but after all he represented only his own stern genius, and the victorious army which he had created; and when he died, and in the rivalries of his generals the power of that army was neutralized, England, by a kind of irresistible gravitation, returned to that position of defined and prescriptive freedom which had been elaborated during the long course of the middle ages.

3. At the Restoration (1660), the courtiers, wits, and poets returned from exile not uninfluenced, whether for good or evil, by their long sojourn abroad; the Anglican clergy saw their church established on a firmer footing than ever; and their Puritan adversaries, ejected and silenced, passed below the surface of society, and secretly organized the earlier varieties of that many-headed British dissent which now numbers nearly half the people of England among its adherents. The theatres were reopened; and every loyal subject—to prove himself no Puritan —tried to be as wild, reckless, and dissolute as possible. Yet in the course of years the defeated party, with changed tactics indeed, and in a soberer mood, began to make itself felt. Instead of asking for a theocracy, they now agitated for toleration; and, renouncing their republicanism as impracticable, they took up the watchword of constitutional reform. The Puritans and Roundheads of the civil war reappear towards the close of Charles II.'s reign under the more permanent appellation of the *Whig party*.

One of the points in which the party was found least altered after its transformation was its bitter and traditional hostility

to the Church of Rome. Hence, after it became known that
the heir-presumptive to the crown, James Duke of York, had
.changed his religion, the Whigs formed the design of excluding
him on that ground from the throne, and placing the crown
upon the head of the next Protestant heir. The party of the
court and the cavaliers (who began about this time to be called
Tories) vigorously opposed the scheme, and with success. James
II. succeeded in 1685, and immediately began to take measures
for the relief of Catholics from the many disabilities under
which they laboured. But he pursued his object with all the
indiscretion and unfairness habitual to his family. Though the
Whigs had been defeated and cowed,—though the great majority
of the nation desired to be loyal,—though the Anglican clergy
in particular had committed themselves irrevocably to the position that a king ought to be obeyed, no matter to what lengths
he might go in tyranny,—James so managed matters as almost to
compel the divines to eat their own words, and, by forfeiting the
affection and confidence of the people, to throw the game into
the hands of the Whigs. The Revolution came; James II.
was expelled; the Act of Settlement was passed; and the Catholics of England again became an obscure and persecuted
minority, which for a hundred years almost disappears from the
public gaze and from the page of history.

Under William III., from 1688 to 1700, there was a lull, comparatively speaking, in political affairs. The Toleration Act,
passed in 1689, amounted to a formal renunciation of the claim
of the state—on account of which so much blood had been
shed in this and the previous century—to impose religious uniformity upon its subjects. Towards the middle of William's
reign the Tories began to recover from the stunning effects of
the moral shock which they had sustained at the Revolution;
and the modern system of parliamentary government, though
complicated for a time by the question of Jacobitism, began to
develope its outlines out of the strife of the opposing parties.

Having thus reviewed the course of events, we proceed to
describe the development of ideas, as expressed in literature,
during the same period.

Poetry before the Restoration; Jonson: The Fantastic School; Cowley, Crashaw, &c.; Milton, Marvell.

4. Under the Stuarts the court still, as in the days of Elizabeth, opened its gates gladly to the poets and playwrights.
Jonson's chief literary employment during his later years was
the composition of masques for the entertainment of the king

and royal family. That quarrelsome, reckless, intemperate man,
whose pedantry must have been insufferable to his contemporaries had it not been relieved by such flashes of wit, such a flow
of graceful simple feeling, outlived by many years the friends
of his youth, and died, almost an old man, in 1637. His beautiful pastoral drama of the *Sad Shepherd* was left unfinished
at his death. To a collection of his miscellaneous poems he
gave the strange title of ' Underwoods.' No. XV. is the famous
epitaph on the Countess of Pembroke :—

> Underneath this sable herse
> Lies the subject of all verse,
> Sidney's sister, Pembroke's mother ;
> Death, ere thou hast slain another,
> Learn'd, and fair, and good as she,
> Time shall throw a dart at thee !

A diligent reader of Jonson's masques will find, scattered up
and down them, some of the airiest and prettiest songs in the
world. ' Rise, Cynthia, rise,' is one of these ; another is the
merry catch in the *Masque of Oberon*, beginning—

> Buz, quoth the blue flie,
> Hum, quoth the bee ;
> Buz and hum they cry,
> And so do we.

Among the numerous epigrams, this is noteworthy :—

> Underneath this stone doth lie
> As much beauty as could die ;
> Which in life did harbour give
> To more virtue than doth live.

The famous song ' To Celia,' which begins—

> Drink to me, only, with thine eyes,
> And I will pledge with mine—

is No. 9 in the group of poems called *The Forest*. The elegiac
verses addressed ' To the memory of my beloved master, Wm.
Shakspeare, and what he hath left us,' are interesting. Jonson's
love of his subject seems to be genuine, and to transport him out
of himself. Here occurs the fine line :—

> He was not of an age, but for all time.

The refinement,—the true *gentleness* of Shakspere's nature
are glanced at in the following lines, which may be compared
with what Lydgate wrote of Chaucer (*ante*, ch. i. § 71) :—

Look how the father's face
Lives in his offspring; even so the race
Of Shakspeare's mind and manners brightly shines
In his well-turnèd and true-filèd lines:
In each of which he seems to shake a lance
As brandished at the eyes of ignorance.
Sweet Swan of Avon! what a sight it were
To see thee in our water yet appear,
And make those flights upon the banks of Thames
That so did take Eliza and our James!

5. The younger race of poets belonged nearly all to what has been termed by Dryden and Dr. Johnson the Metaphysical school, the founder of which in England was Donne. But in fact this style of writing was of Italian parentage, and was brought in by the Neapolitan Marini.[1] Tired of the endless imitations of the ancients, which, except when a great genius like that of Tasso broke through all conventional rules, had ever since the revival of learning fettered the poetic taste of Italy, Marini resolved to launch out boldly in a new career of invention, and to give to the world whatever his keen wit and lively fancy might prompt to him. He is described by Sismondi[2] as 'the celebrated innovator on classic Italian taste, who first seduced the poets of the seventeenth century into that laboured and affected style which his own richness and vivacity of imagination were so well calculated to recommend. The most whimsical comparisons, pompous and overwrought descriptions, with a species of poetical punning and research, were soon esteemed, under his authority, as beauties of the very first order.' Marini resided for some years in France, and it was in that country that he produced his *Adone*. His influence upon French poetry was as great as upon Italian, but the vigour and freedom which it communicated were perhaps more than counterbalanced by the false taste which it encouraged. The same may be said of his influence upon our own poets. Milton alone had too much originality and inherent force to be carried away in the stream; but the most popular poets of the day,— Donne, Cowley, Crashaw, Waller, Cleveland, and even Dryden in his earlier efforts—gave in to the prevailing fashion, and instead of simple, natural images, studded their poems with *conceits* (concetti). This explains why Cowley was rated by his contemporaries as the greatest poet of his day, since every age has its favourite fashions, in literature as in costume; and those who conform to them receive more praise than those who assert

---

[1] Born 1569, died 1625; author of the *Adone* and the *Sospetto di Herode*.
[2] *Literature of the South of Europe* (Roscoe), vol. ii. p. 262.

their independence. Thus Clarendon [1] speaks of Cowley as having 'made a flight beyond all men;' and Denham, in the elegy which he wrote on him, compares him with Shakspere, Jonson, and Fletcher, to the disadvantage of the three older poets. A few specimens will, however, better illustrate the Metaphysical, or, as we should prefer to term it, the Fantastic manner, than pages of explanation. The first is from Donne's metrical epistles : describing a sea-voyage, he says :—

> There note they the ship's sicknesses,--the mast
> Shaked with an ague, and the hold and waist
> With a salt dropsy clogged.

Cleveland compares the stopping of a fountain to a change in the devolution of an estate :—

> As an obstructed fountain's head
>   Cuts the entail off from the streams,
> And brooks are disinherited ;
>   Honour and beauty are mere dreams,
> Since Charles and Mary lost their beams.

Cowley talks of a trembling sky and a startled sun : in the *Davideis,* Envy thus addresses Lucifer :—

> Do thou but threat, loud storms shall make reply,
> And thunder echo to the *trembling* sky ;
> Whilst raging seas swell to so bold a height,
> As shall the fire's proud element affright.
> Th' old drudging sun, from his long-beaten way,
> Shall at thy voice *start*, and misguide the day, &c.

Dryden, in his youthful elegy on Lord Hastings, who died of the small-pox, describes that malady under various figures :—

> Blisters with pride swelled, which through's flesh did sprout
> Like rose-buds, stuck in the lily-skin about.
> Each little pimple had a tear in it,
> To wail the fault its rising did commit.

To such a pitch of extravagance did talented men proceed in their endeavour to write in the fashion, in their straining after the much-admired *conceits !*

6. Of Donne, who died in 1631, we have already spoken.[1] The other poets just mentioned of the Fantastic school, namely, Cowley, Crashaw, Waller, and Cleveland, together with Thomas Carew, Robert Herrick, Sir John Suckling, Richard Lovelace, George Herbert, Sir John Denham, and Francis Quarles, were all ardent royalists. **Cowley,** like Horace driven from Athens,—

> Dura sed emovere loco me tempora grato,—

---

[1] *Autobiography,* vol. i. p. 80.   [1] See p. 182.

was dislodged from both Universities in turn by the victorious arms of the Parliament, and, attaching himself to the suite of Henrietta Maria, was employed by her at Paris for many years as a confidential secretary. After his return to England in 1656, he published his entire poems, consisting of *Miscellanies, Anacreontics,*[1] *Pindaric Odes,* the *Mistress,* and the *Davideis.* In the preface he advised peaceful submission to the existing Government; and this tenderness to 'the usurpation' was maliciously remembered against him after the restoration of monarchy. He was fully included in the act of oblivion which Charles II. is said to have extended to his *friends.* His last years were spent in retirement at Chertsey. He died in 1667, from the effects of a cold caught by staying too long among his labourers in the hay-field.

It will be more easy to assign his proper rank to Cowley, if one remembers that he had a remarkably quick and apprehensive understanding, but a feeble character. One reads a few of his minor pieces, and is struck by the penetrating power of his wit, and dazzled by the daring flights of his imagination; one conceives such a man to be capable of the greatest things. Yet it is not so; a native weakness prevents him from soaring with a sustained flight; the hue of his resolution is ever 'sicklied o'er with the pale cast of thought;' or rather his resolution is not of that tried and stable quality at the outset which would enable it to brush away subsequent and conflicting impulses from its path. He began the *Davideis* at Cambridge, with the idea of producing a great epic poem on a scriptural subject; but he completed no more than four cantos, and then gave up the design. It needed a more stern determination than his to carry through such a work to a successful issue. He felt this, nor doubted that the right poet would be found. He says of the *Davideis,* 'I shall be ambitious of no other fruit for this weak and imperfect attempt of mine, but the opening of a way to the courage and industry of some other persons, who may be better able to perform it thoroughly and successfully.' As in this preface (written in 1656) he was endeavouring to conciliate the party in power, it seems not unlikely that in this passage he actually refers to Milton, who in more than one of his prose works had spoken of his wish and intention to take up the harp some day, and sing to the Divine honour, 'an elaborate song for generations.'

There was something in Cowley of extraordinary power, both to kindle affection and to disarm malice; never was any

---

[1] See Crit. Sect. ch. 1., *Lyrical Poetry,* § 62. ·

man more truly loved by his friends; and this personal charm may explain in part their excessive admiration of his genius. But he, if left to himself, preferred solitude; professing always, says his biographer, Sprat, 'that he went out of the world, as it was man's, into the same world, as it was nature's, and as it was God's.' He once wrote,—

> All wretched and too solitary he
> Who loves not his own company.
> He'll feel the weight of 't many a day,
> Unless he call in sin or vanity
> To help to bear 't away.

In truth a mind so active and penetrating as his could never allow time to hang heavy, or be unemployed. When, for example, upon his return to England, during the Protectorate, his friends advised him to study medicine, his compliance with their advice, instead of leading him to a profitable practice, carried him no farther than the Pharmacopœa; the subject of *herbs* so fascinated him, that he wandered on from the consideration of their medicinal, to that of their general properties, and thence to the study of their modes and conditions of growth. From *herbs* he passed on to *flowers*; which in turn suggested the study of *trees*, first those of the orchard, next those of the forest. The result was a Latin poem in six books, *Of Plants*, a work of wonderful cleverness and brilliancy. Several hands gladly engaged in translating it into English.

7. This remarkable fertility and brilliancy of wit is perhaps still better shown by another work, a Latin play, *Naufragium Joculare*, 'The Comic Shipwreck,' which he wrote and caused to be acted at Cambridge, in his twentieth year. It is in the style of Terence; and the dialogue proceeds with an easy flow of jest, anecdote, and repartee, which exhibits Cowley's linguistic resources in a most remarkable light. His only other dramatic attempts were, *Love's Riddle*, a pastoral comedy, which he composed while still a Westminster boy, and *The Cutter of Coleman Street*, a prose comedy of no great merit.

His shorter poems have now to be considered; and it is among these that we shall find what may approach nearest to a justification of the praises of his contemporaries. As to the *Mistress*, a collection of love poems, Cowley, if his own account may be believed, wrote them, not in the character of a lover impelled to clothe his feelings and wishes in song, but rather in that of a professional verse-maker; for poets, he says, 'are never thought freemen of their company, without paying some duties, and obliging themselves to be true to love.' These poems accordingly may be taken for metrical exercises, displaying much ingenuity but no living power. One, however, which is very gracefully and happily expressed, and more carefully rimed and measured than is the author's wont, shall be given at a future page.[1] But it was the daring flight which he essayed in his Pindaric odes that most dazzled and charmed the age. This style, which Dryden often tried, and Pope and Gray occasionally, was, he tells us, accidentally suggested to him; the works of Pindar having chanced to fall in his way at a time when no other books were to be had, and the compulsory familiarity thus occasioned having led to a deliberate preference for Pindar's irregular metres. But even if this was the correct account of it, it is certain that the permitted lawlessness of the metre, in which long and short lines are mingled together haphazard, and rimes are either coupled, alternate, or even more widely separated, was peculiarly suitable to the vehement rush of thoughts which was ever pressing for utterance through Cowley's brain, and which no adequate solidity of judgment controlled or sifted. But Cowley is not even regular in dealing with irregularity; while many of his 'Pindariques' preserve a wild harmony of their own amidst all their flings and sallies, which is enough to satisfy the critical ear, there are others in which lines occur that trail their huge length laboriously along like wounded snakes, and by no possible humouring or contraction of the syllables can be reduced to harmony. Take, for instance, the conclusion of the ode to Mr. Hobbes—a really fine poem; what mortal ear can tolerate the last line?—

And that which never is to die, for ever must be young.

Dryden's correcter ear, when he Pindaricized, scarcely ever suffered him to make such slips.

The subjects of Cowley's Pindaric odes are very various. Sometimes he translates or imitates Pindar or Horace; sometimes he devotes them to the cause of philosophy, dedicating one to Hobbes, another to the Royal Society then recently founded, another to Harvey on his discovery of the circulation of the blood. The ode *To the Duke of Buckingham*, on his marriage with the daughter of Lord Fairfax, possesses some peculiar interest, as bringing before us, in the day of his happy and brilliant youth, the same Villiers whom Dryden satirized under the character of Zimri, and whose end afforded a theme for Pope to moralize upon in his third *Épistle*. He discharged his loyal duty to his prince in the ode *Upon his Majesty's Restoration and Return.* Among all similar compositions of that age, Cowley's Restoration ode is by far the best, because the most genuine. It is true that his loyalty makes him depart

---

[1] See Crit. Sect. ch. I., *Lyrical Poetry*, § 60.

from truth, when Charles II., or his father, or any other Stuart
is in the case, almost as much as Dryden. But such exaggeration is more excusable in the older poet, who had suffered long
years for the cause which he now saw triumphant, and whose
loyal logic seems to have almost honestly reasoned thus :—
' Being the rightful king, he *must* be all that is excellent.'
With even greater sincerity, one cannot doubt, Cowley abhorred
the Protector, with whom he had never, like Dryden, or Waller,
or Milton, been brought into close contact. In a prose *Discourse
concerning the Government of Oliver Cromwell* he burst forth
into a set of vigorous stanzas, pathetically deprecating the recurrence of such a horrible tyranny as the nation had just been
freed from :—

> Come the eleventh plague, rather than this should be ;
>   Come sink us rather in the sea ;
> Come rather Pestilence, and reap us down ;
>   Come God's sword rather than our own ;
> Let rather Roman come again,
> Or Saxon, Norman, or the Dane ;
> In all the ills we ever bore,
> We grieved, we sighed, we wept ; we never blushed before.
>
> If for our sins the divine vengeance be
>   Called to the last extremity,
> Let some denouncing Jonas first be sent,
>   To see if England will repent ;
> Methinks at least some prodigy,
> Some dreadful portent from on high,
> Should terribly forewarn the earth,
> As of good princes' deaths, so of a tyrant's birth.

We shall have occasion to notice farther on the very different impressions which this great ruler and his policy left on
Dryden and Milton.[1] One, and that one perhaps the best of
the Pindariques, is called *The Complaint* ; in the language of
decent, but firm and not undignified remonstrance, it speaks of
the neglect in which the gentle poet lay, after his long and faithful service to the court.

A poem called ' A Vote' (*i.e.* a wish or prayer), written
when he was but thirteen, ends with this remarkable stanza :—

> Thus would I double my life's fading space,
> For he that runs it well, twice runs his race ;
>   And in this true delight,
> These, unbought sports, and happy state,
> I would not fear nor wish my fate,
>   But boldly say each night,
> To-morrow let the sun his beams display,
> Or in clouds hide them ; *I have lived to-day*.

[1] See pp. 263 and 267.

As a prose writer, Cowley is copious and easy, with much the same faults that we shall have to notice in Dryden.

8. If, after this examination of his writings, the reader should still ask wherein lies the secret of the extraordinary admiration with which Cowley was regarded by his contemporaries, I can only say that, so far as I can discover, the feeling which his writings excited of difficulties overcome, and various learning employed in the work of composition, was the chief incentive to that admiration. Poetry was then looked upon as a kind of art or craft, in which no one could or ought to excel, who had not been regularly instructed in all the technical details, and through a classical education had become familiar at first-hand with the great poets of antiquity. All these requirements were fulfilled in Cowley, and they were undeniably united to brilliant talents, so that, according to all the prevailing notions of the time, he could not fail to be considered a great poet. Thus it happened that Shakspere, who was thought to have written *easily*, employing little labour and no learning, was ranked, even by able men, below Ben Jonson ; a judgment to our present ideas wholly incomprehensible. Cleveland, for instance, writes as follows, in an elegy on Ben Jonson :—

> Shakspeare may make griefe merry ; Beaumont's style
> Ravish and melt anger into a smile ;
> In winter nights, or after meals, they be,
> I must confess, very good company.
> But thou exact'st our best hours' industry ;
> We may read them,—we ought to study thee ;
> Thy scenes are precepts ; every verse doth give
> Counsel, and teach us not to laugh, but live.

The truth is that the whole doctrine of hero-worship, as we now conceive it, is modern. Whether they would have avowed it or not, the real upshot of the criticisms on poetry passed by most thinking men in the sixteenth and seventeenth centuries, amounted to a reversal of the old maxim, ' poeta nascitur, non fit ; ' they assume on the contrary that ' poeta fit, non nascitur.' The mysterious spontaneity of genius, which constitutes the ineffable charm of the master-pieces of all great artists, and links together in one fraternity Mozart, and Raphael, and Shakspere, was considered by critics of this class rather as a disqualification than otherwise ; they associated and confounded ease of composition with shallowness of endowment, and a stock of classical phraseology with creative power.

9. The lyrics of **Edmund Waller** can never die. When he tried the heroic style, some inherent disqualification for the task —perhaps a want of true inborn dignity—caused him frequently

to sink *per saltum* from the sublime to the ridiculous. What more perfect instance of the bathos could be given than the following lines from his elaborate elegy *Upon the Death of the Lord Protector ?*—

> Our bounds' enlargement was his latest toil,
> Nor hath he left us prisoners to our isle :
> Under the tropics is our language spoke,
> *And part of Flanders hath received our yoke.*

His heroics *To the Queen* are stiff and artificial, while those *To the Queen Mother of France* unpleasantly remind one of the 'Loyal Effusions' of Fitzgerald, so amusingly parodied in the *Rejected Addresses.*   But now turn to the lyrics, and though it cannot be alleged that their taste is always perfect, their diction always faultless, yet we are forced to confess that the author ' cum magnis vixisse,' and has not fallen below his opportunities ; he treads on sure ground while using to cultivated men or polished gifted women the language of graceful, airy compliment; nor are times lacking when a vein of deeper feeling is touched in that ordinarily frivolous heart, and he surprises us by strains pensive, musical, and lingering in the memory like a requiem by Mozart.   The song *To Flavia,* beginning—

> Tis not your beauty can ingage
> My wary heart ;

the well-known lyric, *Go Lovely Rose,* the song *To Chloris,* and that *To a very Young Lady,* are all in their several ways exceedingly charming.   The fine lines *Upon Ben Jonson* are so appropriate to Shakspere, and so *in*appropriate to Jonson, that one could almost believe the heading to be a blunder.   The genius of Jonson was, we are told,—

> nor this, nor that,—but all we find,
> And all we can imagine in mankind.

Towards the close of his long life, the muse of Waller approached with trembling the mysteries of death and personal accountability.   He was past eighty when he wrote these noble lines :—

> When we for age could neither read nor write,
> The subject made us able to indite :
> The seas are quiet when the winds give o'er ;
> So calm are we when passions are no more ;
> For then we know how vain it was to boast
> Of fleeting things, too certain to be lost.
> Clouds of affection from our younger eyes
> Conceal that emptiness which age descries.

> The soul's dark cottage, batter'd and decayed,
> Lets in new light through chinks that time hath made;
> Stronger by weakness, wiser men become,
> As they draw near to their eternal home.
> Leaving the old, both worlds at once they view,
> Who stand upon the threshold of the new.

Waller lived into the reign of James II., dying in the year 1687.

10. **Richard Crashaw** was, like Cowley, ejected from the University of Cambridge by the Puritans, and deprived of his fellowship. He became a Roman Catholic, and, after suffering great hardships from poverty in Paris, was discovered and generously aided by his friend Cowley. He died at Loretto in 1650, and was mourned by Cowley in one of the most moving and beautiful elegies ever written. Besides writing many miscellaneous pieces, he translated the *Sospetto di Herode* of Marini. The unequal texture of his poetry, and his predilection for conceits, have greatly dimmed a poetical reputation which force of thought and depth of feeling might otherwise have rendered a very high one.

Some of the songs of this period seem to be destined to, and may be held to deserve, as enduring a fame as those of Béranger. Such are, besides those by Waller already mentioned, Carew's *He that loves a rosy Cheek*, Lovelace's song *To Althea, from Prison*, Wither's *Shall I, wasting in despair*, and many more. Never before or since has English life so blossomed into song. Scotland has since had her Burns, and Ireland her Moore, but to find the English *chanson* in perfection, we must go back to the seventeenth century.

11. **George Herbert**, the brother of Lord Herbert of Cherbury, is the author of religious poetry, conceived in a vein which reminds one of Southwell. That he was influenced by the older poet is evident from a sonnet, composed in his seventeenth year, in which he rails, exactly in the manner of Southwell, against the abuse by which poetry is enslaved to human instead of Divine love. A collection of his poems, entitled *The Temple*, was published in 1635, two years after his death, and a new series, *A Priest to the Temple*, appeared among his *Remains* in 1652. *The Church Porch*, the introductory poem of the first series, is highly characteristic; the style is sententious, antithetical, often quaint, and a little verbose. But for didactic pithiness it cannot easily be matched; take such lines, for instance, as this, in relation to drunkenness and careless companions:—

> Pick out of tales the mirth, but not the sin;

or this in relation to veracity,—

> Dare to be true. Nothing can need a lie.
> A fault, which needs it most, grows two thereby ;

or, with reference to the common neglect of education,—

> Some till their ground, but let weeds choke their son ;

or,—

> Envy not greatness ; for thou mak'st thereby
> Thyself the less, and so the distance greater.

The collection is closed by *The Church Militant*, a long poem enunciating the singular theory (which was afterwards applied by Berkeley to 'the course of empire'), that religion always has and always will travel westward. On account of the lines,—

> Religion stands on tip-toe in our land,
> Ready to pass to the American strand ;

the Vice-Chancellor at Cambridge refused for some time to license the printing of the work.

12. **Sir Henry Wotton** and **Bishop Corbet** both died before the breaking out of the civil war. Wotton's serious thoughts were given to diplomacy, but he wrote two or three pretty things. His *Farewell to the Vanities of the World* breathes the detachment of a hermit, and the idealism of a Platonist ; yet he took orders late in life to qualify himself for the comfortable post of Provost of Eton. Corbet was a convivial sinner, with plenty of good common-sense ; disposed to be lenient to the Puritans, not on principle, but merely from his hearty bluff English good nature, which would not let him bear hardly on the weak. His poetry, like the man himself, is of a coarse fibre. His *Journey into France*, written in what may be called the 'Sir Thopas'[1] metre, is sorry doggerel. In his *Farewell to the Fairies*, this jovial soul, thirsting for pleasure, sighs for the good old mediæval days of dancing, May-poles, love-making, and all sorts of riotous fun, which the fairies were supposed to patronize.

13. **Thomas Carew**, who had a post in the court of Charles I., was cut off in his prime about the year 1639. His poems, which are mostly amatory, are of a level standard of merit ; none rise very high, and none are altogether bad.[2] He is full of similitudes and conceits, but they are less extravagant than

---

[1] From the 'Rime of Sir Thopas' in the *Canterbury Tales*.
[2] See Crit. Sect. ch. I. § 59.

those of Donne or Crashaw.   He platonizes very prettily in the song—

> Ask me no more where Jove bestows.

The rose-form, which, the philosophers would say, exists, apart from actuality, in the eternal archetype, the one Primal Form which is the cause of all forms, reposes, according to the philosophy of the lover, in the fathomless deep of his lady's mystic and heavenly beauty.

14. **William Drummond**, of Hawthornden, a vain, self-conscious man, with little stamina and much febrile excitability, is the author of a quantity of poems, some of which were published in his lifetime, while the entire series were edited and printed in 1656, a few years after his death, by Edward Philips, Milton's nephew, the author of the *Theatrum Poetarum*.   They consist of 'Teares on the Death of Meliades' (Prince Henry, eldest son of James I.), 'Urania, or Spiritual Poems,' 'Madrigals and Epigrams,' 'Forth Feasting,' 'Flowers of Sion,' and 'Posthumous Poems.'   The first-named piece is an elegy in decasyllabic rime; it first appeared in 1613, and, though of far inferior power, seems to have suggested some of the thoughts and images in Milton's *Lycidas* :—

> Queen of the fields, whose blush makes blush the morn,
> Sweet rose ! a prince's death in purple mourn ;
> O hyacinths, for aye your AI keep still,
> Nay, with more marks of woe, your leaves now fill.

Hence may have come the hint for the bonnet of Comus, 'inwrought with figures dim,' and

> Like to that sanguine flower inscribed with woe.[1]

The poems in *Urania* are of little account ; one stanza of Southwell or Herbert is worth the whole of them. 'Madrigals and Epigrams' are mostly in tripping metres, and on amatory themes. Perhaps the best among Drummond's poems, because it seems to express genuine feeling, is 'Forth Feasting,' written in 1617. The river addresses the king on his visiting Edinburgh, his native city.   The conclusion, which is very spirited, runs as follows :—

> O ! love these bounds where of thy royal stem
> More than a hundred wore a diadem ;
> So ever gold and bays thy brow adorn,
> So never time may see thy race outworn ;
> So of thine own still mayst thou be desired,
> Of strangers feared, redoubted, and admired :
> So memory thee praise, so precious hours
> May character thy name in starry flowers ;
> So may thy high exploits at last make even
> With earth thy empire, glory with the heaven.

[1] *Lycidas*, 106.

15. **John Cleveland** was a violent boisterous Royalist, the Wildrake of real life and literary history. Had his fire and force been supported by a keener and more cultivated intellect, he might have been a great poet. He is best known for his tirades against the Scotch, whom he hated both as Presbyterians and as traitors. The old joke against the Scotch, on account of their attachment to their native land appearing to increase in the ratio of their distance from it, was cleverly expressed by Cleveland in *The Rebell Scot* :—

> Had Cain been Scot, God would have changed his doom ;
> Not forced him wander, but confined him home.

His attachment to episcopacy may be gathered from the following lines, taken from *The Hue and Cry after Sir John Presbyter*.

> Down Dragon-Synod with thy motley ware,
> While we do swagger for the Common Prayer,
> That dove-like embassy, that wings our sense
> To heaven's gate in shape of innocence ;
> Pray for the mitred authors, and defy
> These Demi-casters of Divinitie.
> For when Sir John with Jack-of-all-trades joyns,
> His finger's thicker than the Prelate's loyns.

These lines are a fair illustration of the rough vigour which characterized the man.

16. **Sir John Suckling**, born of a good Middlesex family, was well known as a dissolute courtier and amatory poet in the time of Charles I. When the Scotch Covenanters rose in insurrection in 1639, Suckling raised, mounted, and armed at his own expense a troop of a hundred horse, and presented them to the king. At the affair of Newburn, he and his troop joined in the rapid movement to the rear executed by the English cavalry on that disgraceful day ; and his enemies at court seized the opportunity to write many satirical songs and lampoons at his expense. Some of these may be read in the *Musarum Deliciæ*. Engaging in a plot in 1641 to rescue Strafford from the Tower, Suckling was impeached of high treason by the House of Commons, and had just time to make his escape to France. Finding himself a friendless exile in a foreign land, with broken health and in poverty, poor Suckling took poison, and 'shuffled off this mortal coil,' before the end of 1642. His poems and letters were published in 1646. In his lifetime he had given to the world three plays,[1] in one of which, *Aglaura*, occurs the

---

[1] Suckling's plays are, *Aglaura*, a play with two fifth acts, one of which ends happily, the other tragically ; *The Goblins*, a comedy ; *Brennoralt*, a tragedy ; and *The Sad One* (unfinished), a tragedy.

S

pretty, piquant song, 'Why so pale and wan, fond lover.'
His poems are gay and witty, but he was a careless versifier.
The following lines, taken from a poetical epistle to John
Hales of Eton, the 'ever memorable,' furnish a slight example
of his manner.   He tells his friend to 'bestride the college
steed,' and ride up to town, where he would find wit and
wine—

> Flowing alike, and both divine.
> The sweat of learned Jonson's brain,
> And gentle Shakspeare's easier strain,
> A hackney-coach conveys you to,
> In spite of all that rain can do;
> And for your eighteen pence you sit
> The lord and judge of all fresh wit.

17. **Robert Herrick**, after being ejected by the Parliamenta-
rians from his living in Devonshire, came up to London, and
published his poems under the title of *Hesperides, or Works
both Human and Divine.*

The poems of Herrick are classed by Mr. Hallam among the
'poetry of kisses;' it would be more exact to say that they are
the outcome of a lazy amorous temperament, which cannot or
will not put time to better use.   He candidly tells us that—

> he has seen, and still can prove,
> The lazy man the most doth love.

While the Long Parliament was making war and framing treaties, Herrick could only talk of the 'Parliament of roses;' red-
handed battle was raging in every English county, but he can
only bemoan 'the death that is in Julia's eyes.' Herrick's
melody is not invariably perfect, yet there are not a few of his
little poems—they are all very diminutive—which either have a
beautiful tripping movement, or excel in rhythmic evenness and
sweetness.   The divisions of the collection, after certain opening invocations to gods and goddesses, are—'Amatory Odes,'
'Anacreontic and Bacchanalian,' and an 'Epithalamium.'

18. **Colonel Richard Lovelace** wrote a few pretty things,[1]
one or two of which are to be found in most collections, and
Sir John Denham, the intimate friend of Cowley, wrote the first
English descriptive poem of real merit—*Cooper's Hill.*[2]

Of Denham's other poems the chief part are translations from
Virgil, Cicero, and Mancini. The 'Progress of Learning,' a poem in
Pindaric verse, theorizes, from the point of view of a cavalier, who is
at the same time an admirer of Hobbes, on the obstacles which have

---

[1] See Crit. Sect. ch. I. § 51.   [2] *Ibid.* § 45.

troubled the advance of learning and refinement amongst mankind. The revival of learning, and the discredit fallen on the 'lazy cells where superstition bred,' promised a halcyon period ; but the enemy of mankind, inspiring Loyola, Luther, and Calvin with an infernal spirit of bigotry, had dashed those hopes to the ground. Fanaticism, dislodged from the monasteries, had taken possession of the printing press. Authority had fallen only to give place to sectaries and schisma·ics of a hundred types, all quarrelling with one another, and inflated with spiritual pride and a boundless presumption :—

> But seven wise men the ancient world did know,
> We scarce know seven who think themselves not so.

In a poem on Lord Strafford, Denham calls him

> 'Three kingdoms' wonder, and three kingdoms' fear.'

He also wrote some interesting memorial verses 'On Mr. Abraham Cowley's death, and burial amongst the ancient poets.'

19. **William Habington**, the representative of an old Catholic family settled at Hindlip in Worcestershire, is known as the author of the collection of pretty love-poems and quaint paraphrases on verses in the Psalms published in 1635 under the title of *Castara*. This was the name which he gave to the fair and noble maiden who had won his heart, Lucy Herbert, a daughter of the first Lord Powis. The poetry of Habington is sweet, pleasing, and pure ; this last characteristic distinguishes it favourably from nearly all the love-verses of the period. The tender pacific nature of the man is well shown in the following lines, which come at the end of a poem ' To the Honble. Mr. Wm. G.'

> And tho' my fate conducts me to the shade
> Of humble quiet, my ambition payde
> With safe content, while a pure virgin fame
> Doth raise me trophies in Castara's name ;
> No thought of glory swelling me above
> The hope of being famed for virtuous love ;
> Yet wish I thee, guided by better starres,
> To purchase unsafe honour in the warres,
> Or envied smiles at court ; for thy great race,
> And merits, well may challenge th' highest place ;
> Yet know, what busie path so ere you tread
> To greatnesse, you must sleep among the dead.

20. Only three poets took the Puritan side ; but quality made up for quantity. **John Milton** was born in London in the year 1608. At sixteen he was sent to Cambridge, where he speedily gave proofs of an astonishing vigour and versatility of intellect by the Latin and English compositions, chiefly the former, which he produced in his college years. In spite of the

precedents given by the great Italian poets, Latin was still regarded as the universal and most perfect language, not only for
prose, but for poetry; and the most gifted poets of the time,
Milton and Cowley, followed the example of Vida and Sanazzaro, and tried their ' 'prentice hand' upon hexameters and elegiacs. In these exercises, whatever Dr. Johnson [1] may say,
Milton was singularly successful. So far from his Latin poems
being inferior to those of Cowley, it may be doubted whether he
does not surpass even Vida; for if the latter excels him in elegance and smoothness, yet in the rush of images and ideas, in
idiomatic strength and variety, in everything, in short, that constitutes originality, he is not to be compared to Milton. The
elegy upon Bishop Andrewes is really a marvel, considering that
it was the work of a lad of seventeen.

Milton, however, was a true lover of his native language,
and in his Latin pieces he was but, as it were, preluding and
trying his poetic gift, the full power of which was to be displayed in the forms of his own mother tongue. But he would
write simple unaffected English, and be the slave to no fashionable style; whatever mannerism he was afterwards to give way
to, was to be the offspring of his own studies and peculiar mode
of thought. He expresses this determination in a Vacation
exercise, composed in 1627. Apostrophizing his native language, he says :—

> But haste thee straight to do me once a pleasure,
> And from thy wardrobe bring thy chiefest treasure;
> *Not those new-fangled toys, and trimming sleight,*
> *Which takes our late fantastics with delight;*
> But cull those richest robes, and gay'st attire,
> Which deepest spirits and choicest wits desire.

21. The English language obeyed the invitation, and two
years later appeared the beautiful *Ode to the Nativity.*[2] In
1634 he wrote the masque of *Comus,* which was to be acted at
Ludlow Castle by the children of the Earl of Bridgewater, then
Lord President of Wales. The two brothers and their sister,
travelling homewards, lose their way in a thick forest; the
sister, separated accidentally from her protectors, is met by the
enchanter Comus, under whom is represented the worship of
sense and pleasure. She resists his allurements and refutes his
arguments. Meanwhile the brothers debate the untoward occurrence, the younger being much inclined to fear, while the elder

---

[1] In his *Life of Milton,* Johnson writes with an evident bias of dislike,
which sometimes makes him unfair. His Tory prejudices would not allow him
to be just to the poet who had defended regicide.

[2] See Crit. Sect. ch. I. § 49.

is sustained by his confidence in his sister's virtue and 'saintly chastity.' In the end the sister is found and the enchanter driven away; but his spells have bound her to a magic chair, from which she can only be released by the nymph of the Severn (Sabrina) rising from her watery bed and breaking the charm. The poem represents the triumph of virtue and philosophy over the power of the senses ; the imagery is classical, and Christian ideas, as such, have no place. Yet none can doubt that the morality which triumphs in *Comus* is really the morality of Christ, and not that of the Stoics, or of the classical poets. For many turns of phrase, and even for some ideas, Milton is indebted to Fletcher's lovely pastoral drama of the *Faithful Shepherdess*. But there is a majesty, an austere and stately beauty, about this poem, which are all Milton's own. How noble and lovely, for instance, lines like these—

> Virtue could see to do what Virtue would
> By her own radiant light, though sun and moon
> Were in the flat sea sunk :

or—

> How charming is divine philosophy !
> Not harsh and crabbed, as dull fools suppose,
> But musical as is Apollo's lute,
> And a perpetual feast of nectar'd sweets,
> Where no crude surfeit reigns.

L'Allegro and *Il Penseroso*, fair groups of mirthful and of pensive thoughts, which the town-bred poet, intoxicated with the fresh charm of country life, gives voice to and sings to his lyre, were the fruit of his stay at Horton in Buckinghamshire, between the life at Cambridge and the journey to Italy.

All the rest of the shorter poems (except the Sonnets and two or three Latin pieces) were in like manner composed before the breaking out of the civil war.

22. In 1638 Milton visited Italy, and stayed several months at Florence, Rome, and Naples, mixing familiarly in the literary society of those cities. The Italians were amazed at this prodigy of genius from the remote North, the beauty and grace of whose person recommended his intellectual gifts. The Marquis Manso, the friend of Tasso, said, referring to the well-known anecdote of Pope Gregory, that if his religion were as good as his other qualifications, he would be, ' Non Anglus verum angelus.' Selvaggi, in a Latin distich, anticipated the famous encomium of Dryden,[1] and Salsilli declared that the banks of

---

[1] ' Three poets in three distant ages born,
Greece, Italy, and England, did adorn.

the Thames had produced a greater poet than those of the
Mincio. With Galileo he had an interview at Florence. 'There
was it that I found and visited the famous Galileo, grown old,
a prisoner to the Inquisition.' [1]   The news of the increasing
civil dissensions at home recalled him to England; and after
his return he renounced the Muse, and flung himself with
characteristic energy into the thickest of the strife. The Puritans, who as a class possessed little learning, were at that time
hard pushed by Bishop Hall, Usher, and other episcopalian disputants; when Milton appeared in their ranks, and threw not
only the force and fire of his genius, but his varied and copious
learning, on the yielding side. *Of Reformation in England*
(1641), *Of Prelatical Episcopacy* (1641), *Animadversions on the
Remonstrant's Defence* (1641), *An Apology for Smectymnuus* [2]
(1642), and *The Reason of Church Government urged against
Prelaty* (1641), are the titles of the five treatises or pamphlets
which Milton contributed to this controversy. Of the motives
by which he was animated he gives some account in his *Second
Defence of the People of England* (1654). He says that on
his return from Italy, and after the assembling of the Long
Parliament, 'all mouths began to be opened against the Bishops,'
alleging that 'it was unjust that they alone should differ from
the model of other reformed churches [Geneva, Holland, Scotland, &c.]; that the government of the church should be according to the model of other [Protestant] churches, and particularly the word of God.' His attention and zeal being thus
aroused, he determined, having studied carefully the main questions connected with the relations of Church and State, to lay
aside for a time all other labours, and devote himself to the
Puritan side in this controversy. 'I accordingly wrote two
books to a friend concerning the Reformation of the Church of
England. Afterwards, when two bishops of superior distinction
[Usher and Hall] vindicated their privileges against some principal ministers, I thought that on these topics, to the consideration
of which I was led solely by my love of truth, and my reverence
for Christianity, I should not probably write worse than those
who were contending only for their own emolument and usur-

> The first in loftiness of thought surpassed;
> The next in majesty; in both the last.
> The force of Nature could no further go;
> To make a third, she join'd the former two.'

[1] Areopagitica.
[2] See Crit. Sect. ch. II. § 16. The word Smectymnuus was formed from the
initial letters of the names of five Puritan ministers—Stephen Marshall,
Edmund Calamy, Thomas Young, Matthew Newcomen, and William Spurstow
—who had written a pamphlet attacking episcopacy, to which a powerful
answer had appeared from the pen of Bishop Hall.

pations.' (The offensive bad taste of this last assumption is not, be it remembered, quite so unpardonable in the polemics of the seventeenth century, which teem with scurrilities of every kind, as it would be in those of the nineteenth.) ' I therefore answered the one in two books, of which the first is inscribed Concerning Prelatical Episcopacy, and the other, Concerning the Mode of Ecclesiastical Government ; and I replied to the other in some Animadversions, and soon afterwards in an Apology.' To prove how entirely obsolete these pamphlets have grown (except so far as they contain interesting passages bearing on Milton's own career and literary aims), it is enough to say that they one and all *assume* the truth of the main Protestant positions, as against the Roman Church, and only quarrel about the width of the gulf which should ensue on those positions being granted.

23. Yet, barren as was the strife, so far as regards any theoretical results directly established by it, whoever wishes to understand and feel the greatness of Milton must not fail to study these treatises. His prose was no ' cool element ; ' most often it sparkles and scathes like liquid metal, yet softens here and there, and spreads out into calmer, milder passages, stamped with an inexpressible poetic loveliness. For many years, in this portion of his life, Milton gave himself up to political and religious controversy ; all but one of his prose works were composed between 1640 and the Restoration.

24. Writing of the sonnet, Wordsworth finely says that in Milton's hand,—

> The thing became a trumpet, whence he blew
> Soul-animating strains, alas! too few.

Some of these stirring sonnets were composed during the war. That addressed to Cromwell was written before the battle of Worcester, in 1651, but corrected after it, as appears from an inspection of the original MS. in the library of Trinity College, Cambridge, in which the ninth line originally stood thus,—

> And twenty battles more. Yet much remains, &c.

But the pen has been drawn through the first four words, and over them is written ' And Worcester's laureat wreath ; ' and thus the line stands in all the printed editions.

25. After the king's execution, Milton entered the service of the republican government as Latin secretary, with the duty of conducting the official correspondence with foreign powers. He retained this office under the Protectorate. At the Restoration

an order was given for his prosecution, but ultimately he was allowed to retire unharmed into private life. At this time he was totally blind, having lost his eyesight,—

> over-pliéd
> In Liberty's defence, my noble task,
> Wherewith all Europe rings from side to side:

where he refers to his *Defensio Populi Anglicani*, written in 1651 in reply to the Frenchman Salmasius, or Saumaise. After his retirement, he lived at Bunhill Fields, in the outskirts of London, and took up again the cherished literary ambition of his youth, which had been to write a great poem, founded either upon the national mythology, or on some scriptural subject. There are several allusions to this early bias of his mind in the prose works. Thus, in the *Animadversions, &c.*, he writes : 'And he that now for haste snatches up a plain ungarnished present as a thank-offering to Thee, may then, perhaps, take up a harp and sing Thee an elaborate song to generations.' Also, in the *Reason of Church Government, &c.*, published in the same year, after mentioning the encouragement and praise which the Italian literati had given to his early efforts in verse, 'I began,' he says, 'thus far to assent both to them and divers of my friends here at home, and not less to an inward prompting which now grew daily upon me, that by labour and intense study (which I take to be my portion in this life), joined with the strong propensity of nature, I might, perhaps, leave something so written to after times as they should not willingly let it die.' The whole context of this passage is of great interest for the light it throws on Milton's early conviction of the true nature of the task to which his extraordinary powers constituted his vocation.

26. The *Paradise Lost* [1] was first published in 1667. Although the author—from what cause is unknown—obtained a very scanty remuneration [2] from the publisher, the common supposition, that the sale of the work was extremely slow, is erroneous. Within two years from the date of publication, thirteen hundred copies had been sold, and the second edition was exhausted before 1678. But the name of Milton was too hateful in royalist ears to allow of his admirers giving public expression to their feelings under the Stuarts. Addison's papers in the *Spectator* first made the *Paradise Lost* known to a large number of readers, and established it as a household book and an English classic.

The *Paradise Regained*, in four books, and the sacred drama

---

[1] See Crit. Sect. ch. I., *Epic Poetry*.
[2] Fifteen pounds for the first two editions, numbering three thousand copies.

of *Samson Agonistes*, were both published in 1670. Milton died in 1674, and was buried in the church of St. Giles, Cripplegate.

27. **George Wither**, the second Puritan poet, was a native of Hampshire, and sold his paternal property to raise a troop of horse for the Parliament. The diction of his earlier poems, particularly his beautiful songs, shows little trace of the influence of the Fantastic school; but his religious poetry is full of quaintnesses and conceits.

He is the author of some satires entitled *Abuses Stript and Whipt* (1613), a youthful production, written apparently for the sake of attracting notice. In this he succeeded so well (probably through the offence given by his onslaught against 'clergy-pride' and the ambition of churchmen) that he soon found himself arrested and imprisoned in the Marshalsea. The satires—twenty in number, contained in two books—are written in the heroic couplet like Marston's, and have much the same inharmoniousness of metre and rudeness of diction. While in prison he wrote another satire called the *Scourge*, and also *A Satyre*, dedicated to the king, in which he justified his former efforts. He also wrote in prison the dramatic operetta, if so it may be called, of *The Shepheard's Hunting*, which, Mr. Campbell thinks, contains the finest touches that ever came from his hasty and irregular pen. It is in five eclogues, and is evidently modelled on the *Shepheard's Calendar* of Spenser.

28. The third poet, **Andrew Marvell**, who was assistant to Milton for eighteen months in the office of Latin secretary, and represented the borough of Hull in Parliament after the Restoration, was at heart a thorough republican. He was a formidable political satirist, both in prose and verse, on the Whig-Puritan side, during the reign of Charles II. His miscellaneous poems were published by his widow in 1681.

Some of these are pointed, and not without grace. The ode 'To his coy Mistress' is full of fancy and invention. Were our time unlimited, he says, your coyness were no crime :—

> But at my back I always hear
> Time's wingèd chariot hurrying near ;
> And yonder all before us lie
> Deserts of vast eternity.

The definition of love in the 'Fair Singer,' though belonging to the poetry of conceit, is charmingly clever :—

> As lines, so loves oblique, may well
>   Themselves in every angle greet ;
> But ours so truly parallel
>   Though infinite can never meet.

> Therefore the love which us doth bind,
> But fate so enviously debars,
> Is the conjunction of the mind,
> And opposition of the stars.

The incidents of a distracted time sometimes colour the verse strangely. We have the lover pleading thus with his mistress,—

> O then let me in time *compound*,

(as the poor royalists had to do for their lands)

> And *parly* with those conquering eyes.

His satirical poems are chiefly directed against the Dutch, the Scotch, and the Stuarts. The Dutch had the ill-luck to quarrel with both the great English parties, and the roundhead Marvel attacks them with a bitterness of contemptuous invective which the courtier Dryden could not surpass. One of his satires begins thus,—

> Holland, that scarce deserves the name of land,
> As but th' offscouring of the British sand,
> And so much earth as was contributed
> By English pilots when they heaved the lead—

Poetry after the Restoration : Dryden, Butler, Davenant.

29. The poetry of Milton belongs, according to its spirit, to the period before the Restoration, although much of it was actually composed later. The poets whom we have now to consider belong, both in time and in spirit, to the post-Restoration, or reactionary school. The greatest of them—Dryden—is the most prominent figure in the literary history of the latter part of the seventeenth century; and in describing his career, it will be easy to introduce such mention of his less gifted rivals and contemporaries as our limits will permit us to make.

30. **John Dryden** was the grandson of a Northamptonshire baronet and squire, Sir Erasmus Dryden, of Canons Ashby; but his relations on both sides had adopted Puritan opinions, and he grew up to manhood under Puritan influences. From Westminster School he proceeded, in 1650, to Trinity College, Cambridge. The seven years of his college life are almost a blank in his history. Of Milton we know exactly, from his own pen, how he was employed at the corresponding period; and can form to ourselves a tolerably accurate notion of the earnest ascetic student, with his rapt look and beautiful features, walking in the cloisters or garden of Christ's College. But of Dryden the only fact of any importance that we know is, that his

favourite study at this time was history, not poetry. He had begun, indeed, to string rimes together many years before, his elegy on Lord Hastings having been written in 1649 ; but that feeble and artificial production must have given so little satisfaction, either to himself or to others, that we cannot wonder at his having desisted from writing poetry altogether. How unlike Pope, who

> Lisped in numbers, for the numbers came.

In 1657, he came up to London, probably at the invitation of his kinsman, Sir Gilbert Pickering, who stood high in the favour of Cromwell, being, according to Shadwell, ' Noll's Lord Chamberlain.' Dryden seems to have acted as secretary or amanuensis to Sir Gilbert for about two years. Upon the death of Cromwell, in September 1658, he wrote an elegy, in thirty-six stanzas, commemorating the exploits and great qualities of the Lord Protector. It is written in a manly strain, nor is the eulogy undiscerning. For example,—

> For from all tempers he could service draw ;
> The worth of each, with its alloy, he knew ;
> And as the confidant of Nature, saw
> How she complexions did divide and brew,—

lines which well describe Cromwell's keen discernment of character. At the Restoration, the Cavaliers of course came into power, and the Puritan holders of office were ousted. Among the rest, Sir Gilbert Pickering had to retire into private life, happy to be let off so easily ; and Dryden's regular occupation was gone. At the age of twenty-eight he was thrown entirely on his own resources. Exactly twenty-eight years later, the same mischance befell him ; and on each occasion the largeness and vigour of his intellect enabled him to make head against the spite of fortune. Literature was to be his resource ; the strong impulse of nature urged him with irresistible force to think and to write. But no kind of writing offered the chance of an immediate return, in the shape of temporal maintenance, except the dramatic. To the drama, therefore, Dryden turned, and began to write plays. Between 1662 and 1694 he produced twenty-seven plays, of which twelve were tragedies, four tragi-comedies, eight comedies, and three operas. Perhaps his fame would have suffered but little if he had not written one. Many of them are crammed full—all are more or less tainted— with licentious language and gross allusion ; and even in the finest of the tragedies one misses altogether that deep pathos which forms the inexhaustible charm of *Othello* or of *Œdipus*

Tyrannus, and which Dryden had not *heart* enough to communicate to his work.

31. In 1670 Dryden was appointed poet-laureate, in succession to Sir William Davenant, with a salary of 200*l.* a year,
raised towards the end of Charles II.'s reign to 300*l.*   During
the ten following years he was almost exclusively engaged in
writing, either plays, or critical essays on dramatic subjects.
His acknowledged superiority among men of letters, and the
dread of his satire, caused him to be both envied and hated—
passions which in those turbulent times did not trust to the pen
alone for their gratification.   Dryden received the same sort of
castigation which Pope narrowly escaped, and which Voltaire
met with at the hands of the Duc de Rohan.   The clever profligate Wilmot, Earl of Rochester, who wished to be considered
an arbiter of literary taste, had set up by turns three dramatists
—Settle, Crowne, and Otway—as rivals to Dryden.   But, finding
that the judgment of the public remained intractable, he attacked
Dryden himself in an imitation of Horace, published in 1678.
The poet replied vigorously in the preface to *All for Love.*
Next year appeared Sheffield's *Essay on Satire,* in which Rochester was severely handled.   Supposing Dryden to be the author,
Rochester had him waylaid one evening near Covent Garden, on
his return home from Wills's coffee-house, and severely beaten
by a couple of hired bullies.   In reference to this mishap Lord
Sheffield wrote the following stupid and conceited couplet:—

> Though praised and punished for another's rhymes,
> His own deserve as much applause *sometimes.*

32. In the thick of the excitement about the Popish Plot,
Dryden, by producing his play of the *Spanish Friar,* and thus
pandering to the blind frenzy of the hour, placed himself almost
in a position of antagonism to the Court, since the Whig promoters of the Plot were as little acceptable to Charles as to his
brother.   But he soon after made ample amends by writing
Absalom and Achitophel,—the most perfect and powerful satire
in our language,—in which the schemes of the Whig-Puritan
party, and the characters of its leading men, are exposed and
caricatured.   The occasion was furnished by a plot, matured by
the busy brain of Shaftesbury, for placing on the throne at the
king's death his natural son the Duke of Monmouth, to the exclusion of his brother the Duke of York.   The story of Absalom's rebellion supplied a parallel, singularly close in some
respects, of which Dryden availed himself to the utmost.   Absalom is the Duke of Monmouth, Achitophel, his crafty adviser,

is the Earl of Shaftesbury, David stands for Charles II., Zimri
for the Duke of Buckingham, &c., &c.

In 1682 appeared the *Medal*, another satire on the Whigs,
and a few months later the second part of *Absalom and Achitophel*, of which only about two hundred lines, including the portraits of Settle and Shadwell, are by Dryden, the rest being the
work of an inferior poet, named Nahum Tate,—one of those
jackals that hunt with the lions of literature,—but bearing
marks of considerable revision by the master's hand.   The
Religio Laici, published in the same year, will be spoken of
presently.

In February 1685 Charles II. died.   Dryden, as in duty
bound, mourned the sad event in the *Threnodia Augustalis*, a.
long rambling elegy, in which occur a few fine lines, but which
must be set down on the whole as mendacious, frigid, and profane.   Lamentation is not the keynote of the poem ;—after bewailing the deprivation of so much virtue and benevolence
which the world had sustained in the death of Charles II., the
poet turns with alacrity to celebrate with an Io Pæan the accession of the illustrious James.

33. We are now come to the period of his life at which
Dryden changed his religion.   Upon this much-debated subject,
the reader is referred to the candid examination of the entire
question, which will be found in Sir Walter Scott's life of the
poet.   Scott's theory is, that on the one hand the inner workings
of the poet's mind, as inferred from his writings, at last consistently brought him to embrace the Roman Catholic system;
but that, on the other hand, there were many external incidents.
and circumstances in his position, which, in a proportion impossible to be exactly ascertained, cooperated with those internal
movements to produce the final result.   With regard to the
first point, he quotes the poet's own confession in the *Hind and*
Panther :—

> My thoughtless youth was wing'd with vain desires ;
> My manhood, long misled by wandering fires,
> Followed false lights; and when their glimpse was gone,
> My pride struck out new sparkles of her own.
> Such was I; such by nature still I am ;
> Be Thine the glory, and be mine the shame !

The 'false lights' evidently refer to the Puritan opinions in
which Dryden had been bred up, and the 'sparkles' struck out
by his pride as clearly point to the religious speculations, origi-
nating in his own mind, some of which are disclosed in the
Religio Laici.   This poem, one of the few of Dryden's which

were neither written professionally, nor dedicated to, or suggested by, a patron, betokens a mind dissatisfied with the religion in which it had been brought up, and groping its way
among clashing systems in vain endeavours after light.   To one
whose opinions were so unfixed, who lived, too, at the time when
the great Bossuet was analysing the *Variations of the Protestant
Churches*, and the virtues of Fénelon were the talk of Europe,
it is easy to see that when the time came at which it was his
manifest interest to consider the claims of the religion of the
Court, the arguments in favour of the claims of Rome would
present themselves with more than ordinary force, because they
would not find the ordinary obstacles pre-existing in his mind.
The whole subject is thus summed up in the words of Scott :
'While pointing out circumstances of proof that Dryden's conversion was not made by manner of bargain and sale, but
proceeded upon . . . conviction, it cannot be denied that his
situation as poet-laureate, and his expectations from the king,
must have conduced to his taking his final resolution.   All I
mean to infer from the above statement is, that his interest and
internal conviction led him to the same conclusion.'

34. In 1687, some months after his conversion, Dryden
published the *Hind and Panther*, a controversial allegory in
heroic metre in three books, the Roman Church being represented by the Hind, and the Church of England by the Panther.
Allegory, however, the poem is not, for over the greater portion
of it there is no second meaning in reserve ; the obvious sense is
the only one.   The interlocutors and mute personages are called
by the names of birds and beasts, and that is all.   Instead of
Bossuet and Burnet, we have the Hind and the Panther ; but
the expressions which are put in the mouths of the animals are,
for the most part, precisely those which might have been put in
the mouths of the divines.   In the two following extracts the
rival disputants are introduced to the reader :—

> A milk-white Hind, immortal and unchanged,
> Fed on the lawns, and in the forest ranged;
> Without unspotted, innocent within,
> She feared no danger, for she knew no sin :
> Yet had she oft been chased with horns and hounds,
> And Scythian shafts ; was often forced to fly,
> And doomed to death, though fated not to die.

The Independents, Quakers, Free-thinkers, Anabaptists, Socinians, and Presbyterians, are next enumerated, under the em-
blems of the Bear, the Hare, the Ape, the Boar, the Fox, and
the Wolf.   The Lion, whose business, as king of beasts, is to

keep order in the forest, is, of course, James II.   The Panther
is then introduced :—

> The Panther, sure the noblest next the Hind,
> And fairest creature of the spotted kind ;
> Oh, could her inborn stains be washed away,
> She were too good to be a beast of prey !
> How can I praise or blame, and not offend,
> Or how divide the frailty from the friend ?
> Her faults and virtues lie so mix'd, that she
> Not wholly stands condemn'd nor wholly free.
> Then, like her injur'd Lion, let me speak ;
> He cannot bend her, and he would not break.

The first two books are taken up with doctrinal discussions.
The third opens with a long desultory conversation, partly on
politics, partly on pending or recent theological controversies
(that between Dryden and Stillingfleet, for instance), partly on
church parties and the sincerity of conversions.   The language
put in the mouth of the Hind often jars most absurdly with the
gentle magnanimous nature assigned to her; and in her sallies
and rejoinders the tone of the coarse unscrupulous party-writer
appears without the least disguise.   This conversation is ended
by the Panther proposing to relate the tale of the Swallows.
By these birds the English Catholics are intended, who, following
the foolish counsels of the Martin (Father Petre, James's
trusted adviser), are expelled from their nests, and perish miserably.   A conversation follows on the politics of the Church of
England.   Viewed in the light of subsequent events, the confidence expressed by the Hind in the Panther's immovable adhe-
rence to her non-resistance principles excites a smile.   The Hind
next volunteers the story of the Pigeons, by whom are meant
the Anglican clergy.   Their ringleader, the Buzzard, is a satirical sketch of Burnet, an important actor in the intrigues
which brought on the Revolution.   By following the Buzzard's
counsel, the Pigeons draw down upon themselves the righteous
wrath of the farmer (James II.).   The poem then ends abruptly.

Dryden's marvellous gift of ratiocination in verse is nowhere
so well exemplified as in the *Hind and Panther*.   Gibbon, describing his own mental changes in his *Autobiography*, quotes
from it the celebrated lines—

> To take up half on trust, and half to try,
> Name it not faith, but bungling bigotry.
> Both fool and knave the merchant we may call,
> To pay great sums, and to compound the small.
> For who would break with heaven, and would not break for *all* ?

And where can we find a finer instance of a precise and luminous statement, clothed in a beautiful rhythmic dress, than the following lines supply ?

> One in herself, not rent by schism, but sound,
> Entire, one solid shining diamond ;
> Not sparkles shattered into sects like you,
> One is the Church, and must be, to be true ;
> One central principle of unity,
> As undivided, so from errors free ;
> As one in faith, so one in sanctity.

35. Great was the clamour now raised against Dryden, and many were the answers to the Hind that appeared, among which the *City Mouse and Country Mouse*, the joint production of Prior and Charles Montague (afterwards Earl of Halifax), was the most successful.

The full title of this clever squib was : *The Hind and the Panther ; transversed to the story of the Country Mouse and the City Mouse.* As in the *Rehearsal*, Mr. Bayes (i.e. Dryden) is supposed to join two friends, in order to communicate his new work to them ; he can talk of nothing else. ' Egad,' he says, ' I defy all critics. Thus it begins :

> A milk-white mouse, immortal and unchanged,
> Fed on soft cheese, and o'er the dairy ranged ; ·
> Without unspotted, innocent within,
> She feared no danger, for she knew no ginn.
> *   *   *   *   *   *
> was often forced to fly,
> And doomed to death, though fated not to die.'

' Faith, Mr. Bayes,' says Smith, one of the friends, ' if you were *doomed* to be hanged, whatever you were *fated* to, 'twould give you but small comfort.'

36. At the Revolution, Dryden was dismissed from his office of poet-laureate and royal historiographer, and had the mortification of seeing Shadwell the dramatist, who had been repeatedly the butt of his ridicule,—Shadwell the hero of *Mac-Flecknoe* and the Og of *Absalom and Achitophel*,—promoted to the laurel. For the remainder of his life Dryden was more or less harassed by the ills of poverty, but his genius shone out brighter as the end drew near. *Alexander's Feast*,[1] which has been often pronounced to be the finest lyric in the language, was written in 1697 ; the translation of Virgil appeared in the same year ; and the *Fables*, which are translations from Ovid and Boccaccio, and modernizations of Chaucer, were published in March 1700, only a few weeks before the poet's death.

[1] See Crit. Sect. ch. I. § 63.

Dryden's manner of life was essentially that of a man of letters. He had no taste for field sports, and did not delight in rural solitudes; nor, though he keenly watched the conflicts of parties and the development of political questions, did he ever mix personally in the turmoil of public life. Though not reserved, he was diffident and shy, and was far from cutting that brilliant figure in fashionable society which Pope, though self-educated, and a *parvenu*, succeeded in doing. He rose early, spent all the fore part of the day in his own study reading or writing; then about three o'clock betook himself to Wills's coffee house, the common resort of a crowd of wits, pamphleteers, poets, and critics. There, seated in his own arm-chair, which was moved near the window in summer, and to the fireside in winter, ' glorious John ' drank his bottle of port, and ruled the roast, the undoubted chief of the English literary republic.

37. The other poets in this post-Restoration period deserving of especial mention are, Wentworth Dillon, Earl of Roscommon, author of the *Essay on Translated Verse*, Butler, the author of *Hudibras*, and Sir William Davenant. Both Dryden and Pope praised **Roscommon**,[1]—the former in some fine lines (written on the publication of the *Essay* in 1680), the sense of which was rather closely followed by Pope in his *Essay on Criticism.* In both panegyrics the merit of Roscommon is described to be, that he restored in Britain the authority of ' wit's fundamental laws,' and superseded Shakspere's wild beauties and Milton's ruggedness by establishing the reign of classic elegance, polish, and correctness. In short, Roscommon, although his achievements in these respects were much overrated by his eulogizers,

---

[1] Dryden writes, after mentioning the Italian poets,—

> The French pursued their steps ; and Britain, last,
> In manly sweetness all the rest surpassed.
> The wit of Greece, the majesty of Rome,
> Appear exalted in the'British loom :
> The Muses' empire is restored again
> In Charles's reign, and by Roscommon's pen.

And Pope,—

> But we, brave Britons, foreign laws despised,
> And kept unconquer'd and uncivilized ;
> Fierce for the liberties of wit, and bold,
> We still defied the Romans, as of old :
> Yet some there were among the sounder few,
> Of those who less presumed, and better knew,
> Who durst assert the juster, ancient cause,
> And here restored wit's fundamental laws.
> *   *   *   *   *
> Such was Roscommon, not more learn'd than good,
> With manners generous as his noble blood ;
> To him the wit of Greece and Rome was known,
> And every author's merit but his own.

T

was a kind of forerunner of Pope, and a writer of the classical school.

38. **Samuel Butler**, the son of a Worcestershire farmer, lived for some years in early life in the house of Sir Samuel Luke, one of Cromwell's commanders, who furnished him with the original of *Hudibras*. While staying here he composed his famous satire. Little is known with certainty about his manner of life after the Restoration. It is certain, however, that he was befriended by Buckingham, and by Dryden's patron, the Earl of Dorset, and also that he passed all the latter part of his life in extreme poverty. The king, though he was extremely fond of *Hudibras*, and used constantly to quote from it, suffered the author to starve with his usual selfishness and ingratitude. This famous poem, which is in substance a satire on Puritans and Puritanism, may also be regarded as a burlesque on romances, the influence of *Don Quixote* being apparent; and even as, in a partial sense, a parody on the *Faerie Queene*, the titles to the cantos being clearly imitated from those of Spenser. The political importance of the poem was great. It turned the laugh against those terrible Puritans, a handful of whom had so long held the nation down, and defeated more effectually than cannon-balls or arguments could have done 'the stubborn crew of errant saints,'—

> who build their faith upon
> The holy text of pike and gun ;
> Decide all controversies by
> Infallible artillery ;
> And prove their doctrine orthodox
> By apostolic blows and knocks.

This famous satire is in three parts, containing three cantos each. The mere plot is slight, and may be described in a few words. The knight, Sir Hudibras, who is a Presbyterian, attended by his squire Ralpho, who belongs to the ranks of those formidable sectaries who overturned both king and parliament, sally forth to put down a bear-baiting. They come upon the rabble rout, whom the knight in a long speech bids to disperse. Their leaders, Talgol, Orsin, Trulla, &c., laugh him to scorn: a fight ensues, full of droll ups and downs, in the course of which the bear gets loose and helps Hudibras in putting the crowd to flight. Presently, however, they rally and return to the attack; Trulla defeats and disarms the knight, and he and his squire are laid by the heels in the parish stocks. Here they are visited by 'the widow,' the object of the knight's mercenary affections. A long conversation ensues, of which the upshot is, that in consideration of his swearing to give himself a severe flogging, the widow causes Hudibras to be released from the stocks. Next morning he repairs to the place where he is to perform the promised operation. But scruples arising within him concerning the legality of keeping his oath, he refers the case to Ralpho, who argues powerfully and lengthily in favour of the non-obligation on the knight, being a saint, to keep his oath:—

> For all of us hold this for true,
> No faith is to the wicked due ;
> For truth is precious and divine,
> Too rich a pearl for carnal swine.

Hudibras follows in the same strain ; the idea presently occurs to him of taking the whipping vicariously, which Ralpho approves, but strongly demurs to becoming the substitute himself. The whipping thus falls through ; but doubting whether the widow would not find him out, the knight resolves to go to Sidrophel the conjuror, and have his fortune told. He goes ; but through his speaking contemptuously of Sidrophel's art, a fight ensues, in which the knight is victorious, disarming Sidrophel, kicking his man Whackum out of the house, and departing with much plunder. In the third part the story flags, and at last breaks down altogether. The knight again endeavours to make an impression on the widow's heart, but to no purpose. The second canto dismisses Hudibras from sight altogether, being merely a long tirade against the Puritanic 'saints' and their proceedings in the civil war. In the third and last canto the knight seriously thinks of invoking the arm of the law, and of suing instead of wooing, but first indites an heroical epistle to the widow, with whose epistle in reply the poem ends.

Such is the plot ; but these slight outlines are filled up, so as to compose a poem of more than 11,000 lines, with long dialogues between Hudibras and his squire or the widow, discussing for the most part points of Puritanic casuistry. Thus the whole of the first canto of the second part is taken up with a conversation between Hudibras and the widow, the former urging his love, and insisting on the duty of his fair one to accept him, the latter making various objections and counter-propositions. Again, the second canto of the same part consists chiefly of a discussion between Hudibras and Ralpho on the obligation of oaths, as between the saints and the wicked. For though Hudibras has evidently an insuperable objection to fulfilling his oath to the widow in regard to the whipping, yet he desires to extricate himself from the obligation in such a manner as that his tender and scrupulous conscience may be entirely at rest. Ralpho's earnestness in drawing lines of demarcation between the saints, amongst whom he and his master were of course shining lights, and the sinners, is admirably described :—

> For as on land there is no beast,   ·
> But in some fish at sea's exprest,
> So in the wicked there's no vice,   ·
> Of which the saints have not a spice ;
> And yet that thing that's pious in
> The one, in th' other is a sin.

Again,—

> He that imposes an oath makes it,
> Not he that for convenience takes it ;
> Then how can any man be said
> To break an oath he never made ?

39. **Sir William Davenant,** knighted by the king for services before Gloucester in 1643, is the author of *Gondibert* and a few minor poems.   ·

The story of *Gondibert* is unfinished; in fact, the author himself tells us in a postscript that just one-half of the poem, as it was originally designed, is presented to the reader. The scene is laid in Italy; the principal action is the courtship of the Princess Rhodalind, daughter of Aribert, king of Tuscany, in rivalry for whose love her most powerful suitors, Duke Gondibert and Prince Oswald, engage in internecine strife. Davenant seems to have been a disciple of Hobbes and a necessitarian; we have the sage Astragon in the second book discoursing at great length to the purport of what follows:—

> But penitence appears unnatural;
> For we repent what Nature did persuade,
> And we, lamenting man's continued fall,
> Accuse what Nature necessary made.

Considerable intellectual power and literary skill are evident in the structure of this poem; but as the fictitious narrative is in itself wholly uninteresting, and the springs of passion are not strongly touched, the result is but moderately satisfactory.

Heroic Plays: Dryden, Otway, Lee, Crowne, Behn;—Comedy of Manners, Congreve, Etherege, Wycherley:—Jeremy Collier.

40. The position of the English drama after the Restoration may be explained in a few words. The theatres had been closed ever since the Puritan party had gained the mastery in London, that is, since the year 1643. At the Restoration they were reopened as a matter of course: the king during his long foreign sojourn had become used to and fond of theatrical entertainments; the courtiers ostentatiously shared in the royal taste; and the long-silenced wits were only too glad of a favourable opportunity of displaying their powers. Two theatres were licensed; one, which was under the direct patronage of Charles, was called the King's,—the other, which was patronized by his brother, was known as the Duke's, theatre. **Dryden**, who, as has been mentioned, took to writing plays at this time for a livelihood, attached himself to the former. The taste of the king was for the French school in tragedy, and the Spanish school in comedy; and the influence of both is perceptible in Dryden's plays for many years. He could not, indeed, adopt the French heroic metre—the Alexandrine—for which our language is eminently unsuited; but, retaining the ten-syllable verse of the Elizabethan dramatists, he followed Corneille and Racan in forming it into riming couplets. In the plot and manner of his early pieces the Spanish taste conspicuously prevails. The high-flown sentiment, the daring enterprise, the romantic adventure, of the days of chivalry, still hold their

ground in them,—still please a society which the modern critical
spirit had as yet but partially invaded. These heroic plays of
Dryden's are rightly described by Scott as ' metrical romances in
the form of dramas.' A brief outline of the plot of the *Conquest
of Granada*, the most brilliant and successful among them, will
best explain this definition :—

The scene is laid in the Moorish kingdom of Granada ; the period
is the fifteenth century, about the time of the conquest of Granada by
Ferdinand and Isabella. Almanzor, a peerless and invincible Moorish
knight-errant, who owns no master upon earth, and, amongst other
enormous boasts, is made to say,—

> I am as free as Nature first made man,
> Ere the base laws of servitude began,
> When wild in woods the noble savage ran ;

nor has hitherto stooped to love, breaks in upon a fight between two
Moorish factions at Granada, and by the might of his single arm puts
the combatants to flight. He then offers his services to the Moorish
king Boabdelin.   He transfers his allegiance several times in the
course of the play, from the king to his plotting brother Abdalla, and
back again ; but the side, whichever it is, that he supports, with ease
puts its enemies to the rout. His love, when he once yields to the
passion, is as romantic as his valour. While aiding Abdalla, he takes
captive Almahide, a noble lady betrothed to Boabdelin.   The first
glance from her eyes causes him to fall desperately in love ; but hearing
of her engagement, he magnanimously resolves to release her. Later,
after he has carried his sword to the side of the king, and having provoked Boabdelin by his arrogance to order his guards to fall upon him
has been overpowered and sentenced to die, Almahide obtains his
pardon as the price of her consenting to marry the king immediately.
Hearing this, Almanzor would have killed himself ; but Almahide lays
her command upon him to live, and he obeys. After he has left the
court, and the Christian armies are pressing strongly forward, a word
from her recalls him, and his prowess rolls back for a time the tide of
invasion. In the concluding battle the king is slain, and Almanzor
recognizes in the Spanish general, after nearly killing him, his own
father, from whom he had been separated in infancy. Almahide and
he become Christians, and agree to marry when her year of widowhood
is expired.

Other heroic plays composed by Dryden are, *The Indian
Emperor, or The Conquest of Mexico* (1665), and *Tyrannick
Love, or The Royal Martyr* (1669).

41. Such was the material of which Dryden's tragedies were
composed down to the year 1671,—a notable epoch in his dramatic career. The heroic play, it must be evident, from its
tumid exaggerated style, offered a broad mark for a clever satirist ; and its weak points were accordingly seized with great
effect by the Duke of Buckingham and his coadjutors Sprat and

Butler, in a play produced in that year.   This was the famous comedy of the *Rehearsal*, in which Dryden himself figures under the character of Bayes.   The poet, who, for one of the *genus irritabile*, was singularly free from personal vanity, felt that he had received a home-thrust, remained silent, and speedily abandoned the line of the heroic drama.   But he did not forget his obligations to Buckingham, and repaid them with interest a few years later, when he drew the portrait of Zimri in *Absalom and Achitophel.*

In his *Essay of Dramatic Poesy*, published in 1668, Dryden had earnestly argued that rime, which he calls the most noble verse, is alone fit for tragedy, which he calls the most noble species of composition ; and had therefore by implication condemned the use of blank verse by Shakspere.   But as his judgment grew clearer and his taste more refined, he saw cause for changing his opinion.   Some striking lines in the prologue to the tragedy of *Aurungzebe*, produced in 1675, mark this point in the progress of his mind.   He is inclined, he says, to damn his own play,—

> Not that it's worse than what before he writ,
> But he has now another taste of wit ;
> And, to confess a truth, though out of time,
> Grows weary of his long-loved mistress, Rhyme.
> Passion's too fierce to be in fetters bound,
> And nature flies him like enchanted ground ;
> What verse can do, he has performed in this,
> Which he presumes the most correct of his ;
> But spite of all his pride, a secret shame
> Invades his breast at Shakspeare's sacred name :
> And when he hears his godlike Romans rage,
> He, in a just despair, would quit the stage ;
> And to an age less polished, more unskilled,
> Does with disdain the foremost honours yield.

42. In his next play, *All for Love*, he abandoned rime, and never afterwards returned to it.   The influence of Shakspere becomes more and more perceptible in the later plays, particularly in *Don Sebastian*, the finest of all Dryden's tragedies, produced in 1690.[1]   Thus the attempt to divert the taste of the play-going public from British to French and Spanish models was renounced by the projector himself, and replaced by a steady and continuous effort to raise Shakspere to his just rank in the estimation of his countrymen.   Dryden's last play, *Love*

---

[1] Chief plays of Dryden :—*The Indian Emperor, Conquest of Granada, Aurungzebe, All for Love, Don Sebastian*, tragedies ; the *Rival Ladies* and the *Spanish Friar*, tragi-comedies ; *Sir Martin Mar-all, An Evening's Love*, and *Marriage à la Mode*, comedies.

Triumphant, a tragi-comedy (1693), like his first, the *Wild Gallant* (1663), was a failure. *The State of Innocence* (1675), one of his three operas, is an attempt to dramatize and put into rime the *Paradise Lost*. According to Aubrey, Milton, when Dryden applied to him for permission to treat his epic in this fashion, replied, rather contemptuously, ' Ay, you may *tag* my verses if you will.' The piece was never acted. Shakspere himself was not sacred from the remodelling hand of Dryden, whom poverty drove to shifts and expedients of all kinds. Of *Troilus and Cressida* (1679) Scott writes,[1] ' So far as this play is to be considered as an alteration of Shakspeare, I fear it must be allowed that our author has suppressed some of his finest poetry, and exaggerated some of his worst faults.' In fact, Dryden is coarser than Shakspere, as Shakspere is worse than Chaucer—*ætas parentum, pejor avis, tulit nos nequiores.* Yet in point of regularity, and regard to the unity of plan, Dryden's play is an improvement. So in *All for Love* (1678), a tragedy founded on Shakspere's *Antony and Cleopatra*, it may be deemed an improvement that the action of the play is concentrated at Alexandria, whereas Shakspere diffuses it over Italy, Greece, and Egypt. But *The Tempest* (1657), an alteration of Shakspere's play made by Dryden in conjunction with Davenant, has no redeeming feature. ' The effect produced by the conjunction of these two powerful minds was, that to Shakspere's monster Caliban is added a sister monster, Sycorax ; and a woman who in the original play had never seen a man, is in this brought acquainted with a man that had never seen a woman.'

43. **Thomas Otway** is the author of nine plays, of which six are tragedies and three comedies. The latter are of small account, but among the tragedies *Caius Marius*, the *Orphan*, and *Venice Preserved* hold—especially the last—high rank among English dramas. The generous open character of the gallant Pierre, the treachery of Jaffier, his friend, and the passionate affection of Belvidera, supply tragic elements which Otway has worked into the texture of his play with no ordinary skill. The interest of the piece turns on the concoction and discovery of a plot to overthrow the Venetian senate,—a subject which was doubtless suggested by the tremendous excitement of the Popish Plot, then (1681) in the full swing of its career of imposture, panic, and judicial murder. One of the characters, Antonio, is made to say, ' I'll prove there's a plot with a vengeance. . . . That there is a plot, surely by this time no man that hath eyes or understanding in his head will presume to doubt.' This was the sort of language then continually in the mouths of the vile witnesses for the plot and their supporters in parliament.

44. Poor **Nat. Lee**, a sadly irregular liver, wrote eleven tragedies, besides having a considerable share in two which are ascribed to

[1] Life of Dryden.

Dryden—*Œdipus* and the *Duke of Guise*.   The *Rival Queens* and *Theodosius* are considered his best pieces.   Addison says of him, ' There was none better turned for tragedy than our author, if, instead of favouring the impetuosity of his genius, he had restrained it, and kept it within proper bounds.'   **Thomas Shadwell**, the butt of Dryden's satire as Og in *Absalom and Achitophel*, and again, as MacFlecknoe, the ' true blue Protestant poet,' who supplanted Dryden himself as poet-laureate after the Revolution, wrote sixteen plays, of which thirteen are comedies.   The *Virtuoso* and the *Lancashire Witches* long held their ground on the comic stage.   **Elkanah Settle**, worthless (unless he is much belied) both as a man and as a poet, satirized as Doeg in *Absalom and Achitophel*, wrote fifteen plays, chiefly tragedies, of which the most noted was the *Empress of Morocco*.

45.   **John Crowne** wrote a tragedy of some mark, *Thyestes*, and a comedy which long kept the stage, *Sir Courtley Nice* (1685).   The humour of this play consists in the contrast of character, and bitter antagonism, between Mr. Hothead, the tory and churchman, and Mr. Testimony, the whig and dissenter.   Addison says in the *Freeholder* (No. 34), that when he himself saw this play performed, in 1711, a time when party feeling ran unusually high, the whole audience ' very gravely ranged themselves into two parties, under Hothead and Testimony.'

46.   The plays of Mrs. **Aphra Behn**, fifteen in number, were published in 1702.   One of them, *The Roundheads, or The Good Old Cause*, is founded on the events between Cromwell's death and the Restoration ; the puritans are attacked with coarse but vigorous satire.   At the end of the fifth act, the ' Scotch General ' (Monk) rides roughshod over the city ; the king is proclaimed ; loyal men are wild with joy ; Lady Lambert and Lady Desborough go off with their cavalier lovers ; bonfires are lighted in the streets, with spits, and rumps roasting on them, while the ' mobile ' crowd round the fires, with pots, bottles, and fiddles.   It is no wonder that this play was popular in the reign of Charles II. ; rather it is strange that a subject so susceptible of dramatic treatment, and so sure to excite and interest an audience, was not taken up by Dryden and other dramatists of greater mark than Mrs. Behn.

47.   In comedy a new school arose, of which the tone and form may certainly be traced to the unrivalled genius of Molière.   The ' comedy of manners,' of which Congreve, Etherege, and Wycherley were in our present period the chief representatives, exhibited, in polished and witty prose, the modes of acting, thinking, and talking, prevalent in the fashionable society of the time.   That society was a grossly immoral one, and the plays which reflected its image were no less so.   **Congreve**, the most eminent writer of this school, produced only five plays, one of which, the *Mourning Bride*, is a tragedy.   His comedies are—the *Old Bachelor* (1693), the *Double Dealer* (1694), *Love for Love* (1695), and the *Way of the World* (1700).

48.   *The Mourning Bride* (1697) opens with a passage of familiar sound :—

> Music has charms to soothe a savage breast,
> To soften rocks, or bend a knotted oak.

The unities are preserved in this play. The eloquence of over-mastering passion is finely rendered in the scene where Almeria and Osmyn meet in the place of tombs. The *Old Bachelor* took the town by storm; Halifax showered favours on the stripling who had produced such a masterpiece of wit; he appointed Congreve to a place in the Pipe Office, and to another in the Customs of 600*l.* a year. Dr. Johnson winds up a very acute criticism of this play, in which he shows that the knowledge of mankind which it exhibits at first sight is rather apparent than real, with the words, ' Yet this gay comedy, when all these deductions are made, will still remain the work of very powerful and fertile faculties; the dialogue is quick and sparkling, the incidents such as seize the attention, and the wit so exuberant that it "o'er-informs its tenement."' *The Way of the World* was a failure, and Congreve wrote no more for the stage.

49. **Sir George Etherege** is the author of a once celebrated comedy, *The Man of Mode, or Sir Fopling Flutter*. His first play, *The Comical Revenge, or Love in a Tub* (1664), recommended him to the intimacy of the licentious courtiers of the Restoration, among whom he came to be known as 'gentle George' and 'easy Etherege.' *She would if she could*, another comedy, appeared in 1668.

50. **Wycherley's** *Plain Dealer* (1677) is a disgrace to the man who could write it, and the audience that could endure it. It is a perversion rather than an imitation of Molière's *Misanthrope*, the innocent flirtations of Célimène being replaced by the coarse wantonness of Olivia; while for the eccentric moroseness of Alceste, of which after all a real love of truth and goodness was the motive, we get the surliness of the wretch Manly, who is himself capable of all but the more sneaking crimes, though he is continually railing at the baseness of society. Wycherley's other plays are, *Love in a Wood* (1672), *The Gentleman Dancing-master* (1673), and *The Country Wife* (1675).

51. Towards the end of the seventeenth century the immorality of the stage began to be thought intolerable. In this respect the stage had remained stationary since the Restoration, while the morals of English society had been gradually becoming purer. This general feeling found an exponent in **Jeremy Collier**, a non-juring[1] divine, who wrote in 1698 his *Short View of the Immorality and Profaneness of the Stage*. Both Dryden and Congreve were vigorously assailed in this work on account of their dramatic misdeeds. Dryden magnanimously pleaded guilty to the main charge, in the preface to his *Fables*, published in 1700, although he maintained that Collier had in many places perverted his meaning by his glosses, and was 'too much given to horse-play in his raillery.' ' I will not say,' he continues, 'that *the zeal of God's house has eaten him up*; but I am sure it has devoured some part of his good manners and civility.' After

---

[1] That is, one who refused to take the oath of allegiance to King William.

a time, Collier's attack produced its effect; the public taste
became purer; the intellect of the country became ashamed of
the stage, and turned to cultivate other branches of literature;
and from that time the English drama tended downwards to
that condition of feebleness and inanity which reached its
maximum about a hundred years later.

Learning:—Usher; Selden; Gale, &c.

52. The state of learning in England during this period was
not so high as it has been generally esteemed. Selden says in
his *Table Talk*—'The Jesuits and the lawyers of France, and
the Low Country men, have engrossed all learning. The rest
of the world make nothing but homilies.' He was glancing
here at the eloquent divines, Andrewes, Hall, Taylor, &c.
There was, indeed, abundance of *illustrative*, but little *produc-
tive* learning. The divines above mentioned, in their sermons,
ransack for illustrations the whole series of the Greek and
Latin authors, and show no slight acquaintance with councils
and Fathers; but they use all this learning merely to serve
some immediate purpose; they do not digest or analyse it with
a view to obtaining from it permanent literary results. Usher,
the Irishman, is the chief exception. **James Usher,** one of the
three first matriculated students of Trinity College, Dublin,[1]
upon its opening in 1593, rose to be Protestant primate of
Armagh; but he left Ireland in 1640, and, excusing himself on
the plea of the social confusion which prevailed, never afterwards
returned to it. His treatise, *De Ecclesiarum Britannicarum
Primordiis,* and his celebrated *Annales* (a digest of universal
history from the creation to the destruction of Jerusalem by
Titus), are works of solid learning and research, which even yet
are not superseded. Selden himself possessed a great deal of
abstruse learning; probably no Englishman ever dived so deep
into Rabbinical literature, or was so completely at home in certain branches of antiquarian research. But he cannot be compared with the great Dutchman of the age, Hugo Grotius, whom
he met in controversy,[2] nor with the Spanish Jesuit, Suarez.
He was narrower, more lawyer-like, and less philosophical, than
either of those two great men.

---

[1] Usher actively aided in the formation of the Trinity College Library, and
his MSS., given after his death to the college by Charles II., form a valuable
portion of its collections. See his Life by Aikin.

[2] Grotius wrote a book called *Mare Liberum,* asserting the right of free
fishery in the narrow seas near the English coast, to which Selden replied by
his *Mare Clausum,* denying that right.

53. Among the works of **John Selden**, which were published in three volumes fol. some years after his death, the following are the most important:—

(1) *Jani Anglorum Facies Altera* (1610); an English translation appeared in 1683. This is a sort of 'Constitutional History of England,' but with special political objects, *e.g.* to prove that early English kings resisted 'papal usurpations,' and to justify the national rejection of the Salic law in regard to the succession to the crown. It begins with the 'counterfeit Berosus' (*ante*, ch. iii. § 72), and comes down to 1189.

(2) *On Titles of Honour* (1614). This is a curious antiquarian investigation into the origin of the titles of honour and dignity used in modern Europe.

(3) *Of Tythes* (1618). Selden's object was to show that tithes were not due by divine right, but only in virtue of express legal enactment, authorizing the clergy to demand them. Of course, the clergy were up in arms at a proposition so audacious, and Selden was compelled· to make a formal submission before the Court of High Commission. The statement which he read sounds like a retractation, but, when closely scanned, is found to be only an admission of inopportuneness, coupled with an expression of grief for having given offence to the court and the clergy.

(4) *De Jure Naturali et Gentium, juxta disciplinam Hebræorum* (1640). A treatise on the law of nature and nations. Le Clerc, the first review writer, says that this work is obscure and badly arranged; that Selden only copies the Rabbins, and scarcely ever reasons at all.

(5) *A Dissertation on Fleta* (1647) inquiring into the use of the Roman law in Britain during the Roman occupation, and its disuse in later times.

Selden had a seat in Parliament under James, and in the first four years of Charles I.; in 1640 he was sent to the Long Parliament as the representative of the University of Oxford.

He was imprisoned for several years after 1629, on account of the zeal with which he had espoused the popular side in the disputes of that year. But by the publication of *Mare Clausum* (1635) he regained some degree of favour at court. In the Long Parliament he played the part of a moderator, and after the war broke out seems to have retired from active life. His precious library, which is now one of the chief ornaments of the Bodleian library, was nearly being lost to it; for the testy old bachelor took offence at being required by the library authorities to give a bond before taking out on loan some MS. which he required, and declared that Oxford should have none of his books. But his executors, to whom they were left absolutely, upon the Inner Temple declining to provide a suitable place for their reception, made them over to the university.

Selden's *Table-Talk* was published by his amanuensis a few years after his death, which occurred in 1654. This little book derives great interest from the acuteness and penetration of the mind whose casual or habitual thoughts it illustrates.

54. The names of Gale, Gataker, Potter, and Stanley, are the most respectable that we can produce in the department of scholarship during the remainder of the period. Potter's *Greek*

Antiquities, first published in 1697, was a text-book in all British schools for nearly a century and a half, having been superseded only within these few years by the fuller and more critical treatises for which German thought and erudition have prepared the way. Of Bentley, the prince of English scholars, we shall speak in the next chapter.

Prose Fiction :—' The Pilgrim's Progress;' Oratory.

55. In the department of prose fiction, this period, but for one remarkable work, is absolutely sterile. In the exciting times of Charles I. and the Commonwealth, men were in too earnest a mood to spend much time in the contemplation of imaginary scenes and characters. Nor, during the twenty-eight years which separated the Revolution from the Restoration, had the agitation of society subsided sufficiently to admit of the formation of a novel-reading public, by which term is meant that large class of persons, easy in their circumstances, but victims to *ennui* from the tranquillity and uniformity of their daily avocations, who seek in fiction the excitement which the stability of the social system has banished from their actual life. It must be remembered, also, that the drama was the surest road to popularity for an inventive genius up to the end of the century. Soon afterwards the stage fell into discredit, and the novel immediately appeared to fill the vacant place.

One exception, however, to this rule of sterility is to be found in Bunyan's celebrated *Pilgrim's Progress*. John Bunyan, a native of Elstow, near Bedford, was of obscure origin, and was brought up to the trade of a tinker. His youth, according to his own account, was wild and vicious; but having been impressed by the sermon of a Baptist preacher, at which he was accidentally present, he was led to enter into himself, and gradually reformed his life. Forsaking the Church of England, he joined the Baptists, and became a preacher among them. When, after the Restoration, severe laws were passed against nonconformity, Bunyan, refusing to be silenced, was thrown into Bedford gaol, where he was detained twelve years. Here it was that he wrote his famous allegory, the object of which is to represent, under the figure of a journey taken by a pilgrim, the course of a Christian's life in his passage through this world to the world to come. No original work in the English language has had a greater circulation than the *Pilgrim's Progress*, nor been translated into a greater number of foreign languages. The work was first published complete in 1684; Bunyan died in 1688. It is needless to describe a book so well known; but I may remark that there seems a great falling off in the account of the pilgrimage of Christiana and her sons, as compared with that of the pilgrimage of Christian. In truth it appears from the poetical introduction to the second part, that the good man was excited and elated in spirit in no small degree by the extraordinary reception which his Christian had met with ; he was conscious that greatness had been thrust upon him ; and one misses accordingly in the second part something of the delightful freshness, the naturalness, the entire unconscious devotion of heart and singleness of purpose, which are so conspicuous in the first part. But what simple, equable, sinewy English the ' inspired tinker' writes ! what fulness of the Christian doctrine is in him ! what clear insight into many forms of the Christian character ! what thorough understanding of a vast variety of temptations, fleshly and spiritual !

56. Under the head of Oratory we find scarcely anything deserving of mention. Cromwell's speeches, with their designed ambiguity, their cloudy pietism, their involved long-winded sentences, are hardly readable, in spite of Mr. Carlyle's editorial industry. The speeches given in Clarendon's History are often very interesting ; but the difficulty of knowing how much may be the author's own composition detracts from their value. Pamphlets issued in shoals from the press during all this period.

History and Biography:—Milton, Ludlow, Clarendon, &c.; Wood's 'Athenæ,' Pepys, Evelyn, &c.

57. In our last notice of historical writing, it appeared that in the first quarter of the century the best of our historians had written on the affairs of Turkey and on the ancient world. But as the century wore on, and the shadow of the civil war began to darken the sky, English contemporary history became a subject of such absorbing and pressing interest, that our writers had no thought to spare for that of foreign nations and distant times. Fuller, Milton, Ludlow, May, Whitlocke, Rushworth, and Clarendon,[1] besides many inferior writers, wrote entirely, so far as they were historians at all, upon English affairs. Thomas Fuller, a clergyman of great wit and originality, wrote a *Church History of Britain from the Birth of Jesus Christ until the Year* 1648; this work was published in 1656. Milton's *History of England* is but a fragment, extending 'from the first traditional beginning to the Norman Conquest.' Ludlow was one

---

[1] For some remarks on Clarendon's History, see Crit. Sect. ch. II. § 21.

of Cromwell's generals, and signed the warrant for Charles I.'s execution; his *Memoirs*, written during his exile in Switzerland, relating, for the most part, to events in which he had himself been an actor, were first published after his death in 1698. **John May**, a lawyer, described the civil strife, both in Parliament and in the field, from the parliamentary point of view; his work, published about 1650, is described by Hallam as a kind of contrast to that of Clarendon.   **Bulstrode Whitlocke**, one of the commissioners of the Great Seal under Cromwell, composed some dull, but in many respects important, memoirs, which were first published in 1682.   **Rushworth's** *Historical Collections*—a perfect mine of information—appeared in 1659.   He was a clerk in the House of Commons, and for many years was in the habit of taking notes of 'speeches and passages at conferences in Parliament, and from the king's own mouth what he spoke to both houses, and was upon the stage continually an eye and an ear witness of the greatest transactions.'[1]   His Collections range over the period from 1618 to 1644.

58. Of works subsidiary to history, *e.g.* biographies, personal memoirs, diaries, &c., we meet with a considerable number. The most important among them is the well-known *Athenæ Oxonienses* of **Anthony à Wood**, a 'History of all the writers and bishops educated at Oxford from 1500 to 1695.'   Fuller's biographical work on the *Worthies of England*, containing sketches of about eighteen hundred individuals— among others, of Chaucer, Spenser, and Shakspere—arranged under the several counties of England and Wales, appeared in 1662, the year after his death. **Izaak Walton**, better known for his *Treatise on Angling*, wrote Lives of several eminent Anglican divines, including Hooker, Donne, and Sanderson.   **Baxter's** *Reliquiæ Baxterianæ*, a curious autobiography, confused, however, in arrangement and badly edited, first appeared in 1696.   All the material portions of it are given in Orme's *Life of Baxter*.   The *Diary* of **Samuel Pepys**, Secretary to the Admiralty, extending over the years 1660–1669, was first given to the world in 1825, having lain veiled in its original cipher, till raked out of the MS. repository of the Pepysian Library, and deciphered under the superintendence of Lord Braybrooke.   Andrew Marvell, in his *Seasonable Argument*, printed in 1677, thus disposes of Pepys, who was then member for the borough of Castle Rising:—'Castle Rising: Samuel Pepys, once a taylour, then serving-man to the Lord Sandwitch, now secretary to the Admiralty, got by passes and other illegal wayes 40,000*l*.'   It was not Samuel, however, but

---

[1] Wood's *Athenæ*.

his father, who was the tailor. John Evelyn, a country gentleman, skilled in the mysteries of planting and landscape-gardening, is the author of a *Diary*, first published in 1818, which, among other matters, contains an interesting account of the great fire of London, of which he was an eye-witness. The Parliamentary diary of **Thomas Burton**, member for Westmoreland, first published in 1828, gives short notes, which seem to be well and fairly made, of the principal speeches which he heard in the parliaments that met at Westminster between the years 1656 and 1659.

We have few or no narratives of adventure, by sea or land, to record in connection with this period. A time of civil war concentrates the thoughts and the activity of men upon their own country, just as in the systole of the heart the blood all flows together to the vital centre. In tranquil times, the counter movement—the diastole—sets in, and the energies of many of the most stirring and gifted persons in the nation are turned outwards, and employed over wide and remote areas in the search of excitement, or the investigation of nature.

Theology :—Hall, Jeremy Taylor, Bull, Baxter Penn, &c.

59. This is the Augustan period of Anglican divinity. If we examine the literature of the controversy that raged, in this as in the previous period, between the Church of England and the Puritans, we shall find that, if we put aside the wri'ings of Milton, the episcopalian writers immeasurably excelled their opponents both in talent and learning. **Joseph Hall**, Bishop of Norwich, comes next for mention in order of time after Bishop Andrewes. By his reply to the pamphlet produced by five Puritan ministers, who wrote under the fictitious name of ' Smectymnuus,' [1] he drew upon himself the fierce invectives of Milton. His *Meditations* and *Characters* will be noticed in the next section. Ejected by the Puritans from the see of Norwich in 1643, he retired to a small estate at Higham, where he died at a very advanced age in 1656.

60. **William Chillingworth**, a native of Oxford, received his education at Trinity College in that University, and was elected a fellow in 1628. Making the acquaintance of the Jesuit Fisher, he was convinced by his arguments, made his submission to the Roman Church, and settled at Douay. Laud, who was his godfather, induced him to return in 1631 ; he became again a Protestant, and studying with intense application the questions

[1] See p. 262, *n*.

involved in the controversy between authority and private judgment, he produced in 1637 his treatise entitled *The Religion of Protestants a safe Way to Salvation.* To make the terms of union among Protestant Christians as simple and comprehensive as possible, Chillingworth proposed that the Apostles' Creed should be taken as the universal basis and formula of belief; whoever accepted that was a Christian, and belonged to the Church. He imposed no particular interpretation of this creed, and since it was freely accepted by those who denied the divinity of Christ, Chillingworth thus brought upon himself the suspicion and the charge of Socinianism. He signed the thirty-nine Articles, though with much misgiving, and then obtained preferment in the Established Church; but the tempest of civil war dislodged him, like so many others; and being made prisoner on the surrender of Arundel Castle in 1644 to the parliamentary forces, he died soon afterwards at Chichester.

61. **John Hales,** sometimes called ' the ever memorable,' may be considered as belonging to the same tolerant ' Broad Church ' school, which engaged the later convictions of Chillingworth, and the earlier convictions of Taylor. He was educated at C. C. C., Oxford, and started in life with Calvinist opinions, but is said to have been converted to Arminian sentiments by listening to the debates at the Synod of Dort, in 1618, where he was present as chaplain to the English ambassador. He used to tell his friends, that ' at the· well pressing St. John iii. 16, by Episcopius [a leading divine at Dort], there he bid John Calvin good night.' He was a fellow of Eton and Canon of Windsor, and his winning manners, the ease of his society, his ready wit and vast knowledge, made him a favourite with the poets and courtiers of his day; see *ante,* §16. In his sermons and other writings, he was never weary of inculcating the duty of tolerating our neighbour's honest opinions, and the uncharitableness of inferring that any one will lose salvation on account of any religious belief conscientiously held. His works were published in 1659, three years after his death, under the title of *Golden Remains.*

62. **Jeremy Taylor,** the most eloquent of English writers, was born at Cambridge in 1613. Like nearly all the Anglican divines of this period, he inclined to the tenets of Arminius, a Dutch theologian who died in 1608, and whose opinions were vehemently anathematized after his death by the Calvinistic synod of Dort. If asked *what* precisely the Arminians held, one might answer, as Morley is said to have done [1] when a country

---

[1] Clarendon's *Autobiography.*

squire put him the question, 'All the best bishoprics and
deaneries in England;'—it will be sufficent, however, to say
that Arminianism was a species of Pelagianism, and arose by
way of reaction against the predestinarian extravagances of
the Calvinists. Coleridge gives the following graphic account
of the English Arminians:—'Towards the close of the reign
of our first James, and during the period from the accession
of Charles I. to the restoration of his profligate son, there
arose a party of divines, Arminians (and many of them Latitu-
dinarians) in their creed, but devotees of the throne and the
altar, soaring High Churchmen and ultra Royalists. Much as I
dislike their scheme of doctrine and detest their principles of
government, both in Church and State, I cannot but allow that
they formed a galaxy of learning and talent, and that among
them the Church of England finds her stars of the first magni-
tude. Instead of regarding the Reformation established under
Edward VI. as imperfect, they accused the Reformers, some of
them openly, but all in their private opinions, of having gone
too far; and while they were willing to keep down (and, if they
could not reduce him to a primacy of honour, to keep out) the
Pope, . . . they were zealous to restore the hierarchy, and to
substitute the authority of the Fathers, Canonists, and Councils of the first six or seven centuries, and [some of the] later
Doctors and Schoolmen, for the names of Luther, Melancthon,
Bucer, Calvin, and the systematic theologians who rejected all
testimony but that of their Bible.'[1]

63. Taylor, whose parents were in humble life, was first admitted to a scholarship in Caius College, but afterwards went to
Oxford, was admitted *ad eundem*, and elected fellow of All Souls,
through the influence of Archbishop Laud. When the war
broke out, he was made one of the royal chaplains, and it was at
the request of Charles I. that he wrote his first treatise, *Episcopacy Asserted*. The line of argument in this treatise much
resembles that used by Hooker in his seventh book, and by Hall
in his *Episcopacy by Divine Right*. In the appeal to antiquity,
in order to find arguments for episcopacy against the Presbyterians, Taylor is cogent and copious; he is also strong when (§ 36)
he comments on the intolerable all-embracing strictness of the
Presbyterian jurisdiction, and says that men would be no better
off who should exchange for it the lighter yoke of episcopal government. But when he comes to what was the really 'burning
question' of his day, the enforcement by the bishops of religious
uniformity, his words read like a solemn mockery. The juris-

[1] *Literary Remains*, vol. iii. p. 885.

diction of bishops, he says, is enforced only by excommunication and other church censures. ' But yet this internal compulsory, through the duty of good princes to God, and their favour to the church, *is assisted by the secular arm*, either superadding a temporal penalty in case of contumacy, or some other way abetting the censures of the church, and it ever was so since commonwealths were Christian.'

The war proceeded; Taylor was ejected from his living of Uppingham, and, settling in Wales, supported himself by his pen and by tuition. He now wrote, and published in 1647, his famous *Discourse of the Liberty of Prophesying*, addressed to Christopher Lord Hatton. The position of the different parties in the civil war, at the time when this work appeared, goes far to explain the line of argument pursued in it. It was after Naseby field, and the king was in the hands of the army; the bishops had been banished from their sees, and it seemed that the old prelatical jurisdiction, which had been used so long for the persecution of nonconformists, was now gone past recovery. The five eventful years since the publication of *Episcopacy Asserted* had produced a marked change in Taylor's sentiments, and the successful stand made by the persecuted had effectually opened his eyes to the beauty of toleration. Taking a survey of all religious systems, past and present, he concludes that infallibility nowhere exists on earth, that reason, proceeding upon the safest grounds procurable, is the best judge of controversies that can be obtained, and that till, in exercising their reason, men learn to be unanimous, they should bear with one another's mistakes. He discovers accordingly that ecclesiastical punishments ought to be purely of a spiritual nature, and ought not to touch the person or the goods of the offender. The church, he says (§ 15) may proceed in restraining false opinions, so far as to 'convince by sound doctrine, and put to silence by spiritual censures,' but no farther. Moreover, as the result of the destructive analysis to which he has subjected the history of religion, he concludes, that, while the belief in some few necessary doctrines must still be maintained, unless Christianity is to vanish altogether under the scalpels of its interpreters, those doctrines must be the simplest, most primitive, and most universally received that can be found. The common basis required, Taylor, following Chillingworth, finds in the Apostles' Creed.

64. After the Restoration, Taylor was appointed Protestant Bishop of Down. Episcopacy was now again dominant, and we find Taylor 'disclaiming and disavowing the principle of toleration,' and excusing himself as best he could for his late liberalism. Of his remaining works, the most remarkable are, *Of Holy*

Living and *Of Holy Dying*,[1] devotional treatises, of which it is impossible not to admire the depth of thought, the fervour, and the eloquence. The *Ductor Dubitantium* is a manual of casuistry, and the *Golden Grove* (1654), a collection of prayers and litanies, with an appendix containing hymns for festivals. Taylor died in 1667.

65. The discouraged Puritans felt little inclination to renew those controversies on church government which events had so decisively settled one way; and besides, the great power and commanding influence which the Roman Church progressively acquired during the reign of Louis XIV. alarmed all Protestant bodies on this side into an unacknowledged but valid alliance against the common antagonist. If Baxter thundered from the Presbyterian camp, the Anglican bishops and divines were not less vigilant, copious, and argumentative. **Isaac Barrow** wrote his learned work on *The Supremacy*; and **George Bull**, not yet a bishop, addressed to the Countess of Newburgh his *Vindication of the Church of England from the Errors of the Church of Rome*; and **Burnet**, with an express controversial intention, published in 1679 and 1681 his *History of the Reformation*, for which he received the thanks of both houses of Parliament. However, the most remarkable theological works of the last quarter of the century were rather directed against infidelity, or at least against opinions subsisting on the outermost verge of Christianity, than either against Puritanism or 'Popery.' And these works, as we shall see, form a link of transition between the theology of this age and that of the next, that *seculum rationalisticum*, when theology will have to defend, not the mere outworks and dispensable additions, but the very body of the fortress. Bishop Bull's *Defensio Fidei Nicenæ* (1685) is a systematic endeavour to prove, against the Arian writers who were now beginning to make a stir both abroad and in England, that the Christian writers who lived before the Council of Nice (A.D. 325), in spite of occasional looseness and vagueness of language, held really that very doctrine respecting the . Trinity which is affirmed in the Nicene Creed. The *Judicium Ecclesiæ Catholicæ* (1694) is a work of similar scope; it is to elucidate and set forth the judgment of the Church in every age respecting Christ's divinity. Robert Nelson, a friend of Bull's, sent this work in 1699 to the great Bossuet, Bishop of Meaux; and in a pleasant cordial letter of thanks, Bossuet, after stating that he desired to express not his own sense merely, but that of the French bishops in general, of the obligations under which

---

[1] See Crit. Sect. ch. II. § 40.

' le Docteur Bullus' had laid the Christian world, expressed his surprise that so learned and penetrating a mind could fail to recognize the claims of the existing Catholic Church to his allegiance. Bull replied to these expressions in a short pamphlet called *Corruptions of the Church of Rome*, but Bossuet was dead before it was finished.[1] Bull also wrote *Animadversions* on the works of the Unitarian Gilbert Clarke, and *Harmonia Apostolica* (1669), an attempt to reconcile the passages respecting justification found in the writings of St. Paul and St. James.

66. Touched, perhaps, by the ungenerous attitude which the Church, restored by Presbyterian aid, held towards gagged and persecuted nonconformity, after the passing of the repressive acts consequent upon the Restoration, the purer and nobler minds yearned for some scheme of comprehension, under which, concessions being made on both sides, the greater part of the Nonconformists might be brought within the pale of the Church. Archbishop Leighton, Henry More, Ralph Cudworth, and Bishop Wilkins, were the principal men of this school; they were called Latitudinarian divines. **Leighton**, son of the unhappy Presbyterian who was cruelly mutilated by sentence of the Star Chamber in 1629, was one of the most saintly men that ever gave living and practical proof of the divine power of Christianity. He was on terms of the most intimate friendship with Bishop Burnet, who declares, in the *History of his Own Times*, that he 'reckoned his early knowledge of him, and long and intimate conversation with him, that continued to his death, for twenty-three years, amongst the greatest blessings of his life; for which he knew he must give account to God in the great day, in a most particular manner.' Leighton's chief work is the *Commentary on the First Epistle of St. Peter*, which drew forth the ardent admiration of Coleridge. Of Cudworth and More we shall have to speak in another place.

67. **Pearson** is the author of a well-known exposition of the Apostles' Creed (1659). He was a man of vast learning, fitter, according to Burnet, to be a divine than a bishop. His Vindication of the authenticity of the Epistles of Ignatius is a very masterly production. **Lightfoot's** *Horæ Hebraicæ* and *Harmony of the Four Gospels* are works of a different kind. In these, the writer's profound acquaintance with Rabbinical literature enables him to throw a flood of light on the various Jewish usages and rites current in Palestine at the time of the Christian era, and referred to in the New Testament, as well as upon obscure points in the topography.

68. Two thousand Presbyterian ministers were ejected from

[1] See *The Life of Bishop Bull*, by Nelson.

their parishes in 1662, under the Act of Uniformity. Among them the most eminent was **Richard Baxter**, a voluminous but not very instructive writer, except where he confines himself to themes purely devotional. He is the author of a well-known manual of religious meditation, *The Saint's Everlasting Rest* (1649). In the long series of his controversial writings occur such titles as *A Winding-sheet for Popery* (1657), *The Grotian Religion Discovered* (in which he censures Grotius' leanings towards Rome), *The Certainty of Christianity without Popery* (1672), *Against Revolt to a Foreign Jurisdiction* (1691), &c., &c. Tillotson—no mean authority—says of Baxter, that ' he loved to abound in his own sense, could by no means be brought off his own apprehensions and thoughts, but would have them to be the rule and standard for all other men.'

69. In spite of the political pliancy alleged against him by Lord Macaulay, it may be said that English Protestantism has seldom appeared in so attractive a light as in the character and career of **William Penn**. Joining the rising sect of the Quakers while at Christ Church, this young Buckinghamshire squire steadfastly endured family and social persecution, and frequent imprisonment, for what he deemed the holiest of causes; and became in middle life, through his religious earnestness, conviction, and activity, aided by an exuberant flow of language, a very noteworthy and influential person—a man who would have to be reckoned with. He had for several years thrown himself with characteristic energy into the work of colonizing America, when in 1681 Charles II., in recognition of the services of his father, the Admiral Penn who took Jamaica, granted to him and his heirs ' that province lying on the west side of the river Delaware in North America, formerly belonging to the Dutch, and then called the New Netherlands.' The king changed the name of the province to *Pennsylvania*, and made Penn the absolute proprietor and governor of it. He visited his splendid dominion in 1682, and again in 1699, remaining a year or two each time ; the fruit of these visits was a *Description of Pennsylvania*. But it was in religious treatises and pamphlets that his pen was chiefly employed. Among these the most important is *No Cross No Crown*, written in prison. His steady advocacy of toleration by the State of all ' but those who maintain principles destructive of industry, fidelity, justice, and obedience,' frequently brought on him the imputation of being a concealed Jesuit, and emissary of Rome. Other tracts from his hand are —*The Great Case of Liberty of Conscience, once more briefly debated and defended*, and *A Brief Account of the Rise and Progress of the People called Quakers*. He lived to a good old age, dying in 1718.

Philosophy:—Hobbes, Cudworth, Locke, Harrington, Barclay.

70. Though the philosophical teaching of the English Universities remained *in statu quo* during this period, speculation was common among cultivated minds, and developed in certain branches of inquiry marked and important results. In metaphysics occur the name of Thomas Hobbes, and the still more famous name of John Locke. Political reasoning was earnestly followed by Milton, Hobbes, Sidney, Harrington, Filmer, and Locke. Essay writing was attempted by Feltham, and more successfully by Bishop Hall and Sir Thomas Browne. Lastly, the 'new philosophy,' as it was called in that age, that is, the philosophy of experiment, received a strong impulse through the incorporation, in 1662, of the Royal Society.

Hobbes, the 'philosopher of Malmesbury,' was born in the year of the Spanish Armada, and is said to have owed the nervous timidity of his constitution to the terror with which his mother regarded the approach of the invading host. After a residence of five years at Oxford, he travelled on the continent, and made the acquaintance of several eminent men. Returning to England, he devoted himself to the careful study of the classical historians and poets. He early conceived a dislike to the democratical or movement party of that day, and in 1628 published a translation of *Thucydides,* 'that the follies of the Athenian democrats might be made known to his fellow-citizens.' For the greater portion of his long life, after attaining to manhood, he resided as a tutor or as a friend in the family of the Earls of Devonshire. The stormy opening of the Long Parliament, in 1640, led him to apprehend civil war, from which his timid nature instinctively shrank; he accordingly went over to France, and took up his abode in Paris. Among his philosophical acquaintances, there, were Gassendi and Father Mersenne. The former was as great a sceptic as himself; the latter, he says,[1] once when he was dangerously ill, tried to make him a Roman Catholic, but without the least success. His political treatise, *De Cive,* was published at Paris in 1646. The *Leviathan,* containing his entire philosophical system, appeared in 1651; the *De Corpore,* a physiological work, in 1655, and the *De Homine* in 1658. At the age of eighty he wrote his *Behemoth,* a history of the civil war, and, about the same time, a

---

[1] See his curious Latin autobiography, prefixed to the edition of his works by Sir W. Molesworth.

Latin poem on the rise and growth of the Papal power. In his eighty-seventh year he published a metrical version of the *Odyssey*, and in the following year one of the *Iliad*; both, however, are worthless. He died in 1679, being then ninety-one years old.

71. **Cudworth**, who has been already mentioned as one of the Latitudinarian divines, takes rank among the philosophers on account of his *Intellectual System of the Universe* (1678), a work designed to be in three parts, and to refute three several doctrines which he calls 'Fatalisms.' The first is that of an atheistic fate or necessity, which, with Lucretius, accounts for the material world by the fortuitous meeting and interaction of atoms. The second is that of a divine fate immoral, which admits a God, but denies him to be good or just. The third is that of a divine fate moral, which admits God to be good and just, and allows the reality of moral distinctions, but nevertheless considers all human actions as inevitably concatenated and necessary. But, of these three parts, Cudworth only executed the first, the argument against atheism; nevertheless, as he considered it right always to state the arguments of his adversaries fully and in their own words, his work is one of unwieldy bulk.

72. Few names occur in the history of our literature which are more noteworthy than that of **John Locke**, because there are few writers to whose influence important changes or advances in general opinion, upon divers important questions, can be so certainly and directly attributed. His political doctrines have been persistently carried into practice by his own country ever since his death, and recently by other countries also; and the results have—to outward appearance, at least—been singularly encouraging. By his famous *Essay on the Human Understanding*, he effectually checked the tendency to waste the efforts of the mind in sterile metaphysical discussions, and opened out a track of inquiry which the human mind has earnestly prosecuted ever since, with ever-increasing confidence in the soundness of the method, considered as a testing process, applicable to matters of fact. Lastly, his *Treatise on Education*, from which Rousseau is said to have largely borrowed in his *Emile*, contains the first suggestion of a large number of those improvements, both in the theory and practice of education, which the present age has seen effected.

Locke resided for many years after leaving Oxford in the house of his patron and friend, Lord Shaftesbury, the Achitophel of Dryden's satire, whose character the poet portrayed in those famous lines,—

> Restless, unfixed in principles and place,
> In power unpleased, impatient of disgrace ;
> A fiery soul, which, working out its way,
> Fretted the pigmy body to decay,
> And o'er-informed the tenement of clay.[1]

Sharing the Whig opinions of his patron, Locke came in also for his full share of the enmity of the Court, which even demanded, in 1685, his extradition from the States-General of Holland, to which country he had followed Shaftesbury after his disgrace in 1682. His friends, however, concealed him, and Locke had the satisfaction of returning to England in the fleet of the conquering William of Orange. Strange that of the two greatest literary Englishmen of that day—John Locke and John Dryden—the resemblance of whose portraits must have struck many an observer, the one should date his personal advancement and the triumph of the cause to which he adhered, from the same event which brought dismissal, ruin, and humiliation to the other !

73. Locke's own account of the origin of the *Essay* is interesting. In the prefatory Epistle to the Reader, he says : ' Were it fit to trouble thee with the history of this Essay, I should tell thee that five or six friends, meeting at my chamber, and discoursing on a subject very remote from this, found themselves quickly at a stand, by the difficulties that rose on every side. After we had a while puzzled ourselves, without coming any nearer a resolution of those doubts which perplexed us, it came into my thoughts that we took a wrong course; and that, before we set ourselves upon inquiries of that nature, it was necessary to examine our own abilities, and see what objects our understandings were, or were not, fitted to deal with. This I proposed to the company, who all readily assented ; and thereupon it was agreed that this should be our first inquiry. Some hasty and undigested thoughts on a subject I had never before considered, which I set down against our next meeting, gave the first entrance into this discourse; which, having been thus begun by chance, was continued by intreaty ; written by incoherent parcels ; and, after long intervals of neglect, resumed again, as my humour or occasions permitted ; and at last, in a retirement where an attendance on my health gave me leisure, it was brought into that order thou now seest it.'

The *Essay concerning Human Understanding* is divided into four books. In the first, Locke, leaning towards the tenets of the Peripatetics in earlier, and the materialists in later times,

---

[1] *Absalom and Achitophel*, part i.

endeavoured to disprove the theory of innate ideas or principles. No knowledge, he maintains, is at any time possessed by the human intellect that did not come to it through the senses; *nihil in intellectu quod non prius in sensu.* Leibnitz is said to have completed, and at the same time partially overturned, the aphorism, by adding the words '*præter intellectum ipsum*' (except the intellect itself); the measures and forms of which are inherent in its constitution, and could not have been supplied to it through the senses. In the second book Locke gives his own theory of ideas, showing how they are simple or complex, derived from sensation or reflection, or both, and so on. The third book treats of Words, or Language in general, as the instrument of the understanding. The fourth book is concerning Knowledge and Opinion. The tenth chapter of this book is devoted to the proof of the proposition, that 'we are capable of knowing certainly, that there is a God.'

74. The order in which Locke's principal works appeared was as follows :—his first *Letter on Toleration* was published in Holland in 1688; the *Essay on the Human Understanding* appeared in 1689; the two *Treatises on Government* in 1690; the *Thoughts upon Education* in 1693; and the treatise on the *Reasonableness of Christianity* in 1695. He died unmarried at the house of his friend, Sir Francis Masham, in Essex, in the year 1704.

75. Many remarkable works on political science appeared in this agitated period. Speaking generally, these works represent the opinions of five parties: cavalier Tories, and philosophical Tories; Puritan Whigs, and Constitutional Whigs; and philosophical Republicans. **Sir Robert Filmer**, author of the *Patriarcha*, in which the doctrine of 'the right divine of kings to govern wrong' was pushed to its extreme, was the chief writer of the first party; Hobbes represented the second; Milton and Algernon Sidney the third; Locke the fourth; and Harrington the fifth. Milton's chief political treatises are, the *Tenure of Kings and Magistrates* (1649), and *The ready and easy Way to establish a free Commonwealth* (1660). **Harrington's** *Oceana*, the name by which he designates England, as his imagination painted her after being regenerated by republicanism, was published in 1656. The Protector's government at first refused to allow it to appear, but Cromwell, at the request of his favourite daughter, Elizabeth, gave his consent to the publication, coupled, however, with the dry remark, that 'what he had won by the sword he should not suffer himself to be scribbled out of.' In his travels Harrington had visited Venice, and thought the government of that republic the best and wisest in the world.

The leading idea in the *Oceana* is, that ' empire follows the balance of property.' The late war, he thought, was chiefly attributable, neither to the encroachments of the king nor to the factious conduct of the people, but to a slow and silent change which had taken place in the balance of property in England, rendering the lower gentry and the trading classes relatively wealthier, and therefore more influential, than in previous centuries.

76. The Latin romance of *Argenis* (1622), by **John Barclay,** a Scottish Catholic, contains several chapters which have a political bearing, and are intended to recommend constitutional limited government. The story is partially allegorical, and shadows forth the course of events in France during the last years of Henry III. The Latinity of this work is praised warmly by Coleridge, and more temperately by Hallam.

Essay Writing and Miscellaneous Subjects :—Hall, Feltham, Browne.

77. The examples of Bacon and Burton were followed by several gifted men in this period, who preferred jotting down detached thoughts on a variety of subjects, making, as it were, ' Guesses at Truth ' in a variety of directions, to the labour of concentrating their faculties upon a single intellectual enterprise. Thus Bishop Hall wrote, in the early part of the century, *Three Centuries of Meditations and Vows,* each century containing a hundred short essays or papers.   Feltham's *Resolves* ('resolve,' in the sense of 'solution of a problem '), published in 1637, is a work of the same kind.

78. From the fierce semi-political Christianity of the Puritans, and the official historical Christianity of the Churchmen, it is refreshing to turn to the philosophical and genial system of faith confessed in the *Religio Medici* of the good Sir Thomas Browne.   Browne was a mystic and an idealist ; he loved to plunge into the abysses of some vast thought, such as the Divine wisdom or the Divine eternity, and pursue its mazes until he was forced to cry an ' O altitudo ! ' and instead of being tempted to materialism by the necessary investigations of his profession— investigations which he evidently pursued with keen zest and in perfect steadiness of judgment—he regarded all the secondary laws which he discovered, or beheld in operation, as illustrations of the regular government of the Power, whose personality, and disengaged freedom, and supremacy over the laws through which He ordinarily works, were to him antecedent truths of conscience and reason.   The *Religio Medici,* which had already

appeared in a surreptitious and unauthorized form, was first
published by its author in 1643. In the first few pages, his
tenderness and charity towards the Roman Church, and his
genial and innate repugnance to the spirit of Puritanic bitterness, are made apparent. 'We have reformed from them,' he
says, 'not against them.' His own temper, he admits, inclines
him to the use of form and ceremonial in devotion. 'I am, I
confess, naturally inclined to that which misguided zeal terms
superstition.' 'I could never hear the Ave Mary bell without
an elevation.' On the whole, he finds that no church 'squares
unto his conscience' so well in every respect as the Church of
England, whose Articles he thoroughly embraces, while following his own reason where she and the Scripture are silent.
Though at present free, as he alleges, from the taint of any
heretical opinion, he entertained in his youth various singular
tenets, among which were, the death of the soul together with
the body, until the resurrection of both at the day of judgment;
the ultimate universal restoration of all men, as held by Origen;
and the propriety of prayers for the dead. But he declares that
there was never a time when he found it difficult to believe a
doctrine merely because it transcended and confounded his
reason. 'Methinks there be not impossibilities enough in religion for an active faith.' He can answer all objections with
the maxim of Tertullian, *Certum est quia impossibile est*, and
is glad that he did not live in the age of miracles, when faith
would have been thrust upon him almost without any merit of
his own. He collects (§§15–19) his divinity from two books—
the Bible and Nature. Yet he is not disposed so to deem or
speak of Nature as to veil behind her the immanence and necessary action of God in all her phenomena. 'Nature is the art of
God.' Again, he will not, with the vulgar, ascribe any real
power to chance or fortune; 'it is we that are blind, not fortune;' which is but another name for the settled and prede-
termined evolutions of visible effects from causes the knowledge
of which is inaccessible to us. He could himself (§ 21) produce
a long list of difficulties and objections in the way of faith, many
of which were never before started. But if these objections
breed, at any time, doubts in his mind, he combats such misgivings, 'not in a martial posture, but on his knees.'

From this description of the contents of the first few sections,
the reader may form some notion of the peculiar and most original vein of thought which runs through the book. As the
first part treats of faith, so the second gives the author's meditations on the virtue of charity. A delightful ironical humour
breaks out occasionally, as in the advice which he gives to those

who desire to be strengthened in their own opinions. 'When we desire to be informed, 'tis good to contest with men above ourselves; but to confirm and establish our opinions, 'tis best to argue with judgments below our own, that the frequent spoils and victories over their reasons may settle in ourselves an esteem and confirmed opinion of our own.'

The treatise on vulgar errors, *Pseudodoxia Epidemica*, is an amusing examination of a great number of popular customs and received explanations, which, after holding their ground for ages, during the long night of science and philosophy, were now breaking down on all sides under the attacks of the enfranchised intellect. *The Garden of Cyrus* is an abstruse dissertation on the wonderful virtue and significance of the quincuncial form. This is mere mysticism, and of no more value than the dreams of the Pythagoreans as to the virtue of particular numbers.

79. Among miscellaneous writings, the *Sylva* of **John Evelyn** deserves a prominent place. It is a ' Discourse of Forest Trees, and the propagation of timber in his Majesty's dominions,' and was originally read before the Royal Society in 1662. The parliamentary grantees of royalist estates, feeling their tenure insecure, had made enormous waste of the timber on them, cutting down and selling in all parts of the country. Thus at the Restoration, there was an alarming dearth of good timber for ship-building; and yet the preservation and increase of the fleet were matters of prime necessity. The Admiralty consulted with the King, who referred the matter to the Royal Society, and Evelyn's treatise was the result. It was the first book printed by order of the Society. Evelyn was a great planter himself, and his successors at Wotton, his estate in Surrey, have to this day religiously observed his precepts. The publication of the *Sylva* (1664) led to an immense development of planting all over England.

Another interesting tract, from the same hand, entitled *An Apology for the Royal Party*, in the form of a ' Letter to a person of the late Councel of State,' was written in November, 1659. This was a bold action, for to speak for the King had been prohibited. The indignant vehemence of eloquent invective against the whole Puritan party, Presbyterians, Independents, Quakers, and all, is surprising in the gentle and polished Evelyn.

Physical Science.

80. The present Royal Society, incorporated with a view to the promotion of physical science in 1662, arose out of some scientific meetings held at Oxford in the rooms of Dr. Wilkins,

the President of Wadham College. They soon had the honour of numbering among their fellows the great **Newton**, some of whose principal discoveries were first made known to the world in their *Proceedings*. Newton was educated at Trinity College, Cambridge; in the chapel of which society may be seen a noble statue of him by Roubillac, with the inscription, ' Qui genus humanum ingenio superavit.' A *History of the Royal Society*, by **Thomas Sprat**, afterwards Bishop of Rochester, appeared in 1667.

CHAPTER V.

EIGHTEENTH CENTURY.

1. WE will commence, as in the last period, with a brief summary of the political history.

The opening of the century beheld the firm establishment of the state of things brought in at the Revolution of 1688, by the passing of the Act of Settlement, limiting the succession to the crown to Sophia, wife of the elector of Hanover, and the heirs of her body, being Protestants. Upon the accession of Anne in 1702, a Tory ministry came into power for a short time. But its principal member—the able and unprincipled Godolphin—passed over to the Whigs, and it was Whig policy which engaged the nation in the war of the Spanish succession. Marlborough, the great Whig general, was closely connected with Godolphin by marriage. Everyone has heard of the victories of Blenheim, Ramillies, and Oudenarde. The Whig ministry was dismissed in 1710, and their Tory successors, Harley Earl of Oxford, and St. John Lord Bolingbroke, concluded the peace of Utrecht in 1713. But at the death of Anne in the following year the Tory ministers, who showed symptoms of favouring the claims of the Pretender (the son of James II.), were at once hurled from power, and the long period of Whig rule commenced, which only ended with the resignation of Sir Robert Walpole, in 1742. This celebrated minister practically ruled the country for twenty-one years, from 1721 to 1742, during which period England, through him, preserved peace with foreign powers; and such wars as arose on the continent were shorter and less destructive than they would otherwise have been. But in 1741 the temper of the country had become so warlike that a peace policy was no longer practicable, and Walpole was forced to succumb. The administration which succeeded, in which the leading spirit was that fine scholar and high-minded nobleman, Lord Carteret (afterwards Earl Granville), engaged in the Austrian succession war on the side of Maria Theresa. England played no very distinguished part in this war, the success at Dettingen (1743) being more than counterbalanced by the reverse at Fontenoy

two years later. The intrigues of the Pelhams drove Lord
Granville from office in 1744, and the Duke of Newcastle, with
his brother, Mr. Pelham, formed, with the aid of the leaders of
the opposition, what was called the ' Broad bottom ' ministry.
Newcastle—a man of small ability, but strong in his extensive
parliamentary influence—remained prime minister for twelve
years. In 1745 occurred the insurrection of the Highland clans
in favour of the Prince Charles Edward, grandson of James II.
After defeating the royal troops at Prestonpans, the Prince
marched into England, and penetrated as far as Derby. But,
meeting with no support, he was compelled to retreat, and in the
following year his followers were totally routed by the Duke of
Cumberland at Culloden. The continental war was terminated
by the peace of Aix-la-Chapelle in 1748. At the breaking out
of the Seven Years' War in 1756, in which England was allied
with Frederick of Prussia against France and Russia, the Duke
of Newcastle's incapacity caused everything to miscarry. Minorca was lost, and the Duke of Cumberland capitulated with
his whole army to the French at Closter-seven. Pitt, the great
Commoner, the honest statesman, the terrible and resistless
orator, had to be admitted, though sorely against the king's
will, to a seat in the Cabinet. The force of his genius and the
contagion of his enthusiasm effected a marvellous change; and
the memorable year 1759 witnessed the triumph of the allies at
Minden, the victory of Wolfe on the heights of Abraham, which
led to the conquest of Canada, and the defeat of the French fleet
by Hawke off Belleisle.

2. Pitt had to resign in 1761, making way for the king's
favourite, Lord Bute, who concluded the treaty of Fontainebleau
at the end of 1762, by which Canada, Cape Breton, part of
Louisiana, Florida, the Senegal, and Minorca were ceded to
Britain. For the next twelve years England was universally
regarded as the most powerful and successful nation in Europe.
But the war had been frightfully expensive, and Mr. Grenville,
who was prime minister from 1763 to 1765, conceived in an
unlucky hour the idea that a revenue could be raised from
America, by taxes laid on the colonies by the authority of Parliament. The Repeal of the Stamp Act in 1766 delayed the
bursting of the storm; but fresh attempts at taxation being
made, and resisted by the people of Boston, the war of independence broke out in the year 1775, and, through the help of France,
which allied itself with the new Republic in 1778, resulted in
the recognition by Great Britain of the independence of the
United States in 1783. Lord Chatham, who had all along
condemned the awkward and irritating measures of coercion

employed by the ministry, vainly opposed, in his memorable dying speech in the House of Lords, 'the dismemberment of this ancient monarchy.'

The administration which conducted the American war was presided over by the Tory premier, Lord North, who governed the country for twelve years, from 1770 to 1782. Up to the former date the powers of government had, ever since 1688, been exercised, with the exception of a few brief intervals, by the great Whig families—the Russells, Pelhams, Fitzroys, Bentincks, &c. (together with the commoners whom they selected to assist them)—who prided themselves on having brought about the Revolution. It cannot be denied that on the whole this junto governed with great vigour and success, and that the English aristocracy never showed itself to greater advantage. With the advent of Lord North to power, all was changed. Great questions were handled by little men, and the preponderance of intellectual power remained always on the side of the opposition, which numbered Fox, Burke, Barrè, Dunning, and Sheridan in its ranks. At length, in 1782, Lord North was driven from the helm, and after the brief administrations of the Marquis of Rockingham and Lord Shelburne, and that which resulted from the coalition of Fox with Lord North, the younger Pitt came into power at the end of 1783, and commenced his long and eventful career as prime minister. His policy was at first purely Whig and constitutional, like that of his father; but, after 1789, the attitude which he was compelled to take in relation to the extreme or revolutionary liberalism of France, gradually changed the position of his government to such an extent as to make it practically Tory, as being supported by the Tory party in Parliament and in the country. In the long revolutionary wars, commencing in 1793, England played an essentially conservative part. The English aristocracy, allying itself with the legitimate dynasties of Europe and with the Holy See, fought successfully to save some of the institutions and many of the principles which had been bequeathed by the middle ages, in the tempest of destruction which, issuing from the clubs of Paris, threatened the entire fabric of European society.

General Characteristics:—Pope and Johnson; Poetry from 1700 to 1745: Pope, Addison, Gay, Parnell, Swift, Thomson, Prior, Garth, Blackmore, Defoe, Tickell, Savage, Dyer, A. Philips, J. Philips, Watts, Ramsay.

3. The eighteenth century was a period of repose and stability in England's political history. Saved by her insular position

from the desolating wars which ravaged the continent, and acquiescing in the compromise between theoretical liberty and prescriptive right established at the Revolution of 1688, the nation enjoyed during the whole of the period, except in the Jacobite rising of 1715 and 1745, profound internal peace. Then was the time, it might have been imagined, for the fructification under the most favourable circumstances of whatever germs of thought the philosophy and poetry of preceding ages had implanted in the English mind, in the noblest and purest forms of literature and art.

Such, however, was far from being the case. The literature of the eighteenth century, though occupying a large space to our eyes at the present day, from the proximity of the time and the want of other thinkers who have taken up the ground more satisfactorily, is for the most part essentially of the fugitive sort, and will probably be considered in future ages as not having treated with true appreciation one single subject which it has handled. To speculate upon the cause of this inferiority does not lie within the scope of the present work ; we have simply to note the fact.

The rising of the clans in 1745 divides our period into two nearly equal portions, of the first of which Pope may be taken as the representative author ; of the second, Johnson.

4. **Alexander Pope** was born at the house of his father, a linen merchant, residing in Lombard Street, London, in the year 1688. A sojourn at Lisbon had led to the father's conversion to the Roman Catholic faith, and young Pope was brought up, so far as circumstances would allow, in the rigid belief and practice of his father's creed. His religion excluded him from the public schools and universities of England; his education was therefore private, and not, it would appear, of the best kind. Such as it was, it was not continued long; so that Pope may be considered as eminently a self-taught man—a self-cultivated poet. His poetic gift manifested itself early :—

> As yet a child, nor yet a fool to fame,
> I lisped in numbers, for the numbers came.

The classical poets soon became his chief study and delight, and he valued the moderns in proportion as they had drunk more or less deeply of the classical spirit. The genius of the Gothic or Romantic ages inspired him at this time with no admiration whatever, so that in the retrospect of the poetical and critical masterpieces of past times, which concludes the third book of the *Essay on Criticism*, he can find no bright spot in the thick intellectual darkness, from the downfall of the Western

Empire to the age of Leo X. The only native writers whom he deigns to mention are—Roscommon and Walsh! To the author of the *Essay on Translated Verse* he was indeed largely indebted, not only for the general conception of the *Essay on Criticism*, but even for some of the best expressions in it.[1] Walsh, too, who was a man of fortune, was his patron and kind entertainer, and gratitude led Pope to do him, as a poet, a little more than justice. But in spite of minor blemishes one cannot be blind to the transcendent merits of this production, which, taken as the composition of a youth of twenty or twenty-one, is an intellectual and rhythmical achievement perhaps unparalleled.

5. 'The ultimate impulse which actuated Pope in projecting and composing this remarkable poem, may be traced to his youthful study and intense, passionate admiration of the classic poets. The music of their verse, the grace of their phrase, and the elevation of their thoughts, made deep impressions on that strongly receptive intelligence; he felt that they were still not half so well known by his countrymen as they deserved to be; that their comparative obedience to rules arose out of a real freedom of the spirit, and a pure perception· of the beautiful, with which the English license was incompatible; and he has left a tribute which is itself imperishable to these 'immortal heirs of universal praise,' in the passage commencing at l. 181 of this poem—

> Still green with bays, each ancient altar stands.

Yet it is not to be supposed that his admiration was all spontaneous, and stood in no relation to the general state of culture and tendency of criticism in Europe. Both in Italy and in France the tide had been running strongly for several generations against the Middle Ages and all their works; Christian antiquity was deemed Gothic and rude; and the literary class, clergy and laity alike, fixed its gaze on the art and poetry of the Pagan world. Boileau in France was the eloquent exponent of this feeling; he cared not for Dante, but he bowed to Horace—

> And Boileau still in right of Horace sways.

His *Art Poétique*, the leading principle of which is that critical good sense is the most important of poetical qualities, was doubtless well known to Pope. The controversy in which he had been engaged with

---

[1] Roscommon has, speaking of Dryden—

> 'And with a *brave disorder* shows his art.'

Pope follows with—

> 'From vulgar bounds with *brave disorder* part.'

Again, Roscommon has—

> 'Then make the proper use of each extreme,
> And write with fury, but correct with phlegm.'

Of this Pope's lines are but the echo—

> 'Our critics take a contrary extreme,
> They judge with fury, but correct with phlegm.'

'errault, and which had spread to England—Sir William Temple,
)ryden, and Swift, taking up the one side, and Wootton, Bentley, and
 number of obscure persons, the other—respecting the comparative
 ierits of ancient and modern learning, must have excited a keen
 iterest in the young poet. Dryden himself had written with great
 orce on questions of literary and dramatic criticism; particularly
 1 his *Essay on Dramatic Poesy*, in which he had critically compared
 ie ancient with the modern stage, and the French drama with the
 inglish. The work of Bossu, *Reflections on Epic Poetry*, had been
 :ad with attention beyond the limits of France, and our own Rymer
 ad published in 1694 a translation of Rapin's *Reflections on the Poetics
 ' Aristotle*. John Dennis, about the same time, in *The Impartial
 ritic*, analysed with considerable skill the grounds of Waller's poetic
 :putation, and compared the exigencies of the Greek and English
 ieatres. Lastly, when we consider Pope's extreme sensitiveness—how
 uly he said of himself, 'touch me and no minister so sore,' it may
 em probable that the circumstance of Dennis having spoken un-
 .vourably of his *Pastorals* in clubs and coffee-houses, was some induce-
 ent to him to write a poem which should include a severe castigation
 English critics in general, and John Dennis in particular. [1]

6. In a memorable passage, containing not a few illustrious
 imes, Pope has told us how he came to publish :—

> But why then publish ?   Granville the polite—
> And knowing Walsh, would tell me I could write :
> Well-natured Garth inflamed with early praise,
> And Congreve loved, and Swift endured my lays ;
> The courtly Talbot, Somers, Sheffield, read ;
> E'en mitred Rochester would nod the head :
> And St. John's self (great Dryden's friend before)
> With open arms received one poet more. [2]

ryden he had just seen and no more ('Virgilium tantum vidi'
 his expression), in the last year of the old poet's life, he being
 en a boy of twelve.   He knew Wycherley, the dramatist, then
 iomewhat battered worn-out relic of the gay reign of Charles
 ., and wrote an excellent letter on the occasion of his death in
 16.   His relations to Addison were characteristic on both
 les.   Steele introduced them to each other in 1712, shortly
 er Addison had written a favourable notice of the *Essay on
 iticism* in No. 253 of the *Spectator*.   Several trifling circum-
 .nces which occurred in the three following years conspired to
 :ate an unpleasant state of feeling between them, which was
)ught to a climax in 1715 by the encouragement given by Ad-
 on to his friend Tickell in his project of a rival translation of
)mer.   Pope's version and that by Tickell came out nearly

[1] *Selections from Pope*, p. vi., Longmans, 1876.
[2] *Imitations of Horace*.

x 2

together, and nothing can be clearer than the great superiority of the former. Yet Addison (one cannot but fear, out of jealousy), while praising both translations, pronounced that Tickell's ' had more of Homer.' This was the occasion of Pope's writing that wonderful piece of satire which will be found at a subsequent page.[1] Addison made no direct reply, but a few months later, in a paper published in the *Freeholder*, he spoke in terms of high praise of Pope's translation. The poet's susceptible nature was touched by this generosity, and he, in his turn, immortalized Addison in his fifth satire :—

> And in our days (excuse some courtly stains)
> No whiter page than Addison remains ;
> He from the taste obscene reclaims our youth,
> And sets the passions on the side of truth ;
> Forms the soft bosom with the gentlest art,
> And pours each human virtue in the heart.

Far more close and cordial were the relations between Pope and Swift. Their acquaintance began at the time of Swift's residence in London, between 1710 and 1713. The famous Dean was twenty-one years older than Pope ; but there must have been a strong inherent sympathy between their characters, for they became fast friends at once, and continued so until Swift's mind broke down. Each had all the tastes of the author and man of letters ; each was audacious and satirical ; each saw through, and despised the hollowness of society, though in their different ways each strove to raise himself in it. Swift's ambition was for power ; he wished that his literary successes should serve merely as a basis and vantage-ground whence to scale the high places of the state; Pope's ambition was purely for fame, and he regarded literary success not as a means but as an end. It certainly shows some real elevation of soul in both, that two men, each so irritable, and whose very points of resemblance might have made it easier for them to come into collision, should have remained steady friends for twenty-five years. The utter absence of jealousy in both will perhaps account for the fact. Soon after they became acquainted, Swift was able to do Pope a great service. In 1713, the prospectus of the translation of the *Iliad* appeared ; and Swift, who was at that time a real power in London society, used his opportunities to get the subscription list well filled. Chiefly by his exertions, the list became such a long one, that the proceeds amounted to a small fortune for Pope, and set him at ease on the score of money matters for the

---

[1] See Crit. Sect. ch. I., *Satirical Poetry.*

emainder of his life.   His labours in connection with the trans-
ation of Homer extended from 1713 to 1725.   He employed in
ranslating the *Odyssey* the services of two minor poets, Fenton
nd Broome, so that only one-half of the version is from his own
and.   The *Pastorals*,[1] *Windsor Forest*,[2] and the *Rape of the
ock*[3] appeared in the years 1704, 1713, and 1714 respectively.

7. In 1725 Pope published an edition of Shakspere.   His
reface shows a juster appreciation of the great dramatist than
as then common; yet his own taste pointed too decidedly to
1e French and classical school to admit of his doing full justice
) the chief of the Romantic.   He was the first to amend two
: three corrupt readings by slight and happy alterations,
hich have since been generally adopted.   Such is his substi-
ition of 'south' for the old reading 'sound,' in the lines in
welfth Night—

> Oh ! it came o'er mine ear like the sweet *south*
> That breathes over a bank of violets ;

1d of 'strides' for 'sides' (and Tarquin's ravishing '*strides*')
Macbeth.

8. The first three books of the *Dunciad*, which was dedicated
Swift, appeared anonymously in 1728.   In it the poet re-
nges himself on a number of obscure poets and feeble critics,
10 had—though not without provocation—attacked and li-
lled him.   The very obscurity of these individuals detracts
ich from the permanent interest of the satire.   The persons
d parties introduced by Dryden in his *Absalom and Achitophel*
cupied elevated situations upon the public stage, and, as the
tire itself is conceived and composed in a corresponding strain
elevation, it is probable that, so long as English history inte-
its us, that satire will be read.   But the Cookes, Curlls, Con-
1ens, and other personages of the *Dunciad*, are to us simple
nes which suggest no ideas ; and even the intellectual mastery
the author, great though it be, is hardly so evident to us as
) frantic vindictiveness which strains every nerve to say the
)st wounding and humiliating things.

9. The *Essay on Man* appeared anonymously in 1732.   It
s the fruit of Pope's familiar intercourse with the sceptic
rd Bolingbroke, and reflects in the popular literature the opi-
ns of a philosophical school presently to be noticed.   No poem
the language contains a greater number of single lines which
7e passed into proverbs.[4]

---

[1] See Crit. Sect. ch. I. § 43.   [2] *Ibid.* § 46.   [3] *Ib.* § 13.
   [4] For example—
      'A mighty maze, but not without a plan.'
      'The proper study of mankind is man.'

Mandeville and others had recently impugned the benevolence and sanctity of the Deity by pointing out a variety of evils and imperfections in the system of things, and asserting that these were necessary to the welfare and stability of human society. This is the whole argument of the *Fable of the Bees.* Pope in his Essay undertakes to 'vindicate the ways of God to man.' And how does he do so? *Not*—with regard to physical evil—by admitting that the 'whole creation groaneth and travaileth in pain together,' but connecting its imperfect condition with the original sin and fall of moral agents; *not*—with regard to moral evil—by tracing it to man's abuse of his free will, permitted but not designed by his Creator, and to the ceaseless activity of evil spirits; *but,* by representing evil, moral as well as physical, to be a part of God's providential scheme for the government of the universe, to be in fact not absolutely and essentially evil, but only relatively and incidentally so:—

All partial evil, universal good.

All this was pointed out, shortly after the appearance of the Essay, in a criticism from the pen of Crousaz, a Swiss professor. Warburton, in the commentary which he attached to a new edition of the poem in 1740, replied to the strictures of Crousaz, and with much pains and ingenuity endeavoured to give an innocent meaning to all the apparently questionable passages. Ruffhead, in his Life of Pope, gives it as his opinion that Warburton completely succeeded. Johnson was more clear-sighted. In his Life of Pope, after saying that Bolingbroke supplied the poet with the principles of the Essay, he adds, 'These principles it is not my business to clear from obscurity, dogmatism, or falsehood.' And again—'The positions which he transmitted from Bolingbroke he seems not to have understood, and was pleased with an interpretation which made them orthodox.' But what sense but one is it possible to attach to such passages as the following?—

If plagues or earthquakes break not Heaven's design,
Why then a Borgia or a Catiline?
Who knows, but He, whose hand the lightning forms,
Who heaves old Ocean, and who wings the storms,
Pours fierce ambition in a Cæsar's mind,
Or turns young Ammon loose to scourge mankind?
From pride, from pride, our very reasoning springs;
Account for moral as for natural things:
Why charge we Heaven in those, in these acquit?
In both, to reason right is to submit.

Evidently God is here made not the *permitter* only, but the *designer,* of moral evil. Again—

'The enormous faith of many made for one.'
'Worth makes the man, and want of it the fellow;
    The rest is all but leather or prunella.'
'An honest man's the noblest work of God.'
'Damn'd to everlasting fame.'
'But looks through Nature up to Nature's God.'
'From grave to gay, from lively to severe,' &c. &c.

> Submit—in this or any other sphere,
> Secure to be as blest as thou canst bear.

'rom this dictum, left unguarded as it is, it might be inferred that
irtue, and the acting in obedience to conscience or against it, had
othing to do with man's blessedness.   Again—

> Who sees with equal eye, as God of all,
> A hero perish, or a sparrow fall.

'et we are told, 'You are of more value than many sparrows.'   Phe-
omena in the moral world are here confounded with phenomena in
he natural.   With God there is neither small nor great in a material
ense; so far these lines convey a just lesson.   But how can anything
'hich affects the welfare of a human soul—be it that of a 'hero' or of
pauper—be measured by a standard of material greatness?

Alive to the weak points in the morality of the Essay, Pope wrote
he *Universal Prayer*, as a kind of compendious exposition of the mean-
1g which he desired to be attached to it.   In this he says that the
reator,—

> Binding Nature fast in fate,
> Left free the human will.

'ow this can be reconciled with the suggestion to—

> Account for moral as for natural things,

'arburton never attempted to explain.

Mr. Carruthers, in his Life of Pope, speaks of this controversy as if
could have no interest for people of the present generation, who read
1e Essay for the sake of its brilliant rhetoric and exquisite descriptions,
1d do not trouble themselves about the reasoning.   But whether they
re conscious of it or not, the moral tone of the poem does influence
1en's minds, as the use which is constantly made of certain well-
nown lines sufficiently demonstrates.[1]

10.   The various satirical pieces known as the *Moral Essays*
nd the *Imitations of Horace*,[2] with Prologue and Epilogue,
'ere published between the years 1731 and 1738.   A fourth
ook was added to the *Dunciad* in 1742, and the whole poem
'as re-cast, so as to assign the distinction of king of the dunces

---

[1]   For instance—

> 'For forms of government let fools contest,
> Whate'er is best administered is best ;
> For modes of faith let graceless zealots fight,
> His can't be wrong whose life is in the right.'

and—

> 'Heroes are much the same—the point's agreed—
> From Macedonia's madman to the Swede.'

and—
>   'Whatever is, is right.'

[2]   See Crit. Sect. ch. I., *Satirical Poetry*.

to Colley Cibber, the poet-laureate, instead of Theobald. Pope died in May 1744.

11. Politically, Pope occupied through life a position of much dignity. Both Halifax and Secretary Craggs desired to pension him, but he declined their offers. Thanks to Homer, he could say truly—

> I live and thrive,
> Indebted to no prince or peer alive.

The neutral position which he affected is indicated in the lines—

> In moderation placing all my glory,
> While Tories call me Whig, and Whigs a Tory.

In principle, it seems clear that he preferred the politics of Locke to those of Filmer. This may be inferred from such lines as—

> For sure, if Dulness sees a grateful day,
> 'Tis in the shade of arbitrary sway.
>   *   *   *   *
> May you, my Cam and Isis, preach it long,
> ' The right divine of kings to govern wrong.'

On the other hand, all the friends with whom he was really intimate, Swift, Arbuthnot, Bolingbroke, Marchmont, &c., belonged to the Tory party; a score of passages in his poems show the dislike and disgust with which he regarded the Hanoverian family which had come in under the Act of Settlement; that which attracted him in Johnson (whose *London* appeared on the same day with the *Epilogue to the Satires*) was clearly his strong Jacobite feeling; finally, the Caryl correspondence, lately published for the first time under the editorship of Mr. Elwin, shows Pope to have been influenced by the Catholic, loyalist, and conservative associations which surrounded him in his youth far more than is commonly supposed.

12. Yet, although he remained a Catholic through life, there are many pages of his poetry in which the leaven of that scepticism which pervaded the society in which he moved may be distinctly traced. At the court of the Prince of Wales at Richmond, where Pope was a frequent and welcome guest, free-thinking was in favour, and Tindal, the Deist, was zealously patronized :—

> But art thou one whom new opinions sway,
> One who believes where Tindal leads the way ?

The religious indifferentism which he assumed had undoubtedly many conveniences, in an age when serious and *bonâ fide* Romanism was repressed by every kind of vexatious enal disability, and the literary circle in which he lived was omposed exclusively of Protestants or unbelievers. He styled imself—

> Papist or Protestant, or both between,
> Like good Erasmus, in an honest mean.

Perhaps, too, it may be said, that, independently of exter-al influences, his own highly intellectualized nature predis-osed him to set reason above faith, to value thinkers more than aints. But he would not let himself be driven or persuaded ato any act of formal apostasy. When, upon the death of his ither in 1717, his friend Bishop Atterbury hinted that he was ow free to consult his worldly interests by joining the established hurch, Pope absolutely rejected the proposal—upon singular nd chiefly personal grounds, it is true—but so decidedly as to iake it impossible that the advice should be repeated. As he rew older, Pope's sympathies with the free-thinking school, at east with the rank and file of their writers, seem to have de-lined ; very disrespectful mention is made of them in the *Dun-iad*. Their spokesman is thus introduced in the fourth ook :—

> ' Be that my task,' replies a gloomy clerk,
> Sworn foe to mystery, yet divinely dark ;
> Whose pious hope aspires to see the day
> When moral evidence shall quite decay,
> And damns implicit faith and holy lies,
> Prompt to impose, and fond to dogmatize.

Finally, whatever may have been the aberrations of his life, s closing scene was one of faith and pious resignation. The riest who administered to him the last sacrament 'came out om the dying man, . . . penetrated to the last degree with he state of mind in which he found his penitent, resigned, and rapt up in the love of God and man.' [1] Bolingbroke, like he friends of Béranger on a like occasion, is said to have own into a great fit of passion at hearing of the priest being alled in.

13. The reign of Anne was considered in the last century to e the Augustan age of English literature; nor, when we re-iember the great number of poets who then flourished, the high atronage which many of them received, and the extent to hich literary tastes then pervaded the upper ranks of society, hall we pronounce the term altogether misplaced. At any rate, y contrast to the middle period of the century, its opening was right indeed. Johnson, in the Life of Prior, observes :—' Every-

[1] Carruthers' *Life of Pope.*

thing has its day. Through the reigns of William and Anne no prosperous event passed undignified by poetry. In the last war [the Seven Years' War], when France was disgraced and overpowered in every quarter of the globe, when Spain, coming to her assistance, only shared her calamities, and the name of an Englishman was reverenced through Europe, no poet was heard amidst the general acclamation; the fame of our councillors and heroes was entrusted to the gazetteer.' The genius of Chatham—the heroism of Wolfe—are unsung to this day.

14. **Addison**, the son of a Westmoreland clergyman, was singled out, while yet at Oxford, as a fit object for Government patronage, and sent to travel with a pension. In that learned, but then disloyal, university, a sincere and clever Whig was a phenomenon so rare, that the Whig ministry seem to have thought they could not do too much to encourage the growth of the species. While on the continent, Addison produced several poems in praise of King William, written in the heroic couplet in which Dryden had achieved so much. In 1704 he celebrated in *The Campaign* [1] the battle of Blenheim. For this he was rewarded with the post of Commissioner of Appeals. His well-known hymns—'The spacious firmament on high,' and 'The Lord my pasture shall prepare'—though the imagery is unreal, have yet a certain mingled sweetness and force about them, which will not let them be easily forgotten. His dramatic and prose works will be noticed presently.

15. The poet **Gay** was also dependent on patrons, but they were in his case private noblemen, not ministers of State. This kindly-natured man, whom Pope describes as—

> In wit a man, simplicity a child,

belong to the race of careless, thoughtless poets described by Horace, who are ill fitted to battle with the world. But the Duke and Duchess of Queensberry took him into their house during the later years of his life, and managed his affairs for him, thus relieving him from the embarrassments which beset him. He died at the early age of forty-four.

Gay is the author of *Rural Sports*, a poem in heroic metre, answering to the description of the 'lesser epic;' of *The Fan*, a mock-heroic poem in three books, evidently suggested by Pope's *Rape of the Lock*; of the *Shepherd's Week*, a burlesque upon the *Pastorals* of Ambrose Philips; and of *Trivia*, a sort of humorous didactic poem on the art of walking the streets of London. None of these poems rise above mediocrity, though each presents certain points of interest. It is in right of his inimitable songs and ballads that Gay's name still lives

---

[1] See Crit. Sect. ch. I. § 12.

and will live. Among these are, 'All in the Downs,' ''Twas when the seas were roaring,' the gloriously absurd ballad of 'Molly Mog,' a story of a Quaker's courtship called 'The Espousal,' 'Newgate's Garland,' and others. His well-known *Fables* are neatly and flowingly turned, and that is all.[1]

16. **Parnell** is now only remembered as the author of the *Hermit*, a poem of which the design is to inculcate a belief that, in spite of adverse appearances, the events which befall beings endowed with free-will are all providentially pre-arranged.   He was the friend of Harley, Earl of Oxford, to whom Pope sent the edition of his poems, of which he superintended the publication after his death, recommending them to the fallen statesman in a few graceful lines, musical but weighty, such as Pope alone could write.

17. **Swift**, to whom Pope dedicated the *Dunciad*, in the well-known lines—

> Oh ! thou, whatever title please thine ear,
> Dean, Drapier, Bickerstaff, or Gulliver ;
> Whether thou choose Cervantes' serious air,
> Or laugh and shake in Rabelais' easy chair ;
> Or praise the court, or magnify mankind,
> Or thy grieved country's copper chains unbind—

was a copious writer in verse no less than in prose.   His poems extend to nearly twice the length of those of Thomson, and consist of Odes, Epistles, Epigrams, Songs, Satires, and Epitaphs.

Of Swift's poetry he has himself taken care that much should not be said in praise.   A man of his powers could have written a great satire or didactic poem which would have delighted the world.   But he loathed the world, and therefore did not wish to delight it; and because the general taste of the age was in favour of the serious character and dignified movement of heroic verse, he carefully avoided that metre, and wrote nearly all his poetry in jingling careless octosyllabics.   Most of his poems, which are very numerous, are essentially of a fugitive character.   Many short epigrammatic things were written with a diamond ring on inn-windows, a practice of which he was very fond.   Many take the form of sallies and rejoinders, passing to and fro between the Dean and one or other of his lively Dublin friends.   Many are addressed to Stella,[2] or written in her honour.   One of the longest, *Cadenus and Vanessa*, was addressed to Esther Vanhomrigh, the lady whose intellectual education was directed by Swift, and who conceived an ardent passion for him, which he described, while he checked, in this poem.   The disappointment of her hopes, added to the discovery of his private marriage to Stella, brought poor Vanessa to her grave.

[1] See Crit. Sect. ch. I. § 25.
[2] The real name of Stella was Hester Johnson ; this lady lived in Swift's house for twenty-eight years, but is said, even after her marriage to him in 1716, never to have seen him except before a third person.

A long and unclouded friendship subsisted between Swift and Pope; they corresponded regularly, and their letters have been published.

18. **James Thomson**, the author of the *Seasons*,[1] was the son of a Scotch Presbyterian minister.   Showing a bias to literature, he was advised to repair to the great stage of London, ' a place too wide for the operation of petty competition and private malignity, where merit might soon become conspicuous, and would find friends as soon as it became reputable to befriend it.' [2] The proceeds of the sale of *Winter* were all that he had to depend upon for some time after his arrival in the metropolis.   By degrees he acquired a reputation, and a fair share of patronage, from which only his invincible laziness prevented him from reaping greater benefit.   Pope countenanced his tragedy of *Agamemnon* by coming to it the first night, and expressed his personal regard for him in a poetical epistle.   Besides the *Seasons*, he wrote *Liberty*—a tedious, high-flown production, which no one read, even at its first appearance; *Britannia*, an attack on Sir Robert Walpole's government; and *The Castle of Indolence*.[3] After Walpole's downfall, he obtained a sinecure place through the influence of his friend Lyttleton, but did not long enjoy it, dying, after a short illness, in 1748.

19. **Matthew Prior**, a native of Dorsetshire, from an obscure origin rose to considerable eminence, both literary and political. In early life he was a Whig, and first came into notice as the author, jointly with Charles Montague, of the *City Mouse and Country Mouse*.   In 1701 he ratted to the Tories, and made himself so useful to the party as to be selected to manage several delicate negotiations with foreign Powers, in particular that which resulted in the treaty of Utrecht.   His behaviour on this occasion exposed him, though it would appear unjustly, to heavy charges from the Whig ministry which came into power in 1714, and he was thrown into prison, and kept there for more than two years.   His old associates probably considered him as a renegade, and dealt out to him an unusual measure of severity.

There is much that is sprightly and pointed in Prior's loyal odes, which he designed to rival those which Boileau was composing at the same time in honour of the Grand Monarque, Louis XIV.   But it is in his epigrams and 'verses of society' that Prior is most successful. How charmingly, for instance, has he turned the stanzas in which he describes his doubtful cure by Dr. Radcliffe, or those upon a lady refusing to continue a dispute with him, or the lines upon 'The Lady's Looking-glass'!   How manly, English, and sensible is the advice to a

[1] See Crit. Sect. ch. I. § 47.   [2] Johnson.
[3] See Crit. Sect. ch. I. § 24.

ealous husband in the 'Padlock' not to immure his wife or set spies
)ver her, as they did abroad, but give her free liberty to range over this
wretched world, and see how hollow and false it is! This poem ends
with some far-famed lines:—

> Be to her faults a little blind,
> Be to her virtues very kind;
> Let all her ways be unconfined,
> And clap your padlock—on her mind.

n his longer poems Prior was less successful. His *Henry and Emma*,
in amplified re-cast of the old ballad of *The Nut-brown Mayde*, is
admirably versified, and contains at least one line which is a part of
our current sententious or proverbial speech:—

> That air and harmony of shape express,
> *Fine by degrees and beautifully less;*

)ut most people would prefer to its artificial strains the greater brevity,
lirectness, and distinctness of the old ballad. But the immense service
which Dryden had rendered to English poetry, in imparting to the
ieroic couplet a smooth rapidity, as well as an air of lofty audacity,
which it had not known before, is noticeable in all the best heroics of
'rior and Addison. *Alma, or The Progress of the Mind,* in three cantos,
s a satirical account in Hudibrastic verse of the vagaries with which
he mind, at different periods of life, and acting through, or controlled
)y, different parts of the animal economy, troubles her possessor. There
s something cynical, and tending to materialism, in the tone of this
)oem, which was written towards the close of Prior's life. His last
nd most ambitious effort was *Solomon,* a didactic poem in three parts.
t is a soliloquy, and represents the royal sage as searching by turns
hrough every province, and to the utmost bounds, of knowledge,
leasure, and power, and finding in the end that all was 'vanity and
exation of spirit.'

20. **Congreve** the dramatist left a number of pretty songs,
nd some Pindaric poems of more or less merit. In a 'Discourse
n the Pindaric Ode' prefixed to an ode addressed to Queen
Iary, he drew attention to the fact that this kind of poetry had
s metrical laws, and was not the mere chaotic fruit of lawless
nagination, as English writers seemed to think; in it the 'tria
tesichori,' the strophe, antistrophe, and epode, ought to be
:rictly observed. There is a pretty extravagance in the follow-
ig distich:—

> See, see, she wakes, Sabina wakes!
> And now the sun begins to rise;
> Less glorious is the morn that breaks
> From his bright beams, than her fair eyes.

> With light united, day they give,
> But different fates ere night fulfil;
> How many by his warmth will live!
> How many will her coldness kill!

21. **Charles Montague** (*ante*, ch. IV. § 35), after being the leader of the house of Commons under William III., was created Earl of Halifax in 1714. His staunch Whiggism assumes a not unattractive form in *The Man of Honour* (1687), in which he shows that English gentlemen *cannot* stoop to do what James requires :—

> Our lives and fortunes freely we'll expose,
> Honour alone we cannot, must not lose.

Some manly lines, imitated from a passage in the sixth Æneid, occur farther on. Other nations, he says, may till a more fertile soil, and have more taste in the arts, than we :—

> But to instruct the mind, to arm the soul
> With virtue which no dangers can control ;
> Exalt the thought, a speedy courage lend,
> That horror cannot shake, or pleasure bend :
> These are the English arts,—these we profess,
> To be the same in misery and success ;
> To teach oppressors law, assist the good,
> Relieve the wretched, and subdue the proud.

22. Of 'well-natured **Garth**,' author of the mock-heroic poem, the *Dispensary*, the idea of which he took from Boileau's *Lutrin*, we can only say that he was a physician, and a staunch adherent to Revolution principles during the reign of Anne, for which he was rewarded with a due share of professional emolument, when his party came into power in 1714. He was an original member of the Kit-cat Club, 'generally mentioned as a set of wits ; in reality, the patriots that saved Britain.' [1]

The *Dispensary* is about a bitter quarrel which broke out in the year 1687, between the College of Physicians and the apothecaries, concerning the erection of a dispensary in London. Perhaps the subject is somewhat dull ; granting, however, that the conception was a good one, the execution lags considerably behind it ; as a whole, the poem is heavy, and far too long.

23. **Sir Richard Blackmore** was another patriotic poet. He was the city physician, and was knighted by King William.

Blackmore has met, chiefly from his own faults, with harder measure than he deserves. The sarcasms of Pope and Dryden raise the impression that Blackmore can never have written anything but what was lumbering, inane, and in the worst possible taste. Yet let anyone, without prejudice, take up *The Creation*, and read a couple of hundred lines, and he will probably own that it is a very different sort of poem from what he had expected. It is by no means dull, or heavy, or sopo-

---

[1] Horace Walpole's *Anecdotes of Painting*.

ific; the lines spin along with great fluency and animation, though not
xactly sparkling as they go.   The plan is thoroughly conceived and
igested, and the argument ably and lucidly, if not always cogently
ustained.· But Blackmore was ruined, as a literary man, by his enor-
ious self-confidence and utter want of measure or judgment.   He
ttacked with indiscriminating fury the atheists, free-thinkers, wits,
nd critics of his day, as if these names were interchangeable; and
aturally he met with no mercy from the two last.   The characters
f staunch Whig and somewhat narrow pietist are blended in him in
ie oddest manner. His lack of judgment is illustrated by his con-
nuing to write and publish epic poems (*Eliza, Alfred, Prince Arthur,*
c.), long after the world had ceased to read them.   Yet it would be
njust to judge by these of *The Creation* (1712), respecting which
ddison's eulogy,[1] though it gives all the lights without the shadows,
. not so entirely extravagant as it seems at first reading.

24. **Defoe** must be named in this connection, on account of his once
.mous satire, *The True-born Englishman.* His motive for writing it
as the indignation which he felt at what he called English ingratitude,
i showing itself in the attacks continually made on William and his
utch guards as *foreigners,* and in the peevish discontented air which
ost Englishmen wore after so great a deliverance. The composition
of a very coarse kind; and the satire stands to those of Dryden in
iout the same relation as the *Morning Advertiser,* the organ of the
iblicans, does to the *Times.* The strange opening is well known :—

> Wherever God erects a house of prayer,
> The devil always builds a chapel there ;
> And 'twill be found upon examination,
> The latter has the largest congregation.

iis must be understood as ironical : for Defoe was himself a Dissenter.
ie vigorous lines entitled ' A Hymn to the Pillory ' were written at
e time when Defoe was condemned to that ignominious punishment
r writing the ironical pamphlet, *The Shortest Way with the Dissenters.*

25. **Nicholas Rowe,** whose translation of Lucan's *Pharsalia* Johnson,
th hyperbolic praise, calls ' one of the greatest productions of English
etry,' wrote an ' Epistle to Flavia ' (in which he attacks Dryden for
ving corrupted not only the stage but the English language, by the
rew of foreign words ' which he had brought into it), and also some
storal ballads which have much grace and melody. ' Colin's Com-
aint ' is among these ; it opens—

> Despairing beside a clear stream,
> A shepherd forsaken was laid ;
> And while a false nymph was his theme,
> A willow supported his head.

e sees where Shenstone got his manner.

26. **Thomas Tickell** resided for many years at Oxford, being a fellow
Queen's College. Although a Whig and an adherent of Addison, he
the author of some spasmodic stanzas, worthy of the most uncom-
mising upholder of the divine right of kings, entitled ' Thoughts

---

[1] *The Spectator,* No. 339.

occasioned by a Picture of the Trial of Charles I.,' in which lines such
as the following occur,—

> Such boding thoughts did guilty conscience dart,
> A pledge of hell to dying Cromwell's heart !

Tickell's version of the first book of the Iliad has been already noticed.
Among his other poems, which are not numerous, I find only two
worth naming—the ballad of 'Colin and Lucy,' and the memorial
lines upon Addison. The ballad is pretty, but the story improbable ;
Colin having jilted Lucy, she dies of a broken heart; the coffin containing her remains meets the marriage procession ; the faithless Colin
is struck with remorse, and dies immediately ; they occupy the same
grave.   Do not these lines sound like an echo from our nurseries ?

> I hear a voice you cannot hear,
>   Which says I must not stay ;
> I see a hand you cannot see,
>   Which beckons me away.

27. The unhappy history of **Richard Savage** has been detailed at
length by Dr. Johnson in one of the longest and most masterly of his
poetical biographies.[1]   His life and character were blighted by the
circumstances of his birth and rearing.   To these he refers only too
plainly and pointedly in his poem of *The Bastard*, a very forcible piece
of writing containing a line often quoted :—

> He lives to build, not boast, a generous race ;
> No tenth transmitter of a foolish face.

His principal work was *The Wanderer*, a moral or didactic poem in
five cantos (1729), containing many materials and rudiments of thought,
half worked up as it were, which one recognizes again, transformed
after passing through the fiery crucible of a great mind, in Pope's
Essay on Man.   Savage, like most of the English poets of the eighteenth
century, employed the heroic metre for the majority of his compositions, dazzled by the glory and success with which Dryden and Pope
had employed it.

28. **John Dyer,** who after failing as a painter became a clergyman
late in life, is, or was, known as the author of *Grongar Hill* (1727)
and *The Fleece* (1757).   The latter is in blank verse, and totally worthless ; the former, however, is a pretty poem of description and reflection, breathing that intoxicating sense of natural beauty which never
fails to awaken in us some sympathy, and an answering feeling of
reality.   These lines may serve as a specimen :—

> Ever charming, ever new,
> When will the landscape tire the view ?
> The fountain's fall, the river's flow,
> The woody valleys warm and low,
> The windy summit, wild and high,
> Roughly rushing on the sky !

---

[1] *Lives of the Poets.*

The pleasant seat, the ruined tower,
The naked rock, the shady bower;
The town and village, dome and farm,
Each give each a double charm,
As pearls upon an Ethiop's arm.

29. **Ambrose Philips,** a Cambridge man and a zealous Whig, became a hack writer in London. His *Six Pastorals* are rubbish; nevertheless they were dogmatically praised, probably on party grounds, by Steele in the *Guardian.* This was in the year 1713. Pope, who some years before had published pastorals that were really worth something, but had attracted scarcely any notice, in a later *Guardian,* No. 40, ironically continued in the same tone, but by instituting a regular comparison between his own pastorals and those of Philips, exposed effectually the silliness and emptiness of the latter. Philips, when he had discovered the cheat, was exceedingly angry, and is said to have hung up a rod at Button's (the club frequented by Addison), with which he threatened to chastise Pope. Thereby he but increased his punishment; for Pope not only got Gay to write the burlesque mentioned above, in ridicule of the *Six Pastorals,* but affixed to his enemy the nickname of 'Namby-pamby Philips,' which is too just and appropriate ever to be forgotten while Philips himself is remembered. Ambrose also wrote the tragedy of *The Distressed Mother,* founded on the *Andromaque* of Racine; this is named with partial praise by Addison in No. 335 of the *Spectator;* it is the play which Sir Roger de Coverley sees performed on the night of his visit to the theatre.

30. **John Philips** wrote the *Splendid Shilling,* a mock-heroic poem in blank verse, in which the design of parodying the *Paradise Lost* is apparent. *Cider* and *Blenheim* are also in blank verse, a preference due to the author's serious admiration of the English epic. In fact, he seems to have been the earliest genuine *literary* admirer of Milton

31. **Isaac Watts,** educated as a Dissenter, was employed for some years as an Independent minister; but his health failed, and he was received into the house of a generous friend, Sir Thomas Abney of Stoke Newington, where he spent the last thirty-six years of his life. He is the author of three books of *Lyric Poems,* or *Horæ Lyricæ,* mostly of a devotional and serious cast, though the friend of the Revolution and Hanoverian succession comes out strongly here and there; and of *Divine Songs,* for children. His *Hymns and Spiritual Songs* are the well-known 'Watts's Hymns.'

32. **Allan Ramsay,** of Scotch extraction on his father's, of English on his mother's side, settled in Edinburgh as a wig-maker about the year 1710. He joined a society of wits and literary dilettanti, called the Easy Club; and many of his poems were composed to enliven their social gatherings. The work on which his reputation rests, *The Gentle Shepherd,* is a story of real country life in Scotland, in the form of a riming pastoral drama. The dialect is the Lowland Scotch, and the sentiments natural and suitable to the persons represented; the story is clearly told, and pleasing in itself; in short, there is nothing to find fault with in the poem; the only thing wanting is that life-giving touch of genius, which, present alike in the artificial pastorals of Pope and the artless songs of Burns, forbids true poetry to die.

Y

The Drama, 1700–1745 :—Addison, Rowe, Thomson, Young, Southern, Steele.   Prose Comedy :—Farquhar, Vanbrugh, Cibber, Centlivre ; 'The Beggar's Opera.'

33. Since the appearance of Congreve's *Mourning Bride*, a tragedy of the old school, no tragic work had been produced deserving of mention up to the year 1713.   By that time the classic drama of France, the masterpieces of Corneille and Racine, had become thoroughly known and appreciated in England ; and, in the absence of any native writers of great original power, it was natural that our dramatists, both in tragedy and comedy, should model their plays upon the French pattern.   This is the case with **Addison's** celebrated tragedy of *Cato*.[1]   It was projected and partly written in the year 1703 ; but Addison had laid it aside, and only finished and brought it on the stage in 1713, at the urgent request of his political associates.   *Cato* is in form a strictly classic play ; the unities are observed, and all admixture of comic matter is avoided, as carefully as in any play of Racine's.   The brilliant prologue was written by Pope.   The play met with signal success, because it was applauded by both political parties, the Whigs cheering the frequent allusions to liberty and patriotism, the Tories echoing back the cheers, because they did not choose to be thought more friendly to tyranny than their opponents.

34. **Rowe** produced several tolerable tragedies, one of which, the *Fair Penitent* (1703), is a re-cast of Massinger's *Fatal Dowry*.   His *Jane Shore* is an attempt to write a tragedy in the manner of Shakspere.   *Ulysses* and *Lady Jane Grey*, and a comedy named *The Biter*, were failures.   **Thomson**, the author of the *Seasons*, wrote the tragedy of *Sophonisba*,[2] in the style of *Cato*.   The success of this play is said to have been marred by a ridiculous circumstance.   There is an absurdly flat line,

Oh Sophonisba ! Sophonisba, O !

at the recital of which a wag in the pit called out

Oh Jemmy Thomson ! Jemmy Thomson, O !

The parody was for some days in everyone's mouth, and made the continued representation of the play impossible.   **Young,** the author of the *Night Thoughts*, wrote several tragedies,

---

[1] See Crit. Sect. ch. I. §§ 10.
[2] Thomson also; wrote the tragedies of *Agamemnon* (1788) and *Tancred and Sigismunda* (1745).

among which *Revenge*, produced in 1721, still keeps possession of the stage.

35. **Southern**, an Irishman, produced, near the beginning of his long career, two tragedies, *The Fatal Secret* and *Oroonoko* (1692), which for many years held their place on the stage. He was notorious for his adroitness in dealing with managers and booksellers, whence he is addressed by Pope as—

> Tom, whom Heaven sent down to raise
> The price of prologues and of plays.

He is praised by Hallam for having been the first English writer to speak with abhorrence, in his *Oroonoko*, of the slave trade. However, neither the thoughts nor the style of his tragedies rise above the commonplace.

36. **Steele's** comedies of *The Tender Husband* and *The Conscious Lovers* (1721), produced at a long interval of time, achieved a marked success. The plot of the last-named play is slight, and has few or no turns; but there is a good recognition scene at the end. The humour of the editor of the *Tatler* is not wanting; take for instance this little passage from the fifth act :—

Myrtle. But is he directly a trader at this time?

Cimberton. There is no hiding the disgrace, sir; he trades to all parts of the world.

Myrtle. We never had one of our family before, who descended from persons that did anything.

37. The 'Comedy of Manners,' in prose, of which the first suggestion clearly came from the admirable works of Molière, had been successfully tried, as we have seen, by Etherege, Wycherley, and Congreve, in the preceding period. To the same school of writers belonged, in this period, Farquhar, Vanbrugh, and Cibber. Farquhar, a native of Londonderry, is the author of *The Constant Couple* (1700), *Sir Harry Wildair* (1701), and *The Beaux' Stratagem*, the latter written on the bed of sickness to which neglect and want had brought him, and from which he sank into an untimely grave, in his thirtieth year. **Sir John Vanbrugh** wrote the famous comedies of *The Provoked Wife* and *The Provoked Husband*, the latter being left unfinished at his death and completed by Cibber. **Colley Cibber**, a German by extraction, was not only a dramatist, but an actor and theatrical manager. He has left us, in the *Apology for his own Life*, published in 1740, an amusing account of his own bustling, frivolous life, as well as of the state of the stage from the Restoration down to his own time, adding life-like sketches of the principal actors and actresses. His play of *The Nonjuror* (1718), altered by Bickersteth so as to assail the dissenters instead of the Nonjurors, and renamed *The Hypocrite*, contains the celebrated characters of Dr. Cantwell and Mawworm.

Mrs. Centlivre produced a number of comedies in the same period, which commanded a temporary popularity. The best of these (and a truly excellent comedy it is), is *A Bold Stroke for a Wife* (1718); in it first appears that well-known personage, the 'real Simon Pure.' As an acting play, the *Busy Body* has also great merit; one of the characters is an inquisitive meddlesome blundering fellow called *Marplot*; hence comes that now familiar word.

38. In the work of Cibber just mentioned there is a complaint that the Continental taste for opera had lately extended to England, to the detriment of the legitimate drama. **Gay's** *Beggar's Opera* was a clever attempt to gratify this taste by an operatic production truly British in every sense. The subject is the unhappy loves of Captain Macheath, the chief of a gang of highwaymen, and Polly Peachum, the daughter of a worthy who combines the functions of thief-taker and receiver of stolen goods. The attractiveness of the piece was greatly enhanced by the introduction of a number of beautiful popular airs; indeed, but for these, the coarseness of the plot and the grossness of much of the language would have ere now condemned it, in spite of all its wit and drollery. There is no recitative, as in a modern opera; its place is supplied by colloquial prose. The opera was first produced, with enormous applause, in 1727.

Learning, 1700–1745 :—Bentley, Lardner.

39. The greatest of English scholars flourished at the same time with Pope and Swift, and fell under the satire of both. **Richard Bentley** was a native of Yorkshire, and received his education at Cambridge, where he rose to be Master of Trinity College in 1700. The famous controversy between him and Boyle on the Epistles of Phalaris occurred in the last years of the seventeenth century, but we delayed to notice it until we could present a general view of Bentley's literary career. The dispute arose in this way :—Sir William Temple, taking up the discussion which had been carried on between Boileau and Perrault on the comparative merits of ancient and modern authors, sided with Boileau against the moderns, and, amongst other things, adduced the Epistles of Phalaris (which he supposed to be the genuine production of the tyrant of Agrigentum, who roasted Perillus in a brazen bull) as an instance of a work which in its kind was unapproached by any modern writer. Dr. Aldrich, author of the well-known Treatise on Logic, who

was then Dean of Christ Church, was induced by Temple's praise to determine upon preparing a new edition of the Epistles for the press. He committed this task to young Charles Boyle, great nephew of the celebrated natural philosopher, Robert Boyle. A MS. in the King's Library, of which Bentley was then librarian, had to be consulted. Bentley, though he lent the MS., is said to have behaved ungraciously in the matter, and refused sufficient time for its collation. In the preface to his edition of the Epistles, which appeared in 1695, Boyle complained of the alleged discourtesy. Bentley then examined the Epistles carefully; and the result was that when Wotton, in reply to Temple, published his *Reflections on Ancient and Modern Learning*, a dissertation was appended to the work, in which Bentley demonstrated that the Epistles could not possibly be the work of Phalaris, but were the forgery of a later age. In proving his point he was lavish of the supercilious and contemptuous language to which his arrogant temper naturally impelled him. Nettled at this sharp attack, the Oxford scholars clubbed their wits and their learning together; Atterbury, Smallridge, and Friend, had each a hand in the composition of the reply, which, published still under the name of Boyle, was expected to establish Phalaris in the authorship of the Epistles, and to cover Bentley with confusion. For a long time the great critic was silent; he was supposed to be vanquished, and to feel that he was so. But in 1699 appeared the *Dissertation on the Epistles of Phalaris*, the finest piece of erudite criticism that has ever proceeded from an English pen. By an analysis of the language of the Epistles, Bentley proved that they were written, not in Sicilian, but in Attic Greek, and that of a period many centuries later than the age of Phalaris; while, by bringing to bear his intimate knowledge of the whole range of Greek literature upon various topographical and historical statements which they contained, he demonstrated that towns were named which were not built, and events alluded to which had not occurred, in the lifetime of their reputed author. The controversy was now at an end; his opponents promised a reply, but it was never forthcoming.

Bentley, however, with all his wit and penetration, was without that realizing power of imagination which the greatest German critics of our days, such as the brothers Grimm, have united to the former qualities; he was an acute, but not a genial critic. His edition of the *Paradise Lost*, published in 1732, is an astonishing production. Pope's lines upon it in the *Dunciad*—

Not that I'd tear all beauties from his book,
Like slashing Bentley, with his desperate hook—

are not too severe. Among his other works are editions of Horace and Terence, to the latter of which is prefixed a valuable dissertation on the Terentian metres.

40. **Nathaniel Lardner,** a dissenting divine, published, between 1730 and 1757, a bulky work, the fruit of great learning and painstaking research, entitled the *Credibility of the Gospel History*. Lardner was himself an Arian, but his book furnished Paley afterwards with the materials for his popular *View of the Evidences of Christianity*.

Prose Fiction, Oratory, Pamphlets, Miscellanies, 1700–1745 :—Swift, Defoe, Steele, Addison.

41. Under the first head we have **Swift's** satirical romance (first published anonymously in 1726), the *Travels of Lemuel Gulliver*, including the Voyages to Lilliput, Brobdingnag, Laputa, and the country of the Houyhnhnms. The first sketch of the work occurs in *Martinus Scriblerus*, the joint production of Pope, Swift, and Arbuthnot. But Swift soon took the sole execution of the idea into his own hands, and renouncing personal satire, to which Pope was so much addicted, made this extraordinary work the vehicle for his generalizing contempt and hatred of mankind. This tone of mind, as Scott observes, gains upon the author as he proceeds, until, in the Voyage to the Houyhnhnms, he can only depict his fellow-men under the degrading and disgusting lineaments of the Yahoos. *The True History* of Lucian and Rabelais' *Voyage of Pantagruel* furnished Swift with a few suggestions, but, in the main, this is a purely original work.

42. Internal peace and security, prolonged through many years, while enormously augmenting the national wealth, occasioned the rise, about the middle of the present period, of that large class of readers to whom so much of modern literature is addressed—persons having leisure to read, and money to buy books, but who demand from literature rather amusement than instruction, and care less for being excited to think than for being made to enjoy. The stage, especially after Jeremy Collier's attacks upon it, became ever less competent to satisfy the wants of this class, or gratify this new kind of intellectual appetite. The periodical miscellany, the rise of which will be described presently, was the first kind of provision made for this purpose. When Addison and his numerous imitators had written themselves out, and the style had become tiresome, a new and more permanent provision arose in the modern novel.

The first of the English novelists[1] was **Daniel Defoe**, born in
.661. After a long and busy career as a political writer, he was
'erging on his sixtieth year, when, as a sort of relaxation from
iis serious labours, he tried his hand at prose fiction. The *Life
md Adventures of Robinson Crusoe*, founded on the true story
f Alexander Selkirk, a sailor cast by a shipwreck on the unin-
iabited island of Juan Fernandez, appeared in 1719. It was
ollowed by *Religious Courtship, The History of Colonel Jack,
Memoirs of a Cavalier, Moll Flanders, Captain Singleton*, and
everal others. It was Defoe's humour to throw the utmost
·ossible air of reality over every one of his fictions, so as to
·alm it off on the reader as a narrative of facts. Thus the
amous physician, Dr. Mead, is said to have been taken in by
he pretended *Journal of the Great Plague*, and Lord Chatham
o have recommended the *Memoirs of a Cavalier* as the best
·uthentic account of the civil war.

43. No oratory worthy of notice dates from this period. On
he other hand, pamphleteers and political satirists abounded.
)n the Whig side, Defoe wrote an ironical pamphlet, *The
!hortest Way with the Dissenters* (1702), which the House of
·ommons, then running over with Tory and High Church
·eeling, voted scandalous and seditious; he was fined, pilloried,
·nd imprisoned. From the same cause several of his other poli-
·ical writings were at the time considered libellous, and exposed
·im to persecution; to escape which, he, late in life, renounced
·olitical discussion, and indemnified himself for being debarred
·rom describing the busy world of fact by creating a new world,
·a semblance hardly less real, out of his own prolific fancy. On
he Tory side more powerful pens were engaged. No pamphlet
·ver produced a greater immediate effect than Swift's *Conduct
f the Allies*, written in 1712, in order to persuade the nation to
·, peace. 'It is boasted that between November and January
·leven thousand were sold; a great number at that time, when
·re were not yet a nation of readers. To its propagation cer ·
·ainly no agency of power and influence was wanting. It
·urnished arguments for conversation, speeches for debate, and
·aaterials for parliamentary resolutions.'[2] This was followed by
!eflections on the Barrier Treaty, published later in the same
·ear, and *The Public Spirit of the Whigs*, written in answer to
·teele's *Crisis*, in 1714. The *Examiner*, which had been com-

---

[1] This description is not, I think, impugned by the fact that Mrs. Aphra
!ehn, in the reign of Charles II., published several short stories or novelettes
Oroonoko, The Fair Jilt, Agnes de Castro, &c.) not one of which attains the
·ength of a hundred pages.
[2] Johnson's *Life of Swift*.

menced by Prior, and had provoked Addison to start a counter publication in the *Whig Examiner*, was taken up by Swift soon after his introduction to Harley in October 1710, and continued till about the middle of the next year.   In all these productions Swift, who had commenced life as a Whig, writes with the usual rancour of a political renegade.   Differently aimed, but equally effective, were the famous *Drapier's Letters*.   The following were the circumstances which gave the occasion to them :—

Since the Treaty of Limerick, in 1691, Ireland had been treated in many respects as a conquered country.   This was indeed unreservedly and openly the case, so far as the mass of the population were concerned ; but the Irish Protestants also were compelled to share in the national humiliation.   When some enterprising men had established, about the year 1700, an Irish woollen manufacture, the commercial jealousies of England were aroused, and an act was passed, which, by prohibiting the exportation of Irish woollens to any other country but England, destroyed the rising industry.   This was but one out of a number of oppressive acts under which Irishmen chafed, but in vain. Swift's haughty temper rose against the indignities offered to his country, and he only waited for an opportunity to strike a blow. That opportunity was given by the proceedings connected with Wood's contract for supplying a copper coinage, to circulate only in Ireland.   Commercially speaking, it was ultimately proved that the new coinage was calculated to benefit Ireland, not to injure her.   The coins were assayed at the Mint, under the superintendence of no less a person than Sir Isaac Newton, and proved to be of the proper weight and fineness.   But the way in which the thing was done was, and deservedly, the cause of offence.   The privilege of coining money, which had always been considered to appertain to the royal prerogative, was in this instance, without the consent or even knowledge of the Lord Lieutenant or the Irish Privy Council, delegated to an obscure Englishman, who had obtained the preference over other competitors by paying court to the king's mistress.   It was this heaping of insult upon injury which excited the ferment in the Irish mind, of which the memorable Drapier availed himself. The first letter appeared some time in the year 1724.   In it and the two following letters Swift artfully confined himself to those objections and accusations which were open to the perception of all classes of the people.   He declared that the new coins were of base metal ;—he pulled Wood's character to pieces ;—he asserted that the inevitable consequence of the introduction of the new coinage would be the disappearance of all the gold and silver from Ireland.   Such charges as these came home to the

eelings and understanding of the lowest and most ignorant of
his readers, and the excitement which they caused was tremendous. In the fourth and following letters Swift followed up the
attack by opening up the general question of the wrongs and
humiliations which Ireland had to suffer from England. A pro-
clamation was vainly issued by the Irish Government, offering a
reward of 300*l.* to anyone who would disclose the author of the
Drapier's fourth letter. The danger was great, but Sir Robert
Valpole was equal to the occasion. He first tried a compromise,
but without success, and then wisely cancelled the obnoxious
contract. From this period to his death Swift was the idol of
the Irish people. He said once to a Protestant dignitary, in the
course of an altercation, 'If I were but to hold up my little
finger, the mob would tear you to pieces.'

44. **Arbuthnot,** the joint author, with Pope and Swift, of
Martinus Scriblerus, of whom Swift exclaimed, 'Oh, if the
world had a dozen Arbuthnots, I would burn my [Gulliver's]
Travels!'—wrote, about the year 1709, the telling poetical
satire named the *History of John Bull,* levelled against the
Godolphin ministry.

The great war in which Europe was involved was represented by a law-suit carried on by John Bull against my Lord
Strutt (the King of Spain): Nicholas Frog and Esquire South
(the Dutch republic and the Emperor) being parties to the suit
on the one side,—John paying their expenses; and Lewis Ba-
bon (the king of France) on the other. John Bull's attorney,
Humphrey Hocus (Duke of Marlborough), contrives so to manage
his suit for him as to plunge him in a bottomless gulf of expense.
Addison replied with *The Late Trial and Conviction of Count
Tariff* (1713), an attack on the Tory ministry for submitting to
disadvantageous terms at the peace of Utrecht. But the humour
here is not so broad and hearty as in the *History of John Bull,*
which yet evidently served it for a model.

45. From this period dates the rise of the periodical miscellany.[1] To **Richard Steele,** an Irishman, who was employed by
the Whig Government to write the *Gazette* during the Spanish
accession war, the nature of his employment suggested the design of the *Tatler,* a tri-weekly sheet, giving the latest items of
news, and following them up with a tale or essay. To this periodical **Addison** soon began to contribute papers, and continued
write for it nearly to the end. The first number appeared

[1] Usually, but not very correctly, called the periodical *essay*; a word
which can hardly be stretched so as to include the allegories, sketches of
manners and characters, tales, gossiping letters, &c., with which the *Tatler* and
Spectator abound.

on the 22nd April 1709, the last on the 2nd January 1711. The success of the *Tatler* being decisive, it was followed up by the *Spectator* (1711-2), the plan of which, 'as far as it regards the feigned person of the author and of the several persons who compose his club, was projected' by Addison 'in concert with Sir Richard Steele.' [1] In the first number, which was from the pen of Addison, the imaginary projector of the undertaking gives a portrait of himself that is full of strokes of delicate humour; how from childhood he had ' distinguished himself by a most profound silence,' and in mature age lived in the world ' rather as a *Spectator* of mankind than as one of the species.' He announces his intention of publishing ' a sheet full of thoughts' every morning; repudiates political aims; declares that he will preserve a tone and character of rigid impartiality; invites epistolary assistance from the public; and requests that letters may be addressed to the Spectator at ' Mr. Buckley's in Little Britain.' No. 2, by Steele, contains sketches of the different persons composing the Spectator's club; (literature supposed itself hardly able to hold its ground in those days without its clubs :) the fine old country gentleman, Sir Roger de Coverley; the retired merchant, Sir Andrew Freeport; Capt. Sentry, the old soldier; Will Honeycomb, the beau;—besides a stage-bitten barrister, and a clergyman. There is no doubt that Addison believed himself to be engaged in an important work, tending to humanize and elevate his countrymen :—'It was said of Socrates that he brought philosophy down from heaven to inhabit among men; and I should be ambitious to have it said of me, that I have brought philosophy out of closets and libraries, schools and colleges, to dwell in clubs and assemblies, at tea-tables and in coffee-houses.' [2]

By turning to fresh intellectual fields the minds of the upper classes—the people in good society—to whom the theatre was now a forbidden or despised excitement, Addison did without doubt allay much restlessness, still or amuse many feverish longings. The millennium, it seemed, was not to come yet awhile; the fifth monarchy was not to be yet established; no, nor was the world to become a great Armida's garden of pleasure and jollity; nor did blind loyalty to the true prince commend itself now even to the heart, much less to the reason. Robbed of its ideals, disenchanted, and in heavy cheer, the English mind, though not profoundly interested, read these pleasant chatty discoursings about things in general, and allowed itself to be

---

[1] See the preface to Addison's works, by Tickell.
[2] *Spectator*, No. 10.

used, and half forgot its spiritual perplexities. Nothing was
tled by these papers, nothing really probed to the bottom ;
t they taught, with much light grace and humour, lessons of
)d sense, tolerance, and moderation ; and their popularity
)ved that the lesson was relished.

The *Spectator* extended to 635 numbers, including the eighty
the resumed issue in 1714 Upon its suspension in De-
nber 1712, the *Guardian* took its place. Of the 271 papers
the *Tatler*, Steele wrote 188, Addison 42, and both con-
ntly 36. Of 635 *Spectators*, Addison wrote 274, Steele 240,
stace Budgell 37, and John Hughes 11; and of 175 *Guar-
ns*, Steele wrote 82, and Addison 53. Several *Tatlers* were
itributed by Swift, and a few *Spectators* and *Guardians* by
pe.

Among the subjects treated of in the *Spectator* are the fol-
/ing : — Masquerades, clubs, operas, vulgar superstitions,
)sts, devotees, the shortness of life (in the famous ' Vision of
rzah,' No. 159), and the poetical merits of Milton's *Paradise
st*, in an elaborate criticism, extending over seventeen num-
s, written by Addison.

46. At the end of 1715 Addison commenced writing the
eeholder, at the rate of two papers a week, and continued it
the middle of the next year. ' This was undertaken in the
ence of the established Government ; sometimes with argu-
nt, sometimes with mirth. In argument he had many
ials ; but his humour was singular and matchless. Bigotry
elf must be delighted with the Tory fox-hunter.' [1]

The daily miscellany passed by insensible degrees into infe-
r hands, and at last became insufferably dull. From the
ture of the case, intellectual gifts are required to recommend
s style, with which the novel can dispense. There are ten
sons who can write a tale which people will read, for one who
i compose a passable criticism, or a *jeu d'esprit*, or seize the
itive traits of some popular habit, vice, or caprice. Even
i importation of politics, as in the *Freeholder*, failed to give a
manent animation. So, after the town had been deluged for
ne time with small witticisms and criticisms that had no
nt or sap in them, the style was agreed on all hands to be a
isance, and was discontinued. Some years later it was revived
Dr. Johnson, as we shall see.

[1] Johnson.

Works of Satire and Humour: Swift.

47. It will be remembered [1] that Swift's patron, Sir William Temple, took a leading part in the discussion upon the relative merits of ancient and modern authors. Swift himself struck in on the same side, in the brilliant satire of the *Battle of the Books*,[2] which was written in 1697, but not published till 1704. In this controversy the great wits, both in France and England, were all of one mind in claiming the palm for the ancients. It was, perhaps, with some reference to it that Pope, in the *Essay on Criticism*, burst forth into the magnificent encomium in honour of the great poets of antiquity, beginning,

Still green with bays each ancient altar stands, &c.

In the reaction towards the mediæval and Gothic antiquity which marked the close of the last and the beginning of the present century, this enthusiasm for Greece and Rome was much abated. At present there are symptoms of a partial revival of the feeling.

48. The *Tale of a Tub* was also published in 1704, though written in 1696. The title is explained by Swift to mean, that, as sailors throw out a tub to a whale, to keep him amused, and prevent him from running foul of their ship, so, in this treatise, his object is to afford such temporary diversion to the wits and free-thinkers of the day (who drew their arguments from the *Leviathan* of Hobbes) as may restrain them from injuring the state by propagating wild theories in religion and politics. The allegory of the three brothers, and the general character and tendency of this extraordinary book, will be examined in the second part of the present work.[3]

History, 1700–1745 :—Burnet, Rapin.

49. Burnet's *History of his Own Times*, closing with the year 1713, was published soon after his death in 1715. Burnet was a Scotchman, and a very decided Whig. Exiled by James II., he attached himself to the Prince of Orange, and was actively engaged in all the intrigues which paved the way for the Revolution. The *History of his Own Times*, though ill-arranged and inaccurate, is yet, owing to its contemporary character, a valuable original source of information for the period between the Restoration and 1713. Rapin, a French refugee, published

---

[1] See p. 824.   [2] See Crit. Sect. ch. II. § 7.   [3] *Ibid.* § 6.

in 1725 the best complete history of England that had as yet appeared. It was translated twice, and long remained a standard work.

Of the theology and philosophy of the period we reserve our sketch till after we have examined the progress of general literature between 1745 and 1800.

Johnson.   Poetry, 1745–1800 :—Gray, Glover, Akenside, Young, Shenstone, Collins, Mason, Warton, Churchill, Falconer, Chatterton, Beattie, Goldsmith, Cowper, Burns, Darwin, Walcot, Gifford, Bloomfield.

50. The grand yet grotesque figure of Samuel Johnson holds the central place among the writers of the second half of the eighteenth century. In all literary réunions he took the undisputed lead, by the power and brilliancy of his conversation, which, indeed, as recorded by Boswell, is a more valuable possession than any, or all, of his published works. His influence upon England was eminently conservative; his manly good sense, his moral courage, his wit, readiness, and force as a disputant, were all exerted to keep English society where it was, and prevent the ideas of Voltaire and Rousseau from gaining ground. His success was signal. Not that there were wanting on the other side either gifted minds, or an impressible audience; Hume, Gibbon, and Priestley were sceptics of no mean order of ability; and Boswell's own example [1] shows that, had there been no counteracting force at work, an enthusiastic admiration for Rousseau might easily have become fashionable in England. But while Johnson lived and talked, the revolutionary party could never gain that mastery in the intellectual arena, and that ascendency in society, which it had obtained in France. After his death the writings of Burke carried on the sort of conservative propaganda which he had initiated.

Johnson was born at Lichfield, in the year 1709. His father was a native of Derbyshire, but had settled in Lichfield as a bookseller. After having received the rudiments of a classical education at various country schools, he was entered at Pembroke College, Oxford, in the year 1728. His father about this time suffered heavy losses in business, in consequence of which Johnson had to struggle for many years against the deepest poverty. Nor was either his mental or bodily constitution so healthful and vigorous as to compensate for the frowns of for-

---

[1] See Hume's *Autobiography.*

tune. He seems to have inherited from his mother's family the disease of scrofula, or the king's evil, for which he was taken up to London, at the age of three years, to be touched by Queen Anne—the ancient superstition concerning the efficacy of the royal touch not having then wholly died out. His mind was a prey during life to that most mysterious malady, hypochondria, which exhibited itself in a morbid melancholy, varying at different times in intensity, but never completely shaken off—and also in an incessant haunting fear of insanity. Under the complicated miseries of his condition, religion constantly sustained him, and deserted him not, till, at the age of seventy-five, full of years and honours, his much-tried and long-suffering soul was released. In his boyhood, he tells us, he had got into a habit of wandering about the fields on Sundays reading, instead of going to church, and the religious lessons early taught him by his mother were considerably dimmed; but at Oxford, the work of that excellent man, though somewhat cloudy writer, William Law, entitled *A Serious Call to a Holy Life*, fell into his hands, and made so profound an impression upon him, that from that time forward, though he used to lament the short-comings in his practice, religion was ever, in the main, the actuating principle of his life.

After leaving Oxford, he held a situation as undermaster in a grammar-school for some months. But this was a kind of work for which he was utterly unfitted, and he was compelled to give it up. He went to Birmingham, where he obtained some trifling literary work. In 1735 he married a Mrs. Porter, a widow, and soon after, as a means of subsistence, opened a boarding-school, in which, however, he failed. He now resolved to try his fortune in London. He settled there with his wife in 1737, and supported himself for many years by writing—principally by his contributions to the *Gentleman's Magazine*, which had been established by Cave about the year 1730, and is still carried on. His Plan of a Dictionary of the English Language was published in 1747. The price stipulated for from the booksellers was 1,575*l.*, and the work was to be completed in three years. The *Rambler*, a series of papers on miscellaneous subjects, on the model of the *Spectator*, was commenced by him in 1750, and concluded in 1752. This and various other works, which appeared from time to time, joined to his unrivalled excellence as a talker, which made his company eagerly sought after by persons of all ranks, gradually won for Johnson a considerable reputation; and, after the accession of George III., he received, through the kindness of Lord Bute, a pension of 300*l.* a year. This was in 1762. He continued to reside in London—with but short intervals, on the occasions of his tours to the Hebrides, to Wales, and to France—till his death in 1784.

51. Johnson's works—excepting the *Dictionary*, a tragedy called *Irene*, a few poems, the *Lives of the Poets*,[1] some other biographies, and a short novel, the famous *Rasselas*—consist of essays, very multifarious in their scope, discussing questions of politics, manners, trade, agriculture, art, and criticism. The bulk of these were composed for the *Rambler*, the *Idler*, and the *Adventurer*. His prose style, cumbrous, antithetical, and pompous, yet in his hands possessing generally great dignity and strength, and sometimes even, as in *Rasselas*, rising to remarkable beauty and nobleness, was so influential upon the men of his day that it caused a complete revolution, for a time, in English style, and by no means for the better ; since inferior men, though they could easily appropriate its peculiarities or defects—its long words, its balanced clauses, its laboured antitheses—could not with equal ease emulate its excellences.

Among Johnson's poems, the satire called *London*, an imitation of the third satire of Juvenal, and the beautiful didactic poem on *The Vanity of Human Wishes*, are the most deserving of notice.

52. **Gray**, the son of a scrivener in London, was educated and lived the greater part of his life at Cambridge. In the small volume of his poems there are several pieces which have gained a permanent place in our literature. The *Bard*,[2] the *Progress of Poesy*, and the Ode *On a distant Prospect of Eton College*, are all, in their different ways, excellent. As a writer he was indolent and fastidious ; to the former quality we probably owe it that his writings are so few, to the latter that many of them are so excellent. The famous *Elegy in a Country Churchyard* was first published in a magazine in 1750. The melancholy beauty of these lovely lines is enhanced by the severity and purity of the style.

53. **Richard Glover**, the son of a London merchant, produced the first edition of his blank verse epic, *Leonidas*, in 1737. It has not much merit, but at the time of its first appearance was extravagantly praised for political and party reasons ; since every high-flown sentiment in praise of patriotism, disinterestedness, and love of liberty, was interpreted by the Opposition into a damning reflection on the corrupt practices, and the truckling spirit towards foreigners, by which Sir Robert Walpole's government was supposed to be characterised. In its present finished state, as a poem of twelve books, it first came out in 1770. *The Athenaid*, a sequel to the *Leonidas*, and in the same metre, but extending to thirty books, was published after the author's death

---

[1] See Crit. Sect. ch. II. § 30.   [2] *Ibid.* ch. I. § 57.

in 1785 : it is a dull versified chronicle of the successes gained by the Athenians in the Persian war. The ballad of *Hosier's Ghost* is the only composition of Glover's that is worth remembering.

54. **Mark Akenside** was the son of a butcher at Newcastle-on-Tyne. The poem by which he is best known, the *Pleasures of Imagination* (1744), was suggested by a series of papers on the same subject (Nos. 411–421), contributed by Addison to the *Spectator*. But the analysis of the pleasurable feelings which are awakened in the mind by whatever excites the imagination, though suitable enough as a subject for an essay, becomes insupportable when carried on through a poem of more than two thousand blank verses. Akenside had no sense of humour and no wit, but was an ardent lover of nature ; he may be called a second-rate Wordsworth, whose style that of some of his *Odes* much resembles. He was an ardent politician, and attached himself to the faction, which, assuming the name of 'the patriots,' inveighed so long against the government of Sir Robert Walpole. Finding, after Sir Robert's fall, that everything remained much the same as before, Akenside wrote his *Epistle to Curio* (1744) in which, addressing Pulteney, he charges him with having betrayed the just expectations of the country ; this was afterwards altered into the *Ode to Curio.* Lord Macaulay, exaggerating as was his wont, calls the *Epistle* the best thing that Akenside ever wrote, but sets down the *Ode* as worthless.

55. The *Night Thoughts* [1] of **Young** appeared between the years 1742 and 1746. This didactic poem, which has been read and praised beyond its deserts, is in blank verse, and is said to have been inspired by the melancholy into which the poet was plunged by the death, within three years, of his wife and her two children. Moralizing forms the staple of the poem, just as philosophizing forms the staple of Wordsworth's *Excursion*, and microscopic description of Crabbe's *Borough* ; but tales are inserted here and there by way of episode, just as in the other two poems mentioned. There is a fine, fluent, sermonizing vein about Young ; but a flavour of cant hangs about his most ambitious efforts. To use a phrase of the day, he is a sad ' Philistine ; ' and through the admiration long felt or professed for him, his influence must have much tended to propagate false taste. The work is divided into nine *Nights*, the headings of some of which will serve to indicate its general character ; they are—' On Life, Death, and Immortality,' ' Narcissa,' ' The Christian Triumph,' ' The Infidel Reclaimed,' ' Virtue's Apology,' &c. A few lines occur here and there, stamped with a terseness and significance which have made them almost, if not quite, proverbial ; such are—

> Procrastination is the thief of time ;

and—

> Pigmies are pigmies still, though perched on Alps :
> And pyramids are pyramids, in vales.

---

[1] The full title is, ' The Complaint ; or, Night Thoughts on Life, Death, and Immortality.'

In philosophy, Young was a follower of Berkeley, whose idealism he reproduces at some length in the sixth *Night* :—

> Objects are but the occasion ; ours th' exploit :
> Ours is the cloth, the pencil, and the paint,
> Which Nature's admirable picture draws,
> And beautifies creation's ample dome.

In theology he leans on Butler, speaking of—

> A scheme analogy pronounced so true,
> Analogy, man's surest guide below.

Young found an ardent admirer, and even in part a translator, in Ganganelli, Pope Clement XIV., a man prone like himself to bow before the power and splendour of this world. His *Odes* are worth very little ; many of them teem with fulsome praise of George II. and the House of Hanover.

56. **Shenstone,** a native of Halesowen, near Birmingham, not far from which lay his beautiful little estate of ' The Leasowes,' which is still shown to the curious traveller, published his poem of *The School-mistress* in the year 1741. It is in the Spenserian stanza, and affects an antique dress of language ; but it has really very little merit. Shenstone was a vain and frivolous, yet withal querulous, person ; his poems are full of complaints that his estate is too small to admit of his gratifying his refined tastes. Some of his ballads, *e.g.* ' Valentine's Day,' and ' Jemmy Dawson,' have some pretty and pathetic stanzas. The ' Pastoral Ballad ' is a charming piece of pretty trifling.[1]

57. **Collins,** the son of a hatter in Chichester, published his once famous *Odes* in 1746. Nor can these ever be entirely forgotten, so beautiful is the diction, so clear and profound are the thoughts. With some occasional exaggeration and over-luxuriance, this author's language is for the most part exquisitely musical and refined. The odes ' To Simplicity,' on ' The Manners,' and on ' The Passions,' are among those most deserving of notice.

58. **Mason,** the friend of Gray, wrote in 1748 a poem, called *Isis,* containing a petulant attack upon the University of Oxford as the nursery of Jacobitism and disaffection. This drew forth a brilliant reply, the *Triumph of Isis,* from Thomas Warton, then a young student at Trinity College, Oxford, and afterwards distinguished as the historian of English poetry. Mason wrote a number of Odes, and also tried his hand at satire in the ' Heroic Epistle to Sir William Chambers,' which, however, has more ill-nature than wit. We shall meet with him again as a dramatist.

59. **Churchill,** the son of an Essex clergyman, took orders, married, obtained preferment, and appeared to be on the high road to a deanery, when the example of a good-for-nothing school-fellow,[2] an innate thirst of pleasure, a loose moral frame, and an

---

[1] See Crit. Sect. ch. I. § 48.
[2] Robert Lloyd, author of *The Actor,* a poem which had attracted much notice.

z

irritable vanity, turned him aside into the perilous career of the satirist and the wit.   He flung off his gown, and after a first unsuccessful attempt with *The Conclave*, a satire on the Dean and Chapter of Westminster, obtained at a bound all the notoriety which he desired by the publication of the *Rosciad* (1761). This is a clever personal satire on the actors who then trod the London stage, with many dramatic criticisms not without value. By the sale of this, and of the *Apology for the Rosciad*, published soon after, he cleared more than a thousand pounds.   This success completely turned his head; he produced poem after poem with great rapidity, endeavouring to rival the satirico-didactic vein of Pope; allied himself closely with the demagogue Wilkes; fell into profligate ways; and died of fever at Boulogne in 1764, bankrupt in health, money, and good name.   Among his many poems I shall single out for mention, *Night*, and the *Prophecy of Famine*.   The former, dedicated to Lloyd, appeared at the end of 1761 ; its purpose is to vindicate himself and his friends from the attacks which were levelled against them on the score of irregular life.   It is spirited and clever, reminding the reader often of Pope's *Imitations of Horace*, but just without that marvellous preternatural element which makes the one an immortal work of genius, the other a brilliant but ephemeral copy of verses.   These lines are a good specimen :—

> What is't to us, if taxes rise or fall ?
> Thanks to our fortune, we pay none at all.
> Let muckworms, who in dirty acres deal,
> Lament those hardships which we cannot feel.
> His grace who smarts may bellow if he please ;
> But must I bellow too, who sit at ease ?
> By custom safe, the poet's numbers flow
> Free as the light and air some years ago ;
> No statesman e'er will think it worth his pains
> To tax our labours and excise our brains :
> Burthens like these vile earthly buildings bear ;
> No tribute's laid on castles in the air.

In the *Prophecy of Famine*, which appeared in 1763, the chief wit lies in his ascribing to the Scotch, against whom the satire is aimed, exactly the opposite virtues to their (supposed) notorious bad qualities.   But there is no proper arrangement ; one often does not see what he is driving at ; he seems to have written straight on as notions rose in his head, without having formed a clear intellectual plan.   The goddess of Famine, after the battle of Culloden, is supposed to prophesy to two Scotch shepherd boys—Jockey and Sawney—the elevation of Lord Bute to the premiership, the exaltation of the whole nation consequent thereupon, and their fattening at England's expense.

60. **Falconer**, a Scotch sailor, published his descriptive poem of the *Shipwreck*, in heroic verse, in 1762. It is too laboured and artificial to command permanent popularity. The author was himself lost at sea a few years afterwards.

The publication of Percy's *Reliques of Ancient English Poetry*, in 1765, was one of the first symptoms of that great literary and religious reaction from classical to Christian antiquity, the waves of which have since spread so far. Naïve old ballads, such as 'Chevy Chase' for instance, which had stirred the blood of Sir Philip Sidney two hundred years before, were resuscitated from their long sleep, and supplied to imaginative youth towards the close of the century a mental food quite different from that on which their fathers and grandfathers had been reared.

61. **Chatterton**, 'the wondrous boy that perished in his prime,' belonged to a family which for several generations had supplied the sexton of the noble church of St. Mary Redcliffe, at Bristol. In an old muniment-room above the north porch, the boy had come across mouldering parchment records connected with the ancient history of the church, and the strange idea seized him of attributing poems of his own composition to an imaginary monk, whom he called Rowley, of the fifteenth century, and pretending that he had found the original MSS. of these poems in the muniment-room. His forgeries met with considerable acceptance in the west of England, but he was foiled in an attempt to palm off some of them upon Horace Walpole. He came up to London in 1770, and, after a vain attempt to support himself by the pen, died there in the course of a few months, while yet in his eighteenth year—according to one account by taking poison, according to another of actual starvation. A few years later, a celebrated and keenly contested controversy arose concerning the genuineness of the Rowley poems.

62. **Beattie** produced the first canto of his *Minstrel* in 1771. I think that Mr. Craik[1] is unjust to this poem when he says that, in comparison with Thomson's *Castle of Indolence*, it is like gilding compared to gold. Beattie had not the same power of luscious delineation, nor the same command over language, which belonged to Thomson; yet, on the other hand, he sometimes rises to a strain of manly force and dignity which was beyond the compass of the other. The metre is the Spenserian stanza; the tone is like that of Gray in the *Elegy*; it is the chord struck by Rousseau, the superiority of simple unbought pleasures to luxury and pomp, of nature to art, &c. The great defect of the poem is its want of plot. The following is one of the finest stanzas:—

> For know, to man as candidate for heaven,
>   The voice of the Eternal said, Be free;
> And this Divine prerogative to thee
>   Doth virtue, happiness, and heaven convey;
> For virtue is the child of liberty,
>   And happiness of virtue; nor can they
> Be free to keep the path, who are not free to stray.

63. **Goldsmith's** poems are few in number, but several are

---

[1] *History of English Literature*, v. 170.

of rare merit. More than one recent biography has made known the story of the failures, the sorrows, the erratic youth of this child of genius, who retained his Irish heedlessness, generosity, sensibility, and elasticity to the last moment of his life. His didactic poem, *The Traveller*, appeared in 1765, at which time he had long been settled in London, doing miscellaneous literary work for the booksellers. Both the form and the philosophy of this poem (which teaches that the constituents of human happiness vary with climate, place, and circumstance) bespeak strongly the influence of Pope. Great intellectual growth is visible in the *Deserted Village* (1771). We have the same charming type of the village pastor, 'passing rich on forty pounds a year,' which is presented to us in the *Vicar of Wakefield* ; but the poet strikes here a deeper and graver key, when, in lines to which the walls of St. Stephen's have so often re-echoed, he bewails the extension of the English and Irish *latifundia*,[1] and the decay of the peasantry :—

> Ill fares the land, to hastening ills a prey.
> Where wealth accumulates, and men decay :
> Princes and lords may flourish or may fade ;
> A breath can make them, as a breath has made :
> But a bold peasantry, their country's pride,
> When once destroyed, can never be supplied.

All Goldsmith's drollery comes out in the *Elegy on Madame Blaise*, and that *On a Mad Dog* ; all his wit, rapidity, and luminous discernment in the *Retaliation*, a series of imaginary epitaphs on his chief friends, among whom are included Burke, Garrick, and Sir Joshua Reynolds.

64. **Cowper** was designed by his father for the bar, but after a time, his unfitness for that profession becoming manifest, he was appointed to a clerkship in the House of Lords. But an overpowering nervousness prevented him from discharging the duties of the post ; he resigned it, and went to live in the country, which he never afterwards left. He formed an intimate friendship with a man of great force of character and fervid piety, the Rev. John Newton, curate of Olney. In the poems of his first volume, published in 1782, this friend's influence is very manifest. These poems consist chiefly of some long didactic compositions of several hundred lines each, in blank verse, entitled, *Table Talk, The Progress of Error, Truth, Expostulation, Hope, Charity, Conversation*, and *Retirement*. Their tone is generally desponding, and leaning to the side of censure ;

---

[1] The name given to the vast landed estates of the Roman nobles.

he declaims against the novelists and the mischief they cause, indulges in a tirade against the press, and talks of 'the free-thinkers' brutal roar.' Yet there is so much grace and delicacy and lightness of touch, even in most of the censure, and he is so every inch a gentleman everywhere and always, that an affectionate admiration for the writer predominates over every other feeling. *Tirocinium* appeared in 1784; it is an earnest attack on the public-school system, on the ground of its demora-lising influence on character. There are many vigorous lines, and some cutting satire, as in the line—

> The parson knows enough who knows a duke.

There is also a beautiful tribute to John Bunyan, whom he will not name, lest a name then generally despised should awaken only derision.

His second volume, containing *The Task*, appeared in 1785. This is a didactic or reflective poem, in six books. The poet, having been asked to write a poem on a *sofa*, commences with a sketch of the history of *seats*, which he tells with a mild humour, reminding one of the playfulness of a kitten, graceful and pretty, and never vulgar, though sometimes trivial. After having come down to the creation of the sofa, fancy bears him away to his school days, when he roved along Thames' bank till tired, and needed no *sofa* when he returned; then he becomes dreamy, traces his life down the stream of time to the present hour, noting what has made him happy, stilled his nerves, strengthened his health, raised his spirits, or kept them at least from sinking; and finds that it has ever been the free communion with Nature in the country. Many charming descriptive passages are inter-woven in all this. The tale of 'Crazy Kate' is admirably told. Then he maunders on about the gipsies; then launches—if the word is not too vehement—into a tirade against town life, in which occurs the well-known line—

> God made the country, and man made the town.

An additional shade of melancholy and despondency is evidently thrown over the poet's mind by the humiliations which England about this time had to brook—the treaty of Fontainebleau, the loss of America.

Among the smaller poems, the merry history of 'John Gilpin' is familiar to everyone. The 'Negro's Complaint' was written to expose the cruelties of the African slave trade. The stanzas on 'Boadicea' are finely expressed, and with a more *sus'ained* elevation than is usual with him, for Cowper's *art is*

certainly very defective; he seems hardly to have believed that
poetry had any rules at all. His versification is careless, and to
rhythm and choice of words he pays far too little attention;
weak and trivial are continually annexed to weighty lines. This
is noticeable even in that admirable poem, 'On the receipt of
my Mother's Picture.' Though his vein is usually serious, he
has a genuine native humour which can be frolicsome when it
pleases. For an example, take some of his lines 'On a Mis-
chievous Bull,' which the owner sold at the poet's instance :—

> Ah ! I could pity thee, exiled
>   From this secure retreat ;
> I would not lose it to be styled
>   The happiest of the great.
>
> But thou canst taste no calm delight ;
>   Thy pleasure is to show
> Thy magnanimity in fight,
>   Thy prowess : therefore go—
>
> I care not whether east or north,
>   So I no more may find thee ;
> The angry muse thus sings thee forth,
>   And claps the gate behind thee.

The 'Castaway' is exquisite in its mournful pathos, and the
'Verses supposed to be written by Alexander Selkirk,' though
in a jingling metre, are full of striking turns of thought which
ensure to them a permanent popularity. Cowper's last work of
any consequence was his translation of the *Iliad*, in blank verse;
this appeared in 1791.

65. In Scotland, where no truly original poet had arisen
since Dunbar, the last forty years of the century witnessed the
bright and brief career of the peasant poet, whose genius shed a
dazzling glow over his country's literature. Many beautiful
songs,[1] mostly of unknown authorship, circulated in Scotland
before the time of Burns; and **Allan Ramsay**, though an imitator as far as the substance of his poetry was concerned, had so
written in the native dialect as to show that original and truly
national forms lay ready for the Scottish poet. With this
foundation to work upon—with the education of a Scottish pri-
mary school, a knowledge of Pope and Shenstone, and a sound,
clear intellect—**Robert Burns** made himself the greatest song-
writer that our literature has ever known.[2] Force pervaded
his whole character; he could do nothing by halves. At the

---

[1] For an interesting account of them see an article by Professor Shairp in
Macmillan's Magazine for May 1861.
[2] See Crit. Sect. ch. I. §§ 53, 61.

age of eighteen, that passion, from which proceeds so much alike of the glory and of the shame of man's existence, developed itself in his burning heart, and remained till death the chief motive power of his thoughts and acts. He fell in love; and then his feelings, as he tells us, spontaneously burst forth in song. Two other strongly-marked tendencies in his character must be mentioned, to which some of his most famous productions may be attributed. The first was his ardent spirit of nationality; the second, his repugnance to, and revolt from, the narrow sectarianism of his age and country. Almost the first book he ever read was the life of Sir William Wallace, the Scottish patriot, whose hiding-places and ambushes, as pointed out by history or local tradition, he visited with a pilgrim's fervour. It was this spirit which produced such poems as—

> Scots wha hae wi' Wallace bled,

or the *Address to the Scottish Members of Parliament*. His repugnance to Presbyterianism—exemplified in such poems as *Holy Willie's Prayer*, the *Dedication to Gavin Hamilton, Esq.*, and the *Address to the Unco Guid, or the Rigidly Righteous*— redounds partly to the disgrace of the system which he satirized, and partly to his own. If he rebelled against the ceremonial and formal, he rebelled no less against the *moral* teaching of Presbyterianism. His protest against religious hypocrisy must be taken in connection with his own licentiousness. His father, an earnest adherent of that creed and system which the son broke away from and despised, though wrestling all his life against poverty and misfortune, endured his troubles with patience, and died in peace, because he had learned the secret of the victory over self. His wondrously gifted son never gained that victory, and the record of his last years presents one of the most sad, disastrous spectacles that it is possible to contemplate.

Burns' first volume of poems was published in 1786, and a second edition appeared in the following year. *Tam o' Shanter*, a fairy story burlesqued, the *Cotter's Saturday Night*, and *The Vision*, are among the most noteworthy pieces in this collection; none of them attain to any great length. After his marriage to Jean Armour, he settled on the farm of Ellisland, uniting the functions of an exciseman to those of a farmer. But the farm proved a bad speculation—

> Spem mentita seges, bos est enectus arando,

and, having received a more lucrative appointment in the excise

Burns gave up Ellisland, and removed to Dumfries. Here the habit of intemperance, to indulgence in which the nature of his employment unhappily supplied more than ordinary temptations, gradually made him its slave; disappointment and self-reproach preyed upon his heart; want stared him in the face; and the greatest of Scottish poets, having become a mere wreck of his former self, sank, in his thirty-seventh year, into an untimely grave.

66. The *Rolliad* was a satirical effusion, commenced in 1784 by several writers belonging to the party of Fox and the recently defeated coalition, and directed against Mr. Pitt and his supporters in Parliament. The chief of these writers was a Dr. Lawrence; he was assisted by George Ellis, a Mr. Fitzpatrick, and two other persons named Richardson and Tickle. The origin of the name was this: Mr. Rolle, the member for Devonshire, in a speech made on the Westminster Scrutiny,[1] had informed the public that he was descended from 'Duke Rollo.' A ludicrous pedigree of 'John Rolle, Esq.,' thereupon appeared, said to be 'extracted from the records of the Herald's Office.' This was followed by the 'Dedication of the Rolliad, an Epic poem in twelve Books,' written by Fitzpatrick, and addressed to Mr. Rolle. Amidst a great deal of sarcastic eulogy, copiously garnished with puns, the dedicator congratulates Mr. Rolle, because, as his ancestor Rollo fought for William the Conqueror,—

> So you with zeal support through each debate
> The conquering *William* [Pitt] of a later date.

After this one would expect the poem itself; but the joke is that there is no poem. The *Rolliad* itself, though affirmed by its critics to have reached the twentieth edition, is wholly imaginary; we only know of it through the supposed extracts from the poem given in the *Criticisms on the Rolliad*, which appeared in twenty-one successive numbers. In these Pitt, Dundas, the India Board, and Warren Hastings, with many other persons and things, were assailed; often with cruel wit and pungent sarcasm; yet it seems that the victims were not sufficiently interesting, nor the satire quite potent enough, to prevent the *Rolliad* from having almost fallen into oblivion.

67. Dr. **Darwin**, an eminent physician, published his *Loves of the Plants* in 1789. In this strange poem there is a great deal about botany and electricity, and the steam engine, and weaving, and cotton-spinning, but nothing about any subject suitable for poetic treatment. Here, for instance, is an invocation to steam:—

> Soon shall thy arm, unconquered Steam, afar
> Drag the slow barge, or drive the rapid car;
> Or, on wide waving wings expanded, bear
> The flying chariot through the fields of air.
> Fair crews triumphant, leaning from above,
> Shall wave their fluttering kerchiefs as they move;
> Or warrior bands alarm the gaping crowd,
> And armies sink beneath the shadowy cloud.

---

[1] Instituted by the Government with the view of unseating Fox for Westminster, after the famous election of 1784.

The *Loves of the Plants* is only a portion of a larger work, entitled *The Botanic Garden.*

68. Dr. **John Wolcot**, better known as 'Peter Pindar,' wrote coarse and fluent satires against the king, the Royal Academicians, Dr. Johnson, James Boswell, Gifford, and others. The *Lousiad*, in which a little incident, said to have occurred at the royal table, is made the subject of a long satirical and mock-heroic poem, appeared in 1785.[1] Gifford, besides a reply to Wolcot, called an 'Epistle to Peter Pindar,' is the author of the *Baviad* (1794) and *Mæviad* (1796), two clever satires on a school of namby-pamby poets and poetesses, called, from the assumed name of their leader, Mr. Robert Merry, Della-Cruscans. Lastly, Robert Bloomfield, a farmer's boy in early life, and then a shoemaker, gave to the world, in 1800, his excellent descriptive poem of *The Farmer's Boy.*

The Drama, 1745–1800 :—Home, Johnson, Moore, Mason, Colman, Murphy, Goldsmith, Foote, Sheridan.

69. The tragic stage resumed in this period, under the able management of Garrick, a portion of its former dignity. But no original tragedies of importance were composed. **Home's** play of *Douglas*, known to all school-boys as the source of that familiar burst of eloquence, beginning,—

> My name is Norval, on the Grampian hills
> My father feeds his flocks, &c. &c.—

appeared in 1757. **Johnson's** tragedy of *Irene*, produced at Drury Lane by Garrick in 1749, was coldly received, owing to the want of sustained tragic interest. When asked how he felt upon the ill success of his tragedy, the sturdy lexicographer replied, 'Like the Monument.' When we have mentioned **Moore's** *Gamester* (1755), celebrated for its deeply affecting catastrophe, and **Mason's** *Elfrida* (1752) and *Caractacus* (1759), our list of tragedies of any note is exhausted.

70. The comedy of manners, as exemplified by the plays of Congreve and Farquhar, had gradually degenerated into the genteel or sentimental comedy, in which **Colman** the elder and **Arthur Murphy** were proficients. **Goldsmith's** *Good-natured Man* (1768) was a clever attempt to bring back the theatrical public to the old way of thinking, which demanded 'little more than nature and humour, in whatever walks of life they were most conspicuous.' Delineation of character was therefore his principal aim. *She Stoops to Conquer*, a piece written on the same plan, appeared, and had a great run, in 1773. **Foote**, the actor, wrote several clever farces between 1752 and 1778, of which the *Liar* and the *Mayor of Garratt* are among the most noted.

[1] See Crit. Sect. ch. I. § 39.

71. **Sheridan,** the son of an Irish actor and a literary lady, after marrying the beautiful actress, Miss Linley, in defiance of a crowd of rivals, and after being for years the life of society at Bath, connected himself with the stage, and produced *The Rivals* in 1775. All his other comedies appeared in the ensuing five years; viz., *The Duenna, The School for Scandal, The Critic,* and *The Trip to Scarborough.* All these plays are in prose, and all, with the exception of *The Duenna,* reflect contemporary manners. In the creation of comic character and the conduct of comic dialogue, Sheridan has never been surpassed. His wit flashes evermore; in such a play as *The Rivals,* the reader is kept in a state of continual hilarious delight by a profusion of sallies, rejoinders, blunders, contrasts, which seem to exhaust all the resources of the ludicrous. Mrs. Malaprop's ' parts of speech ' will raise the laughter of unborn generations, and the choleric generous old father will never find a more perfect representative than Sir Anthony Absolute. In the evolution of his plots he is less happy; nevertheless, in this respect also, he succeeded admirably in *The School for Scandal,* which is by common consent regarded as the most perfect of his plays, and is still an established favourite in our theatres.

Learning, 1745–1800 :—Porson, Lowth, Pococke.

72. The progress of classical and oriental learning owed little to England during this period. The one great name that occurs (Edward Gibbon) will be mentioned when we come to speak of the historians. Sloth and ease reigned at the Universities; and those great foundations, which in the hands of monks and churchmen in former times had never wholly ceased to minister to learning and philosophy, were now the mere haunts of port-drinking fellows, and lazy, mercenary tutors.[1] **Porson,** the delicacy of whose Greek scholarship almost amounted to a sense, and who admirably edited several of the plays of Euripides,—Bishop **Lowth,** author of the *Prælectiones* on Hebrew Poetry, and of a translation of Isaias,—and **Pococke,** the Arabic scholar—are the only learned writers whose works are still of value.

Prose Fiction, 1745–1800 :—Richardson, Fielding, Smollett, Sterne, Goldsmith ; Miss Burney, Mrs. Radcliffe.

73. Favoured, in the manner before explained, by the continued stability of society, the taste for novels grew from year

---

[1] See Gibbon's *Memoirs.*

to year, and was gratified during this period by an abundant
supply of fiction. Richardson, Fielding, Smollett, and Sterne,
worked on at the mine which Defoe had opened. **Richardson**,
who was brought up as a printer, produced his first novel, *Pamela*, in 1740. A natural and almost accidental train of circumstances led to his writing. He had agreed to compose a
collection of specimen letters—a polite letter-writer, in fact—
for two booksellers; and it occurred to him, while engaged in
this task, that the work would be greatly enlivened if the letters
were connected by a thread of narrative. The bookseller applauded
the notion, and he accordingly worked up the true story of a
young woman—the Pamela of the novel—which had come to his
knowledge a few years before. **Henry Fielding**, sprung from
a younger branch of the noble house of Denbigh, wrote his first
novel—*Joseph Andrews*—in 1742, to turn *Pamela* into ridicule.
Richardson's masterpieces, *Clarissa Harlowe* and *Sir Charles
Grandison*, appeared successively in 1748 and 1753; Fielding's
Tom Jones and *Amelia* in 1749 and 1751. **Smollett**, a Scotchman,
wrote, between 1748 and 1771, a number of coarse clever novels
upon the same general plan as those of his English contemporaries; that is, on the plan of 'holding the mirror up to Nature,'
and showing to the age its own likeness without flattery or disguise. The best are *Roderick Random* and *Humphrey Clinker*.

74. In **Sterne**, humour is carried to its farthest point. His
novel of *Tristram Shandy* is like no other novel ever written:
it has no interest of plot or of incident; its merit and value lie,
partly in the humour with which the characters are drawn and
contrasted, partly in that other kind of humour which displays
itself in unexpected transitions and curious trains of thought.
The first two volumes of *Tristram Shandy* appeared in 1759.
The *Sentimental Journey*, being a narrative of a tour in France,
in which the author assumes credit for the utmost delicacy of
sentiment, and the most exquisite refinement of sensibility, was
published shortly before his death in 1768. The character and
life of Sterne have been admirably portrayed by Thackeray, in
his Lectures on the English Humourists.

75. **Johnson's** tale of *Rasselas, Prince of Abyssinia*, appeared
in 1759. In Lord Brougham's *Life of Voltaire*, Johnson is
reported to have said that, had he seen Voltaire's *Candide*,
which appeared shortly before, he should not have written
Rasselas, because both works travel nearly over the same ground.
Nothing, however, can be more different than the tone and
spirit of the tales. Each writer rejects the optimism of Leibnitz,
and pictures a world full of evil and misery; but the Frenchman
founds on this common basis his sneers at religion and at the

doctrine of an overruling Providence, while the Englishman represents the darkest corners of the present life as irradiated by a compensating faith in immortality, which alone can explain their existence.

76. **Goldsmith's** *Vicar of Wakefield*, the book which, by its picturesque presentation of the manners and feelings of simple people, first led Goethe to turn with interest to the study of English literature, was published in 1766. The *Man of Feeling*, by **Henry Mackenzie**, appeared in 1771. Its author, who wrote it while under the potent spell of Sterne's humour and the attraction of Johnson's style, lived far on into the nineteenth century, and learned to feel and confess the superior power of the author of Waverley. The *Man of the World* and *Julia de Roubigné* are later works by the same hand. **Frances Burney** created a sensation by her novel of *Evelina*, published in 1778, 'the best work of fiction that had appeared since the death of Smollett.'[1] It was followed by *Cecilia* (1782), and—at a long interval, both of time and merit—by *Camilla*, in 1796.

77. Between the works just mentioned and the writings of **Godwin**, there is a gulf interposed, such as marks the transition from one epoch of world-history to another. Instead of the moralizing, the sketches of manners, and delineations of character, on which the novelists of this age had till then employed their powers, we meet with impassioned or argumentative attacks upon society itself, as if it were so fatally disordered as to require reconstruction from top to bottom. The design of *Caleb Williams*, published in 1794, is to represent English society as so iniquitously constituted as to enable a man of wealth and position to trample with impunity upon the rights of his inferiors, and, though himself a criminal of the darkest dye, to brave the accusations of his poor and unfriended opponent, and succeed in fixing upon him, though innocent, the brand of guilt. Besides *Caleb Williams*, Godwin wrote the strange romance of *St. Leon*, the hero of which has found the *elixir vitæ*, and describes the descent of his undecaying life from century to century. About the close of the period, Mrs. **Radcliffe** wrote the *Mysteries of Udolpho*, and the *Romance of the Forest*—two thrilling romances of the Kotzebue school, in which stirring and terrible events succeed each other so rapidly, that the reader is, or ought to be, kept in a whirl of horror and excitement from the beginning to the end. **Horace Walpole's** *Castle of Otranto* was meant as a satire upon novels of this class; though, as he relates with great enjoyment, numberless simple-minded novel-readers took it for a serious production of the romantic school.

[1] Macaulay's *Essays*.

Oratory, 1745–1800 :—Chatham, Burke, Sheridan, &c.

78. This is the great age of English eloquence. Perhaps no country in the world ever possessed at one time such a group of orators as that whose voices were heard in Parliament and in Westminster Hall during these fifty years. Chatham, Burke, Fox, Erskine, Pitt, Sheridan, and Grattan! It seemed as if the country could not bring to maturity two kinds of imaginative genius at once;—the age of the great poets—of Milton, Dryden, and Pope—passes away before the age of the great orators begins. Our limits will only permit us to advert to a few celebrated orations. Everyone has heard of the last speech of the great Lord Chatham, in April 1778, 'the expiring tones of that mighty voice when he protested against the dismemberment of this ancient monarchy, and prayed that if England must fall, she might fall with honour.'[1] The eloquence of **Burke**—

> Who, too deep for his hearers, still went on refining,
> And thought of convincing when they thought of dining[2]—

though it often flew over the heads of those to whom it was addressed, was to be the admiration and delight of unborn generations. The speech on the conciliation of America (1775), that addressed to the electors of Bristol (1780),[3] that on the Nabob of Arcot's debts (1785), and those delivered on the impeachment of Warren Hastings (1788), may be considered his greatest efforts. Upon a subject connected with, and leading to, this impeachment—the conduct of Warren Hastings to the Begums of Oude—Sheridan delivered, in 1787, a speech which was unfortunately not reported, but which appears to have made a more profound and permanent impression upon the hearers than any speech recorded in the annals of Parliament. 'Mr. Windham, twenty years later, said that the speech deserved all its fame, and was, in spite of some faults of taste, such as were seldom wanting either in the literary or the parliamentary performances of Sheridan, the finest that had been delivered within the memory of man.'[4] Grattan during many years was the foremost among a number of distinguished orators who sat in the Irish parliament ; and his fiery eloquence, exerted at a period when England lay weakened and humiliated by her failure in America, extorted for that body, in 1782, the concession of legislative independence. Pitt's speech on the

[1] Arnold's *Roman History*, vol. i.　　[2] From Goldsmith's 'Retaliation.'
[3] See Crit. Sect. ch. II. § 14.
[4] Macaulay's *Essays* ; article, 'Warren Hastings.'

India Bill in 1784, explaining and defending his proposal of the system of double government, which has been lately (1858) superseded, as well as his speeches on the Slave Trade and the Catholic Relief Bill, though not exactly eloquent, should be read as embodying the views of a great practical statesman upon subjects of deep and permanent interest. Erskine was a cadet of a noble but needy family in Scotland. He crossed the Border early in life, raised himself by his remarkable powers as an advocate to the position of Lord Chancellor, and died on his way back to his native country, in his seventy-third year.

Pamphlets, Miscellanies, 1745-1800 :—Junius, Burke, Johnson, Hawkesworth.

79. The famous *Letters of Junius*, addressed to the *Public Advertiser*, extend over the period from the 21st January 1769, to the 21st January 1772. Under his impenetrable mask, the writer first attacks the different members of the ministry of the Duke of Grafton, to whom, as premier, eleven of the letters are addressed, in which the life and character, both public and private, of the minister are exposed with keen and merciless satire. The thirty-fifth letter is addressed to the King, and concludes with the well-known daring words, ' The prince, who imitates their [the Stuarts'] conduct, should be warned by their example; and while he plumes himself upon the security of his title to the crown, should remember that, as it was acquired by one revolution, it may be lost by another.' The mystery about the authorship, which volumes have been written to elucidate, has without doubt contributed to the fame of the Letters. The opinions, however, of the best judges have been of late years converging to a settled belief, that Sir **Philip Francis**, a leading opposition member in the House of Commons, was Junius; and that no other person could have been.

80. Johnson is the author of four pamphlets, all on the Tory side in politics. He was often taunted with writing in favour of the reigning dynasty, by which he had been pensioned, while his real sympathies lay with the house of Stuart. But while his feelings were Jacobite, commonsense induced him to put up with the reigning family. He said, that if holding up his little finger would have given the victory at Culloden to Prince Charles Edward, he was not sure that he would have held it up. And he jokingly told Boswell, that ' the pleasures of cursing the House of Hanover, and drinking King James's health, were amply overbalanced by three hundred pounds a

year.' The *False Alarm* appeared in 1770;—the *Thoughts on the late Transactions respecting the Falkland Islands* (in which there is a well-known invective against Junius) in the following year. The *Patriot* came out in 1774, and *Taxation no Tyranny* in 1775. This last pamphlet was written at the desire of the incapable and obstinate ministry of Lord North, as a reply to the Resolutions and Address of the American Congress. This tirade against brave men for defending their liberties in the style of their English forefathers, shows how mischievously a great mind may be blinded by the indulgence of unexamined prejudices.

81. The longer political writings of **Burke** we shall consider as contributions to political science, and treat under the head of philosophy. The remaining treatises may be divided into four classes,—as relating, 1. to general home politics, 2. to colonial affairs, 3. to French and foreign affairs, 4. to the position and claims of the Irish Catholics. Among the tracts of the first class, the *Sketch of a Negro Code* (1792), an attempt to mediate between the planters and the abolitionists, by proposing to place the slave trade under stringent regulations, and concurrently to raise the condition of the negroes in the West Indies by a series of humane measures, borrowed mostly from the Spanish code, deserves special mention for its far-sighted wisdom. His tracts on American affairs were, like his speeches, on the side of conciliation and concession. Upon the subject of the French Revolution he felt so keenly, that his dislike of the policy deepened into estrangement from the persons of its English sympathizers. He broke with his old friend Fox, and refused to see him even when lying on the bed of mortal sickness. The last of the four letters *On a Regicide Peace* is dated in 1797, the year of his death, and the MS. was found unfinished, as if the composition had been arrested only by physical inability to proceed. Against the penal laws then weighing upon the Irish Catholics, he spoke and wrote with a generous pertinacity. The memory of his mother had perhaps as much to do with this as the native enlightenment and capacity of his mind. His writings on this question, in its various aspects, extend over more than thirty years of his life, from 1766 to 1797. His last *Letter on the Affairs of Ireland* was written but a few months before his death. He avows that he has not 'power enough of mind or body to bring out his sentiments with their natural force,' but adds—'I do not wish to have it concealed that I am of the same opinion to my last breath which I entertained when my faculties were at the best.'

82. The commencement of the *Rambler* in March 1750, marked an attempt on the part of **Johnson** to revive the

periodical miscellany, which had sunk into disrepute since the death of Addison. Of all the papers in the *Rambler*, from the commencement to the concluding number, dated 2nd March 1752, only three were not from the pen of Johnson. Although many single papers were admirable, the miscellany was pervaded by a certain cumbrousness and monotony, which prevented it from obtaining a popularity comparable to that of the *Spectator.* The *Adventurer* was commenced by Dr. **Hawkesworth** in 1753. In that and the following year Johnson furnished a few articles for it, signed with the letter T. The *Idler*, which was even less successful than the *Rambler*, was carried on during two years, from April 1758 to April 1760. All but twelve of the hundred and three articles were written by Johnson. For many years afterwards this style of writing remained unattempted.

Historians, 1745–1800 :—Hume, Robertson, Gibbon, Russell, Mitford, Warton. Biographers—Boswell, &c.

83. The best, or at any rate the best known, historical compositions in our literature, date from this period. The Scottish philosopher **David Hume**, availing himself of the materials which had been collected by Carte, the author of the *Life of Ormond*, published, between the years 1754 and 1762, his *History of England*. The reigns of the Stuarts were the first portion published; in the treatment of which his anti-puritanic tone much offended the Whig party, and for some years interfered with the circulation of the book. Johnson was probably right when he said that 'Hume would never have written a history had not Voltaire written one before him.' For the *Siècle de Louis XIV.* appeared before 1753, and the influence of the *Essai sur les Mœurs* is clearly traceable in Hume's later volumes. **William Robertson**—a Scottish Presbyterian minister, who rose to be Principal of the University of Edinburgh—wrote his *History of Scotland during the Reigns of Queen Mary and King James VI.* in 1759. In 1769 appeared his *History of the Emperor Charles V.*, and in 1777 his *History of America.* As his first work had procured for Dr. Robertson a brilliant reputation in his own country, so his histories of Charles V. and of America extended his fame to foreign lands. The former was translated by M. Suard in France; the latter, after receiving the warm approbation of the Royal Academy of History at Madrid, was about to be translated into Spanish, when the government, not wishing their American administration to be brought under discussion, interfered with a prohibition.

84. **Edward Gibbon**, who was descended from an ancient family in Kent, was born in 1737. While at Oxford, he became a Catholic from reading the works of Parsons and Bossuet. His father immediately sent him to Lausanne, to be under the care of a Calvinist minister, whose prudent management, seconded as it was by the absence of all opposing influences, in a few months effected his reconversion to Protestantism. For the rest of his life he was a 'philosopher,' as the eighteenth century understood the term; in other words, a disbeliever in revealed religion. Concerning the origin of his celebrated work, he says:—'It was at Rome, on the 15th October, 1764, as I sat musing amidst the ruins of the Capitol, while the bare-footed friars were singing vespers in the Temple of Jupiter, that the idea of writing the decline and fall of the city first started to my mind. But my original plan was circumscribed to the decay of the city rather than of the empire; and . . . some years elapsed . . . before I was seriously engaged in the execution of that laborious work.'[1] The several volumes of the History appeared between 1776 and 1787. The work was translated into several languages, and Gibbon obtained by European consent a place among the historians of the first rank.[2]

85. Among the minor historians of the period, the chief were **Goldsmith**, the author of short popular histories of Greece, Rome, and England; **Russell**, whose *History of Modern Europe* appeared between 1779 and 1784, and has been continued by Coote and others down to our own times; and **Mitford**, in whose *History of Greece*, the first volume of which was published in 1784, the Tory sentiments of the author find a vent in the continual disparagement of the Athenian democracy. **Thomas Warton's** *History of English Poetry*, a work of great learning and to this day of unimpaired authority, was published between 1774 and 1781. It comes down to the age of Elizabeth. If all her Professors of Poetry had so well repaid her patronage, the literary reputation of Oxford would have been more considerable than it is.

Among works subsidiary to history, the chief were—in Biography, Johnson's *Lives of the Poets* (1781), a dull *Life of Pope* by Ruffhead, Hume's *Autobiography*, edited by Adam Smith (1777), and **Boswell's** *Life of Johnson* (1791). The records of seafaring enterprise were enriched by the *Voyages* of the great Captain Cook (1773–1784), of Byron, and Vancouver.

---

[1] Memoirs, p. 198.   [1] See Crit. Sect. ch. II. § 25.

Theology, 1700–1800 :—the Deists; Toland, Collins, and others; answers of Bentley, Berkeley, Butler, and Warburton; Methodism, Middleton, Challoner.

86. The English theological literature of this century includes some remarkable works. On account of its celebrity rather than its merit, a few words may be given to the sermon of Dr. **Sacheverell** (1709), which overturned the Whig ministry. It was entitled 'The Perils of False Brethren.' It is a full-mouthed, voluble, roaring production; one long 'damnatory clause' from the beginning to the end; logic it spurns, yet has a certain weight, as proceeding from a solid and imperious, no less than passionate nature. Godolphin (whom he compares to Volpone in Ben Jonson's play of *The Fox*), the dissenters, and the Whig party in general, are bitterly assailed and denounced.

A series of open or covert attacks upon Christianity, proceeding from the school of writers known as the English Deists, began to appear about the beginning of the century. **Toland** led the way with his *Christianity not Mysterious*, in 1702; and the series was closed by Bolingbroke's posthumous works, published in 1752, by which time the temper of the public mind was so much altered that Bolingbroke's scoffs at religion hardly aroused any other feelings but those of impatience and indignation. Collins, Tindal, Chubb, Wollaston, and others, took part in the anti-christian enterprise. In order to reply to them, the Protestant divines were compelled to take different ground from that which their predecessors had chosen in the two previous centuries. Hooker, Andrewes, Laud, Taylor, and the rest of the High Church school, had based the obligation of religious belief to a large extent upon Church authority. But their opponents had replied, that if that principle were admitted, it was impossible to justify the separation from Rome. The Puritans of the old school had set up the Scriptures, as constituting by themselves an infallible religious oracle. But the notorious, important, and interminable differences of interpretation which divided the Biblical party, had discredited this method of appeal. The Quakers and other ultra-Puritans, discarding both Church authority and the letter of Scripture, had imagined that they had found, in a certain inward spiritual illumination residing in the souls of believers, the unerring religious guide which all men desired. But the monstrous profaneness and extravagance to which this doctrine of the inward light had often conducted its adherents, had brought this expedient also into discredit. The only course left for the divines was to found the duty of accepting Christianity upon the dictates of common sense and reason. The Deists urged that the Christian doctrines were irrational; the divines met them on their own ground, and contended that, on the contrary, revelation was in itself so antecedently probable, and was supported by so many solid proofs, that it was but the part of prudence and good sense to accept it. The *reasonableness* of Christianity—the *evidences* for Christianity—the *proofs* of revelation—such was the tenor of all their replies. It has well been called a rationalizing age—Seculum Rationalisticum.

87. Among the crowd of publications issued by the Christian apologists, there are three or four which have obtained a permanent place in general literature. The first is **Bentley's** *Phileleutherus Lipsiensis* (1713), written in answer to **Collins'** *Discourse on Free Thinking*. This is a short and masterly tract, in which the great Aristarch proved, with reference to some cavilling objections which Collins had derived from the variety of readings in the manuscripts, that the text of the New Testament was on the whole in a better and sounder state than that of any of the Greek classical authors.

88. The second is Bishop **Berkeley's** *Alciphron*, published in 1732. This treatise is singularly delightful reading. The beauty of the language, the ease and artless graces of the style, the lucidity of the reasoning, the fairness shown to the other side (for Berkeley always treats his opponents like a gentleman, and gives them credit for sincerity, not with supercilious and censorious arrogance, like such writers as Bishop Warburton), are among its many excellences. In form it is a dialogue, carried on between Dion, Euphranor, and Crito, the defenders of the Christian doctrine and the principles of morals, and Alciphron and Lysicles, the representatives of free-thinking, or, as Euphranor names them in imitation of Cicero, 'minute philosophers.' Alciphron frankly avows that the progress of free inquiry has led him to disbelieve in the existence of God, and the reality of moral distinctions; he is, however, gradually driven from position after position by the ingenious questionings, *Socratico more*, of Euphranor and Crito, and, after a long and stubborn contest, allows himself to be vanquished by the force of truth.

89. The third is the *Analogy of Religion, both Natural and Revealed, to the Constitution and Course of Nature* (1736), by Bishop **Butler**. Of this profound and difficult piece of argumentation, the exact force and bearing of which can only be mastered by close and continuous study, some notion as to the general scope can be derived from the summary, found near the

conclusion, of the principal objections against religion to which answers have been attempted in the book. The first of these objections is taken from the tardiness and gradual elaboration of the plan of salvation; to which it is answered that such also is the rule in nature, gradual change—'continuity,' as we now call it—being distinctive of the evolution of God's cosmical plan. The second stumbles at the appointment of a Mediator; to which the consideration is opposed, how God does in point of fact, from day to day, appoint others as the instruments of His mercies to us. The third proceeds from those who are stag- gered by the doctrine of redemption, and suggests that reforma- tion is the natural and reasonable remedy for moral delinquency; to which it is answered, among other things, that even the heathen instinct told them that this was insufficient, and led them to the remedy of sacrifice. The fourth is taken from the light of Christianity not being universal, nor its evidence so strong as might possibly have been given us; its force is weak- ened or rebutted, by observing, first, how God dispenses His ordinary gifts in such great variety, both of degrees and kinds, amongst creatures of the same species, and even to the same individuals at different times; secondly, how 'the evidence upon which we are naturally appointed to act in common matters, throughout a very great part of life, is doubtful in a high degree.' 'Probability,' says Butler in another place, 'is the guide of life.'

As against the Deists, the controversy was now decided. It was abundantly proved that the fact of a revelation was, if not demonstrable, yet so exceedingly probable that no prudent mind could reject it, and that the Christian ethics were not incon- sistent with, but a continuation and expansion of, natural mo- rality. Deism accordingly fell into disrepute in England about the middle of the century. But in France the works of some of the English Deists became known through the translations of Diderot and the Encyclopædists, and doubtless cooperated with those of Voltaire in causing the outburst of irreligion which followed the Revolution of 1789.

90. One more of these apologetic works must be mentioned, the *Divine Legation of Moses*, by Bishop **Warburton** (1743). This writer, known for his arrogant temper, to whom Mallet addressed a pamphlet inscribed 'To the most Impudent Man alive,' had considerable intellectual gifts. His friendship with Pope, whose *Essay on Man* he defended against the censures of Crousaz, first brought him into notice. The favour of Queen Caroline, whose discerning eye real merit or genius seldom es- caped, raised him to the episcopal bench. The full title of the

controversial work above mentioned is, 'The Divine Legation of Moses demonstrated on the Principles of a Religious Deist from the Omission of the Doctrine of a Future State of Reward and Punishment in the Jewish Dispensation.' The introduction is in the form of a 'Dedication to the Free-Thinkers,' in which, while protesting against the buffoonery, scurrility, and other unfair arts which the anti-Christian writers employed in controversy, Warburton carefully guards himself from the supposition of being hostile to the freedom of the press. 'No generous and sincere advocate of religion,' he says, 'would desire an adversary whom the laws had before disarmed.' [1]

91. The rise of Methodism dates from about 1730. It was a reaction against the coldness and dryness of the current Protestant theology, which has been described as 'polished as marble, but also as lifeless and cold.' With its multiplied 'proofs' and 'evidences,' and appeals to reason, it had failed to make Christianity better known or more loved by its generation; its authors are constantly bewailing the inefficacy of their own arguments, and the increasing corruption of the age. Methodism appealed to the heart, thereby to awaken the conscience and influence the will; and this is the secret of its astonishing success. It originated in the prayer-meetings of a few devoutly disposed young men at Oxford, whom Wesley joined, and among whom he at once became the leading spirit. He was himself much influenced by Count Zinzendorf, the founder of Moravianism; but his large and sagacious mind refused to entangle itself in mysticism; and, after a curious debate, they parted, and each went his own way. After fruitlessly endeavouring for many years to accommodate the new movement to the forms of the Establishment, Wesley organized an independent system of ministerial work and government for the sect which he had called into existence. After the middle of the century multitudes of human beings commenced to crowd around the newly-opened manufacturing and mining centres in the northern counties. Neither they nor their employers took much thought about their religious concerns. Hampered by their legal status, and traditionally suspicious of anything approaching to enthusiasm, the clergy of the Established Church neglected this new demand on their charity;—and miners and factory hands would have grown up as pagans in a Christian land, had not the Wesleyan irregulars flung themselves into the breach, and endeavoured to bring the Gospel, according to their understanding

---

[1] The materials of the above sketch are partly taken from an able paper by Mr. Pattison in the volume of *Essays and Reviews.*

of it, within the reach of these untended flocks. The movement
obtained a vast extension, and has of course a literature to
represent it; but from its sectarian position the literature of
Methodism is, to use an American phrase, *sectional* merely; it
possesses no permanent or general interest. Wesley himself,
and perhaps Fletcher of Madeley, are the only exceptions.

92. Conyers Middleton wrote in 1729 his *Letter from Rome,*
in which he attempted to derive all the ceremonies of the Roman
ritual from the Pagan religion which it had supplanted. An
able reply, *The Catholic Christian Instructed*, was written by
Challoner (1737), to the effect that Middleton's averments were
in part untrue, in part true, but not to the purpose of his argument, since an external resemblance between a Pagan and a
Christian rite was of no importance, provided the inward meaning of the two were different.

The excellent Bishop Challoner was converted in early youth by
the teaching of John Gother. Many years of his life were passed in
the English college at Douai; in 1741 he came over to England to
take charge of the southern district, with the title of Bishop of Debra,
in partibus. He died in his ninetieth year in 1781, saddened by the
ruin and confusion wrought by the No-Popery riots of the previous
year. Among his numerous works, chiefly controversial and devotional,
none has a higher value than the *Memoirs of Missionary Priests* (1742);
it contains numberless details which would otherwise have been lost
respecting the labours and sufferings of Catholic priests employed on
the English mission, from the change of religion down to the bishop's
own time.

Philosophy, 1700–1800:—Berkeley, Hume, Reid, Butler, Hutcheson, Adam Smith, Hartley, Tucker, Priestley, Paley.

93. Nothing more than a meagre outline of the history of
philosophy in this period can here be attempted. Those who
devoted themselves to philosophical studies were numerous;
this, in fact, up to past the middle of the century, was the
fashionable and favourite pursuit with the educated classes.
The most famous work of the greatest poet of the age, Pope's
Essay on Man, is a metaphysico-moral treatise in heroic verse.
The philosophers may be classed under various heads: we have
the Sensational school, founded by Locke, of whom we have
already spoken; the Idealists, represented by Bishop Berkeley;
the Sceptical school, founded by Hume; the Common-sense or
Scotch school, comprising the names of Reid, Brown, and
Dugald Stewart; and the Moralists, represented by Butler,
Smith, and Paley.

There are few philosophers whose personal character it is

more agreeable to contemplate than **George Berkeley**, the Protestant Bishop of Cloyne. He was born in 1684 at Kilevin, in the county of Kilkenny, and educated at Trinity College, Dublin, where he obtained a fellowship in 1707. About four years later he went over to London, where he was received with open arms. There seems to have been something so winning about his personal address, that criticism, when it questioned his positions, forgot its usual bitterness ; and extraordinary natural gifts seemed for once to have aroused no envy in the beholder. Pope, whose satire was so unsparing, ascribes

> To Berkeley every virtue under heaven ;

and Atterbury, after an interview with him, said, 'So much understanding, so much knowledge, so much innocence, and such humility, I did not think had been the portion of any but angels, till I saw this gentleman.'[1]

Of Berkeley's share in the controversy with the Deists, we have already spoken. His *Principles of Human Knowledge*, published in 1710, contains the idealist system for which his name is chiefly remembered.[2] In devising this, his aim was still practical ; he hoped to cut the ground away from beneath the rationalizing assailants of Christianity by proving that the existence of the material universe, the supposed invariable laws of which were set up by the sceptics as inconsistent with revelation, was in itself problematical, since all that we can know directly respecting it is the *ideas* which we form of it, which ideas *may*, after all, be delusive. His other philosophical works are, *Hylas and Philonous, Siris, or Reflections on Tar-water*, and a *Theory of Vision*. Sir James Mackintosh was of opinion that Berkeley's works were beyond dispute the finest models of philosophical style since Cicero.

94. **David Hume**, born at Edinburgh in 1711, was educated for the bar. He was never married. He enjoyed through life perfect health, and was gifted with unflagging spirits, and a cheerful amiable disposition. His passions were not naturally strong, and his sound judgment and good sense enabled him to keep them under control. He died in 1776.

Hume's chief philosophical works are contained in two volumes of Essays and Treatises. The first volume consists of *Essays Moral, Political, and Literary*, in two parts, originally published in 1742 and 1752 respectively. The second volume contains the *Inquiry concerning Human Understanding*,[3] and

---

[1] Mackintosh's *Dissertation on Ethical Philosophy*, article ' Berkeley.'
[2] See Crit. Sect. ch. II. § 45.   [3] *Ibid.* § 46.

other treatises, the whole of which are a revised condensation of the *Treatise on Human Nature*, published in 1738, and spoken of in the advertisement to the Essays and Treatises as a 'juvenile work,' for which the author declined to be responsible in his riper years. In these treatises Hume propounds his theory of universal scepticism. Berkeley had denied matter, or the mysterious somewhat inferred by philosophers to exist beneath the sensible properties of objects; and Hume went yet further, and denied *mind*, the substance in which successive sensations and reflections are supposed to inhere. That we do perceive, and do reflect, is, he admitted, certain; but what that is which perceives and reflects, whether it has any independent being of itself, apart from the series of impressions of which it is the subject, is a point altogether obscure, and on which, he maintained, our faculties have no means of determining. Philosophy was thus placed in a dilemma, and became impossible.[1]

95. The Scotch or common-sense school has received ample justice at the hands of Cousin in his *Cours de Philosophie Moderne*. Its rise dates from the appearance of **Reid's** *Inquiry into the Human Mind upon the Principles of Common Sense*, published in 1764. As a reaction against the idealism of Berkeley and the scepticism of Hume, the rise of the common-sense school was natural enough. It said in effect—'We have a rough general notion of the existence of matter outside and independently of ourselves, of which no subtlety can deprive us; and the instinctive impulse which we feel to put faith in the results of our mental operations is an irrefragable proof, and the best that can be given, of the reasonableness of that faith.'

96. Among the moralists of the period **Butler** holds the highest place. The fact of the existence in the mind of disinterested affections and dispositions, pointing to the good of others, which Hobbes had denied, Butler, in those admirable *Sermons* preached in the Rolls Chapel, has incontrovertibly established. 'In these sermons he has taught truths more capable of being exactly distinguished from the doctrines of his predecessors, more satisfactorily established by him, more comprehensively applied to particulars, more rationally connected with each other, and therefore more worthy the name of discovery, than any with which we are acquainted; if we ought not, with some hesitation, to accept the first steps of the Grecian philosophers towards a "Theory of Morals." '[2] **Hutcheson,** an Irishman, author of an *Inquiry into Beauty and Virtue* and other

[1] See Lewes's *History of Philosophy*.
[2] Mackintosh's *Dissertation*, p. 191.

works, followed in the same track of thought. Hume's *Inquiry concerning the Principles of Morals* was considered by himself to be the best of his writings ; it is, at any rate, the least para-doxical. **Adam Smith**, in his *Theory of Moral Sentiments*, published in 1759, follows Hume in holding the principle of *sympathy* to be the chief source of our moral feelings and judg-ments. **Hartley**, in his remarkable book, *Observations on Man* (1749), teaches that the development of the moral faculty within us is mainly effected through the principle of the *association* of ideas, a term first applied in this sense by Locke. **Tucker's** *Light of Nature* is chiefly metaphysical : so far as he touches on morals, he shows a disposition to return to the selfish theory, in opposition to the view of disinterested moral feelings introduced by Butler. **Priestley**, who, brought up as a Calvinist, embraced Unitarian opinions, and sympathized with the French revolution, adopted in his *Illustrations of Philosophical Necessity* the belief as to the inevitable character of human actions which Auguste Comte has extended widely in our own times. In his *Institutes of Natural and Revealed Religion* Priestley's entire system is laid bare. But neither as theologian nor as philosopher will he be remembered so long as for his claim to a place in the temple of Science, in right of his discovery of oxygen. Lastly, **William Paley**, following Tucker, elaborated in his *Moral and Political Philosophy*, published in 1785, his well-known system of Utili-tarianism : ' Virtue,' he said, ' is the doing good to mankind, in obedience to the will of God, and for the sake of everlasting happiness.' Mackintosh remarks that it follows, as a necessary consequence from this proposition, that ' every act which flows from generosity or benevolence is a vice.'

Political Science :—Burke, Godwin, Paine.

97. Hume's political writings, on the Origin of Government, the Protestant succession, the Idea of a Perfect Commonwealth, &c., &c., form a large portion of the two volumes of Essays and Treatises already mentioned. Hume regards political science as a speculative philosopher ; in **Burke**, the knowledge and the tendencies of the philosopher, the jurist, the statesman, and the patriot, appear all united. The fundamental idea of his political philosophy was, that civil liberty was rather prescriptive than theoretic ; that Order implied Progress, and Progress presup-posed Order ; that in a political society the rights of its members were not absolute and unconditional, but strictly relative to, and to be sought 'in conformity with, the existing constitution of that society. These views are put forth in the most masterly

and eloquent manner in his *Reflections on the Revolution in France*, published in 1790.

Among those who supported in this country the political theories of the French Jacobins and Rousseau, the most eminent were **William Godwin** and **Thomas Paine.** The former published his *Inquiry concerning Political Justice* in 1793; the latter was living in America during the war of independence, and, by the publication of his periodical tracts entitled *Common Sense*, contributed not a little to chase away the despondency which was beginning at one time to prevail among the colonists, and to define their position and political aims. The *Rights of Man* appeared in 1792, and the *Age of Reason*, a work conceived in the extremest French freethinking spirit, in 1794.

Political Economy :—Adam Smith ; Criticism :—Burke, Reynolds, Walpole.

98. The science of Political Economy was, if not invented, at least enlarged, simplified, and systematized by **Adam Smith**, in his celebrated *Inquiry into the Nature and Causes of the Wealth of Nations* (1776). The late rise of this science may be ascribed to several causes;—to the contempt with which the ancient Greek philosophers regarded the whole business of money-getting; to the aversion entertained by the philosophers of later schools for *luxury*, as the great depraver of morals, whence they would be little disposed to analyse the sources of that wealth, the accumulation of which made luxury possible; lastly, to the circumstance, that during the middle ages the clergy were the sole educators of society, and were not likely to undertake the study of phenomena which lay quite out of their track of thought and action. Only when the laity came to be generally educated, and began to reflect intelligently upon the principles and laws involved in the every-day operations of the temporal life, could a science of wealth become possible.

Certain peculiarities about the East Indian trade of the seventeenth century, which consisted chiefly in the exchange of silks and other Indian manufactures for bullion, gave occasion to a number of pamphlets, in which the true principles of commerce were gradually developed. But what was called the 'mercantile system' was long the favourite doctrine both with statesmen and economists, and, indeed, is even yet not quite exploded. By this was meant a system of cunning devices, having for their object, by repressing trade in one direction, and encouraging it in another, to leave the community at the end of each year more plentifully supplied with the precious metals (in which alone wealth was then supposed to consist) than at the end of the preceding. The tradition of over-government, which had come down from the Roman empire, joined to the narrow corporate spirit which had arisen among the great trading cities. of the middle ages, led naturally to such views of national economy. Everyone knows what efforts it has cost in our own days to establish the simple principle of commercial freedom—the right to 'buy in the cheapest and sell in the dearest market.' That this principle has at last prevailed, and that money, in so far as it is not itself a mere commodity, is now regarded, not as wealth, but as the variable representative of wealth, is mainly due to the great work of Adam Smith.

99. **Burke** published in 1756 his celebrated philosophical *Essay* on the origin of our ideas of the *Sublime and Beautiful.* He was then a young man, and had studied philosophy in the sensuous school of Locke; at a later period of his life, he would probably have imported into his essay some of the transcendental ideas which had been brought to light in the interval, and for which his mind presented a towardly and congenial soil. The analysis of those impressions on the mind which raise the emotion. of the sublime or that of the beautiful is carefully and ingeniously made; the logic is generally sound, and if the theory does. not seem to be incontrovertibly established as a whole, the illustrative reasoning employed in support of it is, for the most part, striking, picturesque, and true. The reader may find it difficult. to understand how these two judgments can be mutually consistent; yet it is perfectly intelligible. The theory, for instance, which makes the emotion of the sublime inseparably associated with the sense of the terrible (terror, 'the common stock of everything that is sublime,' part ii. sect. 5), is not quite proved, for he gives magnificence—such as that of the starry heavens—as a source of the sublime, without showing (indeed, it would be difficult to show) that whatever was magnificent was necessarily also terrible. But at the same time he proves, with great ingenuity and completeness, that in a great many cases, when the emotion of the sublime is present, the element of terror is, if not a necessary condition, at any rate a concomitant and influential circumstance. His theory of the beautiful is equally ingenious, but perhaps still more disputable. By beauty, he means (part iii. sect. 1) 'that quality, or those qualities in bodies by which they cause love or some passion similar to it.' He labours at. length to prove that beauty does not depend upon proportion, nor upon fitness for the end designed; but that it does chiefly depend' on the five following properties :—1, smallness; 2, smoothness; 3, gradual variation; 4, delicacy; 5, mild tone in colour. That.

the emotion of beauty is unconnected with the perception of harmony or proportion, is certainly a bold assertion.　However, even if the analysis were ever so accurate and perfect, it might still be maintained that the treatise contains little that is really valuable towards the formation of a sound system of criticism, either in æsthetics or literature.　The reason is briefly this—that the quality which men chiefly look for in works of art and literature is that which is variously named genius, greatness, nobleness, distinction, the ideal, &c.; where this quality is absent, all Burke's formal criteria for testing the presence of the sublime or the beautiful may be complied with, and yet the work will remain intrinsically insignificant.　As applied to nature, the analysis may perhaps be of more value; because the mystery of infinity forms the background to each natural scene; the divine calm of the universe is behind the mountain peak or the rolling surf, and furnishes punctually, and in all cases, that element of nobleness which, in the works of man, is present only in the higher souls.　Hence, there being no fear that we shall ever find Nature, if we understand her, mean, or trivial, or superficial, as we often find the human artist,—we may properly concentrate our attention on the sources of the particular emotions which her scenes excite; and among these particular emotions those of the sublime and beautiful are second to none in power.

100.　**Sir Joshua Reynolds'** excellent *Discourses on Painting*, or rather the first part of them, appeared in 1779.　**Horace Walpole's** *Anecdotes of Painting*, compiled from the unwieldy collections of Virtue on the lives and works of British artists, were published between the years 1761 and 1771.

101.　The *Letters* of **Lord Chesterfield** to his natural son, Philip Stanhope, were published soon after the writer's death in 1773.　Johnson, who never forgave Lord Chesterfield for having treated him, at a time when he stood in great need of patronage, with coldness and neglect, said that the Letters 'taught the morals of a courtesan, and the manners of a dancing-master.' There is more point than truth in this censure.　There might have been some awkwardness in writing about morals, considering to whom the letters were addressed; the subject of conduct, therefore, in regard to great matters, is not touched upon; but good conduct in little things, self-denial in trifles,—in a word, all that constitutes good breeding,—is enforced with much grace and propriety.　Johnson himself was only too vulnerable on this head; Lord Chesterfield describes him in the Letters under the character of a 'respectable Hottentot.'

CHAPTER VI.

MODERN TIMES.

1800–1850.

Ruling Ideas : Theory of the Spontaneous in Poetry.

1. As no summary which our limits would permit us to give-
.of the political events between 1800 and 1850 could add mate-
rially to the student's knowledge respecting a period so recent,
we shall omit here the historical sketch which we prefixed to
each of the two preceding chapters.

At once, from the opening of the nineteenth century, we
meet with originality and with energetic convictions; the deepest problems are sounded with the utmost freedom : decorum
gives place to earnestness; and principles are mutually confronted instead of forms. We speak of England only ; the
change to which we refer set in at an earlier period in France
and Germany. In the main, the chief pervading movement of society may be described as one of reaction against
the ideas of the eighteenth century. Those ideas were, in brief,
Rationalism and Formalism, both in literature and in politics.
Pope, for instance, was a rationalist, and also a formalist, in both
respects. In his views of society, he took the excellence of no
institution for granted—he would not admit that antiquity
in itself constituted a claim to reverence; on the contrary, his
turn of mind disposed him to try all things, old and new, by the
test of their rationality, and to ridicule the multiplicity of forms
and usages—some marking ideas originally irrational, others
whose meaning, once clear and true, had been lost or obscured
through the change of circumstances—which encumbered the public life of his time. Yet he was, at the same time, a political formalist in this sense, that he desired no sweeping changes, and was
quite content that the social system should work on as it was. It
suited him, and that was enough for his somewhat selfish philosophy. Again, in literature he was a rationalist, and also a
formalist ; but here in a good sense. For in literary, as in all
other art, the *form* is of prime importance ; and his destructive
logic, while it crushed bad forms, bound him to develope his.

powers in strict conformity to good ones. Now the reaction
against these ideas was twofold. The conservative reaction,
while it pleaded the claims of prescription, denounced the aberrations of reason, and endeavoured to vindicate or resuscitate
the ideas lying at the base of existing political society, which the
rationalism of the eighteenth century had sapped, rebelled at the
same time against the arbitrary rules with which—not Pope
himself, but his followers—had fettered literature. The liberal,
or revolutionary reaction, while, accepting the destructive rationalism of the eighteenth century, it scouted its political
formalism as weak and inconsistent, joined the conservative
school in rebelling against the reign of the arbitrary and the
formal in literature. This, then, is the point of contact between
Scott and the conservative school on the one hand, and Coleridge, Godwin, Byron, Shelley, and the rest of the revolutionary
school on the other. They were all agreed that literature, and
especially poetry, was becoming a cold, lifeless affair, conforming
to all the rules and proprieties, but divorced from living nature,
and the warm spontaneity of the heart. They imagined that
the extravagant and exclusive admiration of the classical models
had occasioned this mischief; and fixing their eyes on the rude
yet grand beginnings of modern society, which the spectacle of
the feudal ages presented to them, they thought that by imbuing
themselves with the spirit of romance and chivalry—by coming
into moral contact with the robust faith and energetic passions
of a race not yet sophisticated by civilization—they would wake
up within themselves the great original forces of the human
spirit—forces which, once set in motion, would develope congenial literary forms, produced, not by the *labor limœ*, but by a
true inspiration.

Especially in poetry was this the case. To the artificial,
mechanical, didactic school, which Pope's successors had made
intolerable, was now opposed a counter theory of the poetic
function, which we may call the theory of the Spontaneous. As
light flows from the stars, or perfume from flowers—as the
nightingale cannot help singing, nor the bee refrain from making
honey;—so, according to this theory, poetry is the spontaneous
emanation of a musical and beautiful soul. 'The poet is born,
and is not made;' and so is it with his poetry. To pretend to
construct a beautiful poem, is as if one were to try to construct
a tree. Something dead and wooden will be the result in either
case. In a poet, effort is tantamount to condemnation; for it
implies the absence of inspiration. For the same reason, to be
consciously didactic is incompatible with the true poetic gift. For
whatever of great value comes from a poet, is not that which he

wills to say, but that which he cannot help saying—that which some higher power—call it nature or what you will—dictates through his lips as through an oracle.

2. This theory, which certainly had many attractions and contained much truth, led to various important results. It drove away from Helicon many versifiers who had no business there, by depriving them of an audience. The Beatties, Akensides, Youngs, and Darwins, who had inflicted their dullness on the last century, under the impression that it was poetry—a delusion shared by their readers—had to 'pale their ineffectual fire' and decamp, when their soporific productions were confronted with the startling and direct utterances of the disciples of the Spontaneous. On the other hand, the theory produced new mischiefs and generated new mistakes. It did not silence inferior poets; but they were of a different class from what they had been before. It was not now the moralist or the dabbler in philosophy, who, imagining himself to have important information to convey to mankind, and aiming at delighting while he instructed, constructed his epic, or ode, or metrical essay, as the medium of communication. It was rather the man gifted with a fatal facility of rime—with a mind teeming with trivial thoughts and corresponding words—who was misled by the new theory into confounding the rapidity of his conceptions with the spontaneity of genius, and into thinking revision or curtailment of them a kind of treason to the divine afflatus. Such writers generally produced two or three pretty pieces, written at their brightest moments, amidst a miscellaneous heap of 'fugitive poems'—rightly so called—which were good for little or nothing. Upon real genius the theory acted both for good and for evil. Social success, upon which even the best poets of the eighteenth century had set the highest value, was despised by the higher minds of the new school. They loved to commune with Nature and their own souls in solitude, believing that here was the source of true poetic inspiration. The resulting forms were, so far as they went, most beautiful and faultless in art; they were worthy of the profound and beautiful thoughts which they embodied. In diction, rhythm, proportion, melody—in everything, in short, that constitutes beauty of form —no poems ever composed attained to greater perfection than Shelley's *Skylark* or Keats' *Hyperion*. Yet these forms, after all, were not of the highest order. The judgment of many generations has assigned the palm of superiority among poetic forms to the Epos and the Drama; yet in neither of these did the school of poets of which we speak achieve any success of moment. This was probably due to the influence of the theory

which we are considering. The truth is, that no extensive and complex poem was ever composed without large help from that constructive faculty, which it was the object of the theory to depreciate. Even Shakspere, whom it is—or was—the fashion to consider as a wild, irregular poet, writing from impulse, and careless of art, is known to have carefully altered and re-arranged some of his plays—*Hamlet*, for instance—and by so doing to have greatly raised their poetic value. Virgil—Tasso—Dante—must all have expended a great amount of dry intellectual labour upon their respective masterpieces, in order to harmonize the parts and perfect the forms of expression. The bright moments are transitory, even with minds endowed with the highest order of imagination; but by means of this labour—

> tasks in hours of insight willed
> May be in hours of gloom fulfilled.

But this truth was obscured, or but dimly visible, to minds which viewed poetry in the light we have described. Even Scott—true worker though he was—may be held to have produced poems not commensurate with the power that was in him, owing to a want of due pains in construction, attributable to the influence of the prevalent ideas.

Poetry :—Sir Walter Scott, Keats, Shelley, Byron, Crabbe, Coleridge, Southey, Campbell, Wordsworth, Hood, Hogg, &c.

3. The *Life of Scott*, edited by his son-in-law, Lockhart, opens with a remarkable fragment of autobiography. Unhappily, it extends to no more than sixty pages, and conducts us and the writer only to the epoch when, his education being finished, he was about to launch forth into the world; but these few manly and modest pages contain a record of the early years of a great life, which cannot easily be matched in interest. **Walter Scott** was born at Edinburgh on August 15, 1771. His father, descended from the border family or clan of Scott, of which the chieftain was the Duke of Buccleuch, was a writer to the signet, that is, a solicitor belonging to the highest branch of his profession. A lameness in the right leg, first contracted when he was eighteen months old, was the cause of his being sent away to pass in the country many of those years which most boys pass at school. He was fond of reading, and the books which touched his fancy or his feelings made an indelible impression on him. Forty years later he remembered the deep delight with which, at the age of thirteen, stretched under a

plane tree in a garden sloping down to the Tweed at Kelso, he had first read Percy's *Reliques of Ancient Poetry*. 'From this time,' he says, 'the love of natural beauty, more especially when combined with ancient ruins, or the remains of our fathers' piety or splendour, became with me an insatiable passion, which, if circumstances had permitted, I would willingly have gratified by travelling over half the globe.' When he was nineteen years old, his father gave him his choice, whether to adopt his own profession, or to be called to the bar. Scott preferred the latter; he studied the Scotch law with that conscientious and cheerful diligence which distinguished him through life, and began to practise as an advocate in 1792, with fair prospects of professional success. But the bent of nature was too strong for him: literature engrossed more and more of his time and thoughts; and his first publication, in 1796, of translations of *Lenore* and other German poems by Bürger, was soon followed by various contributions to Lewis' *Tales of Wonder*, and by the compilation of the *Minstrelsy of the Scottish Border*, many pieces in which are original, in the year 1802. In 1797 he had married Charlotte Carpenter (or Charpentier), and settled at Lasswade on the Esk, near 'classic Hawthornden.' Foreseeing that he would never succeed at the bar, he obtained in 1799, through the influence of the Duke of Buccleuch, the appointment of Sheriff of Selkirkshire, to which, in 1806, was added a clerkship in the Court of Session, with a salary of 1,300*l.* a year. Both these appointments, which involved magisterial and official duties of a rather burdensome nature, always most punctually and conscientiously discharged, Scott held till within a year before his death.

4. A mind so active and powerful as that of Scott could not remain unaffected by the wild ferment of spirits caused by the breaking out of the French Revolution. But in the main, the foundations of his moral and spiritual being remained unshaken by those tempests. His robust common sense taught him to attend to his own business in preference to devoting himself to the universal interests of mankind; and his love of what was ancient and possessed historic fame—his fondness for local and family traditions—and the predilection which he had for the manners and ideas of the days of chivalry—made the levelling doctrines of the Revolution especially hateful to him. It was otherwise with most of the poets, his contemporaries. Wordsworth, after taking his degree at Cambridge, in 1791—a ceremony for which he showed his contempt by devoting the preceding week to the perusal of *Clarissa Harlowe*—went over to France, and, during a residence there of thirteen months,

formed an intimacy with Beaupuis, a Girondist general, and with many of the Brissotins at Paris. Southey, upon whose smaller brain and livelier temperament the French ideas acted so powerfully as to throw him completely off his balance, wrote the dramatic sketch of *Wat Tyler*—a highly explosive and seditious production—while at Oxford in 1794, and for some time seriously contemplated joining Coleridge in establishing a Pantisocratic community ' on the banks of the Susquehanna.' Coleridge, whose teeming brain produced in later life so many systems, or fragments of systems, was in 1794 full of his wonderful scheme of ' Pantisocracy,' an anticipation of the phalanstères of Fourier, and the Icaria of Cabet. In his ode to *Fire, Famine, and Slaughter*, published in 1798, the Jacobin poet discharges the full vials of his wrath on Mr. Pitt, as the chief opponent of the progress of revolution. The three weird sisters, after expressing their deep obligations to the British statesman, exchange ideas on the subject of the best mode of rewarding him. Famine will gnaw the multitude till they ' seize him and his brood;'—Slaughter will make them ' tear him limb from limb.' But Fire taxes their gratitude with poverty of resource :—

> And is this all that you can do
> For him who did so much for you?
> *   *   *   *   *
> I alone am faithful; I
> Cling to him everlastingly.

In 1804 Scott removed to Ashestiel, a house overlooking the Tweed, near Selkirk, for the more convenient discharge of his magisterial duties. The *locale* is brought picturesquely before us in the introduction to the first canto of *Marmion :*—

> Late, gazing down the steepy linn,
> That hems our little garden in,
> Low in its dark and narrow glen,
> You scarce the rivulet might ken,
> So thick the tangled green-wood grew,
> So feeble trilled the streamlet through :
> Now, murmuring hoarse, and frequent seen
> Through bush and brier, no longer green,
> An angry brook, it sweeps the glade,
> Brawls over rock and wild cascade,
> And, foaming brown with double speed,
> Hurries its waters to the Tweed.

5. Early in 1805 appeared the *Lay of the Last Minstrel*, the first of the series of Scott's romantic poems. Its composition was due to a suggestion of the beautiful Duchess of Buccleuch, who, upon hearing for the first time the wild border legend of

Gilpin Horner, turned to Scott, and said, ' Why not embody it
in a poem ? ' The *Lay* at once obtained a prodigious popularity.[1]
Marmion was published in 1808, and severely criticized soon
after by Jeffrey in the *Edinburgh Review*. Scott's soreness
under the infliction, united to his growing aversion for the
politics of the *Edinburgh*, led him to concentrate all his
energies upon the establishment of a rival review, and the
Quarterly was accordingly set on foot in 1809. The *Lady of the
Lake* appeared in 1810.[2]   Of these three poems Lockhart says :
' The *Lay* is generally considered as the most natural and
original, *Marmion* as the most powerful and splendid, and the
Lady of the Lake as the most interesting, romantic, picturesque,
and graceful.' The *Lay*, however, was not entirely original.
Scott himself, in the preface to the edition of 1829, acknow-
ledges the obligation under which he lay to Coleridge's poem of
Christabel. This striking fragment, he says, ' from the singularly irregular structure of the stanzas, and the liberty which it
allows the author to adapt the sound to the sense, seemed to
me exactly suited to such an extravaganza as I meditated on
the subject of Gilpin Horner. . . . It was in *Christabel*
that I first found [this measure] used in serious poetry, and it
is to Mr. Coleridge that I am bound to make the acknowledgment due from the pupil to his master.'

6. His other romantic poems, the *Vision of Don Roderick,
Rokeby*, the *Lord of the Isles*, the *Bridal of Triermain*, and
Harold the Dauntless—all published between 1811 and 1817—
manifest a progressive declension. Scott was heartily tired of
Harold before it was finished, and worked off the concluding
portion in an agony of impatience and dissatisfaction. When
asked some years later why he had given up writing poetry,
he simply said, ' Because Byron *bet* me.' Byron had returned
from his long ramble over the coasts and islands of the Mediterranean in 1811, and in the course of the five following years
he published his Oriental Tales—the *Bride of Abydos*, the
Giaour, the *Siege of Corinth*, the *Corsair*,[3] *Lara*, and *Parisina*,
which, by their highly coloured scenes and impassioned sentiment, made Scott's poetry appear by comparison tame and pale.
Writing to the Countess Purgstall in 1821, he says : ' In truth,
I have given up poetry ; . . . besides, I felt the prudence of
giving way before the more forcible and powerful genius of
Byron ; ' and would, moreover, he adds, hesitate ' to exhibit in
my own person the sublime attitude of the dying gladiator ; '
alluding to the well-known passage in *Childe Harold*.

---

[1] See Crit. Sect. ch. I. §§ 26, 54.   [2] *Ibid*, § 27.   [3] *Ibid*, § 28.

B B 2

7. But in 1814 Scott struck out a new path, in which neither Byron nor any other living man could keep pace with him. Ransacking an old cabinet, he happened one day, in the spring of that year, to lay his hand on an old unfinished MS., containing a fragment of a tale on the rising of the clans in 1745, which he had written some years before, but, feeling dissatisfied with, had put by. He now read it over, and thought that something could be made of it. He finished the tale in six weeks, and published it anonymously, under the title of *Waverley, or a Tale of Sixty Years since.* The impression which it created was prodigious. *Waverley* was soon followed by *Guy Mannering* and the *Antiquary.* Between 1816 and 1826 appeared seventeen other novels from the same practised hand; but it was Scott's humour still to preserve the anonymous; and though many literary men felt all along a moral certainty that the author of *Waverley* was, and could be, no other than the author of *Marmion,* and Mr. Adolphus wrote in 1820 an extremely ingenious pamphlet,[1] establishing the identity of the two almost to demonstration, yet the public had been so mystified, that it was not till the occasion of a public dinner at Edinburgh in 1827, when Scott made a formal avowal of his responsibility as the author of the entire series,[2] that all uncertainty was removed.

The noble and generous nature of Scott nowhere appears more conspicuously than in the history of his relations with the other eminent poets of his time. Byron, stung by the unsparing criticisms to which Jeffrey subjected his youthful effusions[3] in the *Edinburgh Review,* had replied by his *English Bards and Scotch Reviewers,*[4] in which, including Scott among the poets of the Lake school, he had made him the object of a petulant and unfounded invective. Scott alludes to this attack from the 'young whelp of a lord' in many of his letters, but evidently without the slightest feeling of bitterness. When he visited London in the spring of 1815, and was enthusiastically received by the generation just grown to manhood, which had been fed by his verse, he became acquainted with Byron, and their mutual liking was so strong that the acquaintance in the course of a few weeks almost grew into intimacy. They met for the last time in the autumn of the same year, after Scott's return from Waterloo. Of Coleridge Scott always spoke with interest and admiration, and endeavoured to serve him more than once. With Southey he kept up a pretty constant correspondence, and,

---

[1] *Letters on the Authorship of Waverley.* [2] See Crit. Sect. ch. II. § 4.
[3] The *Hours of Idleness.* [4] *Ibid.* ch. I. § 86.

besides serving him in other ways, procured the laureateship
for him in 1813, after having declined it for himself. Towards
Hogg, the Ettrick shepherd, whose touchy and irritable pride
would have provoked any less generous patron, his kindness
was unvarying and indefatigable.   With Moore he became
acquainted on the occasion of his visit to Ireland in 1825, and
received him at Abbotsford later in the same year.   The Irish
poet made a very favourable impression.   Scott says in his
diary—'There is a manly frankness, with perfect ease and good
breeding, about him, which is delightful.   Not the least touch
of the poet or the pedant. A little, very little man ; . . . but
not insignificant, like Lewis. . . . His countenance is plain
but expressive ;—so .very animated, especially in speaking or
singing, that it is far more interesting than the finest features
could have made it.' Of Scott's intercourse with Sir Humphry
Davy—himself a thorough poet in nature—Lockhart relates an
amusing anecdote :—'Scott, Davy, the biographer, and a rough
Scotch friend of Sir Walter's, named Laidlaw, were together in
Abbotsford in 1820; the two latter being silent and admiring
listeners during the splendid colloquies of the poet and the philosopher. .At last Laidlaw broke out with—"Gude preserve
us ; this is a very superior occasion !   Eh, sirs ! I wonder if
Shakspere and Bacon ever met to screw ilk other up !"'

8. In 1826 occurred the crash of Scott's fortunes, through
the failure of the houses of Constable and Ballantyne.   With
the Ballantynes, who were printers, Scott had been in partnership since 1805, though even his dearest friends were ignorant
of the fact.   How bravely he bore himself in the midst of the
utter ruin which came upon him—how strenuously he applied
his wonderful powers of thought and work to the task of
retrieving his position—how he struggled on till health, faculties, and life itself gave way—these are matters which belong
to the story of the man rather than the author.   The novels
and other works composed between 1826 and his death in 1832,
though they fill very many volumes, manifest a progressive
decline of power.   *Woodstock* was in preparation at the time
when the stroke came ; but there is no falling off in the concluding portion, such as might tell of the agonies of mind through
which the writer was passing.   To *Woodstock*, however, succeeded *Anne of Geierstein*, the *Fair Maid of Perth*, *Count Robert
of Paris*, and *Castle Dangerous*, all of which, or at any rate the
last two, betoken a gradual obscuration and failure of the powers
of imagination and invention.   In 1827 he published a *Life of
Napoleon Bonaparte*. A work on *Demonology and Witchcraft*,
and the *Tales of a Grandfather*, nearly complete the list.   In

the summer of 1832 he visited Italy in a frigate which the Government placed at his disposal, to recruit, if that were possible, the vital energies of a frame which, massive and muscular as was the mould in which nature had cast it, was now undermined and worn out by care and excessive toil. But it was too late; and feeling that the end was near, Scott hurried homewards to breathe his last in his beloved native land. After gradually sinking for two months, he expired at Abbotsford in the midst of his children, on the afternoon of a calm September day in 1832.

We proceed to name the principal works of the other poets, mentioning them in the order of their deaths.

9. **Keats** in his short life contributed many noble compositions to English poetry. His soul thirsted for beauty; his creed —the substance of his religion—was

> That first in beauty should be first in might.[1]

But he was poor, of mean origin, weak in health, scantily befriended: he could not always shut out the external world with its hard unlovely realities; like Mulciber, who

> Dropt from the zenith like a falling star
> On Lemnos, th' Ægean isle,—

he was sometimes driven out of the heaven of imagination, and then he fell at once into the depths of dejection. He died in his twenty-seventh year, and wished his epitaph to be, 'Here lies one whose name was writ in water.' His first work, *Endymion*, and his last, *Hyperion*, may be regarded, the former as an expansion, the latter as an interpretation, of portions of the mythology of Greece. *Hyperion* is a fragment; in it the sublimity of the colossal shapes of the Titans, contrasted with the glorious beauty of the younger gods, bespeaks an imagination worthy of Dante. The *Eve of St. Agnes* belongs to a different vein of ideas; the legends and superstitions of the middle age furnish its subject and its colouring.

10. **Percy Bysshe Shelley,** born in 1792, embraced with fervour, even from his schoolboy days, both the destructive and the constructive ideas of the revolutionary school. He was enthusiastically convinced that the great majority of mankind was, and with trifling exceptions had always been, enslaved by custom, by low material thoughts, by tyranny, and by superstition, and he no less fervently believed in the perfectibility of the individual and of society, as the result of the bursting of

---

[1] From *Hyperion*.

these bonds, and of a philosophical and philanthropic system of education. *Queen Mab*, written when he was eighteen, but never published with his consent, represents the revolutionary fever when at its utmost heat; the court, the camp, the state, the Church, all are incurably corrupt; faith is the clinging curse which poisons the cup of human happiness; when that is torn up by the roots, and all institutions now in being have been abolished, then earth may become the 'reality of heaven;' there will then be free scope for the dominion of love, and reason and passion will desist from their long combat. The metre is rime-less and irregular; but there are bursts of eloquent rushing verse, which for soul-fraught music cannot be surpassed. The *Revolt of Islam* (1817), a poem in twelve cantos, in the Spenserian stanza, though it has most beautiful passages, fails to rivet the interest through insufficiency of plot. It too has for its general drift the utter corruption and rottenness of all that is, involving the necessity, for a nation that desired truly to live, of breaking the chains of faith and custom by which it was held. *Peter Bell the Third* (1819) is a satirical attack upon Wordsworth, who had grown, in Shelley's opinion, far too conservative. To a mind like Shelley's it may be conceived how great was the attraction of the story of Prometheus, the great Titan who re-belled against the gods. To this attraction we owe the drama of *Prometheus Unbound*. His tragedy of *The Cenci*, written at Rome in 1820, shows great dramatic power, but the nature of the story renders it impossible that it should be represented on the stage. The lyrical drama of *Hellas*, written in 1821, was suggested by the efforts which the insurgent Greeks were then making to shake off the yoke of their Turkish tyrants.[1] *Adonais* is a wonderfully beautiful elegy on his friend Keats. The *Masque of Anarchy* (1819) was written upon the news reaching him of what has been called the 'Manchester Massacre.' *Epipsychidion* (1821) is very lovely, but obscure. These are nearly all the longer poems. It is by his shorter pieces that Shelley is best known—*The Cloud, To a Skylark, The Sensitive Plant, Stanzas written in dejection near Naples,* and many others—in which that quality of ethereal and all-transmuting imagination, which especially distinguishes him from other poets, is most conspicuous. Having lived the last four years of his life in Italy, Shelley met with a premature death by drowning, in the Gulf of Spezzia, in the year 1822.

11. **Byron** represents the universal reaction of the nineteenth century against the ideas of the eighteenth. We have seen the

---

[1] See Crit. Sect. ch. I. § 57.

literary reaction exemplified in Scott; but the protest of Byron was more comprehensive, and reached to deeper regions of thought. Moody and misanthropical, he rejected the whole manner of thought of his predecessors; and the scepticism of the eighteenth century suited him as little as its popular belief. Unbelievers of the class of Hume and Gibbon did not *suffer* on account of being without faith; their turn of mind was Epicurean; the world of sense and intelligence furnished them with as much of enjoyment as they required, and they had no quarrel with the social order which secured to them the tranquil possession of their daily pleasures. But Byron had a mind of that daring and impetuous temper which, while it rushes into the path of doubt suggested by cooler heads, presently recoils from the consequences of his own act, and shudders at the moral desolation which scepticism spreads over his life. He proclaimed to the world his misery and despair; and everywhere his words seemed to touch a sympathetic chord throughout the cultivated society of Europe. In *Childe Harold*—a poem of reflection and sentiment, of which the first two cantos were published in 1812 —and also in the dramas of *Manfred* and *Cain*, the peculiar characteristics of Byron's genius are most forcibly represented.

In these poems, and also in those mentioned on a former page[1]—besides the splendour of the diction, the beauty of the versification, the richness of the unaccustomed imagery, and in some cases the interest of the narrative,—a personal element mingled, which must be noticed as having much to do with the hold they obtained upon readers of all nations. Byron was generally supposed to be—

> himself the great sublime he drew.

In Conrad, or in Hugo, or in Lara, the reader thought he could trace the unconquerable pride, the romantic gloom, nay even some portion of the exterior semblance, of the man whom, in spite of protestations, all the world believed to have drawn his own portrait in Childe Harold. The turbulent, haughty, passionate, imperial soul of Byron seemed to breathe forth from the page; and this was, and still is, the secret of its charm.

The *Hours of Idleness*, his first work, written in 1807 when he was but nineteen, are poems truly juvenile, and show little promise of the power and versatility to which his mind afterwards attained. The satire of *English Bards and Scotch Reviewers*, already referred to, was written in 1809. All the leading

---

[1] See p. 371.

poets of the day came under the lash ; but to all, except Southey,
he subsequently made the *amende honorable* in some way or
other.　With the laureate he was never on good terms ; and
their mutual dislike broke out at various times into furious dis-
cord.　Byron could not forgive in Southey, whose opinions in
youth had been so wild and Jacobinical, the intolerant toryism
of his manhood.　Southey's feelings towards Byron seem to have
been a mixture of dread, dislike, and disapproval.　In the preface to the *Vision of Judgment*, a poem on the death of George
III., Southey spoke with great severity of the ' Satanic school '
of authors, and their leading spirit, alluding to Byron's *Don
Juan*, which had recently appeared anonymously.　This led to
a fierce literary warfare, conducted in the columns of newspapers
and in other modes, which Byron would have cut short by a
challenge, but his friends dissuaded him from sending it.　It is
little creditable to Southey that the most acrimonious and insult-
ing of all his letters appeared in the *Courier* a few months after
Byron had died in Missolonghi, a martyr to the cause of the
liberty of Greece.

The *Prisoner of Chillon*, a soliloquy placed in the mouth of
Bonnivard, whom, for his championship of the rights and liberty
of Geneva, the Duke of Savoy imprisoned for six years (1530–
36) in the castle of Chillon on the lake of Geneva, appeared in
1816.　The tale of *Mazeppa*, a Cossack chief distinguished in
the wars of Charles XII., and *Beppo*, belong to the year 1818.
Assailed and censured on every side, when his wife, who had
gone on a visit to her father's house, expressed her intention of
not returning to him, Byron left England in 1816, and saw his
native land no more.　How he lived in Italy it is painful to
think ; so bright and powerful a spirit, degraded by the indulgence of pride and passion to a state of such deep moral defile-
ment !　*Don Juan* appeared, by two or three cantos at a time,
between the years 1819 and 1824.　It was meant, Byron tells
us, ' to be a little quietly facetious upon everything.'　The readiness, fulness, and variety of Byron's mind are placed by this
work in the clearest light; nor less the unbounded audacity of
his temper, and his contempt for all ordinary restraints.　The
metre is the same as the *ottava rima* of the Italian poets.　Byron
died in 1824.

12.　There is no English poet of whom it is more difficult to
express an opinion in few words than of **Crabbe**.　His poems
often raise our admiration; but they also much too frequently
provoke our derision.　For though the powers of his mind were
very considerable, yet they were attended with a kind of æsthetic
blindness, a want of discernment, a deficient sense of what was

fit to be said and what was not; thus he was often led to mix up in the strangest manner what was vulgar and trivial with what was dignified and serious. He was a man of a robust intelligence, but bereft, at least in his ordinary moods, of the finer and more delicate intuitions. The inequality thence arising appears, I think, in all his poems, except 'Sir Eustace Grey.'

His early publications, *The Library, The Village*, and *The Newspaper*, all in heroic verse, date from the eighteenth century. *The Village* was read and revised in the year 1783 by the venerable Samuel Johnson, then in his seventy-fourth year, and owes to him the finest lines that it contains.[1] The collection of poems published in 1807 contained 'The Parish Register,' 'The Hall of Justice,' and 'Sir Eustace Grey.' The first of these is in three parts, which treat of baptisms, marriages, and burials respectively. 'Sir Eustace Grey,' a poem written in stanzas of short lines, is the story, told by himself, of an inmate of a mad-house, whom cruel injuries and the passions of an unbridled youth had bereft of reason, but whom religious meditation and faith have partially restored.

The Borough (1809), an heroic poem in a series of letters, unveils the modes of life of an English seaside town. This must certainly have been the poem which suggested the parody on Crabbe in the *Rejected Addresses*. The author's ridiculous anxiety to avoid giving any offence to any one is scarcely ex-aggerated in the parody, which makes him say, 'My profession has taught me carefully to avoid causing any annoyance, how-ever trivial, to any individual, however foolish or wicked.' The sudden drops into the region of bathos are quite startling, and have a most comic effect. For example :—

> Nor angler we on our wide stream descry,
> But one poor dredger, where his oysters lie :
> He, cold and wet, and driving with the tide,
> Beats his weak arms against his tarry side,
> *Then drains the remnant of diluted gin,*
> To aid the warmth that languishes within.

Such imbecilities are the more provoking, because they alternate with really fine descriptive passages, such as that on the sea and strand which may be found in the same letter. A set of *Tales*, twenty-one in number, treating to a great extent of subjects similar to those handled in the *Borough*, appeared in

[1] ' Must sleepy bards the flattering dream prolong,
Mechanic echoes of the Mantuan song ?
From truth and nature shall we widely stray,
Where Virgil, not where fancy, leads the way ? '

1812. The *Tales of the Hall* (1819) have more of a regular
plan than any other of the author's works. Two brothers, meeting late in life at the hall of their native village, which has been
purchased by the elder brother, relate to each other passages of
their past experience. These tales are composed in a more equable
strain of language and thought than the *Borough*. They never
rise very high certainly; they are prosaic and commonplace in
the flow of narrative; the moralizing is often threadbare : but
they keep clear of the ridiculous lapses which have been noticed
in the former work. The character-painting is the best thing
about them, being sometimes very close and minute, and evinc-
ing much subtlety of appreciation.

13. **Coleridge**, the 'noticeable man with large grey eyes,'[1]
whose equal in original power of genius has rarely appeared
amongst men, published his first volume of poems in 1796. His
project of a Pantisocratic community, to be founded in America,
has been already noticed.[2] Visionary as it was, he received
Southey's announcement of his withdrawal from the scheme with
a tempest of indignation. For some years after his marriage
with the sister of Southey's wife, he supported himself by
writing for the newspapers and other literary work. Feeble
health, and an excessive nervous sensibility, led him, about the
year 1799, to commence the practice of taking opium, and he
was enslaved to this miserable habit for twelve or fourteen
years. Its paralysing effects on the mind and character none
better knew, or has more accurately described, than himself.
What impression he produced at this period upon others may be
gathered from a passage in one of Southey's letters, written in
1804. 'Coleridge,' he says, 'is worse in body than you seem to
believe; but the main cause is the management of himself, or
rather want of management. His mind is in a perpetual St.
Vitus's dance—eternal activity without action. At times, he
feels mortified that he should have done so little, but this feeling
never produces any exertion. I will begin to-morrow, he says,
and thus he has been all his life long letting to-day slip. . . .
Poor fellow ! there is no one thing which gives me so much pain
as the witnessing such a waste of unequalled power.'

Coleridge's poetical works fill three small volumes, and consist of *Juvenile Poems, Sibylline Leaves*, the *Ancient Mariner,
Christabel*, and the plays of *Remorse, Zapolya*, and *Wallenstein*—
the last being a translation of the play of Schiller. Coleridge's
latter years were passed under the roof of Mr. Gillman, a surgeon
at Highgate. One who then sought his society has drawn the

---

[1] Wordsworth.   [2] See p. 370.

following picture of the white-haired sage in the evening of his chequered life :—

Coleridge sat on the brow of Highgate Hill, in those years, looking down on London and its smoke tumult, like a sage escaped from the inanity of life's battle, attracting towards him the thoughts of innumerable brave souls still engaged there. His express contributions to poetry, philosophy, or any specific province of human literature or enlightenment had been small and sadly intermittent; but he had, especially among young inquiring men, a higher than literary, a kind of prophetic or magician, character. . . . A sublime man; who alone in those dark days, had saved his crown of spiritual manhood; escaping from the black materialisms and revolutionary deluges, with 'God, Freedom, and Immortality' still his; a king of men. The practical intellects of the world did not much heed him, or carelessly reckoned him a metaphysical dreamer; but to the rising spirits of the young generation he had this dusky sublime character; and sat there as a kind of *Magus*, girt in mystery and enigma, his Dodona oak-grove (Mr. Gillman's house at Highgate) whispering strange things, uncertain whether oracles or jargon.[1]

Mr. Carlyle goes on to speak of the disappointing and hazy character of Coleridge's conversation, copious and rich as it was, and occasionally running clear into glorious passages of light and beauty. Such, indeed, is the general effect of his life, and of all that he ever did. One takes up the *Biographia Literaria* (1817), imagining that one will at least find some consistent and intelligible account of the time, place, motive, and other circumstances bearing upon the composition of his different works; but there is scarcely anything of the kind. The book possesses an interest of its own, on account of the subtle criticism upon Wordsworth's poetry and poetical principles, which occupies the chief portion of it; but when you have arrived at the end of all introductory matter, and at the point where the biography should commence, the book is done; it is all preliminaries—a solid porch to an air-drawn temple. Coleridge died in 1834.

14. **Southey** left Oxford as a marked man on account of his extreme revolutionary sympathies, and, being unwilling to take orders, and unable, from want of means, to study medicine, was obliged, as he tells us, 'perforce to enter the muster-roll of authors.' The prevailing taste for what was extravagant and romantic, exemplified in Mrs. Radcliffe's novels and Kotzebue's plays, perhaps led him to select a wild Arabian legend as the groundwork of his first considerable poem, *Thalaba the Destroyer*, published in 1801. *Thalaba*, like Shelley's *Queen Mab*, is written in irregular Pindaric strophes without rime. *Madoc*, an epic poem in blank verse, founded on the legend of a

[1] Carlyle's *Life of Sterling.*

voyage made by a Welsh prince to America in the twelfth century, and of his founding a colony there, appeared in 1805 ; and
the *Curse of Kehama*, in which are represented the awful forms.
of the Hindu Pantheon, and the vast and gorgeous imagery of
the Hindu poetry, in 1811. *Roderic, the last of the Goths*
(1814), a long narrative poem in blank verse, celebrates the fall
of the Visigothic monarchy in Spain. The *Vision of Judgment*
(1820), in English hexameters, is a lament over the death of
George III., whom it leaves in the safe enjoyment of Paradise.
A Tale of Paraguay, as it was under Jesuit management, appeared in 1824. Besides these larger works, Southey wrote a
multitude of minor poems. His characteristics as an author are,
indefatigable industry, great skill at manipulating and shaping
his materials, extraordinary facility of expression, and considerable powers of reflection and imagination. Nor can humour be denied him, though he had sometimes an unfortunate way of exhibiting it at the expense of the religious beliefs and practices of
other nations. In 1803 Southey settled at Greta Hall, near
Keswick ; and here the remainder of his life was spent, in the
incessant prosecution of his various literary undertakings. After
the death of his wife, in 1837, he became an altered man. ' So
completely,' he writes, ' was she part of myself, that the separation makes me feel like a different creature. While she was
herself I had no sense of growing old.' After his second marriage in 1839, his mind began gradually to fail, and the lamp of
reason at last went entirely out. In this sad condition he died
in the year 1843.

15. **Thomas Campbell**, though born in Glasgow, was a
Highlander both in blood and nature. His *Pleasures of Hope*
(1799) was certainly the best continuation of the lines of thought
marked out by Pope and the moralists, that had appeared since
the time of Goldsmith. The poem has little plan, as might be
expected from the nature of the subject. It contains a sensational passage concerning slavery, accompanied by the fervent
hope that it may some day be abolished. There are also some fine
lines on fallen Poland, and a masterly sketch of the cheerless
creed of the materialist, which is described in order to be rejected. Some lines occur that are now familiar to every ear ; *e.g.*

> What though my winged hours of bliss have been
> *Like angel-visits, few and far between.*

And,—

> *'Tis distance lends enchantment to the view.*

But the *Pleasures of Hope* is, after all, of the nature of a prize
poem, though a brilliant one. Campbell's genius is most attract-

ive in those poems in which his loving Celtic nature has free play. Such are 'O'Connor's Child,' 'Lochiel's Warning,' 'The Exile of Erin,' and ' Lord Ullin's Daughter ;' in all of which, but especially in the first-named, the tenderness, grace, and passion of the Celtic race shine forth with inexpressible beauty. And the childlike simplicity of love and sorrow,—dwelling on minute circumstances,—homish, clannish, gregarious, unselfish,—not sturdily self-reliant, but yearning towards others, and feeling its own being incomplete without them,—all this, so eminently Celtic in its character, is exhibited in the 'Soldier's Dream.' *Gertrude of Wyoming* (1809), a tale of Pennsylvania, written in the Spenserian stanza, is soft and musical in its versification, but deficient in sustained epic interest. If Campbell had understood his own temperament, which tended to be dreamy and meditative, he would surely not have selected such a dreamy lingering measure as the Spenserian stanza for a *narrative* poem. His martial and patriotic songs, ' Hohenlinden,' 'The Battle of the Baltic,' 'Ye Mariners of England,' are rapid and spirit-stirring, but full of faults of expression. ' The Last Man' is interesting from the nature of the subject : it gives us the soliloquy of the last representative of the human race uttered from among tombs upon the crumbling earth ; but the effort is more ambitious than successful, and many expressions and images are overstrained. Campbell died in 1844.

16. To **Wordsworth**, from his very childhood, life seems to have been a dream of beauty, a continual rapture. Those accesses of intellectual passion, those ardours of intellectual love, which come but seldom to most men, and usually in the maturity of their powers, were to him an habitual experience almost from the cradle. This it was that made him say, ' The child is father of the man ;' this explains such passages as the following in the ode on the ' Intimations of Immortality,' which else might sound like mere mysticism :—

> Not in entire forgetfulness,
> Nor yet in utter nakedness,
> But trailing clouds of glory, do we come
> From God, who is our home :
> Heaven lies about us in our infancy !
> Shades of the prison-house begin to close
> Upon the growing boy,
> But he beholds the light, and whence it flows,
> He sees it in his joy ;
> The youth, who daily farther from the east
> Must travel, still is Nature's priest,
> And by the vision splendid
> Is on his way attended ;

> At length the man perceives it die away,
> And fade into the light of common day.

His whole being was moulded in a singularly perfect balance; the 'sound mind in the sound body' was never more strikingly exemplified than in him. To keen senses acting in a healthy and hardy frame, he joined the warmest moral emotions and the most extended moral sympathies, together with a synthesis of the finest intellectual faculties, crowned by the gift of an imagination the most vivid and the most penetrating. This imagination he himself regarded as the royal faculty, by which he was to achieve whatever it was given him to do, calling it—

> but another name for absolute power
> And clearest insight, amplitude of mind,
> And Reason in her most exalted mood.[1]

Born on the edge of a mountain district, he had been familiar from the first with all that is lovely and all that is awful in the aspects of nature; deep and tender sympathies bound him always to the lot of his fellow-creatures, especially the poor and the simple; unceasing reflection was his delight, and as it were one of the conditions of his existence. It was therefore upon no vacant or sluggish mind that the cry of revolutionary France burst, in her hour of regeneration. He was less shaken than others, because he had already seen in his reveries the possibility of better things for human society than it had yet attained to, better than even the Revolution promised to provide :

> If at the first great outbreak I rejoiced
> Less than might well befit my youth, the cause
> In part lay here, that unto me the events
> Seemed nothing out of nature's certain course,
> A gift that was come rather late than soon.[2]

He visited France immediately after leaving Cambridge in 1792, and remained there above a year. At Orleans he formed an intimacy with an officer of Girondist opinions, who afterwards, as General Beaupuis, fell in battle with the royalists near the Loire :—

> He on his part, accoutred for the worst,
> He perished fighting, in supreme command,
> Upon the borders of the unhappy Loire,
> For liberty, against deluded men,
> His fellow-countrymen ; and yet most blessed
> In this, that he the fate of later times
> Lived not to see, nor what we now behold,
> Who have as ardent hearts as he had then.[3]

---

[1] The *Prelude*, conclusion.   [2] *Ibid.* book ix.   [3] *Ibid.*

With Beaupuis the poet talked over the oppressions of the old *régime*, and speculated hopefully on the new model of a regenerated society, which an uprisen people, whose natural virtues would be now free to exert themselves and find the career which they required, was about to exhibit to the world. Yet even in that hour of elation Wordsworth was saddened by the sight of an untenanted and roofless convent :—

> In spite of those heart-bracing colloquies,
> In spite of real fervour, and of that
> Less genuine and wrought up within myself,
> I could not but bewail a wrong so harsh,
> And for the matin-bell to sound no more
> Grieved, and the twilight taper, and the cross,
> High on the topmost pinnacle.[1]

Compelled to return to England in 1793, he repaired erelong to his beloved mountains, and in the same year produced his first work, containing the 'Evening Walk,' and 'Descriptive Sketches, taken during a pedestrian tour among the Alps,'— poems in which echoes of Pope, Goldsmith, and Crabbe are more apparent than any very decided indications of genius. At this period, England joined in the war against France; and Wordsworth's moral nature—the whole frame of his aspirations and sympathies—received a rude shock. He was even meditating a return to France, and the devotion of all his energies to political action. Perplexed and disappointed, he was in some danger of becoming permanently soured and morose. But from this state his admirable sister, who was now become his constant companion, raised him, and drew him gently towards the true and destined path for his footsteps,—the vocation of a poet :—

> She whispered still that brightness would return ;
> She, in the midst of all, preserved me still
> A poet, made me seek beneath that name,
> And that alone, my office upon earth.[2]

But neither the brother nor the sister had at this time any patrimony. This want, however, was supplied in a singular way, at the very moment when it began to be urgent, by the bequest of a young friend of the name of Calvert, whom Wordsworth had tenderly nursed through the last weeks of a decline. This was in 1794; and the pair, accustomed to the austere simplicity and plain fare of the North, lived contentedly upon this bequest (which did not exceed nine hundred pounds) for eight or nine years. In 1802, when this resource was nearly exhausted, the succession of a new Lord Lonsdale brought with

---

[1] The *Prelude*, book ix.   [2] *Ibid.* book xi.

it the payment of their patrimony, long unjustly withheld. Wordsworth then married, and settled at Grasmere. During this period his poetry, as De Quincey says, was 'trampled upon ;' and he had no other permanent resource for a livelihood. But in 1807 he received from Lord Lonsdale the appointment of distributor of stamps for the counties of Cumberland and Westmoreland, and was set free thenceforward from pecuniary anxieties. Shelley, in his *Peter Bell the Third*, sneers at Wordsworth as a pensioner bought over by the Tories ; but the taunt was false and groundless. Some few persons in England were wise enough to see that Wordsworth's function in this world was to write, and at the same time happy enough to have it in their power to say to him, 'Write, and you shall be fed.' Among these few were Calvert and Lord Lonsdale. It is hard to see how Wordsworth's mental and moral independence was more compromised by accepting an office from the lord lieutenant of his county, than was Shelley's by his deriving his income from landed property, the secure tenure of which depended upon the repression of Jacobinical projects at home and abroad.

17. In 1798 appeared the *Lyrical Ballads*, to which a few pieces were contributed by Coleridge and Southey. Again, in 1800 and 1807, collections of detached poems appeared, and in 1814 was published the *Excursion*. This is the second part of a larger poem which was to have been entitled *The Recluse*, and to have been in three parts. The third part was only planned ; of the first, only one book was ever written. A long poem in fourteen books, called *The Prelude*, written in 1804, was not given to the world till 1850. It contains a history of the growth and workings of the poet's mind, up to 'the point when he was emboldened to hope that his faculties were sufficiently matured for entering upon the arduous labour which he had proposed to himself,' that namely of 'constructing a literary work that might live,' a philosophical poem containing views of man, nature, and society. This great work, the storehouse of his deepest and wisest thoughts, the author himself compared to a Gothic church, the *Prelude* to the ante-chapel of this church, and all his minor poems to 'the little cells, oratories, and sepulchral recesses ordinarily included in such edifices.'

18. Of the general plan of the *Excursion*, I must try to give the outline. In the first book the poet meets the 'Wanderer,' a Scotch pedlar, who, having by hard work earned enough to make him independent of his trade, wanders continually from place to place, feeding his contemplative spirit on the varied physical aspects, or moral themes, which nature and human life supply. The Wanderer conducts him to the remote valley,

where dwells the 'Solitary,' a man who after having lived some years with an adored wife and two children, and then seen them die before his eyes,—having perplexed his brain with a thousand jarring tenets of religion and philosophy,—having hailed with rapture the revolution in France, and groaned over the repression of the manifold activities which it had elicited by the hard hand of military power,—now, in cynical despondency, unsocial and friendless, longs for the hour of death:—

> Such a stream
> Is human life; and so the spirit fares
> In the best quiet to her course allowed;
> And such is mine,—save only for a hope
> That my particular current soon will reach
> The unfathomable gulf, where all is still.

In the fourth book, 'Despondency Corrected,' the Wanderer, with the true eloquence of a noble enthusiasm, endeavours to remove the morbid hopelessness of his friend by unfolding his views of the immense potentiality for good which every human existence, not utterly corrupted, contains within itself; by enlarging on the blessings which, in every age and every land, religious hope, and even, were no better thing obtainable, superstitious reverence, have bestowed upon men: blessings more real than any which modern science—apt to be blind to the higher while keenly conscious of the lower truth—confers on its disciples; lastly, by pointing out the practical courses and methods of discipline which, in his judgment, lead to the perfection of the individual being. The beautiful ideal of human perfection here presented to us differs from that which we find in the pages of the New Testament perhaps only in this, that it implies an *intellectual* activity and culture possible only to the few, and must therefore for ever be unattainable by those unequal and imperfectly balanced characters who constitute, nevertheless, the chief portion of mankind. To such characters Christianity alone opens out the means of reaching the highest grade of perfection compatible with their nature.

In the later books, from the fifth to the ninth inclusive, the chief figure is that of the 'Pastor,' who relates to the personages already introduced numerous anecdotes drawn from the experience of his mountain parish. Among these is the story of 'wonderful Walker,' the good pastor of Seathwaite, in the Vale of Duddon, which parish he held for sixty-six years.

Among Wordsworth's minor poems I will mention, as especially characteristic of his genius, 'Laodamia,' 'Matthew,' the 'Primrose of the Rock,' the 'Solitary Reaper,' the 'Evening

Voluntaries,' the sonnets on the River Duddon, and 'Yarrow Unvisited.'

19. **Moore**, though of humble parentage, was enabled by his own striking talents, and by the self-denying and intelligent exertions of his excellent mother, to receive and profit by the best education that was to be obtained in his native Ireland. He went up to London in 1799 to study for the bar, with little money in his purse, but furnished with an introduction to Lord Moira, and with the manuscript of his translation of *Anacreon*. Through Lord Moira he was presented to the Prince Regent, and permitted to dedicate his translation to him. The work appeared, and of course delighted the gay and jovial circle at Carlton House. Moore thus obtained the requisite start in London society, and his own wit and social tact accomplished the rest. Through Lord Moira's interest he was appointed, in 1803, to the Registrarship of the Bermudas. But he could not long endure the solitude and storms of the 'vexed Bermoothes,' and, leaving his office to be discharged by a deputy, he returned, after a tour in the United States, to England. Some of his prettiest lyrics, *e.g.*, the 'Indian Bark' and the 'Lake of the Dismal Swamp,' are memorials of the American journey. In the poems of *Corruption, Intolerance*, and *The Sceptic*, published in 1808 and 1809, he tried his hand at moral satire, in imitation of Pope. But the *rôle* of a *censor morum* was ill suited to the cheerful, convivial temper of Tom Moore; and, though there are plenty of witty and stinging lines in these satires,[1] they achieved no great success.

He found at all times his most abundant source of inspiration in the thought of his suffering country, whose sorrows he lamented in many a lovely elegy, and whose oppression he denounced in many a noble lyric. Even in that poem which, as a work of art, must be regarded as his masterpiece,—I mean *Lalla Rookh*,—a work in which the reader is transported to the palaces of Delhi and the gardens of Cashmere, Moore himself tells us that he vainly strove, in several abortive attempts, to rise to the height of his own original conception, until the thought struck him of embodying in his poem a sketch of the history of the Ghebers or fire-worshippers of Persia, a persecuted race who, like the Irish, had preserved the faith of their forefathers through centuries of oppression, and whose nationality had never been wholly crushed out by Moslem rule. *Lalla Rookh* (1817) consists of four tales, 'The Veiled Prophet of

---

[1] For instance—

But bees, on flowers alighting, cease their hum ;
So, settling upon places, Whigs grow dumb.

Khorassan,' 'Paradise and the Peri,'[1] 'The Fire-worshippers,' and 'The Light of the Haram.' A slight thread of prose narrative, gracefully and wittily told, connects them, inasmuch as they are all recited by Feramorz, a young poet of Cashmere, for the entertainment of Lalla Rookh, daughter of the Emperor Aurungzebe, while she is journeying from Delhi to Cashmere to wed her affianced lord, the prince of Bucharia. Fadladeen, the chamberlain of the princess's household, criticizes each poem after it has been recited in a very lively and slashing manner. As a political satirist, Moore, on the Liberal side, was quite as cutting and far more copious than Canning, or Frere, or Maginn, on the Tory side. His 'Political Epistles' are of various dates; among them is the far-famed 'Epistle of the Prince Regent to the Duke of York,' in which the 'first gentleman in Europe' is made to say; partly in his own very words :—

> I am proud to declare, I have no predilections;
> And my heart is a sieve, where some scattered affections
> Are just danced about for a moment or two,
> And the *finer* they are, the more sure to run through.

The Fudge Family in Paris (1818), and *Fables for the Holy Alliance* (1819), were designed to stem the tide of reaction, which, after the end of the great war, seemed likely to replace the throne and the altar in their old supremacy. *The Twopenny Post-bag*, a collection of imaginary intercepted letters, put into verse, in one of which there is a playful hit at Walter Scott, who had just published 'Rokeby,' dates from 1813. But all that was highest and purest in Moore's nature is best seen in his *Irish Melodies* (1807–34), in which he appears as the true Tyrtæus of his beloved Ireland. His *Sacred Songs* (1816) are less interesting. In his later years, Moore took to prose writing; compiled the *Life of Sheridan* (1825), and the *Life and Letters of Lord Byron* (1830); and also produced *The Epicurean*, a *History of Ireland*, the *Memoirs of Captain Rock*, and the *Travels of an Irish Gentleman in search of a Religion.* His mind, like Southey's, was gone for several years before his death, which occurred in 1852.

20. **Thomas Hood** was a man of rare powers. Pathos, sensibility, indignation against wrong, enthusiasm for human improvement—all these were his; but the refracting medium of his intelligence was so peculiarly constituted, that he could seldom express his feelings except through witty and humorous forms. However gravely the sentence begins, you know that you will probably have to hold your sides

---

[1] See Crit. Sect., ch. I. § 29.

before it is ended. The following well-known stanza is really a type
of his genius :—

> Mild light, and by degrees, should be the plan
>   To cure the dark and erring mind ;
> But who would rush at a benighted man,
>   *And give him two black eyes for being blind ?*

His first work was *Whims and Oddities*, followed by the *Comic Annual*,
commenced in 1830, and *Up the Rhine* (1838). The wonderful ' Song
of the Shirt ' (1843) was nearly his last effort. He died of a chronic
disease of the lungs in 1845. His works have been published in a
collective form within the last few years.

From the long roll of minor poets, the publication of whose works
falls within the first half of the century, I select a few names.

21. **Hogg**, the ' Ettrick Shepherd,' wrote *The Queen's Wake* (1813),
which, says Mr. Chambers, ' consists of a collection of tales and ballads
supposed to be sung to Mary Queen of Scots by the native bards of
Scotland, assembled at a royal wake at Holyrood.' Mrs. **Hemans** published in] 1828 *Records of Women*, and afterwards *National Lyrics,
Scenes and Hymns of Life*, and other works. Many of her songs are
instinct with genuine feeling, and breathe a thrilling music. Miss
Landon, once so widely known as L. E. L., is the authoress of ' The
Improvisatrice,' ' The Lost Pleiad,' and a multitude of other lyrics now
seldom read. **James** and **Horace Smith** were the authors of the *Rejected Addresses* (1812), a collection of parodies of the style of the
principal living poets. Those on Crabbe, Byron, and Southey, are especially telling. A copious didactic vein is exhibited in the moral
poems of **James Montgomery**, author of *Greenland* (1819), *The Pelican
Island*, and other poems. **Robert Pollok's** *Course of Time* (1827), however feeble and faulty as a poem, was so exactly adapted to the level
of culture in the religious classes of Scotland, that it obtained an extraordinary popularity, having passed through more than twenty
editions. It consists of ten books of blank verse : the subjects handled
are much the same as those met with in Young's *Night Thoughts*.
Kirke White's few poems were for a time made famous through the
publication of his *Remains* by Southey, soon after his death in 1806.
The small posthumous volume of poems by Bishop **Heber** contains,
besides his Oxford prize poem of ' Palestine,' several good hymns and
elegantly turned lyrics.

22. The artist Haydon, complaining of the presumptuous tone of the
art-criticisms volunteered by **Leigh Hunt,** said that he was a man endowed ' with a smattering of everything and mastery of nothing.'
There is much truth in the remark ; this brilliant ' old boy,' the friend
of Shelley and of Byron, could impart neither enough wit to his magazines, nor enough charm to his poems, to make them live. There was
something both of Hood and Lamb in him ; but he seems to have
lacked the power and fibre of the one, the tenderness and profound
humour of the other. Among his poems *A Jar of Honey from Mount
Hybla*, and the *Story of Rimini*, deserve special mention. His various
magazines, the *Examiner*, the *Indicator*, the *Liberal*, &c., were, finan-
cially, all failures ; yet they contain the fruits of much keen observation
and many clever criticisms, all written in a spirit of what is called
advanced Liberalism. The character of Leigh Hunt, as ' Mr. Skimpole,'

was drawn with cruel satire by his protégé Charles Dickens in his story of *Bleak House*. Hunt died in his seventy-sixth year in 1859. His *Autobiography*, published a few months before his death, is a lively and instructive record of the experiences of a struggling life.

THE DRAMA.   1800–1850.

Byron, Sheridan Knowles, Joanna Baillie.

23. During the present century the stage, considered as a field for literary energy, has greatly declined even below the point at which it stood a hundred years ago. Why this is so, it would not be easy to explain; but there is no doubt as to the fact, that the dramas written by men of genius within the last sixty years have generally proved ill-adapted for the stage, while the authors of the successful plays have not been men of genius. The *Doom of Devergoil* and *Auchindrane* by Scott, the tragedy of *Remorse* by Coleridge, that of *The Cenci* by Shelley, Godwin's play of *Antonio*, and Miss Edgeworth's *Comic Dramas*, were all dramatic failures : either they were originally unsuited for the modern stage, or, when produced upon it, obtained little or no success. On the other hand, the *Virginius*, the *Hunchback*, the *Wife*, &c., &c., of Sheridan Knowles, the farces of O'Keefe, and the comedies of Morton and Reynolds, being, it would seem, better adapted to the temper, taste, and capacity of the play-going public than the works of greater men, brought success and popularity to their authors. The *Manfred* of Lord Byron, published as ' a dramatic poem ' (1817), was no more intended for the stage than Goethe's *Faust*, by which it was evidently suggested. Of *Cain*, and *Heaven and Earth*, published as ' mysteries,' the same may be said. On the other hand, the tragedies of *Sardanapalus* and *Marino Faliero* were designed to be acting plays. The plays of Joanna Baillie, intended to be illustrative of the stronger passions of the mind, appeared between 1798 and 1836. Two or three of them only were brought on the stage, and were but coldly received, being deficient in those various and vivid hues of reality which assimilate a drama to the experience of life.

Prose Writers, 1800–1850.

24. We can give only the briefest summary of what has been done in the principal departments of prose writing during this period. In Prose Fiction, besides the Waverley novels, which have been already noticed, must be specified **Jane**

Austen's admirable tales of common life—*Pride and Prejudice*,[1] *Mansfield Park, Northanger Abbey*, &c.—which their beautiful and too short-lived authoress commenced as a sort of protest against the romantic and extravagant nonsense of Mrs. Radcliffe's novels; and **Miss Edgeworth's** hardly less admirable stories of Irish life and character. In Oratory, though this period falls far below that which preceded it, we may name the speeches of Canning, Sheil, O'Connell, and Sir Robert Peel. In political writing and pamphleteering, the chief names are—**William Cobbett**, with his strong sense and English heartiness, author of the *Englishman's Register*—Scott (whose political squib—the *Letters of Malachi Malagrowther*—had the effect of arresting the progress of a measure upon which the ministry had resolved)—Southey—and Sydney Smith. In Journalism, the present period witnessed the growth of a great and vital change, whereby the most influential portion of a newspaper is no longer, as it was in the days of Junius, the columns containing the letters of well-informed correspondents, but the leading articles representing the opinions of the newspaper itself. In prose satire, the inexhaustible yet kindly wit of Sydney Smith has furnished us with some incomparable productions; witness *Peter Plymley's Letters*,[2] his articles on Christianity in Hindostan, and his letter to the *Times* on Pennsylvanian repudiation. In History, we have the Greek histories of Mitford, Thirlwall, and Grote, the unfinished Roman history of Arnold, the English histories of Lingard and Hallam, and the work similarly named (though 'History of the Revolution and of the reign of William III.' would be an exacter title) by Lord Macaulay. Mr. Hallam's *View of the State of Europe during the Middle Ages* (1818) gave a stimulus to historical research, in more than one field which for ages had been, whether arrogantly or ignorantly, overlooked. In Biography—out of a countless array of works—may be particularized the lives of Scott, Wilberforce, and Arnold, compiled respectively by Lockhart, the brothers Archdeacon Wilberforce and the Bishop of Oxford, and Dr. Stanley. As to the other works subsidiary to history—such as accounts of Voyages and Travels —their name is legion; yet perhaps none of their authors has achieved a literary distinction comparable to that which was conferred on Lamartine by his *Voyage en Orient*. In Theology, we have the works of Robert Hall and Rowland Hill, representing the Dissenting and Low Church sections; those of Arnold, Whately, and Hampden, representing what are sometimes

---

[1] See Crit. Sect., ch. II. § 5.   [2] *Ibid.* § 11.

called Broad Church, or Liberal, opinions; those of Froude, Pusey, Davison, Keble, Sewell, &c., representing various sections of the great High Church party; and lastly, on the Catholic side, those of Milner, Dr. Doyle—the incomparable 'J.K.L.'—Wiseman, and Newman. In Philosophy, we have the metaphysical fragments of Coleridge, the ethical philosophy of Bentham, the logic of Whately and Mill, and the political economy of the last-mentioned writers, and also Ricardo and Harriet Martineau. Among the essay-writers must be singled out Charles Lamb, author of the *Essays of Elia*, which appeared in 1823. In other departments of thought and theory, *e.g.*, Criticism, we have the literary criticism of Hazlitt and Thackeray, and the art-criticism of Mr. Ruskin.

CRITICAL SECTION.

CHAPTER I.

POETRY.

Definition of Literature—Classification of Poetical Compositions.

1. ENGLISH LITERATURE is now to be considered under that which is its most natural and legitimate arrangement; that arrangement, namely, of which the principle is, not sequence in time, but affinity in subject; and which aims, by comparing together works of the same kind, to arrive with greater ease and certainty than is possible by the chronological method, at a just estimate of their relative merits. To effect this critical aim, it is evident that a classification of the works which compose a literature is an essential prerequisite. This we shall now proceed to do. With the critical process, for which the proposed classification is to serve as the foundation, we shall, in the present work, be able to make but scanty progress. Some portions of it we shall attempt, with the view rather of illustrating the conveniences of the method, than of seriously undertaking to fill in the vast outline which will be furnished by the classification.

First of all, what is literature? In the most extended sense of the word, it may be taken for the whole written thought of man; and in the same acceptation a national literature is the whole written thought of a particular nation. But this definition is too wide for our present purpose; it would include such books as *Fearne on Contingent Remainders*, and such periodicals as the *Lancet* or the *Shipping Gazette*. If the student of literature were called upon to examine the stores of thought and knowledge which the different professions have collected and published, each for the use of its own members, his task would be endless. We must abstract, therefore, all works addressed, owing to the speciality of their subject-matter, to particular classes of men; *e.g.*, law books, medical books, works on moral theology, rubrical works, &c.—in short, all strictly professional literature. Again, the above definition would include all scientific works, which would be practically inconvenient, and would tend to obscure the really marked distinction that exists between literature and science. We must further abstract, therefore, all works in which the words are used as ciphers or signs for the purpose of communicating objective truth, not as organs of the writer's personality. All strictly scientific works are thus excluded. In popularized science, exemplified by such books as the *Architecture of the Heavens,* or the *Vestiges of the Natural History of the Creation,* the personal element comes into play; such books, are, therefore, rightly classed as literature. What remains after these deductions is literature in the strict or narrower sense; that is, the assemblage of those works which are neither addressed to particular classes, nor use words merely as the signs of *things*, but which, treating of subjects that interest man as man, and using words as the vehicles and exponents of *thoughts*, appeal to the general human intellect and to the common human heart.

2. Literature, thus defined, may be divided into—

(1) Poetry.

(2) Prose writings.

For the present, we shall confine our attention to poetry. The subject is so vast as not to be easily manageable, and many of the different kinds slide into each other by such insensible gradations, that any classification must be to a certain extent arbitrary; still the following division may, perhaps, be found useful. Poetry may be classed under eleven designations— 1. Epic, 2. Dramatic, 3. Heroic, 4. Narrative, 5. Didactic, 6. Satirical and Humorous, 7. Descriptive and Pastoral, 8. Lyrical (including ballads and sonnets), 9. Elegiac, 10. Epistles, 11. Miscellaneous Poems; the latter class including all those pieces—very numerous in modern times—which cannot be conveniently referred to any of the former heads, but which we shall endeavour further to subdivide upon some rational principle.

Epic Poetry:—'Paradise Lost;' Minor Epic Poems.

3. The epic poem has ever been regarded as in its nature the most noble of all poetic performances. Its essential properties were laid down by Aristotle in the Poetics more than two thousand years ago, and they have not varied since. For, as Pope says,—

> These rules of old, discovered not devised,
> Are nature still, but nature methodized.

The subject of the epic poem must be some one, great, complex action. The principal personages must belong to the high places of society, and must be grand and elevated in their ideas. The measure must be of a sonorous dignity befitting the subject. The action is developed by a mixture of dialogue, soliloquy, and narrative. Briefly to express its main requisites,—the epic poem treats of one, great, complex action, in a grand style, and with fulness of detail.

4. English literature possesses one great epic poem—Milton's *Paradise Lost*. Not a few of our poets have wooed the epic muse; and the results are seen in such poems as Cowley's *Davideis*, Blackmore's *Prince Arthur*, Glover's *Leonidas*, and Wilkie's *Epigoniad*. But these productions do not deserve a serious examination. The *Leonidas*, which is in blank verse, possesses a certain rhetorical dignity, but has not enough of variety and poetic truth to interest deeply any but juvenile readers. Pope's translation of the *Iliad* may in a certain sense be called an English epic; for while it would be vain to seek in it for the true Homeric spirit and manner, the translator has, in compensation, adorned it with many excellences of his own. It abounds with passages which notably illustrate Pope's best qualities;—his wonderful intellectual vigour, his terseness, brilliancy, and ingenuity. But we shall have other and better opportunities of noticing these characteristics of that great poet.

The first regular criticism on the *Paradise Lost* is found in the *Spectator*, in a series of articles written by Addison. Addison compares Milton's poem to the *Iliad* and the *Æneid*, first with respect to the choice of subject, secondly to the mode of treatment, and in both particulars he gives the palm to Milton.

Dr. Johnson, in his Life of Milton, speaks in more discriminating terms:—

'The defects and faults of *Paradise Lost*—for faults and defects every work of man must have—it is the business of impartial criticism to discover. As, in displaying the excellence of Milton, I have not made long quotations, because of selecting beauties there had been no end, I shall in the same general manner mention that which seems to deserve censure; for what Englishman can take delight in transcribing passages, which, if they lessen the reputation of Milton, diminish in some degree the honour of our country?'

Coleridge, in his *Literary Remains*, gives a criticism of the

Paradise Lost, parts of which are valuable. He appears to rank Milton as an epic poet above Homer and above Dante. Lastly, Mr. Hallam, in his *History of European Literature*, while he does not fail to point out several defects in *Paradise Lost*, which Addison and other critics had overlooked, yet inclines to place the poem, as a whole, above the *Divina Commedia* of Dante.

. 5. In our examination of the poem, we shall consider,— 1. the choice of a subject; 2. the artistic structure of the work; 3. details in the mode of treatment, whether relating to personages, or events, or poetical scenery; 4. the style, metre, and language of the poem.

(1) With regard to the choice of subject, it has been repeatedly commended in the highest terms. Coleridge, for instance, says, 'In Homer, the supposed importance of the subject, as the first effort of confederated Greece, is an afterthought of the critics; and the interest, such as it is, derived from the events themselves, as distinguished from the manner of representing them, is very languid to all but Greeks. It is a Greek poem. The superiority of the *Paradise Lost* is obvious in this respect, that the interest transcends the limits of a nation.'

There cannot, of course, be two opinions with regard to the importance and universal interest of the subject of the *Paradise Lost*, considered in itself; but whether it is a surpassingly good subject for an epic poem is a different question. One obvious difficulty connected with it is its brevity and deficiency in incident: it is not sufficiently *complex*. Compare the subjects chosen by Homer, Virgil, and Tasso. The Wrath of Achilles— its causes—its consequences—its implacability in spite of the most urgent entreaties—its final appeasement, and the partial reparation of the calamities to which it had led, form one entire whole, the development of which admits of an inexhaustible variety in the management of the details. Similarly, the settlement of Æneas in Italy, involving an account, by way of episode, in the 2nd and 3rd books of the *Æneid*, of the circumstances under which he had been driven from Troy, with a description of the obstacles which were interposed to that settlement, whether by divine or human agency, and of the means by which these obstacles were finally overcome, and the end foreshadowed from the commencement attained—this subject again, though forming one whole, and capable of being embraced in a single complex conception, presents an indefinite number of parts and incidents suitable for poetic treatment. In both cases, tradition supplied the poet with a large original stock of materials, upon which again his imagination was free to react, and either invent, modify, or suppress, according to the require-

ments of his art. In Tasso's great epic, the subject of which
is the triumphant conclusion of the first Crusade, and the deliverance of Jerusalem from the unbelievers, the materials are
evidently so abundant that the poet's skill has to be exercised
in selection rather than in expansion. Now, let us see how the
case stands with regard to Milton's subject. Here the materials
consist of the first three chapters in the Book of Genesis, and a
few verses in the Apocalypse; there is absolutely nothing more.
But it may be said that, as Tasso has invented many incidents,
and Virgil also, so Milton had full liberty to amplify, out of the
resources of his own imagination, the brief and simple notices
by which Scripture conveys the narrative of the Fall of Man.
Here, however, his subject hampers him, and rightly so. The
subjects taken by Virgil and Tasso fall within the range of
ordinary human experience; whatever they might invent, therefore, in addition to the materials which they had to their hands,
provided it were conceived with true poetic feeling, and were of
a piece with the other portions of the poem, would be strictly
homogeneous with the entire subject-matter. But the nature of
Milton's subject did not allow him this liberty of amplification
and expansion. That which is recorded of the fall of man forms
a unique chapter in history; all experience presents us with
nothing like it; and the danger is, lest if we add anything of
our own to the brief narrative of Scripture, we at last, without
intending it, produce something quite unlike our original. That
Milton felt this difficulty is clear, for he has avoided as much as
possible inventing any new incident, and, to gain the length
required for an epic poem, has introduced numerous long
dialogues and descriptive passages.

(2) The internal structure of this poem, as a work of art,
has been admired by more than one distinguished critic. There
is, Coleridge observes, a *totality* observable in the *Paradise Lost* :
—it has a definite beginning, middle, and end, such as few other
epic poems can boast of. The first line of the poem speaks of the
disobedience of our first parents; the evil power which led them
to disobey is then referred to ; and the circumstances of its revolt and overthrow are briefly given. The steps by which Satan
proceeds on his mission of temptation are described in the
second and third books. In the fourth, Adam and Eve are first
introduced. Part of the fifth, the sixth, seventh, and eighth
books are episodical, and contain the story in detail of the war
in heaven between the good and the rebel angels, the final overthrow and expulsion of the latter, and the creation of the earth
and man. All this is related to Adam by the angel Raphael, to
serve him by way of warning, lest he also should fall into the

sin of disobedience and revolt. In the ninth book occurs the account of the actual transgression. In the tenth we have the sentence pronounced, and some of the immediate consequences of the fall described. The greater part of the eleventh and twelfth books is again episodical, being the unfolding to Adam, by the Archangel Michael, partly in vision, partly by way of narrative, of the future fortunes of his descendants. At the end of the twelfth book we have the expulsion of Adam and Eve out of Paradise, with which the poem naturally closes.

The *Paradise Lost* thus forms one connected whole, and it is worked out with great vigour and carefulness of treatment throughout. Many passages, especially at the beginnings of the books, have a character of unsurpassed dignity and sublimity; the language, though often rough or harsh, and sometimes grammatically faulty, is never feeble or wordy; and a varied learning supplies the poet with abundant material for simile and illustration. Still the difficulty before mentioned, as inherent in the choice of the subject, seems to extend its evil influence over the structure of the poem. The fact of his materials being so scanty obliged Milton to have recourse to episodes; hence the long narratives of Raphael and Michael. Through nearly six entire books, out of the twelve of which the poem is composed, the main action is interrupted and in suspense;—a thing which it is difficult to justify upon any rules of poetic art. For what is an episode? It is a story within a story; it is to an epic poem what a parenthesis is to a sentence,—and just as a parenthesis, unless carefully managed, and kept within narrow limits, is likely to obscure the meaning of the main sentence, so an episode, if too long, or unskilfully dovetailed into the rest of the work, is apt to introduce a certain confusion into an epic poem. Let us observe the manner in which the father of poetry—he who, in the words of Horace,

——nil molitur ineptè ;

of whom Pope says : [1]—

> Thence form your judgment, thence your maxims bring,
> And trace the Muses upward to their spring ;

—let us see how far Homer indulged in episode. The use of the episode is twofold : it serves either to make known to the reader events antecedent or subsequent in time to the action of the piece, or to describe contemporary matters, which, though connected with, are not essential to, and do not help forward, the main action. A long narrative of what is past, and a long

[1] *Essay on Criticism*, I.

prophecy of what is to come, are therefore both alike episodical:
of the former we have an example in the second and third books
of the *Æneid*; of the latter, in the eleventh and twelfth books
of the *Paradise Lost*. As an instance of the contemporary episode, we may take the story of Olinda and Sofronio, in the second canto of the *Gerusalemme Liberata*. Now Homer, although
in the *Iliad* he informs us of many circumstances connected with
the siege of Troy which had happened before the date when the
poem commences, seems purposely to avoid communicating them
in a formal episode. He scatters and interweaves these notices
of past events in the progress of the main action so naturally,
yet with such perfection of art, that he gains the same object
which is the pretext for historical episodes with other poets,
but without that interruption and suspension of the main design,
which, however skilfully managed, seem hardly consistent with
epical perfection. Thus Achilles, in the long speech in the ninth
book to the envoys who are entreating him to succour the defeated Greeks, introduces, without effort, an account of much of
the previous history of the great siege. So again Diomede, in
the second book, when dissuading the Greeks from embarking
and returning home, refers naturally to the events which occurred at Aulis before the expedition started, in a few lines, which,
as it were, present to us the whole theory of the siege in the
clearest light. Homer, therefore, strictly speaking, avoids in the
Iliad.the use of the episode altogether. Virgil, on the other
hand, adopts it; the second and third books of the *Æneid* are
an episodical narrative, in which Æneas relates to Dido the closing scenes at Troy and his own subsequent adventures in the
Mediterranean. Tasso uses the episode very sparingly, and pre-
fers the contemporary to the historical form. But when we
come to the *Paradise Lost*, we find that nearly half the poem
is episodical. Several disadvantages hence arise. First of all,
the fact implies a defect in point of art; since the action or story
developed either in a dramatic or an epic poem ought to be so important and so complete in itself as not to require the introduction
of explanatory or decorative statements nearly as long as the
progressive portions of the poem. If the episode be explanatory, it proves that the story is not sufficiently clear, simple,
and complete for epic purposes; if decorative, that it is not
important enough to engross the reader's attention without
the addition of extraneous matter. In either case, the art is
defective. Again, this arrangement is the source of confusion
and obscurity. A reader not very well acquainted with the
peculiar structure of the poem, opens the *Paradise Lost* at
hazard, and finds himself, to his astonishment—in a work whose

subject is the loss of Paradise—carried back to the creation of light, or forward to the building of the tower of Babel.

6. (3) We are now to consider in some detail how Milton has treated his subject; how he has dealt with the difficulties which seem inherent in the selection. A certain degree of amplification—the materials being so scanty—was unavoidable :—has he managed the amplification successfully ? In some instances he certainly has; for example, in the account of the temptation of Eve in the ninth book, the logic of which is very ingeniously wrought out by supposing the serpent to ascribe his power of speech and newly-awakened intelligence to the effects of partaking of the fruit of the forbidden tree; and by putting into his mouth various plausible arguments designed to satisfy Eve as to the motives of the Divine prohibition. But in other passages we cannot but think that the amplification has been unsuccessful. For example, take the war in heaven. In the Apocalypse (ch. xii.) it is mentioned in these few words : ' And there was war in heaven :—Michael and his angels fought with the dragon ; and the dragon fought and his angels, and they prevailed not ; neither was their place found any more in heaven. And the great dragon was cast out, that old serpent, who is called the Devil and Satan, who seduceth the whole world : and he was cast unto the earth, and his angels were cast out with him.' Such, and no more than this, was the knowledge imparted in prophetic vision to the inspired apostle in Patmos regarding these supernatural events. Milton has expanded this brief text marvellously ; the narrative of the revolt and war in heaven takes up two entire books. And strange work indeed he has made of it ! The actual material swords and spears—the invention of cannons, cannon-balls, and gunpowder by the rebel angels—the grim puritanical pleasantry which is put in the mouth of Satan when first making proof of this notable discovery, just such as one might fancy issuing from the lips of Cromwell or Ireton on giving orders to batter down a cathedral, —the hurling of mountains at one another by the adverse hosts, a conceit borrowed from Greek mythology and the war of the Titans against the gods,—

> Ter sunt conati imponere Pelio Ossam
> Scilicet, atque Ossæ frondosum involvere Olympum;

lastly, the vivid description, exceedingly fine and poetical in its way, of the chariot of the Messiah going forth to battle, drawn by four cherubic shapes; all this, though fitting and appropriate enough if the subject were the gods of Olympus or of Valhalla, grates discordantly upon our feelings when it is presented as a suitable picture of the mysterious event which we call the Fall of the Angels, and as an expansion of the particulars recorded in the sacred text. In truth, Milton is nowhere so solemn and impressive as in those passages where he reproduces almost *verbatim* the exact words of Scripture, *e.g.*, in the passage in the tenth book, describing the judgment passed upon man after his transgression. Where he gives the freest play to his invention, the result is least happy. The dialogues in heaven, to say nothing of the undisguised Arianism which disfigures them, are either painful or simply absurd, according as one regards them seriously or not. Pope, whose discernment nothing escaped, has touched this weak point in his *Imitations of Horace*.[1] Hallam himself has admitted that a certain grossness and materialism attach to Milton's heaven and heavenly inhabitants, far unlike the pure and ethereal colours with which Dante invests the angels and blessed spirits presented in his *Paradiso*.

Turning now to the personal element in the poem, we find, as Johnson shows at length, that as the subject chosen is beyond the sphere of human experience, so the characters described are deficient in human interest. So far as this is not the case, it arises from Milton's having broken through the trammels which the fundamental conditions of his subject imposed on him. Of all the personages in the *Paradise Lost*, there is none whose proceedings interest us, and even whose sufferings engage our sympathies, like those of Satan. But this is because he is not represented as the Bible represents him—namely, as the type and essential principle of all that is evil and hateful. There seems to be a conflict in the mind of Milton between the Scriptural type of Satan and the Greek conception of Prometheus. The fallen archangel, driven from heaven and doomed to everlasting misery by superior power, yet with will unconquered and unconquerable, cannot but recall the image of the mighty Titan chained to the rock by the vengeance of Jove, yet unalterably defiant and erect in soul. It is clear that the character of Satan had greater charms for Milton's imagination, and is therefore presented more prominently, and worked out with more care, than any other in the poem. Devoted himself to the cause of insurrection on earth, he sympathizes against his will with the author of rebellion in heaven. Against his will; for he seems to be well aware and to be continually reminding himself that Satan ought to be represented as purely evil, yet he constantly places language in his mouth which is inconsistent with such a conception. For instance:

---

[1] 'In quibbles angel and archangel join,' &c.

> Yet not for those,
> Nor what the potent victor in his rage
> Can else inflict, do I repent or change,
> Though changed in outward lustre, that fixed mind
> And high disdain from sense of injured merit,
> That with the mightiest urged me to contend.

Is not this much more like Shelley's Prometheus than the Satan of the Bible? It has been often said, and it seems true, that the hero or prominent character of the *Paradise Lost* is Satan. Throughout the first three books the attention is fixed upon his proceedings. Even after Adam and Eve are introduced, which is not till the fourth book, the main interest centres upon him; for they are passive—he is active; they are the subject of plots—he the framer of them; they, living on without any definite aim, are represented as falling from their happy state through weakness, and in a sort of helpless predestined manner (we speak, of course, of Milton's representation only, not of the Fall as it was in itself); while he is fixed to one object, fertile in expedients, courageous in danger, and, on the whole, successful in his enterprise. Clearly, Satan is the hero of the *Paradise Lost.* And, apart from the incongruity referred to, the character is drawn in such grand outlines, and presents such a massive strength and sublimity, as none but a great poet could have portrayed. The following lines describe him, when marshalling the hosts of his followers :—

> He, above the rest
> In shape and gesture proudly eminent,
> Stood like a tower; his form had not yet lost
> All its original brightness, nor appeared
> Less than archangel ruined, and the excess
> Of glory obscured; as when the sun, new risen,
> Looks through the horizontal misty air,
> Shorn of his beams; or from behind the moon,
> In dim eclipse, disastrous twilight sheds
> On half the nations, and with fear of change
> Perplexes monarchs. Darken'd so, yet shone
> Above them all th' archangel.

He consoles himself for his banishment from heaven with reflections worthy of a Stoic philosopher :—

> —— Farewell, happy fields,
> Where joy for ever dwells ! Hail, horrors, hail,
> Infernal world, and thou profoundest hell,
> Receive thy new possessor; one who brings
> A mind not to be changed by place or time:
> The mind is its own place, and in itself
> Can make a heaven of hell, a hell of heaven.
> What matter where, if I be still the same,
> And what I should be; all but less than he

> Whom thunder hath made greater ?   Here at least
> We shall be free ; the Almighty hath not built
> Here for his envy ; will not drive us hence ;
> Here we may reign secure, and, in my choice,
> To reign is worth ambition, though in hell ;
> Better to reign in hell, than serve in heaven.

In much of the portraiture of Adam, Milton seems to be unconsciously describing himself. His manly beauty, his imperious claim to absolute rule over the weaker sex, the grasp of his intellect, and the delight he feels in its exercise, his strength of will, yet susceptibility to the influence of female charms,—all these characteristics, assigned by the poet to Adam, are well known to have in an eminent degree belonged to himself. Eve, on the other hand, is represented as a soft, yielding, fascinating being, who, with all her attractions, is, in moral and intellectual things, rather a hindrance than a help to her nobler consort ;— and there are many suppressed taunts and thinly-veiled allusions, which, while they illustrate Milton's somewhat Oriental view of woman's relation to man, can scarcely be misunderstood as glancing at his own domestic trials. To illustrate what has been said, we will quote a few passages. The first is one of surpassing beauty :—

> Two of far nobler shape, erect and tall,
> God-like erect, with native honour clad,
> In naked majesty, seem'd lords of all ;
> And worthy seem'd ; for in their looks divine
> The image of their glorious Maker shone :
> *   *   *   *   *   *
> For contemplation he and valour formed ;
> For softness she, and sweet attractive grace ;
> He for God only, she for God in him :
> His fair large front and eye sublime declared
> Absolute rule ; and hyacinthine locks
> Round from his parted forelock manly hung
> Clustering, but not beneath his shoulders broad. (Book iv.)

Eve thus unfolds her conception of the relation in which she stands to Adam :—

> To whom thus Eve, with perfect beauty adorn'd :
> ' My author and disposer, what thou bidd'st
> Unargued I obey ; so God ordains ;
> God is thy law, thou mine ;—to know no more
> Is woman's happiest knowledge and her praise.'   (Ibid.)

Adam, while expressing the same view, owns the invincibility of woman's charm :—

For well I understand in the prime end
Of nature her the inferior, in the mind
And inward faculties, which most excel ;
In outward also her resembling less
His image who made both, and less expressing
The character of that dominion given
O'er other creatures ; yet when I approach
Her loveliness, so absolute she seems,
And in herself complete, so well to know
Her own, that what she wills to do or say
Seems wisest, virtuousest, discreetest, best;
All higher knowledge in her presence falls
Degraded ; wisdom in discourse with her
Loses discountenanced, and like folly shows.   (Book viii.)

Even in the Fall, Adam is enticed but not deceived :—

—— He scrupled not to eat
Against his better knowledge; not deceived,
But fondly overcome with female charm.   (Book ix.)

Is there not, again, a touch of autobiography in the reproaches
which Adam heaps upon Eve in the following lines ?—

—— This mischief had not then befallen,
And more that shall befall ; innumerable
Disturbances on earth through female snares,
And straight conjunction with this sex ; for either
He never shall find out fit mate, but such
As some misfortune brings him, or mistake ;
Or whom he wishes most shall seldom gain
Through her perverseness, but shall see her gained
By a far worse; &c.   (Book x.)

Eve's submission makes her stern lord relent. It is well known
that Milton's first wife, in similar suppliant guise, appeased his
resentment, and obtained her pardon :—

She ended weeping; and her lowly plight
Immovable, till peace obtained from fault
Acknowledged and deplored, in Adam wrought
Commiseration ; soon his heart relented
Towards her, his life so late, and sole delight,
Now at his feet submissive in distress.   (Ibid.)

The seraph Abdiel is one of the grandest of poetic creations.
Led away at first in the ranks of the rebel angels, he recoils
with horror when he learns the full scope of their revolt, and
returns to the courts of heaven :—

So spake the seraph Abdiel, faithful found
Among the faithless, faithful only he ;

> Among innumerable false, unmoved,
> Unshaken, unseduced, unterrified,
> His loyalty he kept, his love, his zeal:
> Nor number nor example with him wrought
> To swerve from truth, or change his constant mind,
> Though single.　From amidst them forth he passed,
> Long way through hostile scorn, which he sustained
> Superior, nor of violence feared aught;
> And with retorted scorn, his back he turned
> On those proud towers to swift destruction doomed. (Book v.)

By *poetical scenery* is meant the imaginary framework in space in which the poem is set,—the stage with its accessories, on which the characters move, and the action is performed.　In the *Paradise Lost*, as in the *Divina Commedia*, this is no narrower than the entire compass of the heavens and the earth. But there is a remarkable difference between them, which, in point of art, operates to the disadvantage of the English poet. In the fourteenth century no one doubted the truth of the Ptolemaic system, and Dante's astronomy is as stable and self-consistent as his theology.　The earth is motionless at the centre; round it, fixed in concentric spheres, revolve the 'seven planets,' of which the Moon is the first and the Sun the fourth: enclosing these follow in succession the sphere of the fixed stars, that of the empyrean, and that described as the *primum mobile*.　The geography of the Inferno, an abyss in the form of an inverted cone, extending downwards in successive steps to the centre of the earth, and that of the Purgatorio, a mountain at the Antipodes, rising in the form of a proper cone by similar steps, till the summit is reached whence purified souls are admitted to the lowest sphere of the Paradiso, are equally logical and distinct.　But in the seventeenth century the Copernican system was rapidly gaining the belief of all intelligent men, and Milton, in his poem, wavers between the old astronomy and the new.　In the first three books the Ptolemaic system prevails; upon any other, Satan's expedition in search of the new-created earth becomes unintelligible.　After struggling through Chaos he lands upon the outermost of the spheres that enclose the earth :—

> Meanwhile upon the firm opacous globe
> Of this round world, whose first convex divides
> The luminous inferior orbs, enclosed
> From Chaos and the inroad of darkness old,
> Satan alighted walks.　　　　　(Book iii.)

Hither 'fly all things transitory and vain;' hither come the 'eremites and friars' whom Milton regards with true Puritanic aversion, and those who thought to make sure of Paradise by putting on the Franciscan or Dominican habit on their death-bed :—

> They pass the planets seven, and pass the fixed,
> And that crystalline sphere whose balance weighs
> The trepidation talked, and that first moved.

On his way down from hence to the earth, Satan, still in accordance with the Ptolemaic system, passes through the fixed stars and visits the sun.   But in subsequent parts of the poem an astronomy is suggested which revolutionizes the face of the universe, and gives us the uncomfortable feeling that all that has gone before is unreal.   The stability of the earth is first questioned in the fourth book :—

> —— Uriel to his charge
> Returned on that bright beam, whose point now raised
> Bore him slope downward to the sun, now fallen
> Beneath the Azores ; whether the prime orb,
> Incredible how swift, had thither rolled
> Diurnal, *or this less volubil earth,*
> *By shorter flight to the east, had left him there.*

In the eighth book, Adam questions Raphael as to the celestial motions, but is doubtfully answered ; upon either theory, he is told, the goodness and wisdom of God can be justified ; yet the archangel's words imply some preference for the Copernican system :—

> —— What if the sun
> Be centre to the world, and other stars,
> By his attractive virtue and their own
> Incited, dance about him various rounds ?
> *   *   *   *   *   *
> Or save the sun his labour, and that swift
> Nocturnal and diurnal rhomb supposed,
> Invisible else above all stars, the wheel
> Of day and night ; *which needs not thy belief,*
> *If earth, industrious of herself, fetch day*
> *Travelling east,* and with her part averse
> From the sun's beam meet night ——

7. (4) It remains to say a few words upon the style, metre, and language of the poem. The grandeur, pregnancy, and nobleness of the first are indisputable.   It is, however, often rugged or harsh, owing to the frequency of defects in the versification.   It is distinguished by the great length of the sentences : the thread of thought winding on through many a parenthesis or subordinate clause, now involving, now evolving itself, yet always firmly grasped, and resulting in grammar as

sound as the intellectual conception is distinct. This quality of
style is perhaps attributable to Milton's blindness; he could not
write down as he composed, nor could an amanuensis be always
at hand; he therefore may have acted on the principle that one
long sentence is more easily remembered than two or three short
ones.

A series of admirable papers upon Milton's versification
may be found in Johnson's *Rambler*.[1] To it the reader is referred, the subject being not of a kind to admit of cursory
treatment.

The language of the poem does not come up to the standard
of the purest English writers of the period. It is difficult to
understand how Milton, having the works of Bacon, Shakspere,
and Hooker before him, could think himself justified in using the
strange and barbarous Latinisms which disfigure the *Paradise
Lost*. Such terms as 'procinct,' 'battalious,' 'parle,' and such
usages, or rather usurpations, of words, as 'frequent' in the
sense of 'crowded,' 'pontifical' in the sense of 'bridge-making,'
'obvious' for 'meeting,' 'dissipation' for 'dispersion,' and 'pretended' for 'drawn before' (Lat. *prætentus*), were never employed by English writers before Milton, and have never been
employed since.

Nor does he import Latin words only, but Latin, and even
Greek, constructions. Examples of Greek idioms are, 'And
knew not eating death,' and 'O miserable of happy' (ἄθλιος ἐκ
μακαρίου). Latin idioms occur frequently, and sometimes cause
obscurity, because, through the absence of inflexions in English,
the same collocation of words which is perfectly clear in Latin is
often capable of two or three different meanings in English. A few
examples are subjoined: 'Or hear'st thou rather' (*i.e.* would'st
thou rather be addressed as) 'pure ethereal stream:'—'Of pure
now purer air Meets his approach;'—'So as not either to provoke, or dread New war provoked' (where it is not clear at first
sight whether 'provoked' should be rendered by '*suscitatum*'
or '*lacessitos*');—'How camest thou speakable of mute:' &c.

After all, it is easy to be hypercritical in these matters. The
defence, however, of such a minute analysis lies in the fact of its
being exercised on a work truly great. We notice the flaws in
a diamond, because it is a diamond. No one would take the
trouble to point out the grammatical or metrical slips in Blackmore's *Creation*. It is from the conviction that the renown of
the *Paradise Lost* is, and deserves to be, imperishable, that
critics do not fear to show that it is wrong to regard it with a

[1] Nos. 86, 88, 90, 94.

blind, indiscriminate admiration. Of the father of poetry himself it was said—

—Aliquando bonus dormitat Homerus. .

In a note are given a few passages from the poem, which have passed into proverbs, current sayings, or standard quotations.[1]

Dramatic Poetry : Its Kinds ; Shakspere, Addison, Milton.

8. Invented by the Greeks, the drama attained in their hands a perfection which it has never since surpassed. To them we owe the designations of Tragedy and Comedy, the definition of each kind according to its nature and end, and the division into acts. The leading characteristics of dramatic composition have remained unaltered ever since ; but the Greek definition of Tragedy was gradually restricted, that of Comedy enlarged, so that it became necessary to invent other names for intermediate or inferior kinds. With the Greeks, a tragedy meant 'the representation of a serious, complete, and important action,' and might involve a transition from calamity to prosperity, as well as from prosperity to calamity.[2] By a comedy was meant a representation, tending to excite laughter, of mean and ridiculous actions. Thus the *Eumenides* of Æschylus, the *Philoctetes* of Sophocles, and the *Alcestis*, *Helena*, and others of Euripides, though called tragedies, do not end *tragically* in the modern sense, but the reverse. But by degrees it came to be considered that every tragedy must have a disastrous catastrophe, so that a new term—tragi-comedy—which seems to have first arisen in Spain, was invented to suit those dramas in which, though the main action was serious, the conclusion was happy. As Tragedy assumed a narrower meaning, Comedy obtained one pro-

---

[1] Awake, arise, or be for ever fallen.

With ruin upon ruin, rout on rout,
Confusion worse confounded :—

—— At whose sight all the stars
Hide their diminished heads :—

Not to know me, argues yourselves unknown ;—

—— Still govern thou my song,
Urania, and *fit audience find, though few.*

—— With a smile that glowed
Celestial rosy red—

And over them triumphant Death his dart
Shook, but delayed to strike.

[2] Aristot. *Poet.* 6.

portionably more extensive. Of this a notable illustration is found in Dante, who, though he did not understand by the 'tragic style' what we understand by it, but merely the style of grand and sublime poems, such as the Æneid, yet named his own great work *La Commedia*, as intending to rank it with a great variety of poems in the middle or ordinary style, not sublime enough to be tragic, and not pathetic enough to be elegiac. In England, the term Comedy was used all through the Elizabethan age in a loose sense, which would embrace anything between a tragi-comedy and a farce. Thus the *Merchant of Venice* is reckoned among the *comedies* of Shakspere, though, except for the admixture of comic matter in the minor characters, it is, in the Greek sense, just as much a tragedy as the *Alcestis*. In the seventeenth century, the term began to be restricted to plays in which comic or satirical matter preponderated. A shorter and more unpretending species, in one or at most two acts, in which any sort of contrivance or trick was permissible in order to raise a laugh, so that the action were not taken out of the sphere of real life, was invented under the name of Farce in the eighteenth century.

9. The best and most characteristic of English plays belong to what is called the *Romantic* drama. The Classical and the Romantic drama represent two prevalent modes of thought, or streams of opinion, which, parting from each other and becoming strongly contrasted soon after the revival of letters, have ever since contended for the empire of the human mind in Europe. The readers of Mr. Ruskin's striking books will have learnt a great deal about these modes of thought, and will, perhaps, have imbibed too unqualified a dislike for the one, and reverence for the other. Referring those who desire a full exposition to the pages of that eloquent writer, we must be content with saying here, that the Classical drama was cast in the Græco-Roman mould, and subjected to the rules of construction (the dramatic unities) which the ancient dramatists observed; its authors being generally men who were deeply imbued with the classical spirit, to a degree which made them recoil with aversion and contempt from the spirit and the products of the ages that had intervened between themselves and the antiquity which they loved. On the other hand, the Romantic drama, though it borrowed much of its formal part (*e.g.*, the division into acts, the prologue and epilogue, the occasional choruses, &c.) from the ancients, was founded upon and grew out of the Romance literature of the middle ages,—its authors being generally imbued with the spirit of Christian Europe, such as the mingled influences of Christianity and feudalism had formed it. National

before all,—writing for audiences in whom taste and fine intelligence were scantily developed, but in whom imagination and feeling were strong, and faith habitual, the dramatists of this school were led to reject the strict rules of which Athenian culture exacted the observance. To gratify the national pride of their hearers, they dramatized large portions of their past history, and in so doing scrupled not to violate the unity of action. They observed, indeed, this rule in their tragedies—at least in the best of them—but utterly disregarded the minor unities of time and place, because they knew that they could trust to the imagination of their hearers to supply any shortcomings in the external illusion. In the play of *Macbeth* many years elapse, and the scene is shifted from Scotland to England and back again without the smallest hesitation. The result is, that Art gains in one way and loses in another. We are spared the tedious narratives which are rendered necessary in the classical drama by the strict limits of time within which the action is bounded. On the other hand, the impression produced, being less concentrated, is usually feebler and less determinate.

It would be a waste of time to enter here, in that cursory way which alone our limits would allow, into any critical discussion of the dramatic genius of Shakspere. The greatest modern critics in all countries have undertaken the task,—a fact sufficient of itself to dispense us from the attempt. Among the numerous treatises, large and small—by Coleridge, Hazlitt, Mrs. Jameson, Guizot, Tieck, Schlegel, Ulrici, &c.—each containing much that is valuable, we would single out Guizot's as embodying, in the most compact and convenient form, the results of the highest criticism on Shakspere himself, on his time, and on his work.

10. Our literature possesses but few dramas of the Classical school, and those not of the highest order. The most celebrated specimen, perhaps, is Addison's *Cato*. But weak and prosaic lines abound in it, such as

> Cato, I've orders to expostulate ;

or,

> Why will you rive my heart with such expressions ?

and the scenes between the lovers are stiff and frigid. Yet the play is not without fine passages ; as when the noble Roman who has borne unmoved the tidings of the death of his son, weeps over the anticipated ruin of his country :—

> 'Tis Rome requires our tears ;
> The mistress of the world, the seat of empire,

> The nurse of heroes, the delight of gods,
> That humbled the proud tyrants of the earth,
> And set the nations free,—Rome is no more !

On the whole, Cato's character is finely drawn, and well adapted to call forth the powers of a first-rate actor. His soliloquy at the end, beginning

> It must be so ;—Plato, thou reasonest well, &c.

has been justly praised.

The play contains several well-known lines, *e.g.*

> The woman that deliberates is lost.

> 'Tis not in mortals to command success,
> But we'll do more, Sempronius ; we'll deserve it.

> Curse on his virtues ! they've undone his country.

> When vice prevails, and impious men bear sway,
> The post of honour is a private station.

Heroic and Mock-Heroic Poetry : ' The Bruce ;' ' The Campaign ;' 'The Rape of the Lock.'

11. As the unity of the epic poem is derived from its being the evolution of one great complex action, so the unity of the heroic poem proceeds from its being the record of all or some of the great actions of an individual hero. Like the epic, it requires a serious and dignified form of expression ; and consequently, in English, employs nearly always, either the heroic couplet, or a stanza of not less than seven lines. Heroic poetry has produced no works of extraordinary merit in any literature. When the hero is living, the registration of his exploits is apt to become fulsome ; when dead, tedious. Boileau has perhaps succeeded best ; the heroic poems which Addison produced in honour of Marlborough and William III., in hope to emulate the author of the *Epître au Roi*, are mere rant and fustian in comparison. Our earliest heroic poem, *The Bruce* of Barbour[1]— is, perhaps, the best ; but the short romance metre in which it is written much injures its effect. A better specimen of Barbour's style cannot be selected than the often-quoted passage on Freedom :—

> A ! fredome is a noble thing !
> Fredome mayss man to have liking :
> Fredome all solace to man givis ;
> He livys at ease, that freely livys !

---

[1] See ch. I. I§ 84.

A noble hart may have none ease,
Na ellys nocht that may him please,
Gif fredome failyhe; for fre liking
Is yharnyt[1] ower all other thing.
Na he, that aye has livyt fre,
May nocht knaw weill the propyrtè,
The angyr, na the wrechyt dome,[2]
That is couplyt to foul thyrldome.[3]
Bot gif he had assayit it,
Then all perquer[4] he suld it wyt;
And suld think fredome mar to pryss,
Than all the gold in warld that is.
Thus contrar thingis ever mar,
Discoweryngis of the tothir are[5]
And he that thryll[6] is, has nocht his :
All that he has embandownyt is
Till[7] his lord, quhat evir he be,
Yet has he nocht sa mekill fre ·
As fre wyl to live, or do
That at hys hart hym drawis to.

12. Addison's heroic poem, *The Campaign*, contains the well-known simile of the angel, which called forth the admiration and munificence of Godolphin. The story runs as follows :— In 1704, shortly after the battle of Blenheim, Godolphin, then Lord Treasurer, happening to meet Lord Halifax, complained that the great victory had not been properly celebrated in verse, and inquired if he knew of any poet to whom this important task could be safely intrusted. Halifax replied that he did indeed know of a gentleman thoroughly competent to discharge this duty, but that the individual he referred to had received of late such scanty recognition of his talents and patriotism, that he doubted if he would be willing to undertake it. Lord Godolphin replied that Lord Halifax might rest assured, that whoever might be named should not go unrewarded for his trouble. Upon which Halifax named Addison. Godolphin sent a common friend to Addison, who immediately undertook to confer immortality on the Duke of Marlborough. The poem called *The Campaign* was the result. Godolphin saw the manuscript when the poet had got as far as the once celebrated simile of the Angel, which runs thus :—

So when an Angel, by divine command,
With rising tempests shakes a guilty land,
Such as of late o'er pale Britannia past,
Calm and serene he drives the furious blast,
And, pleased the Almighty's orders to perform,
Rides in the whirlwind, and directs the storm.

---

[1] Yearned for.   [2] Wretched doom.   [3] Thraldom.   [4] Perfectly.
[5] Meaning 'explain their opposites.'   [6] Thrall.   [7] To.

Lord Godolphin, it is said,[1] was so delighted with this not very reverent simile, that he immediately made Addison a Commissioner of Appeals. But this favourable judgment of the poem has been reversed by later criticism. *The Campaign*, taken as a whole, is turgid yet feeble, pretentious yet dull; it has few of the excellences, and nearly all the faults, which heroic verse can have.

13. With the heroic we may class its travestie, the mock-heroic. And here the inimitable poem of the *Rape of the Lock* will occur to everyone, in which Pope, with admirable skill, and perfect mastery over all the resources of literary art, has created an artistic whole, faultless no less in proportion and keeping than in the finish of the parts, which, in its kind, remains un-approached by anything in English, and probably in European, literature. The slight incident on which the poem was founded is well known. Among the triflers who fluttered round the sovereign at Hampton Court,

> Where thou, great Anna, whom three realms obey,
> Dost sometimes counsel take, and sometimes tea,

were Belinda (Miss Arabella Fermor), and the Baron (Lord Petre). Small-talk, badinage, flirtation, scandal,—

> At every word a reputation dies—

are insufficient to fill the vacant hours, and for these 'idle hands' some mischief is soon found to do. The Baron, borrow-ing a pair of scissors from one of the maids of honour, Clarissa, audaciously cuts off one of the two curling locks of Belinda's back hair :—

> Just then Clarissa drew, with tempting grace,
> A two-edg'd weapon from her shining case :
> So ladies in romance assist their knight,
> Present the spear and arm him for the fight.
> He takes the gift with reverence, and extends
> The little engine on his fingers' ends ;
> This just behind Belinda's neck he spread,
> As o'er the fragrant steams she bent her head.
> Swift to the lock a thousand sprites repair,
> A thousand wings, by turns, blow back the hair !
> And thrice they twitch'd the diamond in her ear ;
> Thrice she look'd back, and thrice the foe drew near.
> Just in that instant, anxious Ariel sought
> The close recesses of the virgin's thought,
> As, on the nosegay in her breast reclined,
> He watch'd the ideas rising in her mind ;

---

[1] See the *Biographia Britannica*.

Sudden he view'd, in spite of all her art,
An earthly lover lurking at her heart.
Amazed, confused, he found his power expired,
Resign'd to fate, and with a sigh retired.
    The peer now spreads the glittering forfex wide,
To enclose the lock ; now joins it to divide.
E'en then, before the fatal engine closed,
A wretched sylph too fondly interposed ;
Fate urged the shears, and cut the sylph in twain :
(But airy substance soon unites again).
The meeting points the sacred hair dissever
From the fair head, for ever and for ever !

The liberty was resented by the lady, and a breach between the two families was the result, in the hope of healing which Pope wrote this poem. So far the real nearly coincided with the fictitious facts. But Pope, unwilling to leave the matter in an unsettled and indeterminate state—an error which Dryden did not avoid in the *Absalom and Achitophel*—contrived, with the happiest art, to crown the incident with a poetically just and satisfying conclusion. The insulted and enraged Belinda commands her beau, Sir Plume,—

Sir Plume, of amber snuff-box justly vain,
And the nice conduct of a clouded cane,

to extort the lock from the Baron. He makes the attempt, but in vain ; the two parties now muster their forces, and engage in deadly strife, these to keep, those to win back, the lock. Belinda, through the dexterous application of a pinch of snuff, has the Baron at her mercy, and the lock is to be restored. But, lo ! it has vanished, and is hunted for everywhere in vain. Many theories are framed to account for its disappearance, but the poet was privileged to see it wafted upwards to the skies, where, transformed into a comet, sweeping by with ' a radiant trail of hair,' the lover takes it for Venus, and the astrologer for some baleful luminary, foreshowing

The fate of Louis, and the fall of Rome.

Lightness, grace, airy wit, playful rallying, everything, in short, that is most alien to the ordinary characteristics of the English intellect, are found in this poem. It is a keen, sunny satire, without a spark of ill-nature, on the luxury and vanity of a society impregnated with ideas borrowed from the court of the Grand Monarque, from classical revivals, and Renaissance modes of thought. It may be noted that the continual association of contrasted ideas is one of the chief sources of the wit with which the poem flashes and runs over, as with lambent flames of summer lightning. Belinda's guardian sylph cannot discover the nature of the danger which threatens her,—

> Whether the nymph shall break Diana's law,
> Or some frail china jar receive a flaw;
> Or stain her honour, or her new brocade;
> Forget her prayers, or miss a masquerade.

So again,—

> The merchant from the Exchange returns in peace,
> And the long labours of the toilet cease.

And—

> Not louder shrieks to pitying heaven are cast
> When husbands, or when lapdogs, breathe their last.

The trivial is raised to the rank of the important, and, as it were, confounded with it, that both may appear as so much plastic material in the hand of the master. This is the very triumph of art.

Narrative Poetry :—Romances; Tales; Allegories; Romantic Poems; Historical Poems.

14. Narrative poetry is less determinate in form than any of the preceding kinds. The narrative poem so far resembles the epic, that it also is concerned with a particular sequence of human actions, and permits of the intermixture of dialogue and description. It differs from it, in that it does not require either the strict unity or the intrinsic greatness of the epic action. In the epic, the issue of the action is involved in the fundamental circumstances, and is indicated at the very outset. The first two lines of the *Iliad* contain the germ or theme which is expanded and illustrated through the twenty-two books which follow. The course of a narrative poem is in general more like that of real life; events occur and are described which have no obvious internal relation either to each other or to some one ground plan; and a conclusion in which the mind reposes, and desires nothing beyond,—an essential requirement in the epic,—is not to be strictly exacted from the narrative poem. But even if the epic unity of design were observed, the narrative poem would still be distinguishable from the higher kind, either by the inferior greatness of the subject, or by the lower quality of the style. An epic poem, as was said before, treats of one great complex action, in a lofty style, and with fulness of detail. In a narrative poem, it will be invariably found that one of these elements is wanting.

E E

15. It will be convenient to divide narrative poems into five classes : 1. Romances, 2. Tales, 3. Allegories, 4. Romantic poems, 5. Historical poems.

(1) The *Romances*, or Gests, in old English, with which our MS. repositories abound, were mostly translated or imitated from French originals during the thirteenth, fourteenth, and fifteenth centuries. In the former portion of this work a general description was given of these remarkable poems,[1] so that it is unnecessary here to enter upon any questions connected with their origin or subject-matter. We shall now present the reader with an analysis of a curious romance, not belonging to one of the great cycles, which may serve as a sample of the whole class. It is the romance of Sir Isumbras, and is one of those abridged by Ellis.

Sir Isumbras was rich, virtuous, and happy; but in the pride of his heart he was lifted up, and gradually became forgetful of God. An angel appears to him, and denounces punishment. It is like the story of Job : his horses and oxen are struck dead; his castle burnt down; and many of his servants killed. Then, with his wife and three sons, he sets out on a pilgrimage to the Holy Sepulchre. On the way, the two elder children are carried off, one by a lion, the other by a leopard. At last they come to the 'Greekish Sea;' a Saracen fleet sails up; the Soudan is enamoured of the wife, and deprives Sir Isumbras of her by a forced sale, the purchase-money being counted down upon the knight's red mantle. The lady is immediately sent back to the Soudan's dominions in the capacity of Queen. Shortly after this the misery of Sir Isumbras is completed by the abduction of his only remaining son by a unicorn, during a brief interval, in which he was vainly pursuing an eagle which had seized upon the mantle and the gold. In fervent contrition he falls on his knees, and prays to Jesus and the Virgin. He obtains work at a smith's forge, and remains in this employment seven years, during which he forges for himself a suit of armour. A battle between a Christian and a Saracen army takes place not far off; Sir Isumbras takes part in it, and wins the battle by his valour, killing his old acquaintance the Soudan. After his wounds are healed, he takes a scrip and pike, and goes on pilgrimage to the Holy Land. Here he stays seven years in constant labour, mortification, and penance; at last—

> Beside the burgh of Jerusalem
> He set him by a well-stream,
> Sore wepand for his sin;

---

[1] See Prel. Ch. II. § 58.

And as he sat about midnight,
There came an angel fair and bright,
    And brought him bread and wine :
He said, Palmer, wel thou be ;
The King of Heaven greeteth wel thee ;
    Forgiven is sin thine !

He wanders away, and at length arrives at a fair castle, belonging to a rich Queen ; he begs for and receives food and lodging.
The Queen, after a conversation with him, resolves to entertain
the pious palmer in the castle. After a sojourn here of many
months, Sir Isumbras finds one day in an eagle's nest his own
red mantle with the Soudan's gold in it. He bears it to his
chamber, and the recollections it awakens completely overpower
him. He becomes so altered that the Queen, in order to ascertain the cause, has his room broken open, when the sight of the
gold explains all, and mutual recognition ensues. Sir Isumbras
tells his Saracen subjects that they must be forthwith converted.
They, however, object to such summary measures, and rise in
rebellion against him and his Queen, who stand absolutely alone
in the struggle. In the thick of the very unequal contest which
ensues, three knights, mounted respectively on a lion, a leopard,
and a unicorn, come in opportunely to the rescue, and by their
aid Sir Isumbras gains a complete victory. These of course are
his three lost sons. For each he obtains a kingdom ; and, all
uniting their efforts, they live to see the inhabitants of all their
kingdoms converted :—

They lived and died in good intent,
Unto heaven their souls went,
    When that they dead were ;
Jesu Christ, Heaven's King,
Give us aye his blessing,
    And shield us from harm !

Such, or similar to this, is the usual form of conclusion of all
the old romances, even those—as the *Seven Sages*, for instance—
of which the moral tone is extremely questionable.

A portion of the great romance of Arthur has been given to
us in a modern dress by Tennyson. Few readers of poetry are
unacquainted with his beautiful poem of *Morte d'Arthur*, a
modern rendering of the concluding part of the romance bearing
that title. The *Idylls of the King* are renderings of so many
particular passages or episodes in the same great romance. The
source from which the Laureate drew his materials was Sir
Thomas Malory's compilation of the *Historie of King Arthur*;
(see ch. II. § 5).

(2) *Tales* form the second class of narrative poems. The

tale is a poem in which—as a general rule—the agencies are natural; in which the chief interest lies in the story itself, and the manner in which it is unfolded, not in the style, or language, or peculiar humour of the author; lastly, in which neither is the action on a large scale, nor are the chief actors great personages. The earliest, and still by far the best, collection of such tales which English literature possesses, is the *Canterbury Tales* of Chaucer. In connexion with this work, we shall endeavour to draw out in some detail the proofs which it affords of the solidity and originality of Chaucer's genius.

16. In every great writer there is a purely personal element, and there is also a social element;—by the first, which is also the highest in kind, he is what he is, and soars freely in the empyrean of creative imagination; by the second, he is connected with and modified by the society in which he moves, the writers whom he follows or admires, and even the physical characters of the spot of earth where he resides. It is chiefly under these latter relations ·that we propose to consider the genius of Chaucer.

The English society in which he moved was already far beyond those comparatively simple relations which we ascribe to the society of feudal times. In the eyes of an old romance writer, mankind fall naturally and conveniently under these four divisions—sovereign princes, knights, churchmen, and the commonalty. For this fourth, or proletarian class, he entertains a supreme contempt; he regards them as only fit to hew wood and draw water for princes and knights; and nothing delights him more than to paint the ignominious rout and promiscuous slaughter of thousands of this base-born multitude by the hand of a single favourite knight. There certainly was a time—before great cities rose to wealth and obtained franchises, when feudal castles were scattered like hail over the north of Europe, and private war was universal and incessant—at which this picture of society had much truth in it. And as usually happens, the literature which had sprung up under, and which was adapted only to, such a state of things, continued to be produced from the force of habit, after the face of society had become greatly altered. Shutting their eyes to the progress of things around them—overlooking, or else bewailing as an innovation and a degeneracy, the constant accumulation and growing power of wealth obtained by industry, and the consequent rise of new classes of men into social importance—the romance-writers, as a body, continued rather to adapt their translations or original effusions to the atmosphere of the baronial hall, and to the established order of ideas in the knightly understanding, than to seek for sympathy among classes which they dreaded while affecting to despise.

But it is characteristic of genius, first, to have a profound insight into the real; then, boldly to face it; lastly, by the art which is its inseparable companion, to reproduce it under appropriate forms. Thus it was with Chaucer in the England of the fourteenth century. He had no literary models to work by—in his own language at least—except the antiquated and unreal feudal portraits above referred to; but he had sympathies as large as the nature of man, a soul that could not endure a dead form or a mere conventionality, and an intellect which arranged the human beings around him according to their intrinsic qualities,—by what they were rather than by what they were called. He felt, as Burns did, that

> The rank is but the guinea stamp,
> The man's the gowd for a' that.

And accordingly, in that wonderful gallery of portraits, the prologue to the *Canterbury Tales*, we have the existing aspects and classes of English society described with a broad and impartial hand. The Knight is indeed there,—one figure among many; nor does Chaucer, like Cervantes, present him in a ridiculous light; for knighthood in the fourteenth century was still a reality, not a piece of decayed pageantry, as in the sixteenth; but he and his order appear as what they actually were,—that is, as one element in society amongst many; they do not, as in the pages of romance, cast all other orders of laymen into the shade. Churchmen again are, on the whole, represented without partiality and without bitterness; there may be a tinge of Puritanism in the keenness of some of the invectives against ecclesiastical personages, but it is not more than a tinge. On the whole, Chaucer may be truly said to

> Nothing extenuate,
> Nor set down aught in malice;

and if we have an affected Prioress, a roguish Friar, and a hypocritical Pardoner, we have on the other side the Clerk of Oxenford, with his solid worth and learning, and the well-known character of the good parish priest. But besides the knight, the squire, and the ecclesiastical persons, a crowd of other characters come upon the canvas, and take part in the action. There is the Frankelein, the representative of the sturdy, hospitable, somewhat indolent, English freeholder, whom, however, participation in the political and judicial system introduced by the energetic

Norman had made a better and more sterling person than were his Saxon ancestors. Then we have the mixed population of cities, represented by the Merchant, the Man of Law, the Shipman, the Doctour of Physike, and the good Wife of Bath,—all from the middle classes; and by the Haberdasher, the Carpenter, the Webbe (weaver), &c., from the lower. The inferior ranks of the rural population are represented by the Plowman, the Miller, and the Reve.

17. Viewed in this light, as a picture of contemporary society, the Prologue is certainly the most valuable part of the Canterbury Tales. And what does this picture show us? Not that distorted image, which the feudal pride of the great lords, humoured by the sycophancy of the minstrels, had conjured up in the romances, but the real living face of English society, such as Christianity and the mediæval Church, working now for seven centuries upon the various materials submitted to their influence, had gradually fashioned it to be. Doubtless it shows many evils,—the profanation of sacred callings, the abuse of things originally excellent, ill-repressed tendencies to sloth, luxury, and licentiousness. But it shows also a state of things in which every member of society, even the humblest, had recognised rights, and was not sunk beneath the dignity of man : we have the high and the low, the rich and the poor; but the high are not inordinately high, and the low are not debased. The cement of religion binds together the whole social fabric, causing the common sympathies of its members to predominate above the grounds of estrangement.

18. Lastly, let us endeavour to trace the influence of external nature upon Chaucer's poetical development. It must be borne in mind,—indeed, Chaucer's phraseology constantly brings the fact before us,—that to the English poet of the fourteenth century nature was far from being the pruned, tamed, and civilized phenomenon that she was and is to the poets of this and the eighteenth century. Chaucer speaks naturally, not figuratively, of the *greenwood*, by which he means what is now called in the Australian colonies ' the bush,'—that is, the wild woodland country, from which the original forests have never yet been removed by the hand of man. Even in Shakspere's time large portions of England still fell under this category; so that he, too, could naturally sing of the 'greenwood tree,' and found no difficulty in describing, in *As You Like It*, what an Australian would call *bush life*,—that is, life on a free earth and under a free heaven,—not travelling by turnpike roads, nor haunted by the dread of trespass and its penalties, but permitting men to   ge, and, in Shakspere's phrase, ' to fleet the

time carelessly as in the golden world.' This condition of external nature gives a largeness and freshness to the poetry which
arises under it; the scent of the woods and the song of the
birds seem to hang about the verse, and ' sanctify the numbers.'

But, again, observe the ` eminent healthiness, the well-
balanced stability of Chaucer's mind.   He is no sickly natural-
ist; he does not turn with disgust from town life to ' babble o'
green fields;' he neither feels nor affects such a scorn or dis-
approbation of man and society as to be driven to take refuge
in the untarnished loveliness of Nature, in order to find fit
materials for poetical creations.   Human society, no less than
external nature, is in the eyes of Chaucer beautiful and venerable; it, too, comes from the hand of God; it, too, supplies fit
themes for poetry.

With Shakspere and Spenser, but pre-eminently with the
former, the case is much the same.   In Shakspere there is none
of that morbid revulsion against the crimes or littlenesses of
society which drove Byron and Shelley into alienation and
open revolt against it; nor, again, is there that estrangement
from active life and popular movement which makes Wordsworth
the poet of the fields and mountains, not of man.   In the pages
of the great dramatist, who truly ' holds the mirror up to nature,'
not external only but human, we behold society in all its varied
aspects, by turns repellent and attractive, yet in the main as
establishing noble and dignified relations between man and man.

· 19. The following extracts are taken,—one from the *Clerke's*,
the other from the *Nonnes Prestes Tale*. The much-enduring
Grisildes is thus described :—

1.

Among this pore folk there dwelt a man
Which that was holden porest of hem alle ;
But heighe God som tyme senden can
His grace unto a litel oxes stalle.
Janicula men of that thrope him calle.
A doughter had he, fair y-nough to sight,
And Grisildis this yonge mayden hight.

But though this mayden tender were of age,
Yet in the breste of her virginite
Ther was enclosed ripe and sad corrage ;
And in gret reverence and charite
Hir olde pore fader fostered sche :
A few scheep, spynnyng, on the feld sche kept,
Sche nolde not ben ydel til sche slept.

And whanne sche com hom sche wolde brynge
Wortis and other herbis tymes ofte,

The which sche shred and seth[1] for her lyvyng,
And made hir bed ful hard, and nothing softe.
And ay sche kept hir fadres lif on lofte,[2]
With every obeissance and diligence,
That child may do to fadres reverence.

The confusion in the poor widow's household, after the fox
has carried off her cock, Chaunticleere, is thus humorously
described:—

2.

The sely wydow, and hir doughtres two,
Herden these hennys crie and maken wo,
And out at dores starte thay anon,
And saw the fox toward the wood is gone,
And bar upon his bak the cok away ;
They criden 'Out ! harrow and wayleway !
Ha, ha, the fox !' and after him thay ran,
And eek with staves many another man ;
Ran Colle our dogge, and Talbot, and Garlond,
And Malkin with a distaff in hir hond ;
Ran cow and calf, and eek the veray hogges,
So were they fered for berkyng of the dogges,
And schowting of the men and wymmen eke,
Thay ronne that thay thought hir herte breke,
Thay yelleden as feendes doon in helle;
The dokes criden as men wold hem quelle;[3]
The gees for fere flowen over the trees;
Out of the hyve came the swarm of bees;
So hidous was the noyse, a *benedicite!*
Certes he Jakke Straw, and his meynie,[4]
Ne maden schoutes never half so schrille,
Whan that thay wolden eny Flemyng kille,
As thilke day was maad upon the fox.

20. To whatever period of our literature we may turn, a
multitude of Tales present themselves for review. Gower's
Confessio Amantis is in great part composed of them, the
materials being taken from the Gesta Romanorum, or from
collections of French Fabliaux. Dryden's so-called 'Fables'
are merely translations or modernizations of tales by Ovid,
Chaucer, and Boccaccio. The *Knight's Tale, or Palamon and
Arcite*, and the *Nun's Priest's Tale*, are those which he selected
from Chaucer. Falconer's *Shipwreck*, a popular poem in its
day, is hardly worth quoting from. The smooth and sounding
verse betrays the careful student of Pope, but there is no force
of imagination, no depth or lucidity of intellect.

Crabbe's Tales show great narrative and dramatic skill,
and contain some pathetic passages. Perhaps in all of them the

[1] Boiled.
[2] Kept on lofte. *i.e.* sustained, up-*lift*-ed ; from the Anglo-Saxon *lyft*, air.
[3] Kill.   [4] Band or retinue.

moral is pointed with too much pains; the amiable writer had
never felt that the true worth of poetry transcends any set
didactic purpose :—

> O! to what uses shall we put
> The wild wood-flower that simply blows;
> And is there any moral shut
> Within the bosom of the rose? [1]

21. (3) *Allegories.*—According to the etymology of the
word, allegory means the expressing of one thing by means of
another. And this may serve as a loose general definition of
all allegorical writing; for it will embrace, not only the personification of human qualities, which is the ordinary subject of
allegory, but also the application of any material designation
to a subject to which it is properly inapplicable, as when Langlande speaks of the Castle of Caro, and Bunyan of the city of
Destruction and the town of Apostasy. But in addition to
the general notion of medial representation above stated, the
word allegory involves also by usage the idea of a *narrative.*
It embraces two kinds: 1, allegories proper; and 2, fables.
The proper allegory has usually a didactic, but sometimes a
satirical purpose; sometimes, again, it blends satire with instruction. The author of the famous allegorical satire of
Reynard the Fox thus describes at the conclusion (we quote
from Goethe's version) the didactic intention of his satire :—
'Let every one quickly turn himself to wisdom, shun vice and
honour virtue. This is the sense of the poem; in which the
poet has mingled fable and truth, that you may be able to dis-
cern good from evil, and to value wisdom,—that also the
buyers of this book may from the course of the world receive
daily instruction. For so are things constituted; so will they
continue; and thus ends our poem of Reynard's nature and
actions. May the Lord help us to eternal glory! Amen.'
In Langlande's allegorical *Vision of Piers Plowman,* the
satirical purpose so preponderates, that we have thought it best
to class the work under the head of Satire. The great majority
of the allegorical poems of our early writers have didactic aims
more or less definite. The allegory of the *Flower and the
Leaf* has the following symbolical meaning, as Speght in his
argument expresses it :—'They which honour the Flower, a
thing fading with every blast, are such as look after beauty and
worldly pleasure; but they that honour the Leaf, which abideth
with the root notwithstanding the frosts and winter storms, are
they which follow virtue and enduring qualities, without regard

---

[1] Tennyson's *Fairy Princess.*

of worldly respects.' The following extract is from the concluding portion of the poem :—

> 'Now, faire Madame,' quoth I,
> 'If I durst aske, what is the cause and why,
> That knightes have the ensigne of honour,
> Rather by the leafe than the floure?'
>
> 'Soothly, doughter,' quod she, 'this is the trouth:—
> For knightes ever should be persevering,
> To seeke honour without feintise or slouth,
> Fro wele to better in all manner thinge;
> In signe of which, with leaves aye lastinge
> They be rewarded after their degre,
> Whose lusty green may not appaired be,
>
> 'But aye keping their beautè fresh and greene;
> For there nis storme that may hem deface,
> Haile nor snow, winde nor frostes kene;
> Wherefore they have this property and grace.
> And for the floure, within a little space
> Wol they be lost, so simple of nature
> They be, that they no grievance may endure.'

The allegorical works of Lydgate and Hawes have not sufficient merit to require special notice. Some account of Dunbar's
and Lyndsay's allegories was given in our notice of those poets : [1]
an extract from *The Thistle and the Rose* is subjoined :—

> Than callit scho all flouris that grow on field,
>   Discryving all their fassiouns and effeiris;
> Upon the awful THRISSILL scho beheld,
>   And saw him keipit with a busche of speiris;
>   Considering him so able for the weiris,
> A radius crown of rubeis scho him gaif,
> And said, In field go forth, and fend the laif.[2]
>
> And sen thou art a king, thou be discreit;
>   Herb without vertew thou hold nocht of sic pryce,
> As herb of vertew and of odour sweit;
>   And lat no nettil vyle and full of vyce
>   Hir fallow[3] to the goodly flour-de-lyce;
> Nor lat no wyld weid full of churlicheness,
> Compair hir till the lilleis nobilness:
>
> Nor hald no udir flour in sic denty
>   As the fresche Rois, of cullour reid and quhyt;
> For gif thou dois, hurt is thyne honesty,
>   Considering that no flour is so perfyt,
>   So full of blissful angellik bewty,
> Imperiall birth, honour, and dignite.

22. We pass on to the great allegorical masterpiece of the
Elizabethan period,—Spenser's *Faerie Queene.* In this poem

---

[1] P   16.   [2] Defend the rest.   [3] Join herself.

the Gothic or Romantic spirit is even yet more decisively in the ascendant than in the plays of Shakspere, although under the correction of the finer feeling for art which the Renaissance had awakened. The richness of the imagery, the stately beauty of the style,—above all, that nameless and indescribable charm, which a work of true genius always bears about it,—make one forget the undeniable prolixity with which the design is worked out.

Some idea of the nature of the poem, and of the depth and richness of Spenser's imagination, may be gained from the following brief analysis of the twelfth canto of the second book, which contains the *Legend of Sir Guyon, or of Temperance.*

Sir Guyon, under the guidance of a Palmer, is voyaging towards the Bower of Blisse, the abode of Acrasia (Intemperance). The boat has to pass between the Gulf of Greedinesse and a Magnetic mountain. Escaped from these dangers, they coast by the Wandering Islands; then they run the gauntlet between a quicksand and a whirlpool. A 'hideous host' of sea-monsters vainly endeavour to terrify them. Then they sail near the Bay of the Mermaids, who sing more enchantingly than the Sirens; but Guyon turns a deaf ear. At last they reach the desired land, and proceed to the Bower of Blisse. Rejecting the cup of wine tendered by the Dame Excesse, Guyon presses forward through the garden :—

> Eft soones they heard a most melodious sound,
> Of all that might delight a dainty eare,
> Such as attonce might not on living ground,
> Save in this paradise be heard elsewhere :
> Right hard it was for wight that did it heare,
> To read what manner musicke that mote bee ;
> For all that pleasing is to living eare
> Was there consorted in one harmonie ;
> Birds, voices, instruments, winds, waters, all agree.

> The joyous birdes, shrouded in chearefull shade,
> Their notes unto the voice attempred sweet ;
> Th' angelicall soft trembling voices made
> To th' instruments divine respondence meet ;
> The silver-sounding instruments did meet
> With the base murmure of the waters' fall ;
> The waters' fall, with difference discreet,
> Now soft, now loud, unto the wind did call ;
> The gentle warbling wind low answered to all.

Then from the lips of an unseen singer there issues an enthralling Epicurean strain :—

> The whiles some one did chaunt this lovely lay :
> ' Ah ! see, whoso fayre thing dost faine to see,
> In springing flowre the image of thy day !
> Ah ! see the virgin rose, how sweetly she

Doth first peepe forth with bashful modestee,
That fairer seemes the lesse ye see her may !
Lo ! see, soon after how more bold and free
Her bared bosome she doth broad display;
Lo ! see soon after how she fades and falls away !

' So passeth, in the passing of a day,
Of mortall life, the leafe, the bud, the flowre ;
Ne more doth flourish after first decay,
That erst was sought to deck both bed and bowre
Of many a lady, and many a paramoure !
Gather therefore the rose whilst yet is prime,
For soon comes age that will her pride deflowre ;
Gather the rose of love whilst yet is time,
Whilst loving thou mayst loved be with equall crime.'

But Guyon holds on his way unswervingly, and at last comes
upon Acrasia, whom he seizes and binds, together with her
lover, a foolish dissipated youth, with the strangely modern
name of *Verdant.* Then the knight breaks down all those
pleasant bowers 'with vigour pittilesse,' and the Palmer turns
back into their natural shape a crowd of persons, whom Acrasia
had, Circe-like, transformed into animals. So ends the canto.

23. The metre of the *Faerie Queene* was formed by Spenser
from the Italian *ottava rima,* or eight-line stanza (said to have
been invented by Boccaccio), by the addition of a ninth line, two
syllables longer than the rest. This, however, is not the only
distinction, for the internal organization of the two stanzas is
widely different. That of Spenser closely resembles in this
respect the Chaucerian heptastich, the essential character of
both being fixed by the riming of the fifth line to the fourth.
Strike out from the Spenserian stanza the sixth and seventh lines,
riming respectively to the eighth and fifth, and cut off the two
extra syllables in the last line, and you have at once the Chaucerian heptastich. It cannot be denied that the Spenserian is a
more subtly constructed stanza than the *ottava rima;* yet, from
its length, it tends to become unwieldy, and therefore requires
to be managed with the utmost skill. The use of it with Spenser
seems to have become a sort of second nature; when employed
by others, even by so considerable a poet as Byron, it does not
escape from being occasionally wearisome.

24. Thomson, in his *Castle of Indolence,* succeeded remarkably well in imitating the roll of the Spenserian stanza. The
first canto, which, as Dr. Johnson observes, ' opens a scene of
lazy luxury that fills the imagination,' dilates with evident gusto
on the pleasures of a life of indolence. Thomson himself is
described in the following stanza, said to have been written by
Lord

A bard here dwelt, more fat than bard beseems,
Who void of envy, guile, and lust of gain,
On virtue still and virtue's pleasing themes,
Pour'd forth his unpremeditated strain;
The world forsaking with a calm disdain,
Here laugh'd he careless in his easy seat;
Here quaff'd, encircled with the joyous train,
Oft moralizing sage : his ditty sweet
He loathèd much to write, ne carèd to repeat.

In the second canto the haunt of 'lazy luxury' is broken in
upon by the 'Knight of Arts and Industry,' who destroys the
castle, and puts to flight its inmates.

25. The other form of allegorical composition is the *fable*, or
apologue, in which, under the guise of things said or done by the
inferior animals, tendencies in human nature are illustrated,
maxims of practical wisdom enforced, and the besetting vices
and inconsistencies of man exposed. Fables are short, because
they are severally confined to the illustration of a single maxim
or tendency, and would inculcate their moral less strikingly were
the story enveloped in many words. In this kind of composition, the only considerable metrical work in our literature is
Gay's Fables. The idea of versifying Æsop was taken by Gay
from Lafontaine, but executed with far inferior power and grace.
The following is a fair sample of the collection :—

THE TURKEY AND THE ANT.

In other men we faults can spy
And blame the mote that dims their eye,
Each little speck and blemish find;
To our own stronger errors blind.
  A Turkey, tired of common food,
Forsook the barn, and sought the wood;
Behind her ran an infant train,
Collecting here and there a grain.
  'Draw near, my birds !' the mother cries,
'This hill delicious fare supplies;
Behold the busy negro race,
See millions blacken all the place !
Fear not; like me, with freedom eat;
An ant is most delightful meat.
How bless'd, how envy'd were our life,
Could we but 'scape the poulterer's knife !
But man, curs'd man, on turkeys preys,
And Christmas shortens all our days.
Sometimes with oysters we combine,
Sometimes assist the savoury chine;
From the low peasant to the lord,
The Turkey smokes on every board;
Sure men for gluttony are curs'd,
Of the seven deadly sins the worst.'

> An Ant, who climbed beyond her reach,
> Thus answer'd from the neighbouring beech :
>   ' Ere you remark another's sin,
> Bid your own conscience look within :
> Control thy more voracious bill,
> Nor for a breakfast nations kill.'

A variety of other fables and apologues in verse lie scattered over the literary field, some of which are sufficiently spirited and entertaining. Among the best of these are Mrs. Thrale's *Three Warnings*, and Merrick's *Chameleon*.

26. (4) By *Romantic poems*, the name assigned to the fourth subdivision of narrative poetry, we mean poems in which heroic subjects are epically treated, after the manner of the old romances of chivalry, yet in which neither the subject nor the form rises to the true dignity of the epic. Such poems are essentially the fruit of modern times and modern ideas. Between the period of the Renaissance, when the production of metrical romances ceased, and the close of the eighteenth century, the taste of European society preferred, both in art and literature, works modelled upon the masterpieces of Greek and Roman genius, and recoiled with an aversion, more or less sincere, from all that was Gothic or mediæval. In such a period, a romantic poem, had it appeared, would have been crushed by the general ridicule, or smothered under the general neglect. But, towards the close of the eighteenth century, a reaction set in, and the romantic poems of Scott and his imitators are one among many of its fruits.

The *Lay of the Last Minstrel* (1805), the earliest of these productions, exhibits the influence of the old romances much more decidedly than those of later date. Expressions and half lines constantly occur in it, which are transferred unaltered from the older compositions; and the vivid and minute description of Branksome Hall, with which the poem opens, is quite in the style of the old Trouvères :—

> Nine-and-twenty knights of fame
>   Hung their shields in Branksome Hall ;
> Nine-and-twenty squires of name
>   Brought them their steeds to bower from stall ;
>   Nine-and-twenty yeomen tall
>   Waited, duteous, on them all :
>   They were all knights of mettle true,
>   Kinsmen to the bold Buccleuch.
>
> Ten of them were sheathed in steel,
> With belted sword and spur on heel :
> They quitted not their harness bright,
> Neither by day nor yet by night :

> They lay down to rest,
> With corslet laced,
> Pillowed on buckler cold and hard ;
> They carved at the meal
> With gloves of steel,
> And they drank the red wine through the helmet barred.
>
> Ten squires, ten yeomen, mail-clad men,
> Waited the beck of the warders ten ;
> Thirty steeds, both fleet and wight,
> Stood saddled in stable day and night,
> Barbed with frontlet of steel, I trow,
> And with Jedwood-axe at saddle-bow ;
> A hundred more fed free in stall ;
> Such was the custom of Branksome Hall.

27. The popularity of the *Lay* naturally induced Scott to go
on working in the same mine; *Marmion* came out in 1808, and
the *Lady of the Lake* in 1810. *Marmion*, though it has fine
passages, is faulty as a poem. The introductions to the cantos,
addressed to six of his friends, are so long, and touch upon such
a variety of topics, that the impressions they create interfere
with those which the story itself is intended to produce ; nor
have they much intrinsic merit, if we except that to William
Rose, containing the famous memorial lines on Pitt and Fox.
In the *Lady of the Lake*, Scott's poetical style reaches its acme.
Here the romantic tale culminates ; the utmost that can be expected from a kind of poetry far below the highest, and from a
metre essentially inferior to the heroic, is here attained. The
story is conducted with much art ; the characters are interesting ; the scenery glorious ; the versification far less faulty than in
Marmion.

28. **Byron's** Oriental Tales—the *Giaour*, the *Corsair*, the
Bride of Abydos, &c.—are but imitations, with changed scenery
and accessories, of Scott's romantic poems, though they displaced
them for a time in the public favour. But the *Lady of the
Lake* will probably outlive the *Corsair*, because it appeals to
wider and more permanent sympathies. The young, the
vehement, the restless, delight in the latter, because it reflects
and glorifies to their imagination the wild disorder of their own
spirits ; the aged and the calm find little in it to prize or to
commend. But the former poem, besides that 'hurried frankness of composition which pleases soldiers, sailors, and young
people of bold and active disposition,'[1] has attractions also for
the firm even mind of manhood and the pensiveness of age ; the
truth and vividness of its painting, whether of manners or of

---

[1] *Life of Scott: Diary.*

nature, delight the one; the healthy buoyancy of tone, recalling the days of its youthful vigour, pleasantly interests the other.

The following extract is from the well-known Pirate's Song, with which the *Corsair* opens :—

> O'er the glad waters of the dark blue sea,
> Our thoughts as boundless and our souls as free,
> Far as the breeze can bear, the billows foam,
> Survey our empire, and behold our home.
> These are our realms, no limits to their sway—
> Our flag the sceptre all who meet obey.
> Ours the wild life in tumult still to range
> From toil to rest, and joy in every change.
> Oh, who can tell? not thou, luxurious slave!
> Whose soul would sicken o'er the heaving wave!
> Not thou, vain lord of wantonness and ease!
> Whom slumber soothes not—pleasure cannot please.—
> Oh, who can tell, save he whose heart hath tried,
> And danced in triumph o'er the waters wide,
> The exulting sense—the pulse's maddening play,
> That thrills the wanderer of that trackless way;
> That for itself can woo the approaching fight,
> And turn what some deem danger to delight;
> That seeks what cravens shun with more than zeal,
> And where the feebler faint—can only feel :—
> Feel—to the rising bosom's inmost core,
> Its hope awaken and its spirit soar!

29. **Moore's** *Lalla Rookh* is also a Romantic poem, more musical and more equably sustained than those of Byron, but inferior to his in force, and to Scott's both in force and nobleness   One passage we will give ;—it is that in which the Peri, whose admission to Paradise depends upon her finding a gift for the Deity which will be meet for His acceptance, and who has already vainly offered the heart's blood of a hero fallen in his country's defence, and the last sigh of a maiden who had sacrificed her life for her lover,—finds, at last, the acceptable gift in the tear of penitence shed by one who had seemed hardened in crime :—

> But, hark! the vesper-call to prayer,
>   As slow the orb of daylight sets,
> Is rising sweetly on the air
>   From Syria's thousand minarets!
> The boy has started from the bed
> Of flowers, where he had laid his head,
> And down upon the fragrant sod
>   Kneels, with his forehead to the South,
> Lisping the eternal name of God
>   From purity's own cherub mouth,

And looking, while his hands and eyes
Are lifted to the glowing skies,
Like a stray babe of Paradise,
Just lighted on that flowery plain,
And seeking for its home again !
Oh, 'twas a sight—that Heaven—that child—
A scene which might have well beguiled
Ev'n haughty Eblis of a sigh
For glories lost and peace gone by.

And how felt *he*, the wretched man
Reclining there—while memory ran
O'er many a year of guilt and strife,
Flew o'er the dark field of his life,
Nor found one sunny resting-place,
Nor brought him back one branch of grace !
' There *was* a time,' he said, in mild
Heart-humbled tones,—' thou blessed child !
When, young and haply pure as thou,
    I looked and prayed like thee,—but now——'
He hung his head,—each nobler aim
And hope and feeling which had slept
From boyhood's hour, that instant came
    Fresh o'er him, and he wept—he wept !

30. (5) The *Historical Poem* is a metrical narrative of
public events, extending over a period more or less prolonged
of a nation's history. It lies open to the obvious objection
that, if the intention be merely to communicate facts, they can
be more easily and clearly described in prose; if to write something poetically beautiful, the want of unity of plan, and the
restraints which the historical style imposes on the imagination,
must be fatal to success. Hence the riming chronicles of
Lazamon, Robert of Gloucester, and Robert Manning, though
interesting to the *historian* of our literature, are of no value to
the critic. In Dryden's *Annus Mirabilis* the defects of this
style are less apparent, because the narrative is confined to the
events of one year, and that year (1666) was rendered memorable by two great calamities, neither of which was unsusceptible
of poetic treatment—the Great Plague, and the Fire of London.
Yet, after all, the *Annus Mirabilis* is a dull poem; few readers
would now venture upon the interminable series of its lumbering stanzas.

Didactic Poetry:—The 'Hind and Panther;' 'Essay on Man;' 'Essay on Criticism;' 'Vanity of Human Wishes.'

31. We have now arrived at the didactic class of poems,
those, namely, in which it is the express object of the writer to
inculcate some moral lesson, some religious tenet, or some philo-

F F

sophical opinion. Pope's *Essay on Man*, Dryden's *Hind and Panther*, and many other well-known poems, answer to this description.

All, or very nearly all, the Anglo-Saxon poetry composed subsequently to the introduction of Christianity, bears a didactic character. Of Cædmon the Venerable Bede remarks, that he 'never composed an idle verse;' that is to say, his poetical aims were always didactic. A large proportion also of the English poetry produced in the three centuries following the Conquest had direct instruction in view. Most of Chaucer's allegories point to some kind of moral; but the father of our poetry seems to have thought that when a writer desired to be purely and simply didactic, he should employ prose; for the only two of the *Canterbury Tales* which answer to that description—the *Parson's Tale on Penance*, and the *Tale of Melibœus*, enforcing the duty of the forgiveness of injuries—are in prose. Shakspere never wrote a didactic poem; though there is no limit to the suggestiveness and thought-enkindling power of his pregnant lines. The same may be said of Milton; yet, as might be expected from the extreme earnestness of the man, a subordinate didactic purpose is often traceable, not only in the *Paradise Lost* but in the *Comus*, the *Lycidas*, and even the *Sonnets*. The earliest regular didactic poem in the language is the *Hind and Panther* of Dryden, who, it will be remembered, was always a good and ready prose writer, who developed his poetical talent late, and who, but for his marvellous genius for rime, which grew constantly with his years, would have preferred, one might fancy, prose to verse for a religious polemic, as he had preferred it twenty years before for an essay on the Drama. However, we must be thankful that by indulging his genius in this instance, he has left us a very extraordinary specimen of metrical dialectics.

32. Pope's *Essay on Man*, writes Mr. Pattison, 'is a vindication of Providence. The appearances of evil in the world arise from our seeing only a part of the whole. Excesses and contrary qualities are means by which the harmony of the system is procured. The ends of Providence are answered even by our errors and imperfections. God designs happiness to be equal, but realises it through general laws. Virtue only constitutes a happiness which is universally attainable. This happiness through virtue is only reached in society or social order, which is only a part of the general order. The perfection of virtue is a conformity to the order of Providence here, crowned by the hope of full satisfaction hereafter.' At a later page Mr. Pattison, who agrees with several modern critics in

forming a low estimate of the matter of the *Essay*, expresses a strong admiration for the execution. The importance of *style* is hence perceived, which can unite in a common feeling of cordial appreciation minds which estimate in various ways the substance of a work submitted to them. The following passages will enable the reader to form some notion of this perfection of style :—

> Lo ! the poor Indian, whose untutored mind
> Sees God in clouds, or hears him in the wind ;
> His soul proud science never taught to stray
> Far as the solar walk or milky way ;
> Yet simple nature to his hope has given,
> Behind the cloud-topp'd hill, an humbler heaven ;
> Some safer world in depth of woods embraced,
> Some happier island in the watery waste,
> Where slaves once more their native land behold,
> No fiends torment, no Christians thirst for gold.
> To be, contents his natural desire—
> He asks no angel's wing, no seraph's fire ;
> But thinks, admitted to that equal sky,
> His faithful dog shall bear him company.

The optimism, which is the philosophical keynote of the Essay —which Leibnitz had rendered fashionable by his *Theodicea*, and Voltaire was to turn into ridicule in his *Candide*—is thus summed up at the end of the first part :—

> Submit,—in this or any other sphere,
> Secure to be as blest as thou canst bear.
> Safe in the hand of one disposing Power,
> Or in the natal or the mortal hour.
> All Nature is but Art, unknown to thee ;
> All chance, direction which thou canst not see ;
> All discord, harmony not understood ;
> All partial evil, universal good ;
> And, spite of pride, in erring reason's spite,
> One truth is clear—Whatever is, is right.

The following analysis of Fame is from the fourth part :—

> What's fame ?—A fancied life in others' breath,
> A thing beyond us, e'en before our death.
> Just what you hear, you have ; and what's unknown,
> The same (my lord) if Tully's or your own.
> All that we feel of it begins and ends
> In the small circle of our foes and friends ;
> To all beside, as much an empty shade
> As Eugene living, or as Cæsar dead ;
> Alike or when or where they shone or shine,
> Or on the Rubicon or on the Rhine.
> A wit's a feather, and a chief a rod—
> An honest man's the noblest work of God.
> , ...

All fame is foreign but of true desert,
Plays round the head, but comes not to the heart;
One self-approving hour whole years outweighs
Of stupid starers, and of loud huzzas;
And more true joy Marcellus exiled feels,
Than Cæsar with a senate at his heels.

33. The *Essay on Criticism* must also be classed among
didactic poems. In it Pope lays down rules, in emulation of
Horace's famous Epistle *De Arte Poeticâ*, of Boileau's *Art de
Poésie*, and Roscommon's *Essay on Translated Verse*, for the
guidance, not of the writers, but of the critics of poetry. The
depth and sincerity of the admiration with which Pope looked
up to the ancient masters of song, appear from many passages
of this brilliant Essay, particularly from the peroration of the
first part, which, though somewhat marred by the anti-climax
at the end, is replete with a nervous strength—the poet's voice
quivering, as it were, with suppressed emotion, yet not less clear
or musical for the weakness—which it is easier to feel than to
describe.

Still green with bays each ancient altar stands,
Above the reach of sacrilegious hands;
Secure from flames, from envy's fiercer rage,
Destructive war, and all-involving age.
See, from each clime the learn'd their incense bring!
Hear, in all tongues consenting pæans ring!
In praise so just let every voice be joined,
And fill the general chorus of mankind.
Hail, bards triumphant! born in happier days,
Immortal heirs of universal praise!
Whose honours with increase of ages grow,
As streams roll down, enlarging as they flow;
Nations unborn your mighty names shall sound,
And worlds applaud that must not yet be found!
O may some spark of your celestial fire,
The last, the meanest, of your sons inspire,
(That on weak wings from far pursues your flights,
Glows while he reads, but trembles as he writes),
To teach vain wits a science little known,
To admire superior sense, and doubt their own.

34. Johnson's poem on the *Vanity of Human Wishes* is
imitated from the Tenth *Satire* of Juvenal. The striking
passage on Hannibal (expende Hannibalem, &c.) is transferred
to Charles XII. of Sweden. The lines will bear quotation :—

On what foundation stands the warrior's pride,
How just his hopes, let Swedish Charles decide;
A frame of adamant, a soul of fire,
No dangers fright him, and no labours tire;

O'er love, o'er fear, extends his wide domain,
Unconquer'd lord of pleasure and of pain;
No joys to him pacific sceptres yield,
War sounds the trump, he rushes to the field;
Behold surrounding kings their powers combine,
And one capitulate, and one resign;
Peace courts his hand, but spreads her charms in vain;
'Think nothing gained,' he cries, 'till nought remain;
' On Moscow's walls till Gothic standards fly,
' And all be mine beneath the Polar sky.'
The march begins in military state,
And nations on his eye suspended wait;
Sterne Famine guards the solitary coast,
And Winter barricades the realms of Frost;
He comes, nor want nor cold his course delay;—
Hide, blushing Glory, hide Pultowa's day:
The vanquish'd hero leaves his broken bands,
And shows his miseries in distant lands;
Condemn'd a needy supplicant to wait,
While ladies interpose, and slaves debate.
But did not chance at length her error mend?
Did no subverted empire mark his end?
Did rival monarchs give the fatal wound?
Or hostile millions press him to the ground?
His fall was destined to a barren strand,
A petty fortress, and a dubious hand;
He left the name, at which the world grew pale,
To point a moral, or adorn a tale.

Satirical Poetry—Moral, Personal, Political:—Hall, Pope, Byron, Butler, Dryden, Churchill, Wolcot.

35. The didactic poet assumes the office of an educator; the satirist that of a *censor morum*. The first has the same relation to the second which the schools of a country have to its courts of justice. One aims at forming virtue, and imparting wisdom; the other at scourging vice, and exposing folly. According to its proper theory, satire is the Lynch law of a civilised society; it reaches persons and punishes acts which the imperfections of legal justice would leave unchastised. But could not such persons and acts be more efficaciously influenced by warnings of a didactic nature? should they not be left to the philosopher and the divine? The satirist answers, no; there is a class of offenders so case-hardened in vanity and selfishness as to be proof against all serious admonition. To these the dictum applies—

——Ridiculum acri
Fortius et melius magnas plerumque secat res.

The only way of shaming or deterring them is to turn the

world's laugh against them—to analyse their conduct, and show
it up before the public gaze as intrinsically odious and contemptible. He does not expect thereby to effect any moral
improvement in *them*, but rather to shame and deter others who
might be preparing to imitate them; just as a good system of
police is favourable to morality, by diminishing the temptations
and the returns to wrongdoing. The satirist therefore professes
a moral purpose :—

> Hear this and tremble, *you who 'scape the laws*;
> Yes, while I live, no rich or noble knave
> Shall walk the world in credit to his grave;
> To Virtue only and her friends a friend,
> The world beside may murmur or commend.[1]

36. Satirical poetry is divisible into three classes—Moral,
Personal, and Political. By the first is meant that general
satire on contemporary morals and manners, of which Horace,
Juvenal, and Pope furnish us with such admirable examples.
Personal satires are those which are mainly directed against
individuals, as Dryden's *MacFlecknoe*, and *English Bards and
Scotch Reviewers*. Political satires are written in the interest
of a party in the state; the most famous instance is Dryden's
Absalom and Achitophel.

In purely personal satire, the chances are so small in favour
of the chastisement being administered with pure impartiality
and justice, that the world rightly attaches less value to it than
to moral satire. The occasions when personal satire becomes
really terrible, are those when, in the midst of a general moral
satire on prevailing vices or follies, the acts and character of
individuals are introduced by way of *illustrating* the maxims
that have just been enunciated. The attack then has the
appearance of being unpremeditated, as if it had been simply
suggested by the line of reflection into which the poet had
fallen : and its effect is proportionally greater. Pope well
understood this principle, as we shall presently see.

(1) *Moral Satire.* In the Middle Ages, moral satire generally seized upon ecclesiastical abuses. The *Land of Cockaygne*
(assigned by Warton to the end of the eleventh century, but
which must be at least a century later) is a satire on the
indolence and gluttony into which the monastic life, when
relaxed, has occasionally fallen. The *Vision of Piers Plowman*
is in great part satirical, directing its attacks chiefly against the
higher secular clergy.

The satires of Donne and Hall (the first of which received

---

[1] Pope's *Imitations of Horace*.

the honour of modernisation from Pope) are too rough and harsh to have much poetical value. For a specimen of Hall's powers in this way, we take the following picture of a chaplain in a country house, at the end of the sixteenth century :—

> A gentle squire would gladly entertaine
> Into his house some trencher-chapelaine :
> Some willing man that might instruct his sons,
> And that would stand to good conditions.
> First, that he lie upon the truckle-bed,
> Whiles his young maister lieth o'er his head.
> Secondly, that he do, on no default,
> Ever presume to sit above the salt.
> Third, that he never change his trencher twice ;
> Fourth, that he use all common courtesies ;
> Sit bare at meales, and one halfe rise and wait ;
> Last, that he never his young maister beat.
>
> All these observed, he could contented be,
> To give five marks and winter liverie.

Swift's satire, strong and crushing as it is, is so much the less effective, because it seems to spring, not from moral indignation, but from a misanthropical disgust at mankind. Pope excelled in satire, as in everything else that he attempted, and must be ranked with the few really great satirists of all time. Not that his indignant denunciations were not frequently prompted by personal pique and irritated vanity; but his fine taste usually enabled him to mask his personal feelings under the veil, more or less transparent, of a stern and stoical regard for virtue. His satirical writings in verse consist of the four *Moral Essays*, in the form of Epistles, addressed to several persons; the epistle to Dr. Arbuthnot, also called the *Prologue to the Satires*, the *Imitations of Horace* (six in the heroic couplet, and two in octo-syllabics, after the manner of Swift), the *Epilogue to the Satires*, and the *Dunciad*. Of the Moral Essays, the first, *Of the Knowledge and Characters of Men*, is, till just at the close, rather descriptive than satirical. In the second, *On the Characters of Women*, he dashes at once into satire. In contrast to those empty-headed, frivolous fair ones, whose ' true no-meaning puzzles more than wit,' he draws the celebrated character of Sarah Duchess of Marlborough :—

> But what are these to great Atossa's mind,
> Scarce once herself, by turns all womankind ;
> Who, with herself, or others, from her birth
> Finds all her life one warfare upon earth ;
> Shines in exposing knaves and painting fools,
> Yet is whate'er she hates and ridicules.

No thought advances, but her eddy brain
Whisks it about, and down it goes again.
Full sixty years the world has been her trade,
The wisest fool much time has ever made.

. . . .

Offend her, and she knows not to forgive ;
Oblige her, and she'll hate you while you live ;
But die, and she'll adore you—then the bust
And temple rise—then fall again to dust.
Last night her lord was all that's good and great—
A knave this morning, and his will a cheat.
Strange ! by the means defeated of the ends,
By spirit robb'd of power, by warmth of friends,
By wealth of followers ! without one distress,
Sick of herself, through very selfishness !
Atossa, cursed with every granted prayer,
Childless with all her children, wants an heir.
To heirs unknown descends the unguarded store,
Or wanders, heaven-directed, to the poor.

In the third essay, on the *Use of Riches*, after the beautiful
description of the *Man of Ross*, who, with ' five hundred pounds
a year,' made his beneficent influence felt in all the country
round, occurs, by way of contrast, the picture of the closing
scene of Charles II.'s splendid favourite, the second Duke of
Buckingham :—

In the worst inn's worst room, with mat half hung,
The floors of plaster, and the walls of dung,
On once a flock-bed, but repaired with straw,
With tape-tied curtains, never meant to draw,
The George and Garter dangling from that bed
Where tawdry yellow strove with dirty red,
Great Villiers lies—alas ! how changed from him,
That life of pleasure, and that soul of whim !
Gallant and gay, in Cliveden's proud alcove,
The bower of wanton Shrewsbury and love ;
Or just as gay at council, in a ring
Of mimic statesmen, and their merry king.
No wit to flatter left of all his store !
No fool to laugh at, which he valued more ;
There, victor of his health, of fortune, friends,
And fame, this lord of useless thousands ends !

Pope perhaps took up this particular character from the ambition of rivalling Dryden, who, as we shall see presently, wrote
a powerful piece of satire upon Buckingham, in his *Absalom
and Achitophel*. The fourth essay satirises the various kinds
of bad taste, but contains no passages particularly suitable for
citation.

In the *Dunciad* personal satire predominates, but there are passages of more general bearing, in which Pope rises to the full height of the genius. Such a passage is the description of the approach of the empire of Dulness, at the end of the poem :—

> She comes ! she comes ! the sable throne behold
> Of Night primeval, and of Chaos old,
> Before her, Fancy's gilded clouds decay,
> And all its varying rainbows die away.
> Wit shoots in vain his momentary fires,
> The meteor drops, and in a flash expires.
>
> .   .   .   .
>
> See skulking Truth to her old cavern fled,
> Mountains of casuistry heaped o'er her head !
> Philosophy, that lean'd on Heaven before,
> Shrinks to her second cause, and is no more,
> Physic of metaphysic begs defence,
> And metaphysic calls for aid on sense !
> See mystery to mathematics fly !
> In vain ! they gaze, turn giddy, rave, and die.
> Religion, blushing, veils her sacred fires,
> And unawares Morality expires.
> Nor public flame nor private dares to shine :
> Nor human spark is left, nor glimpse divine !
> Lo ! thy dread empire, Chaos ! is restored ;
> Light dies before thy uncreating word :
> Thy hand, great Anarch ! lets the curtain fall ;
> And universal darkness buries all.

(2.) *Personal Satire.* In the epistle to Dr. Arbuthnot— one of the brightest, wittiest, and most forcible productions of the human intellect—after lashing the minor poets of the day, all whom—

> his modest satire bade translate,
> And own'd that nine such poets made a Tate—

the poet proceeds to strike at higher game :—

> Peace to all such ! but were there one whose fires
> True genius kindles, and fair fame inspires :
> Bless'd with each talent, and each art to please,
> And born to write, converse, and live with ease ;
> Should such a man, too fond to rule alone,
> Bear, like the Turk, no brother near the throne,
> View him with scornful, yet with jealous eyes,
> And hate for arts that caused himself to rise ;
> Damn with faint praise, assent with civil leer,
> And without sneering, teach the rest to sneer ;
> Willing to wound, and yet afraid to strike,
> Just hint a fault, and hesitate dislike ;
> Alike reserved to blame or to commend,
> A timorous foe, and a suspicious friend ;
> Dreading e'en fools, by flatterers besieged,
> And so obliging that he ne'er obliged ;

Like Cato, give his little senate laws,
And sit attentive to his own applause;
While wits and templars every sentence raise,
And wonder with a foolish face of praise—
Who but must laugh, if such a man there be?
Who would not weep, if Atticus [1] were he?

It would be easy to multiply extracts from the *Imitations of Horace* which follow; but we must leave the reader to study them for himself. Sketches of his own boyhood—concise but weighty criticisms on English poets—savage attacks on the objects of his hate, Lord Hervey, for instance—and noble descriptions, somewhat jarring therewith, of the ideal dignity and equity of satire,—all this and more will be found in these wonderful productions. The two which are written in the manner of Swift show a marked inferiority to the rest.

In personal satire, the main object is the exposure of an individual or individuals. Skelton's satires on Wolsey are perhaps the earliest example in our literature. Dryden's *MacFlecknoe* is an attack on Shadwell, a rival dramatist and a Whig, and therefore doubly obnoxious to the Tory laureate. Churchill's satires, though much extolled by his contemporaries, have little interest for modern readers. Gifford's *Baviad and Mæviad* is a clever satire in two parts, in the manner of Pope, on the affected poets and poetesses of the Cruscan school; (see ch. v. § 68.) The following extract will give an idea of its merits :—

Lo, Della Crusca! In his closet pent,
He toils to give the crude conception vent;
Abortive thoughts, that right and wrong confound,
Truth sacrificed to letters, sense to sound,
False glare, incongruous images, combine,
And noise and nonsense clatter through the line.
'Tis done. Her house the generous Piozzi lends,
And thither summons her blue-stocking friends;
The summons her blue-stocking friends obey,
Lured by the love of poetry— and tea.

In the *English Bards and Scotch Reviewers*, Byron, with the reckless petulance of youth, held up to ridicule nearly all the poets of his day—Scott, Wordsworth, Southey, Coleridge, Moore, &c. In later life, however, he made ample amends for several of these attacks, to which irritation against the *Edinburgh Review*, and the feeling of power, rather than any serious dislike of his brother poets, had impelled him. The point and spirit of the poem fall off after the first two hundred lines, and

---

[1] Addison.

it becomes at last absolutely tedious. The following extracts
will serve to illustrate the bold and dashing character of this
satire. The first regards Southey :—

> Next see tremendous Thalaba côme on,
> Arabia's monstrous, wild, and wondrous son ;
> Domdaniel's dread destroyer, who o'erthrew
> More mad magicians than the world e'er knew.
> Immortal hero ! all thy foes o'ercome,
> For ever reign—the rival of Tom Thumb !
> Since startled metre fled before thy face,
> Well wert thou doomed the last of all thy race,
> Well might triumphant Genii bear thee hence,
> Illustrious conqueror of common sense !

The next is on Wordsworth :—

> Next comes the dull disciple of thy school,
> That mild apostate from poetic rule,
> The simple Wordsworth—framer of a lay
> As soft as evening in his favourite May.
> Who warns his friend to 'shake off toil and trouble,
> And quit his books, for fear of growing double ;'
> Who, both by precept and example, shows
> That prose is verse, and verse is merely prose ;
> Convincing all by demonstration plain,
> Poetic souls delight in prose insane,
> And Christmas stories, tortured into rhyme,
> Contain the essence of the true sublime.
> Thus, when he tells the Tale of Betty Foy,
> The idiot mother of her ' idiot boy,'
> A moon-struck silly lad who lost his way,
> And like his bard, confounded night with day,
> So close on each pathetic point he dwells,
> And each adventure so sublimely tells,
> That all who view the ' idiot in his glory,'
> Conceive the bard the hero of the story.

37. (3.) Political satire castigates, nominally in the interest
of virtue, but really in the interest of a party, the wicked or
contemptible qualities of the adherents of the opposite faction.
The two most notable exemplifications in our literature are
Butler's *Hudibras* and Dryden's *Absalom and Achitophel.* The
figures of Sir Hudibras and Ralpho—the one intended to represent the military Puritan, half hypocrite, half enthusiast—

> who built his faith upon
> The holy text of pike and gun ;

the other meant to expose a lower type of Puritan character, in
which calculating craft, assuming the mask of devotion without
the reality, made its profit out of the enthusiasm of others—

are satirical creations which, if not equal to Don Quixote and Sancho, can never lose their interest in the country which produced the originals.

The satirical portraits in *Absalom and Achitophel* are drawn with a masterly hand. They include the leading statesmen and politicians of the Whig party towards the end of the reign of Charles II. Some of the characters, though men of mark at the time, have ceased to figure in history ; and the satire on them interests us but little. But the sketches of Shaftesbury, Halifax, Buckingham, and Titus Oates, derive an interest, independently of the skill and vigour of the drawing, from the historical importance of the persons represented. Shaftesbury is thus described :—

> Of these the false Achitophel was first,
> A name to all succeeding ages curst :
> For close designs and crooked counsels fit,
> Sagacious, bold, and turbulent of wit ;

Here follow the lines given above at page 296 ; after which the poet proceeds :—

> A daring pilot in extremity,
> Pleased with the danger when the waves went high,
> He sought the storms ; but for a calm unfit,
> Would steer too nigh the sands, to boast his wit.
> Great wits are sure to madness near allied,
> And thin partitions do their bounds divide ;
> Else why should he, with wealth and honour blest,
> Refuse his age the needful hours of rest ?
> Punish a body which he could not please,
> Bankrupt of life, yet prodigal of ease ;
> And all to leave what with his toil he won
> To that unfeathered two-legged thing, a son ?

Halifax, known as the ' Trimmer,' who defeated the Exclusion Bill, is the subject of a few laudatory lines :—

> Jotham, of piercing wit and pregnant thought ;
> Endowed by nature, and by learning taught
> To move assemblies, who but only tried
> The worse awhile, then chose the better side ;
> Nor chose alone, but turned the balance too,
> So much the weight of one brave man can do.

The following sketch of the Duke of Buckingham may be compared with that by Pope (see p. 440) :—

> Some of their chiefs were princes of the land :
> In the first rank of these did Zimri stand ;
> A man so various, that he seemed to be
> Not one, but all mankind's epitome :

Stiff in opinions, always in the wrong,
Was everything by fits, and nothing long;
But, in the course of one revolving moon,
Was chemist, fiddler, statesman, and buffoon;
Then all for women, painting, rhyming, drinking,
Besides ten thousand freaks that died in thinking.
Blest madman, who could every hour employ
With something new to wish or to enjoy !

.   .   .   .

In squandering wealth was his peculiar art;
Nothing went unrewarded but desert.
Beggared by fools, whom still he found too late,
He had his jest, and they had his estate.
He laughed himself from court ; then sought relief
By forming parties, but could ne'er be chief :
For spite of him, the weight of business fell
On Absalom, and wise Achitophel ;
Thus wicked but in will, of means bereft,
He left no faction, but of that was left.

Oates, the chief witness in the Popish plot of 1680, is the object of a long rolling fire of invective, from which we can only extract a few lines :—

His memory, miraculously great,
Could plots, exceeding man's belief, repeat ;
Which therefore cannot be accounted lies,
For human wit could never such devise.
Some future truths are mingled in his book ;
But where the witness failed, the prophet spoke;
Some things like visionary flight appear :
The spirit caught him up,—the Lord knows where ;
And gave him his rabbinical degree,
Unknown to foreign university.

38. Churchill's *Prophecy of Famine* was an unworthy attack upon the Scotch, written when the author was closely linked with the demagogue John Wilkes, and betokening his influence. The minister, Lord Bute, had given places in England to several of his countrymen; *hinc illæ lachrymæ!* There is no proper arrangement in the poem, no evidence of a concerted plan ; the writer seems to have fired off his small arms just as it might happen, shooting wildly and rapidly, in the vague notion that some of the shot might hit.   In the early portion of the satire, the wit consists, according to Churchill's usual manner, in the ironical ascription to the Scotch of virtues, the bad qualities opposite to which are supposed to be notoriously prominent in their national character.   Two Scotch shepherds, Jockey and Sawney, are then introduced, bewailing, in alternate strophes, the sad condition of their country since the fatal day of Culloden : they are joined by the goddess Famine, who prophesies

the approaching exaltation of the nation through the advent of
a Scotchman (Lord Bute) to power, who will enable his countrymen to fatten upon the riches of England.   The names of
democracy and liberty become hateful in the mouths of Wilkes,
Churchill, and Co., of whom it might truly be said, in the
words of Milton :—

> License they mean when they cry Liberty.

Politically and socially this middle part of the century was
a dull and despicable period, in which the only objects that relieve the gloom are the genuine enthusiasm of Burke, on the
one hand, and the keen, cold, caustic good sense of Horace
Walpole, on the other.   The allusions in Walpole's letters to
Churchill's works, as they successively appeared, are full of
point and truth; in fact, the whole age, in its meanness and
false assumption, its hypocrisy and its corruption, is wonderfully
photographed in the correspondence of that intelligent patrician,
who knew not what reverence was, and was too honest to endure
its counterfeit ; who saw things just as they were, and had the
gift of setting them down just as he saw them.

39. If it be a marked descent from Dryden to Churchill, it
is a still deeper fall from Churchill to Peter Pindar.   John
Wolcot, a native of Devonshire, was educated by his uncle, an
obscure medical practitioner at Fowey, to his own profession.
The natural vulgarity of his mind was never corrected, nor his
irrepressible conceit ever rebuked, by the association with his
betters at a university: in the society of a small country town
he was an oracle, a marvel of genius ; there his sallies were
applauded, his ribaldry mistaken for satire, his obscenity for
humour, and his low smartness for wit.   It would be difficult
to name a literary work exhibiting a more pitiful debasement of
the human intellect than the *Lousiad*, published in 1786.   The
backstairs tattle of the royal household had, it seems, spread
a story that an animal of that description had made its appearance on the king's plate at dinner, who had ordered the heads
of all the cooks and scullions to be shaved in consequence.
Upon this incident, real or imaginary, Wolcot founded what he
calls a heroic-comic poem in five cantos, at the end of which, in
servile imitation of Pope, he makes the Zephyr transport the
animal to the skies, and transform him into a planet, which is
thereupon discovered by Herschel, and solemnly named the
Georgium Sidus.

It may perhaps be said,—Is not Peter Pindar the English
Beaumarchais ;—does he not, like him, turn sham greatness

inside out, and demolish the superstitious awe with which privileged persons and classes are surrounded in the imaginations of the vulgar? No, he is not comparable to Beaumarchais; for Beaumarchais did a solid and necessary work, and he did not. Continental kings, before the French Revolution, however personally despicable they might be, were formidable, because the political system was despotic, because they wielded an enormous power irresponsibly, and could consign to a perpetual dungeon by their *lettres de cachet*, unless prudence restrained them, any private citizen who might offend them. Yet traditional reverence and mistaken piety surrounded these kings with a halo of majesty and sanctity in their people's eyes; he therefore, who undermined this reverence, who exhibited kings and queens as just as miserable forked bipeds, just as silly, greedy, and trifling, as men and women in general, did a good and necessary work, as one of the pioneers of freedom. But in England, in the eighteenth century, kings had no such powers; religious worship, thought, and its expression, were almost entirely free;[1] our political liberties were in the main secure; no king could send an Englishman to prison at his own caprice, or subject him to arbitrary taxation, or deprive him of representation in parliament. What serious harm, then, could the utmost conceivable folly, malignity, and even profligacy, in the king and the royal family do to the people at large? None whatever; there was therefore no object sufficient to justify a satire, no *dignus vindice nodus*. On the other hand, the mere fact of the Hanoverian family being seated on the throne, however it might surround itself with German menials and waiting women like Madame Schwellenberg, whom Wolcot lashes with indignant patriotism,—was tantamount, in the eyes of most Englishmen, to a standing protest on behalf of the right of the people, in the name of the ancient constitution of the country, to resist a tyrannical and arbitrary government; as such it should have made that limited and muzzled royalty sacred from assault.

A man who wrote so much, and whose tongue, as he says of himself,[2]

> So copious in a flux of metre,
> *Labitur et labetur*,

could not but say a good thing occasionally. The postscript to his *Epistle to James Boswell, Esq.*, being a supposed conversation between Dr. Johnson and the author, contains a well-known sally :—

[1] Of course I am not speaking of Ireland.
[2] Apologetic Postscript to *Ode upon Ode*.

P.P. 'I have heard it whispered, Doctor, that, should you die before him, Mr. Boswell means to write your life.'

Johnson. ' Sir, he cannot mean me so irreparable an injury. Which of us shall die first is only known to the Great Disposer of events ; but were I sure that James Boswell would write *my* life, I do not know whether I would not anticipate the measure by taking *his.*'

40. Since Dryden we have had no political satirist comparable to Moore. In the *Fudge Family in Paris,* the letters of Mr. Phelim Fudge to his employer, Lord Castlereagh, are an ironical picture of European society from the point of view of the Holy Alliance. The *Parody on a Celebrated Letter*—that addressed by the Prince Regent to the Duke of York in 1812— is a piece of cutting satire, in which every line has its open or covert sting.

41. Among the many shorter poems which fall under the description of political satire, none has attained greater notoriety than *Lilliburlero,* or better deserved it than the *Vicar of Bray.* The doggerel stanzas of the former were sung all over England about the time of the landing of William III., and are said to have contributed much to stir up the popular hatred against James. The *Vicar of Bray* is a witty narrative of the changes in political sentiment which a beneficed clergyman, whose fundamental principle it is to stick to his benefice, might be supposed to undergo between the reigns of Charles II. and George I. The first and the last stanzas are subjoined :—

> In good King Charles's golden days,
> When loyalty no harm meant,
> A zealous high-church man I was,
> And so I got preferment,
> To teach my flock I never missed,
> Kings are by God appointed,
> And cursed are they that do resist,
> Or touch the Lord's anointed ;
> And this is law, &c.
>
> . . . .
>
> The illustrious house of Hanover,
> And Protestant succession,
> To them I do allegiance swear—
> While they can keep possession,
> For in my faith and loyalty
> I never more will falter,
> And George my lawful King shall be—
> Until the times do alter :
> And this is law, I will maintain,
> Until my dying day, Sir,
> That whatsoever King shall reign,
> I'll be the Vicar of Bray, Sir.

Pastoral Poetry :—Spenser, Browne, Pope, Shenstone.

42. Of the pastoral poetry of Greece, such as we have it in the exquisite *Idylls* of Theocritus, our English specimens are but a weak and pale reflexion. The true pastoral brings us to the sloping brow of the hill, while the goats are browsing below ; and on a rustic seat, opposite a statue of Priapus, we see the herdsmen singing or piping, yet shunning to try their skill in the mid-day heats, because they fear to anger Pan, who then 'rests, being a-weary, from his hunting.'[1]   Even Virgil's *Eclogues*, graceful and musical as they are, possess but a secondary excellence ; they are merely imitations of Theocritus, and do not body forth the real rural life of Italy.   The only English poetry which bears the true pastoral stamp is that of Burns and other Scottish writers ;—and for this reason—that, like the Greek pastoral, it is founded on reality ; it springs out of the actual life and manner of thought of the Scottish peasant. If it is rough-hewn and harsh in comparison with its southern prototype, that is but saying that the Scottish peasant, though not despicably endowed, is neither intellectually nor æsthetically the equal of the Greek.

The chief pastoral poems that we have are Spenser's *Shepherd's Kalendar*, Drayton's *Eclogues*, Browne's *Britannia's Pastorals*, and Pope's and Shenstone's *Pastorals*, besides innumerable shorter pieces.   It is scarcely worth while to make extracts.   Browne's so-called pastorals ought rather to be classed as descriptive poems, since they are destitute of that dramatic character which the true pastoral (which is, in fact, a rudimentary drama) should always possess.

Britannia's Pastorals are in two books, each containing five 'songs' or cantos. A thread of narrative runs through them, but does not furnish much that is interesting, either in character or in incident. The conduct of the story of Marina and her lovers is far too discursive. Each song is introduced by an 'argument,' as in the *Faery Queen*, and the colouring of the whole work is strongly Spenserian. But the digressions and intercalated discussions on all sorts of matters, chiefly however amatory, make it very tedious reading. A true feeling for natural beauty, a special love for the scenery of his native Devon, and a corresponding power of rich and picturesque description, are Browne's chief merits.

43. Pope, in the Introduction to his *Pastorals*, explained his conception of a pastoral poem, as of an ideal picture of the

---

[1] *Theocritus*, Idyll I.

G G

simplicity and virtue,—the artless manners, fresh affections, and natural language of the golden age,—apart alike from courtly refinements and realistic coarseness. In executing this conception he is very happy, especially in the third and fourth pastorals. Shenstone's *Pastoral Ballad* has some delicately-turned phrases; we subjoin a stanza or two :—

> When forced the fair nymph to forego,
>   What anguish I felt at my heart!
> Yet I thought—but it might not be so—
>   'Twas with pain that she saw me depart.
> She gazed, as I slowly withdrew;
>   My path I could hardly discern;
> So sweetly she bade me adieu,
>   I thought that she bade me return.

The nymph proves faithless; and 'disappointment' is the burden of the concluding part or canto of the poem :—

> Alas! from the day that we met,
>   What hope of an end to my woes?
> When I cannot endure to forget
>   The glance that undid my repose.
> Yet time may diminish the pain;
>   The flower, and the shrub, and the tree,
> Which I reared for her pleasure in vain,
>   In time may have comfort for me.

Descriptive Poetry :—'Poly-olbion,' 'Cooper's Hill,' 'The Seasons.'

44. This kind of poetry labours under the want of definite form and scope; it is accumulative, not organic : and consequently is avoided, or but seldom used, by the greater masters of the art. The most bulky specimen of descriptive verse that we possess is Drayton's *Poly-olbion*; the most celebrated, Thomson's *Seasons*. The *Poly-olbion* is a sort of British gazetteer; it describes the most noted spots or towns in every English county, with historical illustrations. The poem shows great imaginative as well as descriptive power; so that one wonders at the patient industry with which a man, whose gifts qualified him for higher things, must have worked out his dull task. The diction is simple and strong, and tends to the Saxon side of the language, as the following extract shows :—

> Of Albion's glorious isle, the wonders whilst I write,
> The sundry varying soils, the pleasures infinite,
> Where heat kills not the cold, nor cold expels the heat,
> The calms too mildly small, nor winds too roughly great,

Nor night doth hinder day, nor day the night doth wrong,
The summer not too short, the winter not too long—
What help shall I invoke to aid my muse the while?
　　Thou genius of the place! this most renowned isle,
Which livedst long before the all-earth-drowning flood,
Whilst yet the earth did swarm with her gigantic brood,
Go thou before me still, thy circling shores about,
Direct my course so right, as with thy hand to show
Which way thy forests range, which way thy rivers flow,
Wise genius, by thy help that so I may descry
How thy fair mountains stand, and how thy valleys lie.

45. *Cooper's Hill*, by Sir John Denham, has the beautiful and often-quoted passage descriptive of the Thames :—

Thames—the most loved of all the Ocean's sons
By his old sire—to his embraces runs,
Hasting to pay his tribute to the sea,
Like mortal life to meet eternity.
Though with those streams he no resemblance hold,
Whose foam is amber, and their gravel gold,
His genius and less guilty wealth to explore,
Search not his bottom, but survey his shore;
O'er which he kindly spreads his spacious wing,
And hatches plenty for the ensuing spring;
Nor then destroys it with too fond a stay,
Like mothers which their infants over-lay,
Nor with a sudden and impetuous wave,
Like profuse kings, resumes the wealth he gave;
No unexpected inundations spoil
The mower's hopes, nor mock the ploughman's toil;
But godlike his unwearied bounty flows;
First loves to do, then loves the good he does;
Nor are his blessings to his banks confined,
But free and common as the sea, or wind,
When he, to boast or to disperse his stores,
Full of the tributes of his grateful shores,
Visits the world, and in his flying towers,
Brings home to us, and makes both Indies ours;
Finds wealth where 'tis, bestows it where it wants,
Cities in deserts, woods in cities, plants;
So that to us no thing, no place is strange,
While his fair bosom is the world's exchange.
O might I flow like thee, and make thy stream
My great example, as it is my theme!
Though deep, yet clear, though gentle, yet not dull,
Strong without rage, without o'erflowing full.

46. Of Pope's *Windsor Forest*, Johnson has remarked, 'The lesign of *Windsor Forest* is evidently taken from *Cooper's Hill*, vith some attention to Waller's poem on *The Park*. . . . . The objection made by Dennis is the want of plan, or a regular sub-ordination of parts terminating in the principal and original

design.   There is this want in most descriptive poems ; because,
as the scenes which they must exhibit successively are all subsisting at the same time, the order in which they are shown
must by necessity be arbitrary, and more is not to be expected
from the last part than the first.'

47. Thomson's *Seasons*, a poem in blank verse, in four
books, bears some resemblance, though no comparison, to Virgil's *Georgics*. The descriptions of the appearances of nature,
the habits of animals, and the manners of men, are generally
given with truthful and vivid delineation. The more ambitious
flights—if a fine panegyric on Peter the Great be excepted—in
which he paints great characters of ancient or modern story, or
philosophises, or plays the moralist—are less successful. Even
in describing nature, Thomson betrays a signal want of imagination ; he saw correctly what was before him—the outward
shows of things—but never had a glimpse of

> The light that never *was* on sea or land,
> The inspiration, and the poet's dream.

There are passages from which the author might be set
down as a pantheist ; but poets are often inconsistent : and, as
Pope disclaimed the fatalism which seems to be taught by the
Essay on Man, so Thomson might have declined to father the
pantheism which seems to pervade the following lines, if expressed in sober prose :—

> What is this mighty breath, ye sages, say,
> That in a powerful language, felt, not heard,
> Instructs the fowls of heaven, and through their breast
> These arts of love diffuses?   What but God?
> Inspiring God! who, boundless Spirit all,
> And unremitting energy, pervades,
> Adjusts, sustains, and agitates the whole.

A passage at the end of *Spring* contains a well-known line—

> Delightful task! to rear the tender thought,
> To teach the young idea how to shoot,
> To pour the fresh instruction o'er the mind,
> To breathe the enlivening spirit, and to fix
> The generous purpose in the glowing breast.

The lines on the robin, in *Winter*, are in Thomson's best
manner :—

> The fowls of heaven,
> Tamed by the cruel season, crowd around
> The winnowing store, and claim the little boon
> Which Providence assigns them.   One alone,
> The red-breast, sacred to the household gods,

Wisely regardful of the embroiling sky,
In joyless fields and thorny thickets leaves
His shivering mates, and pays to trusted man
His annual visit.   Half-afraid, he first
Against the window beats ; then, brisk, alights
On the warm hearth ; then, hopping o'er the floor,
Eyes all the smiling family askance,
And pecks, and starts, and wonders where he is ;
Till, more familiar grown, the table-crumbs
Attract his slender feet.

Lyrical Poetry :—Devotional, Loyal, Patriotic, Amatory, Bacchanalian, Martial.

48. Lyrical poetry, as its name denotes, implied originally that the words were accompanied by lively music.   A rapid movement, and a corresponding rapidity in the verse, are essential to it.   It is the glowing utterance of minds, not calm and thoughtful, but excited and impassioned ; it appertains, therefore, to the affective and emotional side of human nature, and has nothing to do with the reasoning and meditative side. Wordsworth, in pursuance of a poetical theory, published in his youth a collection of *Lyrical Ballads* ; but they were not lyrical, because there was no passion in them, and much reflexion.   In later life, he wisely changed their designation.

There are certain main lyrical themes, corresponding to the passions and emotions which exercise the most agitating sway over the human heart.   These are, Devotion, Loyalty, Patriotism, Love, Revelry, and War.   We will take each theme separately, and from among the innumerable lyrical compositions which adorn our literature, select a very few, as a sample of the riches of the land.   The task of selection is much facilitated by the publication, some years ago, of *The Golden Treasury*, which is a collection of the best songs and lyrics in the language, carefully edited by Mr. Palgrave.

49. (1.) Among devotional lyrics there is none nobler than Milton's *Christmas Ode.*   Hallam pronounced it to be ' perhaps the finest ode in the English language.'   A certain ruggedness of diction partially disfigures the later stanzas ; but, taking the poem as a whole, the music of the numbers is worthy of the stately yet swift march of the thought.   We must find space for the opening and concluding stanzas :—

It was the winter wild,
While the heaven-born Child

All meanly wrapt in the rude manger lies ;
     Nature in awe to him
     Had doffed her gaudy trim,
With her great Master so to sympathise :
     It was no season then for her
     To wanton with the sun, her lusty paramour.

     Only with speeches fair
     She woos the gentle air
To hide her guilty front with innocent snow ;
     And on her naked shame,
     Pollute with sinful blame,
The saintly veil of maiden white to throw ;
     Confounded that her Maker's eyes
     Should look so near upon her foul deformities.

     But He, her fears to cease,
     Sent down the meek-eyed Peace ;
She, crown'd with olive green, came softly sliding
     Down through the turning sphere,
     His ready harbinger,
With turtle wing the amorous clouds dividing ;
     And, waving wide her myrtle wand,
     She strikes an universal peace through sea and land.

     No war or battle sound
     Was heard the world around,
The idle spear and shield were high uphung ;
     The hookèd chariot stood
     Unstain'd with hostile blood ;
The trumpet spake not to the armèd throng ;
     And kings sat still with awful eye,
     As if they surely knew their sovereign Lord was by.

The discomfiture and flight of the Heathen divinities upon the advent of the Redeemer, and the silence of the oracles, are then described, and the ode concludes with the following stanzas :—

     So when the sun in bed,
     Curtained with cloudy red,
Pillows his chin upon an orient wave,
     The flocking shadows pale
     Troop to the infernal jail,
Each fettered ghost slips to his several grave ;
     And the yellow-skirted fays
     Fly after the night steeds, leaving their moon-loved maze.

     But see, the Virgin blest
     Hath laid her babe to rest ;
Time is, our tedious song should here have ending :
     Heaven's youngest teemèd star
     Hath fixed her polished car,
Her sleeping Lord with handmaid lamp attending ;
     And all about the courtly stable
     Bright harnessed angels sit, in order serviceable.

50. Crashaw's lyrics of devotion are often beautiful, though their effect is injured by the conceits in which he, as a writer of the fantastic school, was wont to indulge. Dryden is the author of a fine paraphrase of the hymn *Veni Creator Spiritus*. Pope's *Messiah* is a lyrical eclogue in imitation of the Fourth Eclogue of Virgil. In his hymn entitled *The Dying Christian to his Soul*, Pope essayed to rival Dryden and Addison in this field also. The effort cannot be pronounced unsuccessful; yet the art and labour are too transparent, and the ejaculations have a slightly theatrical cast :—

> Vital spark of heavenly flame,
> Quit, oh ! quit, this mortal frame ;
> Trembling, hoping, lingering, dying,
> O the pain, the bliss, of dying,
> Cease fond Nature, cease thy strife,
> And let me languish into life.
>
> The world recedes, it disappears ;
> Heaven opens on my eyes ; my ears
>   With sounds seraphic ring ;
> Lend, lend your wings ; I mount ; I fly ;
> O Grave, where is thy victory ?
>   O Death, where is thy sting ?

In the present century Byron and Moore hav each tried their hand at sacred lyrics. The *Hebrew Melodies* o the former, and the *Sacred Melodies* of the latter, contain pieces of great lyrical beauty. In the art of wedding words to sounds, no English poet ever excelled, or perhaps equalled, Moore. The gift is exhibited in the following sacred melody, which is but a sample of a great number, all equally felicitous in this respect :—

> Sound the loud timbrel o'er Egypt's dark sea ;
> Jehovah hath triumph'd ; his people are free.
> Sing ; for the might of the tyrant is broken,
> His chariots, his horsemen, so splendid and brave ;
> How vain was their boasting ! the Lord hath but spoken,
> And chariots and horsemen are sunk in the wave.
>
> Praise to the conqueror, praise to the Lord !
> His word was our arrow, His breath was our sword.
> Who shall return to tell Egypt the story
> Of those she sent forth in the hour of her pride ?
> The Lord but look'd forth from His pillar of glory,
> And all her brave thousands are whelm'd in the tide.

51. (2.) *Loyalty.* Of the loyal songs with which our poetry abounds, certain classes only can be said to possess real excellence. When it is on the winning side, loyalty loses its passion and its pathos ; its effusions tend to become interested, and lie

under the suspicion of servility. It is for this reason that such poems as Dryden's *Astræa Redux* and Addison's heroics in honour of William III. fall flat and cold on the ear. But when loyalty is struggling, or when it is persecuted, it is a noble, because a disinterested, sentiment, and it gives birth to noble poems. In our own history these conditions have been present on two occasions—during the Civil War, and after the Revolution of 1688. The Royalist and the Jacobite songs are therefore the only loyal lyrics which need arrest our attention. Of the former class we shall quote a portion of the well-known lines composed by the gallant Lovelace while in prison :—

> When Love with unconfinèd wings
> Hovers within my gates,
> And my divine Althea brings
> To whisper at the grates;
> When I lie tangled in her hair
> And fettered to her eye,
> The birds that wanton in the air
> Know no such liberty.
>
> When, linnet-like confinèd, I
> With shriller throat shall sing
> The sweetness, mercy, majesty,
> And glories of my King;
> When I shall voice aloud how good
> He is, how great should be,
> Enlargèd winds, that curl the flood,
> Know no such liberty.
>
> Stone walls do not a prison make,
> Nor iron bars a cage;
> Minds innocent and quiet take
> These for an hermitage;
> If I have freedom in my love,
> And in my soul am free,
> Angels alone, that soar above,
> Enjoy such liberty.

52. The Jacobite songs, which are mostly of unknown authorship, are full of spirit and fire, and possess that melancholy charm which belongs to a great cause vainly maintained by high-souled men against an overpowering destiny. We select the following specimen :—[1]

> To daunton me an' me sae young,
> An' gude King James' auldest son!
> O that's the thing that ne'er can be,
> For the man's unborn that will daunton me!

---

[1] From Cromek's *Songs of Nithsdale*.

O set me ance on Scottish land,
An' gie me my braid-sword in my hand,
Wi' my blue bonnet aboon my bree,
An' show me the man that will daunton me.

It's nae the battle's deadly stoure,
Nor friends pruived fause, that'll gar me cower;
But the reckless hand o' povertie,
O ! that alane can daunton me !

High was I born to kingly gear,
But a cuif[1] came in my cap to wear;
But wi' my braid-sword I'll let him see
He's nae the man will daunton me.

The best and most spirited of these Jacobite lyrics are to be found in Ritson's *Collection of Scottish Songs,* or Hogg's *Jacobite Relics.*

53. (3.) *Patriotism.* That *amour sacré de la patrie,* which in all countries is a fruitful theme for the Lyric muse, is among ourselves by no means homogeneous. We have Scotch patriotism, Irish patriotism, and British or Imperial patriotism, and noble lyrics inspired by each. Lastly, as there is a poetical justice, so there is a poetical patriotism—a feeling which usually goes abroad to seek for its objects, and is eloquent upon the wrongs sustained by foreign nationalities. Scotland vents her patriotic fervour in Burns' manly lines, supposed to be addressed by Bruce to his army before the battle of Bannockburn. Her poets find her ancient triumphs over England more soul-inspiring than any of those which her sons have, since the Union, assisted her great neighbour to achieve. For patriotism is intense in proportion to its local concentration ; and zeal for the preservation of the integrity of a great empire, though it may produce the same course of action, is an affair of the reason rather than of the feelings, and therefore less likely to give rise to lyrical developments. Two stanzas from the song above mentioned are subjoined :—

Wha wad be a traitor knave,
Wha wad fill a coward's grave,
Wha sae base as be a slave ?
Coward ! turn and flee !

Wha for Scotland's king and law
Freedom's sword will strongly draw,
Freeman stand or freeman fa'?
Let him follow me ![2]

---

[1] Worthless fellow.
[2] In the first edition, I printed the last line of this stanza, 'Scotsman ! on wi' me !' but otherwise it stood precisely as it now stands. A writer in

54. Sir Walter Scott was by reason and principle a staunch imperialist, and his poem on Waterloo illustrates the general or British element in his patriotism. But how cold and tame it reads compared with the glowing lines which burst from his lips, as his heart broods over the rugged charms of his own Caledonia !—

> Breathes there the man, with soul so dead,
> Who never to himself hath said,
>   This is my own, my native land ?
> Whose heart hath ne'er within him burned,
> As home his footsteps he hath turned,
>   From wandering on a foreign strand ?
> If such there be, go mark him well ;
> For him no minstrel raptures swell ;
> High though his titles, proud his name,
> Boundless his wealth as wish can claim,
> Despite those titles, power, and pelf,
> The wretch concentred all in self,
> Living, shall forfeit fair renown,
> And doubly dying, shall go down
> To the vile dust from whence he sprung,
> Unwept, unhonoured, and unsung.
>   Oh ! Caledonia, stern and wild,
> Meet nurse for a poetic child !
> Land of brown heath and shaggy wood,
> Land of the mountain and the flood,
> Land of my sires ! what mortal hand

the *Museum* charged me with having misquoted this stanza ' so egregiously, as to have produced ludicrous nonsense.' According to him, ' by making the first three lines interrogative, it is implied that *no one* is prepared to draw freedom's sword.' Jehu asked, ' Who is on the Lord's side, who ? ' when he wished to have Jezebel thrown out of the window ; he expected, therefore, to find that *no one* was on the Lord's side, if this new grammatical canon be correct. In other respects, too, the criticism is unlucky. Referring to Allan Cunningham's edition of the poet's works, I find that Burns originally wrote (see his letter to G. Thomson, dated in Sept. 1793),—

> Freeman stand, or freeman fa' ?
> Let him follow me !

The ' ludicrous nonsense,' therefore, produced by the mark of interrogation, must be fathered on the poet himself. This first, and clearly best, version was adapted to the air, ' Hey, tuttie, taitie.' Thomson wrote back, delighted with the words, but objecting to the air which they were set to, and suggesting such alterations in the terminal lines of the stanzas as would adapt the song to the air ' Lewie Gordon.' Burns accepted the suggestion, and, in his next letter, gave an altered version, in which, whether by accident or design, a comma was substituted for the mark of interrogation, so that the stanzas read,—

> Freeman stand, or freeman fa',
> Caledonian ? on wi' me !

Alexander Smith, in his late edition of Burns, retains the mark of interrogation, but prints the terminal lines as they stand in the second version. It seems to me that the first version, representing the original form of this noble theme, should be adhered to in all future editions.

Can e'er untie the filial band,
That knits me to thy rugged strand?
Still, as I view each well-known scene,
Think what is now, and what hath been,
Seems as, to me, of all bereft,
Sole friends thy woods and streams were left;
And thus I love them better still,
Even in extremity of ill.
By Yarrow's streams still let me stray,
Though none shall guide my feeble way;
Still feel the breeze down Ettrick break,
Although it chill my withered cheek;
Still lay my head by Teviot stone,
Though there, forgotten and alone,
The bard may draw his parting groan.

55. Irish patriotism blooms, as might be expected, into verse of a mournful, almost of an elegiac cast. Moore's poetry furnishes us with many specimens, among which the following lines, entitled 'After the Battle,' are not the least beautiful:—

Night closed upon the conqueror's way,
And lightnings showed the distant hill,
Where they who lost that dreadful day
Stood few and faint, but fearless still.
The soldier's hope, the patriot's zeal,
For ever dimmed, for ever crossed;
Oh! who can tell what heroes feel,
When all but life and honour's lost!

The last sad hour of freedom's dream,
And valour's task, moved slowly by,
While mute they watched, till morning's beam
Should rise, and give them light to die!
There is a world where souls are free,
Where tyrants taint not nature's bliss;
If death that world's bright opening be,
Oh! who would live a slave in this?

56. British—if it should not rather be called English—patriotism has produced such poems as Glover's *Hosier's Ghost*, Cowper's *Boadicea*, and Campbell's *Mariners of England*. From the *Boadicea* we extract a portion of the Druid's address to the patriot queen of the Iceni:—

Rome, for empire far renowned,
Tramples on a thousand states;
Soon her pride shall kiss the ground—
Hark! the Gaul is at her gates.

Other Romans shall arise,
Heedless of a soldier's name;
Sounds, not arms, shall win the prize,
Harmony the path to fame.

Then the progeny that springs
From the forests of our land,
Armed with thunder, clad with wings,
Shall a wider world command.

Regions Cæsar never knew
Thy posterity shall sway :
Where his eagles never flew,
None invincible as they.

57. Poetical patriotism inspired Gray's *Bard*, Byron's *Isles
of Greece*, and Shelley's *Hellas*. In the first-named poem, the
last of the Welsh bards, standing on a crag that overhangs the
pass through which King Edward and his army are defiling,
invokes ruin on the race and name of the oppressor of his
country, and at the conclusion of his hymn of vengeful despair
flings himself into the sea. Byron's noble lyric is so well known
that we shall not spoil it by quotation, but prefer to extract
portions of two choruses from Shelley's *Hellas*, in which, with
the enthusiasm of genius, the poet paints an ideal future for
enfranchised and regenerate Greece :—

—— Temples and towers,
Citadels and marts, and they
Who live and die there, have been ours,
And may be thine, and must decay ;
  But Greece and her foundations are
  Built below the tide of war,
  Based on the crystalline sea
  Of thought, and its eternity ;
Her citizens, imperial spirits,
  Rule the present from the past,
On all this world of men inherits
  Their seal is set.

But this is not enough ; Greece herself is to live again :—

A brighter Hellas rears its mountains
  From waves serener far :
A new Penëus rolls its fountains
  Against the morning star,
Where fairer Tempes bloom, there sleep
Young Cyclads on a sunnier deep :

A loftier Argo cleaves the main,
  Fraught with a later prize ;
Another Orpheus sings again,
  And loves, and weeps, and dies.
A new Ulysses leaves once more
Calypso for his native shore.

O write no more the Tale of Troy,
  If earth Death's scroll must be !
Nor mix with Laian rage the joy
  Which dawns upon the free ;

Although a subtler Sphynx renew
Riddles of death Thebes never knew.

Another Athens shall arise,
　And, to remoter time,
Bequeath, like sunset to the skies,
　The splendour of her prime ;
And leave, if nought so bright may live,
All earth can take, or heaven can give.

58. (4.) *Love.* Love songs, or amatory lyrics, may be counted by hundreds in all our poetical collections. Those of Surrey, having been written under the influence of Petrarch, have a classic sound, but are somewhat monotonous. The following sonnet is a specimen much above the average :—

Set me whereas the sun doth parch the green,
Or where his beams do not dissolve the ice ;
In temperate heat, where he is felt and seen ;
In presence prest of people, mad or wise ;
Set me in high, or yet in low degree ;
In longest night, or in the longest day ;
In clearest sky, or where clouds thickest be ;
In lusty youth, or when my hairs are gray ;
Set me in heaven, or earth, or else in hell,
In hill, or dale, or in the foaming flood ;
Thrall, or at large,—alive whereso I dwell,
Sick, or in health, in evil fame or good,—
Hers will I be ; and only with this thought
Content myself, although my chance be nought.

Sir Thomas Wyat is the author of the following elegant stanzas, which have the heading, ' The Lover's Lute cannot be blamed though it sing of his Lady's Unkindness ':—

Blame not my lute ! for he must sound
　Of this or that, as liketh me ;
For lack of wit the lute is bound
　To give such tunes as pleaseth me ;
Though my songs be somewhat strange,
And speak such words as touch thy change,
　　Blame not my lute !
　.　　.　　.　　.　　.　　.

Spite asketh spite, and changing change,
　And falsèd faith must needs be known ;
The fault's so great, the case so strange,
　Of right it must abroad be blown :
Then since that by thine own desert
My songs do tell how true thou art,
　　Blame not my lute !

> Blame but thyself that hast misdone,
>   And well deservèd to have blame;
> Change thou thy way, so evil begone,
>   And then my lute shall sound that same;
> But if till then my fingers play
> By thy desert their wonted way,
>   Blame not my lute!

But with the earlier poets in general, Venus is generally found in close alliance with Bacchus; and the sentiment which inspires their strains is of a grosser kind than that which the refining mystical poets of later times have introduced. Moore in this respect resembles the poets of the Elizabethan and Stuart periods rather than his own contemporaries. We shall give one or two specimens of both styles, beginning with Ben Jonson's graceful lines *To Celia* :—

> Drink to me only with thine eyes,
>   And I will pledge with mine;
> Or leave a kiss but in the cup,
>   And I'll not ask for wine.
> The thirst that from the soul doth rise
>   Doth ask a drink divine;
> But might I of Jove's nectar sup,
>   I would not change for thine.
>
> I sent thee late a rosy wreath,
>   Not so much honouring thee,
> As giving it a hope that there
>   It could not withered be.
> But thou thereon did'st only breathe
>   And sent'st it back to me;
> Since when it grows, and smells, I swear,
>   Not of itself, but thee!

Some of Shakspere's sonnets might well be quoted in this connexion, particularly that beginning, 'Did not the heavenly rhetoric of thine eye?' The exquisite lines which follow occur in *Measure for Measure* :—

> Take, O take those lips away,
> That so sweetly were forsworn,
> And those eyes, the break of day,
> Lights that do mislead the morn;
> But my kisses bring again,
>   Bring again—
> Seals of love, but sealed in vain,
>   Sealed in vain!

59. Marlowe's 'Come live with me and be my love,' and Raleigh's reply, 'If all the world and love were young,' are beautiful specimens of what may be called the pastoral love

song. Waller's ' Go, lovely Rose,' and Carew's ' He that loves
a rosy cheek,' are in all books of extracts; but the latter poet's
' Give me more love or more disdain,' is omitted in *The Golden
Treasury* and several other collections; we shall therefore quote
it :—

> Give me more love, or more disdain;
>   The torrid or the frozen zone
> Bring equal ease unto my pain,
>   The temperate affords me none;
> Either extreme of love or hate
> Is sweeter than a calm estate.
>
> Give me a storm; if it be love,
>   Like Danäe in that golden shower,
> I swim in pleasure; if it prove
>   Disdain—that torrent will devour
> My vulture hopes, and he's possessed
> Of heaven, that's but from hell released;
> Then crown my joys or cure my pain;
> Give me more love or more disdain.

The following extract is from George Wither's poem of *The
Steadfast Shepherd* :—

> Can he prize the tainted posies
>   Which on every breast are worn,
> That may pluck the virgin roses
>   From their never touchèd thorn?
>   I can go rest
>   On her sweet breast,
> That is the pride of Cynthia's train;
>   Then stay thy tongue,
>   Thy mermaid song
> Is all bestowed on me in vain.
>
> He's a fool that basely dallies
>   Where each peasant mates with him;
> Shall I haunt the throngèd vallies,
>   While there's noble hills to climb?
>   No, no, though clowns
>   Are scared with frowns,
> I know the best can but disdain;
>   And those I'll prove,
>   So will thy love
> Be all bestowed on me in vain.

60. Cowley's *Mistress* is a collection of love songs full of bold
or curious figures; of far-fetched fanciful comparisons.   The
following stanzas, entitled *Her Name*, are very musical and
graceful :—

With more than Jewish reverence as yet
  Do I the sacred name conceal ;
When, ye kind stars, ah ! when will it be fit
  This gentle mystery to reveal ?
When will our love be named, and we possess
That christening as a badge of happiness.

So bold as yet no verse of mine has been,
  To wear that gem on any line ;
Nor, till the happy nuptial muse be seen,
  Shall any stanza with it shine.
Rest, mighty Name, till then ; for thou must be
Laid down by her, ere taken up by me.

Then all the fields and woods shall with it ring ;
  Then Echo's burden it shall be ;
Then all the birds in several notes shall sing,
  And all the rivers murmur thee ;
Then every wind the sound shall upward bear,
And softly whisper't to some angel's ear.

Then shall thy Name through all my verse be spread,
  Thick as the flowers in meadows lie.
And, when in future times they shall be read
  (As sure, I think, they will not die),
If any critic doubt that they be mine,
Men by that stamp shall quickly know the coin.

Meanwhile I will not dare to make a name
  To represent thee by ;
Adam, God's nomenclator, could not frame
  One that enough should signify ;
Astræa, or Celia, as unfit would prove
For thee, as 'tis to call the Deity, Jove.

The following stanzas give a favourable idea of the amatory
odes of Herrick :—

'TO THE VIRGINS, TO MAKE MUCH OF TIME.'

Gather ye rosebuds while ye may,
  Old Time is still a-flying ;
And this same flower that smiles to-day,
  To-morrow will be dying.

The glorious lamp of heaven, the sun,
  The higher he's a getting,
The sooner will his race be run,
  And nearer he's to setting.

That age is best which is the first,
  When youth and blood are warmer ;
But being spent, the worse, and worst
  Times still succeed the former.

Then be not coy, but use your time,
And while ye may, go marry;
For having lost but once your prime,
You may for ever tarry.

61. Milton, Dryden, and Pope, furnish us with nothing to quote under this head. When we come to modern times, the difficulty lies in the selection. What treasures of lyrical force and sweetness are contained in the love songs of Burns! We must give at least one example :—

O Mary, at thy window be,
It is the wished, the trysted hour !
Those smiles and glances let me see,
That make the miser's treasure poor ;
How blithely wad I bide the stoure,
A weary slave frae sun to sun,
Could I the rich reward secure,
The lovely Mary Morison.

Yestreen, when to the trembling string
The dance gaed thro' the lighted ha',
To thee my fancy took its wing—
I sat, but neither heard nor saw :
Tho' this was fair, and that was braw,
And yon the toast of a' the town,
I sighed, and said amang them a',
' Ye are na Mary Morison.'

O Mary, canst thou wreck his peace
Wha for thy sake wad gladly dee ?
Or canst thou break that heart of his,
Whase only faut is loving thee ?
If love for love thou wilt nae gie,
At least be pity to me shown ;
A thought ungentle canna be
The thought o' Mary Morison.

In grace and melody, if not in pathos, Moore's love songs may be matched with those of Burns, as the following lines exemplify :—

Take back the virgin page
White and unwritten still ;
Some hand more calm and sage
    That leaf must fill ;
Thoughts come as pure as light,
Pure as even you require,
But oh ! each word I write
    Love turns to fire.

Yet let me keep the book ;
Oft shall my heart renew,
When on its leaves I look,
    Dear thoughts of you.

H H

Like you, 'tis fair and bright;
Like you, too bright and fair
To let wild passion write
    One wrong wish there.

Haply, when from those eyes
Far, far away I roam,
Should calmer thoughts arise
    Towards thee and home,
Fancy may trace some line
Worthy those eyes to meet,
Thoughts that not burn but shine,
    Pure, calm, and sweet.

.   .   .   .   .

Byron's *Maid of Athens*, Shelley's *Epithalamium*, and Coleridge's *Genevieve*, we must be content with naming.

62. (5.) *Revelry.* This is a lyrical theme which has been largely illustrated by our poets, especially by those of the seventeenth century. We must confine ourselves to a single specimen, taken from Cowley :—

The thirsty earth soaks up the rain,
And drinks and gapes for drink again.
The plants suck in the earth, and are
With constant drinking fresh and fair.
The sea itself, which one would think
Should have but little need of drink,
Drinks ten thousand rivers up
So fill'd that they o'erflow the cup.
The busy sun (and one would guess
By his drunken fiery face no less)
Drinks up the sea, and when he's done,
The moon and stars drink up the sun.
They drink and dance by their own light;
They drink and revel all the night.
Nothing in Nature's sober found,
But an eternal health goes round.
Fill up the bowl, then, fill it high,
Fill all the glasses there, for why
Should every creature drink but I ?
Why, men of morals, tell me why ?

63. (6.) *War.* The lyrics of war, whatever may be the reason, are not found in great numbers, nor of extraordinary merit, in English literature. We might mention Campbell's *Hohenlinden* and *Battle of the Baltic*, the stirring ballad of *Count Albert*, and the gathering song *Pibroch of Donuil Dhu*, both by Scott, and Macaulay's ballads of *Naseby* and *Ivry*, and *Lays of Rome*. In Dryden's great lyric, *Alexander's Feast*, the 'mighty master' of the lyre, after successfully preluding upon the themes of love and revelry, thus in a bolder strain summons the hero to war :

Now strike the golden lyre again :
A louder yet, and yet a louder strain :
Break his bands of sleep asunder,
And rouse him like a rattling peal of thunder.
Hark, hark ! the horrid sound
Has raised up his head,
As awaked from the dead,
And amazed, he stares around :
Revenge, revenge ! Timotheus cries,
See the Furies arise !
See the snakes that they rear,
How they hiss in their hair,
And the sparkles that flash from their eyes !
Behold a ghastly band,
Each a torch in his hand !
Those are Grecian ghosts, that in battle were slain,
And unburied remain
Inglorious on the plain ;
Give the vengeance due
To the valiant crew !
Behold how they toss their torches on high,
How they point to the Persian abodes,
And glittering temples of the hostile gods.
The princes applaud with a furious joy,
And the King seized a flambeau with zeal to destroy ;
Thais led the way,
To light him to his prey,
And, like another Helen, fired another Troy !

Elegiac Poetry :—' Fidele,' ' The Castaway,' ' Lycidas,' ' Adonais.'

64. English poetry, in sympathy with the sad and lowering skies of our northern climate, is never more powerful and pathetic than when heard in the accents of mourning. The influences of external nature and of the national temperament dispose our poets to taciturnity and thoughtfulness; and, in a world so full of change and death, thoughtfulness easily passes into sadness. Elegiac poems may be distinguished as objective or subjective, according as their tenor and general aim may be, either simply to occupy themselves with the fortunes, character, and acts of the departed, or to found a train of musings, having reference to self, or at least strongly coloured by the writer's personality, upon the fact of bereavement. Among those of the former class may be specified—the dirge in Cymbeline, Milton's sonnet on Shakspere, Dryden's elegy on Cromwell, Tickell's on Addison, Cowper's lines on the *Loss of the Royal George*, Campbell's *Lord Ullin's Daughter*, the song of Harold in the *Lay of the Last Minstrel*, Cowper's *Castaway*, and Pope's *Elegy*

> And think to burst out into sudden blaze,
> Comes the blind fury with the abhorrèd shears,
> And slits the thin-spun life. 'But not the praise,'
> Phœbus replied, and touched my trembling ears:
> 'Fame is no plant that grows on mortal soil,
> Nor in the glistering foil
> Set off to the world, nor in broad rumour lies:
> But lives, and spreads aloft, by those pure eyes
> And perfect witness of all-seeing Jove;
> As he pronounces lastly on each deed,
> Of so much fame in heaven expect thy meed.'

So also in *Adonais*, which is an elegy on Keats, the glorious imagination of Shelley transports him into regions far beyond the reach of the perturbations of a common grief:—

> The breath whose might I have invoked in song
> Descends on me; my spirit's bark is driven
> Far from the land, far from the trembling throng
> Whose sails were never to the tempest given;
> The massy earth and spherèd skies are riven;
> I am borne darkly, fearfully afar;
> Whilst burning through the inmost veil of Heaven,
> The soul of Adonais, like a star,
> Beacons from the abode where the Eternal are.

67. It would be impossible to give an adequate idea of Gray's famous elegy by a short extract, but the student is recommended to read the entire poem carefully. He will find it eminently subjective in spirit; and may compare it with Hamlet's moralisings over the skull of Yorick. Both may be regarded as products of a mind in which there is a morbid preponderance of the contemplative faculty—the balance not being duly maintained between the impressions from outward objects and the inward operations of the intellect.[1]

Miscellaneous Poems.

68. A large number of poems, chiefly belonging to modern times, still remain unnoticed, because they refuse to be classified under any of the received and long-established designations. This miscellaneous section we propose to divide into—

1. Poems founded on the Passions and Affections.
2. Poems of Sentiment and Reflection.
3. Poems of Imagination and Fancy.
4. Philosophical Poetry.

(1.) Poems of the first kind are evidently of the lyrical

---

[1] See Coleridge's remarks on Hamlet. *Literary Remains*, vol. ii. p. 204.

order, but they are not to be classed among lyrics, because they
are deficient in the excitation of thought and rapidity of movement which the true lyric must exhibit.   They occur in great
numbers in the works of modern poets, and, if a type of excellence in the kind were required, a purer one could not easily be
found than Wordsworth's *Michael.*   Many have seen the unfinished sheepfold in Green Head Ghyll, referred to in the
following lines, which Michael, the old Westmoreland 'statesman,' after the news had come that the son so tenderly cherished
had brought disgrace and peril on his head, had never afterwards the heart to complete :—

> There is a comfort in the strength of love ;
> 'Twill make a thing endurable, which else
> Would overset the brain, or break the heart.
> I have conversed with more than one, who well
> Remember the old Man, and what he was
> Years after he had heard this heavy news.
> His bodily frame had been from youth to age
> Of an unusual strength. Among the rocks
> He went, and still looked up to sun and cloud,
> And listened to the wind ; and, as before;
> Performed all kinds of labour for his sheep,
> And for the land, his small inheritance.
> And to that hollow dell from time to time
> Did he repair, to build the Fold of which
> His flock had need. 'Tis not forgotten yet
> The pity which was then in every heart
> For the old Man— and 'tis believed by all
> That many and many a day he thither went,
> And never lifted up a single stone.
>   There, by the Sheepfold, sometimes was he seen
> Sitting alone, or with his faithful Dog,
> Then old, beside him, lying at his feet.
> The length of full seven years, from time to time,
> He at the building of this Sheepfold wrought,
> And left the work unfinished when he died.
> Three years, or little more, did Isabel
> Survive her Husband : at her death the estate
> Was sold, and went into a stranger's hand.
> The Cottage, which was named the Evening Star,
> Is gone—the ploughshare has been through the ground
> On which it stood ; great changes have been wrought
> In all the neighbourhood ;—yet the oak is left
> That grew beside their door ; and the remains
> Of the unfinished Sheepfold may be seen,
> Beside the boisterous brook of Green Head Ghyll.

Pope's *Eloisa to Abelard,* a poem in which love, pride,
repentance, and despair seem to be striving together for the
mastery, and an overcharged heart seeks relief in bursts of wild

half-frenzied eloquence, must also be placed among poems of this class.

69. (2.) Sentiment may be regarded as the synthesis of thought and feeling; and therefore poems of this second class hold an intermediate place between those founded on the passions and affections, and those in which intellectual faculties are, solely or principally, exercised. They are very numerous in every period of our literary history. Spenser's *Ruines of Time* is an early and very beautiful example. In the midst of a personified presentment of Fame, the wish recorded of Alexander is thus strikingly related :—

> But Fame with golden wing aloft doth flie
> Above the reach of ruinous decay,
> And with brave plumes doth beat the azure skie,
> Admir'd of base-born men from farre away;
> Then whoso will by vertuous deeds assay
> To mount to heaven, on Pegasus must ride,
> And by sweet poet's verse be glorified.
>
> For not to have been dipt in Lethe lake
> Could save the son of Thetis from to die,
> But that blind bard did him immortal make
> With verses, dipp'd in dew of Castalie;
> Which made the Eastern Conquerour to crie,
> ' O fortunate young man, whose vertue found
> So brave a trump, thy noble acts to sound.'

Sir John Davies's poem on the *Immortality of the Soul* may be classed either with the present series, or under the head of didactic poetry. The poetry of Quarles is partly sentimental, partly fantastic. A fine couplet occurs in the poem entitled *Faith* :—

> Brave minds oppressed, should, in despite of Fate,
> Look greatest, like the sun, in lowest state.

The *Soul's Errand*, said to be by Raleigh, Milton's *Penseroso*, Dryden's *Religio Laici*, and Burns' *Cotter's Saturday Night*, are additional examples. Cowper's *Lines on his Mother's Picture* deserve special mention. The chief merits of this celebrated poem are—a remarkable tenderness and purity of feeling; the vividness of imagination with which past scenes and circumstances are represented; and occasionally, dignity of thought couched in graceful expressions. Its demerits are—the egotistic strain which is apt to affect a poet who leads an unemployed and retired life, leading him to dwell on circumstances trivial or vulgar, equally with those of a truly poetical cast, because they interest himself; and a lamentable inequality hence arising —such worthless lines as—

> The biscuit or confectionary plum,

or

> I pricked them into paper with a pin,

occurring side by side with others most musical and suggestive, such as—

> Children not thine have trod my nursery floor,

and

> Time has but half succeeded in his theft—
> Thyself removed, thy power to soothe me left.

70. *Childe Harold's Pilgrimage* must also be ranked with poems of sentiment and reflection; for though in form it resembles a descriptive poem, that which gives it its peculiar character is not the description of any external scenes, but the minute analysis and exhibition of the writer's feelings, reflections, and states of mind. The third canto, for instance, is in a great measure a piece of autobiography. Written in 1816, just after he had been separated from his wife and child, and, amidst a storm of obloquy, had passed into voluntary exile, this canto paints the revolt of Byron's tortured spirit against the world's opinion, to which, while he scorned it, he was to the last a slave. The moral of all the earlier portion is scarcely caricatured by the parody in the *Rejected Addresses* :—

> Woe's me ! the brightest wreaths [Joy] ever gave,
> Are but as flowers that decorate a tomb.
> Man's heart, the mournful urn o'er which they wave,
> Is sacred to despair, its pedestal the grave.

Many lines current in general conversation, but often quoted in ignorance of the source when they come, occur in *Childe Harold.* Few have not heard of those magnificent equivalents by which the skull is described as—

> The dome of thought, the palace of the Soul !

Again, O'Connell's favourite quotation at the Repeal meetings of 1844 is found in the second canto ; it is an invocation to the modern Greeks :—

> Hereditary bondsmen ! know ye not,
> Who would be free, themselves must strike the blow ?

At the ball given in Brussels on the night before the advance on Waterloo, we read that

> all went merry as a marriage bell.

And it is said of the young French general, Marceau, that

——he *had kept*
The whiteness of his soul, and so men o'er him wept.

In this dream-land of sentiment, where the dry light of the intellect is variously coloured and modified by the play of the emotions, the magnificent shadowy ideas of Wordsworth's *Ode on the Intimations of Immortality* find their appropriate home.[1]

71. (3.) Imagination and fancy are both intellectual faculties, and the main function of both is to detect and exhibit the resemblances which exist among objects of sense or intelligence. The difference between them, according to the doctrine of Coleridge, may be generally stated thus : that whereas fancy exhibits only external resemblances, imagination loves to disclose the internal and essential relations which bind together things apparently unlike. Drayton's *Nymphidia* is the creation of a fancy the liveliest and most inventive, but shows little or no imaginative power. On the other hand, Shakspere's *Venus and Adonis*, Milton's *L'Allegro*, and the most perfect among Shelley's poems, are works of imagination. If we analyse the series of comparisons of which Shelley makes his *Skylark* the subject, we shall find that in every case the likeness indicated lies deeper than the surface, and calls into play higher faculties than the mere intellectual reproduction of the impressions of sense :—

> Like a poet hidden
>   In the light of thought,
> Singing hymns unbidden,
>   Till the world is wrought
> To sympathy with hopes and fears it heeded not:
>
> Like a high-born maiden
>   In a palace tower,
> Soothing her love-laden
>   Soul in secret hour
> With music sweet as love, which overflows her bower:
>
> Like a glow-worm golden
>   In a dell of dew,
> Scattering unbeholden
>   Its aërial hue
> Among the flowers and grass, which screen it from the view:
>
> Like a rose embowered
>   In its own green leaves,
> By warm winds deflowered,
>   Till the scent it gives
> Makes faint with too much sweet those heavy-wingèd thieves.

---

[1] See p. 882.

> Sound of vernal showers
> On the twinkling grass,
> Rain-awakened flowers,
> All that ever was
> Joyous, and clear, and fresh, thy music doth surpass.

In the *Cloud*, by the same poet, the imagery is partly fantastic, partly imaginative, as may be seen in the following extract :—

> That orbed maiden, with white fire laden,
> Whom mortals call the moon,
> Glides glimmering o'er my fleece-like floor,
> By the midnight breezes strewn;
> And wherever the beat of her unseen feet,
> Which only the angels hear,
> May have broken the woof of my tent's thin roof,
> The stars peep behind her and peer:
> And I laugh to see them whirl and flee,
> Like a swarm of golden bees,
> When I widen the rent in my wind-built tent,
> Till the calm rivers, lakes, and seas,
> Like strips of the sky fallen through me on high,
> Are each paved with the moon and these.
>
> .   .   .   .
>
> I am the daughter of earth and water,
> And the nursling of the sky:
> I pass through the pores of the ocean and shores;
> I change, but I cannot die.
> For after the rain, when with never a stain,
> The pavilion of heaven is bare,
> And the winds and sunbeams, with their convex gleams,
> Build up the blue dome of air,
> I silently laugh at my own cenotaph,
> And out of the caverns of rain,
> Like a child from the womb, like a ghost from the tomb,
> I arise and unbuild it again.

72. (4.) The philosophical is distinguished from the didactic poem by the absence of a set moral purpose. In the *Essay on Man*, Pope starts with the design of 'vindicating the ways of God;' and whatever may be thought of the mode of vindication, this design is adhered to throughout. Nor, again, does the philosophical poem, like the narrative or epic, embody a definite story, with beginning, middle, and end. Its parts may indeed be connected, as in the case of the *Excursion*, by a slight narrative thread; but its characteristic excellence does not depend upon this, but upon the mode in which the different subjects and personages introduced are philosophically handled, and, it may perhaps be said, on the soundness of the philosophy itself. How far the pursuit of these objects is consistent with the full production of that kind of pleasure which it is the business of poetry to excite, is a question difficult of decision.

CHAPTER II.

PROSE WRITINGS.

1. A ROUGH general classification and description of the subject-matter, with a few critical sketches of particular works, or groups of works, is all that we shall attempt in the present volume.

The prose writings of our literature may be arranged under the following six heads :—

1. Works of fiction.

2. Works of satire, wit, and humour.

3. Oratory ; (with the connected departments of Journal-writing and Pamphleteering).

4. History ; including, besides history proper, biography, and narrative works of all kinds, as subsidiary branches).

5. Theology.

6. Philosophy ; (including, besides philosophy proper, essays and political treatises, and all works of thought and theory, *e.g.* æsthetics and literary criticism).

1. Prose Fiction.

2. By a work of fiction a *narrative* work is always understood. A fiction which describes, not imaginary actions, but an imaginary state of things, such as More's *Utopia*, must be considered as a work of thought and theory, and will fall under our sixth head. Works of fiction, then, or fictitious narratives, are of two kinds—those in which the agencies are natural, and those in which they are not. In the latter case they are called romances, in the former, stories of common life. Romances are either mock or serious ;—and mock romances may be either satirical, humorous, or comic. Stories of common life are divided into tales of adventure and novels ; the novel being in its highest and purest form the correlative in prose of the epic poem in poetry, and, like it, treating of ' one great complex action, in a lofty style, and with fulness of detail.'[1] Whatever be its form,

---

[2] See § 3 in the preceding chapter.

the novel must possess unity of plan, and is thereby distinguishable from the mere tale of adventure or travel, in which this unity is not required. Novels, again, may either refer to the past, in which case they are called historical novels, or to the present. If the latter, they admit of a further sub-division, according to the social level at which the leading characters move, into novels of high life—of middle life—and of low life. Further, there is a cross division applicable to the whole class of novels, into those of the artistic and those of the didactic kind. The following table exhibits the above classification of works of fiction at a glance :—

FICTITIOUS NARRATIVES.

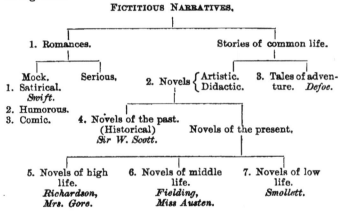

3. (1.) The word 'romance' is here used in a sense which implies that, in works so named, some preternatural or supernatural agency is instrumental in working out the plot. We have not many serious romances in English ; the *Grand Cyrus*, and other delectable productions of Scudéry and Calprenède, were read, admired, and translated amongst us in their day, but do not appear to have been imitated, at least in prose. *St. Leon*, by Godwin, *Frankenstein* or *The Ghost-seer*, by his daughter, Mrs. Shelley, and the *Old English Baron*, by Clara Reeve, are among the principal performances in this kind. The *Phantom Ship*, by Captain Marryat, is a remarkable and beautiful story, founded on the grand old legend of the *Flying Dutchman*. One of the Waverley Novels, the *Monastery*, in which the apparitions of the White Lady of Avenel have an important influence on the development of the story, falls accordingly within the scope of our definition. The most notable

examples of the mock romance are the *Travels of Lemuel Gulliver*. The comic variety is exemplified in the Voyages of Brobdingnag and Lilliput, the satirical in the Voyages to the Houynhnms and Laputa.

(2.) The distinction of novels into artistic and didactic is founded on the different aims which entered into their composition. The artistic novel aims at the beautiful representation of things and persons, such as they really appear in nature, or may be conceived capable of becoming; its purpose is æsthetic, and not moral. Goethe's *Wilhelm Meister* is a celebrated instance. The didactic novel has some special moral lesson in view, which the progress and issue of the story are intended to enforce. Godwin's *Caleb Williams*, Bulwer's *Paul Clifford* and *Eugene Aram*, and the whole class of religious novels, are instances in point.

4. (3.) Among tales of adventure, Defoe's *Robinson Crusoe* bears the palm. Among the many imitations, more or less close, to which that celebrated production has given rise, may be particularised Miss Porter's *Narrative of Sir Edward Seaward*, and Captain Marryat's delightful story of *Masterman Ready*. The *Travels of Anastasius*, by Hope, enjoyed a great reputation fifty years ago.

(4.) Novels of the past are not all necessarily historical novels, since they may relate to supposed events in the *private* life of former ages, whereas by the historical novel is commonly understood a work of which the interest principally turns on the introduction of some personages or events of historic fame. Thus, Bulwer's *Last Days of Pompeii*, in which none of the characters are historical, can only, if at all, claim the title of a historical novel in virtue of the historic catastrophe—the great eruption of Vesuvius, which buried Pompeii in ashes in the reign of Vespasian.

In the historical novel, Sir Walter Scott, the inventor of the style, remains unapproached. Out of twenty-seven novels (omitting short tales), which compose the Waverley series, twenty are historical. The most remote period to which the author has ascended is the eleventh century, the events described in *Count Robert of Paris* being supposed to occur during the first crusade. This, however, is one of the latest and least interesting of the series. The *Betrothed*, the *Talisman*, and *Ivanhoe*, refer to the twelfth century ; the grand romantic personage of Richard Cœur de Lion figuring prominently in both the novels last named. The thirteenth century seems to have had no attractions for our author ; and even in the fourteenth—a period so memorable both in English and Scottish history—he has given us only the *Fair Maid of Perth* and *Castle Dangerous*; the striking story of *Rienzi* was left for Bulwer to appropriate, and work up into an historical fiction of the highest order. In the fifteenth century, the reign of Louis XI. is admirably illustrated in *Quentin Durward*; in which the Duke of Burgundy, Charles the Bold, is presented to us in the plenitude of his power and prosperity; while in *Anne of Geierstein* we see that power humbled to the dust by the arms of the sturdy Switzers. The *Monastery*, with its sequel, the *Abbot*, exhibits the distracted state of Scotland during the religious wars of the sixteenth century. In *Kenilworth*, which belongs to the same period, the scene is laid in England, and the interest centres in Dudley, Earl of Leicester, and the unfortunate Amy Robsart. The seventeenth century must have possessed a peculiar interest for Scott; for the plots of no less than five of his novels are laid in it, and some of these are among the most successful efforts of his genius. The learned fool James I. is introduced in the *Fortunes of Nigel*; the *Legend of Montrose* brings before us the exploits of that gallant but ill-starred chief, and creates for us the admirable portrait of the veteran soldier trained in the Thirty Years' War, under Gustavus Adolphus, the incomparable Major Dalgetty :—Cromwell appears in *Woodstock*; *Peveril of the Peak* illustrates the startling contrasts which existed between the gay immoral society gathered round the court of Charles II., and the terrible Puritan element beneath the surface, crushed down but still formidable;—lastly, in *Old Mortality*, deemed by many to be the author's most perfect production, the plot is connected with the insurrection of the Scottish Covenanters in 1679, and brings before us the haughty form of Claverhouse. Four novels belong to the eighteenth century—*Rob Roy*, the *Heart of Mid-Lothian*, *Waverley*, and *Redgauntlet*. In the first, named, by the happy thought of Constable, Scott's publisher, after a noted Highland freebooter who flourished in the early part of the century, the chief historic interest lies in the admirable art with which the story brings out the contrast then existing between the civilised law-respecting Lowlands, and the confused turbulent state of things a few miles off across the Highland border, where black mail was levied and clannish custom was nearly supreme. In the *Heart of Mid-Lothian* the incidents of the Porteous riots at Edinburgh in 1736 are interwoven with the plot, and Caroline, the generous and strong-minded queen of George II., is associated with her humble petitioner, Jeanie Deans. *Waverley* is a tale of the rising of the clans under the young Pretender in 1745; and *Redgauntlet* refers to a contemplated rising of the English Jacobites a few years later, which the unmanageable obstinacy of the Chevalier stifled in the birth.

5. (5.) In the novel of high life, the chief actors belong to the 'upper ten thousand' of society. Richardson, who was himself the son of a joiner, delighted to paint the manners of this class, to which in all his novels the principal personages belong. As we read them, we associate with Sir Charles Grandisons and Lady G.s, with Harriet Byrons, Lovelaces, and Count Geronimos; an English squire or a foreign nobleman is the meanest company we frequent. Yet Richardson has high excellences; his characters are firmly yet delicately drawn; there is vigorous original outline, filled in and bodied out by a number of fine, almost imperceptible touches: the diction, though often copious to a fault, never sinks to mere verbiage; the story is always naturally and probably evolved; lastly, the author never obtrudes his own personality, but leaves his work before you, to impress you or not, according to its and your own intrinsic qualities. The clever novels of Mrs. Gore have a yet more limited range than those of Richardson; they paint the present generation, and therein only the inhabitants of May Fair, and frequenters of Rotten Row.

(6.) The immense majority of English novels portray the manners and characters which are common in the middle ranks of society. Not to speak of works by living authors—of the *Pickwick Papers* or *Vanity Fair*—all Fielding's novels,[1] *Joseph Andrews*, *Tom Jones*, and *Amelia*, and those of Miss Austen and Miss Edgeworth, belong to this class. *Pride and Prejudice*, by Jane Austen, is the perfect type of a novel of common life; the story so concisely and dramatically told, the language so simple, the shades and half-shades of human character so clearly presented, and the operation of various motives so delicately traced—attest this gifted woman to have been the perfect mistress of her art. Under this head are also included such of Scott's novels as have no historical element, *e.g. Guy Mannering*, the *Antiquary*, the *Bride of Lammermoor*, &c.

(7.) The best specimens in our literature of the novel of low life are by living authors. Which of us has not turned vagrant with little Nell, and dived into the recesses of the Seven Dials with Fagin and the Artful Dodger?[2] *Paul Clifford* also, by Bulwer, belongs to this class; and, in the last century, Smollett's *Roderick Random*, and several of Defoe's novels, which treat principally of uproarious scenes and rough characters, from which the sentimental Richardson would have recoiled in disgust.

[1] For an admirable account of them and their author, see Thackeray's *Lectures on the English Humourists*.
[2] Characters in the *Old Curiosity Shop* and *Oliver Twist*.

2. Works of Satire, Wit, and Humour.

6. Among the best performances of this kind which our literature contains, are the *Tale of a Tub* and the *Battle of the Books* by Swift, Sterne's *Tristram Shandy* and *Sentimental Journey*, and the *Anti-Jacobin* by Canning, Ellis, and Frere.

An explanation has already been given of the title of the first among the works above named.[1] Swift tells us that it was composed when 'his invention was at the height, and his reading fresh in his head.' The 'Epistle dedicated to Prince Posterity' is a fine piece of irony; Dryden is maliciously mentioned in it, as a poet, who, the prince would be surprised to hear, had written many volumes, and made a noise among his contemporaries. The tale itself, such as it is, relates the adventures of the brothers, Peter, Martin,[2] and Jack; and with the sections in which it is carried on, other sections alternate, in which the abuses of learning are exposed. The three brothers, as the names imply, are allegorical, and represent the Roman Catholic, Lutheran, and Calvinistic systems respectively. The book was eagerly read and discussed: a thing little to be wondered at, when a satire, expressed with inconceivable wit and humour, and upon which all the resources of an unquestionably great genius had been expended, was directed against the religious belief and practice of a large portion of the Christian world. But though admired, it was widely condemned. Smalridge, a divine of that age, when taxed with the authorship by Sacheverell, answered with indignation, 'Not all that you and I have in the world, nor all that we ever shall have, should hire me to write the *Tale of a Tub*.' Swift therefore found it necessary to prefix an 'Apology' to the edition of 1709, in which he declared that his meaning had been misinterpreted in many places, and that his real object throughout was to serve pure religion and morality. But if this was his object, he chose a singular way of promoting it. Martin's proceedings, which are represented as rational and right, are disposed of in a page and a half; the rest of the work consists of satirical descriptions of Peter's knavery and mendacity, and of Jack's fanatical extravagance. Of course the general effect of the book is that of a

---

[1] See p. 882.
[2] That by 'Martin' Swift originally meant Lutheranism, and not the Church of England, seems clear from the passage in the Fragment appended to the work, where he speaks of dropping 'the former Martin' and substituting for him 'Lady Bess's Institution,' by which the Church of England could alone be meant. But it is likely that he was not unwilling, at a later period, to have it supposed that 'Martin' stood for the Church of England.

I I

satirical attack on Christianity itself.   Voltaire's strong approval, and recommendation to his followers to peruse it, are conclusive as to the real relation in which it stands to religion. What chiefly delighted him was the vigour of the attacks on Peter.   These, though highly humorous, are coarse, and sometimes revolting, particularly when it is considered that they came from a clergyman.   They show plainly enough that Swift was at the time a cynic and a materialist, and utterly scouted all religion in his secret heart.

7. In the *Battle of the Books*, which is Swift's contribution to the controversy on the respective merits of classical and modern literature (see ch. v. § 47) the ancient and modern books in the Royal Library are represented as engaging each other in a pitched battle.   The Moderns march under various leaders, Cowley and Boileau commanding the light horse, and Descartes and Hobbes leading on the bowmen ; but Milton and Shakspere, indignant at the depreciators of their great masters, take no part in the fray.   The Ancients form a small and compact body, under the command of Homer, Pindar, Plato, &c.   A humorous description of the battle follows, which ends in the Moderns being routed, horse and foot.   A change of style occurs about the middle of the satire, and thence to the end the Homeric manner is parodied very amusingly.

8. The *Anti-Jacobin*, or *Weekly Examiner*, established in 1797 by Canning and his friends, might be classed, according to its form, under the head of Journalism ; but since its professed object was to chastise by ridicule, and so render harmless, the Jacobinical root and-branch aspirations of that portion of the press which had adopted the new French principles, it is properly classed among works of satire and wit.   In performing this self-assigned function, the conductors of the *Anti-Jacobin* did not mince matters ; their language was as violent and abusive as that of their opponents, their accusations as sweeping, and their scrupulosity of assertion not much superior.   But the vigour and wit with which they employed the weapons of sarcasm, irony, and parody, gave them a decided advantage, and have gained for the *Anti-Jacobin* a permanent place in our libraries. Parody was used by Canning in the sonnet upon Mrs. Brownrigg, imitated from Southey's lines on Marten the regicide, and in the famous ballad of the *Needy Knife-Grinder*, suggested by Southey's sapphics.   The prose portion of the paper contained each week three paragraphs headed ' Lies,' ' Misrepresentations,' ' Mistakes,' in which the corresponding delinquencies of the Jacobin press during the preceding week were examined and castigated.   In the second volume Canning introduced the prose

drama of *The Rovers, or the Double Arrangement,* a capital burlesque on Kotzebue's plays, which were then the rage in England.   The virtuous sentiments and loose practice of Kotzebue's heroes and heroines are amusingly exhibited in Matilda and her lover.   Matilda's 'A thought strikes me; let us swear eternal friendship,' is exquisite in its absurdity.

9. Before speaking of works of Humour it is necessary, in order not to confound them with works of Satire, to define the term, humour, with some strictness.   Humour is a peculiar way of regarding persons, actions, and things, in conformity to the peculiar character of the humorist.   It is to be carefully distinguished from wit, which is the quick apprehension of relations between dissimilar ideas—such relations being generally verbal rather than real.   Humour looks beneath the surface; it does not stay among the familiar outsides and semblances of things; it seizes upon strange out-of-the-way relations between ideas, which are real rather than verbal.   In this it resembles imagination; and the humorist must indeed possess this fusing and reuniting faculty in a high degree; but the difference is, that the relations between ideas which his turn of mind leads him to perceive are mostly *odd, strange,* relations, the exhibition of which, while it makes us thoughtful, because the relations are real, not verbal merely, awakens also our sense of the ludicrous.   We may take as an illustration the strange train of ideas in which Hamlet indulges in the scene with the grave-digger, when he 'traces in imagination the noble dust of Alexander, until he finds it stopping a bung-hole.'   Again, the property which has been assigned to humour of looking beneath the surface, involves the power of detecting empty pretension and hypocrisy, however carefully they may be disguised.   Under all the trappings and habiliments with which he seeks to veil his littleness, the humorist still detects the insignificant creature, *man*; and delights, by homely apologue or humiliating comparison, to hold up a mirror in which he may see himself as he is.   This is the direction in which the humorist approaches very near to the satirist, the distinction being that the latter has, while the former has not, a definite moral purpose, genuine or assumed, in lashing and exposing the weaknesses of mankind. Humour is exhibitive, satire didactic.   In humour, as Coleridge says, there is a universalising property ; satire, on the contrary, seizes upon different classes of men, and tends always to personality.   It seems never to have quite lost the memory of the scenes amid which it had its origin—of the holiday licence— the unlimited freedom of heaping abuse and ridicule upon indi-

viduals, which were allowed to the Eleusinian mystics upon their return from the solemn ceremonies of initiation.

10. Sterne, the author of *Tristram Shandy* and the *Sentimental Journey*, is essentially and above all things a humorist. *Tristram Shandy* is ostensibly a fictitious narrative, but it is really a pure work of humour, the narrative being destitute of plot, and the incidents only serving to bring out the humorous traits and notions of the different characters (Mr. Shandy, Uncle Toby, Corporal Trim, &c.) and to give occasion to humorous rhapsodies on the part of the author. In *Tristram Shandy* the humour tends to the side of satire; while in the *Sentimental Journey* it tends to the side of sentiment and pathos. The well-known episode on the dead donkey, and the story of the captive, exhibit this phase of Sterne's humour. We extract the former :—

The mourner was sitting upon a stone bench at the door, with an ass's pannel and its bridle on one side, which he took up from time to time, then laid them down, looked at them, and shook his head. He then took his crust of bread out of his wallet again, as if to eat it, held it some time in his hand, then laid it upon the bit of his ass's bridle, looked wistfully at the little arrangement he had made, and then gave a sigh. The simplicity of his grief drew numbers about him, and La Fleur among the rest, whilst the horses were getting ready ; as I continued sitting in the post-chaise, I could see and hear over their heads.

He said he had come last from Spain, where he had been from the farthest borders of Franconia ; and had got so far on his return home when his ass died. Everyone seemed desirous to know what business could have taken so old and poor a man so far a journey from his own home. It had pleased Heaven, he said, to bless him with three sons, the finest lads in all Germany ; but having in one week lost two of the eldest of them by the small-pox, and the youngest falling ill of the same distemper, he was afraid of being bereft of them all, and made a vow, if Heaven would not take him from him also, he would go, in gratitude, to St. Iago, in Spain. When the mourner got thus far on his story, he stopped to pay nature his tribute, and wept bitterly. He said, Heaven had accepted the conditions, and that he had set out from his cottage with this poor creature, who had been a patient partner of his journey ; that it had ate the same bread with him all the way, and was unto him as a friend.

Everybody who stood about heard the poor fellow with concern ; La Fleur offered him money. The mourner said he did not want it ; it was not the value of the ass, but the loss of him. The ass, he said, he was assured, loved him ; and upon this, he told them a long story of a mischance upon their passage over the Pyrenean mountains, which had separated them from each other three days : during which time the ass had sought him as much as he had sought the ass ; and that they had scarce either ate or drunk till they met. 'Thou hast one comfort, at least,' said I, ' in the loss of thy poor beast : I'm sure thou hast been a merciful master to him.' 'Alas,' said the mourner, ' I thought so when he was alive ; but now that he is dead I think otherwise ; I fear the

weight of myself and my afflictions together have been too much for
him ; they have shortened the poor creature's days, and I fear I have
them to answer for.' 'Shame on the world !' said I to myself. 'Did
we but love each other as this poor soul loved his ass, 'twould be
something.'

11. For pure wit Sydney Smith stands unrivalled among
English prose-writers. He was a sincere and earnest Liberal in
politics, inheriting from Burke, and other leading members of
the opposition to Lord North's government, principles, some
of which they had been the first to establish, while others were
derived from the Puritans of the seventeenth century. In religion
he takes up the utilitarian, common-sense, rationalising tone of
the eighteenth century ; Methodism is, in his eyes, a miserable
imposture—a vulgar fanaticism ; religion, unless rich, respectable, and prudent—unless countenanced by the well-educated
and well-to-do classes, presented itself to him in the light of a
nuisance rather than otherwise. His exertions on behalf of the
enfranchisement of the Irish Catholics ought never to be forgotten. This question forms the subject of *Peter Plymley's
Letters*, written in 1807, in which solid reasoning is conveyed
in a form so piquant, so irresistibly witty and racy, that even
political opponents must have read them with delight. Peter
Plymley writes to his brother Abraham, the Protestant clergyman of a country parish in Ireland ; and, amongst other things,
disposes in the following fashion of the charge—not yet quite
obsolete—which it was then customary to bring against the
Irish Catholics, because they did not, instead of demanding
entire civil and religious equality, overflow with gratitude to
their rulers for the partial relief which they had already obtained. The sixth letter opens thus :—

DEAR ABRAHAM,—What amuses me the most is to hear of the
indulgences which the Catholics have received, and their exorbitance in
not being satisfied with those indulgences. Now, if you complain to
me that a man is obtrusive and shameless in his requests, and that it is
impossible to bring him to reason, I must first of all hear the whole of
your conduct towards him ; for you may have taken from him so much
in the first instance, that, in spite of a long series of restitution, a vast
latitude for petition may still remain behind.

There is a village (no matter where) in which the inhabitants, on
one day in the year, sit down to a dinner prepared at the common
expense : by an extraordinary piece of tyranny (which Lord Hawkes-
bury would call the wisdom of the village ancestors), the inhabitants
of three of the streets, about a hundred years ago, seized upon the inhabitants of the fourth street, bound them hand and foot, laid them
upon their backs, and compelled them to look on while the rest were
stuffing themselves with beef and beer ; the next year the inhabitants
of the persecuted street (though they contributed an equal quota of the
expense) were treated precisely in the same manner. The tyranny

grew into a custom ; and (as the manner of our nature is) it was considered as the most sacred of all duties to keep these poor fellows without their annual dinner. The village was so tenacious of this practice, that nothing could induce them to resign it; every enemy to it was looked upon as a disbeliever in Divine Providence ; any nefarious churchwarden who wished to succeed in his election, had nothing to do but to represent his antagonist as an abolitionist, in order to frustrate his ambition, endanger his life, and throw the village into a state of the most dreadful commotion. By degrees, however, the obnoxious street grew to be so well peopled, and its inhabitants so firmly united, that their oppressors, more afraid of injustice, were more disposed to be just. At the next dinner they are unbound, the year after allowed to sit upright ; then a bit of bread and a glass of water; till, at last, after a long series of concessions, they are emboldened to ask, in pretty plain terms, that they may be allowed to sit down at the bottom of the table, and to fill their bellies as well as the rest. Forthwith a general cry of shame and scandal : ‘Ten years ago, were you not laid upon your backs ? Don't you remember what a great thing you thought it to get a piece of bread ? How thankful you were for cheese-parings ! Have you forgotten that memorable era when the lord of the manor interfered to obtain for you a slice of the public pudding ! And now, with an audacity only equalled by your ingratitude, you have the impudence to ask for knives and forks, and to request, in terms too plain to be mistaken, that you may sit down to table with the rest, and be indulged even with beef and beer. There are not more than half a dozen dishes which we have reserved for ourselves ; the rest has been thrown open to you in the utmost profusion; you have potatoes and carrots, suet dumplings, sops in the pan, and delicious toast and water, in incredible quantities. Beef, mutton, lamb, pork, and veal are ours ; and if you were not the most restless and dissatisfied of human beings, you would never think of aspiring to enjoy them.'

Is not this, my dainty Abraham, the very nonsense and the very insult which is talked to and practised upon the Catholics ?

The temptation to quote just one good thing out of the many hundreds which the lively canon scattered around him is irresistible. It occurs in a note to the third of these same letters of Peter Plymley. ‘Fanaticism,’ says Peter :—

‘ is Mr. Canning's term for the detection of public abuses ; a term invented by him, and adopted by that simious parasite who is always grinning at his heels. Nature descends down to infinite smallness. Mr. Canning has his parasites ; and if you take a large buzzing bluebottle fly, and look at it in a microscope, you may see twenty or thirty little ugly insects crawling about it, which doubtless think their fly to be the bluest, grandest, merriest, most important animal in the universe, and are convinced the world would be at an end if it ceased to buzz.'

3. Oratory, Journalism, Pamphleteering.

12. Oratory is of three kinds : that of the pulpit, that of the bar, and that of the public assembly, or of the tribune, to use a convenient French term.

When the oratory of the pulpit addresses itself to questions purely religious and moral, or when it interprets Scripture, it is called Homiletics, or preaching, and must be considered in connexion with theology. When it deals with political questions, or celebrates the virtues of individuals, it becomes in the strict sense a branch of oratory. The political sermon and the funeral oration are as much a part of eloquence as the advocate's address, or the speech from the hustings ;—the chief difference lying in the conditions of delivery, which give to the pulpit orator leisure for careful preparation, and preclude the possibility of reply.

In this kind of oratory the great names which France can boast of immediately occur to us ;—Boucher and the preachers of the League, Bossuet, Bourdaloue, and Massillon. In English literature we have little that requires notice but the political sermons and funeral orations of Jeremy Taylor, and some sermons by South. Taylor's sermon at the funeral of Archbishop Bramhall has some fine passages ; yet his success in this kind of composition was on the whole inconsiderable.

13. The oratory of the bar differs from that of the pulpit and the tribune in that the conditions under which it exists oblige it ordinarily to take for its guiding and animating lights, not general moral principles, but legal maxims and decisions ; and, even in cases where an appeal to general principles is admissible, to give them always a special and immediate application. A certain relative inferiority hence attaches to this kind of eloquence. It is not ordinarily that of the convinced mind, communicating its convictions to others for some high purpose, whether that be the exhibition of pure truth or the maintenance of the public welfare, or at lowest the defence of party principles, but that of the advocate whose single aim it is to make out his case, and advance the interests of his client. Exceptional cases, however, are not uncommon—as on the trials of eminent public men or notorious criminals—in which the advocate appears as the vindicator of human or divine justice, and discharges a function of great dignity. Of this nature are the orations of Cicero against Verres and Catiline, and, among ourselves, the speeches of Burke on the impeachment of Warren Hastings. But the instances are more common in which lawyers in public trials have been the instruments of royal suspicion or party hate. Never was eloquence more shamefully prostituted than by Coke in his prosecution of Raleigh, or by Bacon when he appeared against his benefactor Essex.

14. The oratory of the public assembly is illustrated in

English literature by a long roll of historic names, some of which are not unlikely to rival in perpetuity of renown the names of the great orators of antiquity. Far above all others rises the eloquence of Burke. The following extract from his *Speech at Bristol previous to the Election* in 1780, refers to the demoralising effects of the penal laws against the Catholics :—

In this situation men not only shrink from the frowns of a stern magistrate, but they are obliged to fly from their very species. The seeds of destruction are sown in civil intercourse, in social habitudes. The blood of wholesome kindred is infected. Their tables and beds are surrounded with snares. All the means given by Providence to make life safe and comfortable are perverted into instruments of terror and torment. This species of universal subserviency, that makes the very servant who waits behind your chair the arbiter of your life and fortune, has such a tendency to degrade and abase mankind, and to deprive them of that assured and liberal state of mind which alone can make us what we ought to be, that I vow to God I would sooner bring myself to put a man to immediate death for opinions I disliked, and so to get rid of the man and his opinions at once, than to fret him with a feverish being, tainted with the gaol distemper of a contagious servitude, to keep him above ground an animated mass of putrefaction, corrupted himself and corrupting all about him.

The eulogium upon Sir George Savile, a little further on, has a terse and classic turn of expression, which our language, from its want of inflexions, has rarely attained to :—

I hope that few things which have a tendency to bless or to adorn life have wholly escaped my observation in my passage through it.   I have sought the acquaintance of that gentleman, and have seen him in all situations.   He is a true genius, with an understanding vigorous, and acute, and refined, and distinguishing even to excess ; and illuminated with a most unbounded, peculiar, and original cast of imagination.   With these he possesses many external and instrumental advantages ; and he makes use of them all.   His fortune is among the largest ; a fortune which, wholly unencumbered as it is with one single charge from luxury, vanity, or excess, sinks under the benevolence of its dispenser. This private benevolence, expanding itself into patriotism, renders his whole being the estate of the public, in which he has not reserved a *peculium* for himself of profit, diversion, or relaxation. During the session, the first in and the last out of the House of Commons, he passes from the senate to the camp ; and seldom seeing the seat of his ancestors, he is always in the senate to serve his country, or in the field to defend it.

----

15. The function of the journalist so far resembles that of the orator, that his object also is to produce immediate conviction or persuasion, with a view to action. But he speaks to his audience through the broad sheet, not by word of mouth. The

extensive use of this mode of address in modern times is attributable, partly to the populousness and geographical extent of modern communities, partly to the increased diffusion of a certain grade of culture, partly also to the invention of a variety of mechanical contrivances, met by corresponding social arrangements, by which the journalist is enabled to address his readers at *regular* and *brief* intervals. At Athens the sovereign people all resided within easy reach of the Pnyx or the Dionysiac theatre, so that the orators who led them could reach them through their ears, and were not compelled, like our journalists, to appeal to citizens living at a distance through the eye. It must be noted that the journalist and the circulator of news, though the two offices are usually combined in practice, have distinct functions in theory. Newspapers originated, as the name itself implies, in the attempt to discharge the humbler office, that of collecting and disseminating news. But as the demand for correct and frequent intelligence increased, and the means of supplying it were also multiplied, the conductors of newspapers naturally seized the opportunity thus afforded them of accompanying their news with their own comments and explanations. It is from the power and social influence which the able use of these opportunities has secured to it that the newspaper press has received the name of the *Fourth Estate*, and that journalism has almost risen to the dignity of a profession. At the present day the journalist sometimes discards the business of a circulator of news altogether—as in the instance of the 'Saturday Review.' The newspaper, as originally understood, is now represented only by government and mercantile gazettes, and similar publications.

16. The pamphlet, whether its ends be political or politico-religious, is equivalent to an elaborate speech, which by means of the printing-press obtains a diffusion immeasurably exceeding that which oral delivery can accomplish. In a country where the press is free, this indirect kind of oratory is sure to be largely resorted to, especially in times of political agitation; and many an eager political theorist, whom compulsory silence would have turned into a conspirator, has relieved his excitement by writing, and proved innocuous as a pamphleteer. The civil war of the seventeenth century, the reign of Anne, and the fifty years terminating in 1835, are the periods at which pamphleteering has most flourished amongst us. We will give a specimen from a work of each period. Few pamphlets composed in the first have much literary value, except the politico-religious tracts of

Milton. The following extract forms a portion of his eulogy upon the Long Parliament in the *Apology for Smectymnuus* :—

With such a majesty had their wisdom begirt itself, that whereas others had levied war to subdue a nation that sought for peace, they sitting here in peace could so many miles extend the force of their single words as to overawe the dissolute stoutness of an armed power, secretly stirred up and almost hired against them. And having by a solemn protestation vowed themselves and the kingdom anew to God and His service, and by a prudent foresight above what their fathers thought on, prevented the dissolution and frustration of their designs by an untimely breaking up; notwithstanding all the treasonous plots against them, all the rumours either of rebellion or invasion, they have not been yet brought to change their constant resolution, ever to think fearlessly of their own safeties, and hopefully of the commonwealth ; which hath gained them such an admiration from all good men that now they hear it as their ordinary surname to be saluted the fathers of their country, and sit as gods among daily petitions and public thanks flowing in upon them. Which doth so little yet exalt them in their own thoughts, that with all gentle affability and courteous acceptance, they both receive and return that tribute of thanks which is tendered them : testifying their zeal and desire to spend themselves as it were piecemeal upon the grievances and wrongs of their distressed nation ; insomuch that the meanest artisans and labourers, at other times also women, and often the younger sort of servants, assembling with their complaints, and that sometimes in a less humble guise than for petitioners, have come with confidence that neither their meanness would be rejected, nor their simplicity contemned, nor yet their urgency distasted, either by the dignity, wisdom, or moderation of that supreme senate : nor did they depart unsatisfied.

17. The next extract is from Swift's *Conduct of the Allies,* a pamphlet published in 1712. By the 'reigning favourites' are meant Godolphin and the Duke and Duchess of Marlborough. The war of the Spanish succession was now practically over ; the ministry which carried it on had been dismissed ; and Swift's object was to reconcile men's minds to the peace which the new ministry were endeavouring to negotiate, by enlarging on the wasteful and corrupt manner in which the nation had been plunged into debt in order to carry on a war which benefited only the allies, the English general, and the capitalists :—

But when the war was thus begun, there soon fell in other incidents here at home, which made the continuance of it necessary for those who were the chief advisers. The Whigs were at that time out of all credit or consideration : the reigning favourites had always carried what was called the Tory principle, at least as high as our constitution could bear ; and most others in great employments were wholly in the Church interest. These last, among whom several were persons of the greatest merit, quality, and consequence, were not able to endure the many instances of pride, insolence, avarice, and ambition, which those favourites began so early to discover, nor to see them presuming to be the sole dispensers of the royal favour. However, their opposition was to no purpose; they wrestled with too great a power, and were soon crushed under it. For those in possession, finding they could never be quiet in their usurpations while others had any credit who were at least upon an equal foot of merit, began to make overtures to the discarded Whigs, who would be content with any terms of accommodation. Thus commenced this *Solemn League and Covenant*, which hath ever since been cultivated with so much zeal and application. The great traders in money were wholly devoted to the Whigs, who had first raised them. The army, the court, and the treasury, continued under the old despotic administration; the Whigs were received into employment, left to manage the parliament, cry down the landed interest, and worry the Church. Meantime our allies, who were not ignorant that all this artificial structure had no true foundation in the hearts of the people, resolved to make their best use of it, as long as it should last. And the General's credit being raised to a great height at home by our success in Flanders, the Dutch began their gradual impositions, lessening their quotas, breaking their stipulations, garrisoning the towns we took for them, without supplying their troops; with many other infringements. All which we were forced to submit to, because the General was *made easy*; because the moneyed men at home were fond of war; because the Whigs were not yet firmly settled: and because that exorbitant degree of power which was built upon a supposed necessity of employing particular persons would go off in a peace. It is needless to add that the emperor and other princes followed the example of the Dutch, and succeeded as well for the same reasons.

18. Among the innumerable tracts and pamphlets produced in the third period, the following passage is selected almost at random; it is from a pamphlet written by Lord Byron in 1821, in the form of a letter to a friend in England, examining the Rev. W. Bowles's strictures on the life and writings of Pope. The passage is interesting as embodying one great poet's deliberate estimate of another :—

Of Pope I have expressed my opinion elsewhere, as also of the effects which the present attempts at poetry have had upon our literature. If any great national or natural convulsion could or should overwhelm your country in such sort as to sweep Great Britain from the kingdoms of the earth, and leave only that—after all, the most living of human things—a *dead language*, to be studied, and read, and imitated by the wise of future and far generations upon foreign shores; if your literature should become the learning of mankind, divested of party cabals, temporary fashions, and national pride and prejudice, an Englishman, anxious that the posterity of strangers should know that there had been such a thing as a British epic and tragedy, might wish for the preservation of Shakspeare and Milton; but the surviving world would snatch Pope from the wreck, and let the rest sink with the people. He is the only poet that never shocks; the only poet whose *faultlessness* has been made his reproach. Cast your eye over his productions; consider their extent, and contemplate their variety—pastoral, passion, mock-heroic, translation, satire, ethics—all excellent, and often perfect.

4. History :—Contemporary and Retrospective.

19. Under this general heading we include true narratives of all kinds. For the faithful record of any actual human experience whatever may be regarded as a work subsidiary to, and promotive of, the end of History proper; which is, the representation of the evolution, either of the general life of mankind (universal history), or of the life of some one nation in particular. Biography of every description is thus included among the departments subsidiary to history. Indeed it has been proved by some late brilliant examples—in the case of Macaulay's England for instance—that the historian who rightly understands his business can glean nearly as much material suitable for his purpose from the lives of private persons as from those of princes, statesmen, or generals. Accounts of voyages and travels are also, though more remotely, subsidiary to history. The observations of an intelligent traveller in civilised countries are obviously of the highest value to the historian. Arthur Young's *Travels in France before the Revolution* and Laing's *Notes of a Traveller* are cases in point. And even the descriptions given by the first explorers of wild uninhabited regions are subsidiary to the history of later generations. To the historian of America, the narrative of Raleigh's blind and struggling progress along the swampy coasts of North Carolina, while engaged in laying the foundations of the colony of Virginia, cannot fail to be of the highest use and interest. So when the history of the Australian Colonies comes to be written, the works of Mitchell, Sturt, Grey, Leichhardt, and other hardy explorers, will assuredly furnish a large portion of the matter of its introductory chapters.

20. History proper is of two kinds: 1, contemporary; 2, retrospective or reflective. A third kind—philosophical history—has been added by some German metaphysicians.[1] By this is meant, the scientific exhibition of the manner in which the state of human society in any given generation inevitably causes, through the operation of physical laws, the state of society found in the next generation. As, however, the life of a nation or of the race is evolved by human actions, and it has not yet been proved, however confidently asserted, by these philosophers, that such actions are subject to physical necessity—in other words, that the human will is not free—those who believe in the opposite doctrines of responsibility and freewill will not

---

[1] See Hegel's *Philosophie der Geschichte.*

be disposed to admit the possibility of history being correctly written upon such a hypothesis.

(1.) Under the description of contemporary history are comprised, in English literature, many works which from the literary point of view are nearly worthless, together with a few which are of rare excellence. The former character applies to the contemporary portions of our old English Chronicles, Fabyan, Hall, Grafton, Holinshed, Stow, &c. Ludlow's and Whitlocke's *Memoirs*, relating to the civil war of Charles I.'s time, though much superior to these, are flat in style, and dull through deficiency of descriptive power. Clarendon's *History of the Great Rebellion* is the most perfect contemporary history that we possess; next to it may be named Burnet's *History of His Own Times*, and Horace Walpole's *Memoirs of the Last Ten Years of the Reign of George II.*

21. Clarendon's history is a work with which the student of our literature should make himself familiar. It is indeed very long, but the theme is one so deeply interesting, and the revolution which it records has so decisively influenced the whole course of our history down to the present day, that he may be excused for spending some time over it. There are many digressions too—Clarendon is partial to them—which if necessary may be omitted. Of course the book is not impartial, nor entirely trustworthy. For not only was the author a keen partisan on the royalist side; he was also a lawyer, and had a legal turn of mind; and was thence disqualified to a certain degree from weighing the conduct and aims of the different parties in even scales. The Puritans on the one hand, and the Catholics on the other, were pursuing objects which the law of the land, in establishing the Church of England, had condemned; and this is reason enough with Clarendon for branding those objects as bad, and their pursuit as criminal. For instance, he thus speaks of the infamous sentence passed on Prynne and his fellow-sufferers, referred to above at p. 241 :—

These three persons (Prynne, Bastwick, and Burton) having been, for several follies and libelling humours, first gently reprehended, and after, for their incorrigibleness, more severely censured and imprisoned, found some means in prison of correspondence, which was not before known to be between them; and to combine themselves in a more pestilent and seditious libel than they had ever before vented; in which the honour of the king, queen, counsellors, and bishops was with equal license blasted and traduced; which was faithfully dispersed by their proselytes in the city. The authors were quickly and easily known, and had indeed too much ingenuity to deny it, and were thereupon brought together to the Star-chamber, *ore tenus*, where they behaved themselves with marvellous insolence, with full confidence demanding ' that the bishops who sat in the court ' (being only the archbishop of Canterbury and the bishop of London), ' might not be present, because they were their enemies, and so parties;' which, how scandalous and ridiculous soever it seemed then there, was good logic and good law two years after in Scotland, and served to banish the bishops of that kingdom both from the council table and the assembly.   Upon a very patient and solemn hearing, in as full a court as ever I saw in that place, without any difference in opinion or dissenting voice, they were all three censured as scandalous, seditious, and infamous persons, ' to lose their ears in the pillory, and to be imprisoned in several gaols during the king's pleasure;' all which was executed with rigour and severity enough.

But whatever defects, whether of matter or manner, may be alleged against this work, the style is so attractive—has such an equable, easy, and dignified flow—that it can never cease to be popular.   Perhaps Clarendon's greatest merit is his skill in character-drawing.   Take, for example, the character of Hampden :—

He was a gentleman of a good family in Buckinghamshire, and born to a fair fortune, and of a most civil and affable demeanour.   In his entrance into the world he indulged to himself all the license in sports, and exercises, and company, which was used by men of the most jolly conversation. Afterwards, he retired to a more reserved and melancholy society, yet preserving his own natural cheerfulness and vivacity, and, above all, a flowing courtesy to all men ; though they who conversed nearly with him found him growing into a dislike of the ecclesiastical government of the Church, yet most believed it rather a dislike of some churchmen, and of some introducements of theirs, which he apprehended might disquiet the public peace.   He was rather of reputation in his own country than of public discourse or fame in the kingdom, before the business of ship-money; but then he grew the argument of all tongues, every man inquiring who and what he was that durst, at his own charge, support the liberty and property of the kingdom, and rescue his country, as he thought, from being made a prey to the court. His carriage throughout this agitation was with that rare temper and modesty, that they who watched him narrowly to find some advantage against his person, to make him less resolute in his cause, were compelled to give him a just testimony. And the judgment that was given against him infinitely more advanced him than the service for which it was given.   When this parliament began (being returned knight of the shire for the county where he lived), the eyes of all men were fixed on him as their *patriæ pater*, and the pilot that must steer the vessel through the tempests and rocks which threatened it.   And I am persuaded his power and interest at that time was greater to do good or hurt than any man's in the kingdom, or than any man in his rank hath had in any time ; for his reputation of honesty was universal, and his affections seemed so publicly guided that no corrupt or private ends could bias them.

After he was among those members accused by the king of high treason, he was much altered ; his nature and carriage seeming much fiercer than it did before. And, without question, when he first drew the sword he threw away the scabbard; for he passionately opposed the overture made by the king for a treaty from Nottingham, and as eminently, any expedients that might have produced any accommodations in this that was at Oxford; and was principally relied on to prevent any infusions which might be made into the Earl of Essex towards peace, or to render them ineffectual if they were made; and was indeed much more relied on by that party than the general himself. In the first entrance into the troubles he undertook the command of a regiment of foot, and performed the duty of a colonel on all occasions most punctually. He was very temperate in diet, and a supreme governor over all his passions and affections, and had thereby a great power over other men's. He was of an industry and vigilance not to be tired out or wearied by the most laborious; and of parts not to be imposed upon by the most subtle or sharp; and of a personal courage equal to his best parts; so that he was an enemy not to be wished wherever he might have been made a friend; and as much to be apprehended where he was so as any man could deserve to be. And therefore his death was no less pleasing to the one party than it was condoled in the other. In a word, what was said of Cinna might well be applied to him—'He had a head to contrive, and a tongue to persuade, and a hand to execute any mischief.' His death, therefore, seemed to be a great deliverance to the nation.

22. Burnet's *Own Times* is a work that is full of inaccuracies, and does not rise above the level of a plain conversational style; it however throws much valuable light on the history of civil transactions in England and Scotland during the latter half of the seventeenth century. This writer also is graphic, and probably faithful, in his delineations of character.

Horace Walpole, son of the Whig statesman, Sir Robert Walpole, had a near view during his long life of the secret machinery by which the state policy of Britain was set in motion; and we have the results of his observation in his *Memoirs* above mentioned, as well as in the lively and lengthy series of his *Letters*. But Horace, though polished and keen, is by no means a genial writer: selfish himself, he did not much believe in human disinterestedness; and without the large intellectual grasp of Gibbon, he was destitute of those strong human sympathies and antipathies which impart a certain interest to the works of much inferior men.

23. (2.) Retrospective history may be either legendary or evidential; by which is meant, history, the statements of which on matters of fact rest on probable moral evidence. The legendary history relates events supposed to occur at distant periods, the evidence for which is mere popular tradition. In such a history, no event, or connexion of events—no names or genealogies—can be accepted as accurately corresponding to reality. Yet, as there are usually certain grains of historic truth deducible from even the most imaginative of these histories, and

as the writers at any rate suppose themselves to be relators of fact not fiction, the reader must not confound this class of works with fictitious narratives. Geoffrey of Monmouth's *Historia Britonum* is a. pure legendary history. All the old English chroniclers begin their histories just as Livy does, with legendary recitals, of which Geoffrey's work is the principal source. In most of them a portion of evidential history succeeds, compiled from the writings of their predecessors. This is followed by the narrative of contemporary events, which is usually the only portion of such works that has any value.

Retrospective histories of the evidential class proceed upon the same principles, whether they treat of ancient or of modern civilisation. The same critical rules are appealed to in each case for the purpose of testing the credibility of the witnesses, ascertaining the dates, or other circumstances connected with the composition of documents—in short, for accomplishing the great end of this kind of historical writing, which is to paint a past age as it really was. We proceed to notice the chief works of this class in English literature, proceeding from ancient to modern history.

24. The *History of the World*, by Raleigh, professes to describe the course of events in the chief countries of the ancient world, from the Creation to the fall of the Macedonian Kingdom in 168 B.C. Some account of the manner in which the design is executed has been given at a previous page.[1] The most remarkable passages are those in which the chivalrous old campaigner illustrates the details of Macedonian or Roman battles, by referring to scenes in his own varied and turbulent life. Now and then the style rises to a very clear and noble strain, as in the following sentences, with which the work concludes :—

By this, which we have already set down, is seen the beginning and end of the three first monarchies of the world, whereof the founders and erectors thought that they could never have ended. That of Rome, which made the fourth, was also at this time almost at the highest. We have left it flourishing in the middle of the field, having rooted up or cut down all that kept it from the eyes and admiration of the world ; but after some continuance, it shall begin to lose the beauty it had ; the storms of ambition shall beat her great boughs and branches one against another, her leaves shall fall off, her limbs wither, and a rabble of barbarous nations enter the field and cut her down.

. . . . .

For the rest, if we seek a reason of the succession and continuance of this boundless ambition in mortal men, we may add to that which hath been already said, that the kings and princes of the world have always laid before them the actions, but not the ends, of those great

[1] See p. 225.

ones which preceded them. They are always transported with the glory of the one, but they never mind the misery of the other, till they find the experience in themselves. They neglect the advice of God, while they enjoy life, or hope it; but they follow the counsel of Death upon his first approach. It is he that puts into man all the wisdom of the world, without speaking a word, which God, with all the words of His law, promises or threats, doth not infuse. Death, which hateth and destroyeth man, is believed; God, which hath made him and loves him, is always deferred. 'I have considered,' saith Solomon, 'all the works that are under the sun, and, behold, all is vanity and vexation of spirit:' but who believes it till Death tells it us? . . . . O eloquent, just, and mighty death? whom none could advise, thou hast persuaded; what none hath dared, thou hast done; and whom all the world hath flattered, thou only hast cast out of the world and despised; thou hast drawn together all the far-stretched greatness, all the pride, cruelty, and ambition of man, and covered it all over with these two narrow words, *Hic jacet!*

25. The vast sweep taken in the *Decline and Fall of the Roman Empire* exhibits Gibbon's wonderful capacity, not only for mastering and reproducing the sequence and connexion of events through a long and obscure period in the principal countries of Europe and Asia, but also for dealing with what may be called the *statics* of the subject, in those detailed, consistent, and luminous pictures which he draws of the state of society as existing in a particular country at a particular time. The main body of the work commences with the reign of Trajan (A.D. 98) and ends with the fall of the Eastern Empire (A.D. 1453); but three supplementary chapters 'review the state and revolutions of the Roman city' (to which, it will be remembered, Gibbon had limited his original design) from the twelfth to the sixteenth century. But though it is difficult to speak too highly of the genius displayed in this memorable work, it must be added that the fidelity of the historical picture which it exhibits is greatly marred by the Sadducean scepticism of the writer. When a Christian bishop or doctor, or a religious king, comes before his field of vision, it is not in Gibbon to be just; he cannot or will not believe that such a man was anything more than a compound of enthusiasm and superstition, in whom morality was always ready to give way to ecclesiastical considerations; and his sneering cavils seem to leave their trail upon the purest virtue, the most exalted heroism, which the times that he writes of produced for the instruction of mankind. He is in thorough sympathy with no one except Julian the Apostate. Again, his ardent attachment to the civilisation and literature of Greece and Rome involved him in a partial blindness and unfairness to the immense importance of the part played by the Teutonic race in modern history; and this unfairness does

K K

certainly, to some extent, affect the general value of his history, considered as a trustworthy picture of a great sequence of events.

Dr. Arnold's unfinished Roman history, based upon that of Niebuhr, extends from the founding of the city to the middle of the second Punic war. Two additional volumes, written at an earlier period but not published till after the author's death, carry on the history of the Roman Commonwealth from the close of the second Punic war to the death of Augustus, with a separate chapter on the reign of Trajan.

Among those who have written the history of England, Scotland, or Ireland, it is impossible to do more than mention a few prominent names.

26. Sir Thomas More's *History of the Reign of Edward V.* is a youthful and rhetorical production, which, according to Horace Walpole, who, in his *Historic Doubts respecting Richard III.*, has sifted the whole matter very ably, will nowhere stand a critical examination and confrontation with the original authorities. Lord Bacon's *History of Henry VII.*, though composed in a homely style, is a masterly work. Men's motives are deeply probed, and their actions wisely weighed; laws and events affecting the course of trade, the progress of agriculture, and the welfare of particular classes of society, are carefully recorded and examined; truth without disguise seems to be the writer's paramount design; and characters are drawn as by an eye that saw all and a hand that could paint all. Milton's *History of England* is a mere fragment. Neal's *History of the Puritans*, and another of *New England*, by the same author, are both valuable works, because carefully based on documentary and oral evidence. But the most eminent historians of the seventeenth century belong to the contemporary class.

In the next century, and down to 1850, we can barely mention the names of Rapin, Carte, Lord Hailes, Belsham, and Adolphus. Hume's clear and manly style would have insured to his *History of England* a longer pre-eminence had not his indolence allowed inaccuracies and a want of references to deform his work. Robertson's *History of Scotland* is pleasant reading, but uncritical. The work similarly entitled by Sir Walter Scott embraces all the earlier portions of the history, from A.D. 80 to the accession of Mary, Queen of Scots, which Robertson had omitted. Moore's *History of Ireland* is a work unworthy of his genius. Lanigan's *Ecclesiastical History of Ireland*, embracing the period from the conversion of the Irish by St. Patrick to the loss of their national independence in the twelfth century, is a calm, dispassionate, and profoundly learned work.

27. No very signal success has been achieved by English writers in compiling histories of modern Continental States. Knolles' *History of the Turks* must be named under this head; and Coxe's *Memoirs of the House of Austria*, and Russell's *Modern Europe*, and Roscoe's *Lorenzo de' Medici*. Here also must be placed Arnold's *Introductory Lectures on Modern History*, which contain several brilliant isolated sketches. One such passage we extract:—

Ten years afterwards there broke out by far the most alarming danger of universal dominion which had ever threatened Europe. The most military people in Europe became engaged in a war for their very existence. Invasion on the frontiers, civil war and all imaginable horrors raging within—the ordinary relations of life went to wrack, and every Frenchman became a soldier. It was a multitude numerous as the hosts of Persia, but animated by the courage and skill and energy of the old Romans. One thing alone was wanting, that which Pyrrhus said the Romans wanted to enable them to conquer the world—a general and a ruler like himself. There was wanted a master hand to restore and maintain peace at home, and to concentrate and direct the immense military resources of France against her foreign enemies. And such an one appeared in Napoleon. Pacifying La Vendée, receiving back the emigrants, restoring the Church, remodelling the law, personally absolute, yet carefully preserving and maintaining all the great points which the nation had won at the Revolution, Napoleon united in himself not only the power but the whole will of France, and that power and will were guided by a genius for war such as Europe had never seen since Cæsar. The effect was absolutely magical. In November 1799 he was made First Consul; he found France humbled by defeats, his Italian conquests lost, his allies invaded, his own frontier threatened. He took the field in May 1800, and in June the whole fortune of the war was changed, and Austria driven out of Lombardy by the victory of Marengo. Still the flood of the tide rose higher and higher, and every successive wave of its advance swept away a kingdom. Earthly state has never reached a prouder pinnacle than when Napoleon, in June 1812, gathered his army at Dresden, and there received the homage of subject kings. And now what was the principal adversary of this tremendous power? by whom was it checked, and resisted, and put down? By none, and by nothing, but the direct and manifest interposition of God! I know of no language so well fitted to describe that victorious advance to Moscow, and the utter humiliation of the retreat, as the language of the prophet with respect to the advance and subsequent destruction of the host of Sennacherib.

28. Orme, Mill, and Elphinstone, are the chief authorities for the history of India. The first two confine their attention to British India, but Elphinstone's work treats chiefly of the times anterior to European occupation. For the history of the colonial dependencies of European States, Robertson (in his *History of America*) and Bryan Edwards, author of a history of Jamaica, are the only names of much importance. Prescott,

Bancroft, and other American writers, have ably taken up that portion of the subject which relates to the American continent.

29. Mr. James and Captain Brenton have written the naval history of Britain. The latter has the advantage in style, the former in accuracy and clearness of arrangement. Sir William Napier's work on the *Peninsular War* is a military history of a high order. The eloquent passage which follows refers to the closing struggle of the battle of Albuera :—

The conduct of a few brave men soon changed this state of affairs. Colonel Robert Arbuthnot, pushing between the double fire of the mistaken troops, arrested that mischief; while Cole, with the fusiliers, flanked by a battalion of the Lusitanian Legion, under Colonel Hawkshawe, mounted the hill, dispersed the lancers, recovered the captured guns, and appeared on the right of Houghton's brigade exactly as Abercrombie passed it on the left.

Such a gallant line, issuing from the midst of the smoke, and rapidly separating itself from the confused and broken multitude, startled the enemy's heavy masses, which were increasing and pressing onwards as to an assured victory : they wavered, hesitated, and then vomiting forth a storm of fire, hastily endeavoured to enlarge their front, while a fearful discharge of grape from their artillery whistled through the British ranks. Myers was killed; Cole, and the three colonels, Ellis, Blakeney, and Hawkshawe, fell wounded ; and the fusilier battalions, struck by the iron tempest, reeled and staggered like sinking ships. Suddenly and sternly recovering, they closed with their terrible enemies, and then was seen with what a strength and majesty the British soldier fights. In vain did Soult by voice and gesture animate his Frenchmen ; in vain did the noblest veterans, extricating themselves from the crowded columns, sacrifice their lives to gain time for the mass to bear up on such a fair field : in vain did the mass itself bear up, and, fiercely striving, fire indiscriminately upon friends and foes, while the horsemen, hovering upon their flank, threatened to charge the advancing line. Nothing could stop that astonishing infantry. No sudden burst of undisciplined valour, no nervous enthusiasm, weakened the stability of their order; their flashing eyes were bent on the dark columns in their front; their measured tread shook the ground; their murderous volleys swept away the head of every formation; their deafening shouts overpowered the dissonant cries which arose from all parts of the tumultuous crowd, as foot by foot, and with a horrid carnage, it was driven by the incessant vigour of the attack to the farthest edge of the hill. In vain did the French reserves, joining with the struggling multitude, endeavour to sustain the fight ; their efforts only increased the irremediable confusion, and the mighty mass, giving way like a loosened cliff, went headlong down the ascent. The rain flowed after in streams discoloured with blood, and fifteen hundred unwounded men, the remnant of six thousand unconquerable British soldiers, stood triumphant on the fatal hill.

Biography : its Divisions ; Diaries, Letters.

30. This branch of literature opens with autobiographies, which, when well executed, constitute its most valuable and

interesting portion. We have little to set by the side of the charming ' Mémoires,' in innumerable volumes, which form so piquant a portion of the literature of France. Scott's fragment of autobiography, printed at the beginning of the *Life* by Lockhart, is admirable ; but unfortunately it is only a fragment, and breaks off when the hero has reached his twentieth year. A similar fragment by Southey, though longer, makes less progress, for it terminates at the fifteenth year ; nor do we much regret its unfinished state. Gibbon's *Memoirs* are much in the French style and manner, and form perhaps the most interesting and best executed autobiography that we possess. Baxter also, Hume, and Priestley, have each given us an account of his life and opinions.

In Biography exclusive of autobiography, we may distinguish—1. general compilations, 2. national compilations, 3. class biographies, 4. personal biographies. Of the first kind, it is to our reproach that until the last few years we have had no specimen deserving of mention. To the *Biographie Universelle* and the *Conversations-Lexicon*, we had for a long time nothing to oppose but the insignificant compilations of Aikin, Grainger, and Gorton. Alexander Chalmers was the first to bring out a biographical dictionary of some pretension, but even in this the omissions are numerous and important.

(2.) Of the second kind, we have the *Biographia Britannica*, a work of great research, though with many serious omissions. The original edition embraced the entire alphabet ; but its defects were so glaring as to determine Dr. Kippis and others to undertake a re-issue of the work upon an enlarged scale ; the new edition, however, was never carried further than the commencement of the letter F. Fuller's *Worthies of England*, noticed at page 286, is a work of the same description.

(3.) Of class biographies—not to mention the Latin works of Leland, Bale, and Pitseus, ' De Illustribus Britanniæ Scriptoribus '—the chief examples are, Walton's *Lives of Anglican Divines* (including Hooker, Donne, and Sanderson), Wood's *Athenæ Oxonienses*, which is a collection of short memoirs of Oxford men, Johnson's *Lives of the Poets*, and Hartley Coleridge's *Biographia Borealis*, or *Lives of Northern Worthies*. From Johnson's account of Gray we extract a passage strongly characteristic of his peculiar style :—

The *Bard* appears, at the first view, to be, as Algarotti and others have remarked, an imitation of the prophecy of Nereus. Algarotti thinks it superior to its original ; and, if preference depends on the imagery and animation of the two poems, his judgment is right. There is in the *Bard* more force, more thought, and more variety. But to copy is less than to invent; and the copy has been unhappily produced at a wrong time. The fiction of Horace was to the Romans credible; but its revival disgusts us with apparent and unconquerable falsehood. *Incredulus odi.*

To select a singular event, and swell it to a giant's bulk by fabulous appendages of spectres and predictions, has little difficulty; for he that forsakes the probable may always find the marvellous. And it has little use; we are affected only as we believe; we are improved only as we find something to be imitated or declined. I do not see that the *Bard* promotes any truth, moral, or political.

His stanzas are too long, especially his epodes; the ode is finished before the ear has learned its measures, and consequently before it can receive pleasure from their consonance and recurrence.

Of the first stanza the abrupt beginning has been celebrated; but technical beauties can give praise only to the inventor. It is in the power of every man to rush abruptly upon his subject that has read the ballad of *Johnny Armstrong*—

> Is there ever a man in all Scotland—

The initial resemblances, or alliterations, 'ruin, ruthless, helm, or hauberk,' are below the grandeur of a poem that endeavours at sublimity.

(4.) Among personal biographies, Boswell's *Life of Johnson* holds confessedly the first place. Next to it in point of literary value, but of equal if not greater intrinsic interest, comes Lockhart's *Life of Scott.* It must be owned that we English have not done that part of our hero-worship particularly well, which consists in writing good lives of our heroes. Shakspeare's life was never written at all. Toland's and Philips' lives of Milton, and Noble's memoirs of Cromwell and his family, all fall far beneath their subjects. Ruffhead's *Life of Pope* is utterly contemptible. Dryden and Swift have fared better, having found a competent and zealous biographer in Scott. Southey also gained much credit by his biographies of Wesley and Nelson; and it may be said generally that during the present century we have done much to make up for our past deficiencies in this department. Scott's *Life of Napoleon* is rather a history of the revolutionary period than a personal memoir. Between 1840 and 1850 the most noteworthy biographies that appeared were Arnold's *Life* by Stanley, and the *Life, Diary, and Letters of Mr. Wilberforce*, edited by his sons.

31. Diaries and letters, if published separately, are to be regarded as so much biographical or historical material. The Diary of Burton (ch. IV. § 58), throws much light on the political history of the time. Those of Samuel Pepys and John Evelyn, in the reign of Charles II., take a more extensive range; we derive from them much curious information as to the literature, art, manners, and morals of that age. The *Diary and Letters of Madame D'Arblay*, the authoress of *Cecilia*, are some-

what disappointing. We have full details of the private life of
the court of George III., at which the lively Frances Burney
figured in the capacity of a waiting-woman to the queen;—but
what a dismal court it was ! what an absence not only of gaiety.
and brilliancy, but even of ordinary refinement ! In collections
of Letters, our literature is rather rich. The correspondence of
Horace Walpole—that prince of letter-writers—with Sir Horace
Mann, the Hon. Seymour Conway, and others, the *Letters and
Speeches of Cromwell*, edited by Mr. Carlyle, and those of
Cowper, by Southey, are among the chief contributions to this
branch of literature. Pope rose in this, as in every other intellectual effort, to the highest excellence ; his Letters to Swift
and others seem to be the perfection of letter-writing.

5. Theology : its Divisions.

32. The general character of English theology, which is of
course chiefly of Protestant authorship, stamps it as controversial
and occasional. Except works of pure learning, its most vigorous and famous productions have all been either defensive or
aggressive. They have also been occasional ; that is, they have
been designed to suit some immediate purpose, and have sprung
out of some special conjuncture of circumstances—differing in
this respect from most of the great works of Roman theologians,
at least in later times, which have usually either been the fruit
of the accumulated study and meditation of years, or have grown
out of systematic courses of lectures.

We may best find a clue through the immense labyrinth of
theological literature, by dividing the subject into several
branches, and then examining the chief works written by English divines in each branch. These divisions may be thus
stated :—1. Doctrinal Theology ; 2. Moral Theology ; 3. Hermeneutics and Biblical Criticism ; 4. Symbolical, 5. Patristic,
6. Rationalising Theology ; 7. Pastoral Theology, or Homiletics ;
8. Devotional Theology. To these it will be convenient to add,
9. Polemics, for the purpose of including a large class of works
which draw successively upon all storehouses of theological
argument to meet the exigencies of controversy, and cannot,
therefore, be fitly classed under any one of the preceding heads.

33. Pure doctrinal discussions have not, on the whole, found
much favour with English divines ; at least, unless we go back
to the subtile doctor, Duns Scotus, Alexander Hales the Irrefragable, and other great British thinkers of the middle age.
An exception, however, must be made to this remark in favour
of the sacramental controversy, on which an immense number

of tracts and treatises have been written.   Upon other doctrinal
topics the important books that exist may be soon enumerated.
They are—Field's *Book of the Church* (1628), Bull's *Defensio
Fidei Nicenæ*, Sherlock's *Vindication of the Doctrine of the
Trinity* (1690), written against the Socinians, Wall on *Infant
Baptism*, and Waterland's *Vindication of Christ's Divinity*
(1719), in reply to the Arian, Dr. Clarke.   Of these works, the
first three date from the seventeenth, the last two from the
eighteenth century.   Dr. Richard Field was a favourite with
James I., who used to say of him, ' Truly this is a *field* which
the Lord hath blessed.'   In his *Book of the Church*, written in
reply to Stapleton and others, after laying down from Scripture
and the Fathers the notes of the true Church, he endeavoured
to show that these notes had been obliterated from the Roman
communion, and were all to be found in the Anglican.   The
discussion is mainly doctrinal, and turns upon the interpretation
of the terms unity, indefectibility, sanctity, &c., in which the
definition of the Church was expressed alike by the High
Church Anglicans and their opponents.

Bishop Bull's famous *Defensio* was primarily intended as a
reply to Petavius, the learned author of the *Rationarium Temporum*, who had remarked that the language held by the
Fathers of the early Church, prior to the Council of Nice,
respecting the divinity of the Son, was often loose, ambiguous,
and even, if the literal meaning of the words were pressed,
heterodox.[1]   This statement had been eagerly seized and made
the most of by Arian and Socinian controversialists.   In opposition both to them and to Petavius, Bull maintains in this
work the perfect orthodoxy, not only of the sentiments, but of
the language of the Ante-Nicene Fathers.   In doing so, Mr.
Hallam considers that he is not always candid or convincing.

Sherlock's *Vindication* is not a work of very high ability,
and it has been said that he lays himself open in it to the
imputation of Tritheism.   Waterland's book against Arianism,
on the other hand, is a very masterly production, and extinguished that opinion in England.   Waterland, who died in
1740, was the last great patristical scholar among Anglican
divines.[2]   But while he makes what use he can of the appeal to
ancient testimonies, the influence exerted by Locke's *Essay* on
all subsequent thinkers may be traced in the closer logic and
more systematic argumentation with which Waterland—as

[1] With reference to these Fathers, the words addressed by St. Augustine to
Theodore the Pelagian should be borne in mind ; ' Vobis nondum litigantibus,
securius loquebantur.'
[2] See Dowling's *Introduction to the Study of Ecclesiastical History.*

compared to the writers of the seventeenth century—deals with the reasonings of Clarke. Wall's treatise on *Infant Baptism* (1705) is a very fair and temperate as well as learned work, the object of which is, first, to prove what was the practice of the early Church with reference to baptism during the first four centuries, and then to urge upon the Baptists, or—as he calls them—Antipædo-Baptists, various considerations touching the evils of disunion, and the ease with which they might, if so disposed, rejoin the Anglican communion.

34. Moral Theology may be generally described as the exhibition of moral science from the religious point of view, and under theological conditions. Casuistry, one of its most important developments, is the application of theology to the solution of difficult questions in morals. Under this head, Taylor's *Ductor Dubitantium* (which he thought the best, but most people regard as the worst of his works), Perkins' *Cases of Conscience*, Sanderson's treatise *De Juramento*, and Forbes' *Theologia Moralis*, are almost the only works that can be named, and none of them is of great celebrity.

35. In Hermeneutics and Biblical criticism much greater things have been effected. Here we have to name Walton's *Polyglott*, consisting of synoptical versions of the Bible in nine languages, and Lightfoot's *Horæ Hebraicæ* and *Harmony of the Four Gospels*. Matthew Pool's *Synopsis Criticorum* is an immense compilation of the principal commentaries of the New Testament. In his bulky *Paraphrase and Annotations on the New Testament*, Hammond appears to be almost overpowered by the fulness and extent of his learning, and unable to wield and master it with the readiness displayed by some of his contemporaries. Leighton's *Commentary on St. Peter* is extolled by Coleridge with an unmeasured laudation, to which neither its learning nor its ability appear sufficiently to entitle it.

36. Symbolical Theology treats of the *Symbola* or confessional formularies of different religious denominations. Moehler's *Symbolik* will immediately occur to the reader as a classic in this branch of divinity. The chief Anglican works of this nature are, Pearson's *Exposition of the Apostles' Creed* (1659), and Burnet's work on the Thirty-nine Articles.

37. But it was in Patristic divinity—that branch which examines, compares, and arranges the testimonies borne by the Fathers and Councils of the early Christian centuries, and more especially in Patristic learning, by which we chiefly mean the task of editing the works of the Fathers—that the Anglican divines gained their greatest distinctions. In this wide field, all that can be done here—and even that may be of some use—is to

indicate a few of the most important works. We may name for instance, Fell's edition of Cyprian, Bishop Potter's edition of Clemens Alexandrinus (a standard work, still unsuperseded), Pearson's *Vindiciæ Epistolarum S. Ignatii* and *Annales Cyprianici*, Beveridge's *Pandectæ Canonum SS. Apostolorum*, a book of immense learning, and Dodwell's *Dissertations* on SS. Cyprian and Irenæus. In ecclesiastical history and antiquities we have Usher's *Annales*, Cave's *Primitive Christianity* (1673), and *Historia Literaria* of ecclesiastical writers, from the Christian era to the fourteenth century, and, above all, Bingham's *Origines Ecclesiasticæ, or Antiquities of the Christian Church* (1708–1722), a work of great research and eminent usefulness. In many of these books there is a controversial element, but in none of them does the writer propose to himself as his main object the establishment of a thesis or the refutation of an opponent; they are not, therefore, to be classed among polemics.

38. The seventeenth century is the great time for the Patristic writers. The rationalising divines date, for the most part, from the eighteenth. The former appealed to antiquity and authority in the discussion of disputed questions, the latter to reason and common sense. Stillingfleet, in his *Origines Sacræ, or a Rational Account of the Grounds of Christian Faith* (1663), directed against Hobbes and the Atheists, and again in his *Rational Account of the Grounds of Protestant Religion* (1681), against the Catholics, took up the new line of controversy, and may be regarded as individually anticipating the *seculum rationalisticum*. Leslie's *Short Method with the Deists* (1694), Butler's *Analogy*, Warburton's *Divine Legation* (1743), Berkeley's *Alciphron*—all of which formed portions of the great debate on Deism—together with Lardner's *Credibility of the Gospels*, and Paley's *Evidences*, the materials for which he took from Lardner, are the chief remaining works to be cited under this head.

39. In Pastoral Theology, or Homiletics, the number of published volumes of sermons defies computation. Among the principal names are—in the seventeenth century, Donne, Andrews, Bramhall, Smith of Queen's, Taylor, Cosin, Hammond, Beveridge, South, and Tillotson; in the eighteenth, Butler, Clarke, Wesley, and Whitfield; in the nineteenth, Robert Hall, Rowland Hill, Chalmers, Arnold, Hare, &c.

40. In Devotional Theology, though the list is, on the whole, a meagre one, some remarkable books have to be named. Such are William Law's *Serious Call to a Holy Life*, the book which made so great an impression on Johnson; Baxter's *Saints' Everlasting Rest* and *Call to the Unconverted*, *The Whole Duty*

of Man, a work of unknown authorship, but precious in the sight of our forefathers a hundred and fifty years ago, and spoken of in that sense in the *Spectator*; lastly, Taylor's moving and eloquent treatises *Of Holy Living* and *Of Holy Dying*. An extract from the latter will enable the reader to form some idea of Taylor's rich and gorgeous style, of the power of his imagination, and the general fulness of his mind. It is upon the shortness of life, and the multitudinous warnings with which it teems, all telling us to prepare to die :—

All the succession of time, all the changes in nature, all the varieties of light and darkness, the thousand thousands of accidents in the world, and every contingency to every man and to every creature, doth preach our funeral sermon, and calls us to look and see how the old sexton, Time, throws up the earth, and digs a grave, where we must lay our sins or our sorrows, and sow our bodies, till they rise again in a fair or an intolerable eternity. Every revolution which the sun makes about the world divides between life and death, and death possesses both those portions by the next morrow; and we are dead to all those months which we have already lived, and we shall never live them over again, and still God makes little periods of our age. First we change our world, when we come from the womb to feel the warmth of the sun; then we sleep and enter into the image of death, in which state we are unconcerned in all the changes of the world; and if our mothers or our nurses die, or a wild-boar destroy our vineyards, or our king is sick, we regard it not, but, during that state, are as disinterested as if our eyes were closed with the clay that weeps in the bowels of the earth. At the end of seven years our teeth fall and die before us, representing a formal prologue to the tragedy, and still every seven years it is odds but we shall finish the last scene; and when nature, or chance, or vice, takes our body in pieces, weakening some parts and loosening others, we taste the grave and the solemnities of our own funeral, first, in those parts that ministered to vice, and, next, in them that served for ornament; and in a short time, even they that served for necessity become useless and entangled, like the wheels of a broken clock. Baldness is but a dressing to our funerals, the proper ornament of mourning, and of a person entered very far into the regions and possession of death; and we have many more of the same signification—grey hairs, rotten teeth, dim eyes, trembling joints, short breath, stiff limbs, wrinkled skin, short memory, decayed appetite. Every day's necessity calls for a reparation of that portion which Death fed on all night when we lay in his lap, and slept in his outer chambers. The very spirits of a man prey upon his daily portion of bread and flesh, and every meal is a rescue from one death, and lays up for another; and while we think a thought we die, and the clock strikes, and reckons on our portion of eternity: we form our words with the breath of our nostrils—we have the less to live upon for every word we speak.

Thus nature calls us to meditate of death by those things which are the instruments of acting it; and God, by all the variety of His providence, makes us see death everywhere, in all variety of circumstances, and dressed up for all the fancies and expectation of every single person. Nature hath given us one harvest every year, but death hath two : and the spring and the autumn send throngs of men and women to charnel-houses; and all the summer long men are recovering from their evils of the spring, till the dog-days come, and then the Sirian star makes the summer deadly; and the fruits of autumn are laid up for all the year's provision, and the man that gathers them eats and surfeits, and dies and needs them not, and himself is laid up for eternity; and he that escapes till winter only stays for another opportunity, which the distempers of that quarter minister to him with great variety. Thus death reigns in all the portions of our time. The autumn with its fruits provides disorders for us, and the winter's cold turns them into sharp diseases, and the spring brings flowers to strew our hearse, and the summer gives green turf and brambles to bind upon our graves.

41. Of works of which the entire form and end are controversial, the quantity is immense. Hooker's *Ecclesiastical Polity*, with the exception of the first book, which we may range with Hallam among contributions to moral and political science, is a vindication of the liturgy and ceremonies of the Church of England, and of her right to impose them, against the attacks of the Puritans. Laud's *Conference with Fisher*, Chillingworth's *Religion of Protestants*, Taylor's *Dissuasive from Popery*, about a dozen treatises, large and small, by Baxter, and Barrow *On the Supremacy*, are some of the most popular productions of this class.

42. The circumstances in which the Catholics of England and Ireland have been placed since English literature emerged from its rude and semi-barbarous beginnings, easily explain the comparative meagreness of their theological literature. Most of the existing works are, as might have been expected, controversial. The writings of Parsons, Allen, Harding, and Walsingham, Stapleton's ponderous tomes, Gother's works and those of the good Bishop Challoner, Arthur O'Leary's *Tracts*, Milner's *End of Controversy*, and some able tracts by Dr. Doyle, mark— if we exclude works by living authors, the Wisemans and Newmans of our own day—some of the most important steps and phases of the great controversy. One or two works of great learning might be named, such as Alford's *Annales Britannici*, or of patient research, as Dodd's *Church History* (originally written by an English priest about the middle of the last century, and republished with corrections by the Rev. Mr. Tierney in 1839), and Alban Butler's *Lives of the Fathers, Martyrs, and other principal Saints*, &c.

6. Philosophy : its Divisions ; Political Science ; Essays ; Criticism.

43. With a brief survey of what English literature has produced under this head, our present task will be concluded.

The term Philosophy, as has been already explained, is here used in a very wide and loose sense, and applied to all works of thought and theory. We commence, however, with the consideration of philosophical works, strictly so called, in examining which we shall endeavour to observe some kind of natural and rational order.

Logic is usually regarded as the fore-court of philosophy, because it is the science which investigates the form of the reasoning principle, philosophy's indispensable instrument, and establishes the conditions of its effective use. The main achievements of English thinkers in this department are, Bacon's *Novum Organum*, Whately's *Elements of Logic*, Mill's *System of Logic*, and Sir William Hamilton's *Lectures*.

Bacon—and in this Mr. Mill has followed him—treated Logic less as a formal science than as a means to an ulterior end, that end being the successful investigation of nature. The rules which the logic of the schools had established for deductive reasoning, though indisputable, were, in Bacon's view, comparatively worthless, because they could not guide the mind in its search after physical laws. They were an instrument for testing the soundness of the knowledge which we had, or thought we had, already, not an instrument facilitating for us the acquisition of new knowledge. It was for this latter purpose that Bacon devised, in the *Novum Organum*, the rules of his new inductive logic. For what he demanded from the science was—not a solution of the problem, ' given certain premisses, to deduce a logical conclusion,' but an analysis of the conditions under which true premisses or propositions, relative to phenomena, might be formed. The human mind being once turned into the track of the investigation of nature, it was obvious that, to prevent waste of labour and rash generalisation, the formation of such a logic was indispensable. Mr. Mill in his *System of Logic*, and Sir John Herschel in his admirable *Discourse on the Study of Natural Philosophy*, have done much to complete the Baconian design.

Whately and Hamilton, on the other hand, have treated logic rather upon its own merits as a formal science, than as a mere instrument of enquiry. Archbishop Whately's *Elements of Logic* exhibit, with beautiful precision of statement and felicity of illustration, the Aristotelian logic in an English dress. Sir W. Hamilton, having in view the cultivation of mental rather than of physical science, subjected the preliminary processes of logic, such as generalisation and predication, to a new and very rigorous analysis, and has in many respects presented the technical parts of the science under a new light.

44. The logical weapon being brightened and made ready for action, the question next occurs, on what subject-matter it is to be employed. The school of physicists employ it at once in the investigation of nature; and the various hypotheses, theories, or laws of physical science, together with natural history and other accumulations of facts gained by observation and experiment, are the collective result. With such labours the student of literature has nothing to do. But for those who devote themselves to philosophy, in the ancient acceptation of the term, as to that study which will lead them to wisdom, the next step, after perfecting the logical weapon, is Psychology, or the study of the human mind. And as this study divides itself into two main branches, that of the moral affections and sentiments, and that of the intellectual faculties, we have a moral and an intellectual philosophy corresponding. The first branch has been cultivated among ourselves by Butler, Adam Smith, Paley, Hume, Hutcheson, and many others. Butler's admirable *Sermons*, preached at the Rolls Chapel, are the most profound and important contributions to Moral Philosophy that our literature possesses. Adam Smith's *Theory of Moral Sentiments*,[1] and Hume's *Enquiry concerning the Principles of Morals*, are also celebrated works. Of these, and of the writings of the other English moralists, the reader will find an account in Sir James Mackintosh's *Dissertation on Ethical Philosophy*.

Locke's famous *Essay on the Human Understanding*, which belongs to that branch of psychology which investigates the intellectual faculties, holds a distinguished place, not only in English but in universal literature. However, Locke examines many other besides purely psychological questions. The Scotch school of philosophers pushed this class of researches very far. Reid, Beattie, Dugald Stewart, and Brown, carefully studied the intellect, and described its various powers. Reid, annoyed and scandalised at the scepticism of Hume, propounded the theory of instincts, and described a great number of intellectual judgments, which Locke and his followers had classed among acquired notions, as original and instinctive. He—but still more Beattie—carried this theory to the length of extravagance, and exposed himself to the ridicule of Priestley in his *Remarks on Dr. Reid's Inquiry*. Hartley's work *On Man* is to a large extent psychological. Lastly, Sir W. Hamilton's Lectures contain probably a more exhaustive analysis of the intellectual processes and powers than the work of any other English writer.

[1] A most interesting account of this work is given in the chapter on the Scottish intellect in the second volume of the late Mr. Buckle's *History of Civilisation*.

45. After distinguishing and describing the powers of the human mind, Philosophy in every past age has been accustomed to proceed to those further enquiries which are termed *meta-physical*, and to ask itself—whence did this complex being which I have just examined take its origin, and what is its destination? in what relation does this finite stand to infinite intelligence? can we know anything of the invisible and supersensual world that surrounds us? Glorious and elevating speculations! which it has become the fashion of modern thinkers to decry as useless, but which, for a certain class of minds—and those not of the meanest capacity—will possess to the end of time an invincible attraction. We can merely enumerate the most important among the works of English metaphysicians. Cudworth's *Intellectual System of the Universe* has for its general object to prove against Hobbes and the atheists the existence and the goodness of God. Henry More, the most eminent among the school known as the Platonising divines of the seventeenth century, is the author of *The Mystery of Godliness, An Antidote against Atheism, Enchiridion Metaphysicum*, and other works, in which, with much that is noble and lofty, we remark too manifest a readiness to put faith, upon insufficient evidence, in any stories that tended to establish the presence of a mystical and supernatural element in human affairs. Berkeley's *Hylas and Philonous*, and *Principles of Human Knowledge*, are the treatises in which his ideal philosophy is expounded. As this philosophy has been much misunderstood, and Reid thought that he had said a clever thing when he had advised Berkeley to test its truth, and the reality of matter, by knocking his head against a post, it may serve a good purpose to extract the following remarks from Lewes's *Biographical History of Philosophy*:—

When Berkeley denied the existence of matter, he meant by 'matter' that unknown *substratum*, the existence of which Locke had declared to be a necessary *inference* from our knowledge of qualities, but the nature of which must ever be altogether hidden from us. Philosophers had assumed the existence of Substance, *i.e.* of a *noumenon* lying underneath all *phenomena*—a substratum supporting all qualities—a *something* in which all accidents *inhere*. This unknown substance Berkeley rejects. It is a mere abstraction, he says. If it is unknown, unknowable, it is a figment, and I will none of it; for it is a figment worse than useless; it is pernicious, as the basis of all atheism. If by matter you understand *that* which is seen, felt, tasted, and touched, then I say matter exists; I am as firm a believer in its existence as any one can be, and *herein I agree with the vulgar*. If, on the contrary, you understand by matter that occult substratum which is *not* seen, *not* felt, *not* tasted, and *not* touched—that of which the senses do not, cannot, inform you—then I say I believe not in the existence of matter, and *herein I differ foom the philosophers and agree with the vulgar*.

In support of this view, Berkeley's own words are presently quoted :—

> I do not argue against the existence of any one thing that we can apprehend either by sensation or reflection. That the things I see with my eyes and touch with my hands do exist, really exist, I make not the least question. The only thing whose existence I deny is that which philosophers call Matter, or corporeal substance. And in doing this there is no damage done to the rest of mankind, who, I dare say, will never miss it.

46. Hume, in his *Enquiry concerning Human Understanding*, begins with some valuable definitions, which may be considered to constitute an improvement, so far as they go, on the terminology of Locke, but ends with proposing ' sceptical doubts,' as applicable to every possible philosophical proposition which the mind can entertain. After Hume, the celebrated Kant in Germany took up the metaphysical debate, and produced his *Kritik der Reinen Vernunft*,[1] a work which makes an epoch in philosophy. Among ourselves Hume was ·feebly answered, upon obvious common-sense grounds, by Reid and his followers; but they were rather psychologists than metaphysicians. Coleridge, whose genius pre-eminently fitted him to excel in metaphysics, left much behind him that is of the highest value, but in a discontinuous sketchy condition, and with large *desiderata*. The *Aids to Reflection* is the work which contains more of his mind upon the deepest questions than any other. The *Friend*, and the *Literary Remains*, while they illustrate to a great extent his metaphysical tenets, belong in form rather to the department of Essays.

Political Science : Filmer, Hobbes, Milton, Burke.

47. Political science, as might have been expected in a country with such an eventful political history, owes much to English thinkers. The conservative and absolutist side has been ably and warmly argued, but on the whole the palm undoubtedly rests with the writers on the liberal and constitutional side. Sir Robert Filmer and the philosopher Hobbes, upon widely different grounds, wrote in support of arbitrary power. In his *Patriarcha*, published in 1680, but written long before, Filmer maintained, not only against Milton and Grotius, but also against St. Thomas and Bellarmine, that men were not born free, but slaves; and that monarchs reigned with a patriarchal, absolute, and unquestionable right, derived, like that of

---

[1] Critique of Pure Reason.

Adam over his own household, immediately from God. Hobbes was an absolutist on quite other grounds. He believed in no divine right of kings ; but he had the lowest possible opinion of subjects, that is, of mankind in general, and thought that to place power in the hands of the masses was the sure way to bring in anarchy. He was therefore in favour of a strong central government, which he would not allow to be thwarted in its task of repression by the licensed meddling of the persons, whether acting directly or by representation, who were subjected to it. Hobbes' political system is unfolded in several of his works, particularly the *De Cive* (1642), the *De Corpore Politico* (1650), and the *Leviathan* (1651).

48. On the other side occur the names of Fortescue in the fifteenth, Milton, Algernon Sidney, Harrington, and Locke in the seventeenth century, and Burke, Godwin, and Payne in the eighteenth ; all of whom were in favour of liberal principles of government, however wide the gulf, in spirit and practical aims, which separated the republican Sidney from the constitutionalist Locke, or the author of the *Rights of Man* from the upholder of the sacredness of prescription. Milton's *Areopagitica*, or *Speech for the Liberty of unlicensed Printing*, though in form a mere pamphlet, is so full of weighty thoughts, which have since been adopted by the reason of civilised Europe, that we prefer to consider it as a contrioution to political science. It is an argument for the freedom of the press, and is perhaps the most eloquent—certainly one of the least rugged—among the prose works of Milton. The following is one of the most important passages. After speaking of the glorious spectacle of a great nation ' renewing her mighty youth,' and producing in boundless profusion the richest fruits of awakened intelligence, he proceeds :—

What should ye do then ? Should ye suppress all this flowery crop of knowledge and new light sprung up and yet springing daily in this city ? Should ye set an oligarchy of twenty engrossers over it, to bring a famine upon our minds again, when we shall know nothing but what is measured to us by their bushel ?[1] Believe it, lords and commons ? they who counsel ye to such a suppression, do as good as bid ye suppress yourselves ; and I will soon show how. If it be desired to know the immediate cause of all this free writing and free speaking, there cannot be assigned a truer than your own mild, and free, and humane government ; it is the liberty, lords and commons, which your own valorous and happy counsels have purchased us ; liberty which is the nurse of all great wits ; this is that which hath ratified and enlightened our spirits like the influence of heaven ; this is that which hath enfranchised, en-

---

[1] The censors of books are compared to those who *engross* or forestall all the corn in the market, and thus create an artificial scarcity.

larged, and lifted up our apprehensions degrees above themselves. Ye cannot make us now less capable, less knowing, less eagerly pursuing of the truth, unless ye first make yourselves, that made us so, less the lovers, less the founders, of our true liberty. We can grow ignorant again, brutish, formal, and slavish, as ye found us; but you then must first become that which ye cannot be, oppressive, arbitrary, and tyrannous, as they were from whom ye have freed us. That our hearts are now more capacious, our thoughts more erected to the research and expectation of greatest and exactest things, is the issue of your own virtue propagated in us : ye cannot suppress that, unless ye reinforce an abrogated and merciless law, that fathers may despatch at will their own children. . . . . Give me the liberty to know, to utter, and to argue freely according to conscience, above all other liberties.

. Locke's two *Treatises on Government* were written as a reply to the *Patriarcha*, and embody the famous doctrine of an 'original compact' between prince and people. An interesting summary of them may be found in Hallam's *Literature of Europe*.

49. Among Burke's political writings, those which contain the clearest and fullest statement of his political philosophy are the *Reflections on the French Revolution*, and the *Appeal from the New to the Old Whigs*. His principles were constitutional and progressive, but anti-revolutionary. The *Appeal*, &c., was occasioned by some slighting notice taken in Parliament of the *Reflections*, as the work of a renegade Whig. Burke endeavours to show that the new Whigs have changed their principles, and not he; that from constitutionalists they have become revolutionists. The following striking passage occurs near the end of the treatise :—

Place, for instance, before your eyes such a man as Montesquieu. Think of a genius not born in every country, or every time ; a man gifted by nature with a penetrating aquiline eye ; with a judgment prepared with the most extensive erudition ; with an herculean robustness of mind, and nerves not to be broken with labour ; a man who could spend twenty years in one pursuit. Think of a man like the universal patriarch in Milton (who had drawn up before him in prophetic vision the whole series of the generations which were to issue from his loins), a man capable of placing in review, after having brought together from the east, the west, the north, and the south, from the coarseness of the rudest barbarism to the most refined and subtle civilisation, all the schemes of government which had ever prevailed amongst mankind, weighing, measuring, collating, and comparing them all, joining fact with theory, and calling into council, upon all this infinite assemblage of things, all the speculations which have fatigued the understandings of profound reasoners in all times!—Let us then consider that all these were but so many preparatory steps to qualify a man—and such a man—tinctured with no national prejudice, with no domestic affection, to admire, and to hold out to the admiration of mankind, the constitution of England ! And shall we Englishmen revoke to such a suit ?

Shall we, when so much more than he has produced remains still to be understood and admired, instead of keeping ourselves in the schools of real science, choose for our teachers men incapable of being taught; whose only claim to know is, that they have never doubted; from whom we can learn nothing but their own indocility; who would teach us to scorn what in the silence of our hearts we ought to adore?

In the *Reflections*, occurs the famous passage on Marie Antoinette and the ' age of chivalry ';—

It is now sixteen or seventeen years since I saw the Queen of France, then the dauphiness, at Versailles; and surely never lighted on this orb, which she hardly seemed to touch, a more delightful vision. I saw her just above the horizon, decorating and cheering the elevated sphere she just began to move in,—glittering like the morning star, full of life, and splendour, and joy. Oh! what a revolution! and what a heart must I have to contemplate without emotion that elevation and that fall! Little did I dream when she added titles of veneration to those of enthusiastic, distant, respectful love, that she should ever be obliged to carry the sharp antidote against disgrace concealed in that bosom; little did I dream that I should live to have seen such disasters fallen upon her in a nation of gallant men, in a nation of men of honour, and of cavaliers. I thought ten thousand swords must have leaped from their scabbards to avenge even a look that threatened her with insult. But the age of chivalry is gone. That of sophisters, economists, and calculators, has succeeded; and the glory of Europe is extinguished for ever. Never, never more shall we behold that generous loyalty to rank and sex, that proud submission, that dignified obedience, that subordination of the heart, which kept alive, even in servitude itself, the spirit of an exalted freedom. The unbought grace of life, the cheap defence of nations, the nurse of manly sentiment and heroic enterprise, is gone! It is gone, that sensibility of principle, that chastity of honour, which felt a stain like a wound, which inspired courage whilst it mitigated ferocity, which ennobled whatever it touched, and under which vice itself lost half its evil, by losing all its grossness.

Essays.

50. An essay, as its name implies, is an endeavour, within definite limits of time and subject, to attain to truth. It is the elucidation by thought of some one single topic, of which the mind had previously possessed an indistinct notion. The essay writer stands at the opposite pole of thought to the system-monger; the first is ever analysing and separating, the second grouping and generalising. This style of writing, speaking generally, was unknown to the middle ages; it arose in the sixteenth century. Nor is the explanation obscure, or far to seek. The general tendency of thought in the middle ages was to *totality*; to regard philosophy as one whole, truth as one, religion as one, nature as one. One of the typical books of the

middle ages—the *Liber Sententiarum*— is a *complete* theology, *corpus* Theologiæ ; it traverses the entire field. But the general tendency of thought in modern times has been to separation and subdivision ; to break up wholes, to mistrust generalisations ; to examine the parts severally, and attain to a perfect knowledge of each individual part, in the hope of ultimately combining the knowledge of particulars into a sound theory of the whole. The same tendency of mind which has in the last three centuries produced and rendered popular so many volumes of essays and detached cogitations in literature, has in the scientific world resulted in the innumerable monographs, reports and papers, by which each enquirer into nature, in his own special department, contributes to the already enormous stock of particular knowledge.

Essays do not include political tracts or pamphlets, from which we may easily distinguish them by considering the difference in the ends proposed. The end of an essay is knowledge ; the end of a political tract or pamphlet, action. Logic appertains to the former, rhetoric to the latter. The essay writer has answered his purpose if he presents to us a new and clearer view of the subject which he handles, and leads us to think upon it. The political writer has answered his purpose if, whatever the view may be which he wishes to enforce, his arguments, whether they be sound or specious, tend to arouse his readers to action in the direction pointed out.

51. The heterogeneous character of the subjects of essays makes it useless, if not impossible, to classify them. An essay may be written about anything whatever which an attentive thinker can place in a new light, or form a plausible theory about ; there would, therefore, be no end to the division and subdivision. We shall merely notice some of the most remarkable collections of essays in our literature. Bacon's essays, concerning which some particulars were noted at page 219 are the earliest in the series. As a specimen, we give a passage from the essay *Of Plantations*, which must have been one of the latest composed, for it is evident from it that the colony of Virginia (founded in 1606) had then been in existence for several years ;—

Plantations are amongst ancient, primitive, and heroical works. When the world was young, it begat more children ; but now it is old, it begets fewer ; for I may justly account new plantations to be the children of former kingdoms. I like a plantation in a pure soil ; that is, where people are not *displanted*, to the end to plant in others. For else it is rather an extirpation than a plantation. Planting of countries is like planting of woods ; for you must make account to lose about twenty years' profit, and expect your recompense in the end. For the principal thing that hath been the destruction of most plantations, hath been the base and hasty drawing of profit in the first years. It is true, speedy profit is not to be neglected, as far as may stand with the good of the plantations, but no farther. It is a shameful and unblessed thing, to take the scum of people, and wicked condemned men, to be the people with whom you plant. And not only so, but it spoileth the plantation; for they will ever live like rogues, and not fall to work, but be lazy, and do mischief, and spend victuals, and be quickly weary, and then certify over to their country, to the discredit of the plantation. . . . . . Consider, likewise, what commodities the soil, where the plantation is, doth naturally yield, that they may someway help to defray the charge of the plantation; so it be not, as was said, to the untimely prejudice of the main business, as it hath fared with tobacco in Virginia. Wood commonly aboundeth but too much; and therefore timber is fit to be one. If there be iron ore, and streams whereupon to set the mills, iron is a brave commodity where wood aboundeth. . . . . For government, let it be in the hands of one, assisted with some counsel; and let them have commission to execute martial laws, with some limitation. And above all, let men make that profit of being in the wilderness, as they have God always, and his service, before their eyes. . . . . . If you plant where savages are, do not only entertain them with trifles and gingles; but use them justly and graciously, with sufficient guard nevertheless; and do not win their favour by helping them to invade their enemies, but for their defence it is not amiss. And send oft of them over to the country that plants, that they may see a better condition than their own, and commend it when they return.

52. Felltham's *Resolves*, Bishop Hall's *Centuries of Meditations and Vows*, and Browne's *Religio Medici*, have all the character of essays: Hume's *Essays, Moral, Political, and Literary*, published in 1742 and 1752, show a remarkable union of practical shrewdness with power of close and searching thought. In our own age, John Foster's *Essays in a Series of Letters to a Friend*, have obtained a high reputation. They are upon ethical subjects, written in a plain strong style, and profoundly reasoned. Lord Macaulay's *Essays*, most of which were originally contributed to the Edinburgh Review, would generally fall, according to the terminology that we have adopted, under the head of Criticism: and the same remark applies to Jeffrey's *Essays*.

Criticism.

53. Criticism may be, 1. philosophical, 2. literary, 3. artistic. Of the first kind, Bacon's *Advancement of Learning* is a splendid instance. After having, in the first book, expatiated in that beautiful language, not more thoughtful than it is imaginative, which he could command at pleasure, upon the dignity and utility of learning, he proceeds in the second part to consider

what are the principal works or acts of merit which tend to promote learning. These, he decides, are conversant with, 1. the places of learning; 2. the books or instruments of learning; 3. the persons of the learned. He then passes in review the chief defects observable in the existing arrangements for the promotion of learning. One of these is, that 'there hath not been, or very rarely been, any public designation of writers or enquirers concerning such parts of knowledge as may appear not to have been already sufficiently laboured or undertaken; unto which point it is an inducement to enter into a view and examination what parts of learning have been prosecuted and what omitted; for the opinion of plenty is among the causes of want, and the great quantity of books maketh a show rather of superfluity than lack; which surcharge, nevertheless, is not to be remedied by making no more books, but by making more good books, which, as the serpent of Moses, might devour the serpents of the enchanters.' The object of the work, therefore, is to institute a critical survey of the entire field of learning, with a view, partly to guide public patronage, partly to stimulate voluntary endeavours to cultivate the waste places indicated. And this survey he proceeds to make, dividing all learning into three branches—history, philosophy, and poetry, and noting what has been done, what overlooked, in each.

54. (2.) In the department of literary criticism, some admirable works have to be named. The earliest and one of the best among these is Sir Philip Sidney's *Defence of Poesie* (mentioned at page 220), from which we must find room for an extract, describing the invigorating moral effects of poetry :—

Now, therein, of all sciences (I speak still of human, and according to the human conceit) is our poet the monarch. For he doth not only show the way, but giveth so sweet a prospect into the way, as will entice any man to enter into it : nay he doth, as if your journey should lie through a fair vineyard, at the very first give you a cluster of grapes, that full of that taste you may long to pass further. He beginneth not with obscure definitions, which must blur the margin with interpretations, and load the memory with doubtfulness, but he cometh to you with words set in delightful proportion, either accompanied with, or prepared for, the well-enchanting skill of music; and with a tale, forsooth, he cometh unto you, with a tale which holdeth children from play, and old men from the chimney corner; and, pretending no more, doth intend the winning of the mind from wickedness to virtue; even as the child is often brought to take most wholesome things, by hiding them in such other as have a pleasant taste; which, if one should begin to tell them the nature of the aloes or rhubarbarum they should receive, would sooner take their physic at their ears than at their mouth : so is it in men (most of whom are childish in the best things till they be cradled in their graves); glad they will be to hear the tales of

Hercules, Achilles, Cyrus, Æneas : and hearing them must needs hear the right description of wisdom, valour, and justice : which if they had been barely (that is to say, philosophically) set out, they would swear they be brought to school again.

The critical passages which occur in Johnson's *Lives of the Poets* appear to be in the main just and sound. Shaksperian criticism has given rise to an entire library of its own. Fielding led the way, by the admiring yet discerning notices of the great dramatist which he introduced in his *Tom Jones.* The prefaces and notes of Pope and Johnson followed; at a later date appeared Hazlitt's *Characters*, and the critical notices in Coleridge's *Literary Remains.*

55. But the greatest achievement of literary criticism that we can point to is Hallam's *Literature of Europe in the Fifteenth, Sixteenth, and Seventeenth Centuries.* This is a book of which the sagacity and the calmness are well matched with the profound erudition. A certain coldness or dryness of tone is often noticeable, which seems not to be wondered at; for it is not easy to imagine that the man who spent so large a portion of his moral existence in surveying the labours and mastering the thoughts of men of the utmost diversity of aspiration and opinion, could have felt a very warm personal interest in any of their systems.

Among works on poetical criticism, we can scarcely err in assigning a high and permanent place to Mr. Thackeray's *Lectures on the English Humourists.*

(3.) In artistic criticism, the same remark might be hazarded as to Mr. Ruskin's *Modern Painters* and *Stones of Venice.* Nothing else of much importance can be named, except Horace Walpole's *Anecdotes of Painting* and Sir Joshua Reynolds' *Lectures.*

APPENDIX.

―・◆・―

ON ENGLISH METRES.

1. THERE exists no work of any authority, so far as I am aware, upon the metres used by our poets, except Dr. Guest's *History of English Rhymes*, which is too long and too intricate for general use. In the absence then of better guidance, the following brief remarks on prosody, and classification of English metres, may be of use to students.

2. Accent is the emphasis which the speaker of a language which he thoroughly understands naturally lays on a particular *syllable* in each word. In conversation or reading, all words are accented except certain particles, which, as being simply links or connecting-rods, the voice desires to pass over as quickly as possible.

3. Every line containing more than three accents is divisible into two *sections*. The break between them is called the pause, or cæsura; it may be indicated by :

[On the basis of the metrical section, Dr. Guest has erected a system of natural prosody for English rhythms, which explains and provides for them far better than the old classical prosody. Accent and contra-position are the soul of the natural system, feet and quantity of the classical system. But Dr. Guest's long and discursive work is not always clear, nor is it methodized so as to serve the purposes of the teacher. Provisionally, therefore, the classical system is retained in the following rules.]

Metre is the arrangement into verse of definite measures of sounds, definitely accented. Thus the hexameter is the arrangement in lines of six equivalent quantities of sound, called feet, each of which consists, or has the value, of two long syllables, and is accented on the first syllable. The English heroic metre, when strictly regular, is the arrangement in rimed couplets of five feet, each foot being equivalent to an iambus (a short and a long syllable), and accented on the *last* syllable. In practice, spondees and trochees are often introduced, the accent is often laid on the *first* syllable of a foot, and there are frequently not more than four, sometimes not more than three, accents in a line.

4. Rime is the regular recurrence in metre of similar sounds. There are four principal kinds : the perfect, the alliterative, the assonantal, and the consonantal. In the perfect rime, the riming syllables

correspond throughout; in other words, they are identical. It is
common in French poetry, but rare in English, e.g.:—

> Selons divers besoins, il est une *science*
> D'etendre les liens de notre con*science.*—MOLIÈRE.

5. The alliterative rime is the correspondence of the initial consonants of the riming syllables. This is the ordinary rhythm of the
Anglo-Saxon, and also of the Scandinavian poetry, e.g.:—

> Eádward kínge, éngla bláford
>
> Sénde sóthfœste sáwle to críste
>
> On gódes wǽra, gást háligne.[1]

These lines, which represent the most common of Anglo-Saxon
rhythms, have each four accents, and either three or two riming syllables, which are always accented. When the riming syllables begin
with vowels, these vowels are usually different, though not always.

6. The assonantal rime is the correspondence of the vowels merely
in the riming syllables. It is of two kinds: in the first the vowel
ends the syllable; in the second, it is followed by a consonant, or a
consonant and vowel. The first kind occurs continually in English
poetry; the second, never; but it is a favonrite rime with the Spanish
poets. Examples:—

> (1) If she seem not so to me,
>   What care I how good she be?
> (2) Ferid los, cavalleros, por amor de carid*a*d;
>   Yo soy Ruy Diaz el Cid, Campeador de Bib*a*r.[2]—
> *Ballad of the Cid.*

7. The consonantal rime is the ordinary rime of English poetry;
it is the correspondence both of the vowel and the *final* consonant, or
consonants, in the riming syllables. Examples:—

> Golden boys and girls all m*u*st,
> Like chimney sweepers, come to d*u*st.

8. All that has been said hitherto applies only to single rimes, the
masculine rime of the Italians. The double, or feminine rime, which
is that commonly used in Italian poetry, is also common with us. The
first syllables form always a consonantal or assonantal (No. 1) rime,
the second syllables a perfect rime. Examples:—

> Ecco da mille voci unitam*en-te,*
> Gerusalemme salutar si *sen-te.*—TASSO. *Geru. Liber.*
>
> And join with thee calm Peace and *Qui-et,*
> Spare Fast, that oft with Gods doth *di-et.*

9. In the triple rime, called *sdrucciola* by the Italians, the first syl-

---

[1] From Guest's *Rhythms*, ii. 70. His translation is,
    King Edward, lord of the Engle,
    Sent his righteous soul to Christ,
    (In God's promise trusting) a spirit holy.
[2] Smite them, knights, for the love of charity;
    I am Ruy Diaz the Cid, champion of Bivar.

lables follow the same rule as in the double rime; the second and third must be, in English poetry at least, perfect rimes. Example :—

> Kings may be blest, but Tam was *glo-ri-ous*,
> O'er all the ills of life vic*to-ri-ous*.

10. Before proceeding further, it is necessary to enumerate the principal kinds of feet used in English poetry. A long syllable is represented by the mark (-), a short syllable by the mark (ˇ).[1] Two short syllables are equivalent to, or have the metrical value of, one long syllable; except at the end of a line, where one, two, and even occasionally three short syllables may be introduced *ex abundanti*, or by way of redundancy; and must be considered as having no metrical value. The feet most used are,—

> The spondee (- -)
> The iambus (ˇ -)
> The trochee (- ˇ)
> The dactyl (- ˇ ˇ)
> The anapæst (ˇ ˇ -)
> The amphiambus[2] (ˇ - ˇ)

English metres may be divided into, 1. the unrimed ; 2. the rimed.

UNRIMED METRES.

11. These, in which a comparatively small portion of our poetry is written, may be quickly disposed of. They are of three kinds, hexameters, blank verse, and choral metres.

(1.) *Hexameters.*—The general rule governing the formation of English hexameters has been already given ; it need only be added, that the last or sixth foot must always be a spondee, and the fifth ordinarily a dactyl, though a spondee is also admissible. Example :—

Felt she in | myriad | springs her | sources | far in the | mountains |

Stirring, col|lecting, | heaving, up|rising, | forth out-|flowing. |—CLOUGH.

This is the only kind of English hexameter which is endurable ; in it, as before observed (§ 3), the accent in each foot is on the first syllable. The words must therefore be so selected that the natural

---

[1] In English poetry, length or quantity depends almost entirely upon accent. Accented syllables are long, unaccented short. In Greek and Latin poetry as is well known, quantity is something intrinsic in each syllable, and depends upon the nature of the vowel and the consonant or consonants following it. Our ears, trained to mark the accents only, take little notice of this kind of quantity ; yet those poets who utterly neglect it, are felt to write roughly and unmelodiously, though most of us could not explain distinctly the grounds of the feeling. A Roman ear could not have endured such a dactyl as *far in the*, because to it the *in* would be made irredeemably long by position. This we scarcely notice ; but even an English ear would stumble at such a dactyl, as e.g., *far midst the*.

[2] Using the analogy of the Homeric δέπας ἀμφικύπελλον I have, for the sake of convenience, substituted this term for the more usual 'amphibrachys,' from which it impossible to form an adjective.

accent in each shall correspond with that required by the metre. If the lines given above. be examined, this rule will be found to be observed; on whatever syllable of a word the metrical accent falls, that syllable will be found to be one which the voice naturally accentuates. Whether this was originally the case with the Greek and Latin hexameters, we do not know. So far as the present accentuation of Greek is concerned, if we admit that it represents the natural accent of the words as used by Homer, we must allow, either that Homer disregarded the natural accents, or that he did not follow our modern rule of invariably placing the metrical accent on the first syllable of each foot. Latin hexameters we pronounce to this day on the principle of always preserving what we suppose to be the *natural* accent of each word, whether that correspond to the metrical accent or not. The second line of the first Æneid is pronounced by us as follows:—

Itáli|am fá|to profu|gus, La|vínaque | vénit.

That is, we disregard the metrical accent, which should fall on the first syllable of each foot (and actually does so in the fifth and sixth), and in reading the line give effect to the natural accents only, as we conceive them, of the words *Italiam, fato, profugus.* When English hexameters were first written, they were constructed in the same manner: they were to be read in the same way as Latin hexameters. The natural accent, except in the last two feet, over-ruled the metrical. Take, for instance, the following lines from Stanihurst's translation of the Æneid :—

Either here | are cou|ching some | troops of | Greekish as|sembly,
Or to crush | our bul|warks this | work is | forged, all | houses
For to pry |, surmoun|ting the | town ; some | practice or | other
Here lurks | of cun|ning ; trust | not this | treacherous | ensign.

If, in reading these lines, we were to observe the rule given in § 3, and now always observed by those who write English hexameters—of placing the accent on the first syllable of each foot,—the effect would be ridiculous, because the natural accent of the words would jar with that which we gave to them. They must therefore be read according to the natural accent; the effect is then rough and unpleasant, but not, as in the other case, absurd. Many hexameters of this description were written by Sidney, Phaier, and others.

12. (2.) *Blank verse.*—This is a continuous metre, consisting, in its most perfect form, of lines containing five iambuses, each iambus being accented on the last syllable. In other words, it is a decasyllabic metre, having the second, fourth, sixth, eighth, and tenth syllables accented. We have not space to discuss here all the variations from this form, which are numerous; but the student will find the subject ably handled in Johnson's papers in the *Rambler* on Milton's versification. The following examples illustrate the principal variations, which affect, 1. the position of the accents; 2. their number; 3. the termination of the line :—

When down | alóng | by plea|sant Tém|pe's stream | (1)

Left for | repén|tance, none | for pár|don left | (2)

In-fi-|nite wráth, | and in|fi-nite despaír | ⎱
⎰ 3
How o-|vercóme | this dire | ca-lam-|ity | ⎰

To the | last sýl-|lable of | recór-|ded time | (4)

Tomor-|row and | tomor|row and | tomor·|row | (5)

Who can | be wise, | amázed, | témperate, | and fu-|rious | (6)

In (1), a strictly regular line, the accents are five in number, and occupy their normal positions. In (2) they are still five, but the first syllable is accented instead of the second. In each of the two examples of (3) there are but four accents, differently placed in each line. In (4) there are but three accents. In (5) there is one, and in (6) two redundant syllables.

13. In most English decasyllabic verse, whether blank or rimed, the line with four accents predominates. It is often possible to find a dozen lines in succession so accented in Shakspere and Milton. But in Pope's decasyllabics, as might be expected from so perfect a versifier, the line with five accents predominates. The effect of the variation in the *position* of the accents is to prevent the monotony which would arise from the perpetual recurrence of iambuses. It answers the same purpose as the free intermixture of dactyls and spondees in the hexameter. The effect of the reduction in the *number* of accents is to quicken the movement of the line. This explains why lines of five accents are the exception, not the rule, in Shakspere: for the dramatic movement, as representing dialogue, and the actual conflict of passions, is essentially more rapid than either the epic or didactic. With less justification Wordsworth in the *Excursion* frequently introduces lines of only three accents, such as,—

> By the deformities of brutish vice.

Such lines can seldom be so managed as to make other than an unpleasing impression on the ear. The license of redundant syllables is allowed in dramatic, but not epic verse. Milton does indeed use it, but sparingly. In eighty lines taken at random from the *Paradise Lost* I have found four instances of redundancy; in the same number of lines similarly taken from the play of *King John*, eighteen instances.

14. (3.) Choral metres may be designated according to the kind of foot which predominates in them. Those used in Southey's *Thalaba* are dactylic or iambic :—

> In the Dom|daniel | caverns,
> Under the | roots of the | ocean ;

and,

> Sail on, | sail on, | quoth Tha-|laba,
> Sail on, | in Al-|lah's name. |

In *Queen Mab* they are iambic, and in the *Strayed Reveller* trochaic :—

> Faster, | faster, |
> O | Circe, | Goddess. |

Rimed Metres.

15. Every English rimed metre is in one of three measures, the iambic, the trochaic, the triple.

Again, all rimed metres are either continuous or in stanzas.

Continuous Verse.

16. I. The following is a list of continuous riming mètres, in iambic measure :—

(1.) Tetrasyllabics; e.g. :—

> The steel | we touch |
> Forced ne'er | so much, |
> Yet still | removes |
> To that | it loves. |—Drayton (in *Guest*).

(2.) Lines of six syllables and three accents; Skeltonical verse. For an example, see ch. ii., § 8.

(3.) Ostosyllabics, having, in strictness, four accents; e.g. :—

> Woe worth | the chase ! | woe worth | the day ! |
> That cost | thy life, | my gal-|lant grey ! |

This metre is extremely common; most of the old romances are in it, as well as Scott's and Byron's romantic poems (except *Lara* and the *Corsair*), *Hudibras*, *Lalla Rookh*, &c.

(4.) Decasyllabics, having, in strictness, five accents. If riming in couplets, they form the famous heroic metre :—

> Awake! | my St. | John, leave | all mea-|ner things |
> To low | ambi-|tion, and | the pride | of kings. |

It is needless to remark that an enormous quantity of verse has been composed in this metre. Sometimes the rimes occur irregularly, as in *Lycidas* :—

> Fame is | the spur | that the | clear spirit | doth raise, |
> ('That last | infir-|mity | of no|ble minds) |
> To scorn | delights | and live | labo-|rious days, | &c.

Endecasyllabics, which constitute the heroic metre of the Italians, fall, in our metrical system, under the description of redundant lines. As exceptions to the decasyllabic rule, they occur very frequently; but still only serve to prove that rule, like other exceptions.

(5.) The Alexandrine, or twelve-syllable metre, having in strictness six accents. This is the metre used by some of our old riming chroniclers, and by Drayton in his *Poly-olbion*; it is also the heroic metre of France; but with us it has fallen into disuse for three centuries. Example.

> The black | and dark|some nights, | the bright | and glad|some days
> Indiff|erent are | to him, | his hope | on God | that stays.
> Drayton (in *Guest*).

(6.) The fourteen-syllable metre, with seven accents. This measure occurs in some old metrical legends, and was used by Chapman in his translation of the Iliad; but it is lumbering and unwieldy, and as such had long been laid aside by our poets, until revived by Mr. F. Newman, who stripped it of rime, and enriched it with a redundant syllable :—

O gen|tle friend! | if thou | and I | from this | encoun|ter sca|ping,
Hereaf|ter might | for e|ver be | from eld | and death | exemp|ted.

The following is from Chapman :—

To all | which Jove's | will gave | effect ; | from whom | strife first | begunne |
Betwixt | Atri|des, king | of men, | and The|tis' god|like sonne. |

17. Combinations of some of these six metres have been occasionally employed, but with indifferent success. Thus Surrey joined the fourteen-syllable metre to the Alexandrine :—

When so|mer took | in hand | the win|ter to | assaile, |
With force | of might | and ver|tue great | his stor|my blasts | to quail. |

18. II. *Trochaics.*—In continuous verse, two trochaic measures are in use: the fifteen syllable and the seven syllable. In the latter, eight-syllable lines, containing four full trochees, are of common occurrence; but the characteristic line of the measure is of seven syllables, and contains three trochees and a long syllable.

(1.) The fifteen-syllable trochaic line is in fact a combination of the eight syllable and the seven syllable. It is not common; the best example of it is *Lockley Hall* :—

Fool! a|gain the | dream, the | fancy ‖ but I | know my | words were | wild. |
But I | count the | grey bar|barian ‖ lower | than the | Christian | child.

(2.) The seven-syllable measure, both in continuous verse, and, as we shall presently see, in stanzas, was a great favourite with Keats and Shelley. In it the latter composed his *Lines written in the Euganean Hills*, and Keats his *Ode on the Poets*, and *The Mermaid Tavern*. Shakspere also used it, as in the lines beginning—

On a | day, a|lack the | day! |

The intermixture of eight-syllable lines is exemplified in the following quotation :—

Thus ye | live on | high, and | then |
On the | earth ye | live a|gain ; |
And the | souls ye | left be|hind you, |
Teach us, | here, the | way to | find you. |

Other mixed measures occasionally occur, as in Shakspere's 'Crabbed Age and Youth,' &c.; which contains fives, sixes, and sevens.

19. III. In *Triple measures* there is but one accent for every three syllables; while in the iambic and trochaic there is one for every two. There is a close analogy between poetry in these measures and music in triple time; a dancing lightness and gliding rapidity are characteristic of both. They are of three kinds, according to the foot which predominates in them—dactylic, anapæstic, and amphi-ambic. I can recollect no instances of the use of a triple measure in

which a line of ordinary length would not give, and by its *novelty* prevents the length of the stanza from being tiresome to the ear. The only objection to this stave is, that the cadence is almost *too* full and rounded ; the break between stanza and stanza which it creates is somewhat more marked than is conformable to the requirements of narrative, if not also of descriptive, verse.

(6.) Another decasyllabic nine-line stanza, of curious construction, is found in Chaucer's *Quene Anelyda and Fals Arcyte*. It has but two rimes, thus arranged :—1, 2, 4, 5, 8 ;—3, 6, 7, 9.

(7.) The sonnet, or fourteen-line decasyllabic stave, of which there are several varieties. The sonnets of Shakspere scarcely deserve the name in a metrical sense, their construction being so inartificial. They have no fewer than seven rimes, and consist merely of three quatrains, with alternating rimes, followed by a riming couplet. All our other poets, so far as I know, follow, in writing sonnets, the Petrarcan model, with some unimportant deviations. The sonnet of Petrarch is composed of two quatrains, with extreme and mean rimes,[1] two in number ; followed by six lines, of which the rimes are arranged in several ways. The most ordinary case is that in which the six lines have but two rimes, and are arranged in three riming couplets. Milton's sonnet *On his Deceased Wife* is an example of this kind. If the six lines have three rimes, they usually follow each other in order, as shown in the following passage, taken from Milton's sonnet to *Cyriack Skinner* :—

> To measure life learn thou betimes, and know
> Towards solid good what leads the nearest way ;
> For other things mild Heaven a time ordains,
> And disapproves that care, though wise in show,
> That with superfluous burden loads the day,
> And when God sends a cheerful hour, refrains.

Other varieties of arrangement may be found in the sonnets of Drummond, Milton, and Wordsworth ; but they only affect the six concluding lines. The two opening quatrains, with their two rimes, and the peculiar arrangement of these rimes, are a fixed element in the sonnet. It has generally, at least in Italian poetry, four, and must never have more than five rimes.

22. It would be tedious to enumerate all the different kinds of staves formed out of octosyllabics, and the combination of these with shorter lines. Three of these staves, the octosyllabic quatrain, the quatrain in eights and sixes, and the quatrain in sixes, with the third line octosyllabic, are commonly called, Long measure, Common measure, and Short measure. The six-line stave, in eights and sixes, was a favourite measure with the old romance-writers. I call it the ' Sir Thopas metre,' because Chaucer uses it for his ' Rime of Sir Thopas,' in the Canterbury Tales. A rough specimen of it may be seen at p. 145. The eight-line stave, formed of two quatrains in eights, or in eights and sixes, with alternating rimes, is also common.

---

[1] That is, rimes connecting the first with the fourth and the second with the third lines.

But enough has now been said to enable the student to recognise and describe for himself any iambic measure that he may meet with.

23. II. Trochaic staves, though much used by our poets, do not present the same well-marked forms as the iambic staves. The predominant line is of seven syllables, that is, contains three trochees and a long syllable. However, octosyllabic lines of four trochees are of constant occurrence in heptasyllabic staves. The six-line stave in sevens, exemplified by the lines at p. 468, by Jonson's *Hymn to Diana* (1), and many other pieces, and the eight-line stave in eights and sevens, exemplified by Glover's *Hosier's Ghost* (2), are perhaps the most important among pure trochaic staves :—

> (1.) Queen and | huntress, | chaste and | fair, &c.
>
> (2.) As near | Porto|bello | lying |
>
> On the | gently | swelling | flood. |

24. A very beautiful metre sometimes results from the combination of a trochaic with an iambic measure. Thus in Shelley's *Skylark* (see p. 474), a trochaic quatrain in sixes and fives is followed by an Alexandrine, the length and weight of which serves beautifully to balance and tone down the light joyousness of the trochaics. Shelley has given us another beautiful combination, that of trochees with dactyls. Example :—

> When the | lamp is | shattered,
>
> The | light in the | dust lies | dead, &c.

25. III. In triple measures, three important staves may be distinguished, the quatrain, the six-line stave, and the eight-line stave. Each of these three again may be either dactylic, anapæstic, or amphiambic, but the last is the most common variety of the three.

(1.) *Quatrains.*—The dactylic quatrain, each line of which contains three dactyls, followed either by a long syllable or a trochee, is not very common. There is an example in one of Byron's *Hebrew Melodies*; the 'Song of Saul before his Last Battle' :—

> Farewell to | others but | never we | part |
> Heir to my | royalty, | son of my | heart ;

and again,—

> Brightest and | best of the | sons of the | morning.—HEBER.

The anapæstic quatrain is distinguishable from the dactylic by the fact of its commencing with an anapæst. In triple measures, the foot with which a poem opens is nearly always a key to its metre. In the following example spondees are mixed with the anapæsts :—

> Not a drum | was heard, | not a fu|neral note.|—WOLFE.

A purer specimen may be found in one of Byron's Hebrew melodies, in which the line contains three anapæsts :—

And the voice | of my mourn|ing is o'er, |

And the moun|tains behold | me no more.|

The amphiambic quatrain, in which each line has either four amphiambuses, or three with an iambus, is the metre of a great number of ballads and songs. The rimes are sometimes coupled, sometimes alternate. Examples:—

I saw from | the beach, when | the morning | was shining, |

A bark o'er | the waters | move glorious|ly on. |—MOORE.

Count Albert | has armed him | the Paynim | among, |
Though | his heart it | was false, yet | his arm it | was strong.
SCOTT.

(2.) The six-line stave, triple measure, is only used, so far as I know, in amphiambic endecasyllabics. Scott's *Lochinvar* is an instance.

(3.) The eight-line stave in the amphiambic tetrameter, or tetrameter catalectic,[1] is a noble measure. Examples:—

Then blame not | the bard if | in pleasure's | soft dream, } &c.—MOORE.

I climbed the | dark brow of | the mighty | Helvellyn. | —SCOTT.

There are also eight-line staves in fives, and in fives and sixes. These are dactylic. Examples:—

Over the | mountains,

And | over the | waves, |

Under the | fountains,

And | under the | graves, &c.
Where shall the | traitor rest, |
He the de|ceiver, | &c.—SCOTT.

A dactylic stave in sixes, fives, and fours, varying in the number of lines, was used by Hood with great effect in his *Bridge of Sighs*:—

One more Un|fortunate |

Weary of | breath |

Rashly im|portunate |

Gone to her | death. |

There are many other varieties, but the rules already given will probably enable the student to name and classify them as he falls in with them.

PINDARIC MEASURES.

26. These hold an intermediate position between stanzas and continuous verse. The Pindaric ode is in three parts—strophe, antistrophe,

---

[1] A line which falls short by one syllable of the full measure of four amphiambuses, is so designated.

and epode; which may be repeated as often as the theme requires. The strophe varies in length, seldom containing more than twenty-eight or fewer than fourteen lines. The antistrophe corresponds to the strophe line for line. The epode may be either longer or shorter than the strophe; each repetition of it must agree, line for line, with the original. Gray's ode, *The Bard*, conforms to these rules; the strophe and antistrophe (each of fourteen lines), and the epode (of twenty lines), are repeated thrice. Congreve also observes the rules (see above, p. 317). The pindariques of Cowley and Dryden are reducible to no rule; they are divided into an arbitrary number of strophes, varying in length from twenty-eight to fourteen lines; the lines are of arbitrary length, and the arrangement of the rimes is arbitrary.

INDEX.

———•◇•———

Abbreviations :—Bp. for bishop ; Abp. for Archbishop; flor. for floruit (flourished) ;
n. for note. When only one date is given it is that of death.

ABE

ABELARD 23, 43
Addison, Jos. (1672–1719)
  307, 314, 322, 329, 412
 His *Cato*, 322, 412 ; *Free-*
 holder, 331 ; *Heroic Poems*,
 414 ; Contributions to *Spec-*
 tator, *Tatler*, &c., 329
Adelard of Bath 39
Adolphus, John (1770–1845) 498
Akenside, Mark (1721–1770) 336
Alcuin (732–804). 2, 8
Aldred, Abp. of York . . . 46
Aldrich, Dr. H. (1647–1710) . 324
Aldhelm (Bp.), (died 709). . 14
Alexandrine Metre, origin of
 the name. 62
Alford, Mich. (1587–1652) . 508
Alfred, King (849–901) . 10, 16
 His Translations, *ib.*
Allegorical Poetry 425
Allegorical Style, rise of . . 97
Allen, Cardinal (1532-1594)170,227
Alliterative Poems 81
Ancren Riwle, The 75
Andreas and Elene . . . 12–14
Andrewes, L. (Bp.) (1555–
 1626) 230
Anselm, St. (1033–1109) . . 22
Anti-Jacobin, The 482
Aquinas, St. Thomas . . . 238

BAL

Arbuthnot, Dr. John (1675–
 1735) 329
Ariosto 171, 197
Arnold, Dr. (1795–1842) 391, 498
Ascham, Roger (1515–1568) 157
 His *Toxophilus* and other
 works 167
Asser (Bp.). 30
Atterbury, F. (Bp.) (1662–
 1731) 325
Aungerville, Richard de (Bp.)
 (1347) 38
Austen, Miss Jane (1775–1817) 391
 Her Novels, 480
Autobiographies 500
Avesbury, Robert de . . . 78
Ayenbite of Inwyt 76

BACON, Francis, Lord Ve-
 rulam (1561–1626)
 His *Essays*, 219, 516 ; *His-*
 tory of Henry VII., 223,
 498 ; Philosophical Works,
 232–8, 509, 517
Bacon, Roger (1214–1292) . 40
Baillie, Joanna (1762–1851) . 390
Baldwin, Wm. (circa 1570) . 142
Bale, John (Bp.) 1495–1563) 161
 His *Kynge Johan*, 194

LIST OF EXTRACTS.

LONDON : PRINTED BY
SPOTTISWOODE AND CO., NEW-STREET SQUARE
AND PARLIAMENT STREET

MARCH 1877.

GENERAL LIST OF WORKS

PUBLISHED BY

Messrs. LONGMANS, GREEN, and CO

PATERNOSTER ROW, LONDON.

———o◦◦◦◦o———

History, Politics, Historical Memoirs, &c.

SKETCHES of OTTOMAN HISTORY. By the Very Rev. R. W. CHURCH, Dean of St. Paul's. 1 vol. crown 8vo. [*Nearly ready.*

The **EASTERN QUESTION.** By the Rev. MALCOLM MACCOLL, M.A. 8vo. [*Nearly ready.*

The **HISTORY of ENGLAND** from the Fall of Wolsey to the Defeat of the Spanish Armada. By JAMES ANTHONY FROUDE, M.A. late Fellow of Exeter College, Oxford.

> LIBRARY EDITION, Twelve Volumes, 8vo. price £8. 18s.
> CABINET EDITION, Twelve Volumes, crown 8vo. price 72s.

The **ENGLISH in IRELAND in the EIGHTEENTH CENTURY.** By JAMES ANTHONY FROUDE, M.A. late Fellow of Exeter College, Oxford. 3 vols. 8vo. price 48s.

The **HISTORY of ENGLAND** from the Accession of James the Second. By Lord MACAULAY.

> STUDENT'S EDITION, 2 vols. crown 8vo. 12s.
> PEOPLE'S EDITION, 4 vols. crown 8vo. 16s.
> CABINET EDITION, 8 vols. post 8vo. 48s.
> LIBRARY EDITION, 5 vols. 8vo. £4.

LORD MACAULAY'S WORKS. Complete and Uniform Library Edition. Edited by his Sister, Lady TREVELYAN. 8 vols. 8vo. with Portrait, price £5. 5s. cloth, or £8. 8s. bound in tree-calf by Rivière.

On **PARLIAMENTARY GOVERNMENT in ENGLAND;** its Origin, Development, and Practical Operation. By ALPHEUS TODD, Librarian of the Legislative Assembly of Canada. 2 vols. 8vo. price £1. 17s.

The **CONSTITUTIONAL HISTORY of ENGLAND,** since the Accession of George III. 1760—1860. By Sir THOMAS ERSKINE MAY, K.C.B. D.C.L. The Fifth Edition, thoroughly revised. 3 vols. crown 8vo. price 18s.

DEMOCRACY in EUROPE; a History. By Sir THOMAS ERSKINE MAY, K.C.B. D.C.L. 2 vols. 8vo. [*In the press.*

JOURNAL of the REIGNS of KING GEORGE IV. and KING WILLIAM IV. By the late CHARLES C. F. GREVILLE, Esq. Edited by HENRY REEVE, Esq. Fifth Edition. 3 vols. 8vo. 36s.

A

The OXFORD REFORMERS — John Colet, Erasmus, and Thomas More ; being a History of their Fellow-work. By FREDERIC SEEBOHM. Second Edition, enlarged. 8vo. 14s.

LECTURES on the HISTORY of ENGLAND, from the Earliest Times to the Death of King Edward II. By WILLIAM LONGMAN, F.S.A. With Maps and Illustrations. 8vo. 15s.

The HISTORY of the LIFE and TIMES of EDWARD the THIRD. By WILLIAM LONGMAN, F.S.A. With 9 Maps, 8 Plates, and 16 Woodcuts. 2 vols. 8vo. 28s.

INTRODUCTORY LECTURES on MODERN HISTORY. By THOMAS ARNOLD, D.D. 8vo. price 7s. 6d.

WATERLOO LECTURES ; a Study of the Campaign of 1815. By Colonel CHARLES C. CHESNEY, R.E. Third Edition. 8vo. with Map, 10s. 6d.

The LIFE of SIMON DE MONTFORT, EARL of LEICESTER, with special reference to the Parliamentary History of his time. By GEORGE WALTER PROTHERO, M.A. With 2 Maps. Crown 8vo. 9s.

HISTORY of ENGLAND under the DUKE of BUCKINGHAM and CHARLES the FIRST, 1624-1628. By SAMUEL RAWSON GARDINER, late Student of Ch. Ch. 2 vols. 8vo. with Two Maps, price 24s.

The PERSONAL GOVERNMENT of CHARLES I. from the Death of Buckingham to the Declaration of the Judges in favour of Ship Money, 1628-1637. By S. R. GARDINER, late Student of Ch. Ch. 2 vols. 8vo. [In the press.

The SIXTH ORIENTAL MONARCHY; or, the Geography, History, and Antiquities of PARTHIA. By GEORGE RAWLINSON, M.A. Professor of Ancient History in the University of Oxford. Maps and Illustrations. 8vo. 16s.

The SEVENTH GREAT ORIENTAL MONARCHY; or, a History of the SASSANIANS: with Notices, Geographical and Antiquarian. By G. RAWLINSON, M.A. Map and numerous Illustrations. 8vo. price 28s.

ISLAM under the ARABS. By ROBERT DURIE OSBORN, Major in the Bengal Staff Corps. 8vo. 12s.

A HISTORY of GREECE. By the Rev. GEORGE W. COX, M.A. late Scholar of Trinity College, Oxford. VOLS. I. & II. (to the Close of the Peloponnesian War). 8vo. with Maps and Plans, 36s.

GENERAL HISTORY of GREECE to the Death of Alexander the Great; with a Sketch of the Subsequent History to the Present Time. By GEORGE W. COX, M.A. With 11 Maps. Crown 8vo. 7s. 6d.

The HISTORY of ROME. By WILLIAM IHNE. VOLS. I. and II. 8vo. price 30s. The Third Volume is in the press.

GENERAL HISTORY OF ROME from the Foundation of the City to the Fall of Augustulus, B.C. 753—A.D. 476. By the Very Rev. C. MERIVALE, D.D. Dean of Ely. With Five Maps. Crown 8vo. 7s. 6d.

HISTORY of the ROMANS under the EMPIRE. By the Very Rev. C. MERIVALE, D.D. Dean of Ely. 8 vols. post 8vo. 48s.

The FALL of the ROMAN REPUBLIC ; a Short History of the Last Century of the Commonwealth. By the same Author. 12mo. 7s. 6d.

The STUDENT'S MANUAL of the HISTORY of INDIA, from the Earliest Period to the Present. By Colonel MEADOWS TAYLOR, M.R.A.S. M.R.I.A. Second Thousand. Crown 8vo. with Maps, 7s. 6d.

INDIAN POLITY; a View of the System of Administration in India.
By Lieutenant-Colonel GEORGE CHESNEY, Fellow of the University of Calcutta.
8vo. with Map, 21s.

The HISTORY of PRUSSIA, from the Earliest Times to the Present
Day; tracing the Origin and Development of her Military Organisation. By
Captain W. J. WYATT. Vols. I. and II. A.D. 700 to A.D. 1525. 8vo. 36s.

The CHILDHOOD of the ENGLISH NATION; or, the Beginnings
of English History. By ELLA S. ARMITAGE. Fcp. 8vo. 2s. 6d.

POPULAR HISTORY of FRANCE, from the Earliest Times to the
Death of Louis XIV. By ELIZABETH M. SEWELL, Author of 'Amy Herbert' &c.
With 8 Coloured Maps. Crown 8vo. 7s. 6d.

LORD MACAULAY'S CRITICAL and HISTORICAL ESSAYS. CHEAP
EDITION, authorised and complete. Crown 8vo. 3s. 6d.

| CABINET EDITION, 4 vols. post 8vo. 24s. | LIBRARY EDITION, 3 vols. 8vo. 36s. |
| PEOPLE'S EDITION, 2 vols. crown 8vo. 8s. | STUDENT'S EDITION, 1 vol. cr. 8vo. 6s. |

HISTORY of EUROPEAN MORALS, from Augustus to Charlemagne.
By W. E. H. LECKY, M.A. Third Edition. 2 vols. crown 8vo. price 16s.

HISTORY of the RISE and INFLUENCE of the SPIRIT of
RATIONALISM in EUROPE. By W. E. H. LECKY, M.A. Fourth Edition.
2 vols. crown 8vo. price 16s.

The NATIVE RACES of the PACIFIC STATES of NORTH AMERICA.
By HUBERT HOWE BANCROFT. 5 vols. 8vo. with Maps, £6. 5s.

HISTORY of the MONGOLS from the Ninth to the Nineteenth Century. By HENRY H. HOWORTH, F.S.A. VOL. I. *the Mongols Proper and the
Kalmuks;* with Two Coloured Maps. Royal 8vo. 28s.

The HISTORY of PHILOSOPHY, from Thales to Comte.   By
GEORGE HENRY LEWES. Fourth Edition. 2 vols. 8vo. 32s.

The MYTHOLOGY of the ARYAN NATIONS.   By GEORGE W.
Cox, M.A. late Scholar of Trinity College, Oxford,   2 vols. 8vo. 28s.

TALES of ANCIENT GREECE. By GEORGE W. Cox, M.A. late
Scholar of Trinity College, Oxford. Crown 8vo. price 6s. 6d.

HISTORY of CIVILISATION in England and France, Spain and Scotland. By HENRY THOMAS BUCKLE. Latest Edition of the entire Work, with
a complete INDEX. 3 vols. crown 8vo. 24s.

SKETCH of the HISTORY of the CHURCH of ENGLAND to the
Revolution of 1688. By the Right Rev. T. V. SHORT, D.D. sometime Bishop of
St. Asaph. Eighth Edition. Crown 8vo. 7s. 6d.

EPOCHS of ANCIENT HISTORY.   Edited by the Rev. G. W. Cox,
M.A. and jointly by C. SANKEY, M.A. Ten Volumes, each complete in itself,
in fcp. 8vo. with Maps and Indices :—

> BEESLY'S Gracchi, Marius, and Sulla, 2s. 6d.
> CAPES'S Age of the Antonines, 2s. 6d.
> CAPES'S Early Roman Empire, 2s. 6d.
> Cox's Athenian Empire, 2s. 6d.
> Cox's Greeks and Persians, 2s. 6d.
> CURTEIS'S Rise of the Macedonian Empire, 2s. 6d.
> IHNE'S Rome to its Capture by the Gauls, 2s. 6d.
> MERIVALE'S Roman Triumvirates, 2s. 6d.
> SANKEY'S Spartan and Theban Supremacy.   } *In the press.*
> SMITH'S Rome and Carthage, the Punic Wars.

EPOCHS of MODERN HISTORY. Edited by E. E. MORRIS, M.A.
J. S. PHILLPOTTS, B.C.L. and C. COLBECK, M.A. Eleven volumes now published,
each complete in itself, in fcp. 8vo. with Maps and Index : —

> COX's Crusades, 2s. 6d.
> CREIGHTON's Age of Elizabeth, 2s. 6d.
> GAIRDNER's Houses of Lancaster and York, 2s. 6d.
> GARDINER's Puritan Revolution, 2s. 6d.
> GARDINER's Thirty Years' War, 2s. 6d.
> HALE's Fall of the Stuarts, 2s. 6d.
> LUDLOW's War of American Independence, 2s. 6d.
> MORRIS's Age of Queen Anne, 2s. 6d.
> SEEBOHM's Protestant Revolution, 2s. 6d.
> STUBBS's Early Plantagenets, 2s. 6d.
> WARBURTON's Edward III. 2s. 6d.

*** Other Epochs in preparation, in continuation of the Series.

REALITIES of IRISH LIFE. By W. STEUART TRENCH, late Land
Agent in Ireland to the Marquess of Lansdowne, the Marquess of Bath, and
Lord Digby. Cheaper Edition. Crown 8vo. price 2s. 6d.

MAUNDER'S HISTORICAL TREASURY; General Introductory Outlines of Universal History, and a series of Separate Histories. Latest Edition,
revised by the Rev. G. W. COX, M.A. Fcp. 8vo. 6s. cloth, or 10s. 6d. calf.

CATES' and WOODWARD'S ENCYCLOPÆDIA of CHRONOLOGY,
HISTORICAL and BIOGRAPHICAL. 8vo. price 42s.

Biographical Works.

The LIFE and LETTERS of LORD MACAULAY. By his Nephew,
G. OTTO TREVELYAN, M.P. Second Edition, with Additions and Corrections.
2 vols. 8vo. with Portrait, price 36s.

The LIFE of SIR WILLIAM FAIRBAIRN, Bart. F.R.S. Corresponding Member of the National Institute of France, &c. Partly written by
himself; edited and completed by WILLIAM POLE, F.R.S. 8vo. Portrait, 18s.

ARTHUR SCHOPENHAUER, his LIFE and his PHILOSOPHY.
By HELEN ZIMMERN. Post 8vo. with Portrait, 7s. 6d.

The LIFE and LETTERS of MOZART. Translated from the German
Biography of Dr. LUDWIG NOHL by Lady WALLACE. 2 vols. post 8vo. with
Portraits of Mozart and his Sister.   [Nearly ready.

FELIX MENDELSSOHN'S LETTERS from ITALY and SWITZER-
LAND, and Letters from 1833 to 1847. Translated by Lady WALLACE. With
Portrait, 2 vols. crown 8vo. 5s. each.

The LIFE of ROBERT FRAMPTON, D.D. Bishop of Gloucester,
deprived as a Non-Juror in 1689. Edited by T. SIMPSON EVANS, M.A. Vicar of
Shoreditch. Crown 8vo. Portrait, 10s. 6d.

AUTOBIOGRAPHY. By JOHN STUART MILL. 8vo. price 7s. 6d.

The LIFE of NAPOLEON III. derived from State Records, Unpublished
Family Correspondence, and Personal Testimony. By BLANCHARD JERROLD.
4 vols. 8vo. with numerous Portraits and Facsimiles. VOLS. I. and II. price 18s.
each. The Third Volume is in the press.

ESSAYS in MODERN MILITARY BIOGRAPHY. By CHARLES
CORNWALLIS CHESNEY, Lieutenant-Colonel in the Royal Engineers. 8vo. 12s. 6d.

The MEMOIRS of SIR JOHN RERESBY, of Thrybergh, Bart. M.P.
for York, &c. 1634—1689. Written by Himself. Edited from the Original
Manuscript by JAMES J. CARTWRIGHT, M.A. 8vo. price 21s.

ISAAC CASAUBON, 1559–1614. By Mark Pattison, Rector of Lincoln College, Oxford. 8vo. 18s.

LEADERS of PUBLIC OPINION in IRELAND; Swift, Flood, Grattan, and O'Connell. By W. E. H. Lecky, M.A. New Edition, revised and enlarged. Crown 8vo. price 7s. 6d.

DICTIONARY of GENERAL BIOGRAPHY; containing Concise Memoirs and Notices of the most Eminent Persons of all Countries, from the Earliest Ages. By W. L. R. Cates. Medium 8vo. price 25s.

LIFE of the DUKE of WELLINGTON. By the Rev. G. R. Gleig, M.A. Popular Edition, carefully revised; with copious Additions. Crown 8vo. with Portrait, 5s.

MEMOIRS of SIR HENRY HAVELOCK, K.C.B. By John Clark Marshman. Cabinet Edition, with Portrait. Crown 8vo. price 3s. 6d.

VICISSITUDES of FAMILIES. By Sir J. Bernard Burke, C.B. Ulster King of Arms. New Edition, enlarged. 2 vols. crown 8vo. 21s.

ESSAYS in ECCLESIASTICAL BIOGRAPHY. By the Right Hon. Sir J. Stephen, LL.D. Cabinet Edition. Crown 8vo. 7s. 6d.

MAUNDER'S BIOGRAPHICAL TREASURY. Latest Edition, reconstructed, thoroughly revised, and in great part rewritten; with 1,500 additional Memoirs and Notices, by W. L. R. Cates. Fcp. 8vo. 6s. cloth; 10s. 6d. calf.

LETTERS and LIFE of FRANCIS BACON, including all his Occasional Works. Collected and edited, with a Commentary, by J. Spedding, Trin. Coll. Cantab. Complete in 7 vols. 8vo. £4. 4s.

The LIFE, WORKS, and OPINIONS of HEINRICH HEINE. By William Stigand. 2 vols. 8vo. with Portrait of Heine, price 28s.

BIOGRAPHICAL and CRITICAL ESSAYS, reprinted from Reviews, with Additions and Corrections. Second Edition of the Second Series. By A. Hayward, Q.C. 2 vols. 8vo. price 28s. Third Series, in 1 vol. 8vo. price 14s.

Criticism, Philosophy, Polity, &c.

The LAW of NATIONS considered as INDEPENDENT POLITICAL COMMUNITIES; the Rights and Duties of Nations in Time of War. By Sir Travers Twiss, D.C.L., F.R.S. Second Edition, revised. 8vo. 21s.

CHURCH and STATE: their relations Historically Developed. By T. Heinrich Geffcken, Professor of International Law in the University of Strasburg. Translated and edited with the Author's assistance by E. Fairfax Taylor. 2 vols. 8vo. 42s.

The INSTITUTES of JUSTINIAN; with English Introduction, Translation and Notes. By T. C. Sandars, M.A. Sixth Edition. 8vo. 18s.

A SYSTEMATIC VIEW of the SCIENCE of JURISPRUDENCE. By Sheldon Amos, M.A. Professor of Jurisprudence to the Inns of Court, London. 8vo. price 18s.

A PRIMER of the ENGLISH CONSTITUTION and GOVERNMENT. By Sheldon Amos, M.A. Professor of Jurisprudence to the Inns of Court. Second Edition, revised. Crown 8vo. 6s.

A SKETCH of the HISTORY of TAXES in ENGLAND from the Earliest Times to the Present Day. By STEPHEN DOWELL. VOL. I. to the Civil War 1642. 8vo. 10s. 6d.

OUTLINES of CIVIL PROCEDURE. Being a General View of the Supreme Court of Judicature and of the whole Practice in the Common Law and Chancery Divisions under all the Statutes now in force. By EDWARD STANLEY ROSCOE, Barrister-at-Law. 12mo. price 3s. 6d.

Our NEW JUDICIAL SYSTEM and CIVIL PROCEDURE, as Reconstructed under the Judicature Acts, including the Act of 1876; with Comments on their Effect and Operation. By W. F. FINLASON. Crown 8vo. 10s. 6d.

SOCRATES and the SOCRATIC SCHOOLS. Translated from the German of Dr. E. ZELLER, with the Author's approval, by the Rev. OSWALD J. REICHEL, M.A. Crown 8vo. New Edition in the Press.

The STOICS, EPICUREANS, and SCEPTICS. Translated from the German of Dr. E. ZELLER, with the Author's approval, by OSWALD J. REICHEL, M.A. Crown 8vo. price 14s.

PLATO and the OLDER ACADEMY. Translated from the German of Dr. EDUARD ZELLER by S. FRANCES ALLEYNE and ALFRED GOODWIN, B.A. Fellow of Balliol College, Oxford. Crown 8vo. 18s.

The ETHICS of ARISTOTLE, with Essays and Notes. By Sir A. GRANT, Bart. M.A. LL.D. Third Edition. 2 vols. 8vo. 32s.

The POLITICS of ARISTOTLE; Greek Text, with English Notes. By RICHARD CONGREVE, M.A. 8vo. 18s.

ARISTOTLE'S POLITICS. Books I. III. IV. (VII.) The Greek Text of Bekker, with an English Translation by W. E. BOLLAND, M.A. and Short Introductory Essays by A. LANG, M.A. Crown 8vo. 7s. 6d.

The NICOMACHEAN ETHICS of ARISTOTLE newly translated into English. By R. WILLIAMS, B.A. Fellow and late Lecturer of Merton College, and sometime Student of Christ Church, Oxford. 8vo. 7s. 6d.

ELEMENTS of LOGIC. By R. WHATELY, D.D. sometime Archbishop of Dublin. 8vo. 10s. 6d. Crown 8vo. 4s. 6d.

LOGIC, DEDUCTIVE and INDUCTIVE. By ALEXANDER BAIN, LL.D. In TWO PARTS, crown 8vo. 10s. 6d. Each Part may be had separately:—
PART I. *Deduction*, 4s. PART II. *Induction*, 6s. 6d.

PICTURE LOGIC; an Attempt to Popularise the Science of Reasoning by the combination of Humorous Pictures with Examples of Reasoning taken from Daily Life. By A. SWINBOURNE, B.A. Fcp. 8vo. Woodcuts, 5s.

ELEMENTS of RHETORIC. By R. WHATELY, D.D. sometime Archbishop of Dublin. 8vo. 10s. 6d. Crown 8vo. 4s. 6d.

COMTE'S SYSTEM of POSITIVE POLITY, or TREATISE upon SOCIOLOGY. Translated from the Paris Edition of 1851-1854, and furnished with Analytical Tables of Contents. In Four Volumes, 8vo. each forming in some degree an independent Treatise:—

VOL. I. General View of Positivism and its Introductory Principles. Translated by J. H. BRIDGES, M.B. Price 21s.

VOL. II. The Social Statics, or the Abstract Laws of Human Order. Translated by F. HARRISON, M.A. Price 14s.

VOL. III. The Social Dynamics, or the General Laws of Human Progress (the Philosophy of History). Translated by Professor E. S. BEESLY, M.A. 8vo. 21s.

VOL. IV. The Synthesis of the Future of Mankind. Translated by R. CONGREVE, M.D.; and an Appendix, containing Comte's Early Essays, translated by H. D. Hutton, B.A. [*In the press.*

DEMOCRACY in AMERICA. By ALEXIS DE TOCQUEVILLE. Translated by HENRY REEVE, Esq. 2 vols. crown 8vo. 16s.

On the INFLUENCE of AUTHORITY in MATTERS of OPINION. By the late Sir GEORGE CORNEWALL LEWIS, Bart. 8vo. 14s.

BACON'S ESSAYS with ANNOTATIONS. By R. WHATELY, D.D. late Archbishop of Dublin. Fourth Edition. 8vo. price 10s. 6d.

LORD BACON'S WORKS, collected and edited by J. SPEDDING, M.A. R. L. ELLIS, M.A. and D. D. HEATH. 7 vols. 8vo. price £3. 13s. 6d.

On REPRESENTATIVE GOVERNMENT. By JOHN STUART MILL. Crown 8vo. price 2s.

On LIBERTY. By JOHN STUART MILL. Post 8vo. 7s. 6d. Crown 8vo. price 1s. 4d.

PRINCIPLES of POLITICAL ECONOMY. By JOHN STUART MILL. 2 vols. 8vo. 30s. Or in 1 vol. crown 8vo. price 5s.

ESSAYS on SOME UNSETTLED QUESTIONS of POLITICAL ECONOMY. By JOHN STUART MILL. 8vo. 6s. 6d.

UTILITARIANISM. By JOHN STUART MILL. 8vo. 5s.

DISSERTATIONS and DISCUSSIONS; Political, Philosophical, and Historical. By JOHN STUART MILL. 4 vols. 8vo. price £2. 6s. 6d.

EXAMINATION of Sir. W. HAMILTON'S PHILOSOPHY, and of the Principal Philosophical Questions discussed in his Writings. By JOHN STUART MILL. 8vo. 16s.

A SYSTEM of LOGIC, RATIOCINATIVE and INDUCTIVE. By JOHN STUART MILL. Two vols. 8vo. 25s.

An OUTLINE of the NECESSARY LAWS of THOUGHT; a Treatise on Pure and Applied Logic. By the Most Rev. W. THOMSON, Lord Archbishop of York, D.D. F.R.S. Crown 8vo. price 6s.

PRINCIPLES of ECONOMICAL PHILOSOPHY. By HENRY DUNNING MACLEOD, M.A. Barrister-at-Law. Second Edition. In Two Volumes. VOL. I. 8vo. price 15s. VOL. II. PART I. price 12s. VOL. II. PART II. just ready.

SPEECHES of the RIGHT HON. LORD MACAULAY, corrected by Himself. Crown 8vo. 3s. 6d.

FAMILIES of SPEECH; Four Lectures delivered before the Royal Institution. By the Rev. Canon FARRAR, F.R.S. Crown 8vo. 3s. 6d.

CHAPTERS on LANGUAGE. By the Rev. Canon FARRAR, F.R.S. Crown 8vo. 5s.

HANDBOOK of the ENGLISH LANGUAGE. For the use of Students of the Universities and the Higher Classes in Schools. By R. G. LATHAM, M.A. M.D. Crown 8vo. price 6s.

DICTIONARY of the ENGLISH LANGUAGE. By R. G. LATHAM, M.A. M.D. Abridged from Dr. Latham's Edition of Johnson's English Dictionary, and condensed into One Volume. Medium 8vo. price 24s.

A DICTIONARY of the ENGLISH LANGUAGE. By R. G. LATHAM, M.A. M.D. Founded on the Dictionary of Dr. SAMUEL JOHNSON, as edited by the Rev. H. J. TODD, with numerous Emendations and Additions. In Four Volumes, 4to. price £7.,

ENGLISH SYNONYMES. By E. JANE WHATELY. Edited by Archbishop WHATELY. Fifth Edition. Fcp. 8vo. price 3s.

THESAURUS of ENGLISH WORDS and PHRASES, classified and arranged so as to facilitate the Expression of Ideas, and assist in Literary Composition. By P. M. ROGET, M.D. Crown 8vo. 10s. 6d.

LECTURES on the SCIENCE of LANGUAGE. By F. MAX MÜLLER, M.A. &c. The Eighth Edition. 2 vols. crown 8vo. 16s.

MANUAL of ENGLISH LITERATURE, Historical and Critical. By THOMAS ARNOLD, M.A. Crown 8vo. 7s. 6d.

HISTORICAL and CRITICAL COMMENTARY on the OLD TESTAMENT; with a New Translation. By M. M. KALISCH, Ph.D. VOL. I. *Genesis*, 8vo. 18s. or adapted for the General Reader, 12s. VOL. II. *Exodus*, 15s. or adapted for the General Reader, 12s. VOL. III. *Leviticus*, PART I. 15s. or adapted for the General Reader, 8s. VOL. IV. *Leviticus*, PART II. 15s. or adapted for the General Reader, 8s.

A DICTIONARY of ROMAN and GREEK ANTIQUITIES, with about Two Thousand Engravings on Wood from Ancient Originals, illustrative of the Industrial Arts and Social Life of the Greeks and Romans. By A. RICH, B.A. Third Edition, revised and improved. Crown 8vo. price 7s. 6d.

A LATIN-ENGLISH DICTIONARY. By JOHN T. WHITE, D.D. Oxon. and J. E. RIDDLE, M.A. Oxon. 1 vol. 4to. 28s.

WHITE'S COLLEGE LATIN-ENGLISH DICTIONARY (Intermediate Size), abridged for the use of University Students from the Parent Work (as above). Medium 8vo. 15s.

WHITE'S JUNIOR STUDENT'S COMPLETE LATIN-ENGLISH and ENGLISH-LATIN DICTIONARY. Square 12mo. price 12s.

Separately { The ENGLISH-LATIN DICTIONARY, price 5s. 6d.
{ The LATIN-ENGLISH DICTIONARY, price 7s. 6d.

A LATIN-ENGLISH DICTIONARY, adapted for the Use of Middle-Class Schools. By JOHN T. WHITE, D.D. Oxon. Square fcp. 8vo. price 3s.

An ENGLISH-GREEK LEXICON, containing all the Greek Words used by Writers of good authority. By C. D. YONGE, M.A. 4to. price 21s.

Mr. YONGE'S NEW LEXICON, English and Greek, abridged from his larger work (as above). Square 12mo. price 8s. 6d.

LIDDELL and SCOTT'S GREEK-ENGLISH LEXICON. Sixth Edition. Crown 4to. price 36s.

A LEXICON, GREEK and ENGLISH, abridged from LIDDELL and SCOTT'S *Greek-English Lexicon.* Fourteenth Edition. Square 12mo. 7s. 6d.

A PRACTICAL DICTIONARY of the FRENCH and ENGLISH LANGUAGES. By L. CONTANSEAU. Post 8vo. 7s. 6d.

CONTANSEAU'S POCKET DICTIONARY, French and English, abridged from the above by the Author. Square 18mo. 3s. 6d.

A NEW POCKET DICTIONARY of the GERMAN and ENGLISH LANGUAGES. By F. W. LONGMAN, Balliol College, Oxford. 18mo. 5s.

NEW PRACTICAL DICTIONARY of the GERMAN LANGUAGE; German-English and English-German. By the Rev. W. L. BLACKLEY, M.A. and Dr. CARL MARTIN FRIEDLÄNDER. Post 8vo. 7s. 6d.

Miscellaneous Works and *Popular Metaphysics.*

GERMAN HOME LIFE. Reprinted, with Revision and Additions, from *Fraser's Magazine.* Third Edition. Crown 8vo. 6s.

THE MISCELLANEOUS WORKS of THOMAS ARNOLD, D.D. Late Head Master of Rugby School. 8vo. 7s. 6d.

MISCELLANEOUS and POSTHUMOUS WORKS of the Late HENRY THOMAS BUCKLE. Edited, with a Biographical Notice, by HELEN TAYLOR. 3 vols. 8vo. price 52s. 6d.

MISCELLANEOUS WRITINGS of JOHN CONINGTON, M.A. late Corpus Professor of Latin in the University of Oxford. Edited by J. A. SYMONDS, M.A. With a Memoir by H. J. S. SMITH, M.A. 2 vols. 8vo. 28s.

ESSAYS, CRITICAL and BIOGRAPHICAL. Contributed to the *Edinburgh Review.* By HENRY ROGERS. 2 vols. crown 8vo. price 12s.

ESSAYS on some THEOLOGICAL CONTROVERSIES of the TIME. Contributed chiefly to the *Edinburgh Review.* By HENRY ROGERS. New Edition, with Additions. Crown 8vo. price 6s.

The ESSAYS and CONTRIBUTIONS of A. K. H. B. Uniform Cabinet Edition, in crown 8vo. :—

Recreations of a Country Parson. Two Series, 3s. 6d. each.
The Common-place Philosopher in Town and Country. 3s. 6d.
Leisure Hours in Town. 3s. 6d.
The Autumn Holidays of a Country Parson. 3s. 6d.
Seaside Musings on Sundays and Week-Days. 3s. 6d.
The Graver Thoughts of a Country Parson. Three Series, 3s. 6d. each.
Critical Essays of a Country Parson. 3s. 6d.
Sunday Afternoons in the Parish Church of a University City. 3s. 6d.
Lessons of Middle Age. 3s. 6d.
Counsel and Comfort spoken from a City Pulpit. 3s. 6d.
Changed Aspects of Unchanged Truths. 3s. 6d.
Present-day Thoughts. 3s. 6d.
Landscapes, Churches, and Moralities. 3s. 6d.

SHORT STUDIES on GREAT SUBJECTS. By JAMES ANTHONY FROUDE, M.A. late Fellow of Exeter Coll. Oxford. 2 vols. crown 8vo. price 12s. or 2 vols. demy 8vo. price 24s. Third Series in the press.

SELECTIONS from the WRITINGS of LORD MACAULAY. Edited, with Occasional Explanatory Notes, by GEORGE OTTO TREVELYAN, M.P. Crown 8vo. price 6s.

LORD MACAULAY'S MISCELLANEOUS WRITINGS :—
LIBRARY EDITION. 2 vols. 8vo. Portrait, 21s.
PEOPLE'S EDITION. 1 vol. crown 8vo. 4s. 6d.

LORD MACAULAY'S MISCELLANEOUS WRITINGS and SPEECHES. STUDENT'S EDITION, in crown 8vo. price 6s.

The Rev. SYDNEY SMITH'S MISCELLANEOUS WORKS; including his Contributions to the *Edinburgh Review.* Crown 8vo. 6s.

The WIT and WISDOM of the Rev. SYDNEY SMITH; a Selection of the most memorable Passages in his Writings and Conversation. 16mo. 3s. 6d.

The ECLIPSE of FAITH; or, a Visit to a Religious Sceptic. By HENRY ROGERS. Latest Edition. Fcp. 8vo. price 5s.

DEFENCE of the ECLIPSE of FAITH, by its Author; a rejoinder to Dr. Newman's *Reply.* Latest Edition. Fcp 8vo. price 3s. 6d.

CHIPS from a GERMAN WORKSHOP; Essays on the Science of Religion, on Mythology, Traditions, and Customs, and on the Science of Language. By F. MAX MÜLLER, M.A. &c. 4 vols. 8vo. £2. 18s.

ANALYSIS of the PHENOMENA of the HUMAN MIND. By JAMES MILL. A New Edition, with Notes, Illustrative and Critical, by ALEXANDER BAIN, ANDREW FINDLATER, and GEORGE GROTE. Edited, with additional Notes, by JOHN STUART MILL. 2 vols. 8vo. price 28s.

An INTRODUCTION to MENTAL PHILOSOPHY, on the Inductive Method. By J. D. MORELL, M.A. LL.D. 8vo. 12s.

PHILOSOPHY WITHOUT ASSUMPTIONS. By the Rev. T. P. KIRKMAN, F.R.S. Rector of Croft, near Warrington. 8vo. 10s. 6d.

The SENSES and the INTELLECT. By ALEXANDER BAIN, M.D. Professor of Logic in the University of Aberdeen. Third Edition. 8vo. 15s.

The EMOTIONS and the WILL. By ALEXANDER BAIN, LL.D. Professor of Logic in the University of Aberdeen. Third Edition, thoroughly revised, and in great part re-written. 8vo. price 15s.

MENTAL and MORAL SCIENCE: a Compendium of Psychology and Ethics. By the same Author. Third Edition. Crown 8vo. 10s. 6d. Or separately: PART I. Mental Science, 6s. 6d. PART II. Moral Science, 4s. 6d.

APPARITIONS; a Narrative of Facts. By the Rev. B. W. SAVILE, M.A. Author of 'The Truth of the Bible' &c. Crown 8vo. price 4s. 6d.

HUME'S TREATISE of HUMAN NATURE, Edited, with Notes &c. by T. H. GREEN, Fellow and Tutor, Ball. Coll. and T. H. GROSE, Fellow and Tutor, Queen's Coll. Oxford. 2 vols. 8vo. 28s.

ESSAYS MORAL, POLITICAL, and LITERARY. By DAVID HUME. By the same Editors. 2 vols. 8vo. price 28s.
        ⁎ The above form a complete and uniform Edition of DAVID HUME'S
                Philosophical Works.

The PHILOSOPHY of NECESSITY; or, Natural Law as applicable to Mental, Moral, and Social Science. By CHARLES BRAY. 8vo. 9s.

Astronomy, Meteorology, Popular Geography, &c.

BRINKLEY'S ASTRONOMY. Revised and partly re-written by J. W. STUBBS, D.D. Fellow and Tutor of Trinity College, Dublin, and F. BRUNNOW, Ph.D. Astronomer Royal of Ireland. Crown 8vo. 6s.

OUTLINES of ASTRONOMY. By Sir J. F. W. HERSCHEL, Bart. M.A. Latest Edition, with Plates and Diagrams. Square crown 8vo. 12s.

ESSAYS on ASTRONOMY, a Series of Papers on Planets and Meteors, the Sun and Sun-surrounding Space, Stars and Star-Cloudlets; with a Dissertation on the Transit of Venus. By R. A. PROCTOR, B.A. With Plates and Woodcuts. 8vo. 12s.

THE TRANSITS of VENUS; a Popular Account of Past and Coming Transits, from the first observed by Horrocks A.D. 1639 to the Transit of A.D. 2012. By R. A. PROCTOR, B.A. Second Edition, with 20 Plates (12 coloured) and 38 Woodcuts. Crown 8vo. 8s. 6d.

The **UNIVERSE** and the **COMING TRANSITS** : Presenting Researches into and New Views respecting the Constitution of the Heavens; together with an Investigation of the Conditions of the Coming Transits of Venus. By R. A. PROCTOR, B.A. With 22 Charts and 22 Woodcuts. 8vo. 16s.

The **MOON** ; her Motions, Aspect, Scenery, and Physical Condition. By R. A. PROCTOR, B.A. With Plates, Charts, Woodcuts, and Three Lunar Photographs. Crown 8vo. 15s.

The **SUN**; **RULER, LIGHT, FIRE,** and **LIFE** of the **PLANETARY SYSTEM.** By R. A. PROCTOR, B.A. Third Edition, with 10 Plates (7 coloured) and 107 Figures on Wood. Crown 8vo. 14s.

OTHER WORLDS THAN OURS; the Plurality of Worlds Studied under the Light of Recent Scientific Researches. By R. A. PROCTOR, B.A. Third Edition, with 14 Illustrations. Crown 8vo. 10s. 6d.

The **ORBS AROUND US**; Familiar Essays on the Moon and Planets, Meteors and Comets, the Sun and Coloured Pairs of Stars. By R. A. PROCTOR, B.A. Second Edition, with Charts and 4 Diagrams. Crown 8vo. price 7s. 6d.

SATURN and its **SYSTEM.** By R. A. PROCTOR, B.A. 8vo. with 14 Plates, 14s.

A NEW STAR ATLAS, for the Library, the School, and the Observatory, in Twelve Circular Maps (with Two Index Plates). Intended as a Companion to 'Webb's Celestial Objects for Common Telescopes.' With a Letterpress Introduction on the Study of the Stars, illustrated by 9 Diagrams. By R. A. PROCTOR, B.A. Crown 8vo. 5s.

CELESTIAL OBJECTS for **COMMON TELESCOPES.** By the Rev. T. W. WEBB, M.A. F.R.A.S. Third Edition, revised and enlarged; with Maps, Plate, and Woodcuts. Crown 8vo. price 7s. 6d.

The **MOON,** and the Condition and Configurations of its Surface. By EDMUND NEISON, Fellow of the Royal Astronomical Society, &c. With 26 Maps and 5 Plates. Medium 8vo. 31s. 6d.

SCHELLEN'S SPECTRUM ANALYSIS, in its application to Terrestrial Substances and the Physical Constitution of the Heavenly Bodies. Translated by JANE and C. LASSELL ; edited, with Notes, by W. HUGGINS, LL.D. F.R.S. With 13 Plates (6 coloured) and 223 Woodcuts. 8vo. price 28s.

AIR and **RAIN**; the Beginnings of a Chemical Climatology. By ROBERT ANGUS SMITH, Ph.D. F.R.S. F.C.S. With 8 Illustrations. 8vo. 24s.

AIR and its **RELATIONS** to **LIFE.** By W. N. HARTLEY, F.C.S. Demonstrator of Chemistry at King's College, London. Second Edition, with 66 Woodcuts. Small 8vo. 6s.

DOVE'S LAW of STORMS, considered in connexion with the Ordinary Movements of the Atmosphere. Translated by R. H. SCOTT, M.A. 8vo. 10s. 6d.

The **PUBLIC SCHOOLS ATLAS of MODERN GEOGRAPHY.** In 31 entirely new Coloured Maps. Edited, with an Introduction, by the Rev. G. BUTLER, M.A. Imperial 8vo. or imperial 4to. 5s. cloth.

The **PUBLIC SCHOOLS ATLAS of ANCIENT GEOGRAPHY,** in 28 entirely new Coloured Maps. Edited by the Rev. G. BUTLER, M.A. Imperial 8vo. or imperial 4to. 7s. 6d. cloth.

KEITH JOHNSTON'S GENERAL DICTIONARY of GEOGRAPHY,
Descriptive, Physical, Statistical, and Historical ; forming a complete Gazetteer
of the World. New Edition (1877), revised and corrected. 8vo. price 42s.

MAUNDER'S TREASURY of GEOGRAPHY, Physical, Historical,
Descriptive, and Political. Edited by W. HUGHES, F.R.G.S. Revised Edition,
with 7 Maps and 16 Plates. Fcp. 6s. cloth, or 10s. 6d. bound in calf.

Natural History and Popular Science.

TEXT-BOOKS of SCIENCE, MECHANICAL and PHYSICAL,
adapted for the use of Artisans and of Students in Public and Science Schools.

The following Text-Books in this Series may now be had :—

ANDERSON'S Strength of Materials, small 8vo. 3s. 6d.
ARMSTRONG'S Organic Chemistry, 3s. 6d.
BARRY'S Railway Appliances, 3s. 6d.
BLOXAM'S Metals, 3s. 6d.
GOODEVE'S Elements of Mechanism, 3s. 6d.
———— Principles of Mechanics, 3s. 6d.
GRIFFIN'S Algebra and Trigonometry, 3s. 6d.
JENKIN'S Electricity and Magnetism, 3s. 6d.
MAXWELL'S Theory of Heat, 3s. 6d.
MERRIFIELD'S Technical Arithmetic and Mensuration, 3s. 6d.
MILLER'S Inorganic Chemistry, 3s. 6d.
PREECE & SIVEWRIGHT'S Telegraphy, 3s. 6d.
SHELLEY'S Workshop Appliances, 3s. 6d.
THOMÉ'S Structural and Physiological Botany, 6s.
THORPE'S Quantitative Chemical Analysis, 4s. 6d.
THORPE & MUIR'S Qualitative Analysis, 3s. 6d.
TILDEN'S Chemical Philosophy, 3s. 6d.
UNWIN'S Machine Design, 3s. 6d.
WATSON'S Plane and Solid Geometry, 3s. 6d.

*** Other Text-Books in continuation of this Series are in active preparation.

ELEMENTARY TREATISE on PHYSICS, Experimental and Applied.
Translated and edited from GANOT'S *Éléments de Physique* by E. ATKINSON,
Ph.D. F.C.S. Seventh Edition, revised and enlarged ; with 4 Coloured Plates
and 758 Woodcuts. Post 8vo. 15s.

NATURAL PHILOSOPHY for GENERAL READERS and YOUNG
PERSONS ; being a Course of Physics divested of Mathematical Formulæ
expressed in the language of daily life. Translated from GANOT'S *Cours de
Physique* and by E. ATKINSON, Ph.D. F.C.S. Second Edition, with 2 Plates
and 429 Woodcuts. Crown 8vo. price 7s. 6d.

ARNOTT'S ELEMENTS of PHYSICS or NATURAL PHILOSOPHY.
Seventh Edition, edited by A. BAIN, LL.D. and A. S. TAYLOR, M.D. F.R.S.
Crown 8vo. Woodcuts, 12s. 6d.

HELMHOLTZ'S POPULAR LECTURES on SCIENTIFIC SUBJECTS.
Translated by E. ATKINSON, Ph.D. F.C.S. Professor of Experimental Science,
Staff College. With an Introduction by Professor TYNDALL. 8vo. with nume-
rous Woodcuts, price 12s. 6d.

On the SENSATIONS of TONE as a Physiological Basis for the
Theory of Music. By HERMANN L. F. HELMHOLTZ, M.D. Professor of Physics
in the University of Berlin. Translated, with the Author's sanction, from the
Third German Edition, with Additional Notes and an Additional Appendix, by
ALEXANDER J. ELLIS, F.R.S. &c. 8vo. price 36s.

The **HISTORY of MODERN MUSIC**, a Course of Lectures delivered at the Royal Institution of Great Britain. By JOHN HULLAH, Professor of Vocal Music in Queen's College and Bedford College, and Organist of Charterhouse. 8vo. 8s. 6d.

The **TRANSITION PERIOD of MUSICAL HISTORY**; a Second Course of Lectures on the History of Music from the Beginning of the Seventeenth to the Middle of the Eighteenth Century, delivered at the Royal Institution. By JOHN HULLAH. 8vo. 10s. 6d.

SOUND. By JOHN TYNDALL, LL.D. D.C.L. F.R.S. Third Edition, including Recent Researches on Fog-Signalling; Portrait and Woodcuts. Crown 8vo. 10s. 6d.

HEAT a MODE of MOTION. By JOHN TYNDALL, LL.D. D.C.L. F.R.S. Fifth Edition. Plate and Woodcuts. Crown 8vo. 10s. 6d.

CONTRIBUTIONS to MOLECULAR PHYSICS in the DOMAIN of RADIANT HEAT. By J. TYNDALL, LL.D. D.C.L. F.R.S. With 2 Plates and 31 Woodcuts. 8vo. 16s.

RESEARCHES on DIAMAGNETISM and MAGNE-CRYSTALLIC ACTION; including the Question of Diamagnetic Polarity. By J. TYNDALL M.D. D.C.L. F.R.S. With 6 plates and many Woodcuts. 8vo. 14s.

NOTES of a COURSE of SEVEN LECTURES on ELECTRICAL PHENOMENA and THEORIES, delivered at the Royal Institution, A.D. 1870. By JOHN TYNDALL, LL.D., D.C.L., F.R.S. Crown 8vo. 1s. sewed; 1s. 6d. cloth.

SIX LECTURES on LIGHT delivered in America in 1872 and 1873. By JOHN TYNDALL, LL.D. D.C.L. F.R.S. Second Edition, with Portrait, Plate, and 59 Diagrams. Crown 8vo. 7s. 6d.

NOTES of a COURSE of NINE LECTURES on LIGHT delivered at the Royal Institution, A.D. 1869. By JOHN TYNDALL, LL.D. D.C.L. F.R.S. Crown 8vo. price 1s. sewed, or 1s. 6d. cloth.

FRAGMENTS of SCIENCE. By JOHN TYNDALL, LL.D. D.C.L. F.R.S. Third Edition, with a New Introduction. Crown 8vo. 10s. 6d.

LIGHT SCIENCE for LEISURE HOURS; a Series of Familiar Essays on Scientific Subjects, Natural Phenomena, &c. By R. A. PROCTOR, B.A. First and Second Series. Crown 8vo. 7s. 6d. each.

A TREATISE on MAGNETISM, General and Terrestrial. By HUMPHREY LLOYD, D.D. D.C.L., Provost of Trinity College, Dublin. 8vo. 10s. 6d.

ELEMENTARY TREATISE on the WAVE-THEORY of LIGHT. By HUMPHREY LLOYD, D.D. D.C.L. Provost of Trinity College, Dublin. Third Edition, revised and enlarged. 8vo. price 10s. 6d.

The **CORRELATION of PHYSICAL FORCES.** By the Hon. Sir W. R. GROVE, M.A. F.R.S. one of the Judges of the Court of Common Pleas. Sixth Edition, with other Contributions to Science. 8vo. price 15s.

The **COMPARATIVE ANATOMY and PHYSIOLOGY of the VERTEBRATE ANIMALS.** By RICHARD OWEN, F.R.S. D.C.L. With 1,472 Woodcuts. 3 vols. 8vo. £3. 13s. 6d.

PRINCIPLES of ANIMAL MECHANICS. By the Rev. S. HAUGHTON, F.R.S. Fellow of Trin. Coll. Dubl. M.D. Dubl. and D.C.L. Oxon. Second Edition, with 111 Figures on Wood. 8vo. 21s.

ROCKS CLASSIFIED and DESCRIBED. By BERNHARD VON COTTA. English Edition, by P. H. LAWRENCE; with English, German, and French Synonymes. Post 8vo. 14s.

The ANCIENT STONE IMPLEMENTS, WEAPONS, and ORNA-MENTS of GREAT BRITAIN. By JOHN EVANS, F.R.S. F.S.A. With 2 Plates and 476 Woodcuts. 8vo. price 28s.

The GEOLOGY of ENGLAND and WALES; A Concise Account of the Lithological Characters, Leading Fossils, and Economic Products of the Rocks; with Notes on the Physical Features of the Country. By H. B. WOODWARD, F.G.S. With a Coloured Map and 29 Woodcuts. Crown 8vo. 14s.

The PRIMÆVAL WORLD of SWITZERLAND. By Professor OSWALD HEER, of the University of Zurich. Edited by JAMES HEYWOOD, M.A. F.R.S. President of the Statistical Society. With a Coloured Map, 19 Plates in Lithography and Chromoxylography, and 372 Woodcuts. 2 vols. 8vo. 28s.

The PUZZLE of LIFE and HOW it HAS BEEN PUT TOGETHER: a Short History of Vegetable and Animal Life upon the Earth from the Earliest Times; including an Account of Pre-Historic Man, his Weapons, Tools, and Works. By A. NICOLS, F.R.G.S. With 12 Illustrations. Crown 8vo. 5s.

The ORIGIN of CIVILISATION and the PRIMITIVE CONDITION of MAN; Mental and Social Condition of Savages. By Sir JOHN LUBBOCK, Bart. M.P. F.R.S. Third Edition, with 25 Woodcuts. 8vo. 18s.

BIBLE ANIMALS; being a Description of every Living Creature mentioned in the Scriptures, from the Ape to the Coral. By the Rev. J. G. WOOD, M.A. F.L.S. With about 112 Vignettes on Wood. 8vo. 14s.

HOMES WITHOUT HANDS; a Description of the Habitations of Animals, classed according to their Principle of Construction. By the Rev. J. G. WOOD, M.A. F.L.S. With about 140 Vignettes on Wood. 8vo. 14s.

INSECTS AT HOME; a Popular Account of British Insects, their Structure, Habits, and Transformations. By the Rev. J. G. WOOD, M.A. F.L.S. With upwards of 700 Illustrations. 8vo. price 14s.

INSECTS ABROAD; a Popular Account of Foreign Insects, their Structure, Habits, and Transformations. By J. G. WOOD, M.A. F.L.S. Printed and illustrated uniformly with 'Insects at Home.' 8vo. price 14s.

STRANGE DWELLINGS; a description of the Habitations of Animals, abridged from 'Homes without Hands.' By the Rev. J. G. WOOD, M.A. F.L.S. With about 60 Woodcut Illustrations. Crown 8vo. price 7s. 6d.

OUT of DOORS; a Selection of original Articles on Practical Natural History. By the Rev. J. G. WOOD, M.A. F.L.S. With Eleven Illustrations from Original Designs engraved on Wood by G. Pearson. Crown 8vo. price 7s. 6d.

A FAMILIAR HISTORY of BIRDS. By E. STANLEY, D.D. F.R.S. late Lord Bishop of Norwich. Seventh Edition, with Woodcuts. Fcp.3 s. 6d.

KIRBY and SPENCE'S INTRODUCTION to ENTOMOLOGY, or Elements of the Natural History of Insects. 7th Edition. Crown 8vo. 5s.

The **SEA** and its **LIVING WONDERS**. By Dr. GEORGE HARTWIG. Latest revised Edition. 8vo. with many Illustrations, 10s. 6d.

The **TROPICAL WORLD**. By Dr. GEORGE HARTWIG. With above 160 Illustrations. Latest revised Edition. 8vo. price 10s. 6d.

The **SUBTERRANEAN WORLD**. By Dr. GEORGE HARTWIG. With 3 Maps and about 80 Woodcuts, including 8 full size of page. 8vo. price 10s. 6d.

The **POLAR WORLD**, a Popular Description of Man and Nature in the Arctic and Antarctic Regions of the Globe. By Dr. GEORGE HARTWIG. With 8 Chromoxylographs, 3 Maps, and 85 Woodcuts. 8vo. 10s. 6d.

THE AERIAL WORLD. By Dr. G. HARTWIG. New Edition, with 8 Chromoxylographs and 60 Woodcut Illustrations. 8vo. price 21s.

MAUNDER'S TREASURY of NATURAL HISTORY, or Popular Dictionary of Birds, Beasts, Fishes, Reptiles, Insects, and Creeping Things. With above 900 Woodcuts. Fcp. 8vo. price 6s. cloth, or 10s. 6d. bound in calf.

MAUNDER'S SCIENTIFIC and LITERARY TREASURY. New Edition, thoroughly revised and in great part rewritten, with above 1,000 new Articles, by J. Y. JOHNSON. Fcp. 8vo. 6s. cloth, or 10s. 6d. calf.

BRANDE'S DICTIONARY of SCIENCE, LITERATURE, and ART. Re-edited by the Rev. GEORGE W. COX, M.A. late Scholar of Trinity College, Oxford; assisted by Contributors of eminent Scientific and Literary Acquirements. New Edition, revised. 3 vols. medium 8vo. 63s.

HANDBOOK of HARDY TREES, SHRUBS, and HERBACEOUS PLANTS, containing Descriptions, Native Countries, &c. of a Selection of the Best Species in Cultivation; together with Cultural Details, Comparative Hardiness, Suitability for Particular Positions, &c. By W. B. HEMSLEY. With 264 Original Woodcuts. Medium 8vo. 12s.

DECAISNE and LE MAOUT'S GENERAL SYSTEM of BOTANY, DESCRIPTIVE and ANALYTICAL. Translated by Mrs. HOOKER. The Orders arranged after the Method followed in the Universities and Schools of Great Britain; with an Appendix on the Natural Method, and other Additions, by J. D. HOOKER, F.R.S. &c. Second Thousand, with 5,500 Woodcuts. Imperial 8vo. 31s. 6d.

THOMÉ'S TEXT-BOOK of STRUCTURAL and PHYSIOLOGICAL BOTANY. Translated by A. W. BENNETT, M.A. With Coloured Map and 600 Woodcuts. Small 8vo. 6s.

The **TREASURY of BOTANY**, or Popular Dictionary of the Vegetable Kingdom; including a Glossary of Botanical Terms. Edited by J. LINDLEY, F.R.S. and T. MOORE, F.L.S. assisted by eminent Contributors. With 274 Woodcuts and 20 Steel Plates. Two Parts, fcp. 8vo. 12s. cloth, or 21s. calf.

The **ELEMENTS of BOTANY for FAMILIES and SCHOOLS**. Tenth Edition, revised by THOMAS MOORE, F.L.S. Fcp. 8vo. with 154 Woodcuts, 2s. 6d.

The **ROSE AMATEUR'S GUIDE**. By THOMAS RIVERS. Fourteenth Edition. Fcp. 8vo. 4s.

LOUDON'S ENCYCLOPÆDIA of PLANTS; comprising the Specific Character, Description, Culture, History, &c. of all the Plants found in Great Britain. With upwards of 12,000 Woodcuts. 8vo. 42s.

Chemistry and Physiology.

INTRODUCTION to the STUDY of CHEMICAL PHILOSOPHY; the Principles of Theoretical and Systematic Chemistry. By WILLIAM A. TILDEN, D.Sc. Lond. F.C.S. Lecturer on Chemistry in Clifton College. With 5 Woodcuts. Small 8vo. 3s. 6d.

A DICTIONARY of CHEMISTRY and the Allied Branches of other Sciences. By HENRY WATTS, F.R.S. assisted by eminent Contributors. Seven Volumes, medium 8vo. price £10. 16s. 6d.

SUPPLEMENTARY VOLUME, completing the Record of Chemical Discovery to the year 1876.   [In preparation.

ELEMENTS of CHEMISTRY, Theoretical and Practical. By W. ALLEN MILLER, M.D. late Prof. of Chemistry, King's Coll. London. New Edition. 3 vols. 8vo. PART I. CHEMICAL PHYSICS, 15s. PART II. INORGANIC CHEMISTRY, 21s. PART III. ORGANIC CHEMISTRY, New Edition in the press.

SELECT METHODS in CHEMICAL ANALYSIS, chiefly INOR-GANIC. By WILLIAM CROOKES, F.R.S. With 22 Woodcuts. Crown 8vo. price 12s. 6d.

A PRACTICAL HANDBOOK of DYEING and CALICO PRINTING. By WILLIAM CROOKES, F.R.S. With 11 Page Plates, 49 Specimens of Dyed and Printed Fabrics, and 36 Woodcuts. 8vo. 42s.

ANTHRACEN; its Constitution, Properties, Manufacture, and Derivatives, including Artificial Alizarin, Anthrapurpurin, &c. with their Applications in Dyeing and Printing. By G. AUERBACH. Translated by W. CROOKES, F.R.S. 8vo. 12s.

OUTLINES of PHYSIOLOGY, Human and Comparative. By JOHN MARSHALL, F.R.C.S. Surgeon to the University College Hospital. 2 vols. crown 8vo. with 122 Woodcuts, 32s.

HEALTH in the HOUSE; a Series of Lectures on Elementary Physiology in its application to the Daily Wants of Man and Animals, delivered to the Wives and Children of Working Men in Leeds and Saltaire. By CATHERINE M. BUCKTON. New Edition, revised. Small 8vo. Woodcuts, 2s.

The Fine Arts, and Illustrated Editions.

A DICTIONARY of ARTISTS of the ENGLISH SCHOOL: Painters, Sculptors, Architects, Engravers, and Ornamentists; with Notices of their Lives and Works. By S. REDGRAVE. 8vo. 16s.

MOORE'S LALLA ROOKH, an Oriental Romance, TENNIEL's Edition, with 68 Illustrations from Original Drawings, engraved on Wood by G. Pearson and other Artists. Fcp. 4to. 21s.

MOORE'S IRISH MELODIES, with 161 Steel Plates from Original Drawings by D. MACLISE, R.A. and the whole of the Text engraved on the same Plates. Super-royal 8vo. 21s.

LORD MACAULAY'S LAYS of ANCIENT ROME. With Ninety Original Illustrations engraved on Wood, chiefly after the Antique, from Drawings by G. SCHARF. Fcp. 4to. 21s.

MINIATURE EDITION of LORD MACAULAY'S LAYS of ANCIENT ROME, with the Illustrations (as above) reduced in Lithography. Imp. 16mo. 10s. 6d.

HALF-HOUR LECTURES on the HISTORY and PRACTICE of the FINE and ORNAMENTAL ARTS. By WILLIAM B. SCOTT. Third Edition, with 50 Woodcuts. Crown 8vo. 8s. 6d.

The THREE CATHEDRALS DEDICATED to ST. PAUL, in LONDON; their History from the Foundation of the First Building in the Sixth Century to the Proposals for the Adornment of the Present Cathedral. By WILLIAM LONGMAN, F.A.S. With numerous Illustrations. Square crown 8vo. 21s.

IN FAIRYLAND; Pictures from the Elf-World. By RICHARD DOYLE. With a Poem by W. ALLINGHAM. With Sixteen Plates, containing Thirty-six Designs printed in Colours. Second Edition. Folio, price 15s.

The NEW TESTAMENT, illustrated with Wood Engravings after the Early Masters, chiefly of the Italian School. Crown 4to. 63s. cloth, gilt top; or £5. 5s. elegantly bound in morocco.

SACRED and LEGENDARY ART. By MRS. JAMESON. With numerous Etchings and Engravings on Wood from Early Missals, Mosaics, Illuminated MSS. and other Original Sources.

LEGENDS of the SAINTS and MARTYRS. Latest Edition, with 19 Etchings and 187 Woodcuts. 2 vols. square crown 8vo. 31s. 6d.

LEGENDS of the MONASTIC ORDERS. Latest Edition, with 11 Etchings and 88 Woodcuts. 1 vol. square crown 8vo. 21s.

LEGENDS of the MADONNA. Latest Edition, with 27 Etchings and 165 Woodcuts. 1 vol. square crown 8vo. 21s.

The HISTORY of OUR LORD, with that of his Types and Precursors. Completed by Lady EASTLAKE. Latest Edition, with 31 Etchings and 281 Woodcuts. 2 vols. square crown 8vo. 42s.

The Useful Arts, Manufactures, &c.

GWILT'S ENCYCLOPÆDIA of ARCHITECTURE, with above 1,600 Engravings on Wood. New Edition, revised and enlarged by WYATT PAPWORTH. 8vo. 52s. 6d.

HINTS on HOUSEHOLD TASTE in FURNITURE, UPHOLSTERY, and other Details. By CHARLES L. EASTLAKE, Architect. Third Edition, with about 90 Illustrations. Square crown 8vo. 14s.

INDUSTRIAL CHEMISTRY; a Manual for Manufacturers and for use in Colleges or Technical Schools. Being a Translation of Professors Stohmann and Engler's German Edition of PAYEN'S *Précis de Chimie Industrielle,* by Dr. J. D. BARRY. Edited and supplemented by B. H. PAUL, Ph.D. 8vo. with Plates and Woodcuts. [*In the press.*

B

URE'S DICTIONARY of ARTS, MANUFACTURES, and MINES.
Seventh Edition, rewritten and enlarged by ROBERT HUNT, F.R.S. assisted by numerous Contributors eminent in Science and the Arts, and familiar with Manufactures. With above 2,100 Woodcuts. 3 vols. medium 8vo. £5 5s.

VOL. IV. Supplementary, completing all the Departments of the Dictionary to the year 1877, is preparing for publication.

HANDBOOK of PRACTICAL TELEGRAPHY. By R. S. CULLEY, Memb. Inst. C.E. Engineer-in-Chief of Telegraphs to the Post Office. Sixth Edition, with 144 Woodcuts and 5 Plates. 8vo. price 16s.

ENCYCLOPÆDIA of CIVIL ENGINEERING, Historical, Theoretical, and Practical. By E. CRESY, C.E. With above 3,000 Woodcuts. 8vo. 42s.

The AMATEUR MECHANIC'S PRACTICAL HANDBOOK; describing the different Tools required in the Workshop, the uses of them, and how to use them, with examples of different kinds of work, &c. with full Descriptions and Drawings. By A. H. G. HOBSON. With 33 Woodcuts. Crown 8vo. 2s. 6d.

The ENGINEER'S VALUING ASSISTANT. By H. D. HOSKOLD, Civil and Mining Engineer, 16 years Mining Engineer to the Dean Forest Iron Company. 8vo.   [In the press.

The WHITWORTH MEASURING MACHINE; including Descriptions of the Surface Plates, Gauges, and other Measuring Instruments made by Sir JOSEPH WHITWORTH, Bart. By T. M. GOODEVE, M.A. and C. P. B. SHELLEY, C.E. Fcp. 4to. with 4 Plates and 44 Woodcuts.   [Nearly ready.

TREATISE on MILLS and MILLWORK. By Sir W. FAIRBAIRN, Bart. F.R.S. New Edition, with 18 Plates and 322 Woodcuts. 2 vols. 8vo. 32s.

USEFUL INFORMATION for ENGINEERS. By Sir W. FAIRBAIRN, Bart. F.R.S. Revised Edition, with Illustrations. 3 vols. crown 8vo. price 31s. 6d.

The APPLICATION of CAST and WROUGHT IRON to Building Purposes. By Sir W. FAIRBAIRN, Bart. F.R.S. Fourth Edition, enlarged; with 6 Plates and 118 Woodcuts. 8vo. price 16s.

The THEORY of STRAINS in GIRDERS and similar Structures, with Observations on the application of Theory to Practice, and Tables of the Strength and other Properties of Materials. By BINDON B. STONEY, M.A. M. Inst. C.E. Second Edition, royal 8vo. with 5 Plates and 123 Woodcuts, 36s.

A TREATISE on the STEAM ENGINE, in its various Applications to Mines, Mills, Steam Navigation, Railways, and Agriculture. By J. BOURNE, C.E. With Portrait, 37 Plates, and 546 Woodcuts. 4to. 42s.

CATECHISM of the STEAM ENGINE, in its various Applications to Mines, Mills, Steam Navigation, Railways, and Agriculture. By the same Author. With 89 Woodcuts. Fcp. 8vo. 6s.

HANDBOOK of the STEAM ENGINE. By the same Author, forming a KEY to the Catechism of the Steam Engine, with 67 Woodcuts. Fcp. 9s.

BOURNE'S RECENT IMPROVEMENTS in the STEAM ENGINE in its various applications to Mines, Mills, Steam Navigation, Railways, and Agriculture. By JOHN BOURNE, C.E. With 124 Woodcuts. Fcp. 8vo. 6s.

LATHES and TURNING, Simple, Mechanical, and Ornamental. By W. HENRY NORTHCOTT. Second Edition, with 338 Illustrations. 8vo. 18s.

PRACTICAL TREATISE on METALLURGY, adapted from the last German Edition of Professor KERL's *Metallurgy* by W. CROOKES, F.R.S. &c. and E. BÖHRIG, Ph.D. M.E. With 625 Woodcuts. 3 vols. 8vo. price £4 19s.

MITCHELL'S MANUAL of PRACTICAL ASSAYING. Fourth Edition, for the most part rewritten, with all the recent Discoveries incorporated, by W. CROOKES, F.R.S. With 199 Woodcuts. 8vo. 31s. 6d.

LOUDON'S ENCYCLOPÆDIA of AGRICULTURE: comprising the Laying-out, Improvement, and Management of Landed Property, and the Cultivation and Economy of Agricultural Produce. With 1,100 Woodcuts. 8vo. 21s.

LOUDON'S ENCYCLOPÆDIA of GARDENING: comprising the Theory and Practice of Horticulture, Floriculture, Arboriculture, and Landscape Gardening. With 1,000 Woodcuts. 8vo. 21s.

Religious and *Moral Works.*

CHRISTIAN LIFE, its COURSE, its HINDRANCES, and its HELPS; Sermons preached mostly in the Chapel of Rugby School. By the late THOMAS ARNOLD, D.D. 8vo. 7s. 6d.

CHRISTIAN LIFE, its HOPES, its FEARS, and its CLOSE; Sermons preached mostly in the Chapel of Rugby School. By the late THOMAS ARNOLD, D.D. 8vo. 7s. 6d.

SERMONS chiefly on the INTERPRETATION of SCRIPTURE. By the late THOMAS ARNOLD, D.D. 8vo. price 7s. 6d.

SERMONS preached in the Chapel of Rugby School; with an Address before Confirmation. By the late THOMAS ARNOLD, D.D. Fcp. 8vo. 3s. 6d.

THREE ESSAYS on RELIGION: Nature; the Utility of Religion; Theism. By JOHN STUART MILL. 8vo. price 10s. 6d.

INTRODUCTION to the SCIENCE of RELIGION. Four Lectures delivered at the Royal Institution; with Two Essays on False Analogies and the Philosophy of Mythology. By F. MAX MÜLLER, M.A. Crown 8vo. 10s. 6d.

SUPERNATURAL RELIGION; an Inquiry into the Reality of Divine Revelation. Sixth Edition. 2 vols. 8vo. 24s.

BEHIND the VEIL; an Outline of Bible Metaphysics compared with Ancient and Modern Thought. By the Rev. T. GRIFFITH, M.A. Prebendary of St. Paul's. 8vo. 10s. 6d.

The TRIDENT, the CRESCENT, and the CROSS; a View of the Religious History of India during the Hindu, Buddhist, Mohammedan, and Christian Periods. By the Rev. J. VAUGHAN, Nineteen Years a Missionary of the C.M.S. in Calcutta. 8vo. 9s. 6d.

B 2

The PRIMITIVE and CATHOLIC FAITH in Relation to the Church of England. By the Rev. B. W. SAVILE, M.A. 8vo; price 7s.

SYNONYMS of the OLD TESTAMENT, their BEARING on CHRISTIAN FAITH and PRACTICE. By the Rev. R. B. GIRDLESTONE, M.A. 8vo. 15s.

An INTRODUCTION to the THEOLOGY of the CHURCH of ENGLAND, in an Exposition of the Thirty-nine Articles. By the Rev. T. P. BOULTBEE, LL.D. Fcp. 8vo. price 6s.

An EXPOSITION of the 39 ARTICLES, Historical and Doctrinal. By E. HAROLD BROWNE, D.D. Lord Bishop of Winchester. 8vo. 16s.

The LIFE and LETTERS of ST. PAUL, including a New English Translation of the Epistles. By the Rev. W. J. CONYBEARE, M.A. and the Very Rev. JOHN SAUL HOWSON, D.D. Dean of Chester. Copiously illustrated with Landscape Views, Maps, Plans, Charts, Coins, and Vignettes.

> Library Edition, with all the Original Illustrations, Maps, Landscapes on Steel, Woodcuts, &c. 2 vols. 4to. 42s.

> Intermediate Edition, with a Selection of Maps, Plates, and Woodcuts. 2 vols. square crown 8vo. 21s.

> Student's Edition, revised and condensed, with 46 Illustrations and Maps. 1 vol. crown 8vo. price 9s. .

HISTORY of the REFORMATION in EUROPE in the TIME of CALVIN. By the Rev. J. H. MERLE D'AUBIGNÉ, D.D. Translated by W. L. R. CATES. (In Eight Volumes.) 7 vols. 8vo. price £5. 11s.

VOL. VIII. translated by W. L. R. CATES, completing the English Edition of the Rev. Dr. D'AUBIGNÉ's History of the Reformation in the time of CALVIN, is in the press.

NEW TESTAMENT COMMENTARIES. By the Rev. W. A. O'CONOR, B.A. Rector of St. Simon and St. Jude, Manchester. Crown 8vo.

> Epistle to the Romans, price 3s. 6d.

> Epistle to the Hebrews, 4s. 6d.

> St. John's Gospel, 10s. 6d.

A CRITICAL and GRAMMATICAL COMMENTARY on ST. PAUL'S Epistles. By C. J. ELLICOTT. D.D. Lord Bishop of Gloucester and Bristol. 8vo.

GALATIANS, Fourth Edition, 8s. 6d.

EPHESIANS, Fourth Edition, 8s. 6d.

PASTORAL EPISTLES, Fourth Edition, 10s. 6d.

PHILIPPIANS, COLOSSIANS, and PHILEMON, Third Edition, 10s. 6d.

THESSALONIANS, Third Edition, 7s. 6d.

HISTORICAL LECTURES on the LIFE of OUR LORD. By C. J. ELLICOTT, D.D. Bishop of Gloucester and Bristol. Sixth Edition. 8vo. 12s.

EVIDENCE of the TRUTH of the CHRISTIAN RELIGION derived from the Literal Fulfilment of Prophecy. By ALEXANDER KEITH, D.D. 37th Edition, with Plates, in square 8vo. 12s. 6d.; 39th Edition, in post 8vo. 6s.

HISTORY of ISRAEL. By H. EWALD, late Professor of the Univ. of Göttingen. Translated by J. E. CARPENTER, M.A., with a Preface by RUSSELL MARTINEAU, M.A. 5 vols. 8vo. 63s.

The ANTIQUITIES of ISRAEL. By HEINRICH EWALD, late Professor of the University of Göttingen. Translated from the German by HENRY SHAEN SOLLY, M.A. 8vo. price 12s. 6d.

The PROPHETS and PROPHECY of ISRAEL; An Historical and Critical Inquiry. By Dr. A. KUENEN, Prof. of Theol. in the Univ. of Leyden. Translated from the Dutch by the Rev. A. MILROY, M.A. with an Introduction by J. MUIR, D.C.L. 8vo. 21s.

MYTHOLOGY among the HEBREWS, its Historical Development; Researches bearing on the Science of Mythology and the History of Religion. By IGNAZ GOLDZIHER, Ph.D. Member of the Hungarian Academy of Sciences. Translated by RUSSELL MARTINEAU, M.A. 8vo. 16s.

The TREASURY of BIBLE KNOWLEDGE; being a Dictionary of the Books, Persons, Places, Events, and other matters of which mention is made in Holy Scripture. By Rev. J. AYRE, M.A. With Maps, 16 Plates, and numerous Woodcuts. Fcp. 8vo. price 6s. cloth, or 10s. 6d. neatly bound in calf.

LECTURES on the PENTATEUCH and the MOABITE STONE. By the Right Rev. J. W. COLENSO, D.D. Bishop of Natal. 8vo. 12s.

The PENTATEUCH and BOOK of JOSHUA CRITICALLY EXAMINED. By the Right Rev. J. W. COLENSO, D.D. Bishop of Natal. Crown 8vo. 6s.

An INTRODUCTION to the STUDY of the NEW TESTAMENT, Critical, Exegetical, and Theological. By the Rev. S. DAVIDSON, D.D. LL.D. 2 vols. 8vo. price 30s.

SOME QUESTIONS of the DAY. By the Author of 'Amy Herbert.' Crown 8vo. price 2s. 6d.

THOUGHTS for the AGE. By the Author of 'Amy Herbert,' &c. Fcp. 8vo, price 3s. 6d.

PASSING THOUGHTS on RELIGION. By ELIZABETH M. SEWELL. Fcp. 8vo. 3s. 6d.

SELF-EXAMINATION before CONFIRMATION. By ELIZABETH M. SEWELL. 32mo. 1s. 6d.

PREPARATION for the HOLY COMMUNION; the Devotions chiefly from the Works of JEREMY TAYLOR. By Miss SEWELL. 32mo. 3s.

LYRA GERMANICA, Hymns translated from the German by Miss C. WINKWORTH. Fcp. 8vo. price 5s.

SPIRITUAL SONGS for the SUNDAYS and HOLIDAYS throughout the Year. By J. S. B. MONSELL, LL.D. Fcp.8vo. 5s. 18mo. 2s.

HOURS of THOUGHT on SACRED THINGS; a Volume of Sermons.
By JAMES MARTINEAU, D.D. LL.D. Crown 8vo. 7s. 6d.

ENDEAVOURS after the CHRISTIAN LIFE; Discourses. By the
Rev. J. MARTINEAU, LL.D. Fifth Edition. Crown 8vo. 7s. 6d.

HYMNS of PRAISE and PRAYER, collected and edited by the Rev.
J. MARTINEAU, LL.D. Crown 8vo. 4s. 6d. 32mo. 1s. 6d.

The TYPES of GENESIS, briefly considered as revealing the Develop-
ment of Human Nature. By ANDREW JUKES. Third Edition. Crown 8vo. 7s. 6d.

The SECOND DEATH and the RESTITUTION of ALL THINGS;
with some Preliminary Remarks on the Nature and Inspiration of Holy Scripture. By ANDREW JUKES. Fourth Edition. Crown 8vo. 3s. 6d.

WHATELY'S INTRODUCTORY LESSONS on the CHRISTIAN
Evidences. 18mo. 6d.

BISHOP JEREMY TAYLOR'S ENTIRE WORKS. With Life by
BISHOP HEBER. Revised and corrected by the Rev. C. P. EDEN. Complete in
Ten Volumes, 8vo. cloth, price £5. 5s.

Travels, Voyages, &c.

A YEAR in WESTERN FRANCE. By M. BETHAM-EDWARDS. With
Frontispiece View of the Hôtel de Ville, La Rochelle. Crown 8vo. 10s. 6d.

JOURNAL of a RESIDENCE in VIENNA and BERLIN during the
eventful Winter, 1805-6. By the late HENRY REEVE, M.D. Published by his
SON. Crown 8vo. price 8s. 6d.

The INDIAN ALPS, and How we Crossed them : being a Narrative
of Two Years' Residence in the Eastern Himalayas, and Two Months' Tour
into the Interior. By a Lady PIONEER. With Illustrations from Drawings
by the Author. Imperial 8vo. 42s.

TYROL and the TYROLESE; being an Account of the People and
the Land, in their Social, Sporting, and Mountaineering Aspects. By W. A.
BAILLIE GROHMAN. With numerous Illustrations Crown 8vo. 14s.

'The FROSTY CAUCASUS;' An Account of a Walk through Part of
the Range, and of an Ascent of Elbruz in the Summer of 1874. By F. C. GROVE.
With Eight Illustrations and a Map. Crown 8vo. 15s.

A THOUSAND MILES up the NILE, being a JOURNEY through
EGYPT and NUBIA to the SECOND CATARACT By AMELIA B. EDWARDS.
With Eighty Illustrations from Drawings by the Author, Two Maps, Plans,
Facsimiles, &c. Imperial 8vo. price 42s.

OVER the SEA and FAR AWAY; being a Narrative of a Ramble
round the World. By THOMAS WOODBINE HINCHLIFF, M.A. F.R.G.S. President
of the Alpine Club. With 14 full-page Illustrations. Medium 8vo. 21s.

THROUGH BOSNIA and the HERZEGOVINA on FOOT during the
INSURRECTION ; with an Historical Review of Bosnia, and a Glimpse at
the Croats, Slavonians, and the Ancient Republic of Ragusa. By A. J. EVANS,
B.A. F.S.A. Second Edition, with Map and 58 Wood Engravings. 8vo. 18s.

DISCOVERIES at EPHESUS, including the Site and Remains of the Great Temple of Diana. By J. T. WOOD, F.S.A. With 27 Lithographic Plates and 42 Engravings on Wood. Imperial 8vo. price 63s.

MEMORIALS of the DISCOVERY and EARLY SETTLEMENT of the BERMUDAS or SOMERS ISLANDS, from 1615 to 1685. Compiled from the Colonial Records and other original sources. By Major-General J. H. LEFROY, R.A. C.B. F.R.S. &c. Governor of the Bermudas. 8vo. with Map. [In the press.

ITALIAN ALPS; Sketches in the Mountains of Ticino, Lombardy, the Trentino, and Venetia. By DOUGLAS W. FRESHFIELD, Editor of 'The Alpine Journal.' Square crown 8vo. with Maps and Illustrations, price 15s.

The RIFLE and the HOUND in CEYLON. By Sir SAMUEL W. BAKER, M.A. F.R.G.S. With Illustrations. Crown 8vo. 7s. 6d.

EIGHT YEARS in CEYLON. By Sir SAMUEL W. BAKER, M.A. F.R.G.S. With Illustrations Crown 8vo. 7s. 6d.

TWO YEARS IN FIJI, a Descriptive Narrative of a Residence in the Fijian Group of Islands; with some Account of the Fortunes of Foreign Settlers and Colonists up to the Time of the British Annexation. By LITTON FORBES, M.D. F.R.G.S. Crown 8vo. 8s. 6d.

UNTRODDEN PEAKS and UNFREQUENTED VALLEYS; a Midsummer Ramble among the Dolomites. By AMELIA B. EDWARDS. With a Map and 27 Wood Engravings. Medium 8vo. 21s.

The DOLOMITE MOUNTAINS; Excursions through Tyrol, Carinthia, Carniola, and Friuli, 1861-1863. By J. GILBERT and G. C. CHURCHILL, F.R.G.S. With numerous Illustrations. Square crown 8vo. 21s.

The ALPINE CLUB MAP of SWITZERLAND, with parts of the Neighbouring Countries, on the Scale of Four Miles to an Inch. Edited by R. C. NICHOLS, F.S.A. F.R.G.S. In Four Sheets, price 42s. or mounted in a case, 52s. 6d. Each Sheet may be had separately, price 12s. or mounted in a case, 15s.

MAP of the CHAIN of MONT BLANC, from an Actual Survey in 1863-1864. By ADAMS-REILLY, F.R.G.S. M.A.C. Published under the Authority of the Alpine Club. In Chromolithography on extra stout drawing-paper 28in. × 17in. price 10s. or mounted on canvas in a folding case, 12s. 6d.

HOW to SEE NORWAY. By Captain J. R. CAMPBELL. With Map and 5 Woodcuts. Fcp. 8vo. price 5s.

GUIDE to the PYRENEES, for the use of Mountaineers. By CHARLES PACKE. With Map and Illustrations. Crown 8vo. 7s. 6d.

The ALPINE GUIDE. By JOHN BALL, M.R.I.A. late President of the Alpine Club. 3 vols. post 8vo. Thoroughly Revised Editions, with Maps and Illustrations:—I. *Western Alps*, 6s. 6d. II. *Central Alps*, 7s. 6d. III. *Eastern Alps*, 10s. 6d. Or in Ten Parts, price 2s. 6d. each.

INTRODUCTION on ALPINE TRAVELLING in GENERAL, and on the Geology of the Alps, price 1s. Each of the Three Volumes or Parts of the *Alpine Guide* may be had with this INTRODUCTION prefixed, price 1s. extra.

Works of Fiction.

The ATELIER du LYS; or, an Art-Student in the Reign of Terror. By the Author of 'Mademoiselle Mori' Third Edition. 1 vol. crown 8vo. 6s.

NOVELS and TALES. By the Right Hon. the EARL of BEACONS-FIELD. Cabinet Edition, complete in Ten Volumes, crown 8vo. price £3.

LOTHAIR, 6s.	HENRIETTA TEMPLE, 6s.
CONINGSBY, 6s.	CONTARINI FLEMING, &c. 6s.
SYBIL, 6s.	ALROY, IXION, &c. 6s.
TANCRED, 6s.	The YOUNG DUKE, &c. 6s.
VENETIA, 6s.	VIVIAN GREY 6s.

CABINET EDITION of STORIES and TALES by Miss SEWELL:—

AMY HERBERT, 2s. 6d.	IVORS, 2s. 6d.
GERTRUDE, 2s. 6d.	KATHARINE ASHTON, 2s. 6d
The EARL'S DAUGHTER, 2s. 6d.	MARGARET PERCIVAL, 3s. 6d.
EXPERIENCE of LIFE, 2s. 6d.	LANETON PARSONAGE, 3s. 6d,
CLEVE HALL, 2s. 6d.	URSULA, 3s. 6d.

BECKER'S GALLUS; or, Roman Scenes of the Time of Augustus: with Notes and Excursuses. Post 8vo. 7s. 6d.

BECKER'S CHARICLES; a Tale illustrative of Private Life among the Ancient Greeks: with Notes and Excursuses. Post 8vo. 7s. 6d.

HIGGLEDY-PIGGLEDY; or, Stories for Everybody and Everybody's Children. By the Right Hon. E. M. KNATCHBULL-HUGESSEN, M.P. With Nine Illustrations from Designs by R. Doyle. Crown 8vo. 6s.

WHISPERS from FAIRYLAND. By the Right Hon. E. H. KNATCH-BULL-HUGESSEN, M.P. With Nine Illustrations. Crown 8vo. 6s.

The MODERN NOVELIST'S LIBRARY. Each Work, in crown 8vo. complete in a Single Volume:—

LOTHAIR. By the Right Hon. the EARL of BEACONSFIELD. Price 2s. boards, or 2s. 6d. cloth.

ATHERSTONE PRIORY, 2s. boards; 2s. 6d. cloth.

BRAMLEY-MOORE'S SIX SISTERS of the VALLEYS, 2s. boards; 2s. 6d. cloth.

The BURGOMASTER'S FAMILY, 2s. boards; 2s. 6d. cloth.

ELSA, a Tale of the Tyrolean Alps. Translated from the German of WILHELMINE VON HILLERN by Lady WALLACE. 2s. boards; 2s. 6d. cloth.

MADEMOISELLE MORI, 2s. boards; 2s. 6d. cloth.

MELVILLE'S DIGBY GRAND, 2s. boards; 2s. 6d. cloth.

———— GLADIATORS, 2s boards; 2s. 6d. cloth.

———— GOOD FOR NOTHING, 2s. boards; 2s. 6d. cloth.

———— HOLMBY HOUSE, 2s. boards; 2s. 6d. cloth.

———— INTERPRETER, 2s. boards; 2s. 6d. cloth.

———— KATE COVENTRY, 2s. boards; 2s. 6d. cloth.

———— QUEEN'S MARIES, 2s. boards; 2s. 6d. cloth.

———— GENERAL BOUNCE, 2s. boards; 2s. 6d. cloth.

TROLLOPE'S WARDEN, 2s. boards; 2s. 6d. cloth.

————BARCHESTER TOWERS, 2s. boards; 2s. 6d. cloth.

UNAWARES, a Story of an old French Town, 2s. boards.; 2s. 6d. cloth.

Poetry and The Drama.

POEMS. By WILLIAM B. SCOTT. With 17 Etchings by L. A. TADEMA and W. B. SCOTT. Crown 8vo. 15s.

MOORE'S IRISH MELODIES, with 161 Steel Plates from Original Drawings by D. MACLISE, R.A. and the whole of the Text engraved on the same Plates Super-royal 8vo. 21s.

MOORE'S LALLA ROOKH, an Oriental Romance, TENNIEL's Edition, with 68 Illustrations from Original Drawings, engraved on Wood by G. Pearson and other Artists. Fcp. 4to. price 21s.

SOUTHEY'S POETICAL WORKS, with the Author's last Corrections and copyright Additions. Medium 8vo. with Portrait and Vignette, 14s.

LAYS of ANCIENT ROME; with IVRY and the ARMADA. By the Right Hon. Lord MACAULAY. 16mo. with Vignettes, 3s. 6d.

LORD MACAULAY'S LAYS of ANCIENT ROME. With 90 Original tions, chiefly after the Antique, engraved on Wood from Drawings by G. SCHARF. Fcp. 4to. 21s.

MINIATURE EDITION of LORD MACAULAY'S LAYS of ANCIENT ROME, with the Illustrations (as above) reduced in Lithography. Imperial 16mo. price 10s. 6d.

The ÆNEID of VIRGIL translated into English Verse. By JOHN CONINGTON, M.A. Crown 8vo. 9s.

The ILIAD of HOMER, Homometrically translated by C. B. CAYLEY, Translator of Dante's Comedy, &c. 8vo. 12s. 6d.

HORATII OPERA. Library Edition, with Marginal References and English Notes. Edited by the Rev. J. E. YONGE, M.A. 8vo. 21s.

The LYCIDAS and EPITAPHIUM DAMONIS of MILTON. Edited, with Notes and Introduction, by C. S. JERRAM, M.A. Crown 8vo. 2s. 6d.

BEOWULF, a Heroic Poem of the Eighth Century (Anglo-Saxon Text and English Translation), with Introduction, Notes, and Appendix. By THOMAS ARNOLD, M.A. Univ. Coll. Oxford. 8vo. 12s.

BOWDLER'S FAMILY SHAKSPEARE, cheaper Genuine Editions. Medium 8vo. large type, with 36 WOODCUTS, price 14s. Cabinet Edition, with the same Illustrations, 6 vols. fcp. 8vo. price 21s.

POEMS. By JEAN INGELOW. 2 vols. fcp. 8vo. price 10s.

First Series, containing 'DIVIDED,' 'The STAR'S MONUMENT,' &c. Sixteenth Thousand. Fcp. 8vo. price 5s.

Second Series, 'A STORY of DOOM,' 'GLADYS and her ISLAND,' &c. Fifth Thousand. Fcp. 8vo. price 5s.

POEMS by Jean Ingelow. FIRST SERIES, with nearly 100 Illustrations, engraved on Wood by Dalziel Brothers. Fcp. 4to. 21s.

Rural Sports, &c.

DOWN the ROAD; or, Reminiscences of a Gentleman Coachman. By C. T. S. BIRCH REYNARDSON. Second Edition, with Twelve Coloured Illustrations from Paintings by H. Alken. Medium 8vo. 21s.

ANNALS of the ROAD; or, Notes on Mail and Stage Coaching in Great Britain. By CAPTAIN MALET, 18th Hussars. To which are added, Essays on the Road, by NIMROD. With 3 Woodcuts and 10 Coloured Illustrations. Medium 8vo. 21s.

ENCYCLOPÆDIA of RURAL SPORTS; a complete Account, Historical, Practical, and Descriptive, of Hunting, Shooting, Fishing, Racing, and all other Rural and Athletic Sports and Pastimes. By D. P. BLAINE. With above 600 Woodcuts (20 from Designs by JOHN LEECH). 8vo. 21s.

The FLY-FISHER'S ENTOMOLOGY. By ALFRED RONALDS. With coloured Representations of the Natural and Artificial Insect. Sixth Edition, with 20 coloured Plates. 8vo. 14s.

A BOOK on ANGLING; a complete Treatise on the Art of Angling in every branch. By FRANCIS FRANCIS. New Edition, with Portrait and 15 other Plates, plain and coloured. Post 8vo. 15s.

WILCOCKS'S SEA-FISHERMAN; comprising the Chief Methods of Hook and Line Fishing. a Glance at Nets, and Remarks on Boats and Boating. New Edition, with 80 Woodcuts. Post 8vo. 12s. 6d.

HORSES and STABLES. By Colonel F. FITZWYGRAM, XV. the King's Hussars. With Twenty-four Plates of Illustrations, containing very numerous Figures engraved on Wood. 8vo. 10s. 6d.

The HORSE'S FOOT, and HOW to KEEP it SOUND. By W. MILES. With Illustrations. Imperial 8vo. 12s. 6d.

A PLAIN TREATISE on HORSE-SHOEING. By W. MILES. Post 8vo. with Illustrations, 2s. 6d.

STABLES and STABLE-FITTINGS. By W. MILES, Imp. 8vo. with 13 Plates, 15s.

REMARKS on HORSES' TEETH, addressed to Purchasers. By W. MILES. Post 8vo. 1s. 6d.

The HORSE: with a Treatise on Draught. By WILLIAM YOUATT. 8vo. with numerous Woodcuts, 12s. 6d.

The DOG. By WILLIAM YOUATT. 8vo. with numerous Woodcuts, 6s.

The DOG in HEALTH and DISEASE. By STONEHENGE. With 70 Wood Engravings. Square crown 8vo. 7s. 6d.

The GREYHOUND. By STONEHENGE. Revised Edition, with 25 Portraits of Greyhounds. Square crown 8vo. 15s.

The OX; his Diseases and their Treatment: with an Essay on Parturition in the Cow. By J. R. DOBSON. Crown 8vo. with Illustrations, 7s. 6d.

Works of Utility and General Information.

The THEORY and PRACTICE of BANKING. By H. D. MACLEOD, M.A. Barrister-at-Law. Third Edition. 2 vols. 8vo. 26s.

The ELEMENTS of BANKING. By HENRY DUNNING MACLEOD, Esq. M.A. Barrister-at-Law. Crown 8vo. 7s. 6d.

M'CULLOCH'S DICTIONARY, Practical, Theoretical, and Historical, of Commerce and Commercial Navigation. New and revised Edition. 8vo. 63s. Second Supplement, price 3s. 6d.

The CABINET LAWYER; a Popular Digest of the Laws of England, Civil, Criminal, and Constitutional: intended for Practical Use and General Information. Twenty-fifth Edition. Fcp. 8vo. price 9s.

PEWTNER'S COMPREHENSIVE SPECIFIER; a Guide to the Practical Specification of every kind of Building-Artificers' Work, with Forms of Conditions and Agreements. Edited by W. YOUNG. Crown 8vo. 6s.

WILLICH'S POPULAR TABLES for ascertaining according to the Carlisle Table of Mortality the Value of Lifehold, Leasehold, and Church Property, Renewal Fines, Reversions, &c.; also Interest, Legacy, Succession Duty, and various other useful Tables. Eighth Edition. Post 8vo. 10s.

HINTS to MOTHERS on the MANAGEMENT of their HEALTH during the Period of Pregnancy and in the Lying-in Room. By the late THOMAS BULL, M.D. New Edition, revised and improved. Fcp. 8vo. 2s. 6d.

The MATERNAL MANAGEMENT of CHILDREN in HEALTH and Disease. By the late THOMAS BULL, M.D. New Edition, revised and improved. Fcp. 8vo. 2s. 6d.

The THEORY of the MODERN SCIENTIFIC GAME of WHIST. By WILLIAM POLE, F.R.S. Eighth Edition, enlarged. Fcp. 8vo. 2s. 6d.

The CORRECT CARD; or, How to Play at Whist: a Whist Catechism. By Captain A. CAMPBELL-WALKER, F.R.G.S. late 79th Highlanders; Author of 'The Rifle, its Theory and Practice.' New Edition. 32mo. 2s. 6d.

CHESS OPENINGS. By F. W. LONGMAN, Balliol College, Oxford. Second Edition revised. Fcp. 8vo. 2s. 6d.

THREE HUNDRED ORIGINAL CHESS PROBLEMS and STUDIES. By JAMES PIERCE, M.A. and W. T. PIERCE. With numerous Diagrams. Square fcp. 8vo. 7s. 6d. SUPPLEMENT, price 2s. 6d.

A PRACTICAL TREATISE on BREWING; with Formulæ for
Public Brewers, and Instructions for Private Families. By W. BLACK. 8vo.
price 10s. 6d.

MODERN COOKERY for PRIVATE FAMILIES, reduced to a
System of Easy Practice in a Series of carefully-tested Receipts. By ELIZA
ACTON. Newly revised and enlarged; with 8 Plates and 150 Woodcuts. Fcp.
8vo. 6s.

MAUNDER'S TREASURY of KNOWLEDGE and LIBRARY of
Reference; comprising an English Dictionary and Grammar, Universal Gasetteer,
Classical Dictionary, Chronology, Law Dictionary, a synopsis of the Peerage,
useful Tables, &c. Revised Edition. Fcp. 8vo. 6s. cloth, or 10s. 6d. calf.

MAUNDER'S BIOGRAPHICAL TREASURY. Latest Edition, reconstructed, and partly re-written, with above 1,600 additional Memoirs, by W. L. R.
CATES. Fcp. 8vo. 6s.

MAUNDER'S SCIENTIFIC and LITERARY TREASURY; a Popular
Encyclopædia of Science, Literature, and Art. Latest Edition, in part re-written,
with above 1,000 new articles, by J. Y. JOHNSON. Fcp. 8vo. 6s.

MAUNDER'S TREASURY of GEOGRAPHY, Physical, Historical,
Descriptive, and Political. Edited by W. HUGHES, F.R.G.S. With 7 Maps and
16 Plates. Fcp. 8vo. 6s.

MAUNDER'S HISTORICAL TREASURY; General Introductory
Outlines of Universal History, and a Series of Separate Histories. Revised by
the Rev. G. W. COX, M.A. Fcp. 8vo. 6s.

MAUNDER'S TREASURY of NATURAL HISTORY, or Popular
Dictionary of Birds, Beasts, Fishes, Reptiles, Insects, and Creeping Things.
With above 900 Woodcuts. Fcp. 8vo. price 6s. cloth.

MAUNDER'S TREASURY of BOTANY, or Popular Dictionary of the
Vegetable Kingdom; including a Glossary of Botanical Terms. Edited by
J. LINDLEY, F.R.S. and T. MOORE, F.L.S. assisted by eminent Contributors.
With 274 Woodcuts and 20 Steel Plates. Two Parts, fcp. 8vo. 12s. cloth.

MAUNDER'S TREASURY of BIBLE KNOWLEDGE; being a Dictionary of the Books, Persons, Places, Events, and other Matters of which
mention is made in Holy Scripture. Edited by the Rev. J. AYRE, M.A. With
Maps, 16 Plates, and numerous Woodcuts. Fcp. 8vo. price 6s. cloth.

INDEX.

Spottiswoode & Co., Printers, New-street Square, London.